FODOR'S®

SCANDINAVIA
1984

Area Editors: AKE GILLE, ELMER MIKKELSEN, SYLVIE NICKELS,
   PER PRAG
Editorial Contributors: CAROL CHESTER, FRANCES HOWELL, IRA
   MEYER, DAVID TENNANT
Editor: RICHARD MOORE
Assistant Editor: THOMAS CUSSANS
Photographs: PETER BAKER
Drawings: ELIZABETH HAINES
Maps: C. W. BACON, BRYAN WOODFIELD

FODOR'S TRAVEL GUIDES
New York

All the following Guides are current (most of them also in
the Hodder and Stoughton British edition.)

CURRENT FODOR'S COUNTRY AND AREA TITLES:

AUSTRALIA, NEW ZEALAND
AND SOUTH PACIFIC
AUSTRIA
BELGIUM AND
LUXEMBOURG
BERMUDA
BRAZIL
CANADA
CARIBBEAN AND BAHAMAS
CENTRAL AMERICA
EASTERN EUROPE
EGYPT
EUROPE
FRANCE
GERMANY
GREAT BRITAIN
GREECE
HOLLAND
INDIA
IRELAND

ISRAEL
ITALY
JAPAN
JORDAN AND HOLY LAND
KOREA
MEXICO
NORTH AFRICA
PEOPLE'S REPUBLIC
OF CHINA
PORTUGAL
SCANDINAVIA
SCOTLAND
SOUTH AMERICA
SOUTHEAST ASIA
SOVIET UNION
SPAIN
SWITZERLAND
TURKEY
YUGOSLAVIA

CITY GUIDES:

BEIJING, GUANGZHOU, SHANGHAI
CHICAGO
DALLAS AND FORT WORTH
HOUSTON
LONDON
LOS ANGELES
MADRID
MEXICO CITY AND ACAPULCO
NEW ORLEANS
NEW YORK CITY

PARIS
ROME
SAN DIEGO
SAN FRANCISCO
STOCKHOLM, COPENHAGEN,
OSLO, HELSINKI, AND
REYKJAVIK
TOKYO
WASHINGTON, D.C.

FODOR'S BUDGET SERIES:

BUDGET BRITAIN
BUDGET CANADA
BUDGET CARIBBEAN
BUDGET EUROPE
BUDGET FRANCE
BUDGET GERMANY
BUDGET HAWAII

BUDGET ITALY
BUDGET JAPAN
BUDGET MEXICO
BUDGET SCANDINAVIA
BUDGET SPAIN
BUDGET TRAVEL IN AMERICA

USA GUIDES:

ALASKA
CALIFORNIA
CAPE COD
COLORADO
FAR WEST
FLORIDA

HAWAII
NEW ENGLAND
PENNSYLVANIA
SOUTH
TEXAS
USA (in one volume)

MANUFACTURED IN THE UNITED STATES OF AMERICA
10 9 8 7 6 5 4 3 2 1

FOREWORD

Scandinavia is an unusual part of Europe. It is a small group of nations, with interdependent histories, many elements of society and background in common, and yet each fiercely proud of its own national identity; a sort of mini United Nations. It is also a region which offers perhaps the widest variety of holiday opportunities in Europe, ranging from the sophistication of such capitals as Copenhagen and Stockholm, through the calm serenity of clear, ice-blue waters, unpopulated forests and unspoiled countryside to the adventure of the far northern tracts of the Arctic Circle. All this with the genuine friendliness and hospitality of the people themselves into the bargain.

For some years the Scandinavian countries have had the reputation of being very expensive, but now that situation has changed. Sweden especially has dropped many places in the "high-priced league", and now ranks favorably with most other European destinations, as does its neighbor, Norway. (Iceland, by contrast, is plagued with an abnormally high inflation rate, fueled by its traditional dependence on the fishing industry, which is in a bad way.) All these changing factors have greatly influenced the position of Scandinavia on the tourist map, and made it more than ever a serious contender for the attention of anyone who wants a holiday that is out of the ordinary.

The Scandinavian countries are laying increased stress on "active holidays". They have at least two excellent reasons for doing this; their opportunities for open air activities—farm holidays, riding, trekking, camping, fishing—are among the finest in the world; and, secondly, this kind of holiday can be enjoyed at reasonable cost. The sea and the inland waterways add yet another dimension to the huge variety of holiday possibilities, especially the cruises up the fjord coastline, with spectacular views, technicolor sunsets and, if you are lucky, the Northern Lights, all enhancing the relaxed life on board.

Scandinavia is easy to reach and even easier to travel around in. The quality of the hotels, even those in the depths of the country, is almost always high, and there is the added advantage that a great many people speak English well and that none of them are diffident about doing so. Which is no small relief when you consider the tortuosities of Finnish!

We wish to acknowledge and express our thanks for the help we have received from many quarters in the preparation of this new edition.

We are indebted once again to the Directors of the Scandinavian National Tourist Offices in London for their generous cooperation; specifically to Boris Taimitarha of the Finnish Tourist Board and to Phyllis Chapman; to Barbro Hunter of the Swedish National Tourist Office; to Bent Nielson of the Danish Tourist Board; to Knut Sjøvorr of the Norwegian Tourist Board; and to Johann Sigurdsson of the Icelandic Tourist Information Bureau.

In Denmark, Erik Palsgaard, Director of the Danish Tourist Board, and Hanne Bing, Head of the Documentation Department, who has been extremely helpful. In Finland we would like to thank Bengt Pilhström of the Finnish Travel Association and his staff for their assistance. In Norway our gratitude goes to Just Muus-Falck, Director of the Norwegian Tourist Board. In Sweden, most helpful assistance was given by Ella Brehmer of the West Coast Tourist Association and by Gertrude Hallbeck of the Dala Tourist Service.

Finally, we would like to acknowledge the hard work and helpful interest of our team of Area Editors, Sylvie Nickels, Elmer Mikkelsen, Ake Gille and Per Prag, without whom this edition would not have been possible.

All prices quoted in this Guide are based on those available to us at time of writing, mid-1983. Given the volatility of European costs, it is inevitable that changes will have taken place by the time this book becomes available. We trust, therefore, that you will take prices quoted as indicators only, and will double-check to be sure of the latest figures.

*

Errors are bound to creep into any guide. When a hotel closes or a restaurant's chef produces an inferior meal, you may question our recommendation. Let us know, and we will investigate the establishment and the complaint. We welcome your letters which will help us to pinpoint trouble spots.

Our addresses are:
in the USA, Fodor's Travel Guides, 2 Park Ave, New York, NY 10016;
in Europe, Fodor's Travel Guides, 9-10 Market Place, London W1.

We accept advertising in some books, but this does not affect the editor's recommendations. We include advertising because the revenue helps defray the high cost of our annual republishing, and the advertisements themselves provide information for our readers.

THE QE2:
THE MAGIC.

British Registry

QUEEN ELIZABETH 2
GETTING THERE IS HALF THE FUN.

CONTENTS

FACTS
AT YOUR
FINGERTIPS

PLANNING YOUR TRIP

REVALUATION INFLATION. Even though the Scandinavian countries are among the most politically stable in the world, their currencies have not escaped inflation, so the prices we quote throughout this book can be indicative only of costs at the time of writing (mid-1983). Keep a weather eye open for fluctuations in exchange rates, both when planning your trip and while on it.

 WHAT IT WILL COST. This is the most difficult travel question to answer in advance, but it is easier for the Scandinavian countries than for almost anywhere else for two reasons. First, the Scandinavians have no reticence about quoting prices. They realize the first thing the traveler wants to know is how much he will have to spend, and in the folders prepared both by the official tourist organizations and by business, every effort is made to estimate costs for you. Second, the spread between top and bottom accommodations is much less here than elsewhere. The lowest priced facilities are good, and there is a definite limit to the amount of luxury you can add.

Despite inflation and skyrocketing prices it is possible to visit Scandinavia without robbing a bank. Try staying and eating in moderate to inexpensive places; the standards will still be high. You'll learn more about the country itself by seeing the off-beat places, avoiding the tourist traps and generally going local.

We give here some cost information that applies throughout Scandinavia, but for a more detailed breakdown of hotel and restaurant prices, miscellaneous costs, etc., see the *Practical Information* chapter in each country section.

Hotel Rates. There are no official hotel price classifications in any of the Scandinavian countries. In general, rates in the towns and rural areas are somewhat lower than in the major cities.

In Denmark, some hotels in Copenhagen offer reductions between Oct. 1 and April 30, and in provincial towns and seaside resorts between Sept. 1 and May 31.

In Finland, most tourist hotels outside the cities reduce their rates off-season (which varies according to region).

In Iceland, unfortunately, there is no such thing as an inexpensive hotel. Prices in other categories are about the same year round. Note that Icelandic hotel rates are quoted in US $.

A great number of hotels in Norway offer reduced pension terms before and after peak seasons though these are allowed only if you stay for 3 or 5 days or longer. At Christmas and Easter, most hotels charge higher rates.

Double rooms may come to 50% more, in Iceland 60%. The service charge is always included in the rate quoted. In Iceland, the service and tax charge of 20–25% is not always included in the price, and you should check. Breakfast in Denmark, Norway and Finland is usually included in the rate. A supplementary charge for heating in winter, though not unknown, is not customary.

Approximate Single Room Rate.

		Denmark (Dkr)	Finland (Fmk)	Iceland (US $)	Norway (Nkr)	Sweden (Skr)
1st	superior	400–500	270–380	$55–$65	450 up	550
class	reasonable	250–350	170–270	$45–$55	275 up	350
Moderate		200–275	110–170	$30–$45	250 up	225
Inexpensive		150–200	60–110	$18–$27	120 up	150

Hotel checks may reduce hotel expenses by 20% or more. The *Scandinavian Bonus Passport* provides an average discount of 25%, special facilities for children, with over 70 top hotels in Scandinavia participating in the scheme from June 15 to Sept. 1. The *Golden Bonus Passport* provides up to 50% discount and 72 hotels participate (Denmark 21, Norway 28, Sweden 23). Ask your travel agent for details.

In Norway, the *Fjordpass* gives a discount of up to 30%, with 180 hotels and pensions participating. In Finland, the Finn Check scheme covers 165 hotels all over the country, divided into three categories; the checks are valid from June 1 to August 31. The Swedish hotel check is valid May-Sept. at the 440 hotels. It covers bed in a twinbedded room and breakfast.

Throughout Scandinavia there are hundreds of youth hostels, in the cities as well as country districts. Standards are simple but comfortable. Some hostels also serve meals. See *Youth Hostels* on page 19. Hostel prices are uniform throughout each country, approximately: in Denmark: 35–40 Dkr; in Finland: from 18–40 Fmk; in Iceland: $5; in Norway: 30–64 Nkr; in Sweden: 30–40 SEK.

Restaurants throughout the country chapters are generally rated expensive (E), moderate (M), and inexpensive (I). The categories break down approximately as follows:

Denmark:	(E) from 125 Dkr; (M) 75 Dkr–100; (I) 40 Dkr–75
Finland:	(E) from 45 Fmk; (M) 25–50 Fmk; (I) 15–30 Fmk
Iceland:	(E) from Ikr 300; (M) Ikr 135–185; (I) Ikr 65–160
Norway:	(E) from 100 Nkr; (M) from 70 Nkr; (I) from 40 Nkr
Sweden:	(E) from 80 SEK; (M) 40–70 SEK; (I) 30–40 SEK

Broadly speaking, a typical, moderate day should cost you approximately:

Denmark:	597 Dkr
Finland:	288 Fmk
Iceland:	1150 Ikr
Norway:	627 Nkr
Sweden:	550 SEK

WHEN TO GO. The summer season in Scandinavia starts around the middle of May and runs until mid-September. This is the time of the year when the days are longest, when the weather is best, and when every possible facility which will make your trip easier is operating at its peak. Because these months are so popular—the heaviest traffic comes during July and August —you should consider going either early or late. Remember that Scandinavians like to travel too, and if you arrive in mid-summer, hotels and train seats are scarce. Another point is that towns and cities tend to become depopulated in summer and then it's the visitors that take over.

The Winter Season. This should not be overlooked, especially if you are a sports enthusiast. From Christmas through Easter you can ski, ice skate, or sleigh almost anywhere (excluding Denmark, of course), even in the capital cities if you should catch them immediately after a heavier-than-usual snowfall. Moreover, once the summer tourists have fled south, the Scandinavians settle down to concerts, ballets, plays, operas, entertaining, and all the other pursuits which help them to occupy the long winter evenings. If you go at this time of the year, you will see the more typical side of life in the North.

Thrift-Season Travel. This means mainly April and October, and has grown increasingly popular as travelers have come to appreciate the advantages of avoiding the crowded periods. Most plane fares are cheaper and so are hotel rates. Even where prices remain the same, available accommodations are better, but remember that seasonal activities for tourists are not always in full swing. Check dates and if you want to get under the skin of the country, the time to do it is when its inhabitants are going about their regular daily routines. Cottages cost considerably less in April–May and in September. Most hotels in Sweden offer lower rates at weekends and during the summer. The hotelchecks, only sold outside Sweden, are also good bargains during the summer tourist season. For up–to–date information of current rates enquire at the Swedish National Tourist Office in your country.

Special Events. In Finland during **January–February,** you should make the trek to Lapland to watch the thrilling reindeer roundups. In Norway, Holmenkollen Week in early **March** brings ski-jumping to Oslo's doorstep. Walpurgis Night, on the 30th of **April,** heralds the arrival of spring, with much festivity. Uppsala, Sweden, is the scene of much student merry-making. Finland comes perhaps closest to maintaining the spirit of the original festival, where anything was permitted—or almost anything.

Good countries to visit in early **May** are Denmark, for the opening of Copenhagen's famous Tivoli Gardens, and Norway, for blossom time in the fjords . On May 14 the Midnight Sun reappears at Norway's North Cape, and May 17, Constitution Day in that country, is celebrated with children's parades and carnival mood from the Naze to the North Cape—especially lively in Bergen and in Oslo, where the Royal Family takes the children's salute. Mid-

May to mid-**June** is the time of the Scandinavian Festivals of music, drama, and ballet in Bergen, Copenhagen (the Fools festival), and Stockholm.

There may also be late skiers still in Norway, Sweden, and Finland in May, for while the winter sports season officially lasts from December through April, you can keep on skiing in the far north, particularly Swedish and Finnish Lapland, through May and into June. This late spring skiing is the best, for you have the combination of snow and long northern days; but in Norway, avoid scheduling your skiing for Easter week, for that is when all the permanent residents flock en masse to the slopes for their spring skiing. Glacier skiing can be practised in Norway far into June; every year from the end of that month to the beginning of **July,** slalom competitions are held on the glaciers of the Fjord Country in the mountains above Stryn (Nord Fjord), Åndalsnes (Romsdal), and Geiranger, with expert skiers.

On the weekend closest to June 23–24, the festive Midsummer's Eve celebrations are held throughout Scandinavia, with bonfires and dancing in the villages around maypoles. The end of June and beginning of July is the time for the annual international cup races at the yachting center of Hankö, in the outer Oslo Fjord and in July and **August** finishing stages of the tallships race reach Faerder lighthouse, also in Oslo Fjord. Yachtsmen go to Denmark in June, the big sailing season. At this time, too, the Viking Festival takes place in Frederikssund to the northwest of Copenhagen. In July, jazz enthusiasts flock to Denmark for the Copenhagen Jazz Festival.

The biggest celebration of America's Independence Day outside the United States is held on July 4 at Rebild, the Danish-American National Park in North Jutland. During July Stockholm has its "Juliade", with all kinds of events and attractions: sports, theater, music, shows, etc. The international Swedish lawn tennis championships at Båstad, northern Skåne, are held the first July week. Iceland, where the weather is often unreliable all year round, is visited most safely in June and July, and Sweden adds August.

Finland's main summer season of cultural and other events begins in June and ends with the Helsinki Festival from end August to mid-**September.** The Swedish National Commemoration Day is celebrated on June 6, with special festivities in Stockholm in the presence of the King.

Early September is often a good choice for touring the Norwegian fjords, and the best time for the superb fall colors of the far north of Norway, Sweden and Finland (where reindeer roundups in the far north start in the fall). The main Danish festival, Århus Festival Week, takes place in September, with ballet, theater, opera, concerts, exhibitions and sport. This is Denmark's chief artistic event.

The winter season of theaters, concert halls and opera houses in the capitals gets under way so October–April can be a good time to come.

On **December** 10 the Nobel Prizes in physics, chemistry, physiology or medicine, literature and economic science are presented at a gala ceremony in the Stockholm Concert Hall. The Nobel Peace Prize is awarded in Oslo on the same day. Christmas gaiety gets under way in Stockholm on December 13 with the Lucia festival, which is when you see those lovely Swedish girls with the candles in their hair, and is kept up for a month; it's a lively period in Copenhagen, too. Finns enjoy the pre-Christmas period with a series of parties: they call this time *pikkujoulu* or "little Christmas".

CLIMATE. The warm offshore currents of the Gulf Stream prevent extremes of heat or cold, thus dispelling the popular image of Scandinavia as being for the most part a frigid Arctic region. In general, you will find here a combination of the New England and British climates. Summer temperatures in Denmark are cooler (68°F/20°C average) than in New England, and winter temperatures are warmer (30°F/−1°C average). Norway is slightly warmer in summer and cooler in winter than Denmark. Central and southern Sweden and Finland have temperatures similar to New England's. Summers in Scandinavia generally are brighter and sunnier, and winter's colder, than in Britain. Iceland's unpredictable climate is similar to Britain's but colder.

WHERE TO GO. Unless you travel on a package tour, with a fixed itinerary and schedule which you can't modify, it is advantageous to rough out your trip. This gives you an opportunity to decide how much you can comfortably cover in the time, and the limits of your pocketbook. If you travel in mid season you need to make bookings well in advance. For highlights of the individual countries of Scandinavia, see *Practical Information* chapters for each country.

The best way to get an idea of where you want to go is to send for the brochures distributed free by the various national tourist offices. Their addresses are:

In the **U.S.A.:** For Denmark, Finland, Iceland, Norway and Sweden: *Scandinavia National Tourist Office,* 75 Rockefeller Plaza, New York, N.Y. 10019. Also, the *Danish Tourist Board,* P.O. Box 3240, Los Angeles, Calif. 90028-3240. Tel. (213) 906-0646.

In **Britain:** *Danish Tourist Board,* 169 Regent St., London W1R 8PY; *Finnish Tourist Board,* Finland House, 66 Haymarket, London SWIY 4RP; *Iceland Tourist Bureau,* at Icelandair Offices, 73, Grosvenor St., London W1X 9DD; *Norwegian Tourist Board,* 20 Pall Mall, London SW1 5NE; *Swedish National Tourist Office,* 3 Cork St., London W1X 1HA.

HOW TO GO. When you have decided where you want to go, your next step is to consult a good travel agent. If you haven't one, the *American Society of Travel Agents,* 4400 MacArthur Blvd. NW, Washington D.C., 2007; in Canada, *ASTA,* 130 Albert St., Ottawa, Ontario; or the *Association of British Travel Agents,* 55 Newman St., London W1, will advise you. In the United States, it is wise to deal with an agency that is a member of the U.S.-T.O.A. (United States Tour Operators Association) because these companies insure your deposits with them. Offices of the Association are at 211 E 51st St., New York, N.Y. 10022.

Travel abroad today is complex in its details. As the choice of things to do, places to visit, ways of getting there, increases, so does the problem of *knowing* about all these questions. If you wish your agent to book you on a package tour, reserve your transportation and even your first overnight hotel accommodation, his services should cost you nothing. Most carriers and tour operators grant him a fixed commission for saving them the expense of having to open individual offices in every town and city. If you wish him to plan for you an individual itinerary and make all arrangements down to hotel reservations and transfers to and from rail and air terminals, his commissions from carriers won't come close to covering his expenses and he will charge you about 10 or 15 percent of the cost of your itinerary. Many people find this a saving in the long run and well worth the reduced aggravation.

Some suggested travel agents in the **U.S.**:

American Express Co., American Express Plaza, New York, N.Y. 10004
Bennett Tours Inc., 270 Madison Ave., New York, N.Y. 10016
Cartan Travel Bureau, One Crossroads of Commerce, Rolling Meadows, Ill. 60008
Thomas Cook Ltd., 380 Madison Ave., New York, N.Y. 10017
Finnair, 10 East 40 St., New York, N.Y. 10016
Four Winds Travel, 175 Fifth Ave., New York, N.Y. 10010
General Tours, 711 Third Ave., New York, N.Y. 10017.
Globus Gateway, 727 W. 7th. St., Los Angeles, Calif. 90017.
Maupintour, 900 Massachusetts St., Lawrence, Kan. 66044
Olson Travelworld, Ltd., P.O. Box 92734, Los Angeles, Calif. 90009.
Scandinavian Airlines System, 638 Fifth Ave., New York, N.Y. 10020
Travellers Intl., 530 Fifth Ave., New York, N.Y. 10036
Unitours/Club Universe, 1671 Wilshire Blvd., Los Angeles, Calif. 90017.

in Canada:
Lawson Tours, 2 Carlton St., Toronto, Ontario.
UTL Holidays Tours, Suite 452, 1253 McGill College Ave., Montreal, Quebec.

in Britain:
Cosmos, Cosmos House, 1 Bromley Common, Bromley, Kent BR2 9LX
DFDS, Latham House, 16 Minories, London EC3N 1AN.
Fred Olsen Travel, 11 Conduit St., London W1R OLS.
Finlandia, 49 Whitcomb St., London WC2
Norway Only, 126 Sunbridge Rd., Bradford BD1 2SX.
Norwegian State Railways, 21–24 Cockspur St., London SW1Y 5DA
Prins Ferries, 17 Charles St., London Wl.
Regent Holidays, Regent House, Regent St., Shanklin PO37 7AE, Isle of Wight
Scantours Ltd., 8 Spring Gdns., Trafalgar Sq., London SW1A 2BG
Tjaereborg Ltd., 7–8 Conduit St., London W1R 9TG
Tor Line, 34 Panton St., London SWl.
Twickenham Travel Ltd., 84 Hampton Rd., Twickenham, Middlesex.

Sampling the tours: *Thomas Cook's* 14-day Viking tour of southern Norway and Sweden, plus Copenhagen, fully escorted, starts at $1,465, plus air fare. *American Express's* 15-day *Northern Lights* tour covers Norway, Sweden and Denmark, from $1,000 plus air fare.

Maupintour have 6 different programs covering Scandinavia, 15 and 22 days, ranging in price from about $1,530 (excluding air fare).

Travellers International's 22-day *Viking Vacations* tour takes in Norway, Sweden, Finland, Leningrad and Moscow, and ends in Copenhagen. Costs are from $1,330 (excluding air fare).

American Express's 17-day *Viking* visits Norway, Sweden and Finland, including an overnight on a Baltic steamer, at rates from $1,030 plus air fare.

Bennett's 15-day *Scandinavian Viking Lands* starts from Copenhagen then goes to Sweden and Norway, also for $1,030 plus air fare.

Tjaereborg is a Danish company, now also operating from the U.K. They offer visits to Scandinavia at very competitive prices, since they deal directly with the public, cutting out the middleman.

Regent Holidays feature a 15-day *Camping Expedition* combining the main sights with the wild Icelandic interior for from £475, and a more conventional *Focus on Life Coach Tour* for from £660.

The fly/drive arrangements of *Regent Holidays* and *Twickenham Travel* combined with camping or summer hotels are also good value.

TRAVEL FOR THE HANDICAPPED PERSON. A useful source of valuable information in this specialized field is *Access to the World,* by Louise Weiss, available from *Facts on File,* 460 Park Ave. S., New York, N.Y. 10016 ($14.95). Organizations are: the *Society for the Promotion of Travel for the Handicapped,* 26 Court St., Brooklyn, N.Y. 11242; the *Travel Information Center, Moss Rehabilitation Hospital,* 12th St. and Tabor Rd., Philadelphia, Pa. 19141.

Evergreen Travel Service, 19505 44th Ave., West Lynnwood, Washington 98036; *Kasheta Travel Inc.,* 948 Atlantic Ave., Baldwin Harbor, N.Y. 11510; *Hill Travel House,* 470 Howe Ave., Sacramento, California 95825 are among several agencies specializing in such travel.

The major source for information in Britain is the *Royal Association for Disability and Rehabilitation,* 25 Mortimer St., London W1N 8AB., who have an extremely helpful publication, *Holidays for the Handicapped.* Information is also provided by *Mobility International,* 62 Union St., London SE1 1TD. *Access in Norway,* available from 68B Castlebar Rd., Ealing, London W5, is also very helpful. The *Norwegian Tourist Board* publish a folder, listing hotels with special facilities for the handicapped. A Danish hotel guide for disabled persons is available from: *Landsforeningen of Vanføre,* Hans Knudsens Plads 1, DK-2100 Copenhagen Ø. The Swedish Tourist Board, Box 74 73, S-10392 Stockholm, publishes *Hotels in Sweden* with information on facilities for the disabled.

STUDENTS. There are two main sources of information on foreign study opportunities and on student and youth travel abroad. *The Council on International Educational Exchange,* 205 East 42nd St., New York, N.Y. 10017, for summer study, travel and work programs, travel services for high school and college students and a free booklet on charter flights. Their *Whole World Handbook* is the best single listing of both work and study possibilities abroad. *The Institute of International Education,* 809 United Nations Plaza, New York, N.Y. 10017, for information on study opportunities abroad and scholarships and fellowships for international study and training. *Vacation Study Abroad* is a complete directory of foreign study programs. *U.S. College-Sponsored Programs Abroad* gives details on foreign study programs run by American schools for academic credit.

TRAVEL DOCUMENTS. Apply several months in advance of your expected departure date.

U.S. residents may apply in person to the U.S. Passport Agency in various cities (see the Federal Government listings in the White Pages of the telephone directory), to local County Courthouses, or at selected Post Offices nationwide. If you have a previous passport obtained within the last eight years you may also apply by mail. You will need 1) proof of citizenship, such as a birth certificate; 2) two identical photographs, in either black and white or color, on non-glossy paper and taken within the past six months; 3) $35 for the passport itself plus a $7 processing fee if you are applying in person (no processing fee when applying by mail) for those 18 years and older, or if you are under 18, $20 for the passport plus a $7 processing fee if you are applying in person (again, no extra fee when applying by mail). Adult passports are valid for 10 years, others for five years; 4) proof of identity such as a driver's license, previous passport, any governmental ID card, or a copy of an income tax return. When you receive your passport, write down its number, date and place of issue separately; if it is later lost or stolen, notify either the nearest American Consul or the Passport Office, Department of State, Washington D.C. 20524, as well as the local police.

If a resident alien, file a Treasury Sailing Permit, Form 1040 C, or if a non-resident alien, file Form 1040 NR certifying that Federal taxes have been paid: apply to your District Director of Internal Revenue for this. You will need to present your alien registration card, passport, travel tickets, latest tax records and current payroll receipts. To return to the United States, resident aliens with green cards must file Form I-131 if you have been abroad for more than one year. Apply for it at least six weeks before departure in person at the nearest office of the Immigration and Naturalization Service, or by mail to the Immigration and Naturalization Service, Washington, D.C.

British subjects: apply on forms obtainable from your travel agency or local main post office. The application should be sent to the Passport Office for your area (as indicated on the guidance form).

Apply about 5 weeks before the passport is required. The regional Passport Offices are located in London, Liverpool, Peterborough, Glasgow, and Newport (Gwent). The application must be countersigned by your bank manager, or a solicitor, barrister, doctor, clergyman, or Justice of the Peace who knows you. Enclose two photos and a fee of £11.

British Visitor's Passport. The simplified form of passport has advantages for the once-in-a-while tourist to Scandinavia and most other European countries. Valid for one year and not renewable, it costs £5.50. Application must be made in person at a main post office and two passport photographs are required—no other formalities.

Visas. Not required of British or American citizens for a stay under 3 months. For visa and entry/exit purposes, the five Scandinavian countries are considered as a single unit.

Health Certificate. Not required for entry into Scandinavia. Neither the United States, Canada nor Britain require a certificate of vaccination prior to re-entry but because of frequent changes in law we suggest you check before you leave. Have your doctor fill in the standard form which comes with your passport or get one from an airline or travel agent. Take the form with you to present on re-entering.

CUSTOMS WHEN LEAVING HOME. If you propose to take on your holiday any *foreign-made* articles, such as cameras, binoculars, expensive timepieces and the like, it is wise to put with your travel documents the receipt from the retailer or some other evidence that the item was bought in your home country. If you bought the article on a previous holiday abroad and have already paid duty on it, carry with you the receipt for this. Otherwise, on returning home, you may be charged duty (for Britons, VAT as well).

WHAT TO TAKE. On transatlantic air routes, the free baggage allowance is now based on *size* rather than weight. In first class, you may check in two pieces, each one up to 62 inches overall measurement (height plus length plus width); in economy class, 2 pieces, neither one over 62 inches, both together not over 106 inches. Underseat (carry-on) baggage is up to 45 inches for both classes. Inside Europe the criterion is still weight.

However, it is wise to travel light anyway. It simplifies going through customs, makes registering and checking baggage unnecessary, lets you take fast autorail trains with room for hand baggage only, and is a lifesaver if you go to those places where there are no porters. The principle is not to take more than you can carry yourself (unless you travel by car). It's a good idea to pack the bulk of your things in one large bag and put everything you need for overnight, or for two or three nights, in a smaller one, to obviate packing and repacking at brief stops.

Travelers' checks are the best way to safeguard your travel funds. In the U.S., *Bank of America, First National City, Republic Bank of Dallas,* and *Perera Co.* issue checks only in U.S. dollars; *Thomas Cook* issues checks in U.S. dollars, British pounds and Australian dollars; *Bank of Tokyo* in U.S. dollars and Japanese yen; *Barclay's Bank* in dollars and pounds; and *American Express* in U.S. and Canadian dollars, French and Swiss francs, British pounds, German marks and Japanese yen. In the U.S., Barclay's checks are free, while other brands have a service charge of 1%.

British visitors can use the *Eurocheque Encashment* card (entitles you to change up to £100 a day) or the Midland Bank's *Uniform Cheque Card* (allows you to obtain, or pay in, local currency).

Clothing. The Scandinavian climate from June through mid-September is ideal. The days are pleasantly warm rather than oppressively hot, and it's a rare night when the temperature won't be just right for sleeping. Normal summer clothing with a generous sprinkling of sports clothes will suffice, but remember that sweaters and good stout shoes or boots should be included if you are going into the mountains. Don't forget the light topcoat or raincoat.

During April, May and October you will likely need heavier clothing at times than at home, although spring and autumn can be intermittently balmy. Winters are cold, of course, but because of efficient central heating systems, you may actually be more comfortable than in the frugally-heated hotels and offices of "southern" Europe. It is better to wear several layers of lighter clothing that can be removed or replaced as required. Mosquitoes, especially in the far north, can be a real nuisance from the end of June to early August; take some repellent with you.

Leave room for bargains. Many products, especially handmade goods, can be bought more cheaply, quality for quality, in the places you may visit than at home. This is your opportunity to stock up in the cheapest market. This part of the world is renowned for its furs; pelts and neckpieces are particularly good buys. Most of the bargains in Scandinavia, however, are not the sort of things you would be carrying with you normally (porcelain, silver, steelware, glass) so it will not affect your packing unless you want to leave room for these items on the return trip. Large shops will usually arrange to send purchases to your ship or directly to your home.

 AIR TRAVEL. Some Useful Hints. The great majority of travelers today will cover some part of their journey by air. The huge pressure on the airlines, especially at the peak holiday seasons, creates problems that the traveler of only a few years ago never knew. Here are a few suggestions that should make your trip just a little easier.

—**Health Pointers.** Sleep well before you leave
—Plan to arrive at your normal bedtime

—Go easy on the food and alcohol on board
—Wear loose comfortable clothes
—Wrap yourself in a blanket to sleep—the body temperature drops
—Take it easy for 24 hours after arrival (especially after a big time change): no important meetings immediately.

Photography. Those once-in-a-lifetime holiday films are vulnerable to the X-ray security machines on airports. At some, such as London's Heathrow, extra-powerful equipment is used; on most the machines are of the "low-doses" type. Both can cause films to be "fogged", and the more often the film passes through such machines, the more the fog can build up.

Warning notices are displayed sometimes, and passengers are advised to remove film—or cameras with film in them—for a hand check. But many airport authorities will not allow hand inspection and insist that all luggage pass through the detection devices.

There are two steps you should follow. First, ask for a hand-inspection whenever you can. Second, buy one or more *Filmashield* lead-laminated bags, which are manufactured by the American SIMA Products Group. These will protect films from low-dosage X-rays, but should not be relied on against the more powerful machines. The bags are also available in Britain.

Baggage Handling.—Don't pack valuables—jewelry, important papers, money and traveler's checks. They should be close to you at all times
—Lock each item and put name and address labels both inside and outside
—Ensure that the check-in clerk puts the correct destination on the baggage tag and fixes it on properly
—Check that he puts the correct destination on the baggage claim tag attached to your passenger ticket
—Keep your baggage weight within the free allowance—excess weight can prove very expensive
—If, by unlikely chance, your baggage doesn't appear on arrival, tell the airline representative immediately, so they have the details necessary to start their tracing system straightaway

GETTING TO SCANDINAVIA
FROM NORTH AMERICA

 BY AIR. *SAS* (Scandinavian Airlines) operates daily non-stop flights from New York to Copenhagen and Bergen with connecting services to all principal cities in Scandinavia, and indeed to several cities in Europe. The Bergen flights also link up with daily coach tours through the Fjord Country to Oslo and on to Stockholm and Copenhagen.

SAS also operates regular flights from New York to Stockholm, Oslo and Gothenburg, and daily flights from Los Angeles and Seattle to Copenhagen—which saves West Coast residents several hours of flight time and eliminates changing planes in New York. SAS also has flights from Chicago and Anchorage to Copenhagen. Its main U.S. office is at 138–02 Queens Blvd, Jamaica, NY 11435.

Finnair operates non-stop flights from New York to Copenhagen and Helsinki. Its main U.S. office is at 500 Fifth Ave, New York, NY 10036.

Northwest Orient Airlines has services from Minneapolis/St Paul via New York or Boston to Oslo, Copenhagen and Stockholm, linked with its great network of services in the U.S. Its head office is at International Airport, Minneapolis/St Paul, MN 55111.

Air Canada operates regular flights from Toronto and Montreal to Copenhagen.

Air Florida operates regular flights from Miami to Oslo and Stockholm.

AIR FARES. In effect there are now four types of air fare: first class, business, economy and various charters. Charter is the least flexible but it is far cheaper than the others. On regularly scheduled airlines charter group passengers receive economy class service but pay much less for it than their seat neighbors who are traveling as individuals. On purely charter-flight lines, the amenities may be fewer and the flight time longer. In the last couple of years the rules for charter groups have been so relaxed and the scheduled carriers have entered the charter/package field so much that the variety of possibilities now available is far too great to list here. The whole situation is covered in a special publication, the annually-revised *How to Fly for Less: A Consumer's Guide to Low Cost Air Charters and Other Travel Bargains,* by Jens Jurgen, published by Travel Information Bureau, 44 County Line Road, Farmingdale, N.Y. 11735 and priced at around $5, postpaid.

Unless you want stop-overs (see below) you will save greatly by picking one of the various types of excursion or package fares (we must, however, regretfully point out that there are many fewer of these available to Scandinavia than to other parts of Europe). Air fares given here are approximate, check before booking. These are the likely fares from New York to Copenhagen this coming season: first class $3,500; Club (full economy or business) Class $1,950; APEX (in economy class) $775. Charter fares are likely to be around the $600 to $750 mark.

Fares to Stockholm, Oslo, and Helsinki are proportionally higher.

Stopovers. If you are going to Scandinavia, why not stopover en route at Glasgow or London, Dublin or Paris? These and many other European points may be visited without extra charge when you purchase a regular priced ticket from New York to a Scandinavian city.

An ordinary roundtrip can be broadened in scope into a very comprehensive circle trip. This allows you to add many cities which lie off the direct route and saves you paying for separate side trips. Outward bound you might visit Reykjavik, Oslo and Gothenburg. Homeward, you can stop at Amsterdam, Brussels, Paris, London, Birmingham, Manchester and Glasgow. Stopovers are, of course, entirely optional.

BY SEA. The chances of traveling by boat across the Atlantic reduce each year—with direct service to Scandinavia all but non-existent except for a handful of one-way cruises. In the past, sea-lovers had a choice between ocean liners (the number of these in service on transatlantic routes has now diminished to one: Cunard's QE 2) and freighters. The possibilities in the latter category have dwindled almost as drastically. The few cargo ships making the trip and accepting passengers are booked several years ahead. Due to poor U.S.-Soviet relations, Polish and Russian boats may no longer dock at U.S. ports. One agent very familiar with developments in this area cautions that details of the transatlantic travel situation change rapidly: no sooner are the latest schedules off the presses, he claims, than they are outdated.

Nonetheless, the persistent can be rewarded with passage on the rare freighter offering relatively comfortable one-class accommodations for a maximum of 12 people. What they lack in the way of entertainment and refinement these ships make up for by way of informality, relaxation and cost (though flying is almost always cheaper). For details, and to help you choose specialists: *Air Marine Travel Service,* 501 Madison Ave., New York, N.Y. 10022, publisher of the *Trip Log Quick Reference Freighter Guide;* or *Pearl's Freighter Tips,* 175 Great Neck Road, Great Neck, N.Y. 11201. For information on *Cunard* passage: 555 Fifth Ave., New York, N.Y. 10017.

Royal Viking, One Embarcadero Center, San Francisco, CA 94111 or 630 Fifth Ave., New York, N.Y. 10111, has in the past featured at least one cruise between Copenhagen, Denmark and New York—a 21-day trip making 11 stops in Scandinavia, Iceland, Canada and New England. Other trips depart from Scandinavian and English ports and concentrate exclusively on the North Cape.

GETTING TO SCANDINAVIA FROM
GREAT BRITAIN

BY AIR. There are a considerable number of direct flights from London, Manchester, Glasgow and Aberdeen to the major cities. *SAS* and/or *British Airways* have regular services from London to Stavanger, Bergen, Gothenburg, Stockholm, Copenhagen, Århus, and Oslo; *British Caledonian* also flies to Copenhagen; *Dan-Air* fly from London (Gatwick) and also from Newcastle to Bergen and Stavanger.

Finnair and *British Airways* operate daily flights from London to Helsinki. *Icelandair* (Flugleidir) fly from London and Glasgow to Reykjavik regularly.

Fares: The most economic fare is the APEX fare in tourist or economy class. Based on the summer 1983 prices from London these are likely to be as follows: to Copenhagen £165; to Oslo £180; to Stockholm £215; to Reykjavik £245; to Helsinki £250.

Stopovers. U.K. tourists traveling on a regular-priced ticket from London to Copenhagen can use stopovers en route. You may fly first to Brussels and then continue via Düsseldorf, Bremen and Hamburg to the Danish city. Alternatively, you can substitute Amsterdam for Brussels and call at Bremen and Hamburg. An even greater choice of stopovers is available on tickets to other Scandinavian cities. If you're flying to Copenhagen from London (or New York) you get a free return ticket to any airport in Denmark but book your free trip at the time you buy your main ticket. Check with your travel agent for even lower night rates and other special fares.

BY SEA. There are several sea routes from Britain to Scandinavia, the duration of the voyage being from 17 to 38 hours, according to route. All carry cars (see *By Car* below). Details listed are for the summer season.

To Denmark: *DFDS* (United Steamship Co.) has a daily service from Harwich to Esbjerg and three to four times weekly from Newcastle.

To Finland: *United Baltic Corporation* have regular year-round cargo passenger services from Hull and London (Purfleet) to Finnish ports (heavily booked in summer). *Baltic Shipping Co.* has a very occasional service from London to Helsinki. *Finnlines'* mammoth Finnjet, the largest and fastest ship on the Baltic, now covers the Travemünde-Helsinki route in 22 hours. It links with other services, such as *DFDS Prins Ferries'* Harwich-Hamburg route, through to the U.K. Other combination through routes include *DFDS Tor Line* from Harwich to Gothenburg, thence overland to Stockholm and on by *Silja Line* to Turku or Helsinki: total duration about 2 days. See also *From the Continent,* below.

To Norway: *DFDS Danish Seaways* operates regular summer sailings from Newcastle (Tyne Commission Quay) to Stavanger (19 hours) and Bergen (21–25 hours). *Strandfaraskip Ferries* operate a weekly service from Scrabster in northern Scotland to Torshaven in the Faroes and then to Iceland before returning via Bergen and Hanstholm in Denmark. *P & O Ferries* are the agents.

To Sweden: *Tor Line,* twice weekly from Harwich (rail and coach connections from London) to Gothenburg and twice-weekly between Felixstowe and Gothenburg.

To Iceland: The Faroese Coastal Line connects Scotland with the Faroes and Iceland during summer.

Tor Line's mammoth ferry boat with room for 1,200 passengers and 400 cars, and a swimming pool, sauna, disco, etc. on board runs popular trips to Gothenburg, Sweden; also a 10-day pre-booked hotel package, including car transport. *DFDS* have similar packages to Denmark. *Tor Line* and *Prins Ferries* both feature packages to Finland. Prices vary according to season; check before booking. *Fred Olsen Travel Ltd* offer a variety of very attractive packages, well worth exploring.

 BY TRAIN. If you're no sailor and would like to reduce the sea travel to a minimum, there is the Harwich–Hook of Holland boat service (6 hours), with train travel through Holland and Germany: The North West Express leaves London (Liverpoool Street Station) in the morning and gets you to Copenhagen in time for an early breakfast next morning—with connecting day trains to Oslo and Stockholm. The night boat train from London connects with the Holland-Scandinavian Express at Hook of Holland next morning and reaches Copenhagen just after 8 P.M.—with connecting night trains to Oslo and Stockholm.

Shorter crossing still is via Dover–Ostend (3¾ hours), but leaving a much longer train journey via Brussels, Cologne and Hamburg on the Nord Express. From London (Victoria) early afternoon, you reach Copenhagen early next evening, Stockholm or Oslo the following morning.

On all these routes there are full dining car, buffet car or snack bar services for all or most of the way. All cross-Channel and cross-North Sea ferries have both full restaurants and self-service facilities. The night service from Hook of Holland (North West Express) carries couchette cars, but no sleepers. The Nord Express from Brussels has sleeping cars and couchettes.

 BY CAR. You'll find that all the ship services from Britain to Scandinavia take cars, and you drive-on and drive-off all boats including the cross-channel ferries. If you wish to drive through the Continent, the distance from London to Copenhagen via Harwich/Hook is 1100 km, via Dover/Calais 1276 km.

Fares depend to some extent on the number of passengers but, for two passengers plus car, are, one way, approximately: to Denmark: £137, to Norway £125, to Sweden £154. Through rates to Finland by *DFDS Tor Line* are £90 (reductions or free car on ex-Harwich sailings off-season if accompanied by four paying passengers). The *DFDS Prins Ferries/Finnlines* combined route to Finland (see *By Sea*), costs substantially more, but there is a special good–value return rate for the car if there are at least four fare–paying passengers. Through rates are also quoted by *Townsend Thoresen* on their short cross–Channel routes in conjunction with *Finnlines.*

GETTING TO SCANDINAVIA
FROM THE CONTINENT

BY AIR. *SAS* links virtually all major European cities with the Danish capital, Copenhagen. In addition, it has regular non-stop flights to Stockholm from Paris, Frankfurt, Hamburg, Amsterdam and Zürich. Other Scandinavian cities can be reached through Copenhagen. *Finnair* links Helsinki with many European cities.

BY SEA. DFDS Danish Seaways operates twice weekly sailings from Amsterdam to Bergen (30 hours), and weekly sailings to Stavanger (24 hours); also from Amsterdam to Kristiansand (21 hours). Jahre Line operates 6–days–a–week sailings from Kiel in West Germany to Oslo (19 hours). *Tor Line* operate a twice or three times weekly service between Felixstowe and Gothenburg taking 24 hours for the crossing.

Finnlines' Finnjet is the largest and fastest car and passenger ferry on the Baltic, traveling from Travemünde, in northern Germany, to Helsinki in 22 hours. Other regular shipping routes linking Sweden and Finland include *Silja Line* ferries Stockholm–Helsinki, Stockholm–Turku; and *Viking Line* services from Stockholm to Helsinki or, via the Åland Islands, to Turku; and from Kapellskär, via the Åland Islands, to Naantali. *Polish Baltic Shipping Co.* link the Polish Baltic port of Gdansk with Helsinki, via Nynäshamn in Sweden. Hourly sailings link Germany with Denmark on the Puttgarden–Rødby route. More easterly services are the Travemünde–Gedser and the Warnemünde (East Germany)–Gedser Baltic crossings. Each sails about four times a day, in both directions. Other routes link Sweden and Finland across the Gulf of Bothnia: Umeå or Sundsvall to Vaasa.

BY TRAIN. There are frequent daily train services from the principal Continental centers to the Scandinavian countries. Trains are fast, well-equipped, and the majority are electric or diesel expresses. From *Paris* one of the two fastest trains (19 hours) is the Paris–Scandinavian Express, which leaves the Gare du Nord in the early afternoon, is routed via Liège, Aachen, Cologne, and Hamburg, and arrives at Copenhagen the following morning. Connections for Oslo and Stockholm. Taking the same time is the Nord Express, leaving Gare du Nord in the evening, runs via Hamburg–Puttgarden to Copenhagen (the following afternoon) with connections to Oslo (arriving the second morning) and Stockholm the same evening. Both trains carry through first- and second-class sleepers and coaches.

There are good fast express trains from various Italian and Swiss cities to Hamburg with direct connections to Copenhagen. Most of these carry sleeper and couchette accommodations.

BY CAR. During the summer months, ferries link Sassnitz (East Germany) and Travemünde (West Germany) with Malmö/Trelleborg, Sweden. At any railroad station motorists can make reservations for ferries across the Great Belt (Halsskov–Knudshoved) as well as for Kalundborg–Århus, Fynshav–Bøjden, and Puttgarden (Fehmarn)–Rødby services (there are up to 30 daily departures). There is also an all-year service Travemünde–Gedser, (4–5 departures daily in each direction), and Warnemünde–Gedser, (3–4 departures).

DFDS Danish Seaways operates drive-on/off ferries from Amsterdam to Bergen twice weekly (one departure calling at Stavanger), once a week from Amsterdam to Kristiansand, and *Jahre Line* operates a car ferry service 6 days a week between Kiel in West Germany and Oslo.

All routes to Finland listed above (under *By Sea*) are operated by drive-on/off ferries; all of them offer excellent passenger amenities.

There is a weekly sailing during summer from Hanstholm in Jutland via Bergen to Torshavn on the Faroe islands, and then on to Scrabster near Aberdeen, or on to Seydisfjordur in Iceland, operated by *P & O Ferries*.

Advance reservations are strongly advisable, especially in summer.

ARRIVING IN SCANDINAVIA

TIME. Iceland is on Greenwich Mean Time. Denmark, Norway and Sweden are one hour ahead of GMT, but the same as British Summer Time between March and October. Finland is two hours ahead of GMT and one hour ahead of BST. Summer time is under discussion as we write, and arrangements for exact dates have not yet been agreed in some of the Scandinavian countries.

 CUSTOMS. The Scandinavians are reasonable people and their customs formalities are straightforward although complicated somewhat by differences in allowances from non-EEC or EEC countries. Therefore, it's best to check what your allowances will be, not only for the original country of your destination, but also for any other countries, should you be traveling within Scandinavia.

Generally, apart from the usual duty-free categories, cameras, film, medicine and other items for personal use are allowed in reasonable amounts. Firearms, ammunition and plants can be imported only with special permission. Animals must be quarantined.

 MONEY. Taking currency into Scandinavia should cause no difficulty either. Each country is interested primarily only in how much of its own money you have with you. All other currencies may be imported without limit, although you may be asked to declare them when you enter. Always carry a few single dollar bills; they will come in handy for last minute airport shopping or unexpected things like exit taxes.

It is also a good idea to stock up on small denomminnation money for the countries you are going to visit. You can get this in packages of $10, $15, or more, from some banks or look under *Foreign Money Brokers* in the Yellow Pages of any international airport gateway city.

You may take an unlimited amount of kroner into Denmark, but if you carry a very large sum it is advisable to have the amount entered in your passport on entry, as exportation of Danish currency notes in excess of 50,000 kr is only permitted if the amount has previously been brought into Denmark or originates from exchange of foreign currency into Danish currency in Denmark; 5,000 marks out of Finland (special permit required for notes of 500 Fmk.) in addition to all the currency brought in; 500 kronur into or out of Iceland in denominations of 50 or less; unlimited kroner into and 2,000 kroner out of Norway, though in denominations of 100 or less; and 6,000 kronor in or out of Sweden in Swedish banknotes (but not 1,000 kr notes).

All five of the Scandinavian currencies are based on a decimal system. There are 100 øre or öre to the Danish or Norwegian krone, the Swedish krona; 100 aurar to the Icelandic krona, and 100 penni to the Finnish markka. Note that in 1981 Iceland adjusted its currency to New Krona (locally abbreviated to Nkr.), whereby 1 new krona equals 100 old kronur, and new bank notes and coins were introduced.

STAYING IN SCANDINAVIA

LANGUAGE. Danish, Norwegian and Swedish are closely related. The centuries have left their marks, however, and today the relationship is somewhat distant: Danish and Norwegian are first cousins, Swedish is a second cousin, and Icelandic remains the venerable grandfather. Educated Scandinavians understand one another reasonably well but books are almost invariably translated for the benefit of each nation's readers.

Finnish, on the other hand, belongs to an entirely different family of languages; it has precisely no relationship to the other four northern tongues. A small minority of Finns speak Swedish as their mother tongue.

As a general rule you'll have no trouble using English in urban parts of Scandinavia. English is now taught in all schools.

If you are looking up a name in a town or telephone directory, it is worthwhile remembering that the distinctive letters å, ä, ae, ø, and ö encountered in the various Scandinavian countries occur at the *end* of the alphabet in their respective country. In Denmark, changes in orthography have converted *aa* to å in some instances (it is the same letter and both spellings are correct). The letter å or *aa* is pronounced like the aw in "law;" ä like the e in "let;" ö or ø like the u in "fur." The Icelandic "á" is pronounced like "ow", and the *p* like th in "thin". In Norway the word-ending meaning "road" can be either "gata" or "gate". The letters ae, run together, are pronounced like the a in "bad."

HOTELS. If you plan to stay in any of the Scandinavian capitals during July or August, be sure to book accommodation well in advance. Efficient reservation offices are located in the railway stations of major Scandinavian cities, but often they will not be able to offer you more than a very simple, second-class hotel or student accommodation that doubles as tourist lodgings during the summer. It is worth remembering, however, that the latter are often very modern, of a high standard and very reasonable in price. They are usually referred to as "summer hotels".

There are not many hotels of the international super deluxe standard. Such institutions are foreign to the Scandinavian scene where the average citizen takes pride in being middle class. Nearly all are spotlessly clean, and intelligently managed by individuals who will often go out of their way to be helpful; many of them are attractively furnished, reflecting the Scandinavian good taste in matters of design. Especially in the country, you will find simple, even spartan lodgings that radiate genuine pleasure in receiving you as a guest. Summer villas and cottages may be rented (for information consult the local tourist offices).

Holiday resort hotels, mountain and tourist inns: these include some of the best and most popular hotels as well as some of the more modest establishments in holiday areas. It is customary to take *en pension* terms (room and all meals), which are offered for stays of varying lengths—in Sweden generally 3 days or over, in Norway 3 or 5 days or over. Prices full board are roughly equivalent to capital city rates without meals.

A special feature of Scandinavian life is the "mission" hotels. These usually offer a modest standard of comfprt at an even more modest price. The atmosphere is not in any way sectarian.

In all Scandinavian countries holidays on farms can easily be arranged, and they have proved a huge success, particularly with families; but in all, you can be sure of comfortable accommodation at a moderate price. Information from the national tourist offices.

 YOUTH HOSTELS. Most youth hostels are open only from June to Sept., some remain open all year. Standards usually are equivalent to second class hotels; occasionally dormitories are used in summer. Families are welcome. Those who are not members of the national youth hostel association in their own country can get an international guest membership card from a hostel association in Scandinavia (ask at national tourist offices).

For further information write in the U.S. to: *American Youth Hostels,* 1332 I St. NW Washington, D.C. 20005, or 132 Spring St., New York, N.Y. 10021; in Canada: *Canadian Youth Hostels Assoc.,* 333 River Rd., Vanier City, Ottawa, Ontario; in Britain: *Youth Hostels Assoc.,* Trevelyan House, St.Albans, Herts, AL1 2DY.

 **CAMPING.** Scandinavia, both because of the nature of its geography and the habits of its people, is an ideal terrain for enjoying the cheapest and ruggedest forms of traveling. In the principal mountain districts of Norway and Sweden, mountain lodges are located at intervals corresponding to a day's hike (marked trails). Lodges are open usually mid-June to mid-Sept. Refuge huts are located in the wild fell regions of Finnish Lapland; and in Iceland, where hotels will also provide accommodation for travelers with their own sleeping bags at a rate of about $5 per night. In Denmark 500 camp sites are open to campers who bring their own tents or caravans, and about half of the sites also have huts for hire.

For information contact the *Camping Club of Gt. Britain,* 11 Lower Grosvenor Place, London SW1 or the various national tourist offices. Denmark: Friluftsrådet, Skjoldsgade 10, Copenhagen 2100 Ø, or *Dansk Camping Union,* Gammel Kongevej 74, Copenhagen 1850 V; in Norway; *Norwegian Mountain Touring Assoc.,* Stortingsgate 28, Oslo; in Sweden: *Swedish Touring Club,* Box 25, S-10120 Stockholm; in Finland: *Finnish Travel Association Camping Department,* Mikonkatu 25, Helsinki 10. Mobile homes can be rented in Sweden at Hjo and Älvdalen; contact *Inter-Holiday,* Lilla Kungsgatan 1, Gothenburg. *Share-a-car* and Drostgaards Campingbiler in Copenhagen are specialists in car camping rentals. See address in country chapter.

In the U.S., the *National Campers and Hikers Association,* 7172 Transit Road, Buffalo, N.Y. 14221, an affiliate of the *International Federation of Camping and Caravaning,* issues the *Carnet-Camping International Pass.* This acts as an inter-club membership for those camping in western Europe and Scandinavia. In addition to information and special privileges at selected camps, the carnet also provides for personal liability insurance. Membership costs $16 annually; the carnet itself is an additional $4.

 FOOD AND DRINK. Scandinavia has its own distinctive dishes and a number of outstanding restaurants. Full deteails on these will be found in the chapter *Food and Drink* following and in the *Practical Information* sections for each country.

Drinking laws are something else again. In Denmark you can be served liquor at any hour. Liquor in bottles can be bought freely anywhere during normal shopping hours. In Norway, spirits are not served before 3 P.M. in towns, not before 1 P.M. in resort hotels, and never on Sunday! But to make up for this you can purchase any number of bottles at the state-run liquor stores (Vinmonopol). There is no restriction on the amount of wine and spirits you may buy in Sweden at any of the state-owned liquor stores, and the consumption in restaurants is limited only by the discretion of the management. Licensed restaurants in Finland serve spirits without restrictions after midday, with the exception of schnapps, which is never served without food. Before midday, only beer is available, but can also now be bought in supermarkets and cafeterias. Drinks are expensive—whisky in a Swedish restaurant will cost 35 Skr.

 DRINKING WATER. Water is excellent and safe to drink everywhere.
     Pollution Report. Scandinavia generally is remarkably free of water and air pollution and strictly enforced laws aim to keep it that way. These apply both to industrial consortiums and the individual.

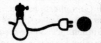 **CLOSING TIMES.** Generally speaking, Scandinavian shops keep about the same hours as their counterparts in Britain and America. Most establishments open at 9 and close between 5 and 6 on weekdays, 1 and 3 on Saturdays. Government offices, as is the trend these days, complete their business at least an hour ahead of commercial enterprises, and banks shut down at 3. Danish banks open from 9.30 to 4 (Thurs. to 6), closed Sat. In Finland, banks are open from 9.30 to 4 (closed Sat.); more extensive hours at Helsinki airport, harbors and main rail station for exchange purposes. In Sweden, banks open from 9.30 to 6 in larger cities, but are closed on Saturdays (as they are in Norway), and usually close at 1 on days before official holidays. Some Stockholm shops are open on Sundays from 1; in Helsinki certain shops are open in the evenings, and Sunday afternoons and evenings. Copenhagen Airport and the Central Station have shops which open until midnight, selling ordinary supermarket items. Banks are open for exchange until 10 P.M. or midnight in three or four places in the city.

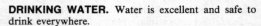 **ELECTRICITY.** Most parts of Scandinavia use 220 volt alternating current. A transformer can be attached to all kinds of electrical appliances you may take with you, but it will be satisfactory only where the appliance has no timing mechanism. The reason for this is that Scandinavian current is 50 cycle

instead of 60 cycle; an electric clock, for example, would run so slowly as to be worthless. Since there may be local variations you should always inquire in advance. The high Scandinavian voltages will burn out electric shavers and traveling irons unless they are properly equipped. Also note that most Scandinavian plugs are a different fit from U.S. plugs.

 READING MATTER AND NEWS. Scandinavia has the highest per capital book consumption in the world, and this fact means that you are seldom more than a few steps from a bookseller. English-language books are sold in every book store of any size, together with works in French, German and other languages. British and American newspapers are distributed in all the larger cities (best reserve your copy with the desk clerk at your hotel), as well as most of the popular and technical magazines. Stockholm dailies, by the way, carry a digest of the latest reports in English during the summer months, as do most Finnish dailies. Danish and Swedish libraries in main cities have foreign books and newspapers. The International Press Center in Stockholm at Sergelstorg has foreign magazines and books.

In Denmark, Radio 2 and 3 broadcast news in English at 8.15 A.M. Monday through Saturday.

In Helsinki you can get the latest news in English by dialing 018, and news of events and entertainment in Helsinki by dialing 058. Finnish Radio broadcast the news in English at 11.10 P.M. and there are other regular English language programs at 10.30 P.M. on Mon., Tues., Fri. and Sat.

In Iceland, a news bulletin in English is broadcast daily at 6 P.M.

In Norway, news in English, French and German (also weather forecast) is given daily on the radio during the summer at about 9.45 A.M.

News and weather forecast on Swedish Radio 3, in English (check newspapers for times). Radio Sweden transmits to the U.S.

 **CINEMAS.** Nearly everywhere in Scandinavia films are shown at fixed hours, usually once in the afternoon and twice during the evening. Unless you arrive on time, you won't be admitted to the theater even though you bought your ticket in advance. In most of the first-run cinemas all seats are reserved and the box-office is open during at least part of the day. The majority of the films are from England or America. Sound-tracks are in English, subtitles in one or another of the Scandinavian languages.

 MEDICAL SERVICES. The I.A.M.A.T. (International Association for Medical Assistance to Travelers) offers you a list of approved English-speaking doctors who have had postgraduate training in the U.S., Canada or Gt. Britain. Membership is free; the scheme is world-wide with many European countries participating. An office call costs $20; house or hotel calls are $30; night and holiday calls are $35. For information apply in the U.S. to 736 Center St., Lewiston, N.Y. 14092; in Canada, 123 Edward St., Toronto M5G 1E2. A similar service is offered by *Intermedic,* 777 Fifth Ave., New York, N.Y. 10017, which also has an initial membership charge of $6 for an individual, $10 for a family, and whose subsequent fee schedule is: office call $20–$30; house or hotel call $30–$40; evenings, holidays, etc. $40–50.

Europ Assistance Ltd. offers unlimited help to its members. There are two plans: one for travelers using tours or making their own trip arrangements, the second for motorists taking their cars abroad. Multi-lingual personnel staff a

24-hr., seven-days-a-week telephone service which brings the aid of a network of medical and other advisors to assist in any emergency. Special medical insurance is part of the plan. Basic prices: £6.10 per person; £18.75 vehicle and driver, up to 5 days; £6.75 for a caravan or trailer. There is special insurance for winter sports. This service is currently only available for British residents. Write to Europ Assistance Ltd., 252 High St., Croydon CR0 1NF, England, for details.

Free Medical Care (or reduced cost treatment) for *British* visitors is available in many European countries. But you have to be prepared with documentation in most cases. One month before leaving Britain, write to your local Department of Health and Social Security office for a Form CM1. Fill this in and return it; you will then get a form E111 to take with you. This form relates to treatment in other EEC countries.

In Denmark, all foreigners staying in the country temporarily are eligible for free treatment in hospitals and casualty wards in case of sudden illness, emergency, or aggravation of a chronic condition, and for prescribed medicines at reduced cost. Doctors may demand cash payment, which will then be refunded by the municipal office. This cash payment refunded by municipal offices applies to British visitors (EEC visitors) only. But hospital treatment is free to all nationalities.

In Finland, treatment is substantially state-subsidized, though not free: maximum state hospital charges are about 28 Fmk., including treatment, doctor's fee and medicine; the cost for a visit to an outpatient clinic, 22 Fmk. The cost for private consultations is naturally higher, and it is advisable to take out the usual forms of health insurance.

In Iceland treatment is state-subsidized; insurance, however, is recommended.

In Norway, British subjects have the same rights to medical aid and help with any expenses for treatment and hospitalization as Norwegians.

In Sweden, American and Canadian citizens will have to pay any charges, as there are no agreements regarding hospital treatment between the countries in question.

TRAVELING IN SCANDINAVIA

BY AIR. SAS and Finnair connect various Scandinavian cities. In Norway, *Braathens* SAFE, and *Wideröe;* in Sweden *Linjeflyg* AB (LIN) have an extensive network of daily services. Approximate fare from Copenhagen to Oslo or Stockholm is 975 Dkr return; using the various discounts available. On certain flights SAS offer reduced return tickets between the Scandinavian capitals, for around SEK 550.

BY SEA OR LAKE. The major boat routes within Scandinavia are operated by car-carrying (as well as passenger) ferries. Services between Sweden and Finland run from Stockholm or nearby ports to Helsinki, Turku and Mariehamn (Åland); Kapellskär (near Stockholm) to Mariehamn and Naantali; also Skellefteå–Pietarsaari, Umeå–Vaasa and Sundsvall–Vaasa.

There are daily sailings between Copenhagen and Oslo. From Jutland in Denmark it is possible to cross directly into Norway and Sweden. Various companies operate from North Jutland to Norway, namely from Frederikshavn to Oslo, Frederikshavn–Larvik, Hanstholm–Arendal, Hanstholm–Kristiansand, and Hirtshals to Kristiansand. From Copenhagen to Sweden only passenger ferries (hydrofoils) leave the city center, but car ferries connect Dragør outside Copenhagen with Limhamn in the south of Sweden. The Elsinore (Helsingør)–Helsingborg route with frequent departures takes both cars and passengers and is the shortest connection available. Other cars ferries provide regular services between Denmark and Sweden, running from Grenå to Varberg or Helsingborg and from Frederikshavn to Gothenburg.

DFDS operates between Copenhagen and Oslo, the Faroe Islands, and Helsinki. P&O Ferries links the Faroes, Bergen (Norway) and Hanstholm (Denmark) with Iceland and Scotland during the summer.

Tours. The most famous of Scandinavian coastal voyages is the 11-day trip from Bergen via North Cape to Kirkenes and return, leaving Bergen daily. A similar round-Iceland voyage takes about a week.

In Norway summer cruises along the fabulous coastline to North Cape and even to Spitsbergen are offered by *Chandris, Cunard, North Star Line, Norwegian American Line* and *Royal Viking Line.* The Telemark Canal, a famous inland waterway, runs from Skien on the Oslo fjord to Dalen among the mountains of Telemark. Also during the summer, the world's oldest paddle steamer, the *Skibladner,* plods its way from Eidsvoll to Lillehammer on Lake Mjøsa, the largest lake in Norway.

In Finland you can cruise for up to a week—over some 700 miles—on Europe's largest lake area, the Saimaa lake region, eating and sleeping on board. There are also interesting trips across the Gulf of Finland from Helsinki to Tallinn in Estonia (visa essential).

In Sweden, there is the delightful trip on the Göta Canal from Gothenburg to Stockholm, through the country's lovely Lake District. The trip takes 3 days and there are several sailings weekly.

HYDROFOILS. There are frequent daily services between Copenhagen and Malmö (35-minute crossing). There is also a hydrofoil service on the Finnish lake of Päijänne.

Hydrofoil boats are widely used in Norway. Stavanger, Haugesund and Bergen on the west coast are linked by hydrofoil services, as are the Ryfylke fjords from Stavanger, the Hardangerfjord from Bergen. Speed boat services, too, from Bergen to the Sognefjord and Nordfjord areas.

BY TRAIN. Rail travel in Scandinavia is to be recommended, not only for the comfort of the majority of the rolling stock, but also its cleanliness and general efficiency of the systems. Speeds may not match those in France or Germany, but the majority of the routes are scenic or have considerable interest. Fares are based on a sliding scale, the farther you travel the cheaper per kilometer it gets. Second-class travel can be undertaken anywhere without any worries as overall standards are high.

Iceland is the only Scandinavian country that is without any rail system at all. The problems created by the nature of its terrain and severe climate make the building of railroads impossible.

From the U.K., Esbjerg, on the west of Jutland, is the arrival point for the ferries from Harwich and Newcastle, with rail services direct to Odense and Copenhagen. Also, there are good connections to Frederikshavn in northern Jutland for the ferries to both Norway and Sweden. Coming from the European mainland the routes are via the Puttgarden–Rødbyhavn train ferry; to Copenhagen via Flensburg to join the Esbjerg line at Fredericia.

From Copenhagen, routes go to Stockholm via the train ferry connecting Helsingør and Helsingborg (Sweden) and also to Gothenburg, Sweden's second city, and to Oslo, the Norwegian capital, again using the train ferry. Three daytime express (and one overnight) trains link Oslo and Stockholm daily and from Malmö, in southern Sweden, there are several fast trains each day to Stockholm, as there are from Gothenburg.

In Norway, the routes from Oslo go south and west to Kristiansand and Stavanger, north and west to Geilo and Bergen, north to Lillehammer, Dombås and Trondheim. From the last another line continues north across the Arctic Circle to Bodø. The line that services Narvik comes from across the border in Sweden and is not directly linked to the main Norwegian system.

In Finland, routes go west from Helsinki to the port of Turku (ferry connections to Sweden and the Åland Islands), east to the Russian border and on to Leningrad, north-west to Tampere and on to Lapland via Oulu. Other routes take the lake and forest regions of central and eastern Finland to Imatra. As the Finnish railroad gauge is "broad", that is 5 ft (152.5 cm) as against the "standard" gauge of 4 ft 8½ in. (143.5 cm) through most of Europe, there are no through trains from the other parts of Scandinavia. But as the Russian gauge is the same, there are through services from the U.S.S.R.

Reduced fares. The railway networks of the four Scandinavian countries—Denmark, Norway, Sweden, and Finland—have combined to offer an excellent runabout ticket called the *Nordturist*. This gives unlimited travel for 21 days on all the railways in these countries, as well as on railway operated bus routes (not in cities), and on ferries operated by the respective railway companies. Considering the vast area which this covers it is one of the best bargains going even if you have to pay extra when on non–railway ferries.

The cost in 2nd class for 21 days is about Dkr. 1,430. In 1st class the price is Dkr. 2,140. The ticket can be purchased either direct from any of the participant railways (identification such as a passport must be shown if you buy it within Scandinavia), or their main agents.

In the U.K. the main issuing agent is the Norwegian State Railways, 21/4 Cockspur Street, London SW1Y 5DA. Good value as the pass is, remember that you need to do quite a lot of traveling to make it worthwhile.

In *Denmark* Rover Tickets are no longer available. Tourists may find the one-month tickets useful. These cost Dkr. 1,400 (2nd class) or Dkr. 1,600 (1st Class), and cover unlimited travel on all domestic Danish DSB–trains, buses and ferries.

In *Sweden,* there are no "runabout" tickets as such for country-wide travel. But in addition to the concessions for the elderly (see below), there are family tickets applicable where three or more members of one family travel together. These give savings of about 25% on standard fares. It is advisable to buy a discount card for 180 SEK, giving you 40% reductions. Buy at any railway station, but remember you'll need a photo. At Stockholm and Gothenburg there are local, 3-day runabout tickets covering city trains, buses, trams and ferries.

In *Norway,* a "bargain rail pass" is available in two versions. A one–way ticket valid for 7 days and covering a distance of up to 750 km (470 miles), which costs $45; and a one–way, 7 day ticket with unlimited mileage costing $60. These tickets are valid all week except Fridays and at Easter. Stop–overs are unlimited, and the tickets can be purchased at any railroad station in Norway.

In *Finland* the *Finnrail Pass* is issued for 8, 15, and 22 days. The 2nd class fare costs 270, 390 and 530 Fmk. respectively. In 1st class the prices are $405, 585 and 795 Fmk.

In *Denmark,* reductions are granted to any "group" of three or more persons traveling together. Other favorable suggestions are *Excursion Tickets* i.e. train ticket and admission to Danish sights, available from DSB at special low rates. In Copenhagen the HT (Copenhagen Transport) offers bargain one-day *tourist tickets* valid for trains and buses in Copenhagen and North Sealand.

Senior Citizens. There are considerable discounts available to travelers over 65. The only proof that is needed is your passport. There is a special low fare in Sweden, probably the lowest in Europe. There are also special rail reductions (often one-way rates for roundtrips). In Finland, senior citizens of over 65 years and disabled persons can get a card at a nominal cost from any railway station entitling them to good reductions. Sweden has no minimum mileage on their bounty, though most others require a trip to be fairly long. There are reductions on much bus and sea travel, too. Ask at the national tourist offices for further details.

A **Eurailpass** is a convenient, all-inclusive ticket that can save you money on over 100,000 miles of railroads and railroad-operated buses, ferries, river and lake steamers, hydrofoils and some Mediterranean crossings in 16 countries of Western Europe. It provides the holder with unlimited travel at rates of: 15 days for $260, 21 days for $330, 1 month for $410, 2 months for $560, 3 months for $680; and a second–class Youthpass (anyone through age 26) fare of 2 months for $370. Children under 12 go for half-fare, under 4 go free. Eurailpass prices cover first-class passage, reservation fees and surcharges for the Trans Europe Express service. Youthpasses are good only for second-class travel. Available only to those residents who live outside Europe or North Africa, the pass must be bought from an authorized agent in the Western hemisphere or Japan *before* you leave for Europe. Apply through your travel agent; or the general agents for North America. *French National Railroads,* Eurorailpass Division, 610 Fifth Ave., New York, N.Y. 10020; or through the *German Federal Railroad,* 11 West 42nd St., New York, N.Y. 10036 and 45 Richmond St. W., Toronto M5H 1Z2, Ontario, Canada. To get full value from your pass, be sure not to have it date-stamped until you actually use it for the first time. For complete details, write to Trains, P.O. Box M, Staten Island, New York 10305.

 PRESERVED STEAM RAILWAYS AND MUSEUMS. All four Scandinavian countries have at least one active steam railway operated by enthusiasts in the summer months. As dates and times of operations of these vary (and also change at fairly short notice in some cases) we advise that you contact both the main tourist offices of the country concerned and also the local offices in the districts where the railways are located.

Sweden. Best of all with seven preserved railways at present.
Österlans Museijarnvag. Brosarp to St. Olaf in Skåne. Standard gauge, about 8½ miles (14 km) long.
Ohs Bruks Jarnveg. Ohs Bruk to Bor in Småland. Narrow gauge, about 9 miles (15 km) long.
Museibanan Anten Gräfsnäs. Anten to Gräfsnäs in Västergötland, not far from Alingsås. Narrow gauge, about 7 miles (11 km) long.
Ostra Sodermanslands Jarnveg. Mariefred to Laggesta. Narrow gauge, about 2½ miles (4 km) long. Has the oldest steam engine, built in 1888.
Roslagens Järnvägar. Uppsala to Faringe in Uppland. Narrow gauge, about 18½ miles (30 km).

Jädraås Tallås Museibanan. Runs in the country near Gävle (see below) for about 22 miles (35 km), making it the longest preserved railway; standard gauge.

Gotlands Hesselby Järnvägar. On the island of Gotland. Narrow gauge, about ¾ mile (1 km) long.

The Swedish Railway Musuem is at the town of Gävle, about 110 miles north of Stockholm. A fact sheet is available at your nearest Tourist Office.

Denmark. One or two private and industrial lines have occasional steam specials. But there are also three preserved railways.

Maribo to Bandholm. On the island of Lolland, standard gauge and about 5 miles (8 km) long. Scenic route with collection of engines and rolling stock.

Mariager to Handest. In Jutland; standard gauge, just under 5 miles (8 km).

Bryrup to Vrads. Again in Jutland, 2 miles (3 km) of standard gauge line.

Helsingør (Elsinore) to Gilleleje. Normal Danish railway route with steam specials in summer.

Vejle to Jelling. In Jutland, runs through beautiful hilly countryside (14 km).

The Danish National Railway Museum is in Odense on the island of Funen.

Norway. There are three preserved railways here.

Setesdalsbanen. Grovane to Breiholen not far from Kristiansand in southern Norway. Narrow gauge, about 3 miles (5 km) long.

Hölandsbanen. Sørumsand to Fossum about 24 miles east of Oslo. Narrow gauge, just under 2½ miles (4 km) long.

Krøderbanen. Kroderen to Vikersund, about 50 km (31 miles) NW of Oslo. Standard gauge, 40 km (25 miles) long.

The Norwegian National Railway Museum is at Hamar, about 80 miles north of Oslo. In summer a narrow gauge engine hauls wooden coaches over a short length of track in the museum grounds.

Finland. *Veturien Ystävät* (Finnish Railway Society); *Humppila–Forssa Railway.* A regular service is operated on a 4½-mile (7 km) stretch of narrow gauge line between Jokioinen and Minkiö; it has three engines, one woodburning. The National Railway Museum of Finland is at Hyvinkää.

BY BUS. Scandinavia depends on buses in the rural areas. Thus it is possible to tour to almost any place you choose by local bus lines. Some buses carry mail and small parcels as well as passengers, and almost all have room for bicycles (mostly free in Denmark) and skis. In Norway many bus services connect with rail and ferry services, which works very well. One of the longest bus services in Europe runs above the Arctic Circle—from Fauske to Kirkenes near the Russian frontier—a trip of 4 days. Iceland's *Omnibus Passport* and *Full Circle Passport* on scheduled bus services offer considerable advantages (see *Practical Information* for Iceland).

BY CAR. (For car ferries see *By Sea* above.) Being motorized is the best way to see a great deal of Scandinavia in a short time. Roads in Denmark are unusually good. In Norway, Sweden and Finland the distances are too great in relation to the population to permit paving much but the main highways between cities and the major long distance routes. Iceland is especially weak in this respect. The only stretch of highway is between Keflavik and Reykjavik and is a toll road. Roads on the outskirts of towns are surfaced, but elsewhere they consist of scraped lava, occasionally disappearing altogether when a riverbed changes course, though there is usually a crossing place. In consequence, although distances are not very great, journeys by road can be time-consuming and this must be allowed for in any itineraries. The completion of the road across the southeast corner of the country has meant the construction of some particularly fine bridges, and there is now a road right round Iceland which has opened up previously inaccessible spots.

Moreover, some roads are narrow by British or American standards, particularly in Norway, where many mountain routes had to be carved out of rock. Thus you can seldom expect to average more than 30 miles an hour. You may drive to the North Cape, 1,400 miles from Oslo, following E6 most of the time. From Kåfjord on the Porsanger Fjord, there is a 45 minute car-ferry service to Honningsvåg, and then 35 km by bus or car to North Cape—the northernmost point of Europe.

You drive on the *right* in all Scandinavian countries. In Denmark, the town speed limit is 37 m.p.h. (60 km.p.h.), in other Scandinavian towns, 31 m.p.h. (50 km.p.h.), except in Iceland, where it is 27 m.p.h. (45 km.p.h.). Denmark has a general limit of 50 m.p.h. (80 km.p.h.), but 60 m.p.h. (100 km.p.h.) on motorways. (Maximum speed for trailers on motorways is 70 km.p.h.) In Iceland, the general limit is 45 m.p.h. (70 km.p.h.), in Norway 50 m.p.h. (80 km.p.h.), in Sweden 56 m.p.h. (90 km.p.h.) and in Finland 50 m.p.h. (80 km.p.h.) in non built-up areas.

As the liquor regulations might lead you to suspect, Scandinavians are strict about drinking. When it comes to driving a car, they are absolutely inflexible. If you are involved in an accident, a blood test is taken as a matter of course, and if you have had more than a mild whisky and soda, you will spend up to 3 weeks in jail. No exceptions are made for anyone, so you'd better take a taxi if you've been out on the town. If you do not wish to drink, turn your empty glass upside down; this signal is universally respected.

Motoring itineraries will be found in the regional chapters, and if you don't want to take your own automobile there are excellent hire facilities (see below). Several firms offer suggested itineraries covered by a flat rental rate. In Sweden, incorrectly parked cars are towed away and dipped headlights used all day.

Documents. For Denmark, Norway, Sweden, and Finland, you need only your national driving license. In Sweden, unless your driving license is issued in English, French, Dutch, Italian, Spanish or German, you must produce a special certificate confirming the authenticity and validity of the license, written in Swedish, English or French. For Iceland, an international license is necessary. Internationally valid third-party insurance (Green Card) is required, except for citizens of EEC countries. Your automobile association can assist you in these matters.

Maps. The Scandinavian touring and automobile clubs will supply you with maps and itineraries. All publish excellent touring books and have branch offices in the larger towns in addition to the following headquarters.

Denmark: *De Forenede Danske Motorejere* (FDM), Blegdamsvej 124, in Copenhagen. The official Geodaetisk Institut maps, available in most bookshops, are among the world's best.

Finland: *The Automobile and Touring Club,* Kansakoulunkatu 10, Helsinki. Excellent maps of Finland on various scales are published by that country's Map Service of the National Board of Survey. They can be obtained from main bookshops in Finland or from the Map Service shop at Eteläesplanadi 10, Helsinki 13.

Iceland: excellent maps are available from the Iceland tourist bureau.

Norway: *Kongelig Norsk Automobilklub* (KNA), Parkveien 68, and *Norges Automobil-Forbund,* Storgate 2, both in Oslo.

Sweden: *Kungliga Automobil Klubben* (KAK), and *Motormännens Riksförbund* (M), Sturegatan 32, in Stockholm.

Fuel prices are subject to increase. The following are approximate indications for super grade per liter; in Denmark: 6.19 Dkr; in Finland 3.54–3.68 Fmk; in Iceland: 12.20 Ikr (regular only); in Norway: 4.60 Nkr (varies in the north); in Sweden: 4.29 Skr (cheaper gas in Sweden can be bought at the self-service stations, open 24 hours; they are fully automated, but you need 10 Skr notes).

Car hire. *Avis* and *Scandinavia Car Rental,* among other firms, offer self-drive cars throughout Scandinavia ranging from Volkswagens to Land-Rovers. In season a special free return of rented cars between Oslo/Bergen, or vice versa, and Oslo/Stockholm/Malmö/Copenhagen is worth your notice. Chauffeur-driven cars are also available. Prices are roughly equivalent to U.S. and U.K. prices. All addresses in *Practical Information* sections for each country. Package fly-drive arrangements with unlimited mileage are also available offering flexibility and advantageous rates.

In Sweden there is a low-price go-as-you-please rental check which can only be bought outside the country. Low rental rates are also offered as part of rail and air packages.

In Iceland, Land-Rovers and minibuses are especially suitable; they cost more and must be booked well in advance. Rental rates are higher than elsewhere here and a sales tax of 20% does nothing to help, but fly-drive arrangements bring costs down.

 CONVERSION TABLES. One of the most confusing experiences for many motorists is their first encounter with the metric system. The following quick conversion table may help to speed you on your way.

Kilometers into Miles. This simple chart will help you to convert to both miles and kilometers. If you want to convert from miles into kilometers read from the center column to the right, if from kilometers into miles, from the center column to the left. Example: 5 miles=8.5 kilometers, 5 kilometers=3.1 miles.

Miles		Kilometers	Miles		Kilometers
0.6	1	1.6	37.3	60	96.6
1.2	2	3.2	43.5	70	112.3
1.9	3	4.8	49.7	80	128.7
2.5	4	6.3	55.9	90	144.8
3.1	5	8.0	62.1	100	160.9
3.7	6	9.6	124.3	200	321.9
4.3	7	11.3	186.4	300	482.8
5.0	8	12.9	248.5	400	643.7
5.6	9	14.5	310.7	500	804.7
6.2	10	16.1	372.8	600	965.6
12.4	20	32.2	434.9	700	1,126.5
18.6	30	48.3	497.1	800	1,287.5
24.8	40	64.4	559.2	900	1,448.4
31.0	50	80.5	621.4	1,000	1,609.3

Motor fuel: an Imperial gallon is approximately 4½ liters; a U.S. gallon about 3¾ liters.

Liters	Imp. gals.	U.S. gals.
1	0.22	0.26
5	1.10	1.32
10	2.20	2.64
20	4.40	5.28
40	8.80	10.56
100	22.01	26.42

Tire pressure: measured in kilograms per square centimeter instead of pounds per square inch; the ratio is approximately 14.2 lbs. to 1 kg.

Lbs per sq. in.	Kg per sq. cm	Lbs per sq. in.	Kg per sq. cm
20	1.406	26	1.828
22	1.547	28	1.969
24	1.687	30	2.109

LEAVING SCANDINAVIA

CUSTOMS RETURNING HOME. Americans who are out of the United States at least 48 hours and have claimed no exemption during the previous 30 days are entitled to bring in duty-free up to $400 worth of articles for bona fide gifts or for their own personal use. Personal purchases must accompany you on your return. The value of each item is determined by the price actually paid (so save your receipts). Every member of a family is entitled to this same exemption, regardless of age, and the allowance can be pooled. For the next $1,000 worth of goods beyond that first $400, inspectors will assess a flat 10% duty, rather than hitting you with different percentages for different types of goods.

Small, duty-free, gifts to friends may be mailed (but not more than one to any address with a written notation on the package, "Unsolicited Gift—value less than $50"). These packages, however, may not include perfumes, tobacco, or liquor.

If your purchases exceed your exemption, list the items that are most expensive under your exemption and pay duty on the cheaper items. Any article you fail to declare cannot latter be claimed under your exemption. To facilitate the actual customs examination it's convenient to pack all your purchases in one suitcase. Remember that use does not exempt an article. That suit or watch that you bought in Europe and then wore there is nonetheless subject to duty when you reenter your own country.

Not more than 100 cigars and 200 cigarettes may be imported duty-free per person, nor more than a liter of wine or liquor (none at all if your passport indicates you are from a "dry" state, or if you are under 21 years of age). Only one bottle of perfume that is trademarked in the United States may be brought in, plus a reasonable quantity of other brands.

Antiques are defined, for customs purposes, as articles over 100 years old and are admitted duty-free. If there's any question of age, you may be asked to supply proof.

Do not bring home foreign meats, fruits, plants, soil, or other agricultural items when you return to the United States. To do so will delay you at the port of entry. It is illegal to bring in foreign agricultural items without permission, because they can spread destructive plant or animal pests and diseases. For more information, read the pamphlet "Customs Hints", or write to: "Quarantines", Department of Agriculture, Federal Center Bldg., Hyattsville, Md. 20782.

Major purchases such as furniture, sets of china, and the like have to be shipped separately, of course. Before you do this, however, consider the pros and cons carefully. Unless you deal with a thoroughly reliable and experienced store, you run the risk that either the goods you ordered won't be sent at all or else will be so poorly packed that they are damaged in transit, two alternatives that you are largely helpless to remedy after your return home. Assuming that you

are dealing with a reputable firm, insist on finding out exactly what the shipping charges will amount to. In many cases, shipments such as these are handed over to customs brokers and freight forwarders in your country whose charges may be in addition to what you have already paid. Americans in particular sometimes find themselves having to pay supplemental charges on shipments whose value may actually be less than the cost of shipping. Make sure, too, that your shipment is insured and that the proper customs documents are attached.

Residents of **Canada** may, after 7 days out of the country, and upon written declaration, claim an exemption of $150 a year plus an allowance of 40 ounces of liquor, 50 cigars, 200 cigarettes and 2 lb of tobacco. Personal gifts should be mailed as "Unsolicited Gift—Value Under $25". For further details, ask for the Canada Customs brochure "I Declare".

British subjects. There are two levels of duty free allowance for people entering the U.K.; one, for goods bought outside the EEC or for goods bought in a duty free shop within the EEC; two, for goods bought in an EEC country but not in a duty free shop.

In the first category you may import duty free: 200 cigarettes or 100 cigarillos or 50 cigars or 250 grammes of tobacco (*Note* if you live outside Europe, these allowances are doubled); plus one liter of alcoholic drinks over 22% vol. (38.8% proof) or two liters of alcoholic drinks not over 22% vol. or fortified or sparkling wine; plus two liters of still table wine; plus 50 grammes of perfume; plus nine fluid ounces of toilet water; plus other goods to the value of £28.

In the second category you may import duty free: 300 cigarettes or 150 cagarillos or 75 cigars or 400 grammes of tobacco; plus 1½ liters of alcoholic drinks over 22% vol. (38.8% proof) or three liters of alcoholic drinks not over 22% vol. or fortified or sparkling wine; plus four liters of still table wine; plus 75 grammes of perfume; plus 13 fluid ounces of toilet water; plus other goods to the value of £120 (*Note* though it is not classified as an alcoholic drink by EEC countries for Customs' purposes and is thus considered part of the "other goods" allowance, you may not import more than 50 liters of beer).

In addition, no animals or pets of any kind may be brought into the U.K. The penalties for doing so are severe and are strictly enforced; there are *no* exceptions. Similarly, fresh meats, plants and vegetables, controlled drugs and firearms and ammunition may not be brought into the U.K. There are no restrictions on the import or export of British and foreign currencies.

 DUTY FREE is not what it once was. You may not be paying tax on your bottle of whiskey or perfume, but you are certainly contributing to somebody's profits. Duty free shops are big business these days and mark ups are often around 100 to 200%. So don't be seduced by the idea that because it's called "duty free", it's a bargain. Very often prices are not much different from your local discount store and in the case of perfume or jewelry they can be even higher.

As a general rule of thumb, duty free stores on the ground offer better value than buying in the air. Also, if you buy duty free goods on a plane, remember that the range is likely to be limited and that if you are paying in a different currency to that of the airline, their rate of exchange often bears only a passing resemblance to the official one.

THE
SCANDINAVIAN
SCENE

Detail from Picture-stone: Gotland, 8th century.

SCANDINAVIAN HISTORY

Exploring Abroad—Pioneering at Home

No two people are likely to agree on just what is meant by the term Scandinavia. Almost everyone would admit that Norway and Sweden are Scandinavian countries, but when it comes to Denmark there are always those who claim that the Danes are more a part of the Continent than the North. Others point out that the Finns belong to an entirely different culture, at least as far as race and language are concerned. Then there's the question of whether or not to include Iceland and Greenland or even the Shetlands and the Orkneys as parts of Scandinavia. As if the debate weren't confused enough already, you're sure to find someone who'll try to prove that Great Britain and the United States are Scandinavian too. After all, a Danish king sat on the English throne, and it wasn't much later that the Normans (or Northmen) crossed the Channel and did it all over again. Similarly, America was discovered by a Scandinavian, and the first president of the United States traced his ancestry back to an early king who lived near Trondheim, Norway. The most devastating way to put an end to this kind of talk is to make reference to the fact that Russia was founded by the Swedes, but it's far safer to stay off the topic completely unless you're planning to leave Scandinavia quite soon.

For whatever consolation it offers, it's worth noting that the situation was just as perplexing a thousand years ago as it is today. When

Denmark, Norway and Sweden first emerge from the mists of pre-history, we find them split up into a great number of small kingdoms constantly fighting with one another. Occasionally local differences would be settled long enough to wage war on a grander scale, but however united or disunited the Scandinavians happened to be at any particular time, at least they were always democratic—everyone had a sword and was permitted to join in the fun. A few of the hardier individuals had so much fun that they went "berserk", that is, they threw off their shirts *(serk)*, cast aside their shields, and went into battle bare-chested and armed only with a club. This was the supreme test of courage, and if you were fortunate enough to survive, you were entitled to move three stools closer to the head of the table.

Presently, of course, nearly everybody was sitting at the head of the table, and although this made things even more democratic than they had been before, it did lead to overcrowding. Since the soil was too poor to afford much of a living, the only solution was to take to the sea, and soon the Scandinavians were rowing and sailing to the corners of the then known world, sometimes even beyond. For more than two centuries, starting about 800 A.D., the Vikings struck fear into the hearts of good Christian men and women. *Vik,* incidentally, still means "creek" or "bay" in Danish, Swedish and Norwegian, and thus the Vikings were "Creeklings", or the people who would suddenly sweep out of a bay to capture some passing vessel. Alternatively, they swept into other people's bays, leaving behind them, among other things, the suffix "wich" in a great number of English placenames. "Wich", of course, is no more than a derivative of *vik.* When they got to France they were called Normans, a word which today is still pronounced the same way as the noun *nordmann* (the "d" is silent), which means a Norwegian.

Anyhow, the Danes were among the first to build themselves an empire. They conquered England about the year 900, and King Canute ruled Denmark and England jointly for 18 years. In fact, Danish power stretched east to the Oder River and north to Skåne, the southern province of Sweden. Meanwhile the Norwegians were exploring the coast of Labrador and colonizing Iceland and Greenland. The Swedes in turn had built trading centres at Novgorod and Kiev, not only laying the foundations of the Russian state but giving it their name, *Rus,* a local word for Swede.

Sea power was the key to the Scandinavian conquests and enabled their sphere of influence to include at one time not only Scandinavia as we know it today, but also most of the British Isles, Greenland and Iceland, the Baltic states, Normandy, Sicily, and parts of the Byzantine Empire. In Constantinople the Varangian Guard, a Viking *corps d'élite,* was the military power behind the throne. The Guard was well paid for its services, and many of the Vikings who took part in it returned home with enough Byzantine gold to support a large army. Thus Harald Hårdråde built up his fortune as Empress Zoe's strong man, returned to Norway, and soon was king. His trip to the East evidently whetted his appetite for travel, because in 1066 he invaded England in an attempt to recapture the English crown. Harald the Norwegian, however, was defeated by Harold the Saxon at Stamford Bridge in a battle which may have contributed to William the Conqueror's victory at Hastings a few months later.

Finland enters the Scandinavian scene at about this time. They had settled their forested, swampy land at about the beginning of the Christian era and history has little to say about them in those early centuries. Now, while Christian knights from France and Britain emigrated to the Holy Land, there to die gloriously while chopping up the infidel, the Swedes decided to start their own "crusade". Around 1160, King Erik marched to Finland, overran the country, and added it to the Swedish crown. Thereafter the Finns were mostly subjects of Sweden for nearly 700 years.

Dawn of the Christian Era

As the Viking Age came to a close, Denmark, Norway and Sweden were adopting the Christian faith. Baptizing, to be sure, was often a violent process, and those who displayed a tepid interest in heaven were sometimes speeded on their way to Valhalla. If the Cross and the sword went hand in hand, so did the Cross and gold. Viking prosperity had been founded as much on trade as on plunder, and as the economic importance of Western Europe increased, some individuals found it expedient to embrace the new faith for business reasons. This fusion of the old paganism with the new religion is nowhere more vivid than in the Scandinavian stave churches, a number of which have survived to the present day. On the top of the tower you will always find a cross, but on the eaves and along the door jamb, dragons and other pagan symbols are carved just for safety's sake. This is not to say that Christianity wasn't taken seriously, but simply that with populations so small and communications so difficult there could be no mass conversion. Instead, the Viking era shades off imperceptibly into the Christian era.

Anglo-Saxon missionaries were instrumental in bringing Christianity to Scandinavia, but during the 13th century the links with the West grew weaker and Scandinavia fell under the pernicious influence of the Hanseatic League. The merchants of Hamburg and Lübeck secured for themselves far-reaching privileges and gradually built up a monopoly of trade all through the Baltic. The Hansa quays in Bergen on Norway's west coast still remain as evidence of the Hanseatic power, and, indeed, Helsinki was founded largely with an eye to destroying this power. Denmark was probably affected the most, since the league's economic control led to political alliances with Pomerania, Mecklenburg, and other German principalities. As trade passed more and more into foreign hands, Scandinavian sea power declined to the vanishing point, and it was nearly 500 years before the rise of an independent America re-opened the seas and made a revival possible.

The Middle Ages

Scandinavian history in the Middle Ages presents a confused picture of succeeding dynasties, recalcitrant earls and scheming bishops. Following the Viking tradition, Danes, Norwegians and Swedes continued to borrow each other's kings and queens with such charming abandon that the student of history is never quite certain who was king of what at any particular time. This friendly custom is still in vogue: Norway's late King Haakon was born a Dane.

After centuries as a Baltic power, Sweden begins to come more and more in conflict with Russia. Denmark follows suit and finds herself embroiled not only with the Russians but with several of the German states, and Norway, having lost a third of her population to the plague in 1349 and 1350, loses her royal dynasty too and unites with Denmark in 1450.

This period is also notable for the Kalmar Union, a step in the direction of unity which, had it succeeded, would have made one nation out of the whole of Scandinavia. From 1389 to 1521, Denmark, Norway and Sweden were joined for years at a time under the same ruler. The Danes were the most powerful element, and for a while Norway and Sweden played distinctly secondary roles. Danish King Christian II even went so far as to attack the Swedes and occupy Stockholm. His policy backfired, however, when he attempted to destroy all opposition by putting a number of prominent Swedes to death in the celebrated massacre of Stockholm in 1520. A few years later the Dano-Swedish union was at an end, and the Swedes, under the leadership of the warrior-king, Gustav Vasa, went from strength to strength.

While Sweden was making herself supreme in the Baltic, the Norwegians found themselves regarded as little better than a Danish province, Danish-speaking officials and a Danish Statholder represented the joint king with such careful attention to duty that even today the Norwegian language, in its written form at least, is almost as close to Danish as American-English is to British-English.

The same was true of Iceland, whose connections with Denmark had lasted since 1380. The intervening centuries saw Iceland suffering at the hands of pirates and from the imposition of a trade monopoly. In 1798, the Althing (believed to be the oldest parliament in the world) met at Thingvellir for the last time and was dissolved in 1800.

Finnish land bordering on the Gulf of Bothnia was populated primarily by descendants of Swedish settlers, and the Swedes came more and more to think of Finland as part of their own country. In 1616 the Finns were granted a measure of local autonomy, but their intense patriotism together with their dreams of independence made any foreign rule unpopular, however temperate it might be.

Romantic Monarchs

The Reformation spread quickly over Scandinavia about the same time that the yoke of the Hanseatic League was being cast off. Denmark accepted the new teachings, and Norway was bound to follow. Sweden's Gustavus Adolphus built a new empire on the shores of the Baltic after brilliant campaigns had neutralised the Danes, the Poles and the Russians, and his entry into the Thirty Years' War saved the Protestant cause in Germany. Some 20 years later, Charles X further consolidated Sweden's position by wresting from Denmark the fertile Swedish provinces of Skåne, Halland and Blekinge, and by bringing the Estonians and the Letts under Swedish rule.

Perhaps the most romantic of all the Swedish soldier-kings was Charles XII, one of the foremost generals of his age and the subject of Voltaire's famous biography. Attacked simultaneously by Russia, Poland and Denmark in 1700, Charles fought a number of brilliant battles, his victory over the Russians at Narva being one of the most spectacular. Forced by unfavourable weather to abandon his march on Moscow, Charles moved south to the Ukraine where his defeat at Poltava in 1709 ended his dreams of a new Swedish empire. The peace settlement saw Sweden stripped of her Baltic conquests, including part of Finland. In a desperate attempt to recoup his losses Charles tried to take Norway, but instead he met a warrior's death.

In the 18th century we find Sweden preoccupied with internal problems, a period which has been called the Age of Liberty. Constitutional reform, the rise of the party system and constant efforts to limit the power of the king are some of the recurring themes of this era. Denmark passed from dependence on Russia to dependence on Germany, a process which reached its story-book climax with Count Struensee. The latter was a German doctor who became the lover of Queen Caroline Matilde, wife of the mad King Christian VII. The Count was responsible for a number of reforms and doubtless would have instituted others had not the reactionary party stepped in and put an end to both his philanthropy and his philandering.

At the same time in Sweden a king, Gustavus III, little known in the outside world except for the fact that he figures as the leading character in Verdi's *Un Ballo in Maschera,* was creating a Golden Age in the arts. Much of Sweden's rich heritage of architecture, painting, sculpture and the theater is due to the patronage of Gustavus and his mother, a sister of Frederick the Great. His life was full of highly colored incidents and his death by no means the least of them.

The 19th and 20th Centuries

The upheavals of the French Revolution had a decisive influence on the history of all the Scandinavian countries, and by the time Napoleon had been sent packing to his exile at St. Helena, Finland had become a Russian Grand Duchy with the Czar as Grand Duke. A French Marshal, Bernadotte, accepted the Swedish crown, and soon received the Norwegian one also. Norway had drawn up a new constitution and declared her independence, but failing to gain the support of the Great Powers, after a short war entered into a voluntary union with Sweden. Denmark, allied with Napoleon during most of these troubled years, was left to reflect on the error of her ways and rebuilt the fleet which she had lost to the English under Nelson.

For the whole of Scandinavia the 19th century was a time of great economic and cultural growth while the rest of Europe was distracted by the bloodshed and chaos of internal unrest. Finland, though increasingly oppressed by Russia, enjoyed a golden age in literature, commerce and the sciences. Norway sublimated the mounting friction with her Swedish partner and raised painting and literature to new heights.

In 1864, however, Denmark was attacked by Germany; when the dust settled, the partly German-speaking provinces of Schleswig and Holstein were gone. Bismarck saw to it that they remained German.

In Iceland, an upsurge of nationalism resulted in the reestablishment of the Althing in 1874. In 1903, Denmark appointed a Minister for Iceland instead of a Governor and an Act of Union was signed between the two countries in 1918. This recognized Iceland as an independent, sovereign state under a common king.

Since 1814, Sweden has avoided being embroiled in any war, instead devoting her energies and talents to developing her own resources. This policy has been so successfully pursued that today she ranks as one of the most prosperous countries in Europe. Peace, hard work and common sense—a rather rare combination of virtues if you stop to reflect a moment—have enabled the Swedes to create for themselves a way of life which is both a model for and the envy of the rest of the world. Today her enlightened system of social services has struck a humane and workable balance between the needs of society as a whole and the liberty of the individual.

Norway started the present century by dissolving her union with Sweden in 1905 and inviting a Danish prince to ascend the throne as Haakon the Seventh. Though neutral during the First World War she put her merchant marine, then the fourth largest in the world, at the service of the Allies—and saw half of it sent to the bottom of the ocean by German torpedoes. The 9th of April, 1940, found her at the mercy of Germany again. Five years of occupation followed, during which her people not only refused to have any part in Hitler's "new order" but staged such a gallant resistance that nearly 600,000 Nazi troops were at one time engaged in keeping her subjugated.

Denmark also fell a victim to Nazi agression on the 9th of April. Her resistance was as universal and as resolute as Norway's, and by the war's end her economic life was nearly ruined. Today she has been rebuilt so well that she is stronger than ever before.

Finland's story, however, is more tragic. During the 19th century her Russian rulers alternated between coaxing and bullying, and when the collapse of Russia ushered in the Bolshevik revolution, she seized her opportunity. After a short and bloody civil war the nationalists, partly with German assistance, won the day, and Finland joined the free nations of the world. With great energy and enterprise she set her house in order and was soon established as one of the model democracies. In the winter of 1939–40 she was attacked by Russia and finally crushed despite a united and heroic struggle. In 1941 when Russia and Germany came to blows, Finland sought to win back some of the territory she had been forced to surrender, an attempt which ended by her having to fight the Germans as well as the Russians. Although she stands solidly with the West today, her position next to Russia is a delicate one, a situation requiring moderation and restraint. Neutrality is her firm stand in all international affairs.

While Denmark was being occupied by Nazi troops during the Second World War, Iceland was occupied by British troops. Within a year, they were relieved by American troops. In 1944, a referendum was held in Iceland that resulted in a 97 per cent vote in favor of repealing the

1918 Act of Union with Denmark. On June 17, 1944, the Republic of Iceland was formally proclaimed and, since then, all Iceland's affairs have been in her own hands.

SCANDINAVIAN DEMOCRACY

It Works!

Democracy is a sadly overworked word these days, with very different connotations east and west of the Curtain. So much so, in fact, that it wouldn't be a bad idea if the political scientists invented another more neutral term. Until they do so, however, we must look beyond the word to the reality for which it stands, an easy task for the visitor to Scandinavia. A thoughtful look at the faces of the people, a glance at their way of life, a sense of their warm-hearted hospitality, and you will come away with a renewed faith in the meaning of freedom.

Compared with the other nations of Western Europe, the northern countries have been free of political upheaval since the war. The late King Haakon of Norway returned from his exile in London to find his reputation immeasurably enhanced among the people whom he had refused to surrender to Nazi oppression. King Christian of Denmark was acclaimed for sharing the occupation with his fellow citizens, a symbol of bravery and dignity during a period of continual crisis. In Sweden, love of king and country and faith in the wisdom of neutrality survived the war unblemished, nor did the Finns think any less of their Field Marshal and President, Carl Gustaf Mannerheim, because of his leadership during and after a war which brought them so much tragedy. This is not to say that recovery has been a quick or simple process for any of these countries. Quite the contrary; few nations have made such united and heroic efforts to recoup their losses.

Scandinavian history is singularly free of revolution and tyranny. Although parliamentary government matured only a bit over a hundred years ago, respect for the rights of the individual, a distrust of hasty reform, and affection for institutions and systems of proven worth have long been ingrained in the Nordic character. Autocratic kings have been curiosities who didn't last very long, probably because the theory of divine right never caught on among people used to ruling themselves. Since Viking times, the king has been regarded as first among equals, and if he couldn't lead, well, someone was found who could.

On first thought it sometimes seems incongruous that countries famous for their moderate brand of socialism should at the same time believe in royalty. The answer to this paradox requires no metaphysics, as you'll discover when you brush elbows with the Swedish king in a Stockholm theater lobby, when you meet the Danish royal family cycling along a rustic lane, or when you learn that the Norwegian Crown Prince underwent all the hardships of a military winter exercise along with the other youths. If you stop and stare, you may be accused of intruding on their privacy. The fact of the matter is that these monarchs provide the stabilizing influence, free from all party ties, and the continuity which the Scandinavians appreciate. It's probably no exaggeration to say that if the crown were abolished in any of the three countries, the king would be the favoured candidate for president.

Parliamentary government has equally ancient and honorable traditions in the history of the North. At Thingvellir, in Iceland, the world's first parliament, called the Althing, was set up in 930 and has been going almost ever since. The old Viking *tings* were the forerunners of the present-day national assemblies. At these gatherings of the chief men of the kingdom, which were attended by representatives from every province, the king would debate with his subjects such questions as the raising of taxes and the passing of laws.

Today every adult votes in general elections. Women acquired the franchise earlier in Scandinavia than anywhere else in the world and serve not only in Parliament but in the Cabinet. Perhaps operating on the theory that the fairer sex is also competent the Danes have appointed ladies as Ministers of Trade and Ecclesiastical Affairs, whereas the Norwegians chose one to head the Ministry of Family Affairs and Consumers' Interests.

In every sphere of life sex equality is the accepted principle. Even the Church, in Denmark, Norway and Sweden, has thrown its doors open to man's better half. In spite of the mere males' not infrequent antipathy to being looked down upon by females—albeit from a pulpit—several such feminine preachers have already been ordained. Other lasses readily find jobs as wireless operators on board merchant ships, no doubt revelling in the thought that their words echo halfway around the world.

Untroubled by what's happening to the short waves, the average Scandinavian will probably point with most pride to the system of social security under which he lives. There is no question in his mind that the state has just as great an obligation to safeguard the welfare of the private citizen as has the private citizen the duty of pulling his full weight for the common weal. Instead of each rowing separately, they row together, and the resulting wave has swept far beyond their own shores. The practical fruits of this belief are found in unemployment insurance, care of the aged and infirm, free education, free dental treatment for school children, maternity benefits, and a host of other measures which, however commonplace they may be in the North, are still hotly debated in other countries considered no less democratic.

Nobility and Equality

In the eyes of the state all are equal. Sweden and Denmark still have counts and barons, but the privileges of the nobility were done away with a century or more ago. Norway went a step farther and abolished titles and privileges both. Equality is, of course, more than a matter of form. The services of medical specialists are available to rich and poor alike, and there are enough thoroughly trained doctors to assure everyone of getting the best that money and science can provide. Scandinavian hospitals and clinics are models of efficiency as well as architecture; thus it is no accident that the physicians they train rank at the top of their profession. Nor is it a freak that the Scandinavian countries consistently lead other nations in such dry but revealing matters as health statistics and mortality tables.

Higher education is similarly open to all. The fisherman's son from Norway's Lofoten Islands, the farmer's daughter from Jutland, the lumberman's children from the forests of Finnish Karelia, and the steelworker's boy from Luleå, all have the best educational facilities open to them and—what is more—take full advantage of them. Brains are thought of as a national asset, like anything else, and the idea of letting them go to waste, apart from the human injustice involved, strikes the Scandinavian with horror.

The principle of equality extends even to the illegitimate child, whose rights and benefits are regarded as being unimpaired by the life-style of its parents: if necessary, the mother and baby receive aid from the state.

Among the duties owed to society by the Scandinavian citizen is that of defending his country in time of war. All the armies are based on conscription, and every able-bodied male is called up for a period of at least six months' training at the age of 18 or 19. The only "regulars" are, practically speaking, those officers and noncommissioned officers who act as instructors, general staff, and the like. The Scandinavians were long committed to a policy of pacifism and neutrality, and, convinced that no one would attack this peaceful corner of the globe, they allowed their state of national preparedness to drop lower and lower. World War II put an abrupt end to the illusion that virtue was any defence against tanks and bombers. Since 1945, Norway and Denmark have seen fit to join the West in a military alliance, although Sweden, the best-armed of the five, continues to believe in the policy of neutrality which she has pursued so successfully in the past. Finland, sharing a long frontier with Soviet Russia, is a special case. With her armed forces drastically limited by the 1947 peace treaty, she has directed her energies towards humanitarian affairs, such as providing a venue for major international conferences on strategic arms limitation, and the like.

The humanitarianism which finds its expression in social legislation to protect the rights of the worker, the mother, and the child, had its champion in the international field in the person of Fridtjof Nansen, the Norwegian explorer. Besides organizing relief for millions of starving Russians at the end of World War I, he instituted the famous Nansen passport, which gave extra-national status to countless refugees. While others scoffed or passed resolutions, Nansen went quietly to work, always accomplishing the seemingly impossible, such as, for example, population exchanges between Greece and Turkey. Both the League of Nations and the United Nations have been wholeheartedly supported by the Scandinavians, as evidenced by the fact that the last president of the League and the first two secretaries-general of the UN have come from the North.

No less inspiring are the Nobel Peace Prizes, instituted by the Swedish inventor of dynamite, and awarded, usually every year, for outstanding work in the cause of peace. Another great Swede, Count Bernadotte, gave his life in the service of the United Nations while acting as mediator between Arabs and Jews in Palestine. The Danes, for their part, took thousands of under-nourished children into their homes after World War II and restored them to health before returning them to their parents. Nor does this idealism flag where national interests are involved. Norway and Denmark became involved in a dispute over Greenland during the Thirties. The case was submitted for arbitration to the International Court of Justice at The Hague, and never for a moment was the issue allowed to embitter relations between the two countries. Sweden and Finland were equally reasonable in a similar dispute of the Åland Islands.

Moderation and Politics

Parliamentary government and the party system were achieved in Scandinavia in the 19th century. At first there were two parties, corresponding more or less to the English Conservatives and Liberals, plus a strong agrarian faction. Since the beginning of the 20th century, however, socialist parties, representing the increasing number of industrial workers, have made great headway, and with the exception of Norway where the government is conservative, they dominate Scandinavian politics. Four or five parties are the general rule, under an electoral system which discourages the formation of splinter groups and the dissipation of parliamentary power. Finland is an exception in having around ten parties, covering all shades of politics from Conservative to Communist. The Communist vote has gradually declined since the early Sixties, though it still runs more or less level with the Conservative and Center parties behind the leading Social Democrats.

There is no self-conscious proletariat in Scandinavia, just as there is no large group of ultra-rich. Springing largely from peasant origins, the Scandinavians have brought something of the countryman's shrewd, unhurried rhythm into public life, a fact which sometimes irritates those who prefer the slick and the quick.

Freedom of the press is an essential feature of the Scandinavian scene. The Swedish constitution includes it among the four basic laws which date back to 1809. Each country being relatively small, even the largest newspaper has a proportionally limited circulation and thus cannot hope to be a financial and political power behind the scenes, as is often the case in larger nations. As a result, the news is presented more impartially and factually.

All five countries are careful to maintain a strict constitutional distinction between the legislative, the judiciary, and the executive powers. In the main their constitutions reflect some of the ideas and ideals which inspired the American Declaration of Independence and the French Revolution. Nor is this surprising when we remember that Sweden's constitution dates from 1809, and that a French Marshal—Bernadotte—was elected regent at that time, succeeding to the throne as King Carl Johan in 1818. Norway's constitution was drawn up in 1814, and Denmark followed suit in 1849 while the wind of revolution was still sweeping across Europe. Although blood flowed freely on the Continent during this period, reform was a peaceful process in Scandinavia. In place of military parades, Norway, for example, commemorates Constitution Day by a procession of school children carrying the national flag, a symbol of unity.

An interesting feature in present Danish political life is provided by the 10-year-old Progressive Party, whose primary aim was initially the complete abolition of income tax. Though this happy event has not yet come to pass, social and cultural welfare subsidies have been perceptibly reduced by the state aiming to ease the growing discontent with the excessive cost of welfare benefits. At the same time interest in and control of public personalities' spending and fringe benefits has also increased.

Nevertheless, in a world where democracy is increasingly being considered unworkable, the Scandinavians, despite their high taxation seem to prove that individual liberty in a structured society is still a viable proposition.

THE SCANDINAVIAN
ECONOMY

Riches from Land and Sea

by
SYLVIE NICKELS

Nature's most lavish gift to Scandinavia was beautiful scenery: mountains and forests, lakes and skerries, fjords and waterfalls. Since no country can survive on beauty alone, however, it is fortuitous that most of these natural features can be translated one way or another into terms of hard cash to help buy all the things these Nordic countries cannot supply themselves. Thus, the Swedish match that has lit your cigarette or pipe far beyond the borders of Scandinavia, the Norwegian brisling sardine or Danish bacon that probably has a place in your larder, and the Finnish pulp that may have gone into your daily newspaper are essentially the products of highly specialized industries. Indeed, specialization is a Scandinavian specialty. And though they, too, have had to learn increasingly to diversify, they have simply carried this same talent through into a broader range of goods.

47

In many respects Scandinavia has been lucky. Industrialization which, in other parts of the world, spread like a blight across the land, came late to this quiet corner. This has not only spared her the social problems which slums and depressed areas entail, but has also enabled her to profit from the errors of others. Of course, these northern countries are as vulnerable as anyone else to the far-reaching repercussions of such international factors as the oil crisis, and each has been affected and has reacted in its own way. Even Norway, now blossoming as a major oil producer, has found that new wealth brings problems of a different kind in its wake.

The Scandinavian Success Story

In less than a century, Sweden has established herself as one of the Great Powers of the iron and steel industries. In fact, her iron ore deposits are among the largest in Europe and are to be found in two separate districts: central Sweden and, more importantly, in the Kiruna-Malmberget region of Swedish Lapland. This major source lies on the railroad from Luleå to the ice-free port of Narvik in northern Norway, so that the ore is blasted from the mountains and can be loaded directly on the railway wagons for export. The iron also feeds the famous Swedish steel industry, and engineering products provide her main exports, from ball bearings to ships and motor cars; the latter especially have won increasing popularity abroad for their sturdy reliability. Indeed, the whole trend of Swedish foreign trade since the 1950s has changed towards the increase of manufactures and the proportionate decline of raw materials as dominant features of her exports.

Sweden has no coalfields of any significance and has to import all her oil. But vast resources of hydro-electric power provide 14% of all the energy she needs. The power comes from a profusion of waterfalls and fast rivers, while some of the numerous lakes serve as splendid natural regulating reservoirs. Sweden has specialized in the transmission of electricity over long distances, and even exports it to Denmark by means of submarine cables. Not surprisingly, she has also made a specialty of electrical equipment; the first electric rolling mill in the world was built by a Swede, Danielsson, in 1894, and in the telephone industry the name of Ericson enjoys world renown. Nobel, perhaps best known as the founder of the trust which bears his name and distributes awards for services to peace, literature and the sciences, was the inventor of dynamite. Other Swedish inventions are the Primus stove and the domestic refrigerator, both creating flourishing industries.

Most dominantly visible of all Sweden's natural resources are the vast forests which cover over half her land area and which provide the raw materials for about one-fifth of her exports—a proportion which used to be much higher until the dramatic increase in exports of engineering products. Timber, pulp and paper are the forests' chief offspring, but they also contribute in a major way to the important chemical industry. Another significant subsidiary is the match industry which, in the days of Ivar Kreuger, was the hub of a world organization.

In a world increasingly concerned with recycling waste, incidentally, it is interesting to note how the Swedes have really got down to tackling the problem. The collection of household and commercial waste paper has now been made compulsory by law and is effective almost everywhere.

Construction is another branch in which the Swedes have had enormous success, selling "know-how" and whole projects overseas, from hotels and office blocks in East Europe to hydro-electric plants in Kenya and the design for Kuwait's water supply system.

Recent estimates by the Swedish National Institute of Economic Research, however, show that all is not as enviable as one might have supposed in Sweden's economic situation. Considerable sums of emergency aid have been pumped into such ailing industries as shipbuilding and the merging of three major steel producers into one company, with a 75% government holding, is among other measures aimed at curbing the economic slide. Improved exports have been matched by rising imports and the general international recession has not helped, though at 3% Sweden's unemployment is still quite low. To improve her competitiveness, Sweden devalued the krona by 16% in October 1982. She has also reduced her value-added tax, and the rise in consumer prices is dropping. For the immediate future the restrictive economic policy of recent years is being tempered to stimulate production and investment in a further effort to cut accumulated deficits.

Harvesting the Sea

Just next door, with her tremendous coastline and difficult mountainous interior, Norway has at all times turned to the sea. Recently, the ocean has taken on a quite new significance, with the exploitation, still in its relative infancy, of North Sea oil in which Norway may have the richest share. The experts estimate, for example, that in 1982 oil and gas exports were 53 billion kr. (or over 50% of total exports) and, backed by a general improvement in the export of processed goods, resulted in an enviable drop in Norway's trade deficit. However, overdependence on oil, especially with unpredictable oil prices, has its dangers as has been shown by the forecasts of declining revenues in the immediate future. Additionally, although the potential rewards are great, the cost of acquiring them is very high indeed for a country with slender resources. Right from the beginning the Norwegian state has been heavily involved in Norway's share of North Sea oil, laudably holding the view that such riches there are should be used to help create employment in non-oil spheres and to improve the standard of living for all. It has moved cautiously and it remains to be seen what the future holds. The Norwegians, in the meantime, are developing a high degree of expertise in offshore engineering and in servicing the needs of the new industry, an expertise which can be and is an exportable "product" to other nations engaged in similar ventures. She has also become the world's largest builder of drilling rigs.

Other aspects of the sea are major features of Norway's economy. Cornerstone of this has long been her up-to-date merchant navy, fifth largest in the world, totalling over 21,000,000 gross tons and thus giving a figure of tons per head of population far in excess of any other country in the world. Following the oil crisis and general recession, the owners of Norway's massive fleet of carriers have found life rather less rosy as many tankers lay idle and net foreign freight earnings began to drop dramatically. Recently, however, there have been signs of a marked improvement in the freight market of which Norway has taken full advantage. The ship-building industry in Norway, as elsewhere, has felt the pinch as buyers paused to think again, but a long tradition of maritime skills has given Norwegian shipping a better chance than most of weathering even the storms of world economy.

With the growing scarcity of Antarctic whales, Norway has withdrawn from that particular scene, but her fishing fleets have long been active in many other waters. The North Atlantic Drift (Gulf Stream), for example, which acts as a sort of hot water bottle to the Scandinavian peninsula, also attracts great shoals of cod, herring and other species to the banks off Norway's west coast. Her exports of dried fish—stockfish and klipfish—to the Latin countries originated in the Middle Ages and have since extended to many other parts of the world. Deep-frozen fish and the products of the canning industry all boost the country's foreign earnings. By-products include oil and fishmeal fertilizers.

Grandly scenic as it is, Norway has the greatest proportion of agriculturally unproductive land in Scandinavia, excepting Iceland. About a quarter of it is covered by forests, with pine and spruce predominating and contributing in a small way to the country's export total. Apart from one mine in Spitzbergen, Norway has no coal, but a variety of other mineral deposits, among which are copper, pyrites and iron ore. Silver has also been mined in some places since the early 17th century.

In terms of hydro-electricity, she is even better off than Sweden; the total capacity of water power resources capable of economic development is estimated at 120,000 million kwh a year, about 58% of which was harnessed by the end of 1974. In the field of electrical power produced (and consumed) per inhabitant, Norway ranks first in the world, and the availability of cheap electricity has been directly responsible for the creation of a number of industries, notably the electro-chemical and electro-metallurgical industries.

Unexpected Industry

Denmark, surprising as it may be to many, is a thoroughly industrial country. In fact, the proportion of the working population employed in agriculture was 7.6% in 1980 and agricultural exports provided only 28% of the total in 1981. That said, this branch is one of the most efficiently organized anywhere in the world. Though farms may have decreased in number, they have increased in size and, unlike those in many other countries, they must now survive and thrive without direct government subsidies. A recent tendency has been the drop in dairy products and rise in arable and pig farming.

There is hardly any need to emphasize the fame of Danish butter, cheese, bacon and many other agricultural products, nor the excellence of Danish beer. What may be less well-known is the scope of Danish industry, particularly manufacturing, which accounts for about two-thirds of the country's exports. Despite declining world trade, these exports have continued to rise, especially with the developing countries. The Danes have their own special philosophy when it comes to industry, and it has paid off. Its backbone is made up of small or medium-sized firms who have concentrated on high quality goods aimed at small markets, rather than trying to compete with the big industrial powers on mass markets scales. Such firms help each other, especially when it comes to overseas promotion and marketing.

The largest branch is machinery. In fact, of all diesel-driven ships in the world, 25–30% have engines made in Denmark or under Danish license. Many other export items are agro-based, such as farming and dairy machinery; yet others have developed from expertise in such fields as electronics and pharmaceuticals. The latter is another important offshoot of agriculture: the Danes, for example, are the world's largest exporters of insulin (based mainly on pig pancreas) for the treatment of diabetes. Danish furniture, pottery and ceramics have had world renown for many years. Textiles and clothing, only minor exports in 1960, now account for 6.5% of manufactured products. Denmark, by the way, is the only Scandinavian member of the EEC, though all her Nordic neighbors have agreements of some kind with the Community. She also has her own sector of the North Sea, from which developing oil and gas production will contribute decisively to her economic future.

More Forests and Fish

Across the waters of the Baltic Sea, Finland has won the admiration of the rest of the world for her energy and determination in recovering from the ill effects of two wars and the loss of some of her best agricultural and industrial districts. The huge forests cover an even greater proportion of her land area (over 70%) than in Sweden, and the countless lakes and rivers provide cheap transportation from lumber camp to factory. The Finns refer to the forests as their "green gold" and, indeed, wood-based products have traditionally provided the main items of her gross national product and of her exports.

In fact, their relative importance has declined sharply of recent years (around 40% of total exports in 1982, compared with over 70% in the early 1960s), but this is largely due to dramatic developments in other spheres. Since the end of World War II, for example, Finland's metal-working and machine industries have developed enormously, accounting now for over 30% of her exports. Fashion goods and design products have also gained increasing ground abroad, and contributed nearly 8% of exports in 1980. Chemicals accounted for over 11%.

One of the more recent Finnish exports is "know-how", with Finnish technicians advising on the construction of industrial plants all over the world. Finnish companies now operate more than 60 production plants in 20 foreign countries, ranging from tractors in Brazil, radiosondes in Argentina and South Africa, to lifts in France, and textiles, glass and plastics in Canada.

From the point of view of power resources, Finland is less well off than her neighbors, for many of her rivers are slow or too remote. Thus she continues to rely heavily on oil imports, largely from the U.S.S.R., but also increasingly from the Middle East. Agriculturally, she is able to provide her population with most of the necessities of life. The promotion of peat production in the 1980s (Finland is one of the world's major sources of this natural fuel) is also an interesting development, primarily aimed to meet a proportion of the needs of community heating plants and industry.

And finally, there is Iceland. Flung out there in mid-Atlantic, Iceland's long preoccupation with her fishery limits, her negotiations and disputes with other countries—notably Britain—are more easy to understand when one realizes that she depends on fish to the tune of about 75% of her exports. Not so long ago, this figure was even higher, reaching nearly 90% as recently as 1969, for Iceland's other natural resources were either nonexistent or unexploited. They are in any case few, but the most important is the one most lacking in so much of the rest of the world; and that is energy.

Iceland has huge untapped sources of both hydro-electric and thermal power, the latter trapped in enormous hot subterranean pockets of this volcanic country. With the exploitation of these resources now under way, she has energy for sale, and many interested foreign customers, and it is just because of this exploitation that the Icelandic economy is already much less dependent on fish. Thus, manufactures powered by these resources accounted for a fifth of her exports in 1980—12.2% in aluminium ingot alone. As usual, this kind of exploitation requires enormous investment so it is no rapid answer to Iceland's economic problems which include the highest rate of inflation in the Western world. However, she also has one of the lowest unemployment rates.

Cooperation between the Scandinavian countries has always been at a high level. Another feature is the way in which private enterprise and state ownership manage to run side by side, and the relatively advanced level of increased worker responsibility (and reward) in many companies. That the economy of these northern lands is as sound as it is anywhere in an uncertain world is best proved by the standard of living which is enjoyed by all levels. Average wages are high by any standards, while a premium is placed on training and scientific research. Taxes are also high, as is the cost of living; but this is surely not too hard a price to pay for an enviable absence of poverty and distress.

CREATIVE SCANDINAVIA

Inspired Introspection

Many important forces unite Scandinavians, but there are many significant differences between Danes, Finns, Norwegians and Swedes. Painters tend to use different color tones, writers choose different subjects and musicians strike other tones. Danes, Norwegians and Swedes can read each other's languages without too much trouble, but as soon as the languages are spoken the problems of communication can be considerable. On several occasions when Danish entertainment shows have been televised on the Swedish network, the Swedish Broadcasting Company has received numerous protests from viewers who have demanded subtitles in future. Studies of audience reaction reveal that more than 50 percent of the viewers have trouble with the "foreign" language.

In Finland, Swedish and Finnish are the official languages though they are quite dissimilar. Swedish has always been the language of a minority, yet it was the language of administration and culture until the latter part of the 19th century. Today the Swedo-Finns account for only 6.3 percent of the population, while only 15 percent of the entire population is considered bilingual. Linguistically, most Finns are isolated from the rest of the world.

Outstanding creative Scandinavians have often been meditative, serious, melancholy and suffered from feelings of isolation. Some have found that the small, tightknit coteries in Scandinavia stifled their talents. At the same time, their work has nearly always been deeply rooted in the ways, climate and atmosphere of their part of Scandinavia.

Scandinavian Literature

Runic inscriptions are regarded as the earliest traces of literature. Most of the rune stones date from between the 9th and 12th centuries, and usually convey concise, factual information about the lives of chieftains, warriors and priests. By the 12th century Nordic paganism was combined with the newly introduced Christianity; Thor was superseded by Christ, but pagan and Christian symbols and views appeared side by side.

The history of Norse literature began after the establishment of Christianity and the adoption of the Latin alphabet. By this time, mainly because of internal strife in Norway, the literary center in the Norse world had shifted to the colony of Iceland, where the major part of what we call Old Norse literature was written down. The most celebrated Icelandic historian was Snorri Sturluson, famed for his *Heimskringla,* and in the middle of the 17th century a bishop in Iceland discovered collections of lays about Scandinavian gods and heroes which he later called the *Elder Edda.* The bishop had no intention of allowing scholars to read his treasures, but when his only daughter was seduced by a young priest, the bishop wanted revenge. He offered to donate the *Elder Edda* and several other important manuscripts to the Danish king, provided the young priest was punished. He evidently was, because old Icelandic manuscripts have been a subject of heated debate at regular intervals during the past four decades.

During the Middle Ages priests and monks set about recording the histories of the nations. Among the major works were sixteen books by Saxo Grammaticus, a Dane, who recorded the oral pagan legends and heroic poems; one of these was the story of Hamlet.

Christianity made the most profound effect on Sweden. In the latter part of the 13th century Petrus de Dacia, a Dominican monk, traveled to Cologne, where he met a young peasant girl. For fourteen years he corresponded with her and expressed his intense love. The importance of Petrus was overshadowed by Saint Birgitta and her nine books of *Revelations.* She was the first outstanding woman in Scandinavia and was canonized.

Until the 18th century, Scandinavian literature, aside from folklore, displayed only a minimum of national independence. The Scandinavians were profoundly influenced by the mainstreams of culture on the Continent and in England, but they felt an increasing desire to express themselves in their own languages.

The economy and daily life of Norway and Denmark differed, but culturally they comprised one unit. Throughout the 18th century most books by Norwegians and Danes were published in Copenhagen. Consequently, both countries have argued over claims to the talents of Ludvig Holberg, the 18th-century playwright who is regarded as the Molière of Scandinavian literature. Statues of Holberg are prominently displayed in front of the Royal Theater, Copenhagen (often called the house that Holberg built) and the National Theater, Oslo.

Born and brought up in Norway, Holberg moved to Copenhagen, which became his home for the rest of his life. He was a rationalist, a neo-classicist, a skeptic and a monarchist. In his works he expressed the dominant philosophical, literary and political views of the Age of Reason. When the Royal Theater in Copenhagen opened, the first play performed was Holberg's *The Political Tinker*. He went on almost single-handedly to supply the theater with a repertoire, and within two years wrote some 26 comedies. The importance of Holberg's comedies can hardly be overrated. With them he literally put Denmark on the map and made Danish literature a part of European culture.

Not long after Holberg, Denmark's possibly most gifted lyrical poet emerged. Johannes Ewald was an exponent of pre-romanticism. He was the first poet to delve into Scandinavian antiquity and discover the treasurers of the myths, the works of Saxo Grammaticus, the medieval ballads and the sagas. One of his poems later became the Danish National Anthem.

Linnaeus and Swedenborg

After the defeat and death of Charles XII, Sweden was reduced from a great power to a minor one. During the 18th century some of the nation's most creative men devoted themselves to the sciences. Although Carl Linnaeus was primarily a natural scientist, his compact style of writing made a strong impact on literary men. Linnaeus's contemporaries had been writing in an impersonal style, marked by French classicism, while he chose to express himself in a highly personal manner.

The other great Swedish international figure during this period was Emanuel Swedenborg who began as a scientist, became a religious mystic and then wrote his visionary revelations of Heaven and Hell in Latin. When the rationalists took over in the later part of the 18th century, superstitions and mysticism were harshly criticized by such poets as Johan Kellgren, a disciple of Voltaire.

Gustav III had dreams of creating a "golden age" of Swedish cultural life similar to that of Louis XIV. Contemporary authors were under the influence of the Age of Reason, while Gustav III wanted patriotic writers with nationalistic ideas. The importance of Gustav III cannot be overrated. He tried to improve the status of culture in the country, and founded the Swedish Academy, the Royal Opera, the Royal Ballet, the Drottningholm Theater and a number of other institutions that still play a significant part in the cultural life of Sweden.

The most outstanding poet of the period and possibly Sweden's greatest, Carl Michael Bellman, was invited to entertain at the court of Gustav III, but he was never considered a candidate for the Swedish Academy. Bellman set his lyrics to contemporary songs and folk songs. His Bible parodies, satires, drinking songs and lyrics about Stockholm revealed a striking realism and impressionism.

The romantic movement in Scandinavia came from Germany. The pioneer and leader in Denmark was Adam Oehlenschläger, the tragedian and poet. N. F. S. Grundtvig, hymn-writer, politician, philologist and romantic poet, is mostly remembered for his ideas on education, society, the Church and general welfare, which were inspired by his patriotism and faith in the common man.

Kierkegaard and Andersen

The other outstanding Danish religious figure of this period was Søren Kierkegaard. Grundtvig emphasized the importance of fellowship. In contrast, Kierkegaard was an arch individualist who revolted against Hegelism and considered a system of thought possible, but not a system of existence. He felt that Hegelism eliminated the personality of the individual. One of Kierkegaard's most important experiences was his broken engagement to his beloved Regine Olsen. Two weeks after breaking the engagement, Kierkegaard traveled to Berlin, where he began to write. Within the next ten years he wrote the greater part of his voluminous output.

A third major Danish writer from the romantic period was Hans Christian Andersen, whose works have reached much greater audiences than any other Scandinavian. His fairy-tales quickly reached the rest of Europe, America and even crossed the Great Wall of China, a feat few European writers have achieved.

Many of Andersen's fairy-tales were not merely products of his imagination: they were often allegorical stories of his life and experiences. He pictured himself as an ugly duckling grown into a beautiful swan that flew into a pond where children came with their parents to feed it. This symbolized his life from a youth of poverty to the time he became famous and fêted by royalty and leading dignitaries at home and abroad.

Kierkegaard did not exert a profound influence in Scandinavia until Georg Brandes, Denmark's greatest critic, published a book about him in 1877. Brandes, who had learned a great deal from the literary criticism and psychological approach of Frenchmen Taine and Sainte-Beuve, exerted a greater influence than anyone else on Scandinavian literature after 1870. He led the naturalism movement from which he disassociated himself twenty years later when he became a champion of Nietzsche.

Towards the end of the 18th century the Norwegian writers in Copenhagen formed a society with nationalistic aims. The first major writer of new Norway was Henrik Wergeland. He fought to liberate his country from the influences of Swedish politics and the Norwegian language from the dominating influence of Danish. A most important literary manifestation of the belated romantic movement in Norway was the interest in old ballads and folk tales. Inspired by these trends Jørgen Moe and Peter Christen Asbjørnsen got together and collected a large number of folk tales. One of their major problems was language. Standard Norwegian was practically indistinguishable from Danish, while the original dialects of the stories would have made them incomprehensible to the majority of educated Norwegians. Moe and Asbjørnsen chose a middle way.

In his plays and poems Björnstjerne Björnson combined an interest in Norway's past with the problems of his own time. He was probably Norway's greatest interpreter of patriotism. Björnson chose to fight for his ideals in the thick of the battle in Norway. Henrik Ibsen, on the other hand, found the atmosphere in Norway too uncomfortable and spent most of his time abroad. Both authors were influenced by Brandes and debated Norwegian problems in their works. Ibsen was also influenced by Kierkegaard's claim that the individual should not compromise.

Through his skillfully molded plays, Ibsen became one of the world's great playwrights and his dramatic technique became a model for playwrights throughout the world, but in 1903 Björnson was awarded a Nobel prize that should have gone to Ibsen.

Ushered in by poet Per Daniel Amadeus Atterbom, the Swedish romantic movement gained its outstanding representative in poet Esaias Tegnér whose best known work was *Frithiofs Saga,* an epic poem of Viking love. Though later generations have reacted rather strongly against the romantics, two authors have survived the changes of taste. They are C. J. L. Almquist who wrote mostly in prose and Erik Stagnelius, a mystic poet.

By 1809, when Swedish rule came to an end and Finland became an autonomous Grand Duchy within the Russian Empire, the Finnish national romantic movement developed quickly. Finns became increasingly anxious to get Finnish recognized as an official language on an equal footing with Swedish. Elias Lönnrot made numerous expeditions to Karelia to collect the folk poetry from which he compiled the national epic *The Kalevala.* The linguistic endeavors of Lönnrot and others founded Finnish language literature.

At the same time Swedo-Finn Johan Ludvig Runeberg objected to the overly romantic trends in Swedish literature and played an important part in setting up standards of poetic realism. Even though Runeberg wrote in Swedish he became recognized as Finland's national poet—largely through his *Tales of Ensign Stål,* a cycle of poems that portrayed the Finno-Russian War of 1808–09. The opening poem in the cycle, *Our Land,* is the Finnish National Anthem. Though Runeberg is called Finland's national poet, the most respected and honored Finnish author of the period is Aleksis Kivi whose novel *The Seven Brothers* is a classic. Kivi is also considered the father of Finnish drama. Eino Leino is perhaps the most talented of the Finnish language poets. Profoundly influenced by *The Kalevala,* Leino was a spokesman for Finnish independence and the independence of the individual.

The 20th Century

One of the top Danish writers to be influenced by Georg Brandes was novelist J. P. Jacobsen who was a sort of Danish Flaubert. He received a European reputation through his novels *Marie Grubbe* and *Niels Lyhne.* Two outstanding naturalistic writers were Herman Bang and Henrik Pontoppidan who, in 1917, shared a Nobel prize in literature with Karl Gjellerup, now considered a minor Danish author. Another disciple of Brandes was poet Holger Drachmann, who later gave up his role as a revolutionary and became an anti-bourgeois, anti-orthodox individualist, later turning conservative and romantic.

Two major 20th-century Danish writers were Martin Andersen Nexø and Johannes V. Jensen. Nexø is often regarded as the Gorki of Danish literature. He devoted his literary talents to the cause of the working classes. Johannes V. Jensen, a North Jutlander, reacted against naturalism and established himself as a teller of tales. Though his "myths" had little anthropological value, they often made moving and stimulating reading. Jensen, who has been called a Danish Kipling, was awarded a Nobel prize in 1944. Other major Danish writers of the 20th century include poet, novelist and critic Tom Kristensen, novelist Jacob Paludan, psychological novelist and playwright H. C. Branner, playwrights Kaj Munk, C. E. Soya and Kjell Abell, novelist and short-story writer Karen Blixen (known in the English speaking world as Isak Dinesen), poet Paul La Cour, novelist Martin A. Hansen, poet-novelist Tove Ditlevsen and Faroese novelist William Heinesen. The versatile Piet Hein is known not only for his "Grooks" (epigrams full of simple truths), but also as a designer, architect and inventor.

Modern Swedish literature was started through the works of August Strindberg. Though mostly known abroad as a playwright, Strindberg was also a most talented novelist and short-story writer. Everything he wrote—and he wrote enormously—was characterized by spontaneity, straightforwardness, compactness and eruptiveness. Regrettably, his translators have seldom been able to convey his shattering intensity. Strindberg was driven and fascinated by extremes. He was truly and enthusiastically carried away by his loves which were always mixed with hate. He was opposed to feminists, whom he regarded as his rivals and enemies, and felt that the woman's place was in the home, but he married three women who had no intention of giving up their careers. As a writer, he experimented constantly, and thus became an idol for quite dissimiliar authors.

Strindberg was much too controversial a figure to be elected a member of the Swedish Academy or be discussed as a candidate for a Nobel prize. The first Swedish author to receive the literary award was Selma Lagerlöf (1909) who gained the most widespread popularity of any Swedish fiction writer. Against a background of frightening and fantastic tales, she described the battle between good and evil. The first critic to recognize her talent was Brandes. Other Swedish authors who have received Nobel prizes are Verner von Heidenstam (1916), Erik Axel Karlfeldt (1931) and Pär Lagerkvist (1951).

Gustaf Fröding is often regarded as the uncrowned king of Swedish poetry. A daydreamer, Fröding often viewed himself with sarcasm. He saw himself as a clown, the local drunkard poet or a mountain troll who was too ugly to court a young princess. Fröding also had a keen sense of humor.

Pär Lagerkvist, novelist, playwright and poet, revolted against the realistic theater of Ibsen and found inspiration in the post-Inferno works of Strindberg. He has called himself "a religious atheist". In contrast, novelist Hjalmar Bergman depicted a neurotic world with imagination and humor. The epic tradition has been continued by Vilhelm Moberg whose four novels about a group of peasants who left

Sweden to start a new life in the United States belong to the major works in the genre.

Moberg, Eyvind Johnson and Harry Martinson had working-class backgrounds. Johnson has written intellectual, allegorical novels; Martinson has reacted against the dangers of the modern age. Other major contemporary writers include poets Gunnar Ekelöf, Hjalmar Gullberg, Erik Lindegren and Karl Vennberg and novelists Lars Ahlin, Lars Gyllensten and Sara Lidman. Also, the well-known playwright and movie maker, Ingmar Bergman.

Still somewhat caught up in Norwegian romanticism Knut Hamsun believed in the possibilities of the agricultural development of Norway. He received a Nobel prize (1917) for his novel *The Growth of the Soil* in which he praised the life of the peasant. Hamsun blamed much of the rootlessness of the modern age on the United States and England. During the two World Wars, he was an outspoken supporter of Germany.

Hamsun and Sigrid Undset are the two Norwegian authors of this century who have drawn the greatest of attention abroad. After first dealing with Oslo middle-class women and their problems, Sigrid Undset turned to the late Middle Ages in Norway: *Kristin Lavransdatter* and *Olav Audunssøn and His Children* brought her world fame and a Nobel prize in 1928.

There are several prominent, contemporary writers in Norway. They include novelists Tarje Vesaas, Cora Sandel and Johan Borgen. Agnar Mykle gained a great deal of attention when his novel *The Song of the Red Ruby* was tried as pornography. The book was banned (1957) in Norway, but the ban was lifted about a year later. As a result, Mykle's novel received much more publicity than it deserved.

The forte of Swedo-Finnish authors has been poetry. Several of the leading modernists were Swedo-Finns, such as Edith Södergran and Elmer Diktonius. Finnish language authors were not very interested in the avant-garde Swedo-Finns. They devoted their attention to securing the foundation of the Finnish language and expressing pride over Finland's independence, won in 1917. The authors were often the inspirers and interpreters of national sentiments.

After Finland's defeat in the second Finno-Russian War (1941–44), Frans Eemil Sillanpää, the only Finnish author who has been awarded a Nobel prize (1939), reverted to memories of childhood. Mika Waltari, who had written a large number of novels about Finland, sought historical subjects in Mediterranean countries and the younger generation took a more cynical view of patriotism and Finland's conditional freedom, which was—and still is—dependent on a sensitive relationship with the Soviet Union.

At the end of World War II, Finland's literary trends were a generation behind the rest of Scandinavia, but in the post-war decades the Finns have been quickly catching up. Without question the most popular writer is Väinö Linna, whose last four novels have sold more than a million copies in Finland alone. Linna has put his finger on some of the sensitive roots of the youthful republic of Finland. His novel *The Unknown Soldier,* a brutally realistic description of the second Finno-Russian war, marked the first change in attitude towards Finland's idealized past. Veijo Meri, Christer Kihlmann and Hannu Salama are other modern Finnish authors to look out for.

Though most Scandinavian writers are cut off from the rest of the world because of language, they have strikingly large and appreciative audiences in their own nations. Furthermore, the Scandinavian welfare states regularly increase their support of the arts. Authors can achieve numerous forms of awards, scholarships and financial grants; they also receive small amounts for their books in public libraries.

Painting and Sculpture

The geographical position of Scandinavia has kept it on the outskirts of the main trends of art. Scandinavian art has developed basically along the lines of European art, and the impulses have generally come from Western Europe and reached the northern countries directly or by way of Germany. Russian influences are noticeable in Finland.

Norwegian painting and sculpture dates back to the days of the Vikings. The famous Oseberg and Gokstad ships are excellent examples of skilful and talented carvings and decorations.

Medieval mural art, which was practised throughout Scandinavia, reached its highest peak in the province of Uppland, north of Stockholm, in the 15th and 16th centuries. At Täby church, built about 1300, the paintings are by Albertus Pictor, an outstanding mural artist of the period.

The 17th century was an important period for architecture in Sweden, while painting reached a high point a century later. Two rococo painters Alexander Roslin and Carl Gustaf Pilo gained prominence abroad. Sweden's first major sculptor, Johan Tobias Sergel, was also active at this time.

The only Danish artist who has gained world fame was sculptor Bertel Thorvaldsen. Danish art has a distinct character, deeply rooted in the ways and manners of the people. There is usually a tone of restrained simplicity. Of importance to Danish painting was Christoffer Wilhelm Eckersberg, "the father of Danish painting", who pioneered the naturalism that dominated art during the 19th century.

Romanticism was the dominant reaction of Swedish art to the Industrial Revolution. By the last two decades of the 19th century painters tried to convey an everyday naturalism. The new trends first became visible in landscape painting. Carl Fredrik Hill, often referred to as "the genius of Swedish landscape painters", sought a form of pure art. While Hill's contemporaries had difficulty appreciating his work, they also showed little understanding for Ernst Josephson, the other great Swedish painter of the period. Prince Eugen, youngest son of King Oscar II, was a landscape painter of note. His home, Waldermarsudde, is now open to the public.

Finnish art came into its own during the latter part of the 19th century. Albert Edelfelt was the first Finnish painter to gain recognition in Europe. Naturalism came to Finland in the 1880s but it was strongly colored by the national romanticism of *The Kalevala*. Edelfelt was the first to depict realistically the people and the life of his times. The central figure in the Finnish national romantic movement was

Akseli Gallén-Kallela, a painter and graphic artist, whose home in a Helsinki suburb has been turned into a charming and interesting museum. After a journey to Karelia, Gallén-Kallela changed his style from naturalism to romantic realism. Later he developed gradually towards an abstract style. Helena Schjerfbeck, who was almost entirely cut off from foreign influences, developed a subjective simplified style of her own, characterized by an abstract purity of line and sparse use of color. Pekka Halonen, Eero Järnefelt and Hugo Simberg are other leading painters born in the 1860s and 1870s. Some of Hugo Simberg's somber works are in Tampere Cathedral.

Modern Art

The romantic school in Norway, with its somewhat idealized and remote concept of Norwegian landscapes, prevailed until the end of the 19th century, when Edvard Munch created a "revolution" with his radical impressionism. An Edvard Munch museum opened in 1960 in Oslo and it belongs to one of the sights visitors should not miss. Munch started as a realist after which he went through periods of mysticism, symbolism, Nordic expressionism and finally impressionism.

In the early part of the 20th century a group of Matisse pupils—the most prominent of whom was Isaac Grünewald—emerged. Partly in opposition to the new radical efforts, a group of Swedish artists appeared around 1910 with paintings full of naivism, which was more closely related to romanticism and German expressionism than to the elegance of Matisse or the cubist forms of Picasso. Two major expressionists are Siri Derkert and Vera Nilsson. Evert Lundquist employs a personal expressionistic style. Primitivism stems from Sven Erixson and Bror Hjorth who often find inspiration in older Swedish folk art. Hjorth is also one of Sweden's major sculptors of this century. Other outstanding sculptors include Carl Eldh, Carl Milles and Arne Jones.

Sam Vanni and Kain Tapper are among Finland's interesting modern artists. In the field of sculpture, her first outstanding artist was Wäinö Aaltonen. His striking busts in bronze and granite can be seen in many parts of the country. Aimo Tukiainen, whose equestrian statue of Gustaf Mannerheim is across the street from the Finnish Parliament building, is another well-known artist. Two women are among other distinguished modern sculptors: Laila Pullinen and Eila Hiltunen. The latter's Sibelius Monument in Helsinki is among her many striking works.

In Finland, as elsewhere in Scandinavia, the appreciation of art is not a minority interest. Almost every home is embellished with some original paintings, or smaller pieces of sculpture, and their owners will be fully aware of who created them. Equally, they will be able to tell you the name of the designer of that glass bowl or decanter on the dresser or that piece of ceramic on the table. This widespread interest has given rise to many art and design exhibitions, of which the summer-long one of Summer-Pinx at Sysmä in central Finland is a good example, combining the new works of known and unknown artists and sculptors. It is partly held in the open air in a delightful lake and forest setting. Another, held during alternate summers (years with uneven numbers) is Purnu, near Orivesi, on the shore of Lake Koljonselkä, set in a luxuriant park.

J. F. Willumsen, painter, sculptor, ceramist and architect, has been one of the most controversial figures in Danish art. The basis of his art was naturalism, expressed with a dynamic visionary power. Another artist, Asger Jorn was a member of the COBRA group, which was founded in opposition to the painters of the modernistic Paris school, whom they considered too bound in composition and thought. Consequently, his paintings have a freer and revolutionary originality.

Norwegian sculptor Gustav Vigeland holds a unique position. Though his project suffers somewhat from elephantiasis, a large collection of his works covers Frogner public park in Oslo. Vigeland designed the overall layout of the park as well as the smaller details such as the lanterns and gates.

The interest in art is clearly manifested by the large number of galleries. Though there are few outstanding artists, the average standard is noticeably high. There is almost a direct ratio between the interest in art and the affluency of the Scandinavian nations. Each of the governments have either passed or are discussing plans to lay aside a certain percentage of the building costs for public buildings for "artistic decorations". Cities and communities also pay for much art.

Architecture and City Planning

The extensive forests of Scandinavia have naturally resulted in wood being a predominant architectural feature. From the time of the 12th-century stave churches in Norway (of which there are still some twenty in existence) to the present day, country buildings are mostly beautifully-designed wooden structures. The early churches of Denmark, though simpler, were also built with wood.

The reign of the Danish king, Christian IV (1588–1648), was characterized by a great deal of building. Some of the better known structures are Rosenborg Palace in Copenhagen, the Stock Exchange (a long building with a spire of dragon's tails), and Frederiksborg Castle in North Zealand. The most extraordinary of the buildings from the days of Christian IV is the Round Tower in Copenhagen, a church tower and an observatory combined. At his death, Christian IV left his country rich in monumental buildings, but impoverished by misguided policies.

The 17th century was a period of considerable activity in Sweden. The two most prominent architects were Jean de la Vallée and Nicodemus Tessin the elder, whose most important commission was to build a country palace, Drottningholm, for Dowager Queen Hedvig Eleonora.

The tide of architecture within Scandinavia had earlier run from Denmark to Sweden, but towards the end of the 17th century it moved in the reverse direction. The man who brought about this change was Nicodemus Tessin the younger. His greatest project was the Royal Palace in Stockholm. Inspired by the Rome of Sixtus V and by the Paris and Versailles of Louis XIV, Tessin planned the palace to be the center piece in an extensive scheme that called for remolding the whole northern section of Stockholm. Only part of his plans became a reality as funds were needed to finance the wars of Charles XII.

National romanticism during the 19th century also left its mark on building. Holm Munthe was a Norwegian architect who was anxious to make use of the "laft" construction of the old country buildings and the decorative effects of the stave churches. The most picturesque examples still in existence are the Frognerseter Restaurant and Holmenkollen Tourist Hotel. Soon buildings became burdened with overly elaborate carvings on roof ridges and over-hanging roofs.

The traditional forms of building have exerted an enormous influence on contemporary Norwegian architecture. This can be seen in Magnus Poulsson's Gravberget Church. Along with Arnstein Arneberg, Poulsson drew up the plans for Oslo's City Hall.

Shortly after Finland came under Russian rule and the capital city was moved from Turku to the small town of Helsinki, a large number of public buildings had to be built. Around 1815, a grand center was planned for the expanding city which was to surpass all earlier Scandinavian dimensions. Responsible for this venture were Johan Ehrenström and Carl Engel who created the area round Senate Square in empire style, including the Cathedral, the University, the University Library, the Old Town Hall, the Foreign Office and other government buildings in the area.

It has often been said that Finland is the most far off country in Europe. Even Norway and the Soviet Union are in some respects in closer touch with the mainstreams of European culture than Finland. This, combined with the nation's relative poverty and sparse population, made it difficult for Finnish architects in previous centuries to borrow features of stone architecture from abroad. There are almost touching examples of how 18th-century church builders tried to adapt Swedish stone structures to Finnish timber. Wooden structures still dominate sections of some Finnish towns.

It was also the lack of foreign contacts and influences and the familiarity with severe simplicity that enabled Finnish architects to develop their own styles that suited new technological and social conditions. When men like Eliel Saarinen and Lars Sonck started on their careers in the 1880s, they were not held back by deeply rooted public likes and dislikes. In fact, the development of modern architecture has been formed by specialists who have workèd largely independently of the tastes of the general public. Finnish patriotism in the 20th century has been another force that has inspired the creative talents of the young nation to search into the past for things specifically Finnish and safeguard them.

Interesting comparisons can be made between Saarinen's national romantic Railroad Station in Helsinki and Ragnar Östberg's national romantic City Hall in Stockholm, Johan Sirén's Finnish Parliament Building and Tengbom's Stockholm Concert Hall. In 1920 Saarinen won second prize in the Chicago Tribune's Tower competition and his design revolutionized skyscraper architecture in the United States. Two years later Saarinen emigrated to the United States, where he directed the founding of the Cranbrook Academy of Art.

In the 1920s, the late Alvar Aalto won the Paimio Sanatorium competition. Since then this famous architect designed well-known structures in many parts of the world, but Finland remained his base of operations. Aalto's furniture designs have also received much acclaim. Among numerous other projects, his associates continue his work on plans for the re-development of Helsinki.

Other outstanding Finnish architects include Erik Bryggman, Viljo Rewell (who designed the Toronto City Hall), Yrjö Lindegren, Aarne Ervi, Kaija and Heikki Sirén, Aarno Ruusuvuori, Reima Pietilä and many others. Almost any Finnish town can provide fine examples of what these architects can do with the basic theme of four walls and a roof.

In 1900 Swedish architect Ragnar Östberg wondered how long Swedes would continue to be fascinated by foreign things. Östberg's attitude signals the coming of Swedish national romanticism, also called "brick architecture". Examples of this trend include numerous Stockholm structures: Engelbrekt church by Israel Wahlman (1914), the Stadium, inspired by the wall embracing the city of Visby on Gotland, built for the 1912 Olympics by Torben Grut and the City Hall by Östberg (1923).

Swedish architecture first began to attract international attention shortly after the turn of the century. Swedish architects were not only interested in the visual qualities of their structures, but they also sought solutions to adapting their buildings to the changing social conditions in the country.

The major characteristics of modern Swedish architecture at its best are a well-balanced combination of practicability and adaption to natural surroundings.

The new age of architecture was launched at the Stockholm Exhibition of 1930, where a large number of architects participated with whole villas, terrace houses, apartments, etc., in a unified environment. The framework of the whole, the arrangement of the exhibition, the halls and the restaurant were designed by Gunnar Asplund, the pioneer of modern architecture in Sweden. Among the display apartments that gained attention was one designed by Gustaf Clason.

Many downtown areas in Swedish cities are being torn down and re-developed, but the tempo is somewhat dependent on the labor market. The new downtown areas can be regarded as showcases of the current trends in Swedish architecture, Stockholm proving a magnificent example.

Scandinavian Design

Industrial art is to Scandinavia what painting is to Holland and music to Austria. A prime reason may be that the climate—the cold, long and dark winters—makes the home an exceptionally important part of Scandinavian life. Another factor has been the government-supported campaigns aimed at developing and improving the taste of the general public. The first of these was launched in Sweden in 1919 with the slogan "more beautiful things for everyday use". Industrialization came late to Scandinavia and was still in its early stages at this time. Consequently, industrialization and the new concepts of design joined forces spontaneously.

Scandinavians feel that harmony in home decorating has almost a therapeutic effect on citizens. Most designers have regarded the practicability of articles as being paramount. They seldom create art objects that cannot be put to use. This attitude can be regarded as an expression of the Scandinavian welfare states.

Danish industrial art first attracted international attention in 1889, when Royal Copenhagen, the oldest factory in the country (founded 1775), was awarded a *grand prix* for underglaze-painted porcelain at the World Fair in Paris. In 1900 the other major Danish porcelain factory, Bing and Gøndahl, was equally honored for ceramics designed by J. F. Willumsen. These two awards immediately gave Denmark an international name in the field. Early in the 20th century Danish silver became world renowned through the work of Georg Jensen, a gifted artist and craftsman. In 1925 the Swedish Orrefors glassworks were awarded a gold medal in Paris for their art glass.

Until the mid-Twenties decorative art dominated the field. At this time the trend turned towards utilitarian objects and Scandinavian art, handicraft and industrial art secured its international reputation during the 1930s.

The Scandinavians turned from the free pictorial style towards a textural ceramic style, which was most clearly manifested in stoneware. In Denmark the Saxbo stoneware of Nathalie Krebs was a striking example of the new trends. At the same time, Kay Bojesen, who was an apprentice of Georg Jensen, placed an increasing emphasis on the simplicity and purposefulness of silverware, though Bojesen's most popular—if not most important and most remarkable—contributions have been as a "woodsmith". His wooden toys and souvenirs are sold throughout the world.

While the Danes have gone in more for art ceramics, the Swedes have paid more attention to utility wares. Artists like Carl Malmsten, Wilhelm Kåge, Arthur Percy, Elsa Gullberg and Gunnar Nylund have pioneered Swedish applied art. The prime goal was to design practical, beautiful and inexpensive wares for the average home, but they also made individual pieces of a more exclusive nature.

Though the art of making glass dates back to the 16th century in Sweden, it did not gain international recognition until the 20th century. Most of the many glassworks are clustered closely together in the forests in the province of Småland. Much of the credit for the success of Swedish glass is due to the Orrefors glassworks, which produces everything from simple everyday ware to large ornamental objects. Kosta, the oldest glassworks in the country (founded in 1741), is a vital and successful company with an illustrious past. Still another expression of the democratic trends in Swedish industrial art is stainless steel flatware.

The Wärtsilä-Arabia factory largely dominates ceramics in Finland. Established in 1874, it is the largest of its kind in Europe today. Though the major part of its production consists of bathroom and sanitary porcelain, its art ceramics belong to the most outstanding in Scandinavia or anywhere else. Kaj Franck, Kyllikki Salmenhaara, Birger

Kaipiainen and Francesca Lindh are among the designers who have contributed to Arabia's creations.

Finland has also gained an international reputation in glassware, notably through its Nuutajärvi glassworks (an independent member of the Wärtsilä group) and the Karhula Iittala company. Timo Sarpaneva and Tapio Wirkkala are two great names in glass design.

Finland's "ryijy" rugs date back to the 15th century, but like many other aspects of contemporary Finland, they were revived in the wave of national romanticism at the turn of the century. Originally, they were used as a coarse, strong and heavy cover which seal hunters and deep-sea fishermen used instead of fur skins. Eventually the pile became shorter and the rugs lighter and more ornamental and became festive tapestries during the 18–19th century. In textiles, Dora Jung, Marjatta Metsovaara and Uhra Simberg-Ehrström are among several outstanding designers.

Strangely enough, the Danes, who live in an agricultural country with a minimum of trees have led the way in modern furniture and woodwork. The functional furniture movement was championed by Kaare Klint, who was appointed head of the furniture department at the Academy of Art's school in architecture in 1924. Klint objected to furniture being designed as ornamental woodwork; he believed it should be conceived with its future use as a guide post. Though Swedish furniture seldom reaches the artistic peaks of Danish furniture, there is a greater choice of quality products for the average pocket-book in Sweden. Finnish architect Alvar Aalto has devoted a great deal of attention to what he calls "architecture accessories"—furniture and interior decorating details. Ilmari Tapiovaara is another great name in Finnish furniture design.

Music

The first Swedish composer of importance emerged in the early part of the 18th century. He was Johan Helmich Roman. The Gustavian opera period was largely created through the efforts of Gustav III and highlighted by foreign performers. The revival of interest in folk music, stimulated by romanticism in the early part of the 19th century, gave Scandinavian music independent character for the first time. Inspired by a meeting with Richard Nordraak, Norway's first national romantic composer, Edvard Grieg set out to develop his own style. Norway's wealth of folk music became his major source of inspiration, and he also wrote music to the works of several major Norwegian writers—one of his best known works was written for Ibsen's play *Peer Gynt*. Grieg was the first Scandinavian composer to reach a world-wide audience.

Grieg studied in Copenhagen with Niels Gade, the leading Danish romantic, whose first symphony had its first performance at the Leipzig Gewandhaus, where Gade served as joint conductor with Mendelssohn. In the latter part of the romantic period Carl Nielsen was Denmark's greatest composer. The principal features of his works were a melody based on a clear and predominantly diatonic interval sequence, a strong and pure harmony that was often inspired by church modes and an exuberant, eruptive rhythm. Vagn Holmboe, probably the most gifted modern composer in Denmark, is considered Carl Nielsen's successor, with his string quartets and symphonies attempting to unite and keep together inconsistent components.

Without question Scandinavia's greatest composer was Finland's Jean Sibelius. His works are often divided into three major periods. The first is his "Kalevala period" because he was profoundly influenced by the Finnish epic. It is figured to have lasted through his First and Second Symphonies. The next was his "classical" period and covers his works from the Third through the Fifth Symphony. The third includes his Sixth and Seventh Symphonies. The weight and loneliness conveyed by much of his music reflects an aspect of Scandinavia. Other notable Finnish composers include Erkki Melartin, Selim Palmgren, Leevi Madetoja and Uuno Klami.

While Sibelius was one of the greatest composers of his time and his works were well known to musicians throughout the world, Swedish composer Hugo Alfvén gained a certain popularity for his lively instrumentations that earned him the name of "a Swedish Richard Strauss". His *Midsummer Vigil* was one of his better known works. Vilhelm Steenhammar composed "Sverige" (Sweden), based on a poem by Heidenstam, which became an important patriotic song.

The beginnings of modern Swedish music date from about 1920. The generation of composers who emerged—particularly Hilding Rosenberg and Gösta Nystroem—took completely different roads from those that had been used previously in Swedish music. They revolted against national romanticism and were drawn to men like Schönberg, Stravinsky and Honegger. Karl-Birger Blomdahl belonged to a younger generation. Among other works, he composed the modernistic opera *Aniara*, based on a long poem by Harry Martinson.

Science and Exploration

Since the days of the Vikings Scandinavians have traveled and explored the world. Leif Eriksson sailed from Norway for Greenland, but he was driven off course and arrived at what he called "Vinland", which is believed to have been somewhere on the northeastern coast of North America. Early in the 18th century Vitus Bering, a Danish navigator, discovered the Bering Sea and the Bering Straits. Other Danes started the colonization of Greenland about this time.

During the past century numerous Scandinavians have explored the Arctic and Antarctic regions. Knud Rasmussen, the Dane, explored the regions from Greenland to Alaska. Peter Freuchen participated in several of Rasmussen's expeditions and wrote a number of entertaining books.

A. E. Nordenskiöld, a Swede, was the first to clear the North East Passage (1878–79), making possible the circumnavigation of the Old World. The first attempt to fly to the North Pole was carried out by S. A. André, a Swede, whose balloon went down in the Arctic wastes in 1897. Sven Hedin, the famed Swedish explorer of Tibet, made his first expedition in 1894–97 and his last in 1938.

Norwegian Fridtjof Nansen skied across Greenland in 42 days in 1888. Later he made an attempt to reach the North Pole with dog teams, skis and kayaks. In later years, Nansen devoted himself to humanitarian work, most especially for prisoners of war and other victims after World War I. In 1923 he was awarded a Nobel Peace Prize.

Between 1903 and 1906 Roald Amundsen, a Norwegian, led an expedition through the North West Passage to Nome, Alaska. He was also the first to reach the South Pole, in December 1911.

Thor Heyerdahl, another Norwegian, became famous when he set out in 1947 with five other men on his unique and daring crossing of the Pacific on a balsa raft *Kon Tiki*. The 4,300 mile voyage from Peru to the Polynesian islands was undertaken to prove Heyerdahl's theory that the people on these islands had originally come from South America. Since then, Heyerdahl has undertaken equally bold journeys across other oceans.

The earliest of the major Scandinavian scientists was Danish Tycho Brahe, an outstanding astronomer. He made a series of observations which for his time were exceptionally accurate and comprehensive. His observations of planets, most particularly the orbit of Mars, were of prime importance as they formed the foundation on which Kepler, an assistant to Brahe, based his three laws of planetary motion. Niels Steensen is known to all medical men through Steno's duct. His pioneer work on the muscles of vertebrates and the anatomy of fishes was also important. During the 17th century Danish Ole Rømer discovered the finite velocity of light.

Carl Linnaeus became Sweden's foremost natural scientist through his plant classifications that revolutionized botany. Several of his disciples set off on expeditions to many parts of the world. Half a century later Sweden had another outstanding scientist, Jöns Jakob Berzelius, whose system of chemical formulation is used universally. He may also be considered a pioneer in nuclear research.

In the first half of the 19th century the leading figure in the exact sciences was the great Danish physicist Hans Christian Ørsted, who is chiefly known for his discovery of the magnetic field of the electric current, which started a new era in the science of electricity and magnetism.

Danish physicists Niels and Aage Bohr (father and son) are respected by scientists everywhere for their nuclear research. Alfred Nobel and his experiments with dynamite, Gustaf Dalén and his AGA sun valve and Sven Wingquist and his ball bearing are important Swedish contributors to modern science.

SHOPPING IN SCANDINAVIA

Fresh Ideas for Modern Living

In the field of modern design the Scandinavians probably lead the rest of the world. "Scandinavian modern", for instance, is a guarantee of first-rate craftsmanship, elegance, simplicity, and skilful blending of the functional with the aesthetic. National associations working in cooperation with local institutions, often through the medium of mobile exhibitions, have done a tremendous amount to educate popular taste, and in all five of the Scandinavian countries applied art has become a national tradition.

Recognizing that art as well as bread is a necessary ingredient of the full life, Scandinavian craftsmen have ceased to cater for the tastes of an exclusive and wealthy upper class. Instead, the trend has been to concentrate on the needs of the ordinary person and to train him to distinguish the good from the bad. At the same time, due emphasis has been placed on the values of hand craftsmanship and traditional designs. Again there are national associations which encourage home handicrafts, preserve the purity and authenticity of classical styles, and provide outlets for the products of native artists.

Admiring and owning artistic things are only the first steps in appreciation of the arts, according to the Scandinavian way of looking at it. Equally important is participation in some artistic activity, and thus it is no accident that so many Scandinavians weave on their own looms, knit, paint, mold pottery, carve wood, or work in silver and pewter.

It is interesting to note that the ideals of Scandinavian industrial design and applied arts were inspired by England's William Morris. Like him, the Scandinavians endeavor to extend the work of the craftsman to mass-produced goods in every branch of industry. Book-bindings, carpets, furniture, textiles, wallpapers, everyday glass and chinaware all show the influence of this effort. Denmark's Holmegaard glassworks and the Royal Porcelain Factory are well known, the latter for its development of underglaze, a new departure in porcelain. Norway has its Hadelands glass factory (which manufactures everything from windowpanes to exquisite etched goblets) and the Porsgrund Porcelain Works. Nuutajärvi and Iittala & Karhula produce some of Finland's best glass, and the Arabia Pottery Works just outside of Helsinki is one of the world's biggest. Probably best known of all are the Swedish names of Orrefors, Kosta, or Strömbergshyttan for glass, and Gustavsberg or Rörstrand for ceramics. Special guided tours are constantly arranged to take visitors through these and other factories.

Shopping Around

Provided money is no object, shopping in Scandinavia can be a delight. And whether money is a major factor or not, at least you can always be sure that Scandinavian quality and workmanship will give you full value for money. It's a good idea to compare before actually buying because prices vary considerably; as a rule you'll find them higher in specialty shops than in department stores, and in the fashionable or "old" part of town rather than in the commercial center. You can get the best of both worlds by window shopping, getting some ideas in the fashionable streets then buying in the more reasonably priced ones. Individual stores and trade names are listed in the country chapters; there are some justly famous ones that shouldn't be missed even if you only buy a token gift there.

One bright idea is to visit the local design center; here you will find the latest innovations by up-and-coming craftsmen and prices that occasionally are within reach of a visitor's modest budget.

Service everywhere is generally quick and gracious (English is spoken in most places and some department stores provide guides for foreign visitors); you're encouraged to browse around . . . and wait your turn. Most stores offer tax rebates on goods above a certain minimum value shipped (or taken) out of the country.

Designs for Living

Many of Scandinavia's traditional offerings (crystal, silver, porcelain, home furnishings, furniture, textiles, furs, etc.) can be found in all five countries, and you can hardly go wrong if you mix your countries up so to speak, but as a general guide you might bear in mind the following choices:

Denmark: porcelain, silver, design furniture, fabrics, wallpaper, furs, baroque pottery

Finland: design furniture, handwoven textiles, fashion design, furs, metal and semi-precious jewelry, art glass, wooden toys, candles, Lapp slippers and caps

Iceland: handmade clothing, sheepskins, lava ceramics

Norway: Saga mink, Norwegian blue fox, jewelry (especially inlaid enamel on silver or gold), crystal, ceramics, pewter, woodcarvings and sweaters.

Sweden: crystal, silver jewelry, stainless steel, home furnishings, leather goods, woodcarvings, candles, paintings.

In the past there have been stories of one Scandinavian country on the brink of war with another because a certain striking design appeared to have been pirated. It is almost impossible to copyright any kind of artistic creation, and when an area is superbly creative as Scandinavia, there must always be a large degree of overlap in the design of goods appearing on the market. However much this might worry the Scandinavians themselves, the end result for the shopper is one of enormous variety. Just wandering around a big department store in Helsinki or Stockholm can be a happily frustrating experience, there is so much to choose from and almost all of it has that indefinable feeling of being heirloom material. If your taste is for the delicate or the massive, the textured or the elegantly smooth, the traditional or the Martian, you will find exactly what you have always wanted to possess somewhere along the line.

In case you're thinking big, it might interest you to know that Denmark manufactures first-rate industrial machinery, Finland fabulous pre-fab houses, Norway fleet racing boats, Sweden perfect precision instruments and the safest car; and that doesn't exhaust the possibilities by a long chalk. Go and see for yourself, and worry about your bank manager when you get home.

SPORTS IN SCANDINAVIA

Of Sun and Ships and Skiing-Wax

The people of Scandinavia enjoy one inestimable boon; natural surroundings which provide both ample elbow room and unequalled opportunities for a variety of sports and open-air pursuits. Their favorite sports have in fact been dictated or suggested by their surroundings: skiing, mountaineering, sailing and angling are blessedly free of codes and conventions. The games which are subject to the tyranny of the white line—such as tennis and football—are latterday importations. For the Scandinavians as for the old Vikings, what counts is the individual performance, man striving against man or overcoming the forces of nature, rather than the team games of more populous countries.

Winter Sports

The valley of Morgedal in the mountains of Telemark claims—and rightly so, say the pundits—to be the cradle of modern skiing, and it is fitting that we should deal with Norway first.

From the tender age when he (or she) first starts to walk, the Norwegian boy (or girl) is given a pair of skis. The typically Norwegian ski sports are ski jumping, long distance races, and cross-country touring. In recent years, however, Norway has become increasingly alive to the thrills of downhill and slalom racing, for which her mountains are ideal.

The season lasts from the end of December to the middle of April, and the best known resorts are situated along the Oslo-Bergen Railway, the Dovre Railway (the Gudbrandsdal valley), in the Jotunheim Mountains (typical alpine country), and in the districts of Telemark and Valdres. Some 200 hotels, pensions, and skiing chalets cater to the needs of the visitors. All inclusive, first-class accommodation at the very best winter sports resorts is available at bargain rates. Oslo, Norway's capital, is the oldest and still the largest winter sports center in the world. Trondheim, Norway's third town, affords similar opportunities for winter sports, and in the far north, Narvik, with its mile-long aerial cablelift and impressive mountains, affords skiing that will thrill experts and novices alike. At most resorts, instructors are also at hand for lessons or conducted tours. Though skiing equipment (skis, poles, bindings and boots) can usually be hired, the price of these items is comparatively small and the quality excellent in Norway, and it is well worth buying your own at your town of arrival.

The most delightful period of the year for skiing is the early spring, when the days are already getting long, the mountain snow is at its silkiest, and the sun turns you mahogany brown in a matter of days. Don't, however, try to go skiing in Norway during Easter week, unless you have reserved accommodation: the Saturday before Palm Sunday sees practically the entire urban population of Norway converging with the single-mindedness of a colony of termite ants on their favorite haunts, eager to forget the winter darkness. Hotels and huts are crammed to capacity, and trains and buses bulge with sun-and-snow-worshippers. It is a good plan to book for the period after Easter, or if Easter comes particularly late, the period just before.

Should you come to Oslo on business and find your days taken up with sordid commercial matters, you will still be able to enjoy all the skiing you want, for the capital of Norway is in the happy position of possessing an unrivaled winter sports playground at its very doorstep. An electric railway will whisk you up to the hills above the city. Here you will find two excellent slalom hills, generously floodlit, with ski lifts. If you prefer skiing along an undulating forest trail, you will find a three-mile circular track, likewise floodlit, constructed for business men like yourself. If you wish to increase your proficiency, the famous Tomm Murstad School of Skiing, two minutes' walk from the terminal station, will take you in hand. In the vicinity of Oslo there are well-run ski centers at Kirkerudbakken (Baerum) and Ingierkollen (Oppegård).

Winter and spring provide most Norwegians with all the skiing they want, but summer skiing is available in a great many places. At Stryn, at the northern end of the Jotunheim Mountains (about eight hours from Oslo) there is an annual slalom and downhill competition held around midsummer day. If you want something out of the ordinary, you might try the mountains of Swedish Lapland in May and June, when the Arctic daylight has banished the darkness, and the sun blazes down. But remember to bring your sunsuit, as this will usually prove the most suitable attire.

Sweden's Riksgränsen in Lapland is a first-rate resort, and other Swedish centers that offer the enthusiast all he could possibly desire are Vålådalen, Storlien, Sälen, and Åre. Finland has Rovaniemi, Kusamo, Pyhätunturi, Saariselkä, Pallastunturi, and Kilpisjärvi, in Finnish Lapland, for spring skiing, and Lahti, Koli, Jyväskylä, Kuopio, and Aulanko, farther south, for winter and Easter skiing.

Practically every little village throughout Norway, Sweden and Finland has its weekly ski competitions. In Norway ski jumping takes pride of place, while the dictates of terrain make for a greater emphasis on ski racing in Sweden and Finland. The Holmenkollen competitions, with all the Alpine and Nordic events, attract skiers from as far afield as Chile and Japan. On a fine Sunday in March the series culminates with the ski jumping competitions on the Holmenkollen hill just outside Oslo, where 100,000 spectators gather to cheer their idols. The traditional picture has been that of the Swedes and Finns carrying off most of the long-distance races, while Norway maintained her supremacy in ski jumping. In recent years, the Norwegians alternate with the Finns and Swedes in taking first place at these Nordic events.

At the more expensive hotels one is expected to wear a lounge suit or dinner jacket in the evenings, but on the whole, Scandinavian winter sports resorts are not as dressy as other European centers. For skiing purposes it is better to be warm and comfortable than chic, but bring a windproof jacket, trousers and mittens, and don't forget dark glasses and tan lotion.

Before the first snow falls, autumn frosts cover the lakes and rivers of Scandinavia (this doesn't go for Denmark) with ice, and skates are hunted up in attics and lumber rooms, to be used until skiing begins. Though Norway produced Sonia Henie, skating runs a poor second to skiing. At the more international winter sports hotels you will probably find a skating rink, but you are not likely to find many Norwegians skimming over the ice. In Norway, Sweden and Finland, however, there are a number of speed skaters, whose races attract large and enthusiastic crowds. In fact, speed skating meets are public attraction number one from the spectators' point of view in Norway, and enjoy nearly the same prestige in Sweden and Finland. Two skaters race at a time, crossing over in the back straight on each lap, so that laps are run alternately on the outside and inside of the bend. The effortless grace and precision of these human machines, reeling off lap after lap to a time schedule which is adjusted to tenths of a second is worth watching.

Ice hockey and bandy, the special Scandinavian ball game played on ice, are the most popular team games on skates. Here the Swedes are fairly sure to beat their Finnish and Norwegian rivals.

Trotting races on the ice are Scandinavia's own form of winter horse-racing, and the horse (or reindeer in Lapland) also comes into its own in the romantic sleigh ride which most mountain hotels will arrange on suitable moonlit nights. Then there is the sport of *skikjoring,* which consists of being towed on skis by a horse or car: not entirely simple, as you will discover when you reach a steep downhill stretch, and spend a few anxious seconds wondering what happens when you catch up with your speedy tower. The expert skier will swerve to the left or the right, while the novice takes a middle course. This is not to be recommended.

Before we leave the snow and the ice, we should mention the facilities which exist for the thrilling sport of ice-yachting on the fjords and lakes of Finland and Sweden, as well as the creeks and inlets of their Baltic coastline. Winter fishing through holes in the ice of frozen lakes has its enthusiastic following, too. No picture of the winter scene would be complete without mentioning the ubiquitous *spark,* which can only be described as a snow scooter, and looks like a kitchen chair on runners. These are an endless source of delight to children and very useful in helping grandma to get her parcels home from the village store. Less romantic are the noisy motorized sledges which can now be rented in a number of centers though happily their use is often quite strictly controlled.

Summer Sports

In recent years the Swedes have produced a number of national teams which have earned the respect of the world's football fans, and several of their leading players have received tempting offers to turn professional from prominent Italian, Spanish and South American clubs. The other countries, though for the moment eclipsed on the football field by the scintillating Swedes, are not many goals behind; but it certainly seems that Sweden has established a comfortable lead in most branches of summer sport. Perhaps we should warn the British rugby football enthusiasts and the American football fan that the brand referred to is, of course, association or "soccer".

The comparatively short summer and the absence of good grass lawns might persuade you that tennis is not much played in Scandinavia. It certainly cannot compare with California or the Riviera in this respect, but Bästad near Halmstad tries. A great many fine indoor courts enable the game to be played all the year round. Björn Borg, the young superstar and top-ranking international player is Swedish. The Swedes and Finns also excel in racing drivers: the late Ronnie Peterson was a great champion. Athletics are enormously popular and many an international prize and Olympic medal has found its way to Scandinavia. The late Paavo Nurmi and, very recently, Lasse Viren are only two who have won fame for Finland with their remarkable achievements on the track.

The many charming seaside resorts which dot the North Sea and Baltic coasts of the Scandinavian countries are first-rate centers for the yachtsman, as well as the mere bather. Yachting is about as close to being a people's sport in Scandinavia as it is possible to make this pastime, in other lands usually reserved for the wealthy. From Scandinavian designers we have a number of world famous boats, such as the "Dragon" and the "I.O.D." (International One Design), fast, elegant and seaworthy craft popular the world over. June, July and August are the regatta months, with international contests taking place chiefly around the outer Oslo Fjord, Stockholm and its archipelago, and the Danish Kattegat coast.

The chances of hiring a boat are rather slim, whatever the advertisements may lead you to believe, as not many people would risk entrusting such a personal thing as a sailing boat to a complete stranger, whatever the financial inducement. A few enterprising Norwegians, Swedes and Danes have opened sailing schools for courses of seamanship, which include a good grounding in what the budding yachtsman ought to know, as well as a cruise on board a sloop. Full particulars of schools and courses available to non-Scandinavians can be obtained on application to the various National Yachting Associations. Of course, if you are a member of a recognized foreign yacht club you will have no difficulty in getting introductions, and should be all set for some invigorating weeks afloat. You will soon discover that the almost total absence of tides, coupled with the steep shelving of the coast, obviates any chance of waking up next morning to find you are high and dry on a mudbank. Moreover, the great fringe of islands big and small which runs like a protective screen along practically the entire coastlines of the four major Scandinavian countries provides stable conditions.

Exploring and Camping

Summertime also finds an army of campers and cyclists setting off for the wide open spaces of Scandinavia. From the plateaus of farthest Lapland to the beaches of Denmark, along the fjords, the lakes and the rivers, in the mountains and in the forests, they pitch their tents, toss their pancakes or throw their capers. The Youth Hostel Associations of each country have built a chain of stations throughout the length and breadth of Scandinavia, enabling the cyclist, hiker, or motorist who does not aim to camp out to spend a cheap and enjoyable holiday. For a few kroner, a bed can be obtained for the night, while the same sum procures a wholesome meal. The more adventurous will bend their steps towards the mountains, where good inexpensive accommodation can be found in the tourist huts and chalets of the national or local associations. Routes are invariably well-marked with cairns, but in case of doubt always obtain information from a local expert, and never forget that map and compass are essential when touring or climbing in the mountains. Even in midsummer it is apt to be chilly anywhere above 3,000 feet, so bring a set of warm winter woolies to be on the safe side. Don't imagine that a pair of stout shoes will stand up to the wear and tear of this sort of holiday. Nothing but a pair of strong boots will do.

Norway offers mountain climbing for the expert on a par with anything in Europe. Although most peaks have been climbed, there is still scope for making new and difficult routes. The principal mountain ranges are found in Jotunheimen, Sunnmøre, Romsdal, Trollheimen, Nordmøre, Lofoten and Lyngen.

An Angler's Paradise

The possibilities of Scandinavia as a holiday center for anglers were first discovered in the 19th century by enterprising English sportsmen, who came to the western fjords of Norway and returned to tell their friends in the stately homes of England and Scotland about the gargantuan trout and salmon they had gaffed. Thus began what has become an annual pilgrimage of British—and later American—sportsmen to the waters of Norway. Later on, Finland and Sweden were added to the list. While the western fjords still retain their popularity as salmon fishing centers, with the Laerdal River in the lead, the charms of remoter Lapland are making this part of Scandinavia increasingly popular.

Some of the more expensive hotels catering to the fly fisherman own their own beats, the use of which is reserved for hotel guests, but you can enjoy first-rate sport merely by purchasing a fishing card from the local policeman. The inexpensive "Angling in Norway", available through the Norwegian Tourist Board, deals minutely with all the famous salmon waters and contains a wealth of useful information about trout fishing. There is also a chapter on sea fishing, a popular and rewarding sport. In Denmark there are many waters frequented by anglers, and the charge for a license is minimal. The Swedish Kattegat resorts south of Gothenburg are also becoming centers for this fascinating form of big game fishing.

Even Cricket!

Canoeing is another great summer pastime and, in Finland, guided canoe trips are organized through several wilderness areas by the Finland Canoe Association. Facilities for horse riding, too, have increased considerably in recent years.

There are some excellent golf courses in Sweden, where the game is very popular: Boskogen, site of two Scandinavian Opens, chic Barsebäck, beautiful Mölle, Rya by the sea, Ven's island course, prestigious Hovås, Lidingö near Stockholm, Falsterbo and dozens more. A unique experience is playing golf in Sweden's far north under the midnight sun: start around midnight and finish at 4 A.M. for a change. Denmark too has around 40 courses, most of which, because of her milder climate, are open all year; Rungsted is probably the best, Elsinore has a nice course, as does nearby Gilleleje, and the island of Bornholm. Norway's best-known course is Bogstad near Oslo and there are others near main cities, most in typically dramatic Norwegian surroundings. Finland has a few courses, and Iceland only two (both near Reykjavik) to offer the follower of the Royal and Ancient Game.

Curiously enough Denmark has one claim to a special place among the Scandinavian countries, as it is the only one where cricket is played regularly by a small but keen coterie, whose doings are faithfully recorded in the leading Copenhagen dailies. It is a baffling experience, unless you are in the know, to find a corner of the sports page devoted to accounts of their matches.

Horse-racing is hardly a typical Scandinavianism, though in Oslo and Copenhagen weekly race meetings are held from May to October and at the Täby track, north of Stockholm, every week of the year. Far more popular are the trotting races, which help to encourage the breeding of good light draughthorses so essential in agricultural communities.

Hunting for Moose and Deer

Norway, Finland, and Sweden offer excellent opportunities for hunting various kinds of game. Moose of a species called elk in England are hunted in Finland from mid-October to mid-December, in Norway during the first ten days of October, and in Sweden for four days in early September or October, depending on the province. Wild reindeer may be shot in Norway during September, while fallow deer are stalked in Denmark from September through December. It is now forbidden to shoot polar bears in Spitzbergen waters.

Although trophies belong to the hunter, the meat and the hides usually belong to the owner of the hunting grounds. Rifles and ammunition may be imported for hunting, but special licenses are required. Costs are high. For further information write to Pal Mariassy, Grevgatan 28, Stockholm, Sweden, or Sverek, S–17193 Solna.

The Scandinavian attitude toward sport is in every way a sound one, reminiscent in a sense of the old Greek ideals. The desire to win is not allowed to rob the contestant of delight in the sport for its own sake. Nor is sport commercialized to the same extent as in larger and more populous countries. Moreover, sport is democratic. A man takes up a sport because it appeals to him, without giving more than a passing thought to his purse. Naturally the bus conductor who wants to take up sailing doesn't invest in a 12-metre yacht, but contents himself with a less pretentious model. But he gets the same amount of fun out of it. Fun is what the Scandinavian gets out of his sport in full measure. A well-known story about a Dane who came to Norway to ski will illustrate the spirit far better than a dozen articles. The Dane was putting on his skis outside the hotel for the very first time in his life and was desperately trying to get his boots into the bindings, without noticing that he had the skis on backwards. "You've got those skis turned the wrong way," remarked a Norwegian, who was attempting to be helpful. "How the hell do you know which way I'm going?" retorted the Dane.

FOOD AND DRINK

How to Skål and Survive

Although the Viking custom of drinking toasts out of somebody else's skull went out of fashion quite some time ago, it's only fair to warn you, as a visitor to Scandinavia, that you're still in danger of losing your head. Nor need you be on guard against bearded men carrying spears. The threat is more subtle, as you'll discover when you first slide your feet under a Scandinavian table.

When Do We Eat?

The first thing which will puzzle you as you edge uncertainly towards the *spisesal* (dining room) is the question of mealtimes. Breakfast, of course, is a natural, and is consumed sometime between the early morning bath and a glance at the newspaper. But now the difficulty begins. The next meal of the day defies definition. Some Anglo-Saxons are tempted to call it dinner, counting the sandwiches and glass of milk that many businessmen eat at their desks around noon as lunch. There are even those who stick by this theory doggedly, refusing to notice that the clatter of silverware against china, which starts up around 4.30 P.M. and becomes deafening towards 6.00 P.M., has completely disappeared, in Norway at least, by the dinner hour. The Scandinavians, being practical people, avoid the dispute by calling it

79

middag. We advise you to do the same, thereby working for peace in a troubled world.

Instead of sowing discord, the Scandinavians are interested merely in making maximum use of the long and bright summer evenings. Accordingly, families sit down to the main meal of the day as soon as father comes home from work, somewhere towards the tag end of the afternoon. The great advantage of this arrangement is that, once *middag* is over, everyone is free for the rest of the day. If you come hotfoot from South Dakota or South Kensington with a hatful of introductions to near relations or business acquaintances, you can turn this custom into a game. Don't refuse three or four dinner invitations you received for the same day. Just fix a different hour for each.

While you have your napkin unfolded and are wondering who's going to eat all that food, we should urge you to save some room for *aftens* or supper, the final meal of the day, not counting incidental snacks. This may be no more than cakes and coffee or it may consist of no less than a complete cold buffet, depending on the circumstances and whether or not your eyes have the socially-accepted glaze. No one is looked down upon for starting this as early as 7.00 P.M. although, at a formal party, it might well not appear until midnight.

With this overall timetable in mind, let's get down to particular dishes. The typically Scandinavian breakfast is more varied than the typical English or American one. The larger hotels, accustomed to catering especially to visitors from abroad, will be able to offer you bacon and eggs, though this honorable combination is not indigenous to the Scandinavian ménage. Instead, eggs, cheese, cold meats, herrings in a number of guises, jams, and fruit are all likely to make their appearance, in addition to less usual items such as cereals, porridge, hot meatballs, and salad. These you'll discover together with a great variety of bread, many kinds rarely found in other countries. One of them, *Knekkebrød,* is of the hard, unleavened type which you've undoubtedly seen elsewhere under the proprietary name of Ry King. Unless you specify otherwise, your egg will normally be served soft-boiled and still in its shell.

By the time you've tried everything, chances are you'll have a solid foundation which will carry you through to mid-afternoon. But if you find your fancy gradually turning towards throughts of food along about noon, you have a number of choices. In most of the bigger cities there are sidewalk stands displaying signs reading *Pølser* or *Varm Korv.* At these you will be able to buy hot dogs, often wrapped in what looks like a pancake instead of a roll. They are smaller than what you're used to, and you will probably agree that they taste better.

If all you want is something cool, look for another kind of sidewalk stand, marked *Is* or *Glass.* The name has nothing to do with the verb "to be" or with windowpanes, but informs you that here you can have ice cream.

The Mysterious Open Sandwich

Failing both of these (and still assuming you're interested), make for the nearest restaurant. If you see the word *smørbrød,* you're in luck, for this is Scandinavia's most typical dish. The word means simply, "butter-bread", but there's nothing simple about it, as you'll discover when the waiter hands you a menu listing dozens of varieties.

Smørbrød is the rich uncle of its English or American nephew, the sandwich. Unlike the anonymous sort of thing served at garden parties or railway stations, it is a single-decker, and presents its offering naked and unashamed. Lobster, smoked salmon, prawns, shrimps, smoked herrings, all appropriately and artistically garnished, cold turkey, chicken, roast beef, pork, a host of sausages, cheeses, eggs, and salads, all tastefully and appetizingly arranged. Variously called *smörgås* by the Swedes and *voileipä* by the Finns, three of them taken with a cool lager are generally considered an excellent lunch, whether or not you abandon all caution and succumb to a piece of pastry for dessert. Hot food is available too, if you are still hungry.

Wherever you may be in Scandinavia, the sea is never far off, and this is a good thing to remember when you sit down to *middag*. Perhaps because the fish served in restaurants and hotels is invariably fresh, the Scandinavians are all great fish-eaters. Whatever the reason, their seafood dishes are justly renowned for their variety and excellence. Lobster, salmon, and trout are great favorites, but you will also have your choice of cured herrings, crayfish, crab, oysters, shrimps, prawns, hake, eel, and other seaborne morsels. Boiled cod may sound unromantic, yet you'll find it transformed when served *à la Scandinave* with melted butter and parsley. In the summer the Swedes and Finns indulge in traditional crayfish weeks when you can go on eating these succulent little creatures until your conscience begins to bother you. In Denmark you'll compare the Limfjord oysters to the best that Baltimore or Colchester has to offer.

Then there are a number of fish dishes which only the bolder spirits are advised to try. The first of these is *rakørret,* which is trout that, like Keats' wine, has "lain long years in the deep-delved earth". There is actually much more to the preparation of this highly odiferous *spécialité de la maison* than burying it in the backyard, but it is undoubtedly an acquired taste. Next comes *surströmming,* another form of man's inhumanity to fish, except that this time it's a herring who suffers. As the name suggests, the taste is distinctly sour; that is, if you get that far. The third of our "don'ts" for cautious gourmets is *lutefisk,* which is codfish steeped in a lye of potash. The finished product has the consistency of frog spawn and a taste which can only be experienced and not described. The Norwegians who eat this "delicacy" anesthetize themselves with such copious drams of *akvavit* one might suspect that the *lutefisk* is only an excuse.

While we are on the subject of dishes which should be approached circumspectly, we may as well complete the story with a mention of *geitost* or goat's cheese, which has the hue of scrubbing soap or milk chocolate and the texture of plastic wood. Give it a try anyhow; you'll be called on for your own opinion sooner or later. And if you are too disappointed, all the Scandinavian countries produce excellent imitations of such well-known favorites as Roquefort, Camembert, Gruyère, and even England's Stilton. Danish Blue is another local variety with which no cheese-lover could possibly quarrel.

Scandinavian cooks use margarine or butter for their cooking, and not oil as the Latins do. Game and roasts are usually served with a cream sauce which is delicious. In some cases, sour cream is used, and *ryper* (a variety of grouse or ptarmigan) prepared with this sauce and accompanied by cranberry jam is a rare treat.

By now you are doubtless wondering what has happened to the renowned Swedish *smörgåsbord.* It's doing fine, thank you. But let me first explain to the uninitiated that the *smörgåsbord* (called *voileipäpöytä* by the Finns) is a very special *hors d'oeuvre,* offering the diner a stupendous number of small dishes, each more calculated than the last to whet his appetite and make him forget all rash resolutions to respect his waistline. The beauty of this institution is that it contains no *pièce de résistance* to dominate the table. You roam at will like the honey bee, savoring here a morsel of smoked eel, there a little lobster, and roving through the delicacies of the animal kingdom, with regular rounds of *akvavit* and beer to give you fresh incentive. These days, the *smörgåsbord* is seldom the prelude to a four-course dinner in private homes, but some restaurants feature it as a specialty, maybe on a certain day in the week.

Desserts do not run to the English or American pattern. Neither the English pudding nor the American ice cream desserts are as prevalent as soufflés, large, tiered cream cakes, and berries in season. Strawberries reach the table somewhere around the end of June and manage to survive for a commendable number of weeks. Later on in the year, Finland, Norway and Sweden offer a delicious wild berry which is hardly known elsewhere, the cloudberry, called *suomuurain* or *lakka* in Finnish, *hjortron* in Sweden, and *multer* in Norway. In appearance rather like an overgrown unripe raspberry, it has a delicate aroma which is unique. Incidentally, the Finns make a delicious liqueur from the juice of this berry.

Speaking of liquid refreshments, we should note that the Scandinavians are coffee-drinkers rather than tea-drinkers, and they make their coffee good and strong, in the best Continental tradition. In Denmark and Norway, coffee is somewhat expensive, and families who drink a lot have to make up for it with some sort of substitute. This trend has, of course, resulted in an increase in tea-drinking, but on the whole the Scandinavians have not yet acquired the English touch. So be sure to emphasize that you want your tea strong. Don't expect to find that the cult of tea has made the Scandinavians tea-conscious. The buttered toast, crumpets and muffins of Belgravia have no afternoon counterpart in Bergen or Bornholm. Instead, look for a restaurant-type of place with the sign *"Konditori"* over the door. The waitress will bring cakes to your table along with tea, coffee, milk or a soft drink. You'll be hard put to choose among the several delicious varieties.

Skål

Scandinavia's local brand of firewater is known as *akvavit,* and a glass of this is known in Denmark, Sweden and Finland as *snaps,* whereas the Norwegians call it a *dram.* Served at the beginning of the main meal of the day—at the *hors d'oeuvre* stage, or occasionally with the first course—it is invariably taken with a beer chaser. *Akvavit* emphatically is not a drink for the tyro toper and you'll find it takes a little practice to attain proficiency in the local ritual of gulping it down without falling off your chair. The mysteries of the *skål* or toast, apart from regional variations, are too complicated to explain here, but you won't go far wrong if you stick to the following procedure.

First, at the start of any meal, wait for someone to give the signal. At a formal party, the host, after clearing his throat ominously or belaboring the nearest piece of china or crystal with a soup spoon, will seize his glass and launch into a *velkommen til bords* speech. All this means is "welcome to the table" and you may even find it a gracious gesture of hospitality. Anyhow, the crucial thing is to listen intently for the word *skål*. This is your cue. Seizing your own glass, you hold it firmly in a position of tantalizing proximity to your parched lips, though preferably far enough away from your nose to avoid asphyxiation. Then you nod your head north, south, east, and west as you echo *"skål"*. Now, and not a moment sooner, your *akvavit* starts its downward journey. This is the supreme test. As all hell breaks loose somewhere in your gullet, you may be tempted to reach convulsively for the beaker of cool beer that beckons by your plate. Not so the trained snapser. He returns his glass to its original position just south of his chin, nods blandly to the four points of the compass while simulating an air of complete indifference to the fires consuming within, and then sends a mouthful of malt brew in pursuit of the *akvavit*.

When the urge to wet your whistle descends on you, don't try a surreptitious drink on your own, but pick up your glass boldly, fix a fellow diner with a purposeful stare, pronounce the word *"skål"*, and proceed as above. Anyone is fair game for this except your hostess; after all, someone has to keep track of the time. Apart from achieving a drink, you will undoubtedly have won the undying gratitude of your friend across the table, who was almost certainly contemplating a similar move. Remember that husbands are expected to *skål* their wives, who, if slighted, are entitled to collect a pair of stockings by way of damages.

Although there are so many striking points of similarity between the food and drink of each of the Scandinavian countries, it is surprising that in a few unimportant details, which only indirectly affect the table, there should be some startling discrepancies. For example, one may say without any risk of offending the Swedes and the Danes, that the Finns and Norwegians make infinitely better dessert and eating chocolate. On the other hand, the Danish Aalborg akvavit and the Swedish Norrland akvavit can be said to be the best of its kind—but the Norwegians have gone one step further by producing their *linje akevitt*, which is stored in huge sherry vats of American white oak, and then sent on Norwegian cargo liners to Australia and back. It is said that the rolling of the ship, combined with the change of climate when crossing the Equator—the "Linje"—adds an unusual flavor to the "scalplifter." Lager beer in Scandinavia is of top quality, whether you drink Danish Carlsberg or Tuborg or Norwegian Ringnes or Schou, all of which are exported around the world.

Apart from these minor exceptions, you will find that the Scandinavians have elevated the culinary arts to a high place among the graces which add flavor to life. Wherever you dine you will discover that the serving is on a par with the cuisine. Helpings are generous, dishes and drinks which are supposed to be hot really are hot, and iced drinks never arrive in a semitepid state. This is only natural where hospitality is regarded as one of the supreme virtues.

After finishing a meal in Scandinavia, it is a time-honored custom for the hostess to stand near the door of the dining room. The guests, one by one, shake her hand on their way into the living room and pronounce the words, *"takk for maten"*. Badly translated, this means "thank you for the food". A phrase well-worn by usage, perhaps, but nonetheless welcome from those who have dined well in congenial company.

DENMARK

PRELUDE TO DENMARK

The Fairytale Land

The Danes aren't a frivolous folk, and nowadays very few are farmers. They worked hard in the 19th century to make their not specially fertile soil productive, and in the 20th they've worked even harder to build up a series of industries based on virtually nothing beyond their own brains. But however hard they work they certainly know how to relax and enjoy life.

They've a glorious history behind them. At one time or another they're ruled the whole of Norway and Sweden as well as parts of Germany, territories to the east of the Baltic, and most of England. They still rule Greenland, an island larger than Australia. One of their Viking forbears may well have sailed to America centuries before Columbus. The Danes know all this, and are naturally proud of such a heritage. Unlike most nations, however, they don't feel obliged to keep on boasting about it. They're extremely modest. Above all, they're realists, and know they have to live in the present and the future—not the past.

Efficiency and good management, they well know, are the keynotes of success. So you can be certain that when a Dane says something will be done it will be done exactly as promised, and on time. But there's no coldness in this efficiency. The Danes welcome visitors to their trim and lovely land with extraordinary warmth and generosity, especially the British, whom they feel to be brothers or at least close cousins, the Americans, whose country has received so many Danish immigrants, and everyone else who speaks the language of Britain and America. They like to be happy. Hard-working and cheerful, the Danes are inveterate optimists and extract a full measure of enjoyment from each passing day and the visitor from abroad ought to be able to do likewise.

You might also consider Denmark as a gateway to the rest of Scandinavia and take advantage of the comprehensive and reasonably-priced guided tours arranged by Danish travel agencies; see Useful Addresses on page 123 for names and addresses.

PRACTICAL INFORMATION FOR DENMARK

WHAT WILL IT COST. Below we give some indication of price costs in Denmark; however with the present unstable world currency situation these figures can only be approximate. But Denmark is a small country and you can explore it without making Copenhagen your base: hotel prices are considerably lower outside the capital and North Zealand, though they are rising at the North Sea coastal resorts. The cheapest areas are probably Funen and Jutland. A stay in a country inn is a good bet, and here you will have the best chance of meeting the Danes; rooms will be clean and comfortable, but often there are no private bathrooms.

Hotel Room, Half Double. (including VAT and service)

	1st class superior	1st class reasonable	Moderate	Inexpensive
Copenhagen	400 Dkr	250 Dkr	175 Dkr	125 Dkr
Provincial town, resort	300	150	125	100
Rural	250	125	100	75

Other local prices are: a bottle of wine, 90 Dkr; a glass of snaps, 12–15 Dkr; cinema ticket, 35; opera ticket from 40. Try at least once the smørrebrød (cold buffet), 65–80 Dkr.

Examples of food prices are: beef, 125 Dkr per lb.; butter, 18 per lb.; milk 6 per liter. Mineral water is 3 Dkr, and beer 5 per bottle (extra 1 Dkr for non-returnable bottle). Cigarettes are expensive, about 20 Dkr for a pack of 20.

Denmark's living standards are among the highest in Europe, with high social security: but the Danish worker pays for it, with 50% of gross income being paid out in various taxes, and many prices are realistic, not subsidized.

Restaurant prices are about 25–40 Dkr for breakfast, 40–65 Dkr for an inexpensive meal, 100–125 Dkr for a moderate dinner (or expensive lunch); 125 Dkr and up is expensive, (excluding beverages).

A Typical Day For One Person.

Room in moderate Copenhagen hotel (half double)	200 Dkr
Breakfast	35
Lunch, popular restaurant	60
Dinner	125
Transportation (bus, train)	35
Theater or cinema ticket	50
Cigarettes (pack of 20)	20
Coffee (cafeteria)	10
Beer (bottle) in bar	12
Miscellaneous	50
	597 Dkr

TIPPING. Because of the introduction of a 22% value added tax, tipping, except for *very* special services, has been banished from hotels and restaurants. All prices are now fully inclusive and you are specifically requested *not* to give tips in these establishments.

Checkrooms, washrooms and shoeshines have fixed charges, to which no additions should be made. Barbers are not tipped, though beauty parlor assistants may be given 1–2 Dkr if their service is good. Tipping is not regular for guides in castles, etc. Ushers should never be tipped. Taxi drivers are happy with 10%. You might note that Danes, on the whole, consider tipping patronizing, so use some tact if doing so.

WHEN TO COME. Minorities are sometimes right. Most visitors come to Denmark during the months of July and August, while the wiser minority chooses May, June or September. The few enjoy themselves in comfort. While the summer congestion in hotels is terrific, the "season" for Copenhagen and for big hotels throughout the country now lasts virtually the year round.

In *May,* the Tivoli Gardens open, the most famous amusement park in the world. With the end of *June* the summer season reaches its height. Everybody in Copenhagen goes to the country, everyone from the country goes to Copenhagen, and visitors from abroad go everywhere. The beaches are thronged. During the summer, some 30–40 music festivals take place in Denmark. Among the best known are the Organ Festival in Sorø, the Beat Festival in Roskilde, the Chamber Music Festival at the old Egeskov Castle in Southfunen, and the traditional Viking Festival in Frederikssund.

In *September,* Tivoli closes, and the Royal Theater opens with ballet, opera and classical drama. The Queen returns to town, and the Royal Guards start marching through the city at noon on their way to Amalienborg Palace to relieve the sentries.

WHAT TO SEE. Highlights of Denmark Biggest city is Copenhagen, one of the most delightful capitals of the world. Another town you might want to see is Odense, the city of Hans Christian Andersen, on the island of Funen (Fyn), which also offers a beautiful landscape and a great number of medieval castles and manor houses. For the picturesque, visit AErø, a small island south of Funen, with the tiny, fairy-tale town of AErøskøbing.

The peninsula of Jutland also has many places well worth visiting: Århus, the principal town, with its "Old Town", open-air museum, cathedral, university, town hall, and beautiful surroundings; other larger towns such as Aalborg, Randers, Vejle, Esbjerg, and the ancient towns of Ribe, Ebeltoft, and Mariager. Manor houses are dotted all over, and scenic landscapes vary from the moors in the west to the hilly eastern Jutland.

The island of Møn, south of Zealand, with the 400-foot-high beechwood-clad chalk cliffs; and the island of Bornholm in the Baltic Sea is a gem that enjoys more sunny hours than anywhere else in Denmark.

HOW TO GET ABOUT. Although one of the smallest countries in Europe, Denmark has a widespread **railroad** system with over 1,250 miles (2,000 km) of routes plus 125 miles (200 km) of ferries. Standards of comfort and cleanliness are high. From Copenhagen to the main cities of Funen and Jutland there are fast *Inter-City* trains (shown as "IC" in timetables) and also slightly faster *lyntog* trains (shown as "L" in timetables). All services which use the Great Belt (Zealand to Funen) ferries require seat reservations; other trains do not. From Copenhagen, train travel to Odense takes about 3 to 3½ hours; to Esbjerg about 4½ hours; to Århus about 5 hours. Most long-distance trains have refreshment facilities.

There is also an efficient **bus** network, which is often the only means of public transportation. As a rule, rail and bus tickets are not interchangeable, but many buses do connect with train services, particularly those serving rural areas. Many larger towns arrange bus trips to various places of interest locally and in the surrounding countryside. The Fairytale Tours of Denmark take you in three days through charming "unexplored" Denmark, from Copenhagen to Århus or Frederikshavn. Departures daily from June through August.

Modern passenger **steamers** link Copenhagen with Rønne (on the island of Bornholm, 8 hours) daily. Day and night services operate in summer, in winter, night services only. There are ferry services across the Sound between Denmark and Sweden, and also to Norway.

Air service includes daily domestic departures to and from Copenhagen. Flying time inside Denmark is less than an hour. Visitors arriving in Copenhagen from a non-Scandinavian airport are transported by air to a provincial airport without extra charge.

Between Kastrup Airport and Copenhagen air terminal (in Central Station) there are frequent coaches. Ordinary city buses are cheaper—(routes 32, 32H), Town Hall Square; (route 9), Kongens Nytorv and Østerport; (route 38E), Valby Station.

You can hire a private plane through *Copenhagen Airtaxi,* and *Beeline Flight Academy,* Copenhagen Airport, DK–4000, Roskilde.

 MOTORING. Denmark's small size, charming countryside and excellent roads make it an ideal country for touring by car. You may either bring your own or rent one upon arrival. Bridges, connecting many of the islands, are toll-free; fares on automobile ferries are moderate, while the driver often travels free of charge on inland routes. For motorists who wish to see Denmark, but have only limited time at their disposal, we suggest the following itinerary (which may also be adapted for travel by bus or train). For car hire agencies see *Useful Addresses* for Copenhagen following.

Route 1: *North Jutland.* Esbjerg-Ringkøbing-Holstebro-Thisted-Aalborg. Distance, about 186 miles (300 km).

Route 2: *East and South Jutland.* Hadsund-Mariager-Randers-Rosenholm-Århus-Skanderborg-Horsens-Vejle-Ribe. Distance, about 167 miles (263 km).

Route 3: *South Jutland and Funen.* Tønder-Sønderborg-Fynshav-Bøjden-Faaborg ferry-Svendborg-Langeland-Erø-Odense (or route 4). Distance, about 123 miles (197 km).

Route 4: *Funen and Zealand.* Odense-Nyborg-Halsskov ferry-Ringsted-Roskilde-Copenhagen.Distance, about 86 miles (138 km).

Route 5: *South Funen, Lolland, Falster and Zealand.* Langeland-Tårs ferry-Nysted-Nykøbing-Vordingborg-Køge-Copenhagen. Distance, about 120 miles (192 km).

Assuming that the majority of motorists will cross from Britain to Esbjerg, it would be convenient to follow routes 1 to 3, with 4 and 5 interchangeable to or from Copenhagen back to Esbjerg. Travelers arriving overland from Germany can start with route 3, follow 4 and 5, then take 2 and 1 in reverse, to return them to the German frontier. Ferry arrivals at Rødbyhavn from Puttgarden slot naturally into route 5. DFDS offer very good short break packages.

Traffic Rules: There is a general town speed limit of 37 m.p.h (60 km.p.h.), outside towns the maximum is 50 m.p.h. (80 km.p.h.) and on motorways 60 m.p.h. (100 km.p.h.). Trailers 45 m.p.h. (70 km.p.h.), also on motorways. Seat belts are compulsory.

In every town with time-limited parking restrictions you are required to use a parking disc unless you're parked at a meter. You can get a parking disc at FDM, banks, tourist offices, police stations and some shops. Place the pointer on the time of arrival in the right front window of your car and beware of exceeding the time allowance (or of parking your car illegally) as the police do come by and have cars towed away. A circular blue sign with red rim and cross means no stopping at all. Parking on country highways and motorways is prohibited.

Avoid driving in the narrow streets of Copenhagen between the Kongens Nytorv and the Town Hall Square as direct throughway is almost impossible.

SPORTS. Denmark's extensive coastline, fjords, sounds, and rivers make it ideal for **water sports** of all types. Opportunities for **swimming** are numerous, but ask about unfrequented spots because of possible strong currents. Best beaches are those of Fanø, the west coast of Jutland up to Skagen, Juelsminde, Kerteminde, Nyborg, the north coast of Zealand, and Falster, but there are many others.

For **sailing,** there are the waters in the Sound, around southern Funen, and in the East Jutland fjords. **Rowing, canoeing,** and **kayaking** are favorite activities. In addition to the popular kayak trip down the river Gudenå are those down the Mølleå (about 20 miles) in North Zealand, the Suså trip (may be varied from 8–28 miles) in South Zealand, and a fjord and coastal trip at Naestved.

For **fishing,** salmon may be caught near Bornholm and in Storstrømmen from Vordingborg between May 1 and Sept. 30. Freshwater anglers will find salmon, trout, perch and pike (license required). Fishing tours on the Sound are arranged from Skovshoved Harbor; ask the Copenhagen tourist office for details.

Tennis courts and **riding** clubs are found almost everywhere, and there are excellent **golf courses** at the principal tourist centers. Spectator sports include **football** (soccer), except during the summer months, **cycling** races, and **horseracing**—tracks for flat races and trotting races are operated at Copenhagen, Aalborg, Århus, Odense. Bjaeverskov (Køge), south of Copenhagen, Nykøbing Falster, Billund (South Jutland), Almindingen (Bornholm), and Skive. There are hundreds of outstandingly good **campsites** that may also be used by trailers.

MEET THE DANES. *Friends Overseas,* an American-Scandinavian organization receives hundreds of letters each year from Scandinavians who would like to meet American tourists and introduce them to their families, friends and cities. Americans are given the names and addresses of those Scandinavian members and are expected to write before leaving the States, allowing sufficient time for return correspondence. For further information, please send self-addressed stamped envelope to: Friends Overseas, 68–04 Dartmouth Street, Forest Hills, New York 11375.

HINTS FOR BUSINESSMEN. In Denmark, normal business and office hours are from about 9.0 A.M. to 4.0 P.M., but you should be prepared for an invitation to dinner as an extension of your business appointment.

If you have a good business connection, he will usually be able to supply you with secretarial help, if necessary. If not, you can find a secretary through one of the secretarial agencies. In Copenhagen, try Competance, tel. 11 16 19, or Manpower, tel. 11 78 00. A secretary can be sent to your hotel room or you can take your material to the agency office. Secretarial services cost from 95 Dkr per hour, for a minimum of 4 hours. It is also possible to hire an interpreter from Translatørforeningen, tel. 12 60 44. Hours: 10–2; outside these hours an answering machine will take messages.

There is a public telex booth at the Copenhagen main telegraph office at Købmagergade 37 from where it is possible to telex direct to the U.K., U.S.A. and Canada.

 THEATERS, MUSIC, EXHIBITIONS. In addition to the special events and festivals, many seasonal and year-round attractions are offered. Most of the theatrical and musical activity centers about Copenhagen, but Aalborg, Århus and Odense also maintain permanent theaters and municipal orchestras. The theater season generally runs from September 1 to the end of May, while houses offering revues and other light entertainment are open during the summer months as well. Copenhagen, one of Europe's liveliest capitals, is the place for night life, and in the larger towns also you'll find nightclubs and night bars as well as restaurants with floorshows and dance bands providing music for your dancing or listening mood. Art and design exhibitions, flower shows, dog shows, and a host of similar displays flourish in the capital and in the larger provincial towns all year around—most towns on Funen, for example, have museums including works of local artists.

 FOOD. A "Danish Breakfast" consists of coffee or tea, 4–5 kinds of bread served with generous slabs of butter, marmalade, and a glass of milk. For your coffee break try a Danish pastry.

The Danes eat their lunch around noon. Most of them, from the humblest to the most exalted, take their packets of sandwiches to work with them. At some hotels and restaurants, particularly outside of Copenhagen, that astonishing institution known as "cold table" holds sway at lunch time. This consists of an enormous table groaning with an assortment of fish and cold meat or fowl. These may be boiled, pickled, fried, or roasted. The Danish way of coping with these is to take a piece of bread and delicately pile on the fish or meat together with pickles and relishes of various kinds. The result is *smørrebrød*. Don't charge into the fray too recklessly, because a hot dish usually follows if you are taking the set lunch.

Many restaurants offer a lengthy list of *smørrebrød* and you just check your choice. (The fresh shrimp, salmon, varied species of herring, roast beef with onions topped by a fried egg, are all specialties to be recommended.) There are columns for rye bread *(rugbrød)* and wheat bread *(franskbrød)*. Three per person is par. If you don't find a particular restaurant's list offered to you with the daily menu, just ask for it.

A good tip to remember is that many country inns cater for guests who bring their own sandwiches. These usually have a notice *Madkurve kan medbringes* or *Medbragt mad kan spises her.* All you have to do is to order a bottle of beer and ask for "service". You will then be provided, without charge, with a plate, knife, fork, pepper and salt. If you also order coffee after your repast, you will be doubly welcome.

The Danes eat their dinner around 6.00 P.M. Having dinner so early makes it possible for them to go out on a spree, or just out, that much sooner. It also makes it possible for them to have something more to eat from 9.00 P.M. onwards, usually tea or coffee and cakes. But you don't have to do likewise, since the principal restaurants are open all evening. Danish meats are superb and vegetables always fresh. Potatoes are sometimes eaten in great quantities.

There are 50 or more varieties of Danish beer made by as many breweries, and the best known come from Carlsberg and Tuborg. Most popular is Pilsner, a light beer, but there is also Lager, a darker beer. (What is called "Lager" in Britain is called "Pilsner" in Denmark.) Each of these varieties has a stronger brother. The strong brother of Pilsner is "Gold Export", and the strong brother of Lager has several names, depending on the brewery that makes it. Among the popular Danish-made spirits and liqueurs are Cloc Liqueur, Cherry Heering, and the cherry wine *Kijafa*.

The national drink of Scandinavia is popularly called *snaps,* the famous Aalborg Aquavit. This is neither an aperitif, a cocktail nor a liqueur, but is meant to be drunk with food, preferably with a beer chaser. Some claim they drink it for the good of their tummies. *Snaps* at room temperature tastes vile, which is why it is served icy cold and should never be sipped or left to get warm. Knock it back and damn the consequences. Remember that snaps goes with cold food, particularly herrings and cheese, not hot.

 HOTELS. In Copenhagen the high season runs from May 1st to end October, in the seaside resorts and provincial towns from June 15 to August 20. Off-season hotel prices are lower in Copenhagen, but this is not the general practice elsewhere, although some seaside resorts and new hotels may offer reductions. Your best bet is to avoid peak-period travel and to ask for the off-season rates. For rates in the respective hotel categories, consult the Facts At Your Fingertips section at the start of the book under the heading *Hotels.* In Copenhagen, as a rule, breakfast is included in the room price unless indicated, but some hotels will ask you during the high season to take half or full pension rates.

Like the other Scandinavian countries, Denmark has a number of "Mission Hotels". These always offer better accommodation than their modest price would indicate. Most serve beer and wine, no spirits.

One final point. Instead of using blankets and top sheets, you will find that the Danes sleep under a bag of feathers enveloped in a sheet bag. This permits no adjustment during occasional heat waves, and you will either swelter or do without bed clothes. Moreover, the bag of feathers doesn't tuck in at the bottom, probably because being tucked in gives the Danes claustrophobia. Again you are confronted with a choice between having cold shoulders or cold feet. If you get desperate, you can remove the outer case of the feather bag, use it as a top sheet and the bedspread as a blanket. After a few days however, you will love this bag of feathers (eiderdowns) so much that you will buy one and take it home with you.

 CAMPING. Camping passes are compulsory at all approved sites in Denmark. International passes (carnets) issued by Alliance Internationale de Tourisme (A.I.T.) or by Fédération Internationale de Camping et de Caravanning (F.I.C.C.) are fully valid in Denmark. If a camper from abroad is not in possession of a camping pass issued by one of these organizations, he may, on production of passport, obtain a temporary camping pass. This pass is valid for all approved sites in Denmark for a price of 19 Dkr and is valid for the rest of the year for the holder and his family. Temporary camping passes are issued by the campwardens of the approved sites. For the official list with information on camping sites in Denmark, apply to *DFDS Travel,* Latham House, 16 Minories, London EC3N 1AN, or any bookseller or campsite in Denmark (price 33 Dkr). Denmark has over 500 officially recognized sites, many of extraordinarily high quality. Nearly 70 are open all year, with heated public rooms.

If you are without tent or trailer you may stay in a youth hostel. Like the camping sites they are usually of a high standard, but a yearly issued guide also tells about the facilities of the hostel. Many contain family rooms and they can usually provide you with breakfast upon request. A hosteller's carnet is compulsory.

 CLOTHING. Normal summer clothing will usually suffice in the Danish summer, but you may risk a cold day, so don't forget a sweater and good shoes. Danes are rather informal about clothing, at bathing resorts both sexes may wear shorts, also in summer restaurants. In larger towns and Copenhagen, count on daily clothing in restaurants, cinemas and theaters, no need to wear a dinner jacket, lounge suit, tie or long dress, except in very fashionable restaurants, or unless you go to the theater to be seen rather than to see. If you visit Denmark between mid-June and mid-August, count on more rain than before or after that period, but bring your raincoat and umbrella in any case.

 CHILDREN. Student babysitters are available, also guided children's sightseeing tours. Babysitter agency: Minerva, Åkrogen 20, DK–2600 Glostrup. Tel. 02–45 90 45 or 02–45 90 64 or ask your hotel porter.

Hotels provide cots, highchairs, feeding bottles, etc. Traveling with children is easy.

 HANDICAPPED TOURISTS. To ensure a comfortable and enjoyable stay in Denmark, it is best to book far in advance to secure a room in a suitable hotel. Public transportation cannot admit wheelchairs, except for the S-trains and some of the long distance trains. *Landsforeningen af Vanføre* (National Association of Disabled Persons), Hans Knudsens Plads 1, DK–2100 Copenhagen Ø can advise on any problems associated with holidays for the handicapped. They have also issued a pamphlet, entitled *Hotelguide for the Handicapped,* which lists hotels throughout the country that are able to offer facilities for handicapped guests. Hotels marked (H) in the listings are those catering to the totally wheelchair-bound guests. The Danish Tourist Board's publication *Access in Denmark—a Tourist Guide for the Disabled* contains practical information on transportation, accommodations, access to sights and attractions, etc.

 MAIL. All mail goes airmail to Britain at no extra charge. Letters to Britain, ordinary: 2.50 Dkr up to 20 grams, 8.00 up to 100 grams. Letters to U.S. and Canada, ordinary: 3.50 Dkr up to 20 grams, 8.00 up to 100 grams, including airmail to U.S. and Canada (no extra charge for letters up to 5 grams, you need not write "5 g" but can use "by airmail" or the like—this is a change from earlier practice). Postcards: Britain 2.50 Dkr, U.S. and Canada 2.70 Dkr, airmail included. Domestic: letters and postcards 2.50 Dkr. These charges are liable to change during 1984.

Cables. Telegrams and cables are sent from the telegraph office, not from the post offices as in Britain. Regular, per word to U.S.A. and Canada 3.00 Dkr,

Britain 1.50 Dkr, minimum 7 words, basic fee 45 Dkr. (as per April 1983). To cable by phone dial 0022 for domestic destinations, 0023 for Britain, 0024 for overseas.

 TELEPHONES. All automatic (6 digits). If calling outside your area code (see the White Pages), dial area code plus exchange (central Copenhagen is code 01, outskirts 02). All domestic calls are cheaper from 8.00 P.M. to 8.00 A.M. Direct dialing to the U.K. (00944), U.S.A. and Canada (0091 except to Alaska and Hawaii) is now possible.

 CONVENIENT CONVENIENCES. You can count on finding public lavatories on larger squares in Copenhagen and on the market place of minor towns. Trains outside Copenhagen have facilities which may be common to both sexes. With the possible exception of stations, the hygienic standard is satisfactory. D or DAMER is ladies, H or HERRER is for men.

COPENHAGEN

Scandinavia's Fun Capital

The center of Danish fun is Copenhagen, biggest and happiest of the Scandinavian capitals and by almost unanimous agreement one of the liveliest cities of Europe. More than a million Danes, a quarter of the country's population, live and let live here. The city, on the island of Zealand, is just as flat as the sea that embraces it, as flat as the rest of Denmark, which averages only 98 feet above sea level. (This is why every second inhabitant has a bicycle.)

When is the best time to come? "Even in winter", wrote one Scottish editor, "Copenhagen is an ideal summer resort." A Danish journalist was more objective about his own country. "Denmark was never intended to be inhabited in winter," wrote he. So much for the ambiguous nature of reality. On the subject there is no argument: Denmark is lovely in summer, autumn and spring. May marks the liberation from the bonds of the long northern winter. On May 4, flickering candles flame in the windows of Denmark to celebrate the liberation in 1945. The next day there are celebrations in every Danish town from southern Jutland to the far reaches of Bornholm. The circus comes to Copenhagen, too, in May; the amusement park, Bakken, opens in the Klampenborg Forest in April, Tivoli comes alive on May 1st, and Denmark begins to rock like the yachts between Elsinore and Copenhagen, warming up for that water carnival known as "Round Sealand" in late June—the world's biggest sea yacht race (1,600 participants last year). The Royal Danish Ballet end their season, and June comes to a climax on June 23 with Midsummer's Eve, a night of outdoor dancing, singing, feasting, bonfires and fireworks, transforming the whole nation into one big carnival. Try to celebrate this night along the Sound. You'll never forget the unreal summer twilight, streaked with rockets edged with a thousand fires along the shores of the Kattegat, as though Sweden and Denmark were both aflame.

With the end of June, everyone enjoys the long, sunflooded days and short balmy nights in Denmark. Make your reservations early; the Danes will do the rest.

The Lie of the Land

Many visitors find it odd that Denmark's capital should be on the extreme eastern edge of one of the country's larger islands, only a few miles from Sweden. But the reason is simple. Historically, Copenhagen was the capital not only of Denmark in its modern form, but also of Norway and southern Sweden and other Baltic territories. As a well-sheltered port with immediate access to the high seas—large ships still sail from the city center—Copenhagen in days gone by was an ideally situated capital.

Being on the coast, free from too much heavy industry and from many coal fires and furnaces, Copenhagen is a cleaner capital than most. Though it lacks a background of mountains to set it off, view-points from which it can be admired, hills to which its houses can cling, and though much of it has had to be rebuilt, Copenhagen remains a charming city.

Exploring Copenhagen

If you suggest to someone that, although Copenhagen has a history stretching back to the 11th century, the city really doesn't look very old, you are likely to get the reply, "Considering it's been bashed about by the Swedes a few times, ravaged by a number of fires and bombarded by the British, that's hardly surprising." Strategically located on the Sound connecting the Baltic with the Kattegat and the North Sea, Copenhagen was just a small village ceaselessly harassed by Wendian pirates until the middle of the 12th century. But in 1167 Bishop Absalon, warrior and politician as well as priest, like many contemporary clerics, decided to protect the infant village by building a castle on the small central island known as Slotsholmen.

Shortly thereafter the town adopted the name of Køpmannaehafn (Merchants' Haven), and proceeded to grow apace within its protecting walls. In the 15th century, the king came to live in Copenhagen and a university was started. Increasing in both size and importance little by little, the prosperous city entered upon a great period of expansion with the accession of King Christian IV (1588–1648) to the throne. This man of extraordinary energy was possessed with a passion for building. Whenever he could take time off from waging wars, he started some new project, and even today so many of his works remain that whenever there's a question about who erected what, Christian gets the credit. Rosenborg Castle, the Round Tower, and the Stock Exchange with its exotic dragon spire, were all inspired by him. He also gave the town an arsenal and a naval dock, and put up the "Nyboder", or rows of small houses which are still inhabited by naval personnel and pensioners.

In 1659, when Swedish King Carl Gustaf tried to put an end to the continual Dano-Swedish wars by the simple strategy of conquering Denmark outright, Copenhagen found itself in a difficult situation. The town was besieged and everyone, including Frederik III, took a hand at defending it. After attempting to take the city by storm, the Swedes were routed and driven back to their own shores. This same Frederik thereupon built the Citadel near Langelinie, which served the reverse of its intended function in 1940 when the Germans initiated their occupation of Denmark by capturing the old fortifications.

Back in 1728 and 1795, fires swept Copenhagen and destroyed vast portions of it. The devastation had scarcely been repaired when a British fleet twice bombarded the city during the Napoleonic Wars in 1801 and 1807. Fortunately the palaces survived—Amalienborg, Christiansborg and Rosenborg—and the vacant sites undoubtedly provided opportunities for rebuilding that might not otherwise have been undertaken. After the Napoleonic Wars, Denmark enjoyed relative peace and Copenhagen expanded far beyond the ramparts and water fortifications. Industries such as brewing, shipbuilding and manufacturing hardware became immensely profitable, and the city grew from a population of 130,000 in 1850 to its present size of well over a million inhabitants, suburbs included.

Strolls About Town

With this partial introduction to the Copenhagen scene, the time has come to sally forth into the bewildering jumble of winding streets, unexpected canals and multitudinous buildings which are the distinguishing features of the Danish capital. The average visitor from abroad, as he steps out of the Central Station into the warm sun of a summer morning, is likely to be a bit baffled at the start. As we've already pointed out, there is a serious scarcity of distinguishing landmarks by which the new arrival can easily chart his course through this intricate city. While it's true that Copenhagen a few years back seemed to be largely a collection of charmingly distinctive spires, there are now so many tall modern buildings that you can no longer see them. And to top it off, about the time you are at last getting yourself oriented, you are so unnerved by the sudden appearance of a platoon of bicyclists bearing down upon you that all idea of where you are or where you intended to go is just as precipitously driven from your head.

Any attempt to plot out some interesting tours for the person bent on discovering the "real" Copenhagen is fraught with danger. Assuming that you master your fear of two-wheeled traffic and have provided yourself with a suitable map, it's more than possible that you'll start off in the wrong direction and be so captivated by what you see that you won't detect your error until you've gone several blocks out of your

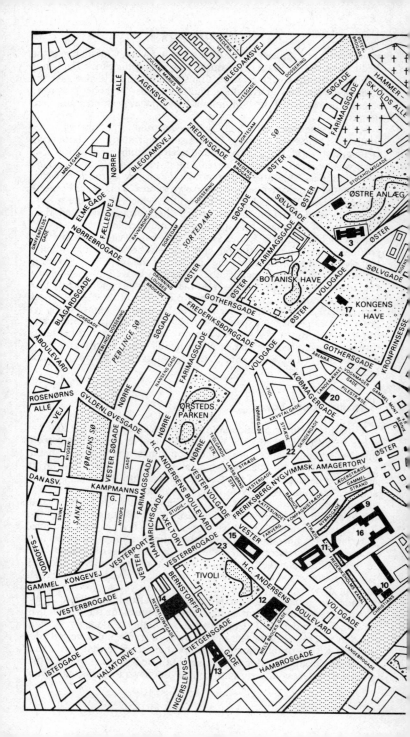

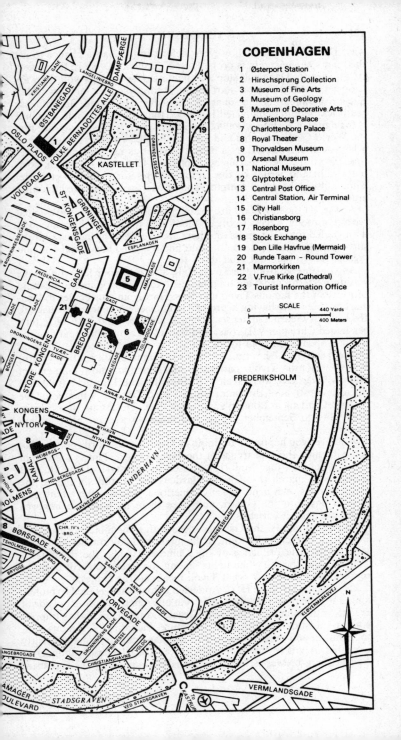

COPENHAGEN

1 Østerport Station
2 Hirschsprung Collection
3 Museum of Fine Arts
4 Museum of Geology
5 Museum of Decorative Arts
6 Amalienborg Palace
7 Charlottenborg Palace
8 Royal Theater
9 Thorvaldsen Museum
10 Arsenal Museum
11 National Museum
12 Glyptoteket
13 Central Post Office
14 Central Station, Air Terminal
15 City Hall
16 Christiansborg
17 Rosenborg
18 Stock Exchange
19 Den Lille Havfrue (Mermaid)
20 Runde Taarn – Round Tower
21 Marmorkirken
22 V.Frue Kirke (Cathedral)
23 Tourist Information Office

SCALE

0 ———————— 440 Yards
0 ———————— 400 Meters

way. Don't be alarmed, however—before you've had a chance to get the points of the compass properly unscrambled, it's more than likely that a friendly Dane will stop and politely offer to show you the way.

So let's plunge in and start at the Rådhuspladsen, or Town Hall Square. Dominating the square is the Town Hall itself, an immense red-brick building completed in 1905. High above the main entrance is the figure of Bishop Absalon, founder of the city. Inside you see first the World Clock invented and built by Jens Olsen. Then you come to a large hall surrounded by a balcony, which is used for official functions. Here there are marble busts of Hans Christian Andersen, poet, playwright and writer of the famous stories for children, of Bertel Thorvaldsen, the noted sculptor, and of Martin Nyrop, the building's architect.

Above, on the first floor, are the council chamber and the municipal reception room. Access to the 350-foot-high tower only in connection with guided tours. From its top there are fine views of the city and the surrounding countryside. You might find it a good idea to take advantage of this to plan out your day's tour.

As you emerge from the Town Hall, a turn to your left would take you up Vesterbrogade, and in a moment you would come to the main entrance of the famous Tivoli Gardens. Hardly anyone comes to Denmark without first having heard of Tivoli Gardens. These date back to 1843, when Georg Carstensen, Danish architect and man of letters, persuaded Christian VIII to let him lay out an amusement park on the site of Copenhagen's old fortifications. "If only people are allowed to amuse themselves," he argued, "they will forget to talk politics." Within a few months Tivoli, patterned after London's now long-extinct Vauxhall Gardens, was a reality. In 1951 the wheel turned a full circle when the Festival of Britain organizers used Tivoli as a model for the Festival Gardens in London's Battersea Park. During its short season from May to September, Tivoli welcomes an average of 4 million visitors.

Whatever you happen to be doing in Tivoli, on a Saturday or Sunday you will enjoy the appearance of the Tivoli Guard. This is a group of toytown soldiers (age limit 17) dressed in the style of the Queen's Guard, who march through the Gardens several times a day to the music of their own band. Keen competition precedes the admittance of each boy into the Guard, and once there he holds an honored position among his friends.

On certain nights, the Gardens close with a magnificent display of fireworks. As rockets fly to meet the moon and colorful set pieces vie with the electric brilliance of the Chinese Pagoda, the illuminated fountain, and the fairy-like lights among the trees, you will begin to appreciate something of what Tivoli means to the Danes.

Just beyond Tivoli, in H. C. Andersen's Boulevard, is the Glyptotek, containing the most complete collection of French sculpture outside of France, with remarkable pieces by Degas, Gauguin, and other Impressionists; outstanding Egyptian sculpture including a famous hippopotamus; and much Greek and Roman statuary, magnificently presented. A gift to the municipality from Carl Jacobsen, founder of the Carlsberg breweries, the museum is maintained by the Carlsberg

Foundation, which has done so much to further cultural and scientific activities in Denmark. The first thing that strikes your eye as you walk into the winter garden is Kai Nielsen's Watermother, serenely watching the 14 marble babies who tumble over her sculptured body.

Close to the Glyptotek looms the city Police Court, an austere, somber building completed in the 1920s. The Police Court is now closed, and you cannot walk into the courtyard direct from the street. Tourists are, however, welcome to apply to the information stand (8 A.M.–4 P.M.), *Polititorvet,* for permission to visit the courtyard. If you do go in you will be surprised by the beautiful columned courtyard in Roman style with a giant bronze statue of the hero, Justice, stamping out Satan.

Returning again on to Vesterbrogade on your right is the SAS building, containing the Royal Hotel, and on the left is the Central Station with Air Terminal. In the center of the street you'll see an obelisk commemorating the freeing of the Danish peasants from the feudal yoke in 1788. Just beyond, in the black Vesterport building, is the Permanent Exhibition of Danish Arts and Crafts, where the best works of most of Denmark's contemporary artists are displayed and sold. A 5-minute walk from here, along Vesterbrogade, brings you to the City Museum. Outside is a model of medieval Copenhagen, while inside are exhibits depicting the city's history. The first part of the Absalonsgade in connection with the City Museum will be re-erected in its late-19th-century state with old sidewalks and gaslights and, of course, no motorized vehicles.

Up Strøget to Christiansborg

But our path lies in the opposite direction. Instead of turning left as we leave the Town Hall, we turn right and arrive shortly at a series of streets running eastwards from the square and collectively known as "Strøget". This is Copenhagen's Bond Street or Fifth Avenue, now for pedestrians only. Not far along Frederiksberggade, the first one, we come to a double square, the northern half of which is called Gammeltorv and the southern, Nytorv. The most interesting thing about these twin squares is the splendid fountain in the middle of the former. On April 16, the Queen's birthday, children are brought here to see the "golden apples dance". These golden apples are gilded metal balls which "dance" on the jets of water.

Looking to the right from the Nytorv half of this square, you may be able to see a spot of water to the south. A few steps in this direction bring you to Rådhusstraede and then to Frederiksholms Canal, where you'll find the entrance to one of Copenhagen's most fascinating places, the National Museum, built in the 1740s for Crown Prince Frederik, who later became King Frederik V. Inside you can see the world's finest collection of Stone Age tools and runic stones dating from the Viking period. Note particularly the beautiful Hindsgavl Dagger, fashioned and used several thousand years before the birth of Christ. You can also get some idea of Viking camp life, the ships with which they traveled all over the world, and their unusual burial mounds in which it was the custom to put a jug of liquor beside the body of the deceased to assure him happiness in heaven.

One of the featured exhibits in the Historical Music section is a number of Bronze Age *lur,* unusual musical instruments between four and six feet in length, which were popular 3,000 years ago; 36 lurs or fragments have thus far been found in peat bogs all over Denmark. The museum offers for sale interesting silver and bronze replicas of certain of the exhibits.

Directly across the bridge from the National Museum is Christiansborg Palace, seat of the Folketing, or Danish parliament, and the Supreme Court. This is where Bishop Absalon built his first fortress in 1167. Its ruins can be visited under the present building, which is the sixth on this site. From 1441 until the fire of 1794 Christiansborg was used as a royal residence.

On the same island with the palace are clustered a number of other important buildings. Set in an idyllic garden is the Royal Library, with Denmark's largest collection of books, newspapers, incunabula and manuscripts, including the earliest records of Viking expeditions to America and Greenland. On one side of the library is Tøjhuset, Copenhagen's arms museum, with outstanding displays of uniforms, weapons, and armor, in an arched hall nearly 200 yards long.

Børsen, Round Tower and University

On the other side of the library is the low, red-brick Børsen, former Stock Exchange. This fine example of Renaissance architecture is claimed to be the oldest stock exchange in the world still used for its original purpose, though the main part of the business has now been moved to other premises. Børsen stands in tribute to the skill and originality of Christian IV. Indeed, it is said that he lent a hand in the twisting of the tails of the four dragons that form its spire. Picture this rotund monarch standing on the roof and clad, as shown in his portraits, in what appears to be black velvet outlined with silver braid and an enormous lace collar, wearing white doeskin gauntlets and thigh boots, and sporting a white silk scarf over his blind eye.

Still on Slotsholm island and on the island side of Christiansborg Palace, we come to Thorvaldsen's Museum. Here the great sculptor is buried, surrounded by originals or casts of all his works. Beyond and to the north of this museum we recross the canal over Højbro, or High Bridge.

Let's stand in the middle of Højbro for a moment and look back down the canal to the right. Just across from Børsen is Holmens Kirke, where two of Denmark's greatest naval heroes are entombed. One is Niels Juel, the man who shredded the Swedish fleet at Køge in 1677, and the other is the almost legendary Tordenskjold, who defeated Charles XII of Sweden during the Great Northern War. At the far end of the canal you see Knippelsbro, the big drawbridge leading to the island of Christianshavn. That green and gold spire with the curious spiral staircase winding around it is part of Vor Frelsers Kirke (Our Saviour's Church). After a look inside, you'll find that the excellent view from the tower is well worth the climb.

Christianshavn is one of the oldest quarters of Copenhagen. It is well worth taking a stroll along Christianshavns Kanal to look at the houseboats and the old restored houses. Or you can rent a row-boat and take it along the canal. On fine summer nights you might be lucky enough to get a boat for a moonlight trip.

Returning from Christianshavn, we continue over Højbro to Højbro Plads. Passing the equestrian statue of Bishop Absalon our path lies straight ahead, past Nikolaj Kirke, over Strøget once more, and into Købmagergade. Four blocks up this street—on the right—is the Round Tower, which Christian IV built as an astronomical observatory, not as part of the church to which it is attached. If you are energetic, you can climb to the top by means of an internal spiral ramp. Peter the Great of Russia, so the story goes, drove up in a horse-drawn carriage. Not being an emperor, you will have to walk. If you prefer mental to physical exercise, try solving the Hebrew and Latin rebus printed in letters of gold outside the tower. Translated it means: "Lord, make the King's, Christian the Fourth's, heart faithful and just."

Perhaps this is the place for a few more words about Denmark's amazing warrior-architect-scholar-king. Vitally alive to every new idea, Christian IV was much more than a builder. During his busy life he found time to revolutionize farming, reform the administration of his Norwegian kingdom, create seven new chairs of learning at the University and start trading companies to exploit the fabled riches of the East and discover a Northwest Passage. Even when he went for a walk, he would pull a ruler out of his pocket and check the workmanship of local masons and carpenters.

Across the road from the Round Tower is Regensen, since 1623 a residential college for university students. It is worth pushing aside the heavy door and taking a quick look at the courtyard. The old lime tree there celebrates its birthday with a private May lunch, after which the students "shake hands" with a pair of gloves hung up in its branches.

Strolling up Købmagergade a little farther, we turn left at the second corner. Another long block and we come to the University and Vor Frue Kirke. The University celebrated its 500th anniversary in 1979 with a public feast. The main building, however, was erected in the early 19th century. The scientific faculties have been moved to a new campus at Nørre Faelled behind the Rigshospital, while the humanities have been moved to a new campus at Amager.

Vor Frue Kirke, or Our Lady's Church, has been Copenhagen's cathedral since 1924. Bishop Absalon is believed to have built a chapel here in the early 13th century. Ravaged by fire in 1728 and hit during Nelson's bombardment in 1807, it was restored at the beginning of the 19th century, and again in 1977–79. Bronze statues of Moses and David flank the entrance, and Thorvaldsen's marble sculptures of Christ and the Apostles can be seen inside. The ruins of the first church (1320) can now be seen in the basement, and a small historical collection has been opened on the first floor. On coming out take a turn to the left down Nørregade and, before you know it, you are back at the twin squares of Gammeltorv and Nytorv, our first stop.

Kongens Nytorv to Langelinie

Thus far we have described a large circle in the older part of town. The trip we are about to start upon will take us pretty much in a straight line. It begins at Kongens Nytorv, which lies at the opposite end of Strøget from the Town Hall square. Strøget, you will recall, is the series of streets with different names that comprise Copenhagen's principal shopping district. The better stores are at the end from which we are about to set out.

In the center of Kongens Nytorv is a mounted statue of Christian V. Near the end of June every year, newly matriculated students arrive here in horse-drawn wagonettes and dance gaily around the silent figure of the king. The southern side of the square is flanked by the Royal Theater, featuring ballet and opera as well as classical drama. Next door stands the Theater's annex, popularly called the "Starling Box". The Dutch baroque building of Charlottenborg, which has housed the Danish Academy of Fine Arts since 1754, is also in Kongens Nytorv.

The stretch of water you see running up to Kongens Nytorv is the Nyhavn Canal. Picturesque 18th-century buildings, mostly containing sailors' cafés, crowd along both sides. Out path lies directly ahead, however, down Bredgade to the first turning to the right, Sankt Annae Plads, then the next left into Amaliegade.

Before you stands an imposing colonnade. Although it looks like stone, it is actually made of wood—if you don't believe us, try tapping it. When you've gone through the arches, the square you are in contains the four residences that comprise Amalienborg Palace. The one immediately to the right is used by Queen Margrethe and her family, the following (facing you on the right) is occupied by dowager Queen Ingrid. The Museum of Royal Costumes and Possessions at Amalienborg has now been finally closed (for security reasons). During the autumn and winter, when the Queen lives in Copenhagen, the guards, complete with bearskins and headed by their band, march through the city from the barracks adjoining Rosenborg Castle every day, to relieve the Amalienborg sentries at noon. Colorful, too, is the sight of a royal coach with its scarlet-coated drivers giving the team some brisk trotting exercise through the busy streets.

Turning left out of the palace square we come back to Bredgade. Directly in front of us broods the Marble Church. Perched around the outside are 16 statues of various religious leaders from Moses to Luther, and below them stand other sculptures of outstanding Danish ministers and bishops. The building was completed in 1894, after having lain in ruins since 1770.

We turn right into Bredgade and shortly arrive in front of the Museum of Decorative Arts, once a royal hospital. Art handicraft from the Middle Ages to the present—most notably ceramics, silverware, and Flemish tapestries—is on display, together with collections of musical instruments and Danish memorabilia.

A few steps more take us up to Esplanaden, where there is a small museum with collections from the resistance movement during World War II. There you will also see the Gefion Fountain. Powerfully and dramatically this commemorates the legend of the goddess Gefion, who was promised as much of Sweden as she could plough around in one day. Changing her four sons into oxen, she carved out the island of Zealand. Perhaps there may be an element of truth in the story, for if you look at a map of Sweden you'll see that Lake Vänern is much the same size and shape as Zealand itself.

The park in front of us, alongside Esplanaden, is graced by the English Church standing at its entrance. In the center, surrounded by two rings of moats, is the Kastellet, or Citadel (there are plans to restore it to its original star shape). The grounds are open to the public. Stretching straight ahead of us is the Langelinie Promenade, where foreign navies moor their ships, and all of Copenhagen meets on Sunday afternoon. About halfway along it, the Little Mermaid of Hans Andersen's famous fairy story perches on a rock by the water's edge and gazes wistfully across the harbor.

Jewels, Flowers and Old Masters

The last of our three excursions begins in Kongens Have, the King's Gardens, where little children play around the statue of Hans Christian Andersen. Our objective is the Renaissance-style Rosenborg Palace, now a museum containing not only a breathtaking display of all the Danish crown jewels but also a fine collection of furniture, together with the personal effects of Danish kings from the time of Christian IV, including that monarch's precious pearl-studded saddle.

Just opposite the palace are some 25 acres of botanical gardens, as well as an observatory and mineralogical museum. Across the street from the north end of these gardens we come to Statens Museum for Kunst, the national art gallery, whose liveried doorkeeper sports buckle shoes and a cocked hat on chilly days. In addition to Danish works, you'll find paintings by Rembrandt, Cranach, and Rubens, wood engravings by Dürer, a fine collection of French Impressionists with a remarkable self-portrait by Matisse, and a huge paper cutout made by the artist shortly before his death. Behind the main building is the Hirschsprung Collection, specializing in paintings, drawings, and sculptures by Danish artists of the 19th century.

We have now been through most of the better-known parts of the heart of Copenhagen, but it would be an error to forget that the real heart of any city is the living one. The red-coated postmen, the bearskinned, not over-military-looking Royal Guard, the spirited Tivoli Guard, the cyclists, the Nyhavn rowdies and drunks, the little fat man who delivers the milk all week and then blossoms out as a racehorse owner on Sundays, Queen Margrethe: all these are the real sights of Copenhagen.

Short Excursions Out of Town

When the sun is shining, whether there is spring in the air or snow on the ground, and the Copenhagener wants a few hours in the country the chances are he will go to Dyrehaven, the Deer Park near Klampenborg. Here nearly 2,000 of these timid, graceful animals wander about at complete ease. A golf course, a summer fun-fair (open mid-April to late August) and several all-year-round restaurants occupy the rest of the 3,500 acres of forest, paths and ponds that make up this lovely park. Near the entrance to the park is the Bellevue bathing beach. Farther along the seaside drive from the capital to Elsinore (Helsingør) are a host of luxurious villas and charming places to stop. Also near Elsinore is Denmark's only casino, the Marienlyst Hotel.

Starting from either Lyngby or Holte, you can go for a walk in the woods close by, or else stroll around lakes Lyngbysø and the much larger Furesø. At Lyngby, near Sorgenfri station, you'll find the open-air museum known as Frilandsmuseet. In a park covering 40 acres is a collection of reconstructed old Danish farms, several windmills, and country houses moved here from other parts of Denmark and southern Sweden. The houses are furnished and equipped with the implements and utensils of the period and place they represent.

The Hareskov woods can be reached from Svanemøllen station (train B). From Hareskov you may ramble through the forest to Fiskebaek and have lunch there. Afterwards you might vary your return journey by riding the motorboat to Lyngby or Holte station.

A shorter trip which many enjoy is to Dragør on the island of Amager. This quaint old fishing village, where geese still roam in the crooked streets, has a charm of its very own. The oldest house contains a museum of furniture, costumes, drawings, and model ships. Its chimney is twisted to prevent the Devil finding his way through. The museum in Store Magleby, an old, half-timbered farmhouse, displays Amager furniture, dresses, and needlework.

Another haunt you might enjoy, as much for the trip out as for what you find at your destination, is to Grundtvig's Church. Consecrated in 1940 and built in a style based on the typical Danish village church, this building, with its organ-like façade stands in memory of the poet, clergyman and founder of the Folk High School, whose name it bears.

Contemporary building experiments in modern living have been carried out by subsidized non-profitmaking building societies on suburban sites, unfortunately too far from one another for one tour. Farum Midtpunkt (S-train B from city, or bus 330 from Bellahøj), Galgebakken and neighboring Hyldespjaeldet at Albertslund (train B or bus 123 to Albertslund, bus 141 or 149 from the station, crossing 123), Gadekaeret (Ishøj) and Askerød, Hundige, (trains A or E or bus 121) are the foremost examples.

Denmark Outside Copenhagen

It is generally felt that you must at least see Copenhagen when you visit Denmark, even if there is no time to see anything else. However, there is quite another Denmark outside this busy capital. The provincial regions all have their different characteristics in landscape, inhabitants and experiences to give you.

If you travel by car don't choose the main roads: the secondary roads will prove far more interesting and are of a high standard. Good maps are available from booksellers or gas stations.

If your time is limited you might book a three-day *Fairytale Tour* by bus. Accompanied by an English-speaking guide you will see some of the most important sights and sleep in first-class hotels (included in the tour price). All Fairytale tours start and finish at Copenhagen and are of three-day duration. Places visited are, among others, Odense, Randers, Roskilde etc. Breakfast and dinner are included in the price. The first three-day tour is at the end of May and the last tour is at the beginning of September. Travel bureaux will give you all details.

If you have more time it is a good idea to select a specific region and stay there for some time. Prices are considerably lower outside Copenhagen and North Zealand. You could stay at a country inn, or you could hire a summer cottage—apply well in advance to a regional tourist office stating the price you wish to pay, the area in which you wish to stay and the dates. Weekly rentals from 1,200 Dkr up.

Recently it has also become popular to stay at a farmhouse. You can have a Farmhouse Holiday for 150 Dkr per day full board, and 130 Dkr half board—cheaper for children under 12—or a Carefree Country Holiday at 850–1,150 Dkr per week. Here you do your own housekeeping. Apply to a tourist office covering the area in which you want to stay for either farmhouse-type accommodation. The minimum period of stay for both of these and for the cottages mentioned above is one week. Summer cottages and Carefree Country Holidays reduce their prices out off season (September–May).

If you favor something more sporting try a bicycle holiday. All-inclusive bicycle tours along narrow country lanes enable you to experience the beauty of the Danish countryside. The tours last 3–14 days, and you are supplied with bicycles (although you can bring your own), a map of the route and coupons for meals and overnight stay in a selected country inn (or youth hostel, in the cheapest tour). The daily trips cover 25–30 miles, so you will have a lot of time and children can keep up with the pace, although not on the Round Denmark 14–day tour. Tours are normally operated from May to the end of September, at week prices between 900 and 2,000 Dkr including half or full board, (reductions for children under 12, Denmark Tour excluded).

Another idea is a canoe holiday. In a canoe (max. 3 persons) you paddle down the river Gudenå, Denmark's longest, about 5 hours a day for a week. At your own pace you relax in ever-changing landscapes, make a stop or two as you wish, and camp overnight. The start is at Tørring, north of Vejle and west of Horsens and the final stop is Silkeborg in the lake district. Included in a fee of approximately 1,500 Dkr are canoe rent and transportation to Tørring, paddle, life jackets, tent (or bring your own), camping fees and route description, but no food. Operated from May to October. Shorter trips are arranged down the Karup Å and Skjern Å, also in Jutland.

You can also hire a covered wagon and explore Funen or Langeland. The 2,300 Dkr fee includes horse (and feed), wagon with gas, fridge and sleeping room for four, for a week; food is not included. It is cheaper in the off season, when the weekly rate is 1,600 Dkr. Similar holidays are arranged on Samsø, an island out of the way in Kattegat. These tours are called "Wild West on Samsø".

In all cases go for information and bookings to the local tourist office or write to the Danish Tourist Board in Copenhagen or to Dantourist A/S, Hulgade 21, DK–5700 Svendborg.

PRACTICAL INFORMATION FOR COPENHAGEN

 HOTELS. The hotels in Denmark's capital are numerous and range from the luxurious down to the very plain and modest side-street hotel. During the season (May through Oct.) it is advisable to book your room well in advance, either directly or through your local travel agent. If you happen to come without a reservation, go to the Room Service, situated in Kastrup Airport and the Central Station (Kiosk P); open until after arrival of international night trains in season. Winter, weekdays 9–5 and Saturdays 9–12. For a moderate fee the bureau will find you a room in a hotel if possible, otherwise a private room. During the off-season (Nov.-Apr.) many hotels, especially the new ones, lower their rates considerably. It is therefore advisable when reserving to have the prices confirmed. Hotels designated (BE) charge for breakfast. The budget hotel area is near the central station, around Colbjørnsengade-Helgolandsgade, and best among the cheaper establishments are the so-called Mission Hotels (unlicensed).

Deluxe

D'Angleterre, Kongens Nytorv 34; 246 beds, ranks first among the Copenhagen hotels. Aristocratic, spacious, with excellent food and service. Its sidewalk terrace is a permanent fixture during the tourist season. Bar, restaurant with music, beauty salon, barber shop (BE).

Kong Frederik, Vester Voldgade 23–27, 210 beds; comfortable rooms, fine restaurant, English-type bar.

Royal, Hammerichsgade 1. This modern hotel has the best of Danish architecture, art and furniture used with international experience. 500 beds, all rooms with bath; sauna; restaurant, bar (BE).

Scandinavia, Amager Blvd. 70, 1100 beds, 27 stories high, recent; pool, sauna (BE). Faces old city moats.

Sheraton Copenhagen, Vester Søgade 846 beds, 34 suites. All rooms with TV, sauna (BE).

First Class Superior

Ascot, Studiestraede 57. Centrally located, 95 beds, all rooms with bath; also 13 apartments with 1 to 5 beds.

Codan, Sct. Annaeplads 21, 243 beds, all rooms with bath; ground floor and roof restaurants (BE).

Copenhagen Admiral, Toldbodgade 24, 815 beds in Wiinblad-decorated rooms with modern Danish design in 1780-framed former granary with intact Pomeranian girders. Sauna (BE). Opened 1978.

Imperial, Vester Farimagsgade 9, 331 beds (all rooms with bath). Centrally located, pleasant decoration and furniture. Open-air restaurant famed for good food, cafeteria.

Marina, at Vedbaek north of Copenhagen, 208 beds, all rooms with bath; music; ping-pong, billiards, sauna, near beach and station, or buses 188, 27 and 1 via Klampenborg. Also has 31 apartments of 2–6 beds, bath and kitchen.

SAS Globetrotter Hotel, Engvej 171, near Kastrup Airport. 265 beds. Modern; with restaurant, bar and cafeteria. Bowling and sauna. Bus 9 to Stock Exchange in 15 min.

71 Nyhavn, a former storehouse at this address, converted to hotel; 123 beds, all rooms with bath.

"3 Falke" (Three Falcons), Falkoner Allé 9, 286 beds, in the Frederiksberg section; the name describes the municipal arms. Good bus connections and parking facilities.

First Class Reasonable

Astoria, Banegårdspladsen 4; 155 beds (most rooms with bath), Near Tivoli and the Central Station.

Alexandra, H. C. Andersens Boulevard 8; 116 beds. Close to the Town Hall Square, the center of the capital. Quiet and modest. Restaurant.

Bel Air, Løjtegårdsvej 99, near airport. 430 beds, all rooms with shower or bath. Restaurant, bar, sauna. Bus 34 to Copenhagen in 25 min.

Danhotel, Kastrup Airport, 511 beds, all rooms with bath, some with TV. Bus 32 or 32H to city takes about 30 mins.

Esso Motor Hotel, Kettevej 4. 321 beds, indoor pool, sauna. At Hvidovre, western Copenhagen (BE).

Excelsior, Colbjørnsengade 4, 94 beds. Basic, near Central Station.

Neptun, Sct. Annaeplads 18, 90 beds, all rooms with bath or shower, attractively furnished. Also, 2 apartments with 4 beds, 2000 Dkr per week.

Park, Jarmers Plads 3, 114 beds. Central, redecorated (BE).

Østerport, Oslo Plads 5. 136 beds (some rooms with bath). Bar, music; very fine restaurant with French and Danish specialties.

Moderate

Carlton, Halmtorvet 14, 99 beds, in various room categories. Away from the main streets, but in the "naughty" district.

City, Peder Skramsgade 24. 162 beds. Near the harbor and the Royal Theater. Well furnished, but no rooms with private bath.

Gentofte, Gentoftegade 29, 126 beds, all rooms with shower and toilet. Quiet, on the outskirts. Bus 24 to Nørreport (25 mins.) or train A.

Savoy, Vesterbrogade 34. 138 beds, older.

Skovriderkroen, Strandvejen 235; 48 beds, music, garden. Lovely location near beach; good food (BE). Bus no. 1 to town in about 35 minutes.

Viking, Bredgade 65; 159 beds. Large rooms, but few with private bath. Well managed.

Vestersøhus, Vestersøgade 58, 87 beds, is good for long stays.

Weber, Vesterbrogade 11. 138 beds, some rooms without baths. Central.

Inexpensive

Amager, Amagerbrogade 29; 48 beds. On the way to airport, but still central.

Dragør Faergegård, Dragør, 40 beds, in idyllic fishing resort south of town, near beach and airport. Buses 30 and 33 to Town Hall Square in 40 mins. (BE).

Hotel Esplanaden, Bredgade 78. 92 beds. Very few rooms with private bath. Centrally located near Langelinie and the Citadel. Fine bus and train connections to the city and northern outskirts.

West, Westend 11; 41 beds, simple, few facilities (BE).

Mission Hotels

Missionshotellet, Løngangsstraede 27, largest with 300 beds, located near town hall. Behind the Central Station are the **Hebron,** Helgolandsgade 4, **Nebo,** Istedgade 6 and **Westend,** Helgolandsgade 3. **Ansgar,** Colbjørnsensgade 29.

Hostels

Europe's second biggest youth hostel was opened in 1980 in Copenhagen: **Copenhagen Hostel,** Sjaellandsbroen 55. 448 beds in 2- and 4-bed rooms. Open all year, 3 miles from centre, bus 37 from Holmes Bro. Another possibility in Copenhagen is **Københavns Vandrerhjem,** Herbergsvejen 8, 336 beds, 2 miles from city.

 RESTAURANTS. It is difficult to list Copenhagen restaurants because there are scores of good ones. If you stay in a recommended hotel you may be sure also of the restaurant. A piece of sound advice is to have a look at the menu card before you order favorite dishes so that the bill will not come as a shock (every restaurant must display a priced menu outside the entrance). Lobsters, shrimp, crabs, and salmon are luxury food and just as expensive as in your own country. Many restaurants close at midnight; the larger ones stay open until 2 A.M., but admit no customers after 1 A.M. Standards are so high you can safely wander into almost any of them.

Expensive

Anatole, Gothersgade 35. French cuisine, seasonal specialties. Often full. Closed Sundays.

Baghuset, Gothersgade 13, in the rear, specializes in charcoal-grilled steaks and fish served in 200-year-old former backstage store. Small, nautical, nice bar. Book ahead. Closed Sun.

Bourgognekaelderen, Dr. Tvaergade 2. Lovely old-fashioned basement restaurant. Good fish dishes. Closed Sun.

Hos Jan Hurtigkarl, Dronningens Tvaergade 43. This restaurant is considered to serve the best food in Copenhagen. Also serves meals as French as can be found outside France. Value for money. Closed Sun.

King Hans' Cellar, Vingardsstraede 6. Haute cuisine served in 13th cent surroundings, or in the Oyster Bar. Changing menu according to seasonal dishes. Small, best reserve. Closed Sat. and Sun. May–August.

Krogs Fiskerestaurant, Gammel Strand 38, serves up its fruits of the sea in plusher—and more expensive—surroundings. Try, for example, the dish "Tout de Paris". Closed Sun.

Langelinie Pavillonen, housing the Royal Yacht Club, is excellent for lunches, teas, dinners; magnificent view of the harbor. Evening music and dancing.

Pakhuskaelderen, under Hotel Nyhavn 71. Open grill in former storehouse basement.

St. Gertruds Kloster, Hauser Plads 32. Enjoy a candlelit dinner with more than 50 specialties on the menu and excellent wines in medieval surroundings.

Syv Små Hjem (7 Small Homes), Jernbanegade 4, is a delightful, initmate restaurant with a first-rate wine cellar. Chic. Your food bill is not for the budget-minded, but wine is sold practically at cost.

Viking, in Palace Hotel, is convenient, serves better-than-average meals, and prides itself on serving you quickly.

Moderate

Bee Cee Cafe, Østergade 24, lunch restaurant in the beautiful restored Pistolstraede, an architectural experience. Entrance from Strøget. The restaurant itself is in a basement with modern interior decor and good food. Closed Sun.

Bøf Og Ost, Gråbrødretorv 13, French auberge-tradition, on popular square off Strøget. Closed Sun.

Cheval Blanc, Mikkel Bryggersgade 6. Unpretentious, cozy "inn" with fixed menu and varying "weekly offers". Reasonable prices. Closed Sun.

La Cocotte, Vester Farimagsgade 33. The Hotel Richmond restaurant serves French cuisine in its cosy corners with slate tables and old rustic furniture. Closed Sundays.

Copenhagen Corner in the House of Industry built on Rådhuspladsen. This, the new meeting-place in Copenhagen, was opened in 1979. This is a restaurant with moderate prices and a nice setting, but, according to *Politiken's* food expert, service may be slow. The food is good and the menu always includes a "today's special"—which means that the price is low.

Glyptoteket, Stormgade 35, is across the street from the museum by the same name, revives weary art-lovers with excellent cooking.

Heering, Pilestraede 19. Friendly, attractively decorated café and restaurant.

Victor, Ny Østergade 8. *The* place to go. Restaurant with French-style menu, bar and café.

Østerport, Hotel restaurant, Oslo Plads 5, spanking new décor matches delightful Danish and French cuisine. Cold table is excellent.

Queens Restaurant and Pub, Vestervoldgade 25–27, for English style food and drink.

Streckers Restaurant (also called Beefy's Brother). Highly recommended. In basement, Kompagnistraede 20. Not very impressive from outside, but inside, a pleasant surprise with delicious food. Closed Sun.

Tivolihallen, Vester Voldgade 91. Basement public house from 1850, especially good for home and lunch specialties. Also dinners. Closed weekends.

Inexpensive

Bad København, Studie straede 63. Daily changing homemade buffet in this lunch restaurant attached to a public bath. Closed weekends.

Cafe Lindevang, P. G. Ramms allé 4. Public and cozy lunch restaurant at Frederiksberg (also hot food). Enormous dishes. Closed weekends.

DSB Bistro & Grill, Central Station. Quick restaurant with reasonably priced breakfast, lunch and dinner mainly for the busy traveler. Food fair.

Els, Store Strandstraede 3, near Nyhavn. Founded in first half of 19th century, with mainly original interior. Danish lunch, closed weekends. Best book.

Familiehaverne, Pile Allé 10–18; traditional outdoor restaurant open May to 15 Sept. Near the Zoo.

Gyllen, Nørre Voldgade 2. Unpretentious lunch restaurant near Town Hall Square. Plain, but good. Closed Sun.

Havfruen, Nyhavn 39, in sailors' quarter.

Hos Karl Kik (Slotskaelderen), Fortunstraede 4. Lunch restaurant now run by third generation of Kik family. Specializes in *smørrebrød.* Closed Sundays.

Parnas, Lille Kongensgade 16, where artists meet over music and Danish food.

Tokanten, Vandkunsten 1. Caters primarily for families. Very popular with all ages. Large menu for children.

Vista, Vesterbrogade 40. Cheap restaurant with self-service.

Cafeterias in Magasin, Anva, S&E and Favør department stores close ½ hour before the shop. Wholesome, American-style burgers sold all over town at **Burger King, McDonald's** and others.

 **ENTERTAINMENT.** Copenhagen is without doubt the liveliest city in Scandinavia, if not in Europe. In fact, planning an evening out is always rather a perplexing process because there are so many possibilities. *This Week in Copenhagen* may help you. It is a free publication obtainable from hotels, travel agencies, etc.

As far as the cinema is concerned, you have nearly fifty choices to consider before you even leave your hotel room. The film fare is primarily American and British. Except for children's films, soundtracks are in their original languages with Danish subtitles. Performances begin at fixed hours and seats are usually reserved. No need to tip. No smoking in cinemas.

Copenhagen's theaters play in the Danish language almost exclusively. The Royal Theater, however, offers opera and outstanding ballet in addition to plays and, since tickets are normally in great demand, you should ask your travel agent or the hotel porter to secure reservations for you up to a week before. Most concert tickets (except for Tivoli) are sold at *Wilhelm Hansen,* and ARTE.

During the summer months it is worth remembering that some theaters feature revenues and ballet by international companies. If it's music you wish, the Royal Theater's orchestra (Det Kongelige Kapel) and the Radio Symphony orchestra are outstanding and are often directed by well-known foreign conductors. Famous soloists give recitals from time to time, which are listed in *This Week in Copenhagen.*

 NIGHTLIFE. Still feeling strong? We have a long way to go before we have exhausted Copenhagen's potentialities. All-night membership clubs are now things of the past. About 35 restaurants are permitted to stay open until 5 A.M. (ask your hotel porter or see the newspapers). If you still feel reluctant to go home, the first morning restaurants open at this hour to serve you a nice early breakfast and another drink. For shows, see the *Ekstrabladet* newspaper advertisements. Below listed spots are moderate to expensive and usually have an admittance fee.

CABARET AND DANCING. Lorry Landsbyen, Allegade 7–9, a roofed beer garden restaurant with revues and jazz concerts.

Københavnerkroen, Bernstorffsgade 3, with soloists, entertainment and a public of all ages. No hot food. Closed Sun.

Vin Og Ølgod, Skindergade 45, German beerhouse atmosphere with singing and dancing. Closed Sun.

Bohemians may find their way to the district around Nikolaj Kirke, locally known as "The Minefield". Here there are dozens of small music and dance spots where a beer is the price of admission. One favorite is the inner room of "Lauritz Betjent". Its real name is the *Café Royal,* and it is opposite Christiansborg. *Musikcaféen* and *Vognporten,* both in Magstraede 14, have Danish and foreign folk singers and jazzbands respectively, and dancing. If you want to see the kind of scenes Hogarth painted, you can visit the sailors' dives of Nyhavn. These places are mostly male but not likely to prove dangerous if you go with someone else, are a "good mixer", and stay reasonably sober. One of many is *Hong Kong* at Nyhavn, entrance through the gate across the courtyard. Dancing all day. *Jazzhouse Montmartre* in Copenhagen has for several years beenone of the most famous jazz spots in Europe.

BARS. Hotel Bars of *D'Angleterre, Palace, Kong Frederik, Imperial, Royal,* and *Richmond* are all excellent and frequented by Danes and visitors.

Hviids Vinstue, Kongens Nytorv 19, commonly known as "Smoky Joe's", has an English pub atmosphere. Closed Sun. in summer.

Queen's, Vester Voldgade 25–7, is a popular imitation of an English pub.

Wonder Bar, Studiestraede 69, and **Kakadu Bar,** Colbjørnsensgade 6 (near Central Station) are in quite another class: mostly singles bars.

TIVOLI GARDENS. This world-famous amusement park is open daily from May 1 to mid-September, 10 A.M. (amusements all in operation by 2.30 P.M.) to midnight.

It covers an area of 850,000 square feet. In May, amusements are cheaper, and on some Wednesdays children get free afternoon tickets for a few amusements. **Concert Hall:** Not only does Tivoli lie in the heart of Copenhagen, but during the summer months it is the city's musical center as well. Symphony concerts are given every evening at 7.30 and 9 (sometimes free). Also free daily "proms".

Pantomime Theater: ("Peacock Building" to left of main entrance): Performances every evening except Sun., pantomimes 7.45, ballets 9.45. Pantomimme came to Denmark from Italy via France and England about 150 years ago. This is the only place in the world where traditional pantomime is still performed.

Open-air Stage (in middle of gardens): International variety acts every evening at 7 and 10.30, weekends 5, 7, and 10.

Amusements: In the farthest righthand corner of the gardens ("The Fun Corner") and in "The Alley" behind the scenic railway; open from 2 or 4 until midnight.

Variety Theater Glassalen has a varied program with Danish revues during the summer.

Tivoli Boy Guards: Parade every Sat. and Sun., 6.30 and 8.30.

Fireworks: Weds. and Sats. at 11.45 P.M. on lake and open-air stage. Sun., stage fireworks at 11.15 P.M.

Restaurants: Eating places of all categories; open daily 9 A.M.-midnight. **Divan I** and **Divan II** are noteworthy but by no means inexpensive. Of greater gastronomic interest but no cheaper is **Belle Terrasse.** Over beer and sausages at **Ferry Inn (Faergekroen)** you can join in the folk singing. Also **Perlen, Balkonen** and **Grøften.**

Dancing: Every night from 10-midnight at *Taverna.*

Jazz, Folk: *Slukefter* and *Vise Vers Huset.*

 MUSEUMS. Arranged in alphabetical order for convenience. All times given are summer hours. **Amalienborg Palace,** with its four identical mansions, Changing of the Guard and famous equestrian statue. **Arsenal Museum** (Tøjhuset), Tøjhusgade 3; arms and armor; 1–4 Sun. and holidays 10–4, free. **Copenhagen City Museum** (Bymuseet), Vesterbrogade 59, entrance totally free; guild relics, costumes, paintings and engravings illustrating the history and appearance of the capital through the ages. Also Søren Kierkegaard reliquae; 10–4 and Tues. evenings 7–9, closed Mon., free. **C.L. David Collection,** Kronprinsessegade 30; medieval Islamic pottery, European decorative art from 18th century; daily, except Mon., 1–4. Free.

Glyptoteket, Dantes Plads; antique bronzes, French painting and sculpture; 10–4 in summer; 12–3 in winter (closed Mon.); Wed. and Sun. free.

Hirschsprung Collection, Stockholmsgade 20; 19th-cent. Danish art; 1–4, and winter Wed. 7–10 P.M., closed Mon. and Tues.

Hunting and Forestry Museum (Jagt- & Skovbrugsmuseet), Hørsholm; open 10–4, closed Mon., by bus 84 or faster 75E (weekdays only).

Liberty Museum, Esplanaden; objects pertaining to 1940–45 Danish resistance; 10–4, Sun. to 5, closed Mon.

Museum of Decorative Art (Kunstindustrimuseet), Bredgade 68; collections from Middle Ages to present; 1–4. Closed Mon. Free except Sun., holidays, and July-August.

National Museum, Frederiksholms Kanal 12; collections pertaining to Danish civilization from Stone Age to recent times, ethnographical and coinc collections; all sections Sundays and holidays 10–4, weekdays some sections 10–4 and others 1–4. Closed on Mondays. The Prehistoric and Greenland sections are outstanding. Free.

Open Air Museum (Frilandsmuseet), Sorgenfri, 10–3 or 5 according to season. Oct.-Apr. Sun only. Closed Mon. Bus 84 or S-train CC (weekdays only) or A.

Ordrupgård Collection, Vilvordevej, Charlottenlund; 19th-century French paintings, especially Impressionists; open 1–5, Wed. eve. 7–10; closed Mon. Bus 160 from Klampenborg or Lyngby S-stations.

Rosenborg Castle, Østervoldgade 4a; royal jewels, tapestries, china; 11–3.

State Museum of Art, Sølvgade, the national gallery with Danish and European painters; 10–5, closed Mon. Free.

Theatrical-Historical Museum, Christiansborg Ridebane; Wed., Fri., Sun. 2–4.

Thorvaldsen's Museum, Slotsholmen; works by Danish sculptor, 1170–1844; 10–4, Closed Tues., admission always free.

Zoological Museum, Universitetsparken 15, 10–5, admission free.

 PLACES OF INTEREST. Amalienborg Palace, royal residence in one of four palaces flanking Amalienborg Square; changing of guard at noon.

Aquarium, Charlottenlund (bus 1 or 27), largest in northern Europe; open 10–6, Wed. 10–8.

Bella Centret, on Amager, is the new trade exhibition center; buses 37 and 46.

Christiansborg Castle, Slotsholmen: royal reception rooms, knights' hall, June-Sept. guided tours 12, 2, 4; Sept.–June, at 2 only and closed Sat. Closed Monday all year.

Citadel, 300-year-old Copenhagen fortification, 6 A.M.-10 P.M.

Deer Park, Dyrehaven, near Klampenborg: S-train A or bus 27.

Dragør on Amager, a village settled by Dutch immigrants; bus 30 or 33 from Town Hall Square.

Grundtvigs Church. På Bjerget; 9–5; Sundays 12–4 P.M.

Holmens Church, Holmens Kanal; weekdays 9–2. Saturdays 9–12.

Jens Olsen's World Clock, Town Hall; 10–4, Sat. 10–1.

Kastrup Airport, one of Europe's busiest; bus 32 and 32H from Town Hall Square.

Memorial Park at Ryvangen, wartime Resistance, Tuborgvej, Hellerup; S-train or bus 21; 10 A.M. to sunset.

Parliament, June-Sept.., 10–4, exc. Sat., during Parliament sessions: Sun. only (guided tours).

Round Tower (Rundetårn), Købmagergade; 10–5, Sun. 12–4. Opening times mentioned are shorter in winter season.

Royal Library, Christians Brygge 8; 9 A.M.-7 P.M. weekdays.

Town Hall (Rådhuset), hourly guides 10–3, Sats. 10–12; tower at 11 and 2 P.M., Sat. 11 only.

Zoo, Roskildevej 32; founded in 1859, the oldest and largest zoo in Scandinavia. Open 9 to 6 at the latest, according to season; 9 to 4 winter.

TRANSPORTATION. Copenhagen and its environs are well served by public transport with an extensive **bus** network and an electrified local **railroad** system, the "S" trains, as well as harbor ferries. The whole area is divided into zones which are the basis for the fare structure with facilities for transfer at no extra charge on routes within the zone and in some adjacent zones. Tickets are 5 Dkr per zone (valid for two zones). Free transfers on bus and train inside an area comprising Elsinore, Roskilde, Køge and Copenhagen. Stamp cards (11 trips per card, each trip valid for a minimum of 3 zones) can save money. If you start by train, you must cancel the card (but not full-rate tickets) in the yellow machine at platform entrances. Tourist Tickets (from hotels and rail stations) give one day's unlimited travel in Greater Copenhagen for 25 Dkr or in the whole Metropolitan Area for 50 Dkr. Full details from main tourist office.

Taxis are expensive but all are metered. Tipping is purely optional and rarely even looked for. There are taxi stands in many parts and they also pick up en route. The *Fri* sign means the cab is available for hire. From the city center to the airport costs around 100 Dkr, again subject to change. Useful telephone number for taxis (including those with English-speaking drivers) is 35 35 35.

Motor boat tours are available in the summer in the harbor and canal network, lasting between 30 minutes and an hour.

From May to October, there are various **bus** and **motor coach tours** around the city, to the outer areas including Helsingør (Elsinore) and Hillerød and over to Sweden. Details from the main tourist office and at many hotels.

The energetic can hire a **bicycle** (a favorite mode of transport) from several sources, including Københavns Cykelbørs, Gothersgade 157, and some railway stations. And for romantics, there are **horse-drawn cabs** in the famous Deer Park, and they are now available in the city center. Rather expensive.

CLOSING TIMES. *Banks* are open from 9.30 A.M. to 4 P.M., Saturdays closed (6 P.M. on Thursdays). You can also exchange money outside normal closing hours at the Central Station and at Kastrup Airport. *Shops* usually operate from 9 A.M. to 5.30 P.M., staying open Fridays until 7 or 8 P.M., closing Sat. at 1 or 2 P.M. Supermarkets at Central Station and the Airport open until midnight.

Most *post offices* are open from 10 A.M. to 5 P.M., but the one at the Central Railway Station is open from 9 A.M. to 9 P.M., except on Sun., when it is open 10–4. (The foregoing are all subject to occasional changes so check to be sure.)

SHOPPING. Copenhagen is the home of handwrought silver, furniture, ceramics, materials and wallpapers with bold designs, delicate porcelain, and baroque pottery. As in Stockholm, we would suggest that you first explore a large and varied collection of local offerings before branching out into specialty stores. A budget idea is to shop in the large shopping centers in the suburbs which are often cheaper than inner city stores.

The smallest Danish coin is now 5 øre, consequently prices are all rounded to a multiple of 5 (up or down: if your bill is, for example, 13.72 Dkr, you will be charged 13.70 Dkr; if 25.89, the charge will be 25.90 Dkr).

Note: Provided your purchases are mailed to your own address outside Denmark, you may reclaim the VAT (tax) or MOMS, as it's called in Denmark. Check at the store.

Shopping Centers. *Lyngby Storcenter,* Klampenborgvej, is the expensive exception, where fashionable designs are displayed in rich surroundings. Notice the old-fashioned grocer's shop. (Buses 68 or 84, or trains A and CC.)

To the west is **Rødovre Centrum** (buses 13, 41) and *City 2* at Tåstrup with low price *Obs* and supermarkets and specialty shops (trains B and BB or bus 123 to Tåstrup, then bus 116).

South of town are **Ishøj Bycenter** (with *Bilka* low-price supermarket) and **Hundige Storcenter** with low-price **Bilka** (bus 121 or trains A to Ishøj or E to Hundige).

Design. Near the Central Station at *Den Permanente* (The Permanent Exhibition of Danish Arts and Crafts, which also sells some exhibits) there is a purposeful selection of the finest handwork from all over the country.

A store where you'll find a beautiful and large display of Scandinavian design, plus the best of handicrafts from other countries is *Illum,* Østergade 52, the local Harrods. There are over 70 departments, including porcelain, the best names in Danish and Scandinavian furniture, fabrics and Finnish Rya rugs; a tax-free shipping service, two restaurants, a hairdresser, and credit cards are accepted. A shopper's delight.

Illums Bolighus, Amagertorv 10 (not to be confused with the above store), is *the* Center of Modern Scandinavian Design. If you are interested in some of the most attractive and yet practical things that are being marketed today, this is the spot to visit.

The furniture of Fritz Hansen is well known throughout the world, but you may also have heard the name of Finn Juhl, several of whose chairs have been purchased by the New York Museum of Modern Art. Jens Thuesen and Niels Vodder are also tops.

Ikea, Mårkaervej, Tåstrup (bus 119 from the station), is a huge furniture store with own, often cheaper, designs. *Brugsmøbler,* Albertslund off Highway A1 (bus 123), have specially designed quality furniture at moderate prices.

Silver. You will, of course, be interested to see the home of *Georg Jensen Silver* at Østergade 40. Here you will find the largest collection of Jensen hollowware in the world. Browse among his extensive offerings of gold and silver jewelry and study his permanent exhibit of tables laid with many of the famous patterns in sterling silver and stainless steel.

Danish design achieves beauty by classic lines and graceful forms, and centuries of sensitive craftsmanship are reflected in every piece of contemporary silver. *Hans Hansen* at Amagertorv 16 features stunning flat ware, cigarette boxes, and such.

Peter Hertz, Købmagergade 34, is one of the oldest silversmiths in town and makes most of his pieces to order. He specializes in marvelous place settings and delicate jewelry.

But moderns must first visit *A. Michelsen,* Bredgade 11—their prize-winning cigarette container and silver pitcher, their graceful tubecluster candelabra and the enameled anniversary and enameled Christmas spoons designed each year, are all collectors' items.

A bit further along Bredgade, at number 17, is *A. Dragsted,* whose jewelry and tableware are favorites with the Royal Court.

Porcelain and Glass. The *Royal Copenhagen Porcelain Manufactory* (actually a shop on the original factory site) at Amagertorv 6 might be your next stop. If it is blue anniversary plate or beautiful brown and blue figurines with their fine underglaze you desire, your best bet may be in some antique shop in Kompagnistraede, which runs parallel with Strøgetstraede.

Bing & Grøndahl porcelain is next door and ranks equally high in quality and design. *Rosenthal,* Frederiksberggade 21 has a choice of porcelain and glassware primarily by Scandinavian artists such as Bjørn Wiinblad and Tapio Wirkkala. *Skandinavisk Glas,* Ny Østergade 1 has excellent designs, too.

Holmegaard glassware is on display at Østergade 15, offering everything in Danish design from snaps klukflaske to beautiful opalescent vases. A permanent glass exhibition/museum has been opened.

Arts and Crafts. At Ny Østergade 11 is the *Bjørn Wiinblad House,* with a sales display of the artist's own products.

For native crafts, see *Håndarbejdets Fremme,* Vimmelskaftet 38, which has embroideries, handprinted fabrics, and gleeful trinkets in impeccable taste. Every article is handmade; patterns and materials are also sold.

Clara Waever at Østergade 42 features special embroidery, lace, and linen.

Elling, at Bredgade 24, features materials of fanciful design together with bright printed pieces amusing for a child's room.

In the 1785 Potter's House at Overgaden oven Vandet 10, *P. Brøste* displays modern Danish and foreign arts and crafts.

Hanne Hansen, a fine quality shop at Fiolstraede 19, and *Form & Farve,* Nicolaj Plads 3.

At Bredgade 47, the captivating wooden toys, bowls, and plates of *Kay Bojesen* are on display.

Furs. More mink are raised in Denmark than anywhere else in Europe. And in Copenhagen shops you are assured of quality and style. *A.C. Bang,* Østergade 27 and *Birger Christensen* nearby at number 38; both are purveyors to the Court.

Department Stores. *Magasin du Nord,* a huge, modern department store at Kongens Nytorv is the biggest of its kind in Denmark, with particularly good buys in silver, ceramics, and furs.

Illum, Østergade 52, see above, under *Design.*

Daells Varehus, Nørregade 12, is a smaller store, but offers good quality at extremely reasonable prices. Cash only sales.

Lamps. Famous Danish modern lamp designs can be found at *Egon Christophersen,* Amagerbrogade 211, and *Grundsøe,* Frederikssundsvej 68.

Toys. *Rønberg,* St. Kongensgade 60–62 and Strandvejen 191, and *BR,* a toy chainstore, who have their biggest shop on Frederiksberggade 11 are *Kiddie Wonderlands.* *Rigtigt Legetøj,* Lavendelstraede 5–7, is run by educationalists and sells only educational playthings.

Clothing. *Svend Crone,* Ved Vesterport 9 has men's quality wear at reasonable prices. Less expensive is *Regent,* Vesterbrogade 34 and branches. The *Bee Cee* at Østergade 24 and *Brødrene Andersen,* Østergade 7–9 both have ladies' wear of quality.

More conventional - and cheaper - clothing can be found in many shops on Strøget and, for example, at *Lyngby Storcenter* and *Rødovre Centrum.* At these two centers try the Sven E. There are also many bargains to be found at the Magasin department store.

Interior Decor. If interior decorating is your interest, *Lysberg, Hansen and Therp,* Bredgade 3, has an exclusive boutique with dainty embroideries for your table.

Dahl Jensen, Frederikssundsvej 288, displays dainty porcelain figurines as well as vases with seagulls sketched in pale pinks and purples.

Tutein & Hersaa, Hyskenstraede 12, is a tiny shop specializing in paper lampshades, skilfully pleated to beautify ceiling or wall.

This and That. *Tvillinge Staal A/S,* Frederiksberggade 26, shines with stainless steel cutlery, pitchers, and tools.

Best pewter buys are in the department stores and from the large selection at the *Pewter Center,* Ny Østergade 2.

For luxurious leather goods, beautiful pocketbooks, and bags of every size, try *Johannes Neye,* Vimmelskaftet 28.

The popular Stanwell and Kriswill pipes are made in Denmark and available at all leading shops, including *Wilhelm Jørgensen,* Østergade 61, and *Pibe Dan,* Vestergade 13. *Anne Julie* carves her own collection and sells her products at Vester Voldgade 8.

Bright copper and old brass are also good buys in Copenhagen.

Wander down the Fiolstraede with its antique and second-hand book dealers. For antiques try also *Erik Vejerslev,* Hyskenstraede 7. Old Danish glassware is his specialty.

Junk market held on Saturday mornings (from 8) at Israels Plads (behind the Nørreport Station).

 TELEPHONES. Exchanges are automatic (6 digits) and divided into nine areas. To be connected, dial the exchange (plus the preceding two-digit area code if you exceed your local area). Central Copenhagen code is 01, suburbs are code 02. All domestic calls are half price between 8 P.M. and 8 A.M.

 SPORTS. Copenhagen is a paradise for sportsmen. You can even indulge in some fairly rare ones here: *Archery* is practised at the Valby Sports Grounds May–Oct. Contact leader between 5–6 P.M. (tel. (02) 90 71 72). *Squash rackets:* information on courts and rackets for hire at Svanemøllehallen, tel. 20 77 01. *Cricket* is played by these clubs: A.B., Skovdiget 1; Frem, Valby Idraetspark; K.B., Peter Bangsvej. *Tennis* clubs that allow visitors to become temporary members: B. 93, next to Østerbro Stadium; H.I.K., Hartmannsvej 37 Hellerup; K.B., Peter Bangsvej and Pilealle.

You see *football* (association or soccer) at the Idraetsparken at Østerbro or Valby, Sunday afternoons or evenings, except July. *Bicycle races* take place on the Ordrup track at Charlottenlund, usually on Mon. and Tues. If you want to go *horse riding,* you can hire them at the Deer Park, Klampenborg. In winter *skating* is mainly an outdoor sport; but there are some indoor rinks at Østerbro Stadium and in Hvidovre, and there is skating on Peblingesø.

 GOLF. You have four choices in the vicinity of the capital. The 18-hole *Copenhagen Golf Club* is at Eremitagesletten in the Klampenborg Deer Park, 35 minutes by car or train from Copenhagen. The 18-hole course at the *Rungsted Golfklub* is 30 minutes by car or train from Copenhagen. There is an 18-hole course at *Helsingør Golfklub,* Gl. Hellebaekvej, and an 18-hole course at *Hillerød Golfklub,* Ny Hammersholt, 40 minutes from Copenhagen. Near Copenhagen there are further golf clubs at Kokkedal, Birkerød, Søllerød/Holte. Ask for the special golf pamphlet at the Tourist Information Office.

 HORSERACING is accompanied by totalizator betting in Copenhagen. *Flat racing* takes place between the latter part of April and the middle of December at the Klampenborg Race Course (Bus 27 or S-train C to Klampenborg, then bus 160, or bus 176 from the Station). *Trotting* events are held throughout the year on Suns. and Weds., at the Charlottenlund Race Course (S-train C or bus 1 to Charlottenlund).

SWIMMING. The nearest sandy beach is at Charlottenlund. More popular is the artificial beach a little further north at Bellevue. Go to Klampenborg by S-train C or bus 27 (from Hellerup). Beaches free. Swimming pools, open during the summer are: Gladsaxe Bad, Vandtårnsvej 55, Søborg; Vestbad, Nykaer 26, Rødovre; Bellahøj Friluftsbad, Bellahøjvej; Bavnehøj Friluftsbad, Enghavevej 90; Emdrup Friluftsbad, Bredelandsvej and Sundby Friluftsbad, Sundbyvestervej. South of Dragør (bus 30 or 33) are low meadows alongside the beach, with shallow water (the cleanest near Copenhagen): ideal for children. A 7-km man-made beach is now open to the public at Køge Bugt Strandpark, south of Copenhagen. It is fine, sandy and clean. Bus 121 from Valby Station, or by S-train A to Ishøj or Hundige station and from there by the beach bus (season only) direct to the beach.

 SAILING is a popular sport in Copenhagen, whose waters are ideally suited to it. Visitors who want to participate in this sport can obtain assistance through the big clubs devoted to it, especially: the Royal Danish Yacht Club, tel. 14 87 87; the Copenhagen Amateur Sailing Club, Klubhuset Svanem øllehavnen, tel. 20 71 72. A sailing- or motor-boat can be hired from *Maritim Camping* at Jyllinge, tel. 02–38 83 58, or from *Danish Boat Charter,* Strandvejen 327, Klampenborg, tel. 63 08 00.

 CAMPING. During the summer there are camping facilities at these sites: *Absalon,* on Hwy. A1, 20 minutes by car from city center, open year round; *Naerum,* 10 miles north, off motorway to Elsinore and *Sundbyvester* on Amager island; *Bellahøj,* in Copenhagen (usually crowded); then others of less than top standard. Prices are about 25 Dkr per person, cheaper for children.

 GUIDED VISITS. The *Carlsberg Brewery,* Ny Carlsbergvej 140, may be visited Monday to Friday at 9, 11 and 2.30. The *Tuborg Brewery,* Strandvejen 54, (buses 1 and 21), Monday to Friday any time between 8.30 and 2.30. Guided walking tours (2 hours) with various starting points and routes, July through August. Consult Copenhagen dailies or ask for detailed information at the Tourist Information Office.

 USEFUL ADDRESSES. Embassies: Britain, Kastelsvej 36–40, tel. 26 46 00; Canada, Kristen Bernikowsgade 1, tel. 01–12 22 99; U.S. Dag Hammarskiölds Allé 24, tel. 42 31 44.

Tourist associations: Danish Tourist Board, H.C. Andersens Blvd. 22, weekdays 9–6 or 8, Sun. in season 9–1, tel. 01–11 13 25.

Travel agencies: American Express, Dagmarhus, Amagertorv 18; Wagons-Lits/Cooks, Vesterbrogade 2, Spies Rejsebureau Nyropsgade 41; Viking Nordturist, H.C. Ørsteds vej 70 (coach travels); Tjaereborg Rejser, Rådhuspladsen 75; Dansk Vandrelaug, Kultorvet 7 (hiking and biking); Bennett, Rådhuspladsen 47 (Fairytale Tours and many others. Also Unisol agent).

Automobile club: FDM, Blegdamsvej 124, open 9–5, Sat. 9–12.

Day-and-night pharmacies (Apotek): Vesterbrogade 6C; Amagerbrogade 158.

Dentist (emergencies only): Oslo Plads 14 (at Østerport station).

Car hire: Avis, Kampmannsgade 1, tel. 15 22 99; Hertz, Hammerichsgade 1, tel. 12 77 00; Pitzner, Trommesalen 4, tel. 11 12 34. All have offices at the airport. Share-a-Car, Studiestraede 57, tel. 12 06 43 is cheaper and also hires out campers and tents.

Bus route and timetable information: 54 51 91.

Train seat reservation, carferry bookings: major stations or tel. 14 88 80.

Long distance and international train information: Central Station or tel. 14 17 01.

Flight routes information: SAS, Air Terminal and Airport, or tel. 54 17 01.

Youth organizations: YWCA and YMCA, Amaliegade 24; Youth hostels Assn., Vesterbrogade 39; DIS Students' Traveling Bureau, Skindergade 28.

Church services: Anglican, St. Alban's English Church, Langelinie; Roman Catholic, St. Ansgar (Cathedral), Bredgade 64; Jewish, Synagogue, Krystalgade 12.

ZEALAND AND ITS ISLANDS

Holiday Haunts and History

Next to Copenhagen, Zealand is the part of Denmark that is seen by more visitors than any other. Even so, most visitors see only part of Zealand, a very small part. They miss not only the very beautiful island of Møn but also the interesting and lovely Odsherred region. The classic tour—up the coast of the Sound to Elsinore and Hamlet's castle (Kronborg), down to Fredensborg Castle, on to Frederiksborg Castle, and back to Copenhagen—covers no more than a corner of the rolling and often beautiful country which is Zealand.

Exploring Zealand and Its Islands

Elsinore (Helsingør in Danish) is one of Denmark's oldest towns. Yet it did not achieve any importance until 1429, when Eric decided to impose "sound dues" on all vessels entering or leaving the Baltic. Now it is the Danes who have to pay dues when they cross from one part of their country to the other across the Great Belt on the State Railway ferries. There have been plans of bridges here and a tunnel from Elsinore to Sweden, but they've been put off for the time being.

"Hamlet's town", or "the pleasant corner in Scandinavia", has a rich tradition of trade and shipping. The romantic center of the city with the many idyllic little houses goes back to about 1574 when the monumental Kronborg Castle was built.

Museums and Sights

Erected between 1574 and 1582 by Frederik II, the Renaissance Kronborg Castle is a must. Visit the central yard first and then take a walk on the inner and outer ramparts. The visitable parts of the Castle include a 200-ft-long banqueting hall, a commercial and maritime museum, dungeons and casemates where the sleeping Ogier will awake and fill every Dane with his spirit when Denmark is in danger. The chapel interior is luxurious, and people are still married there. See p. 133 for opening times. There is a long tradition of performances of *Hamlet* in the courtyard, including many by famous interpreters of the role over the years, both English and from other countries.

St. Mary's Church and Carmelite Monastery were both founded in 1430 and are among the foremost examples of Danish medieval architecture. Buxtehude was the organist here 1660–68. Although still partly inhabited, both the former chapter hall and refectory can be visited. Admittance to the church is from 1.30 to 4.30. From September 16 to May 15, 12.30 to 3.30. Guided monastery tours at 2 P.M., from mid-May to mid-Sept., also at 11 A.M. and 3 P.M.

St. Olai Church has been a cathedral since 1961. Started about 1200, it was not completed till 1559. At the north side, walls from the 13th-century church can still be seen. Open 10–5 April to September, 10–3 October to March.

Denmark's Technical Museum contains really noteworthy old technical products from Denmark, e.g. the old Hammel car from 1886, which ran in the London–Brighton race. Nordre Strandvej department is open 10–5 all year, Ole Rømersvej 10–4 all year.

The Øresund Aquarium has on display Sound fauna as seen in 10 different localities, with emphasis also on sea-anemones and crustaceans. Open daily 1–5 mid-May through August, winter, only Sats. and Suns. 1–5.

Marienlyst Castle was built in 1587 as a summer-house for Kronborg, later a dower house for Queen Juliane Marie. Rebuilt 1760, and French-style gardens added. Now a city museum and used for representative occasions. Castle open 12–5 June-Aug.; 1–3 Wed., Fri., Sat. and Sun., Sept.-May, gardens all day.

A contemporary romantic feature occurs when the girls' guard march through Elsinore every Friday during the summer. You can also hear music in late August and early September, when Elsinore has her annual church music festival.

Surroundings

Around Elsinore are a string of quiet seaside resorts with pleasant, sandy beaches inviting you to linger for a day, or longer. On summer Sundays, a veteran railroad goes to Gilleleje instead of the normal "railbus". Vedbaek, Humlebaek (with the fine Louisiana art gallery (open 10–5), Snekkersten to the south. Hellebaek and Hornbaek to the north and Sweden (Helsingborg) to the east. Ferries every 20 minutes.

A Typical Seaside Resort

One example of a vacation village is Tisvildeleje. In winter a fisherman's village, in summer there is an enormous expansion in population. People walk through its only main road with its low, one-story houses, either to the coast and beach behind the dunes, or back to their summer cottages. Or they walk to the funny "railbus" which will take them back to Hillerød and Copenhagen. Other people will throng at the packed parking lot and walk from their cars down to the beach or into the hilly woodland. Some go fishing, others go to the "Troll Forest", a part of the wood with twisted, mysterious pines—if you do the same, you might possibly meet some figures who are clearly *not* trolls; there is a naturist bathing beach nearby. One could instead go inward to Tisvilde or Tibirke and enjoy the village atmosphere.

For the tourist the towns of Hillerød and Fredensborg, only six miles apart, form a unit of the classic tour of north Zealand. South of Hillerød, there's the charming village of Søllerød with its medieval church, terraced yard and thatched-roofed inn. North of Hillerød a belt of fishing-villages are now completely changed into summer bathing resorts. In Hillerød itself is a folk museum in a 200-year-old smallholding, open 2–5 June through August (Closed Mondays), and there is Frederiksborg Castle.

Castles, Museums and Sights

Frederiksborg Castle originates from 1600–20, and was built by Christian IV on his birthplace. This king erected several other architectural gems, but for Frederiksborg he chose the beautiful site between the wide lake on one side and a double moat on the other. After a fire in 1859 the castle was restored with money from the founder of the Carlsberg brewery. Today it is the national-historic museum. The Chapel is famed for its interior and a Compenius-organ from 1610, still in use. Both open 10–5 May to September, 10–4 in October, 11–4 in April, 11–3 from November to March. Organ concerts Thurs., 1.30–2. Before the fire the castle was a royal summer residence, and Danish kings were crowned here—today they are not crowned at all.

Palace Park is French-style, with views to the castle. The Bath (a country seat) is still sometimes in use for royal hunting lunches.

AEbelholt, four miles west, is a monastery with ruins from 1175. Anthropological museum. Closed Mondays. Open 10–4 May to Aug., 1–4 in Sept., Oct. and April weekends 1–4.

Fredensborg is known for its palace and its inn. The palace was built in 1721–3. Today, still a royal palace with 420 rooms grouped around the Dome Hall, it is an exquisite setting for royal parties. Also valuable paintings. Open to visitors in July every 30 minutes from 1 to 5 (guided tours).

The park is one of the most beautiful in Europe, with historic memorials. It runs down to the nearby Lake Esrum. The Marble Garden is the royal family's private garden. Italian baroque sculptures and rose garden. Open to the public when the royal family is not in residence, (i.e. July only). Park open all year.

West of Copenhagen

Selsø Manor, 15 miles north of Roskilde, has been uninhabited since 1829 and is now being restored as a museum by an enthusiastic journalist. You will find a 400-year-old baroque banqueting hall and Louis XVI tapestries. Open only from mid-April to mid-October as there is no heating. West of Roskilde is Odsherred with the main towns Holbaek and Nykøbing. The central part of Holbaek grew up around a 14th-century Blackfriars' convent and the museum is in a late 17th-century building. Surroundings include Tuse Church with frescos from 1450 picturing the childhood of Jesus. Southwest of Holbaek is a miniature Frederiksborg, Løvenborg Castle, erected behind protecting moats in about 1634 (no admission). Tveje Merløse Church south of the town is extraordinary in its architecture, being an example of an early medieval church. It has a restored ceiling and the western end still contains the gallery for the master and mistress.

Nykøbing is the main town in a popular holiday resort area. The western part of this coastal area has a ferry connection with Ebeltoft.

Near the road from Nykøbing to Kalundborg is Dragsholm Castle, built in the 13th century by the Roskilde bishop as a fortress. After the Reformation, the castle was used as a state prison; one of the "guests" was the Earl of Bothwell, who died here in 1578 and is buried in Fårevejle Church. Today the castle serves hotel guests in its restored buildings.

To the west in the bottom of a narrow fjord is Kalundborg, basis for ferries to Samsø and Jutland. Until 1658 the city was strongly fortified, but since its castle was destroyed that year, the strange church is the only unruined part of the fortification.

The Church of Our Lady, from 1170, has a groundplan shaped like a Grecian cross. With its five towers and eastern European patterns it serves—together with wireless masts—as a landmark. The Regional museum is west of the church. Old thatched-roofed houses, especially in Praestegade and Adelgade, where Lindegården houses the local museum with expositions in more than 15 rooms, partly in rococo, as well as a fine collection of local costumes.

Nearby is Røsnaes, with dolmens, windmill, cliffs and lighthouse. Rococo Lerchenborg Castle at Asnaes is situated in a marvelous baroque park with roses and summer concerts.

From Lerchenborg, go south to Slagelse; 3 miles west from town you will find Trelleborg, a Viking fortress which is nearly 1,000 years old. Actually there are two forts, one much larger than the other, each with a huge circular rampart and a moat. The remains of some 30 barracks survive, and one has been reconstructed to show the peculiar, slightly curving shape given to the walls of these 100-ft-long buildings. The site layout is thought to have been influenced by Byzantine models. Slagelse is on the main road between Korsør and Copenhagen.

Returning to Copenhagen along the main road you will pass the towns of Sorø, Ringsted and Roskilde. Sorø is an old Cistercian abbey from the last half of the 12th century. Today it is dominated by the abbey church and its academy serves as a public school. Sorø Church is Denmark's largest abbey church, with the tomb of Bishop Absalon, the founder of Copenhagen, behind the altar. Three kings are buried here and so are two well-known Danish poets, Ludvig Holberg and B. S. Ingemann. The latter rests outside the abbey in the churchyard. Open weekdays 10–5, and on Sundays 2–5, from May to Sept. The Academy, since 1586 a royal school, was from 1623 a noble academy. Destroyed by a fire in 1813 and re-erected 14 years later. Admittance only during academy holiday in summer.

The Suså river nearby (canoeing) and the hilly woodland around the Tystrup-Bavelse lakes are pleasant. Also take a walk round Sorø lake from the Academy. Near Sorø is Zealand's only round church at Bjernede, erected in about 1170, thus introducing the art of brickburning in Denmark.

Ringsted was an important medieval town, and is today a commercial town with 28,000 inhabitants. Its surroundings include the Suså and many historic memorials. St. Benedict's Church was originally a Benedictine abbey; this Romanesque church was the first in Scandinavia to be built from brick. King Valdemar erected it 1160–70 as a monument over his father, Knud Lavard, who had been murdered in 1131. The Roman Church rewarded him by canonizing Knud Lavard, who is the only Danish saint. During the next 200 years the church served as the royal sepulchral chapel. From June to August concerts are held in the church on Tues. afternoons and Wed. evenings. Open from 10–12 (free) and in summer also 1–5.

Roskilde is Zealand's second largest town, with 50,000 inhabitants. A royal residence already in the 10th century, today the 38 royal tombs in the Cathedral still maintain the connection to the royal house. The first Danish railroad stretched from Copenhagen to Roskilde and dates back to 1847. In the Middle Ages the town was the most significant spiritual center in northern Europe, with 12 parish churches and 8 big convents and charitable institutions besides the cathedral. In 1972 it started as another spiritual center through the foundation of Roskilde University, the first Danish university to take up the Anglo-Saxon ideas of basic education as the entrance to higher educations.

Roskilde Cathedral was erected by Bishop Absalon about 1170 on a wooden church 200 years older. It is a most important medieval building, where the Romanesque and Gothic styles intermingle. Add to that the various porches and chapels which have been extended from time to time in the prevailing architectural style and altogether they represent a longitudinal section of Danish building history. The chapels have been added to serve as royal tombs, and today one finds 38 of them here—the latest burial was that of King Frederik IX in 1972. There is also an interesting 500-year-old clock and a pillar on which several royal personages, including Peter the Great and the Duke of Windsor, have marked their heights. Admission (unless a service is in progress) weekdays April-Sept. 9–5.45, Oct.-March 10–3.45, Sundays from 12.30.

The Viking Ship Museum is next. In 1962 five Viking ships were excavated near the museum. They date back to around 1000 A.D. and were sunk in the 11th century to form a barrier for enemy vessels sailing towards Roskilde. You can follow the restoration, and films and sometimes special exhibitions on the excavation are shown. Open from 9 to 5 (6 during June, July and August, from Nov. to March, open only from 10 to 4).

The Fjord (try a cruise with the Veteran ship, the Skjelskør, in summer). Atomic Experimental Station at Risø (4 miles north, not open to the public). Lejre Forsøgscenter is a historical and a working archeological museum and research center (Iron Age Village, Herthadalen) open May through September 10–5. Ledreborg Manor is open in July 11–5, and Sundays in June and August 11–5.

South to Køge and the Cliffs of Møn

Interesting towns in southern Zealand, if you pass near them, are Køge, Naestved, and Vordingborg. Køge boasts more ancient half-timbered houses than any other town in Zealand. The oldest dated (1527) is at Kirkestraede 20. There are also the smithy at Kirkestraede 13, the mayor's house at Brogade 16, the weaver's house on the square, and, in particular, Vestergadegården (Vestergade 16) which is richly carved and has an overhanging first floor.

Køge Bay is the site of two great naval battles between Danes and Swedes. The Danish national anthem refers to the earlier of these two (1677) in its first line, "King Christian stood by the lofty mast", although some sources claim the King observed the engagement from the tower of Køge's St. Nikolai Church. Whatever the facts of the matter may be, this tower did provide a convenient place for hanging pirates.

In the Køge district are a number of fine castles: Gisselfeld, a stunning two-storied Renaissance edifice with a beautiful park; moated on all sides; rococo Bregentved with copper spires and magnificent gardens; Gjorslev, built in 1400 by the Bishop of Roskilde, in the shape of a cross crowned by a tower in the center; Vallø and Vemmetofte, impressive castles, founded as homes for unmarried ladies of rank.

Near Rødvig are the chalk cliffs called Stevns Klint, which are striking, though not as impressive as the ones at Møn, nearly three times higher. The Højerup Church on Stevns Klint, however, has rather a pathetic air about it. Built around 1250, the church found its foundation being undermined by the sea and, so the story goes, moved itself an inch inland every Christmas. Unfortunately this retreat was far too cautious, because first the cemetery and then the choir toppled into the sea. In recent years the church has been restored and the cliffs below it bolstered with masonry to prevent further damage.

Naestved also has a number of half-timbered houses. Boderne is a medieval suite of houses, one of them a museum of art-handicraft. Apostelgården in Riddergade dates from about 1500, and is noteworthy for the figures of Christ and the Twelve Apostles carved under its eaves. There are more old houses in Kompagnistraede, as well as the impressive Gothic church of St. Peder, which has a fresco depicting King Valdemar Atterdag and Queen Helvig. Also of interest is the

15th-century Helligåndshuset (House of the Holy Ghost) containing a museum with regional collections. A mile outside of town, there's Herlufsholm Manor, once an abbey, with a 13th-century chapel. The Holmegård Glassworks makes an interesting visit, while regional handicrafts can be seen in the museum at Stenboderne.

On a small island just south of Naestved is the beautifully furnished castle of Gavnø, privately-owned but open to visitors. The delightful garden has modern sculptures in wood and stone. There is a flower show here in May.

The best Zealand canoe trip (52 miles up the Suså river) starts in Naestved and takes you through the most beautiful part of this island. There are many resting spaces, and canoes with life-jackets can be hired.

Vordingborg, Zealand's most southerly town, is splendidly situated on the Great Stream or Storstrøm, the strait separating Zealand from Falster. Here are the ruins of King Valdemar Atterdag's castle, the place where he died in 1182. Besides an outer wall nearly half a mile long, there is a Goose Tower 115 feet tall (if you include the Golden Goose on top) from which there is a view over to Falster and Møn. Around the castle are extensive grounds, now a botanical garden.

From Vordingborg a 2-mile bridge runs to the island of Falster, whose rich soil is used to grow most of Denmark's sugar beet. Nykøbing is the principal town, with excellent hotels and the House of the Czar, an 18th-century half-timbered structure where Peter the Great stayed in 1716. Another bridge connects with the island of Lolland. There are good sandy beaches about 6 miles away.

Lolland's main attractions are the towns of Maribo and Nysted, the latter known for Ålholm Castle, an old "robbers' castle" from the 12th century. Once a royal dwelling, today especially known for the nearby automobile museum with vintage and veteran cars owned by the Ålholm baron. The cars date from 1896 to 1930 and there are about 250 of them. A steam train from 1850 crosses the castle park and takes the visitors down to the Baltic. Maribo, in the middle of the island, is dominated by the cathedral from the 15th century; originally a Bridgettine abbey. Ruins of the convent are still to be seen. The open-air museum has a farmhouse representing the original regional dwelling. On summer weekends a veteran railway will take passengers to Bandholm on the northern coast over the lands of Knuthenborg Manor. The Knuthenborg Safari Park contains game, botanical sights, a monkey jungle and other safari animals. There is also a children's zoo. You can drive through the park, but take care to keep the windows closed unless you want to be visited by a baboon. Open May to September, 9–6.

From Stubbekøbing on Falster, a short ferry crossing takes you to Bogø, with a dam connected with Møn near Fanefjord. Its white 13th-century church has an overwhelming number of frescos.

A few miles east of Stege, the main town, with its 15th-century gate, is the church at Keldby. This 13th-century church contains a lot of frescos, too, painted between 1275 and 1480. Even the royal wedding between King Valdemar and Queen Helvig in 1340 is pictured here. The third frescoed church is at Elmelunde further east. The nave here dates from about 1075.

The east coast of Møn displays 75-million-year-old chalk cliffs, towering 400 feet above the sea, a great natural sight, seen from the top or the bottom. The 18th-century Liselund Castle with its English-style park and pavilions is nearby.

On your way back to Zealand you can make a detour to Nyord, a dammed island with many 250-year-old unspoiled farmhouses. Cars are not allowed in the hamlet, so you should walk there. Via Stege you reach the main road and the bridge to Zealand.

PRACTICAL INFORMATION
FOR ZEALAND AND ITS ISLANDS

HOW TO GET ABOUT. Trains and buses link Copenhagen with all the important Zealand points: Elsinore, 50 mins.; Hillerød, 40 mins.; Roskilde, 20 mins.; and Køge, 1 hour. For those who are driving, here is a suggested 2-day itinerary for Zealand:

First day: Depart Copenhagen-Elsinore-Fredensborg-Hillerød-Frederiksvaerk-Hundested-Rørvig-Nykøbing-Sjaelland-Fåreveile-Snertinge-(Jyderup)-Kalundborg-(Ruds Vedby)-Slagelse-(Trelleborg)-Skaelskør-Naestved. Distance, 170 miles (272 km).

Second day: Naestved-Vordingborg-(Møn)-Praestø-Fakse-Ladeplads-Vemmetofte-Rødvig-Stevns Klint-Store-Heddinge-Køge-Roskilde-return Copenhagen. Distance, 122 miles (195 km).

WHAT TO SEE. Natural sights: Møn's Cliffs, Stevns Cliffs, and the Pomlenakke woods.

Old houses: at Køge and Naestved.

Interesting buildings: Zealand's only surviving round church (12th century), Bjernede; St. Olai's Church and church of St. Mariae with Carmelite monastery, Elsinore; palace square and church, Hørsholm; the 12th-century, 5-towered church at Kalundborg; St. Nikolai's Church, Køge, and the unique, 2-storied church at Ledøje; the churches at Naestved, Ringsted, and Sorø; cathedrals of Elsinore, Maribo and Roskilde; Viking fortress, Trelleborg; ruins with Goose Tower, Vordingborg.

Other places of interest: Holmegård Glassworks (weekdays 9–1.30, Sats. and Suns. 11 and 3), Holme Olstrup; English-style park at Knuthenborg: Sorø Academy; the veteran car and railroad museum at Ålholm Castle near Nysted.

Museums: Louisiana Art Gallery, Humlebaek; Nivågård Art Gallery, Nivå; Trade and Shipping in Kronborg Castle, Elsinore; Hunting and Forestry, Hørsholm; the National Historical Museum in Frederiksborg Castle, Hillerød; Diocesan, Maribo; House of the Czar, Nykøbing Falster; Helligåndshuset, Naestved; also interesting exhibits in museums of Frederikssund, Frederiksvaerk, Dronningmølle, Holbaek, Kalundborg, Køge.

CASTLES AND MANOR HOUSES. *Bregentved Castle,* gardens open Wed., Sun., and hols., 9–8. *Fredensborg Castle,* 1–5, July 1–31; park all year. *Frederiksborg Castle,* Hillerød, 10–5, May 1 to Sept. 30; 11–4, April; 10–4, October; 11–3, Nov. to March.

Gisselfeld Castle, park open from 10 to 4 or 5 or 6.30 depending on season.

Gjorslev Castle, free admission to park.

Gavnø Castle, near Naestved, flower gardens, chapel and museum open 10–4 or 5, castle with paintings. Season from around May 1 to Sept. 1.

Ålholm Castle and *car museum,* near Nysted, open 10–6 in summer.

Herlufsholm Manor, Naestved, chapel open 11–5, May 1 to Oct. 31.

Jaegerspris Castle, 10–12 and 1–5 Apr. 1 to Oct. 31, and park open daily.

Kronborg Castle, Elsinore, 10–5 May 1 to Sept. 30, 11–4 April and Oct., 11–3 Nov. 1 to Mar. 31.

Lerchenborg Castle near Kalundborg, 18th-century baroque with French-style park (rose garden) and English-style lawns. Andersen collection. Mid-June to mid-Aug. 11–5 (exc. Fri.)

Liselund, on Møn, charming 18th-century manor and park, open all year. Castle open May 1–Oct. 31. Conducted tours weekdays at 10.30, 11, 1.30 and 2, Sun. and hols. also at 4 and 4.30.

Nysø Manor, built in 17th century Dutch style, museum open April to Sept., Wed. and Sat. 2–5, Sun. 10–5.

Pederstrup Manor, May 1–Aug. 31, Tues.–Sun. 10–12 and 1–5. Oct. 1–April 30, 2–4 only. Park open daily. May–Aug; March–April, Sept.–Oct. Tues.–Sun. 2–5; Nov.–Feb. Sat. and Sun. 2–5.

Sparresholm Manor, interesting museum of horsedrawn carriages (drive in them yourself). Daily 10–5 in summer, weekends 10–5 in fall.

Vallø Castle and park near Køge, well worth a visit. Park open daily.

 HOTELS AND RESTAURANTS. The roads running north and south from Copenhagen pass through seaside resorts and small villages, so you can expect accommodations to range in price and comfort accordingly. Remember that the peak season at the seaside places runs from June 15 to August 20, elsewhere from May 1 to September 30. During other months, ask for the off-season rates. Through the Elsinore Tourist Office you can book all over north Zealand. Letters (BE) indicate breakfast extra.

ALBERTSLUND (Taastrup). *Motel Wittrup,* Hwy. A 1, 104 beds, 48 rooms with shower (BE). Moderate.

ELSINORE (Helsingør). Hotels: *Marienlyst,* 398 beds, all rooms with bath; private beach, sauna, roulette, indoor salt pool. Fashionable with music and dance. There are also 63 flats for hire, with kitchenette and bath; each flat sleeps 4 to 6 people. *Meulenborg,* 50 beds, annex, old manor house in extensive grounds with pool, fish ponds and sea fishing, open mid-May through Sept., *Skandia,* 90 beds; *Missionshotellet,* 65 beds, all moderate.

FREDENSBORG. Hotel: *Store Kro,* near castle, all 49 rooms have bath, first class superior. As comfortable as any hotel in Denmark and has unrivaled food, too. Many rooms have terrace.

GLOSTRUP. *Glostrup Park Hotel,* 100 beds, all rooms with bath, fairly expensive; breakfast is included.

GREVE STRAND (between Copenhagen and Køge). **Motel:** *Canteen,* 20 beds, modern and reasonable (BE).

HOLBAEK. Hotels: *Strandparken,* 52 beds, all rooms with bath, in park. First class reasonable.

HORNBAEK. Hotels: *Trouville,* deluxe, 81 beds, all rooms with bath, near beach; pool, sauna, fishing, sailing, music, garden.

JYDERUP. Inns: *Bromølle Kro,* 4 miles south off Roskilde-Kalundborg road, oldest in Denmark (1198), in beautiful surroundings opposite children's amusements. A former host supplemented his income by murdering his sleeping guests, but this hobby isn't practised any longer. *Snertinge Kro,* 3 miles north, is the typical Danish country inn (moderate prices). Both (BE).

KARREBAEKSMINDE. Restaurant: *De hvide Svaner,* old thatched-roofed buildings, first class food.

KØGE. Hotels: *Hvide Hus,* 224 beds, deluxe, has sauna. *Centralhotellet,* 24 beds, moderate. (BE).
Restaurant: *Richters Gård.* Open all year.

KORSØR. Hotels: *Klarskovgård,* 172 beds, all rooms with shower. *Tårnborg-kroen,* 23 beds, 5 doubles with shower, reasonable. (BE).

MARIBO. On island of Lolland. **Hotel:** *Hvide Hus,* 130 beds, first class, modern, has sauna, pool. Breakfast is included.
Restaurant: *Bang's Have,* in lovely surroundings, fine for meals on outings, music Sats all the year round.

MENSTRUP. Hotel: *Menstrup Kro,* 70 beds, in renovated country inn, moderate. Near beach. Homemade country food.

MOGENSTRUP. Hotel: *Mogenstrup Kro,* 85 beds, cozy country inn, renovated, first class reasonable.

MØN. Hotels: Stege: *Skydevaenget,* moderate, (BE), 51 beds. At cliff: *Hunos-øgård,* reasonable, 56 beds, lounge with open fireplace; good cooking, free fishing. Open April–Oct.

MULLERUP HAVN, between Kalundborg and Slagelse. First class camping and holiday center. Marina and individual chalets. *Skipperkroen,* inn with unusual interior. Accommodations in 10 cottages with 6 beds, bath and kitchen.

NAESTVED. Hotels: *Vinhuset,* 65 beds, very pleasant, nightclub, first class reasonable. *Axelhus,* 30 beds, no rooms with private bath, spacious, inexpensive (BE).

NYKØBING (Falster). **Hotel:** *Baltic,* 130 beds, pleasant, moderate.
Motel: *Liselund,* near Hwy. 2, 50 beds, moderate.

NYKØBING. (Sjaelland). **Hotel:** *Odsherred,* 12 beds, inexpensive. (BE).
Restaurant: *Den gyldne Hane,* Havnebyen (on road to Ebeltoft ferry), almost entirely fish dishes. Fresh food, also hotel (18 beds), inexpensive. (BE). *Klintek-roen,* 24 beds, all rooms with bath, moderate (BE).

RINGSTED. Hotels: *Postgården,* old, but modernized, 24 beds. *Casino,* 20 beds; both moderate. Try their "stage-coach luncheon".
Restaurants: *Apotekergården,* exclusive, *Møllekroen,* both good food.

RØNNEDE. Motel: *Axelved,* near town off Mwy. 2, only 18 beds, (BE), moderate.

ROSKILDE. Hotels. Since Roskilde is only 19 miles from Copenhagen, the budget-minded traveler might consider staying overnight here, where prices are considerably lower than in central Copenhagen. *Prindsen,* 70 beds, shrimp a specialty in restaurant. *Risø,* 40 beds, all rooms have bath. Both first class. *Motel B.P.,* Highway A1, 58 beds in modern rooms.

Restaurants: *Kaelderhalsen* is now a discothèque. *Palaecafeen,* with music.

SLAGELSE. Hotel: *Ny Missionshotel,* 60 beds, moderate. *Hotel E2,* 98 beds, first class reasonable, all rooms with bath.

Restaurants: *Centrum* and *Turisten. Anlaegspavillonen* has dancing.

SØLLERØD. Restaurant: *Søllerød Kro,* an old, thatched-roof inn with rustic furniture.

SORØ. Hotel: *Postgaarden,* 44 beds, 9 rooms with bath or shower, moderate.

TISVILDELEJE. Pension: *Helenekilde,* inexpensive summer pension. Half board.

VORDINGBORG. Hotels: *Kong Valdemar,* 150 beds, moderate. Music, dance, garden. *Motel Nafta,* 7 cottages with bath and kitchen, inexpensive. *G1. Masnedøgaard Holiday Center.* Open all year.

SHOPPING. The main road in Roskilde is Algade and its continuation Skomagergade, with the greatest selection of shops. On Saturday mornings you may attend instead the open-air market day.

USEFUL INFORMATION. Tourist information offices exist in every sizeable town; the larger offices also book accommodation. These offices, plus camp and caravan sites are all signposted by the international symbols.

THE CENTRAL ISLANDS

Funen, the Garden of Denmark

Funen (Fyn), like many a Dane, is rather rotund. Not only does it contain some of the country's richest agricultural land, but most of Denmark's fruit grows here as well.

Its capital is Odense, and, despite its inland location, is the nation's fourth largest port by virtue of a ship canal. Next in importance is beautifully situated Svendborg, a busy seaside town and jumping-off place to the smaller islands in the south. This part of Funen has more lovely old castles and manor houses to the square mile than perhaps anywhere else in Europe.

Exploring the Central Islands

Your first acquaintance with Funen might be Nyborg, the terminal for train ferries from Zealand. Newcastle, as its name is in translation, grew up around the castle, which was built in 1179 as a guard against Wendish pirates; its central position in the Danish kingdom led to its use as the meeting place of the Danehof, an early parliament. The first Danish constitution, the Great Charter, was granted here by Erik Glipping in 1282. Ten years later the town got a charter, too, and today it has about 18,000 inhabitants. Contrasting this medieval castle, where plays are performed on the ramparts, are the most modern hotels on Funen.

North of Nyborg is Kerteminde, but make a stopover at Ladby. Here, in an air-conditioned underground burial mound, are preserved the remains of a 1,100-year-old Viking ship, 72 feet long and 9 feet wide. In it was interred a Viking chief together with his arms, his most valuable treasures, 4 hunting dogs, and 11 horses. Kerteminde itself is Funen's most important fishing town, and a picturesque summer resort with old half-timbered buildings in Langegade. Nearby are Viby, an unspoiled hamlet, and Munkebo, which underwent a sudden expansion when the Lindø shipyard was started in the 1950s. Today, this small village 10 miles from Odense, has one of the greatest shipyards in the world.

The two largest towns on the island, Odense and Svendborg, are equally suited as a center for exploring the Danish "butter hole". Odense, a port since 987 although 14 miles from the sea, is the third largest Danish city and above all is known as the birthplace of Hans Christian Andersen, who spent the first 14 years of his life here. The Odense river, where his mother did her laundrywork, runs through Funen Village to the harbor at the narrow fjord leading to the sea.

Museums and Sights

Hans Andersen's probable birthplace at Hans Jensensstraede 39 is today a museum containing his personal belongings, sketches, works and silhouettes, and letters from Dickens and Jenny Lind.

Hans Andersen's childhood home at Munkemøllestraede 3–5 has been described by the writer in *The Story of My Life*. From his 2nd to his 14th year he lived with his parents, the cobbler and the washerwoman in the flat to the right.

St. Canute's Cathedral is Gothic, erected in the 13th century on the site of St. Alban's Church, where King Canute was killed and later canonized. Today he is enshrined here. Two royal tombs are those of King Hans and King Christian II, with their queens. See also Claus Berg's golden 16th-century altarpiece. The font is from 1660. Open 10–5 (Sun. 11.30–12.30) May-Aug., 10–4 weekdays Sept.-Apr.

The Funen Village (Den fynske Landsby), 2 miles south, bus 2, is an open-air museum of 22 Funen country buildings including a water mill and open-air theater with Andersen plays for the children in summer. Return to town along the river (boats, path).

Mønterstraede is a museum street where 4 houses dating from 1547 to 1646 show the town culture and life of those days.

The Diocesan Museum at Jernbanegade 13 has a local prehistoric collection (especially Iron Age) and collection of Funen art, e.g. Jens Juel. Open as Mønterstraede Museum.

The Danish Railway Museum, Dannebrogsgade, displays the State Railway collections: two royal wagons and a Newcastle steam engine from 1869. Open May–Sept. daily 10–4, Oct.–Apr. Sun. only 10–3.

Other places of interest: St. Hans' Church, partly from the 13th century; old houses in Overgade; Zoo; Tivoli; town hall and university (since 1966). Also make a river cruise.

At Nørre Lyndelse, 8 miles south, is the native home of Carl Nielsen, the best-known Danish composer, who recalled his home in *My Childhood in Funen.*

Svendborg and the Southern Isles

To the south is Svendborg and the bordering island of Tåsinge, both beautifully situated on the sea. Svendborg, second largest Funen town, got its town charter in the 13th century. Today it is devoted to industry, commerce and navigation and is ideal for stopovers because of good beaches and "unexplored" surrounding isles. The islands of Tåsinge and Langeland are connected by bridges to Svendborg. The other islands are reached by ship only. Among them, visit AErø and if time allows, Hjortø.

While in Svendborg, visit the Church of St. Nicolas, devoted to the sailors' patron, a Romanesque basilica prior to 1200. Restored 1892, with frescos in the arches. Admittance daily except during services. Museums to visit are:

Anne Hvide's Gård at Fruestraede 3 is the regional museum in the oldest preserved building from 1560, with Middle Ages collections, ship models and local collections. May-Oct. 10–4, winter 1–4.

The Zoological Museum at Dronningemaen 30 has a complete collection of Danish mammals, birds and eggs. Open daily 9–5 April-Sept., winter 10–4.

Thurø is connected by a dam to Funen at the Christiansminde woods. Thurø is an orchard with 1,600 inhabitants and used to be the home of some Danish painters and poets who were inspired by its doll-like village and sailors.

Tåsinge, south of Svendborg, has 5,000 inhabitants. Here and in Svendborg was the setting of Elvira Madigan's romance, and the movie was made on location here. (The tombs are at Landet churchyard). Visit Bregninge Church (panorama from its tower) and the nearby skipper's home with ship models and Elvira Madigan traces. Troense is one of the best preserved Danish villages, with a row of half-timbered houses. The former school is a museum for the shipping which used to be the living of the islanders. Nearby Valdemarsslot castle is from around 1640 and is now a naval museum with much sumptuous furnishing.

Langeland, largest in the archipelago, is connected by bridge and dam to Tåsinge. The main town is Rudkøbing, where H. C. Ørsted, the discoverer of electromagnetism, was born. Today it is dominated by merchants' estates. In Brogade and Østergade are many preserved old houses. South of the town are Ristinge and Bagenkop with good beaches, and ferry to Kiel in Germany. North of Rudkøbing are the 13th-century Tranekaer Castle and Egeløkke Manor, once the living of Bishop Grundtvig, founder of the Danish Folk High School movement in the 19th century. The northernmost village is Lohals (ferry to Korsør). As a whole Langeland is rich in relics of the past, and you can always find a beach.

AErø has two towns, Marstal and AErøskøbing. Had it not been because of its competitor, Marstal would have been famous. Today its museum houses a collection of model ships, and the church interior and small shipyards tell a story of bygone grandeur one or two centuries ago. The town has ferry connection with Rudkøbing. However, the smaller, AErøskøbing has the most to offer the tourist. Even the sparrows sleep in its 17th and 18th-century streets with 36 protected houses. As in Ebeltoft you will find an isolated community, today revived because of tourism. However, you can still see its post office dating from 1749, its wooden pumps and cook house in function, although the latter serves today's requirements better as a public toilet! Also see the bay-windows, the Doll House and the unique collection of bottle ships (750 models), plus Gunnar Hammerich's House with its old furnishing. The attractive church dates from 1756 and has an interesting pulpit with carvings of dubious ladies with fig leaves. The town is still lit by gaslight at night.

When leaving, you can take ferries to Mommark (Als), Faaborg or Svendborg (Funen) or Rudkøbing.

Southern Funen

Along the lanes around Svendborg you find numerous picturesque spots, but one you must visit is Egeskov. The castle here is the best-preserved water castle in Europe. Its name comes from the oak forest which was felled around 1524 to form 30 years later the piles on which was built an impregnable Renaissance castle. It is still impregnable to tourists, but its five gardens and the museum of vintage cars and aircraft can be visited. You are now about halfway between Nyborg and Faaborg, both of which should be seen. On the road to Nyborg is Holckenhavn Manor dating from 1580, where Corfitz Ulfeldt, the most notorious traitor in Danish history, lived with his wife Leonora Christiana, daughter of King Christian IV. Visit the 30-acre park, open 9–4. The chapel (pulpit carvings) is not generally open except by appointment.

On the road from Egeskov to Fåborg is Brahetrolleborg, a Cistercian abbey from 1172, which after the Reformation came under the Crown, and since 1668 a barony. It was here that Johan Ludvig Reventlow let the peasants burn a wooden horse symbolizing his release of them. The 100-acre park is open to the public daily 9–5.

Other interesting châteaux are the somber, moated Broholm; the lovely Renaissance-style Rygård; Hesselagergård, built in 1538 with walls more than six feet thick and encircled by a moat; Glorup, a manor house from 1580, rebuilt in baroque style in the 18th century; Lykkesholm, Hellerup, Ravnholt, and Ørbaeklunde.

Fåborg was a privileged town in the 13th century but damaged by a fire in 1728, which, however, spared many old houses that can still be seen in Vestergade and Holkegade. Moreover, one of five medieval gates survives, and so does the belfry, all that remains of St. Nicolas' Church to which it once belonged. The museum contains the best collection of Funen painters, a private donation, also works by Kai Nielsen, the sculptor who did the controversial "Ymer Well" in the market square. Just east of town is the 600-year-old Kaleko water mill, now a museum. Ferry crossings to either Avernakø with 120 inhabitants (especially recommended at Shrovetide and Whitsuntide), or to Lyø (200 inhabitants). This will show you idyllic landscapes and Lyø Village. There is another ferry to Gelting near Flensburg, and the main road leads west to the Bøjden ferry for Fynshav, on Als. On the way one passes the round church at Horne, the only one of its kind in Funen. With walls 7 feet thick it served both as church and fortress, but today only the core of the building remains. North of Fåborg is a former manor house, now the Hotel Stensgård. Between Fåborg and Assens to the northwest lie the Svanninge Hills, known jokingly as the Funen Alps.

The western coast of Funen offers less of interest than the rest of the island. Assens has a church of minor note and a 17th-century house which was the home of Peter Willemoes. At the age of 18, this Danish hero commanded a battery during the bombardment of Copenhagen with such distinction that Lord Nelson complimented him personally. Middelfart claims to have the only suspension bridge in Denmark, built in 1970, and is worth a stop if only for its Folk Museum at Brogade 6. Just outside of town is Galsklint, a memorial park in honor of British pilots shot down during World War II.

PRACTICAL INFORMATION FOR THE CENTRAL ISLANDS

 HOW TO GET ABOUT. Funen is linked to Jutland by the Little Belt Bridges (at Middelfart) and ferries (Fynshav-Bøjden); to Zealand by ferry (Nyborg-Korsør and Halsskov-Knudshoved); to the island of Langeland via the Tåsinge bridge; and to AErø by ferry. Its main town of Odense may be reached from Copenhagen in 3 hours by "L" train, or more quickly by air. All important towns on the island are served by local trains and buses.

 MOTORING. Roads are wide and well-banked; a detailed regional map is essential if you plan to explore the smaller byways. To avoid delay book ahead for the car on the ferry between Funen and Zealand. *Dantourist* in Svendborg runs a prearranged 8-day tour with half-pension through Middelfart, Svendborg, Odense and Roskilde (start in any of those towns): will cost approximately 2,200 Dkr. The route will also take you to AErø. Route map supplied on booking. Or you could make this 3-day tour from Odense:

First day. Odense, sightseeing (about 3 hours) Ladbyskibet-Kerteminde-Holckenhavn-Ørbaek-Glorup-(Rygård)-Hesselager–Broholm   Manor-Svendborg. Distance, about 50 miles (81 km).

Second day. Excursions from Svendborg to islands of Tåsinge (Valdemar's Castle, Bregninge Church), Langeland (Tranekaer Castle), and AErø.

Third day. Depart Svendborg-Kvaerndrup-Egeskov Castle-Brahetrolleborg Castle-Fåborg-Assens-(Wedelsborg   Castle)-Middelfart-Bogense-(Glavendrup Stone)-Odense. Distance, about 100 miles (160 km).

 WHAT TO SEE. In addition to castles, manors, and pretty villages, Funen offers its visitors such spots of natural beauty as the Beacon Hills (Frøbjerg Bavnehøj) and Svanninge Hills; the Viking ship at Ladby; the Glavendrup Stone with runic inscriptions and Boat Stone, near Bogense; the 13th-century churches of St. Knud at Odense and St. Nicolas at Svendborg; the round church at Horne and Bregninge's church, with magnificent views of the Funen archipelago from its tower. The islands to the south each possess their own intriguing features. Odense was the home of Hans Christian Andersen, and his former house is open to visitors.

  MUSEUMS. Odense: *Hans Andersen's House,* Hans Jensensstraede 39–43; generally open 10–5, June–Aug. 9–7, best check. *Hans Andersen's Childhood Home,* Munkemøllestraede 3; usually open 10–5. *Funen Village* (Den fynske Landsby), 9 to dusk (Nov.-Mar., Sun and hols. only). *Møntergården* in Mønterstraede; open all the year from 10 to 4.

Interesting exhibits in: *Funen Museum,* Bogense; *Fåborg Museum* and *Den gamle Gård* (Old Farmhouse), Fåborg; *Kerteminde Museum; Middelfart Folk Museum; Zoological Museum,* Svendborg: AErøskøbing's *Collections of Bottle and Model Ships* and *Hammerichs Hus; Langeland's Museum,* Rudkøbing.

CASTLES AND MANOR HOUSES. South of Odense are: *Egeskov Castle,* water castle with vintage car and aircraft museum, open Easter to Oct. 10–5, June–Aug. 9–6; park all year. *Nyborg Castle* (Castle of Danehof), closed Mon. except from June to August; open May 1–Sept. 30, 9–6; winter 10–3, closed Dec.–Feb. *Glorup Manor,* park open Sun. 9–6, Thurs. 12–6. *Holckenhavn Manor,* park open daily 9–4. *Broholm Manor* and *Brahetrolleborg. Ryg árd Castle, Hvidkilde Manor,* near Svendborg. *Lykkesholm. Ravnholt Manor,* park open 10–6. *Ørbaeklunde Manor, Steensgård Castle.*

On Tåsinge is 17th-century *Valdemar Slot* (Castle), while *Tranekaer Castle* and *Egeløkke Manor* are all on Langeland.

West of Odense, near Tanderup, is 18th-century *Wedellsborg,* with walls dating from the Middle Ages and large English-style park (open to public); near Middelfart is *Hindsgavl Castle,* park open to public.

HOTELS AND RESTAURANTS. Odense makes an excellent base for exploring the rest of the island. In general, hotels maintain the same rates throughout the year, although some may offer reductions during the off-season (October 1 to April 30) and it is always as well to inquire. By joint arrangement you can stay in one Funen inn and take half-pension in another of about 20 choices (min. 2 days, 200 Dkr). You can also buy an "inn check" for 150 Dkr covering one night's stay and breakfast. The meal coupons are also on sale separately from Dantourist, Svendborg.

AERØSKØBING. Hotels: Best is *AErøhus,* 66 beds, some rooms with bath (BE); half-timbered house, good country-style food, sauna; small *Terrassen* and *Phønix;* all moderate. *Motel Damgården,* Borgnaes, former farm, inexpensive.

ASSENS. Hotels: *Lillebaelt, Marcussen's,* both moderate, some rooms with bath. *Phønix,* inexpensive. All (BE). *Ebberup Kro,* 4 miles east, 22 beds, country-style inn, fishing possibilities, moderate.

FÅBORG. Hotels: *Fåborg Fjord,* recent, moderate, 90 beds. About 3 miles north of Faaborg on the Assens road is the luxurious *Steensgård,* a former manor. *Klinten,* 120 apartments with 6 beds, bath and kitchen. Sauna, pools, weekly rentals. First class. *Falsled Kro,* first class, near Stensgård, charming country inn, with French food and wines. Also English pub, 11 rooms. Superb, expensive food. All (BE).

KERTEMINDE. Hotel: *Tornøes.* 25 beds, garden. Venison in season. Moderate.
Restaurant: *Munkebo Kro,* by main highway, famous for fried eel.

MARSTAL, on AErø Island. The *AErø,* 68 beds, 25 rooms with bath or shower. Moderate, renovated. There are also 5 cottages.

MIDDELFART. Hotel: *Grimmerhus,* Kongebrovej 42, 20 beds, no private bath or comfort, beautifully situated, inexpensive (BE). Closed around Christmas. *Hindsgavl Slot* (manor), in lovely park. Popular for congresses. 1st class reasonable.

NYBORG. Hotels: *Hesselet,* 92 beds, all rooms with bath, deluxe; sauna and pool (BE). *Nyborg Strand,* 400 beds, some rooms with bath, first class. Both on beach, close to 18-hole golf course. *Øksendrup Kro & Motel,* a few miles south, 30 beds, inexpensive. (BE).

Restaurant: *Danehofkroen,* serves good value tourist menu.

ODENSE. Hotels: *Hotel H.C. Andersen,* in new concert house. First class superior. 296 beds, all rooms with bath. *Grand,* 235 beds, 113 rooms with bath; one of Denmark's best, and with fine cuisine, bar; first class superior. *Windsor,* 109 beds, restored with modern, rather expensive rooms. First class. *Hans Tausen,* 90 beds, also restored. First class reasonable. *Frederik VI,* 92 beds, suburban, with garden. Moderate. *Mørkenborg Kro,* 30 beds, on beautiful site 11 miles NW. Has antiques and children's playground; inexpensive (BE).

Motels: Recent *Munkeris,* 91 beds, all rooms with shower. *Odense,* a converted farmhouse, garden in former fruit orchard, delightful; 82 beds in attractive rooms with shower, both moderate and (BE). *Brasilia/Blommenslyst Inn,* 100 beds, all rooms with bath. In park 5 miles west. First class reasonable.

Restaurants: *Den gamle Kro,* lovely timbered inn with charming atmosphere, a long list of specialties; moderate prices. *Den grimme AElling,* steak house. *Franck-A,* moderately-priced meals served in differently-styled interiors. *Under Lindetraet,* vis-à-vis Andersen's house, and *Skoven,* in Hunderup Forest, both are excellent and rather expensive. *Sortebro Kro,* in the Funen Village, for simple and inexpensive fare.

RUDKØBING on Langeland Island. **Hotel:** *Skandinavien,* 15 beds, all rooms with shower; TV-room, inexpensive (BE).

Restaurant: *Spodsbjerg Kro og Badehotel.*

SVENDBORG. Hotels: *Svendborg,* 100 beds, all rooms with bath; music and dance, first class reasonable; *3 Roser,* modern motel, 256 beds (also weekly 4–5 bed apartments with kitchen). All rooms with bath. Free golf and pool. Moderate prices (BE). *AErø,* 18 beds, no private bath, older; restaurant with aeronautical, marine and sailors' rooms. *Stella Maris,* 28 beds, 13 rooms with bath, mission hotel, garden: both inexpensive and (BE).

See also Troense.

Restaurants: *Røde Mølle,* Hvidkilde, in former water mill. Venison a specialty. *Svendborg* hotel restaurant with dancing.

TRANEKAER, on Langeland Island. **Hotel:** *Tranekjaer Gjaestgivergaard,* 32 beds, terrace, first class reasonable. Restaurant with raftered ceiling and open hearths. Venison a specialty in season.

TROENSE, on Tåsinge Island. **Hotel:** *Troense,* 64 beds in new rooms overlooking the Sound. Free golf-course nearby. Moderate.

JUTLAND

Birds, Beaches and Runic Stones

The peninsula of Jutland (Jylland) is the only part of Denmark that is attached to the continent of Europe. Its southern boundary is the frontier with Germany. A tenth of the peninsula consists of moors and sand dunes, the latter being almost entirely along the west coast. The other nine-tenths are devoted to agriculture and, to a much lesser extent, to forestry. Jutland's west, or North Sea, coast has but one deep-water port, Esbjerg, though fishing harbors have been developed in recent years at Hirtshals and Hvide Sande. Apart from Esbjerg, the main fishing ports are still Skagen and Frederikshavn in the extreme northeast of Jutland. The geography of the eastern side is quite unlike that of the western. Along the shore facing Funen are deep, well-wooded fjords running miles inland.

Exploring Jutland

The region of Jutland bordering Germany is one that has been fought over a number of times. When bricks replaced mud and wood as Denmark's chief building material one of the first uses made of them by the Danes was the construction of the Dannevirke wall across the neck of Jutland to keep the Germans out. Today the people try to invite them into Denmark instead, tempting them with nature, open beaches and signboards with German texts. However, the population is mixed, and the provinces of Schleswig (Slesvig in Danish) and Holstein (Holsten) caused many feuds and wars between Denmark and Germany. A plebiscite in 1920 established the present boundary, and today the inhabitants on either side of the border cooperate or compete in such plans as an extra North Sea dike or in making cultural Danish arrangements south of the border. But still some administrative features indicate that this southernmost area has a history of its own.

Traveling north along the east coast, you first meet the island of Als, with Sønderborg, separated by the Sound. On the way you pass Gråsten Castle, rebuilt after a fire in 1757 and since then much restored. Today it serves as summer residence for the Queen's Mother, Queen Ingrid. Just before Als is Dybbøl Mill, perhaps the most revered spot in Denmark and today a national symbol that has been re-erected three times. It is the focal point in a memorial park to the wars in 1848 and 1864. Sønderborg Castle is still intact in spite of the wars; parts of it date back to the 12th century, and it is now a museum. If time allows, the rest of Als is also worth a visit. It bears the mark of the Danfoss factories and of "riding at the ring" festivities in Sønderborg (4 days, starting the second Saturday in July).

Back on the mainland again, the road is set for Åbenrå, an ancient town that has suffered from fire and bombardment through the ages. Take a walk through Slotsgade and Vaegterpladsen and visit the 15th century Brundlund Castle with a restored water mill. North of Åbenrå you meet Knivsbjerg, the tallest South Jutland hill, which served as a German rallying point and was blown up by the Danes during the German occupation. Haderslev is dominated by the cathedral (from about 1265 and later rebuilt). Christiansfeld was founded on April 1, 1773, by Moravian Brethren, who found here a refuge; their observances were similar to those of the Danish church, but with music and handicrafts playing a leading part. The settlement is still special and was awarded a European medal in 1975 for its intact atmosphere. Also visit their church and churchyard, the Field of God, with female burials to the right, male burials to the left.

Our next stop is the medium-sized modern town of Kolding, dominated by the Koldinghus ruin, once a 13th-century royal residence surrounded by a moat. The castle and its chapel were burnt down by Spanish troops in 1808. From 1892 onwards the rooms have gradually been restored and house a historical museum in the castle tower. Fredericia is an important railroad junction, trains from Funen and all parts of Jutland meeting here. Before that, it was an important, though not pleasant fortress, the inhabitants being either soldiers or religious fugitives who were granted religious liberty. The ramparts are well preserved and the central part of town has straight, crossing streets, giving unobstructed fields of fire. Take a walk on the ramparts; the 3½ miles stood the test on July 6, 1849, against the Slesvig army. On the 5th of July every year is a flower pilgrimage to the soldiers' graves, followed the next day by a trooping parade and procession in the uniforms of 1849.

But don't forget the western coast of this region. From Kolding the road will take you back to the frontier district and the old community of Tønder (founded 1243). This town is still known for its exquisite lace. There is a modern art museum, but it is the old museum collections of lace, Dutch tiles, furniture, silver and faience that would probably interest you most. There are many attractive houses and doorways, especially in Østergade, Vestergade and Uldgade. Kristkirken (Christchurch) is richly decorated. Though built in 1591 much of the contents are from an earlier church—a black marble font from 1350, the pews and the pulpit from about 1586. Also notice the handcarved epitaphs dating from 1586 to 1695, and the lectern from 1623 with 18 handcarved biblical scenes. The marshes nearby are unique in Denmark in that dikes protect this region against the periodic floods which formerly caused tremendous damage; even so, the town had to be evacuated as recently as 1976 because of the threat of flooding. Now Danish and German authorities have agreed to build an extra dike. Many couples from abroad know Tønder as a continental Las Vegas or Gretna Green because liberal Danish laws have allowed them to marry here.

Three miles to the west nestles the lovely, thatch-roofed village of Møgeltønder. Its cobbled main street, bordered by old lime trees and 17th-century Frisian houses, is considered the most beautiful village street in Northern Europe. Here, in a 17-acre park, is the 18th-century baroque Schackenborg manor house. The ownership will pass over to Prince Joakim, younger son of Queen Margrethe, when he comes of age. The 12th-century village church, part of the estate, has 16th-century frescos, a Gothic altar-piece sculpted by Flemish artists, an arch dating back to 1240, and an outstanding 13th-century wooden Madonna and Child. The baroque organ (1679) is the oldest church organ still in use in Denmark.

Not far away is the remarkable village of Rudbøl. The Danish-German frontier runs right through its center, though the dividing line is no more substantial than a few metal discs set among the Dutch bricks with which the street is paved. Rudbøl's inn has achieved a certain amount of fame. The building stands in Denmark, but the front entrance is in Germany.

Trip to the Past

The town of Ribe has changed little since the Middle Ages, and its narrow winding streets, its venerable houses and the cathedral have made it a fascinating attraction for visitors from abroad and Danes alike. The 800-year-old cathedral is one of Scandinavia's finest churches, built of Danish brick and stones brought from the Rhine land. The main tower of the cathedral was raised some seven centuries ago by citizens who were as concerned with the defense of their city as with the salvation of their souls. Don't miss the "Cat Head Door" on the south side. According to legend this was provided for the exclusive use of the devil.

The market place features the old inn known as Weis' Stue. In the parlor are panels with biblical pictures and a 400-year-old clock. A carved cupboard is dated 1500, and a candelabrum 1599. Hospitality is the rule of the house.

Many half-timbered houses can be seen in Sønderportsgade, Puggårdsgade and Sortebrødregade, many of them from the 16th century. Ribe's smallest building huddles at Klostergade 72. Other points of interest are the Black Friars Abbey and the church of St. Catharine, both dating from the mid-13th century. The abbey is the best-preserved and most beautiful monastery in Denmark, except for the one at Elsinore. On Slotsbanken you can view all that remains of the huge 12th-century stronghold of Riberhus. Skibbroen is the oldest Danish port. On the quay stands the Floodwave Column, whose marks show the water levels of previous floods—the top level mark is the 1634 flood, which also hit the cathedral. Only the weak dikes prevented two new floods in 1976, when the entire coastal region down to Germany was threatened by a sea a mere 12 yards below the dike top.

In days past, every town was free to set its own legislation, and the legend goes that a mother watching her son being hanged in another Jutland town cried out: "Oh, my boy, thank heaven you were not tried at Ribe." However, female criminals were treated with more consideration in Ribe. The town's legal code declared that a thief of the weaker sex should not be hanged—she was to "be buried alive, because she is a woman".

In 1973 traces of the original Ribe were found north of the river, and these excavations have brought to light coins from c. 700, proving that the town is the oldest in Denmark.

Esbjerg and the Western Islands

In Esbjerg we have a town that, for a change, is not old. It is, in fact, one of Denmark's youngest and is often the first impression of Denmark to Britons arriving by ship. A hundred years ago only 20 people lived here, now there are over 79,000. Apart from being Denmark's main gateway for imports and exports and an important fishing port, it is West Jutland's cultural and school center with folk high school, conservatory and museum. Being the only deep-water port on the west coast of Jutland, the town is also the home of several hundred fishing cutters, and you might visit the yards where they are built. Also interesting is the trip to the fish auction halls, but be sure to get there early if you are to see anything.

Fanø is the northernmost of the three Danish tidal area islands, reached by a 20-minute ferry crossing from Esbjerg. The islanders were known as sea-faring people, and a shipbuilding industry arose about 1760. The first half of the 19th century was a successful time, and the fleet was the second largest, after Copenhagen. The islands still have lots of reminders from this time, goods brought home from Holland and other countries. But since 1850 bathing guests have been the main source of income, Fanø offers some 10 miles of sandy beach. The island has but two main roads, one crosswise and one lengthwise between Nordby (north) and Sønderho (south). Though the minor of those two Sønderho (350 inhabitants) has most to offer in remaining skippers' houses from about 1800; 47 of them are protected. The national costume is unchanged and still in use, at least on Sønderhoday (late July).

South of Fanø is the islet of Mandø. To reach it you have to go by the postal van which will carry you along the road at low tide. 125 people live here, they have their own church from 1727 and an inn (apply ahead if you want a room). Bird lovers would find this islet a paradise.

Rømø is the largest and southernmost of the islands, access is over an 8-mile causeway, and the only main road is supplemented at low tide by the 3 miles-broad beach which is also used by automobiles. 800 people live here where the most characteristic buildings are the commanders' farms from the time of the sea-faring inhabitants. Only a few remain today, one of them (from 1744) is a museum. Rømø church has wrought iron hat pegs above each pew.

Holiday Haunts on the Jutland Coast

Northwest of Esbjerg stretches the promontory known as Blåvand-shuk. From here it is possible to drive for miles through wonderful scenery behind the sea and dunes. After Graerup Strand you motor along some 15 miles of sand before reaching Henne Strand. Continuing in your vehicle with the sea on one side and the lagoon on the other, you reach the old fishing village of Hvide Sande, strategically placed between Ringkøbing Fjord and the North Sea, with a canal and locks. At the northern end of the lagoon you arrive at the North Sea resort of Søndervig.

Skipping about 50 miles of dunes and beach, we stop at Bovbjerg, just beyond Lemvig on the western end of the Limfjord. Here, cliffs 140 feet high tower above the ocean. Until breakwaters were built here in 1909, the sea had cut its way nearly 200 yards inland in less than a century.

If your time is limited and you are not yet tired of sea and sand, you may continue further up north to Thyborøn on the western mouth of the Limfjord and continue on its northern side. However, another longer route inland will offer you more variation and other landscapes and scenery.

From Bovbjerg we continue to the small towns of Lemvig and Struer. Lemvig is terraced in the hilly landscape, and you arrive and depart along hairpin bends. Dominating Struer are the factories of Bang & Olufsen, known the world over for their radio and television products. After Struer and Vinderup is Sahl Church with a magnificent golden altarpiece from about 1200. The gold is, in fact, copper. Not far away is the open air museum at Hjerl Hede, where you'll find several village houses from various regions, one of them dating back to about 1530. At Hjerl Hede is a reconstructed Iron Age house which is occupied in summer. Also visit the magnificent surrounding area around the Flynder-sø lake.

Now it is time to go north along the east side of the Limfjord to visit the Spøttrup Castle which will give you an impression of a medieval manor, erected about 1500 and now owned by the state and made a museum. Notice the thick walls and the knights' hall and watchmen's gallery. The adjoining gardens have been reconstructed according to old descriptions of Middle Age spices and medicinal herbs.

In 1978 a high-level bridge across the Sallingsund gave easier access to the island of Mors in the Limfjord. The bridge runs between the Pain and the Torment (on Mors side), two place-names reminiscent of earlier problems coming to and from the island. The main town is Nykøbing, but the best sights are to be found among the natural sights of Legind Bjerge near the bridge, at Feggeklit, and finally at Hanklit.

We leave Mors across the Vildsund bridge, and via Thisted, where a well-known Danish poet, J. P. Jacobsen, was born. Heading northwest we reach again the North Sea coast at Klitmøller, where the country with its woods and lakes is particularly beautiful. Today it is a favorite summer resort. Off Bulbjerg coast, Denmark lost a major tourist attraction in 1978, when sea undermined the 154-foot-high Skarreklit rock. All that now remains is a fast-eroding stump, and only local postcards tell how it once looked. You may make a detour to Frøstrup, where you can find the northernmost European storks in a private garden. Other birds can be studied inland near Bygholm.

Presently we approach a second beach at Blokhus, another popular West Jutland seaside resort, and further up north the somewhat larger Løkken, Lønstrup and Hirtshals (ferries to Norway). North of Tannisby is Råbjerg Mile, a "drifting" dune, now some 2½ miles inland, which, during the past 400–500 years was moved 10 yards east by the west wind every year. This once fruitful area was the setting of some outdoor scenes in Peter Brook's film of *King Lear* and is today a natural dune desert reached on foot only from Kandestederne.

We have now covered so much of Western Jutland that little remains but the very tip of the peninsula where the waters of the North Sea collide with those of the Kattegat at the spit of Skaw. Just south of this point you find Skagen and Old Skagen, popular both among artists and tourists. There is a church tower buried by sand and a local museum with works by Danish painters who made their reputation here.

Going back south along the east coast we reach Frederikshavn with daily connections to Sweden and Norway. The fishing harbor is one of Denmark's largest. The entire area is popular with holiday-making Danes and is plentifully supplied with summer chalets (some of them for rent) and campsites.

A ferry from Frederikshavn forms the connection to the isle of Laesø, an untouched and unspoiled landscape with rich fauna and 2,600 inhabitants. Byrum's 500 inhabitants live in the biggest town in the middle of the island. If you don't bring your car to Laesø and its beaches, there are bus tours to the various views and the farmhouses with seaweed roofs. On your way you may pass an islander in her national costume richly decorated with forged silver, perhaps the most beautiful in Denmark.

Aalborg

When you reach Aalborg, you have crossed the Limfjord and leave the northern part of Jutland known as Vendsyssel. Aalborg is known for the schnapps produced here, and also the tasty Limfjord oysters which are dredged in the neighborhood. The town is the most important north Jutland town and, together with her twin town north of the fjord, the fourth largest in Denmark. You find charming combinations of new and old, and twisting lanes filled with medieval houses exist side by side with broad modern boulevards. Sights include the magnificent Jens Bang's stone house, a 16th-century cathedral dedicated to the English St. Botolph, the early 16th-century Aalborghus Castle and the early 15th-century Monastery of the Holy Ghost. Aalborghallen, a colossal modern hall in the middle of town, is a magnificent center for concerts and exhibitions. In 1972 the new art museum by the Finnish architect Alvar Aalto with its open-air theater became the home of Danish paintings and sculptures since 1800 and of modern foreign art. East of Aalborg is Denmark's latest university campus, and north of Aalborg and Nørresundby you will find Lindholm Høje, a Viking burial place with 682 graves.

Among the excursions from Aalborg, the one to Himmerland is 100 miles. It takes you past the late 16th-century Lindenborg Castle to Lille Vildmose, a 34-square-mile marsh where the rare black stork can still be found. After 27 miles Hadsund is reached and Mariager Fjord crossed. Following the southern bank inland you arrive in rosefilled Mariager, Denmark's smallest market town, and Hobro at the head of the fjord. Near Hobro is Fyrkat, another 1,000-year-old Viking settlement resembling the one at Trelleborg. Today the settlement is reconstructed. North of Hobro, pay a visit to the delightful, hilly Rold Skov (Forest) and the Rebild Hills in its northern part. Every 4th of July thousands of Danes and Danish-Americans gather here to celebrate America's Independence Day. "Old Glory" and "Dannebrog" wave stoutly in the breeze, flanked by the flags of all the 50 states, and important Americans and Danes are invited to take part in speechmaking and other festivities. Since their purchase by Danish-Americans in 1911, these heather-clad hills have been a national park. In it stands the Lincoln Memorial Cabin, built of logs from the original 13 states. Also in the neighborhood are the Tingbaek Chalk Mines, with the original models of monuments by two well-known Danish sculptors.

1,400-year-old Viborg

Southeast of Hobro is Viborg, an important medieval town. In 1727 this town claimed to be 1,600 years old, tracing its history back to the crowning of Dan, the first king of Denmark. The road to Viborg leads you past the rambling 16th-century manor house of Tjele, known as the setting of many Danish literary works. It was probably more correct, however, when, in 1950, Viborg celebrated 1,400 years of existence as an assize town, 1,000 years as a trading center, 900 years as a bishopric, 800 as a market and 700 years of civic government. As if this were not enough, legends insist that Canute set out from Viborg to conquer England. On sale locally are reproductions, made as cuff links, of a silver coin minted on Canute's orders and inscribed, *Knud, Englands Konge:* Canute, King of England.

Dominating Viborg is its cathedral, at one time the largest granite church in the world. Of the original edifice, built in 1130, only the crypt remains. The cathedral was restored and reopened in 1876 after it had been damaged by fire several times. Its wall-paintings, executed between 1901 and 1913, were the work of a team of artists inspired and supervised by Joakim Skovgaard. Another church worth visiting is Søndre Sogns Kirke, an old monastery with a golden altarpiece (1520) and more than 200 paintings dating from the early 18th century.

About 5 miles south of Viborg you will find some of the loveliest scenery in Denmark. Hald Lake and the rustic heatherclad Dollerup Hills together form a district where it is possible to walk for hours on end and still discover new delights. This region is also known as the "fisherman's paradise".

From Viborg Highway 16 continues to Randers. However, you are recommended to use the longer tour via Rødkaersbro and Bjerringbro which will offer you a beautiful ride along the Gudenå, Denmark's longest river.

Randers and Djursland

Randers occupies a niche in Danish history because it was here in 1340 that Niels Ebbesen killed the German oppressor, Count Gert the Bald, commander of a German army which had occupied almost all of Jutland. Ebbesen's statute stands in front of the Town Hall. The 15th-century St. Morten's Church has been extensively restored. The carved wooden pulpit and screen, the exquisite organ, and the saintly figures have all been re-gilded. One of the most interesting buildings in the narrow streets is the House of the Holy Ghost on Erik Menveds Plads. In the Middle Ages friars from the nearby monastery nursed the sick here. Today it is occupied by the Tourist Association, and on its roof you may notice a cluster of storks' nests. It is considered only a matter of time until the last stork leaves Denmark forever. Today they remain only in very few Jutland spots.

East of Randers lies Djursland, a holiday area which draws people from all over Denmark. Here there are several fine old manor houses, churches, ancient burial places and ruins. Rosenholm Castle, the property of the Rosenkrantz family since its erection in 1560, is an imposing Danish Renaissance structure. The manor, its park and gardens are open to the public from mid-June to August, 10–5. Nearer Randers, Gammel Estrup, a grand 17th-century manor house, is now a museum full of rich period furnishings including an alchemist's cellar; and an agricultural museum. Admission from 10 to 5, May 1–Oct. 31.

About 8 miles southeast of Randers off Highway 10 is the fine baroque manor of Clausholm, set in a beautiful park with terraces and small cascades. From here, Anna Sophie Reventlow, daughter of the High Chancellor, was abducted by King Frederik IV, who married her morganatically and later made her Queen. To the east of the region is its main town, Grenå, ravaged several times in the 17th century by Swedish troops. Today Swedes still invade the town, but because of the ferry route to Varberg in Sweden. It is also possible to go by ferry to Hundested on Zealand, and there is a ferry to the isle of Anholt 27 miles out in the Kattegat.

A Hidden Gem

Anholt is 8½ square miles of unspoiled nature of a very special kind. You will find here Denmark's only desert, natural beauties, 16 miles of beaches, and 2 miles from the harbor the only town with 160 inhabitants. It is possible to walk for hours here watching both the idyllic Anholt Village, the desert consisting of open gravel plains filled with sand, and the viewpoint Sønderbjerg, at 157 feet the highest point on the island. The village has a memorial for Danes who fell against the English in the battle of 1811. To nature-lovers Anholt is a paradise with its many plants and birds. If you cross to the eastern point, Totten, you may be rewarded with the sight of seals.

It is possible to take your car to Anholt, but not necessary since you can drive only to the village. However, since ferry connections are bad, count on an overnight stay in the inn.

Mols and Ebeltoft

Below Djursland stretches the countryside of Mols. The drive to Fuglsø, Agri and Femmøller is magnificent, with rolling hills covered by heather and spruce, sandy roads winding past thatched cottages and peacefully grazing cattle, and dikes everywhere to keep the sea in place. The natives of this region have the reputation of being hillbillies, and an infinite number of stories are told of their simple ways and slow wit.

One place you must be sure to see is Ebeltoft, a miniature town which, like ÆErøskøbing, belongs to the past. Wandering up and down among the winding, cobbled streets lined with quaint old houses, you will imagine that you have walked out of the present into a fairytale. From Mols or Ebeltoft you are also able to see Århus, situated on a broad bay and surrounded by woods.

Århus, Old and New

Århus is Denmark's second largest town. Its history goes back more than 1,000 years, but it is also a modern city with a bustling seaport.

The copper roof and red brick walls of the 13th-century Århus Cathedral, Scandinavia's longest church, can be seen for many miles around. Inside is the largest, most highly carved and richly colored reredos in Denmark. The pulpit dates from 1588, and the early 18th-century organ is particularly fine. Just as remarkable is the Town Hall built between 1938 and 1942. A Danish showpiece, everything about it is impressive: its unusual architecture, its lavish use of glass, its mural-decorated lobby and its immense carpet depicting a stylized map of Århus. Most people either like it or detest it on sight. Behind the Town Hall, and designed not to conflict with it, is the new Concert House, inaugurated in 1982.

The best ties with the past are to be found in another church and the open-air museum. Our Lady's Church and Monastery in Vestergade is the oldest building in the city. The friars' court and a number of fine

Gothic arches can still be seen. In the chapter hall are medieval frescos. South of the town, at the Moesgård manor, is the Århus Museum, which houses the 2,000-year-old Grauballe man, discovered in a peat bog, plus rune stones and an ethnographic collection.

The open-air museum called "The Old Town" (Den gamle By) is a collection of town rather than country houses now brought together in the middle of Århus. Here there are 61 homes, each one furnished and equipped according to its period. With their streets and gardens, their shops and markets, the buildings provide an authentic picture of what life was in the good old days. The houses are populated every year during the Festival Days in the beginning of September, and you are able to taste bread as it was baked in previous times.

The University, started in 1933 and not yet completed, has a spacious 37-acre campus. From the architectural point of view as well as the academic, it has already won an outstanding place for itself in Scandinavia. A corner of the campus grounds houses the new art museum with Danish art since 1770.

Situated on a central spot, Århus is an ideal base for exploring middle Jutland. Some places have already been described but another tour should be made to the Danish lake district.

The Lake District

Silkeborg is a modern town lying on the banks of the river Gudenå west of Århus. It is situated in the middle of some of the loveliest scenery in Denmark. The town has two museums, one housing the 2,000-year-old Tollund man, and another with an art collection with special emphasis on Asger Jorn's pictures, because he was born here.

Surrounded by the river and lakes, it is quite natural to leave Silkeborg by water. The river winds through an area of hills covered with woods and heather. You can make the tour by rowboat, canoe, punt, or if you are less energetic by a paddle-steamer built in 1861. A *must* for anyone in this region is the ascent of Denmark's second highest hill, the 483-foot Sky Mountain (Himmelbjerget). The tower on top, another 80 feet, was inaugurated on Constitution Day, 1875, in commemoration of King Frederik VII.

Country roads run north and south of the lakes in the direction of Skanderborg. Off the southern banks near Rye are the few remaining stones of Øm Monastery. Founded in 1172 by the Cistercian Order, it was once one of the richest monasteries in that part of the world. After the Reformation Frederik II lived here for a while before having it demolished and the stones carried to Skanderborg to be used in the erection of a new castle. The museum there will show you the culture of that time and bones that had been treated surgically by the monks, and coins.

Samsø

Another day trip from Århus could be to the island of Samsø, but the car ferries leave from Hou, northeast of Horsens. Here, on 44 square miles, you can find a cross-section of Danish landscapes. The flora and fauna differs from that which can be found in the rest of Denmark. The Stavns Fjord is a bird sanctuary with many gulls and wading birds. Samsø also has an "English" country house in the shape of Brattingsborg Manor, which was built in 1870. Other sights include the Ballebjerg viewpoint and the village of Nordby, one of the most beautiful Danish villages. Don't forget to visit the village pond surrounded by the houses of the former day laborers, today now used as summer dwellings.

Around Vejle

South of Silkeborg you find Vejle, another town with a beautiful position among water and forest-clad hills. To the east a lovely tree-lined fjord stretches to the Kattegat. A motorway bridge is being built here. North of Vejle is the mysterious Grejs Valley, which you can also see from the train to Jelling. Jelling is the oldest known royal dwelling. King Gorm lived here more than 1,000 years ago with his Queen, and two burial mounds have long been known as the King Mound and the Queen Mound. However, the royal tombs are not under them, but, it seems, in the church itself, rather a strange feature, since they were not Christians. However, on the churchyard you will find "Denmark's Certificate of Baptism", the greater of the two runic stones outside the church. It depicts the oldest figure of Christ in Scandinavia, and the text explains that the stone was erected by King Harald over Gorm, his father, and Thyra, his mother, and that Harald christened the Danes. The event took place in about 960. The minor stone was erected by Gorm as a memorial over his queen.

West of Vejle is the little village of Billund, known because of Legoland, founded by the inventor of the famous Lego construction toy. This amusement park is entirely built of his plastic toy bricks and contains miniature copies of the Amalienborg Palace, an English provincial town, the Mount Rushmore presidents and a Wild West saloon. Plenty of time could be spent here, and when you are tired of playing, go and see the antique dolls collection, dating back to 1580. But the sensation here is "Titania's Palace", originally built by Sir Neville Wilkinson, who started its construction in 1907 as a gift for his daughter. Everything is a correct miniature copy of older models, and includes a bathroom basin, given by Queen Mary, who was herself a dolls house aficionado, which is inscribed "From the Queen of England to the Queen of Fairyland". In 1978 it was sold at Christie's in London to Legoland for £135,000 and was put on display there for the first time in 1979.

The last sight in the neighborhood is at Givskud, further along the Jelling road, where you will find a Lions' Park, where 40 lions live in open surroundings. There are other species to be found here, for instance baboons and a "savanna" with elephants and camels. For the children a mini-farm with animals.

PRACTICAL INFORMATION FOR JUTLAND

WHAT TO SEE. The natural sights of Jutland are many: the dunes and wide sand beaches of Fanø and the west coast from Blåvands Huk to Skagen; the beautiful fjords along the east coast, especially the Vejle Fjord in the center; the countryside around Silkeborg; Dollerup Hills, and Hald Lake near Viborg; the Mols Hills, across the Bay of Århus; the Skaw (Skagen) where the waters of the North Sea and those of the Kattegat merge; the Little Belt, the narrow stretch of water between Jutland and the island of Funen; the Limfjord; the Rebild Hills; Hjerl Hede, a privately-run museum of re-erected old houses in a typical Jutland moorland setting near Skive; Legoland at Billund near Vejle; the coast around Vejle.

Among towns and villages, Ebeltoft and Ribe rate first for unusualness and charm. But Tønder, Møgeltønder, Sønderho, Randers, and Mariager have strong claims of their own.

As for buildings, the more important are: Ribe Cathedral; the castle at Kolding; Jens Bang's house, the Monastery of the Holy Ghost, the castle (Aalborghus), and Museum of Art at Aalborg; the old houses at Randers; the Old Town open-air museum, the cathedral, town hall, and university at Århus; Dybbøl Mill near Sønderborg; the castles of Gammel Estrup and Rosenholm; the Clausholm and Tjele manors; Hvidsten Inn, and Spøttrup Castle.

Other Jutland attractions include the rune stones at Jelling, near Vejle; Rudbøl, where the Danish-German frontier runs down the center of the main street; the storks and the ruins of Øm Abbey.

HOW TO GET ABOUT. From Copenhagen a good way to northern Jutland is by comfortable and frequent car and passenger ferries from Kalundborg to Århus or to Juelsminde, Hundested to Grenå, and, shortest, Sjaellands Odde to Ebeltoft. Cars are carried on all these services. There are also direct flights from the capital to Århus, Billund, Aalborg, Karup, Sønderborg, Skrydstrup and Esbjerg, as well as "L" and "IC" train service (5–6 hours). Buses and trains connect all important points on the peninsula.

MOTORING. Advance bookings are advisable at busy times at least for these car ferry crossings: Sjaellands Odde-Ebeltoft, Grenå-Hundested, which are privately run, and for the state run Kalundborg-Århus. Consult an FDM office or the pamphlet "Car ferries" on timetables, prices and booking. Bookings for the state routes can be made at any major rail station 2 months ahead.

From the Continent (Kruså): Tønder-Møgeltønder-Rudbøl-Skaerbaek (Rømø Island)-Ribe-Esbjerg-ferry to Fanø Island-Hjerting-Varde-Nymindegab-Hvide-Sande-Søndervig-Ringkøbing-Stavning-Skjern-Herning-Silkeborg-Virklund-Himmelbjerget-Emborg (ruins of Øm Abbey)-Skanderborg-Århus-(Samsø Island). Distance, about 260 miles (416 km).

Little Belt Bridge (Route 1 from Copenhagen): Kolding-Agtrup-Skamlingsbanken- Hejlsminde- Christiansfeld- Haderselv- Hoptrup- Åbenrå- Varnaes-Sønderborg-(tour of Als via Augustenborg-Nordborg-Mommark-Kegnaes adds 56 miles)-Dybbøl-Broager-Gråsten-Kruså. Distance, about 100 miles (160 km).

Vendsyssel and Limfjord: Depart Aalborg-Hals-Aså-Saeby-Frederikshavn-The Skaw (Skagen)-Hirtshals-Hjørring-Lønstrup-Børglum Abbey-Løkken-Blokhus-Fjerritslev-(Slettestrand and Svinkløv)-Bygholm Vejle-Øsløs-Thisted-Vildsund-Mors Island-Spøttrup Castle-Hjerl Hede-Mønsted chalkmines-Viborg-Rødkaersbro-Bjerringbro-Randers-Hvidsten Inn-Mariager-Hadsund-Skørping-Rebild Hills-Gravlev-return Aalborg. Distance, about 370 miles (590 km).

 HOTELS AND RESTAURANTS. Inn vouchers are available from Horsens Tourist Office for the majority of Jutland's inns. They cost around 150 Dkr. per night, including breakfast.

AALBORG (Ålborg). Hotels: Among many good hostelries here are the *Hvide Hus,* 361 beds, all rooms with bath, sauna and pool, music in winter periods, and the *Phønix,* 280 beds, traditional, music in winter periods, good food; both first class superior.

Central, 113 beds, some rooms with bath, and *Park,* 97 beds; inexpensive *Missionhotellet Ansgar,* 86 beds. (BE).

Motel: *Scheelsminde,* 90 beds, park, moderate.

Restaurants: At Håbets Gård you find *Peberkvaernen,* a wine bar with plain food at reasonable prices. *Skråen* is a jazz and folk place.

In Jomfru Ane Gade: *Fyrtøjet,* pleasant restaurant, reasonable prices, and *Faklen,* with a carillon, expensive, *Jomfru Ane,* pleasant, expensive.

A good buy is *Regensen,* a steak house with open grill and reasonable prices. *Den Lille* and *Caféen* are both reasonable.

Outside those two locations are *Duus Vinkjaelder,* which serves wine from centuries-old wine cellars under Jens Bang's house, and *Stygge Krumpen.* Moderate to expensive.

Pizzeria Napoli, Borgergade, good food, reasonable. *Kniv og Gaffel,* Maren Turisgade, nice, good food. The same applies to *Restaurant Brix' Gård,* C. B. Obels Plads.

ÅBENRÅ. Hotels: *Grand,* 75 beds, some rooms with bath; sauna; *Hvide Hus,* 98 beds, garden, sauna, both first class. *Missionshotellet,* 30 beds, inexpensive (BE).

About halfway between town and German border on Hwy. 10 is the charming 60-bed *Søgårdhus,* near lake (angling), moderate.

Restaurant: *De 3 Makreller,* quaint cellar restaurant.

ANHOLT. Inn: *Anholt Kro,* inexpensive.

ÅRHUS. Hotels: *Marselis,* 130 beds, bar; *Atlantic* at the harbor, 186 beds, bar, music, dance. Both deluxe. *Ritz,* near station, 92 beds, 63 rooms with bath, clean and well-kept; *Tre Ege,* 64 beds, all rooms with bath; bar, garden (BE); both first class. *Missionshotellet Ansgar,* 233 beds, moderate to first class, garden. At station.

Inexpensive *Kragh,* 25 beds (BE).

Motel: *La Tour,* 90 beds, all rooms with bath, (BE), first class.

Restaurants: One of the finest restaurants in Europe: *De 4 Årstider* (The 4 Seasons) in Åboulevarden, opposite the Magasin department store. French cuisine, excellent food, not cheap.

Next comes *Gammel Åbyhøj* with the same line of food, situated in Åbyhøj Bakke Alle 1.

Also in town are *Tropicana*, Ryesgade, music and floor show; *Klostergården*, Børsen, excellent food. *Café Mahler*, Vestergade 39, is intimate with few tables, excellent food, not cheap; *Kellers Gård*, in center of town, Frederiksgade 84, excellent Danish food.

Near town are *Sjette Frederik's Kro*, Risskov, old inn situated on cliffs above the bay and among woods; *Frederikshøj Kro* at Marselisborg Wood, excellent cuisine at moderate prices. Here also is *Skovmøllen*, an old half-timbered watermill.

EBELTOFT. Hotels: The *Hvide Hus*, modern, 104 beds, rooms with bath and balcony overlooking the bay. Rooftop restaurant, sauna, pool, golf, first class superior. *Molskroen*, 46 beds, First class reasonable.
Restaurants: *Mellem Jyder*, next to old Town Hall; *Den skaeve Kro*.

ESBJERG. Hotels: *Britannia*, 132 beds, all rooms with bath; music at weekends only, first class reasonable. *Bangs*, 55 beds, 38 rooms with bath, breakfast only; *Palads*, 77 rooms, 27 with bath, cheerful, dancing Fris and Sats (BE). *Missionshotellet Ansgar*, 90 beds; *Bell-Inn*, 53 beds; both moderate.
Restaurants: *Bonbonnieren* has dinner-dancing, moderate. *Discothèque Blue Heaven*, Skolegade 20, rather exclusive, with floor show. For the younger set, the *Discothèque Lord Nelson* at Skolegade 31.

FANØ. Hotels: Small *Krogården*, 32 beds (BE), moderate. *Hotel Sønderho*, 16 beds, inexpensive. *Vesterhavet*, 6-bed apartments with bath and kitchen; sauna, pool, weekly rentals, first class. *Hotel Kongen af Danmark*, all rooms with shower, first class reasonable, breakfast only, 96 beds. The *Golfhotel*, 26 beds, no private bath, moderate. *Kellers Hotel*, 26 beds, some with private bath, moderate.

FREDERICIA. Hotels: *Landsoldaten*, 118 beds, bar, music, first class reasonable; *Peter Ågegården*, 16 beds, all rooms with shower, moderate (BE).

FREDERIKSHAVN. Hotels: *Jutlandia*, 196 beds, all rooms with bath, music and dance Fris and Sats only. First class. *Hoffmanns*, 127 beds, 37 rooms with bath, cozy and well-furnished, first class reasonable.
Motel: *Lisboa*, on Hwy. 10, 90 beds, good service, moderate (BE).

GRENÅ. Hotel: *Du Nord*, 180 beds, also apartments with 4 beds, bath and kitchen. first class reasonable. Garden, pool, music, dance.

HADERSLEV. Hotels: first-class *Motel Haderslev*, 66 beds, in park, music, dance Sats in winter only; moderate *Motel Syd*, 46 beds. (BE).

HANSTHOLM. Hotel: *Hanstholm*, unusual cliff setting; 162 beds, most rooms with bath; sauna, pool and golf, garden; first class superior.

HERNING. Hotels: *Eyde*, 163 beds, bar. *Hotel Birkegården*, 112 beds, garden and pool, first class reasonable (BE). *Østergaard's*, 160 beds, all rooms with bath, all first class. *Missionshotellet*, 77 beds, moderate.

HIMMELBJERGET. Hotels: *Landsbykroen*, at Nørre Vissing on Skanderborg-A 15 road. 14 beds in rural surroundings. Possibilities of angling and boat-hire. first class reasonable. *Gl. Rye Kro,* 32 beds in modern wing added to old inn. For anglers. Moderate. (BE).

HORSENS. Hotel: *Bygholm Parkhotel,* 131 beds, 70 rooms with bath, 18th-century castle in idyllic park, first class reasonable (BE). *Jørgensens,* in baroque mansion, 76 beds, 48 rooms with bath, modernized, first class. *Missionshotellet,* 85 beds, 10 rooms with bath, moderate.
Restaurant: *Steak-House Helene,* Spanish style, dance.

HOVBORG. *Hovborg Kro,* 54 beds, small recent hotel, old inn. First class lodgings and food in rural surroundings. Good for anglers.

HVIDSTEN. Restaurant: *Hvidsten Kro,* historic old country inn with picturesque interior, moderate prices; also has 12 beds (BE).

KARUP. Hotel: *Motel Centrum,* 8 beds. Inexpensive (BE). For anglers.

KOLDING. Hotels: *Saxildhus,* 138 beds, some rooms with bath and balconies, near castle, an outstanding hostelry, first class reasonable; bar; music. *Hotel Kolding,* 20 rooms with private bath. Also first class reasonable. 70 beds, bistro, discothèque.
Motel: *Tre Roser,* 61 beds, all rooms with bath. Pool, sauna, garden, park (BE), first class reasonable. Also 4-bed apartments with kitchenette (weekly rentals).
Restaurant: *Kryb-i-Ly,* at Taulov on Kolding-Middelfart highway overlooking Kolding Fjord. Moderate to expensive. Also 50 beds (first class reasonable).

LAESØ. *Carlsen's Hotel,* Vesterø Havn, at ferry berth, 20 beds, inexpensive rooms. Restaurant.
Restaurant: *Bakken* at Byrum.

NYMINDEGAB. Hotel: *Nymindegab Kro,* 63 beds, 12 rooms with bath, overlooking Ringkøbing Fjord, excellent food among magnificent scenery, moderate; sauna, garden. Fishing (BE). Also 5-bed apartments with kitchen (weekly rentals.)

ØSLØS. *Bygholm Holiday Center* in sanctuary between Thisted and Fjerritslev on the Limfjorden. 20 hotel beds plus motel apartments of 4 or 6 beds and shower. Pool and sauna, riding, fishing, own beach. Cafeteria. Camping.

RANDERS. Hotels: *Randers,* 140 beds, all rooms with bath, attractive décor, personalized service, delicious food, one of Denmark's best, first class reasonable. Also *Kongens Ege,* 170 beds, all rooms with bath, first class, night-club.
Restaurants: *Nummer 1,* old-style pub with garden, music. *Øster Tørslev,* 9 miles northeast, modern motel. Inexpensive (BE). All rooms with bath.

RIBE. Hotels: *Dagmar,* 78 beds, 20 rooms with bath, atmospheric 16th-cent. building, fine antiques (BE), moderate.
Weis' Stue, 9 beds, no room with private bath, in a protected 16th century house; interior has the oldest cupboard in Denmark and Dutch tiles (BE). (This inn has been copied by an enthusiastic hotel owner in Maine.)
Inexpensive, as are *Klubben,* (BE). *Sønderjylland,* with 45 and 10 beds respectively.

RINGKØBING. Hotels: *Fjordgården,* 111 beds, all rooms with bath, evening music on summer evenings only, bar, garden, sauna, first class reasonable. *Søndervig Vesterhavsbad,* 44 beds, all rooms with bath; also apartments.

ROLD SKOV. Hotel: *Rold Storkro,* 92 beds, 53 rooms with bath, first class, sauna and pool, garden, angling, hunting (BE).

SAEBY. Hotel: *Motel Oda,* 10 beds (BE). Inexpensive. Open April–Sept. 15. *Pension Åhøj,* 17 beds, moderate.

Inn: *Voerså Kro,* 10 miles south, picturesque surroundings; plain cozy tap room. 12 rooms, music, occasional dancing, folk dancing in summer in garden, moderate (BE), room inexpensive.

SAMSØ. Hotel: *Ballen Hotel,* 25 beds, moderate (BE), garden.

SILKEBORG. Hotels: *Impala,* 79 beds, 41 rooms with bath, fine view, color TV, indoor pool, sauna, garden, music Sats only (BE). *Dania,* 80 beds, 35 rooms with bath, bar, music. Both first class reasonable.

Restaurants: *Dania* has restaurant, bar, and bodega; *La Strada,* on market square, with dancing Sats only.

SKAGEN. Hotels: *Skagen,* 82 beds, all rooms with bath, pool, garden; first class superior; *Brøndums,* 67 beds, 14 rooms with bath; attractive building with garden and music, near beach, Danish "cold table" and fish specialties in restaurant; both first class reasonable.

Gammel Skagen: *Klithotellerne,* 47 apartments with bath and kitchen, moderate.

Restaurants: *Fiskerestauranten,* opposite the fishermen's houses, fish market and boat moorings; all kinds of fish served in traditional atmosphere. *De to Have* (The Two Seas), on the spit of Skaw. These are both summer restaurants.

SKANDERBORG. Hotel: *Skanderborghus,* 82 beds, nearly all rooms with bath, modern, magnificent lakeside location, first class reasonable, but out of town, with sauna and garden (BE).

SØNDERBORG. All hotels are excellent. *Arnkilhus, City, Garni,* and *Park Hotel Lido,* all reasonable, about 20–30 beds. Also moderate to inexpensive are *Alssund, Ansgar* (mission hotel), *Dybbøl Banke* and *Teaterhotellet,* with 54, 90, 30 and 46 beds; all have some rooms with bath.

THISTED. Hotel: *Aalborg,* 48 beds, some rooms with bath. Near swimming-pool, moderate.

TØNDER. Hotels: *Tønderhus,* 58 beds, 31 rooms with bath; *Romantic Hotel,* 70 beds, some rooms with bath, (BE); *Hostrup's,* 39 beds. All moderate.

VEJLE. Hotels: *Australia,* 150 beds, all rooms with bath, bar, first class superior. *Grand,* 63 rooms with bath, bar, first class. *Grejsdalens Hotel,* small with limited facilities but beautifully situated.

Munkebjerg, deluxe, is magnificently located on a fjord, 4 miles east. Pool, sauna, music, garden, bar.

Motel: *Hedegården,* first class, 2 miles from center, 72 beds, all rooms with bath, modern.

160　　　　　　　　　**DENMARK**

Restaurants: *Grand Bistro, Moulin Rouge, Granddisco* and *Flamingo* have dancing.

VIBORG. Hotel: *Missionshotellet,* 73 beds, many rooms with bath, garden, modernized, moderate.

Motels: *Søndersø,* 80 beds, garni, in park, first class reasonable, new. *Kongenshus Hotel,* 19 beds, inexpensive.

Restaurant: *Salonen,* with concerts and dancing. Closed Mon.

Between Viborg and Århus, *Kongensbro Kro* serves simple, typically Danish dishes and has attractive rooms for overnight guests; good fishing and the Gjern automobile museum nearby. Also 26 beds.

 SPORTS. Water sports are understandably popular here. There are over 200 miles of continuous sand beach on the west coast; good bathing can also be had on the eastern side. You can drive on the beach from Løkken to Blokhus as well as the 11-mile stretch of Fanø's coastline. The best known resorts include Skagen, Hirtshals, Løkken, Blokhus, Ålbek, Saeby, Aså, and Hals; Århus and Grenå also have fine beaches.

There's excellent **sailing** on the waters of the East Jutland fjords and the Limfjord, and **fishing** for salmon trout in the West Jutland streams. The river Guden, Denmark's longest, offers wonderful possibilities for a week's **canoeing** or **kayaking** tour from Tørring to Randers.

Aalborg, Århus, Brønderslev, Ebeltoft, Esbjerg, Fanø, Vesterhavsbad, Frederikshavn, Herning, Hobro, Holstebro, Horsens, Kolding, Randers, Silkeborg, Skagen, Skive, Skjern, Vejle and Viborg all have **golf** courses.

 USEFUL ADDRESSES. Tourist information: There are offices in every sizeable town and the larger also book accommodation. **Youth hostelers** should book ahead. **Camp sites** are signposted by the international wigwam signal.

ISLE OF BORNHOLM

The Baltic Hideaway

Far from the rest of Denmark, in the Baltic between Sweden and Poland, is an island 225 miles square. Since 1658, when Jens Kofoed's islanders threw out Swedish troops, the Bornholmers' Danish nationality and feelings have never been doubted. The 93 miles of coastline change from cliffs and rocks to skerries and dunes of the world's finest sand. The flora and fauna is special, too, and here you'll find Almindingen, the third largest forest in Denmark. Bornholm is the only place in Denmark where towns were built on sloping rocks and the independent farmers never settled in villages. There are many special trades connected with a "Bornholmer", hence the word designates an islander, a grandfather clock—or a smoked herring. Today fortified round churches and ruins still bear witness to times not so idyllic.

Exploring Bornholm

You may wonder how so many natural sights could have been put together as on Bornholm. It seems as if the "splendid isolation" also has concentrated and isolated a lot of nature that was not allowed to spread to the rest of Denmark. So even if you have seen other parts of Denmark you will be surprised here.

Rønne

The main city is Rønne, port for ships to Copenhagen, Sweden and Germany (although the latter is rather erratic). When arriving by ship you will be fascinated by the half-timbered tower which appears before you disembark, but the church is young, from 1915–18, and the real half timber is to be found in the streets behind the church. The majority of those houses were built around 1800, though some go back as far as late 17th century. Notice that nearly all houses have but one story, a fact that has given the city a large extension. The most beautiful of the houses is Erichsen's Farm in Laksegade where Holger Drachmann, the poet, and Dr. Zahrtmann, the Bornholm painter, lived.

An interesting museum, the Defense Museum, has been opened at Kastellet in Rønne. On the last Thursday in the month, from April to December, the Rønne Day gives rise to much activity and, among other amenities, free horse-carriage rides are given in the old town.

Jons Kapel and Hammershus

Let us start our island excursions with a visit to the northwest corner. The bicycle is a very popular means of transportation, although many people also travel by car. We pass through Hasle, well suited for discovery walks, and continue to Jons Kapel on the coast. Before reaching it you may make detours to the coast to see tiny Helligpeder and Teglkås.

According to legend, Brother Jon, the monk, lived in a cave on the steep cliff. He gave his sermons from the rock, which since then has borne the name Jon's Chapel (Jons Kapel). He must have had strong legs and lungs, since he lived on a rock 130 feet high and preached from the 72-foot Pulpit rock.

Jons Kapel is halfway between Hasle and the marvellous ruins of the Hammershus Castle. The castle was built about 1255 as a fortress on a strategic spot. The stronghold was in use until 1743, but before that time its importance had decreased. It was occupied by Swedish troops in 1648, but Jens Kofoed, the Bornholm hero, killed its governor and the castle was given back to Denmark. The remaining ruins were protected in 1822, the biggest in North Europe.

At Borrelyng young children would enjoy a visit to the small zoo where there are animals roaming free in a natural environment.

Fashionable Allinge and Sandvig

The dominating Hammerknude with a good view from the lighthouse stands as the northern protection of Bornholm against the sea and enemy ships of earlier days. It also protects the twin towns of Sandvig and Allinge, together with the fashionable district of Bornholm. Here you find most of the hotels, but also several low half-timbered houses, especially in Allinge. In spite of the modern signs of civilization one of the characteristic Bornholm smokehouse chimneys still dominates the town. Also from these towns you can walk along the coast. Tejn and Sandkås further down the north coast are other popular beach resorts.

A Round Church

But, for a change, go inland to Olsker. Its church will serve as your introduction to the four round churches of Bornholm. They were all erected about 1150, and with their shape and thick walls they served a double purpose as both physical and spiritual protection of the poor souls who were often attacked by pirates or enemy armies. The church was defended from the third story. The church at Olsker is the smallest but tallest of the round churches.

Rø and Its Neighborhood

Our next stop is at Rø between Helligdomsklipperne and Rø Plantation. If you choose the Helligdomsklipperne on the coast you will meet a famous rock formation towering up to 72 feet above sea level and filled with crevices, caves and rock columns. It is one of the great natural sights of Bornholm, and in summer it is also possible to see it from the sea. You may then realize why it got its name, which may be translated as the Sanctuary or Sacred Thing.

Rø Plantation is a natural sight of quite another kind. Here as you walk in heather, among trees or on stones, you may meet the black woodpecker or deer. Scenery that you won't forget soon surrounds the artificial lake.

Østerlars and Gudhjem

From Rø we go inland once more, now heading for the greatest of the round churches at Østerlars. This church seems to be the most imposing of all because of the strong buttresses. The structure is the same as we saw at Olsker, only this one is better adorned, and better suited for defense purposes. The nave diameter is about 18 yards.

You will probably understand why generations of painters have visited Gudhjem, whether you see it from the top of the Bokul cliff or from the narrow roads looping down the terraces to the charming little village. The small, well-kept houses have to a great extent been carved out of the rock, and two little harbors and the smokehouses give evidence of the main occupation, at least outside the tourist season.

A Riviera Tour and a Prize Town

Ever been to the Riviera? If so, compare the Bornholm counterpart along the coast road from Gudhjem to Saltune on the Svaneke road. Shortly after leaving the coast a path leads from the Hotel Randkløveskår down to the coast. A little inland you find the Randkløveskår, a narrow gorge between tall rock formations, later dividing into two clefts. Now refreshed we continue along the main road to Svaneke.

In 1975 the Council of Europe awarded a gold medal for the "consistent preservation of the historical character of the typical little port" to the easternmost Danish provincial town, Svaneke. So here you will meet mostly 18th- or 19th-century houses. The harbor was cut into the rock, and steep streets and houses on high plinths show the difficulties of constructing this original fishing-hamlet in the Middle Ages. Two different mills are its landmarks. But it seems that conditions were not so harsh as one might believe, because you find here vines, figs and mulberries.

Inland, between Svaneke and Nexø, you find a peculiar landscape known as the Paradisbakkerne (Paradise Hills). A beautiful view will meet you among the valleys full of rocks, woodland and forest lakes. The best "entrance" to this area is from Klinteby west of Nexø. Map and route descriptions for this area have been worked out to secure the best enjoyment from your visit, where you can only move on foot. Marked tours take 1, 2 or 3 hours respectively.

Sand, Dunes and Beaches

The Bornholm coast, from Nexø to Boderne on the south coast, is the area almost entirely devoted to bathing and water sports, although you will also find beaches on other parts of the coast. Some people even bathe from the rocks. The water is shallow and thus also suited for the children. At Dueodde you find dunes 45 feet high and miles upon miles of beach with the most fine-grained sand in the world. Here is also the 145 feet tall lighthouse with a marvelous view from its top.

Central Bornholm

Let us conclude our visit to the Bornholm landscapes with a glance at the central part. It is dominated by one town, Åkirkeby, and the third largest Danish forest, the Almindingen. Åkirkeby is the oldest town on the island with a municipal charter from 1346 and in the Middle Ages a spiritual center as well. You can see that when visiting the church built in the second half of the 13th century. Both walls and tower are well suited for defense purposes, but the church is not round. The church furniture here is worth studying. The altarpiece and pulpit are Dutch Renaissance from about 1600, and the font belongs to the most outstanding pieces of Scandinavian Romanesque fonts, being of the same age as the church. Eleven arcadian panels depict scenes from the life of Christ, and they are explained with more than 500 runic letters also cut into the sandstone. More runes are to be found on stones in the porch.

The Almindingen is one of the most varied Danish forests, with trees, rocks, lakes and ponds. You find here the Rytterknaegten, Bornholm's highest "mountain" (516 feet!) with the Kongeminde tower, even now, it seems, too low to come above the treetops of this vast area. Near the Rytterknaegten you can take a walk in the Echo Valley (Ekkodalen) with walls 72 feet over you.

The forest is only 10 miles from our starting point, Rønne. On your way back you may make detours to the round churches at Nylars (between Åkirkeby and Rønne) and Nyker northeast of Rønne. The one at Nylars is the best preserved and most decorated of the four Bornholm round churches.

Christiansø

Before leaving Bornholm, you should make a point of crossing to the idyllic island of Christiansø (Christian's Island), the largest of the group of islets that includes Frederiksø, Graesholm, and other smaller rock formations. Originally a bastion, only the towers "Storetårn" and "Lilletårn" remain of the fort, which was started in 1684 and dismantled in 1855. The barracks, street and the gardens, for which the earth was transported in boats, have a distinctive atmosphere of their own. Not only was the foundation of the bastion an architectural achievement, but the flora is also something special, with vines and Southern European plants that are watered only by rain water from the basins. There is no ground water on the island.

Although no longer used as a fortification, all the islets come under the Ministry of Defense, and the 118 inhabitants pay no local taxes. Graesholm is an inaccessible bird sanctuary. It is the only place in Denmark where the razorbill and guillemot breed.

PRACTICAL INFORMATION FOR BORNHOLM

WHEN TO COME. Like every other holiday area in Denmark, Bornholm is crowded from late June till mid-August. Thus, early June is a good month for your trip, and late August is even better. In August and September there are not only more hours of sunshine here than elsewhere, but both the sea and the air are warmer. Music-lovers should come during the music festival from mid-July to mid-August, where Danish and foreign musicians play in the churches throughout the island.

HOW TO GET ABOUT. Bornholm can easily be reached by the large boats that leave Copenhagen for Rønne every night at 11.30 P.M., arriving early the following morning. During the summer there are sailings during the day. Alternatively, SAS will fly you from Copenhagen to Rønne in less than an hour, or, by car, you can cross the Sound to Sweden and take a ferry from Ystad. In summer there are also ferry connections from Germany—Travemünde and Sassnitz (GDR), but check before attempting to use this service, since it varies considerably.

In summer there are bus services on all the main roads. The island of Christiansø may be reached from Allinge, Gudhjem or Svaneke by motorboat or steamer (1½ hours).

MOTORING. In spite of the small area, a 3-day itinerary will give you a lot of sights and impressions. If you are a good biker, you may follow the same route; 150 miles (230 km).

First day. Rønne-Blykobbe Wood-Hasle-Klemensker Rutsker-Baelå Helligpeder-Teglkås-return to Helligpeder and mainroad Hasle-Allinge. Detour off mainroad to Jons Kapel (path). Vang-Finnedalen-Hammershus-Hammerhavnen-(hilly detour to Hammerens Fyr)-Sandvig and Allinge-Olsker-Tejn-along coast road to Rø-Rø Plantation-Rø-(detour to Rutsker Højlyng with Rokkestenen, Rocking Stone). Back to coast road-Hellingdommen (off road, path)-Gudhjem.

Second day. Gudhjem-Østerlars Church-to coast road and east to Randkløve Skår (off road)-(detour to Ypnasted)-Bølshavn-Østermarie Church-Bølshavn-Listed-Svaneke-Ibsker-Årsdale-Nexø-Paradisbakkerne (Paradise Hills)-Bodilsker-Balka Strand-Snogebaek-Dueodde, Poulsker and Pedersker beaches.

Third day. Dueodde-coast road to Pedersker-Åkirkeby-Almindingen Woods (with Ekkodalen (Echo Valley) and Rytterkaegten)-Vestermarie-Nylars-Arnager-Rønne. Eventually detour to Nyker round church.

WHAT TO SEE. Bornholm's Museum and the Defense Museum in Rønne; the old sections of Rønne, Gudhjem, Svaneke, and Nexø; ruins of Hammershus Castle; round churches of Østerlars, Olsker, Nyker, and Nylars; characteristic herring-smokery at Arnager, Gudhjem, Snogebaek, with the recent glassworks at the last two. The rock formations of Jons Kapel on the west coast,

Helligdommen near Rø, and on the east coast between Gudhjem and Svaneke; the sand dunes and enormous beach at Dueodde; Almindingen forest and the view from Rytterknaegten; the woods and wild rock and heather country of Paradise Hills (Paradisbakkerne) near Nexsø; the adjoining island of Christiansø; the zoo at Borrelyng.

 HOTELS AND RESTAURANTS. Bornholm has long been a favorite summer holiday resort of Danes and tourists alike. Recent hotel development has provided plenty of modern accommodation, primarily in Rønne and the coastal resorts. And, of course—as elsewhere in Denmark—you can eat well practically anywhere.

ÅKIRKEBY. Hotel: *Kanns,* 42 beds, all with bath, garden, first class reasonable (BE).

ALLINGE. Hotels: *Abildgård,* at Sandkås, 250 beds, all rooms with shower, tennis, garden, sauna, pool, solarium, half-board terms, first class small apartments with fridge, no cooking; *AEblehaven,* 280 beds in 70 apartments with kitchen; pool, sauna, first class (weekly rentals). See also under Sandvig.
Restaurant: *Grotten,* at Sandkås, dance restaurant, with an underground discothèque set in the rocks.

GUDHJEM. Hotels: *Hotel Helligdommen,* 41 beds, most rooms with bath. First class. *Thern's,* 95 beds, garden; moderate (BE). *Ellebaek,* 46 beds, garden, moderate, pension only.
Restaurant: *Bokulhus,* on top of Bokul rock; fish specialties.

HASLE. Hotel: *Herold,* 40 beds, 14 rooms with bath, harbor view. First class.

NEXØ (Neksø). *Bornholm,* 27 beds, garden, heated pool, on Dueodde beach. Also 4–5-bed apartments with kitchen (weekly rentals). *Balka Strand,* 70 beds, music, dance, garden, pool, and *Balka Søbad,* 320 beds, tennis, garden, sauna, pool; all first class and pension only. *Linds Pension,* 32 beds, limited facilities, inexpensive.
Restaurant: *De tre Søstre* (The Three Sisters) is an excellent place with fish specialties (from split cod to lobster) and entertainment in summer; in winter, a bodega only.

RØNNE. Hotels: *Griffen,* large, new, 284 beds, all rooms with shower, pool, sauna, tennis, deluxe; restaurant with local dishes. Near airport. *Fredensborg,* 128 beds, all rooms with bath and balcony, facing the sea, sauna, beach; in addition there are 12 apartments.
Badehotel, Ryttergården, 224 beds, near beach, with pool and riding, all rooms with bath; plus 35 4–6 bed apartments for weekly rental. First class superior.
Missionshotellet, 210 beds, 110 rooms with bath, moderate, sauna, pool, in town center but charming.
Restaurants: *Rådhuskroen,* in town center, old half-timbered house, excellent smørrebrød, also a few rooms, moderately priced. *De fem Ståuerna,* exclusive fish and steak restaurant in Hotel Fredensborg.

SANDVIG. Summer hotels: *Strandhotellet,* 80 beds, 20 rooms with shower, garden, on the beach, refurnished with modern décor, first class reasonable *pension. Hammersø,* 90 beds, 49 rooms with bath, pension, garden, pool, near beach, first class. *Strandslot,* 110 beds, nearly all rooms with shower, garden, pension, moderate.

Restaurant: *Burgundia,* fish restaurant.

SVANEKE. Hotels: *Siemsens Gård,* 90 beds, 42 rooms with shower, garden, sauna, open May-Nov. *Østersøen,* 35 beds, 5 rooms with shower, garden, both moderate. *Pension Nansens Gård,* 14 beds, limited facilities, inexpensive. Open mid-June to mid-Sept.

Restaurant: *Louisekroen,* Bølshavn, well-prepared food served in stylish atmosphere.

SPORTS. Excellent swimming is possible from flat rocks, the sandy beach that stretches for miles on the south coast, and sizeable sandy beaches to the west. Sea bathing until late September. Gudhjem, Rønne and Sandvig have good swimming pools. *Walking* and *cycling* tours through the countryside are other favorite activities. *Sailing* and *fishing* for salmon in the waters offshore attract the deepsea sportsman, and there's free trout fishing south of Rønne off "Stampen".

SUMMER CHALETS. Bornholm offers quite a number of small holiday homes for renting, many of them very well built and well equipped. The tourist offices in Åkirkeby, Allinge, Nexø, Rønne and Svaneke handle bookings.

SPECIAL ACTIVITIES. Throughout the island you will find a lot of special activities that are run in small factories or are family concerns. They will all be glad to let you get acquainted with their work, so what is listed below is but a selection of where you are welcome. There are two glassworks, one at Snogebaek and the other at Gudhjem.

Ceramics. Rønne: Michael Andersen, L.Hjorth, Johgus and Søholm factories. Ceramic Holidays include visits to potters and instruction; stay at the Hotel Ellebaek in Gudhjem—approximately 2,500 Dkr for a week, with all meals.

Painting Lessons. These can also be had from a local painter at about 85 Dkr per lesson.

Weaving holidays. This is another interesting arrangement, with a prepacked weaving holiday including instruction and all meals and excursions. Materials, which are not expensive, are paid for separately, and accommodations can be booked separately.

Windsurfing holidays. These can be had with expert guidance, including stay and all meals. They cost approximately 3,000 Dkr per week.

All active holidays are arranged by Bornholms Kongresbureau, Snellemark 13, DK-300 Rønne. Tel. (03) 95 12 11.

Bornholm also has a **golf** course at Åkirkeby.

SPECIALTY SHOPS. *Rønne:* Above ceramics factories; Espersen harbor (smoked fish). *Allinge:* Gaveboden (ceramics, glass, trinkets). *Gudhjem:* Keramikstâuan (ceramics and stoneware). *Nexø:* Keramikstâuan. *Snogebaek:* Keramikstâuan; Alkemisterne (local folk art). *Svaneke:* Waldorff (stoneware); I Stalden (ceramics, textiles); Staugård (stoneware, paintings, ceramics).

 USEFUL ADDRESSES. Tourist information: *Allinge,* Hammershusvej 2. *Rønne,* Havnen—and for active holidays and all types of bookings: the above Bornholms Kongresbureau, Snellemark 13, Rønne. Also tourist offices at Gudhjem, Hasle, Nexø, Svaneke, Tejn and Åkirkeby.

FINLAND

PRELUDE TO FINLAND

Suomi, Sauna and Sibelius

Suomi, as the Finns call their native land, is the forgotten country of Europe. Or if not forgotten, misunderstood, for confusion still shrouds many people's ideas of whether she is on this side of the so-called Iron Curtain or that. The answer, most emphatically, is "on this". Finland may have had to wait a long time for her precious independence (until 1917, in fact), but she has learned perhaps better than anyone the art of being friends with all, while still maintaining her fiercely won democratic freedoms. Neutrality is the key to her international success and has enabled her to play a very active part, not least in hosting some of the most important conferences of international concern in modern times.

If you dislike water or trees, it would be absurd to go there, for the permutations on these two themes are pretty well limitless in Finland. Nine percent of the country is covered by a total of 60,000 lakes—a proportion that in some areas rises to 50%. Nearly three-quarters of the rest is clothed in forests. There are low, forested ridges and hills in parts of the south rising to bare-topped fells as you progress north. And scattered about these pleasingly untamed landscapes are modern towns and communities where good architecture and high living standards are the norm.

But, of course, the landscapes are not really so totally untamed. Most of them support flourishing farms and a massive wood and paper industry, which means that the land must be expertly managed to produce the most of what it is best suited for. So the wilderness is still being pushed back, and here on the doorstep of the Arctic a way of life has been evolved which is cosmopolitan and supremely civilized. Small wonder then that no glib generalization can provide the key to unlock this nation's innermost secrets. Not inappropriately, however, it is a Finnish word which comes closest to expressing the essence of the Finnish character. This word, *sisu,* has no equivalent in English. One could say it meant courage or grit, perseverance or determined will, and still not have caught the special savor of what has become Finland's motto in her time of troubles. Rather, it connotes a quality of youth, a readiness to face hardship when necessary, and a taste for testing mental and physical stamina against their own variable elements. It would be wrong, though, to imagine the Finns merely as "tough." Their interest in the arts—their own and the rest of the world's—has produced distinguished contributions especially to literature, music, sculpture, and design, and resulted in a wide-ranging series of festivals for visitors to enjoy.

Linguistically the Finns are related to the Estonians and Hungarians, and these three groups may have migrated westward from some common region in central Russia during a past too dim to be remembered. About the beginning of the Christian era, at any rate, the Finns migrated into the area that is now called Finland, and they are content in the knowledge that they have inhabited the northeastern shores of the Baltic for longer than history records. In appearance, in politics, and in thinking they are part of Scandinavia; in sympathies, in commerce, and in outlook they are part of the West, with whom their cultural and trade ties are very many. Since World War II, they have built up friendly relations with their important Soviet neighbor with whom they have major trading agreements and pacts of (hopefully) mutual non-interference. Certainly, as far as the outside world is concerned, the Finns, whether they speak Finnish or Swedish are Finns wherever their country's interests are concerned.

What are the main charms of Finland? To answer this question with a word is impossible, perhaps because the freshness of the country is as much the work of man as of Nature, and as varied. The historian will speak of the old castles and forts dating back to the days when Finland was in every sense an outpost and when the power of the Hanseatic League was still unbroken. The yachtsmen will tell you of the archipelago along the western and southern coasts where there are sheltered waters and unrivaled sailing. Mention salmon and the fisherman's eyes will light. Reflect for a moment on the size of Finland—larger than the British Isles with just over 4,800,000 people—and you will understand what attracts the hiker and camper waiting to claim one of those 60,000 lakes as his own. The architect will point with pride to a new functionalism blended with grace and dignity, to well-planned cities and towns where the great outdoors still lives. The interior designer will show you the glass, ceramics and textiles that have won the Finns prizes at many an international exhibition. Someone may remind you of the *sauna* or steam bath, the peculiarly Finnish institution which combines good health with good fellowship so aptly that it has spread to most other parts of the world. Someone else might ask you if you knew that the late Paavo Nurmi or, more recently, Lasse Viren are only two of many great athletes and distance runners. The social worker will ask you if you have seen the new hospitals, the schools, the experiments in community welfare and well being.

And from the Finns themselves you can learn the art of enjoying those spacious landscapes bounded by their huge horizons, for no one knows better how to appreciate all they have to offer. Though some of them may dispute it, basically they remain children of Nature who like nothing better than to leave their smart towns and cities and head for the countryside—to walk, fish, swim, sail, pick mushrooms or wild berries in the abundant forests, or simply sit on a granite boulder by some lake shore and contemplate.

It is easy to follow suit. Most hotels, campsites, holiday villages are ideally placed for just these activities. And from any of them you can discover for yourself that view or that painting, that friendly gesture or that bit of hospitality which will always mean Finland for you.

PRACTICAL INFORMATION FOR FINLAND

13·06
5·34
24·00
£2·70

WHAT IT WILL COST. The tables of hotel and restaurant prices, based on 1983 figures, will act as a guide, but it is estimated that prices will increase by about 10% in 1984. Generally speaking, hotel and restaurant prices in Helsinki are about 10% higher than in the provinces.

The standard of living in Finland is high, and so are costs, and taxation, though recently inflation has been kept down. The average weekly wage is about 1,120 Fmk; and the monthly rental for an unfurnished 2-bedroom flat in a good area of Helsinki would be 1,240–1,760 Fmk.

Double Room, Per Person including service and Continental breakfast

	1st class (E)	Moderate (M)	Inexpensive (I)
Helsinki	from 140–250	90–140	50–90
Resort/Provincial town	from 120–200	75–120	40–70

The cost of a single room varies from a little more to a third or even half as much again, especially in the more expensive hotels.

Budget accommodations: An extra bed is available in most hotel rooms for a reasonable extra charge. Self-catering in summer cottages is well organized from 400–2,500 Fmk a week, average about 700–1,200 Fmk. Youth hostels have no age restrictions: from 18–40 Fmk per person per night. Farmhouse holidays are a good buy at 80–140 Fmk a day full board (50–75% reduction for children), including sauna twice a week.

Restaurant Prices.

	1st class (E)	Moderate (M)	Inexpensive (I)
Lunch	from 45	25–35	15–25
Dinner	from 50	30–50	20–30

These are table d'hôte *prices; for* à la carte, *count on two or three times more.*

Some further prices: bottle of good, moderate wine, 28 Fmk (from liquor store); large measure of whiskey, 14.70; haircut (man's), 32; woman's shampoo and set, 60; cinema 20–35; theater, 20–50 (20–40 in provinces); cigarettes (pack of 20), 8.20; sauna (public) per person, 13, privately booked 20–50 per 1 1/2 hours (in hotel).

Bread, 3–5 Fmk a loaf; 1 kilo butter, 31; 1 kilo best beefsteak 50.

A Typical Day for One Person.

Room, breakfast, moderate hotel incl. tax and service	100 Fmk.
Lunch, moderate, with coffee	30
Dinner, moderate, with coffee	40
Public transport (tourist ticket)	22
Taxi (say 3 km)	21
Theater ticket (middle range)	40
Pack of cigarettes	7
1 coffee, popular café	2
1 beer, popular café	6
Miscellaneous	20
	288 Fmk.

TIPPING. Finnish *hotels* add a service charge of 15% to the bill and additional tipping is not taken for granted. *Restaurants* add 14% to the check (15% at weekends and holidays); you can leave the odd change. Give 2–3 Fmk to *doormen* and *checkroom attendants.* It is not necessary to tip *taxi* drivers. *Porters* at railway stations are difficult to find; if you do, the fixed charge is 2 Fmk per bag; 1–2 Fmk for hotel bellhops. *Hairdressers, barbers, theater ushers* do not expect a tip; nor do *guides* round historical sites. A general guideline is that you can tip for good service, but it is not expected.

 WHEN TO COME. The summer season lasts from mid-May to mid-September, reaching its peak in July, but note that some facilities, such as lake traffic, only run from June through August. The skiing season begins in January in the southern parts of the country and lasts until the end of April in the north. When the Finns have a holiday they really go to town, and everything except restaurants closes down: New Year celebrations last through *January* 1. Kalevala Day on 28 *February* is followed by perhaps the greatest holiday of them all: May Day Eve (*vapunaatto* in Finnish) on 30 *April,* a nation-wide jollification that combines Labor Day and student festivities with an emphatic welcome to the return of spring; many people never see their beds this night. *May Day (vappu)* itself is a quieter, family affair, though students and workers have their separate processions. Midsummer Eve (*juhannusaatto*) is another nation-wide celebration held on the weekend closest to *June* 24, when everyone who can leaves for the country for festivities round immense bonfires.

June also marks the beginning of the summer series of Finland Festivals, with the Kuopio Dance and Music Festival, Ilmajoki Music Festival and the Naantali Music Festival. Towards the end of the month and into early *July,* the Jyväskylä Arts Festival offers a varied program of cultural events with a different theme each year. The Savonlinna Opera Festival, with many performances set in the medieval castle, takes up much of July. Coinciding with it is the shorter Pori Jazz Festival followed by the Kaustinen Folk Music Festival and Kuhmo Chamber Music Festival in the second half of the month. In *August,* the Lahti International Organ Festival is followed by the Turku Music Festival, which is devoted to music in all its forms, and the Tampere Theater Summer with a wide variety of both indoor and open-air drama performances. The Helsinki Festival completes the series for two weeks from end August. Other less formal but often "fun" events are dotted about the Finnish summer calendar.

 WHAT TO SEE. Helsinki is an airy city, with the sea much in evidence, a host of islands, fine public buildings and outstanding modern architecture in both center and suburbs. The South Harbor with its open-air morning market and the nearby Senate Square with its neoclassical architecture are "musts". So are the fortress islands of Suomenlinna, the open-air museum of Seurasaari, and the busy shopping areas in and around the Esplanade, Mannerheimintie and Alexanterinkatu. Drive out to Porvoo and see the home of Runeberg, the national poet. Hämeenlinna is the birthplace of Sibelius. Tampere somehow manages to combine beautiful surroundings with bustling industry. For sports, summer and winter, Lahti beckons; Turku's treasures are a cathedral and a castle. Savonlinna is a convenient center from which to visit the Saimaa Lake district and has a famous castle. Jyväskylä in central Finland offers the bustle of a busy woodworking center in the heart of wild forestscapes that are also a superb natural holiday playground. Further north, the Kainuu district is a splendid and rugged area for outdoor enthusiasts, especially hikers and canoe-ists. Kuusamo, a little south of the Arctic Circle, is in another fine region for good fishing, marvellous walking—and a chance to shoot some rapids. North of the Arctic Circle, Lapland offers the wildest, remotest country of all, along with reindeer herds and (in some areas) Finland's Lapp minority. There are comfortable hotels to be found everywhere and, in all towns and many villages, look out for examples of beautiful modern architecture, for which the Finns are world-renowned.

 HOW TO GET ABOUT. All parts of Finland are accessible by one means of transport or another. Because of the watery nature of the landscapes, rail travel can be quite devious though, unusually, rail fares are substantially lower than those for bus travel. Express diesel trains (2 classes) serve all the main routes and include car-carrying trains from Helsinki to Kemi, Oulu and Rovaniemi, and from Turku and Tampere to Rovaniemi. The railway network stops short a little north of the Arctic Circle.

If you are able to work out your detailed itinerary in advance, it is possible to buy tourist tickets combining travel on trains, steamers, buses and planes, offering savings of about 10%. There are also Family Tickets giving substantial reductions on the railways. For foreign visitors only, a Finnrail pass entitles holders to unlimited travel on Finnish State Railways for reduced rates in first- and second-class for periods of 8, 15, or 22 days. The cost for 15 days is 585 Fmk first class, 390 Fmk second class; a supplementary charge of 12 Fmk is obligatory on special express trains and covers an advance seat reservation; on ordinary express trains, seat reservation is recommended at 5 Fmk. Pensioners of over 65 years and the disabled are entitled to reductions. The Eurail Pass, Inter Rail S ticket (men over 65 and women over 60), and Eurail Youth Pass (Student Rail Pass, for those under 26) are valid in Finland, not only for rail travel but also on some sailings to Finland. There is also a Nordic Tourist Ticket by train, giving unlimited travel for 21 days or one month through Denmark, Sweden, Norway and Finland at very reasonable rates, with concessions on some shipping lines.

Road transport is operated by Matkahuolto, a private company that also administers coach stations throughout the country and 500 service points, from which coach tickets can be bought as well as from travel agencies in Finland and some abroad. Passengers are also carried by the yellow, mail-carrying buses of the Post Office which are a familiar sight all over the country.

Finnair maintains a comprehensive air network serving the following points: Helsinki, Ivalo, Joensuu, Jyväskylä, Kajaani, Kemi, Kokkola, Kuopio, Kuusamo, Lappeenranta, Mariehamn, Mikkeli, Oulu, Pietarsaari, Pori, Rovaniemi, Savonlinna, Tampere, Turku, Vaasa, Varkaus. There is a Pensioners' Discount of 50% for anyone over 65 years, and a Family Discount of 25%–75%, according to age, for all except the head of the family. Another bargain is Finnair's Holiday Ticket offering unlimited travel for 15 days on the domestic network for $230, half price for children under 12 years. Air taxis are available in Helsinki and a number of other centers and are very reasonably priced; sightseeing flights can be made from some resorts.

Lake steamers and motor ships, with restaurants on board, ply the inland waterways. Increasingly, trips are organized as cruises, ranging from a few hours or a weekend to several days, but there is still a number of regular schedules (see regional chapters) which you can join or leave at will. A pilotage scheme is available on several lake routes, taking care of the transfer of the motorist's car between terminals at reasonable charges. In addition, there is a hydrofoil service between Lahti and Jyväskylä, and boat services operate on the Saimaa Canal from Lappeenranta.

A summary of trips to the Soviet Union is given in Facts At Your Fingertips (page 23).

Tours: The choice of organized tours, either escorted or not, within Finland has broadened enormously over recent years. There is everything from short trips into the lake districts and extensive grand tours, to professional study journeys covering any subject from architecture and agriculture to metallurgy and meat technology. Many tours combine various forms of travel. Some concentrate on particular aspects of areas, such as the magnificent fall colors in Lapland early in September.

Of particular significance is the great increase in hobby or special interest holidays. Fishing, walking, canoeing and water sports generally are among summer outdoor activities that are particularly well catered for; and, of course, skiing tours in winter. Gold washing in Lapland is one of the less obvious possibilities. If you can make up a small group, the choice is almost limitless, with candlemaking, bakery, gardens and social welfare among the list of subjects currently on offer as tour themes. The choice, of course, varies according to demand, and the latest details can be obtained from the Finnish Tourist Board offices or direct from the Finnish tour operators (see below).

Generally speaking, escorted or all-in individual tours within Finland are rather expensive. The best value is provided by packages, for example, ex-U.K. from which there is a variety of arrangements for between £250–£600 for 7–14 days. With some, travel within Finland is by a combination of different forms of travel and the aim is to show as much of the countryside as possible at relative leisure. In others, costs include the transport of your own car by sea to Finland or the use of a self-drive car on arrival or the freedom of the Finnrail Pass. Farmhouse and self-catering holidays are also featured, as are various tours to the Soviet Union.

 MOTORING. An extensive road-building programme has resulted in a good network of asphalted main roads throughout much of the country. In the south, four-lane motorways grow a little annually. Other major roads have a surface of oil and sand. Where the old dirt roads still remain, as in many parts of the far north and remoter areas, the gravel is often bound with clay and dustlaying chemicals, thus making the surface even and hard; but when it rains these roads can be somewhat slippery, dirty and smelly. In winter all main roads are kept open for traffic and the going is usually good. During the spring thaw (April–early June, according to latitude), some roads are at times impassable or very difficult to negotiate; look out for the road sign *"kelirikko"* which warns you of bad conditions. Another warning sign, with appropriate drawing, concerns elk (moose) and reindeer; take heed for collision with up to 600 kg. of elk is no joke. They are especially active at dusk.

Speed limits are 60, 80, 100 or 120 km per hour, according to the classification of the road and traffic density, and the limit applicable is indicated by signs. If it is not, the basic speed limit is 50 km.p.h. in built-up areas, 80 km.p.h. in the countryside or, on motorways, 120 km.p.h.

At intersections, cars coming from the right have priority. The rights of pedestrians on pedestrian crossings must be rigorously observed. The use of seat belts is now compulsory. *Important:* the laws regarding drinking and driving are very strict. If you exceed the exact limit of .5 milligrams of alcohol in the blood, the penalty is nearly always imprisonment or a heavy fine.

Super gasoline costs 3.54–3.68 Fmk per liter. There is a good network of service stations and repair garages, but it is wise to keep topped up if you are in less populated regions or taking minor roads in wilderness areas.

Car hire: Fly-drive arrangements ex-U.K. are available through airlines and some tour operators, covering return flight, self-drive car with unlimited mileage and, in some cases, Finn Checks for accommodation. These are convenient and good value. Car hire firms in Helsinki, some of whom offer weekly rates with unlimited mileage, are: *Avis,* Fredrikinkatu 36; *Europcar Car Rental,* Mariankatu 24; *Polarpoint,* Hertz International Licensee, Hotel Inter-Continental, Mannerheimintie 46–48; *Finn-Rent,* Hietaniemenkatu 6B; *inter-Rent,* Hitsaajankatu 7.

SEUTULA AIRPORT at Helsinki has spacious modern buildings with good passenger facilities and a frequent coach service to the city taking 30 minutes for the journey. Finnish products can be bought from its food shop and there are counters selling duty-free liquor, tobacco and perfumes. These are not particularly cheap by international standards, except for Finnish vodka. No separate airport tax is charged for international flights. There are regular links with nineteen provincial airports, in each case with coach service provided between the airport and center concerned. Check-in takes place at the airports, not at town terminals.

HOTELS. The standard of *hotels* within each category is usually very high and though no establishment has been classified as deluxe, many would qualify as such in some other countries. The deluxe classification has been avoided in this section because the line between this and many first class (E) hotels is very fine in Finland, where no official form of classification exists. Many establishments belong to one of several big hotel chains. For an indication of the price categories (E), (M) and (I) used throughout this section, see the table earlier in this chapter. All hotels add a service charge of 15% to the room bill. In many hotels, the room price includes a free morning sauna and swim.

A free list of all the hotels in Finland is available from the Finnish Tourist Board and this gives considerable detail of the amenities offered by each, as well as indicating those providing full board. Most hotels also have one room or more for private meetings or small conferences. For specially-equipped congress centers, see "Hints for the Businessman" below.

Most of the *summer hotels* listed in larger centers act as student accommodation at other times of the year; they are usually modern and offer excellent value. Some are run by the students themselves. The lowest price is to be found in a *boarding house (matkustajakoti),* addresses of which can be obtained from local tourist offices.

Especially useful for motorists is the Finn Check scheme which covers 165 hotels throughout the country. Minimum length of trip is 4 overnights; each check costs 100 Fmk and covers accommodation, breakfast and service for one person per night. In top class hotels an additional 45 Fmk is required; in those of lower category, the check also covers the cost of a self-service lunch. Only the first night can be reserved in advance; reservation to the next hotel is free of charge. Some hotel chains have excellent, flexible arrangements, such as those of Rantasipi (PL 210, Jyväskylä) whose fifteen top class establishments are nearly all situated in beautiful natural surroundings.

In the summer, most Finnish families disappear to their *summer cottages,* usually tucked away in the forests by some lake or river shore, or on an island.

Visitors can follow suit by renting a summer cottage, either in a *holiday village* or in a lone situation. The range of weekly rentals is from 400–2500 Fmk, average 700–1200 Fmk. For self-catering, estimate costs at slightly more than in the U.K. Addresses for this type of accommodation are given for each region in the following pages, but a main booking center for the whole country is Lomarengas, Museokatu 3, Helsinki 10.

Another increasingly popular form of accommodation is in *farmhouses* where full board is available at reasonable cost and you have a chance to participate in family life. Such holidays are marketed by several tour operators, and through Suomen 4H-liitto, Bulevardi 28, Helsinki 12, or Lomarengas as above.

Finally there are *youth hostels* —about 140 of them throughout the country, many of them in empty schools with fairly large rooms, but a lot offering "family rooms". There are no age restrictions and the hostels are also open to motorists. Food is not usually provided, but coffee and refreshments are often available. Overnight charges range from 18–40 Fmk. Further details from the Finnish Youth Hostels Association, Yrjönkatu 38B, Helsinki 10.

If you have been looking forward to taking a *sauna* or Finnish bath, here's your chance. Most hotels and holiday villages have them, and one or two a week are included in farmhouse holiday prices.

 FOOD AND DRINKS. Don't be misled by Finland's wild and lonely landscape—the Finns are sophisticated diners, they know food and, what's more, they enjoy it. The food is varied and plentiful. A special Finland Menu is now available in three price categories from some 200 restaurants and cafés throughout the country (list from Finnish Tourist Board offices). In addition the *Lappi à la Carte* leaflet describes three gourmet routes through Finnish Lapland featuring traditional dishes. If you happen to be around from about the end of July to early September, don't miss a crayfish party—when the Finns don bibs and tuck into boiled crayfish, flavored with dill and washed down with fiery Akvavit, right through the white nights. You will also encounter such national specialties as *poronkieltä* (reindeer tongue with lemon sauce), *hiilillä paistettua silakkaa* (Baltic herring grilled over charcoal), *kalakukko* (fish and pork baked in a rye flour crust, specialty of Kuopio), *lihapullia* (meat balls), and *uunijuustoa* (oven cheese). The Finns like good rich desserts, and to digest them they provide some delicate liqueurs, *Lakka* (cloudberry) and *Mesimarja* (Arctic brambleberry). In addition imported spirits (expensive) and wines (reasonable) are available.

Taking account of Finland's cost of living and high standards, you can get a good meal at a reasonable price, especially if you stick to *table d'hôte* menus served between fixed times, which are usually fairly early, particularly in more moderately priced establishments. The number of pleasant snack bars for quick inexpensive refreshments has increased enormously in recent years. The number and range of restaurants specializing in food from different parts of the world has increased greatly, too. What is more, the food is always attractively served.

Drinks increase the bill heavily, but watch your intake anyway, for the measure is large. Beer is served from 9 A.M. onwards and other liquor from noon until the restaurant closes. Beer is now also sold in supermarkets, many cafés and a number of otherwise unlicensed premises. ALKO, the Finnish State Alcohol Monopoly, have many shops where you can buy all kinds of alcoholic drinks. But note the strict laws referred to under "Motoring" relating to drinking and driving. At the other end of the scale, drinking water is safe everywhere, and excellent coffee is drunk in great quantities.

CAMPING. The best way to enjoy Finland's wealth of lake-and-forest scenery is to get out into it. There are camping areas near most cities and throughout the countryside, open to all. About 350 camp sites classified into three grades have been established by various organizations in Finland and, as the Finn has an eye for beauty, most of them have choice locations on the shores of lake, river or sea. Generally, free camping is not allowed without the landowner's permission and it is especially of the utmost importance in this forest-bound land to take the greatest possible care with regard to fire.

Camping is handled by the Finnish Travel Association's Camping Department, Mikonkatu 25, Helsinki 10. A system of Finncamping Checks is sold as part of a package arrangement through some travel agencies. Otherwise the charge is usually in the 16–40 Fmk range per family (two adults, two children, a car and tent or caravan) and, though the services vary, this normally includes facilities for cooking, washing-up and washing. At some sites, those not holding an international camping pass (FICC) must have a national camping card costing 4 Fmk. There are now about 200 sites where caravans can be linked to the electric current (220 V.). Only a few sites have facilities for filling and changing gas bottles, which can be done at most service stations and hardware stores.

A free list of campsites is available from the Finnish Tourist Board offices and most of them are marked on the excellent Suomen Tiekartta (Finnish Road Map) and Autoilijan Tiekartta (Motorist's Road Map) from bookshops or the Automobile and Touring Club in Helsinki.

 SPORTS. Most water sports in Finland take place in one of the 60,000 lakes—or about one for every 80 inhabitants—and some saltwater activities go on in the islands near Helsinki, off the south coast, in the Turku archipelago and the Åland islands. Many of the lakes are connected by waterways providing ample opportunity for **canoeing** and **kayaking.** Canoe safaris of several days' duration are arranged by the Finnish Canoeing Association and on some of these canoes may be rented. You can shoot the rapids in the Rukatunturi area (near Kuusamo) and in northern Karelia, and several loggers' competitions provide exciting spectator sport. In the Saimaa lake districts, there are 2000 km of marked routes suitable for waterborne travel, whether by canoe, **motor boat** or **yacht.** Flotilla sailing is now arranged, notably in the Saimaa lake districts, offering marvelous opportunities to experience the magnificent forest-and waterscapes with the freedom of wind and canvas, under supervision, in the company of like-minded souls. Yachts can be rented in a few centers and, nowadays, there is even a sailing school in Lapland. **Water skiing** and **wind surfing** can be enjoyed in a number of resorts. The northern regions stretching up into Lapland are ideal for **fishing.**

Among the many interesting **hiking** possibilities are the fell areas of Finnish Lapland, where marked routes and refuge huts are provided. A free booklet, *Hiking Routes,* is available from Finnish Tourist Board offices.

Golfing enthusiasts will find 20 courses, of which the best are at Tali Manor (7 km from Helsinki center, 18 holes), Espoo (near Helsinki, 18 holes), Aulanko (9 holes), Tampere (18 holes), Turku (18 holes), Lahti (9 holes) and Oulu (9 holes).

Riding has become very popular, with 110 member clubs of the Finnish Equestrian Federation, most of whom have riding schools.

Cycling is growing in popularity and bicycles can now be hired from quite a number of hotels, holiday villages, campsites, youth hostels and some tourist

A market in Copenhagen, close to
Christiansborg

The Dybbøl Mill in Denmark, protected by 18th-century guns. An alley on the idyllic island of Christiansø, Denmark

Ice fishing—a family treat in Finland,
where perch and pike lurk below, waiting
for lunch

The area around Myvatn in Finland, is ideal
for hikers, bird-watchers and geologists.
Houses, still buried under the lava of the
great Helgafell eruption

offices. In some areas, planned cycling routes of various durations, mainly following old country roads, have been worked out.

Tennis can be played in many places, but hire of rackets is limited.

Baseball with a Finnish accent, *pesäpallo*, is popular enough to have several hundred clubs. **Athletics** probably arouses the most enthusiasm of all, both from the point of view of participation and spectating. **Flying** and **gliding** are also well catered for.

An indication of sports facilities in each region is given under the appropriate sections. Central addresses for further information on each sport are as follows: The *Finnish Equestrian Federation, Finnish Golf Union, Finnish Tennis Association, Finnish Squash Rackets Association, Finnish Yachting Association, Finnish Motor Boat Association* and *the Finnish Canoe Association* are all at Topeliuksenkatu 41 a, Helsinki 25; *Finnish Association of Archers,* Maneesikatu 2, Helsinki 17; *Finnish Waterski Association,* Mr P.J. Barck, Rajalantie 2, 40950 Muurame; *Finnish Aeronautical Association,* Malmi Airport, Helsinki 70. Flotilla sailing is arranged through the *Nautic Center,* Karhusaari, Espoo 10, near Helsinki.

 WINTER SPORTS. The Finns are fervent followers of winter sports. Skiing heads the list and, in this, the Finns tend to concentrate on its more rigorous aspects—jumping and cross-country racing, at which they are always among the first. However, ski tows and ski lifts are increasing yearly and there are good opportunities for downhill enthusiasts, though naturally not to be compared with the range of terrain and amenities of traditional Alpine areas.

A special feature of winter sports in Finland are the well-marked skiing trails of varying lengths which lead from many centers, hotels or holiday villages, and provide easy-to-follow circuits requiring varying degrees of skill and endurance. Some of these are illuminated in the evenings, as are an increasing number of slopes suitable for slalom or downhill skiing.

Ski instruction and the hire of ski equipment are now available in many places. Note, however, that the cost of buying cross-country equipment is very reasonable in Finland.

The top skiing spot is Lahti, site of the chief event of the Finnish winter sports season, the Salpausselkä International Skiing Championships, held in early March. The second most important sports fixture is the Ounasvaara Winter Games held later in March at Rovaniemi. In Lapland, you may also enjoy the unique experience of skijoring behind a reindeer or zipping along in a reindeer-drawn sleigh. Further information on the best skiing possibilities is given for each region in the following pages.

Helsinki is the center for skating and related sports. You'll also find the peculiar Nordic game of bandy—soccer on ice—and ice hockey played in many towns, and ice yachting is practised on some of the lakes. Motor racing on ice, too, has become very popular. Other winter possibilities include fishing through the ice of frozen lakes and skidoo excursions.

Inclusive ski weeks and ski trekking holidays are arranged in many places, including by *Suomen Latu (Finnish Ski Association),* Fabianinkatu 7, Helsinki. Among winter tour operators in Helsinki are: *Finnish Travel Association,* Mikonkatu 25; *Global Travel,* Dagmarinkatu 6; *Kaleva Travel Agency,* Opastinsilta 8B; *Finntourist,* Iso Roobertinkatu 26. They feature both sporting arrangements and Finnish-style Christmas holidays. Or you can do a once-in-a-lifetime 5-day reindeer safari with Lapp guide: details from the above operators or *Lapland Travel,* Pohjanpuistikko 2, Rovaniemi 20.

MEET THE FINNS. Chalet and farmhouse holidays are good ways of getting a special insight into Finland; so are the seminars arranged for English-speaking visitors on different aspects of Finland (such as design, architecture or the Finnish language). Professional study tours on an enormous range of subjects are organized by several travel agencies.

 POSTAL RATES. Up to 20 grams, letters airmail to Britain, 1.50 Fmk; to U.S. and Canada, 2.00 Fmk. Postcards airmail to Britain, 1.30 Fmk; to U.S. and Canada, 1.50 Fmk. Aerograms cost 1.50 Fmk.

 HINTS FOR THE BUSINESSMAN. Many offices start work early and finish early—usually 8 a.m. to 4 or 4.30 p.m.—in many cases closing an hour earlier in summer. In fact, summer can be a difficult time for finding some Finns who take their holidays then and disappear for some weeks into the countryside. If you're told some elusive contact is away "*maalla*", that's just where he or she is! Otherwise, it's rather easier than in many countries to reach "top" people. On the whole Finns are bad at answering letters and good at settling matters on the phone or face to face. You can dial to and from most parts of Europe, remembering that Finland is 2 hours ahead of British time in winter, 1 hour in summer. Note, too, that the Finns go in for early lunches—from 11 a.m. is quite common.

Secretarial or interpreter services can be arranged through main hotels or through a number of agencies or translation bureaux specializing in these. Car hire is efficient and widely available, with possibilities of collecting and leaving the vehicle in different places. The hire of taxi planes is reasonably priced.

There is now a number of excellent purpose-built conference centers where at least 300 delegates can be seated in a single hall or where there are over 20 separate meeting rooms. The standard of technical equipment provided or available is very high, including all kinds of projection equipment, simultaneous translation equipment and, in some cases, closed-circuit TV. The principal centers at present are:

Helsinki and vicinity: Finlandia Hall, Karamzininkatu 4, Helsinki 10; Dipoli Congress Center, Otaniemi, Espoo 15 (9 km from city); Helsinki International Fair Center, Finnish Fair Corporation, PB 24, Helsinki 52; Hotel Presidentti, Eteläinen Rautatiekatu 4, Helsinki 10; Hotel Inter-Continental, Mannerheimintie 46, Helsinki 26; Hotel Kalastajatorppa, Kalastajatorpantie 1, Helsinki 33 (suburb of Munkkiniemi); Korpilampi Forest Lake Hotel, Espoo 97 (23 km from city); Hanasaari Cultural Center, Espoo 10 (7 km from city center).

Hyvinkää: Rantasipi Hyvinkää, 50 km north of Helsinki.

Hämeenlinna: Rantasipi Aulanko Hotel, Aulanko, about 100 km northwest of Helsinki.

Jyväskylä: Hotel Rantasipi Laajavuori, in central Finland.

Rovaniemi: Lappia House, Hallituskatu 11. Almost on the Arctic Circle.

Tampere: Hotel Rosendahl, Pyynikintie 13, Tampere 23.

Turku: Hotel Rantasipi Turku, Pispalantie 7, Turku 51.

In addition, facilities on board several modern ships give possibilities for holding conferences afloat in the Baltic on regular schedules between north Germany or Sweden and Finland.

CONVENIENT CONVENIENCES. These are available in all the usual places, such as rail and bus stations, airports, big stores, restaurants, snack bars, but sometimes standards are not as high as you might expect from a country known for its cleanliness and sense of hygiene. In some places such as Helsinki's main railway station, for example, you will be handed a quota of toilet paper by the attendant as you pay your entrance fee—an odd restriction when you consider that paper is a main Finnish export! On some premises, it is necessary to ask for the key *(avain)*. In most cases, the doors are clearly marked with the appropriate symbol of a man or woman, cock or hen. Otherwise, the words to look out for are *naisille* (for women) and *miehille* (for men). You can expect high standards in all hotels and most restaurants.

USEFUL ADDRESSES (all in Helsinki). **Embassies:** U.S.A., I. Puistotie 14A; Canada, Pohjoisesplanadi 25b; Britain, Uudenmaankatu 16–20.

Tourist information: Helsinki City Tourist Office, Pohjoisesplanadi 19; Hotel Booking Service, Railway Station. Regional and local tourist offices are given under the Regions.

Holiday Villages: Lomarengas, Museokatu 3.

Farmhouse Holidays: Lomarengas; Suomen 4H-liitto, Bulevardi 28.

Travel Bureaux: Area Travel Agency, Kaisaniemenkatu 13A; Finland Travel Bureau, Kaivokatu 10; Finnish Travel Association, Mikonkatu 25; Finntourist, Iso Roobertinkatu 26; Globaltravel, Dagmarinkatu 6; Kaleva Travel Agency, Opastinsilta 8B; Travel Agency Lomamatka, Simonkatu 8; Travek Travel Bureau, Eteläranta 16; Travela (Youth Travel Bureau), Mannerheimintie 5C; AGEBA Special Travel Service, Pohjoisranta 4; Boris Koreneff Travel, Erottajan Parkkihalli.

Finnair: main booking offices at Mannerheimintie 102 and Aleksanterinkatu 17; Air Terminal behind Hotel Inter-Continental, at Töölönkatu 21.

Automobile and Touring Club, Kansakoulukatu 10.

HELSINKI

Broad Avenues and Bright Prospects

If Finland is a young nation, her capital is equally youthful. More-over, embraced on three sides by the sea, it is extremely compact, yet manages to house over 10% of the country's 4¾ million inhabitants.

Helsinki (Helsingfors to the Swedish-speaking minority) is very much a city of the sea, sprawling over peninsulas, curving round bays and spilling out across islands that are linked by bridges, causeways or even by boat to the central hub. This hub fills a chunky peninsula where, somehow, without overcrowding, are to be found the single-chamber Parliament, the leading technical and educational institutes, art galleries, theaters, museums, business houses, the great Sports Stadium (scene of the 1952 Olympic Games), much outstandingly good architecture, the head offices of every big industrial enterprise—in fact all that constitutes the legislative, cultural, scientific, commercial and economic life of the country. And still there is space left for airy parks and broad streets.

Helsinki owes its origin to the chance whims of two monarchs, and its development has largely been the result of a series of accidents. Some 400 years ago King Gustav Vasa of Sweden ordered the citizens of four Finnish towns—Porvoo (Borgå), Tammisaari (Ekenäs), Rauma and Ulvila (Ulfsby)—to leave their homes and proceed to a place on the rapids of the river Vantaa. There they were to build a new town to attract the trade of the Estonian city of Tallinn, thus challenging the power of the Hanseatic League. Like many another city of this period, Helsinki's growth was interrupted by wars, plagues and fires. Not until 1809, when Finland became an autonomous Grand Duchy of Russia, was Helsinki really able to start developing; then three years later, it became the capital of Finland, primarily because the Czar found Turku (Åbo) was too far away from Russia and too close to Sweden to remain the capital of his newly-acquired territory.

The first of the accidents which stimulated the new capital's growth was the Great Fire in Turku. So much of the latter city was gutted that the University was moved bodily to Helsinki, which at once became the cultural as well as the political center of the country. In 1808, thanks to chance again, another Great Fire played a part in the young city's future. This time it was Helsinki that burned, allowing the German-born architect, Carl Ludvig Engel, an opportunity to plan the rebuilding of the city practically house by house and stone by stone. It is to Engel and to his partner, Ehrenström, that Finland must be grateful for her beautiful capital.

Around the Senate Square which Engel designed stand the Cathedral, the University and the State Council Building—a group built in one of the purest styles European architecture can boast. Perhaps it was Engel's inspiration, but from his day Finland has always had good architects. Two of them, Eliel Saarinen and Alvar Aalto, became world famous. You can hardly walk down any street in Helsinki without seeing splendid examples of the work of modern architects whose fame is already spreading beyond the frontiers of Finland, such as Heikki and Kaija Sirén, Rewell, Ervi, Petäjä, Pietilä, Penttilä.

Under the protective shadows of the island fortress of Suomenlinna (Sveaborg), Helsinki developed rapidly during the 19th century. The lovely park-strewn suburb of Töölö, and the island residential districts of Lauttasaari, and Kulosaari came into being quite recently. Still newer suburbs grew up in the post-World War II period, and the city continues to expand, as indeed it must, for like most capitals, it has not enough accommodation for all who wish to live there. This is not the result of poor planning, but rather of the territorial losses suffered by Finland after the war, when 400,000 Finns, living in lands ceded to the Soviet Union by the peace treaty, chose to abandon their homes and possessions—and remain Finns. Many came to live in Helsinki.

Exploring Helsinki

From the visitor's point of view, Helsinki has the virtue of compactness. Once you have oriented yourself and found out where you are on the city map, it will be difficult to get lost. The piers where ships from abroad dock, the railway station and, to a lesser extent, the air terminal, are all in the center of the city. So, however you come, you can start wandering around on foot at once.

It's an idea to begin by finding a good viewpoint from which to make your first survey of the city—such as the top of the Olympic Stadium Tower, the hill of Tähtitorninmäki, or comfortably installed in a top

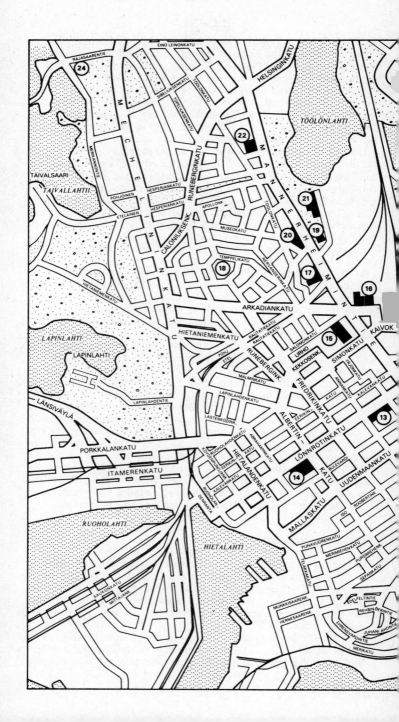

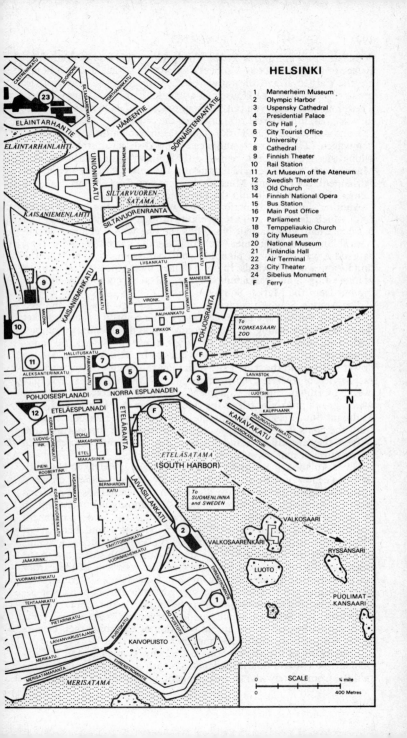

HELSINKI

1 Mannerheim Museum
2 Olympic Harbor
3 Uspensky Cathedral
4 Presidential Palace
5 City Hall
6 City Tourist Office
7 University
8 Cathedral
9 Finnish Theater
10 Rail Station
11 Art Museum of the Ateneum
12 Swedish Theater
13 Old Church
14 Finnish National Opera
15 Bus Station
16 Main Post Office
17 Parliament
18 Temppeliaukio Church
19 City Museum
20 National Museum
21 Finlandia Hall
22 Air Terminal
23 City Theater
24 Sibelius Monument
F Ferry

floor bar or restaurant as in the Torni, Hesperia, Inter-Continental, Palace or Vaakuna hotels. Probably the first buildings you will notice are the Cathedral and the railway station, both in the center of the town, together with the House of Parliament and the Stadium Tower. These four structures you can see from practically anywhere in Helsinki. The great broad street running from the center of town through the city and out to the main Turku road is Mannerheimintie, or Mannerheimvägen. (*Tie* in Finnish, and *vägen* in Swedish, mean street or road.) Along this broad avenue, named after Finland's great hero Marshal Mannerheim, you'll be able to pick out the Post Office, the House of Parliament, the National Museum, the fine new Concert and Congress Center, Finlandia Hall, and the Olympic Stadium.

Another simple introduction to the city is to take the No. 3T or 3B tram which describes a figure of eight through the city, bringing you back to where you started. No. 3T is the one with a commentary in several languages in summer (see "Sightseeing", page 199). After that, as good a way as any of planning your sightseeing is to start in the middle and work outwards. In point of fact, by far the greatest number of interesting sights are contained in the central part of the city, branching out from the Market Square.

The Market Square is down by the South Harbor, a few hundred yards from some of the passenger quays. The colorful openair market flourishes each morning, ending around 1 P.M. and reopening in summer from 3–8, when the emphasis is more on arts and crafts. Grouped around the striking statue of Havis Amanda, by Ville Vallgren, are the flower sellers, and the fruit stalls with their mountains of strawberries, raspberries, blueberries, red currants and red whortleberries. You may even be fortunate enough to find the special cloudberry, *suomuurain,* which grows mostly north of the Arctic Circle and is ripened by the Midnight Sun. Fish are sold at the very edge of the harbor, straight from the boats in which they were caught earlier in the morning and so fresh they are still alive and flipping. Meat and dairy produce is sold in the covered market, just beyond the fish stalls.

Havis Amanda, incidentally, the beautiful lady loved by all Helsinki-ites, is a center of *vapunaatto* (May Day Eve) revelry. She is crowned again and again on this festive night with the white caps of students who wade through the protective moat surrounding her and climb up to embrace her. Another statue of interest is the stone monument commemorating the time in 1833 when Nicolas I and his consort Feodorovna visited Finland. Known as the Empress Stone, it stands just opposite the quay used by the small boats which steam out to the islands of the harbor archipelago. Follow the west side of the harbor southwards, past the arrival quay for ships from Sweden, Germany and Denmark and you come to the pleasant park and district of Kaivopuisto, where most of the embassies are to be found. On the shore, here and elsewhere, you will see small wooden structures from which some Helsinki housewives follow an old tradition of scrubbing their carpets in the sea (or lake, as the case may be).

Leading out of the Market Square are Pohjoisesplanadi and Eteläesplanadi (North and South Esplanades), with gardens running up the middle. Compositely known as Esplanadi, it is a dangerous thoroughfare at four every afternoon when car owners race up the street on their way home from the office. In an hour, peace reigns and Esplanadi becomes a favorite promenade. Lovers of porcelain, fashion and crafts will find here some of the display rooms of Finland's top firms.

Along the edge of the Market Square facing the sea stands the President's Palace, with a sentry in field grey patrolling the entrance. Near it you can see the City Hall and various administrative buildings and behind it towers Helsinki's most famous landmark, the Cathedral. A few steps in the direction of this impressive church bring you to the Senate Square, where facing you is Walter Runeberg's statute of Alexander II of Russia, the enlightened despot who was so well disposed to Finland.

Opposite the Cathedral a lively shopping and entertainments center should open in 1984 or 1985, adding a new dimension to this gracious but rather quiet district. Most of the streets leading off the Senate Square contain government and administrative offices. Snellmaninkatu is named after J. V. Snellman, whose statue stands in front of the Bank of Finland. Known as the awakener of the Finnish national spirit, he was instrumental in persuading the Russian overlords to accept the idea of a separate Finnish currency and officially recognizing the Finnish language. Nearby is the House of the Estates, site of Finland's Parliament during the Russian era, and now occupied by several scientific societies.

Snellmaninkatu leads into the district of the town known as Kruununhaka, a sleepy residential quarter built around the northern harbor, from which regular boats cross to the island of Korkeasaari on which lies Helsinki's zoo.

The Senate Square and Baron Mannerheim

But return to the Senate Square. With your back to the Cathedral and its enormous cupola, look left, and you will see the gleaming "onions" of the Orthodox Uspenski Cathedral towering high above the rocky island of Katajanokka. Connected to the mainland by a bridge, this district houses the customs administration and other port offices.

On January 28, 1951, the great Marshal Baron Carl Gustaf Mannerheim, died in Switzerland. He was flown back to his native land and lay in state in the Cathedral for three days before his state funeral. The citizens of Finland were allowed to pay their last respects to him while he lay there in the dim vastness of this lovely church. Young war widows, children, officers and soldiers, who had fought in Finland's wars against Russia under Mannerheim's leadership, filed past in their thousands, and the only sound was one of weeping. Never in Finland's history has there been such an expression of national feeling.

But let us leave the Senate Square and the "Whitehall district" of Finland, which, quite appropriately, is rather sleepy and slow. Let's take a stroll up Aleksanterinkatu, the main shopping center of Helsinki. At its top end, where it runs into Mannerheimintie, is Stockmann's, Finland's largest department store. At this corner is the famous statue of the Three Smiths by Felix Nylund, a common rendezvous for people who have to meet somewhere in town. Near the center of town, off

Esplanadi, is the permanent Finnish Design Center at Kasarmikatu 19, where there is a changing display of the best in Finnish industrial art. Goods displayed here can be bought in Helsinki's departmental stores.

Where Mannerheimintie meets Esplanadi stands the Swedish Theater where plays are given in the Swedish language. To reach its Finnish-language rival, the older National Theater, you must turn around and go back down Aleksanterinkatu to the first street on your left, which leads into the huge square in front of the railway station, which is also the hub of the city's impressive new metro network. Here, however, the National Theater is overshadowed by the massive station itself, designed by Eliel Saarinen. Although he became an American citizen during the war, Saarinen's last wish was to be buried in his native country. His ashes were flown to Finland in 1950 and interred in the grounds of the beautiful home he built for himself along the shore of lovely Lake Hvitträsk.

Right opposite the Railway Station is the City Center, a complex of shops, restaurants, cafés, with underground passageway of shops leading to the railway station. Also on the opposite side of the Railway Square and facing the National Theater is the Ateneum Art Gallery, which houses specimens of the works of Finland's greatest painters. The paintings of Gallen-Kallela, Hugo Simberg, Albert Edelfelt, Eero Järnefelt, and Magnus Enckell are known far beyond the borders of Finland and are well worth a visit. You'll also find some sculptures by the world-famous Wäinö Aaltonen.

Just behind the railway station stands the General Post Office. The Finns have dubbed it the "post box" because of its yellow color and rectangular shape, which remind them of a Finnish letterbox. Opposite the Post Office is Sokos House which contains a large hotel and restaurant, plus numerous business offices and shops. Nearby is one of Helsinki's latest shopping precincts, Kaivopiha, an attractive oasis linked to the railway station.

The Post Office marks one boundary of the "downtown" part of the capital. From here, following Mannerheimintie, let us go northwards toward Töölö. A stone's throw from where we stand takes us to the House of Parliament, the impressive structure in red granite which seems so striking because of the ample space around it. No rows of flats and business houses crowd in here. The Parliament building looks solid and, if you go inside you will agree that it is solid, built to withstand storms of debate within and criticism from without. It is lavishly and beautifully decorated inside, even to the special caucus room reserved exclusively for the score or more of lady representatives. Finland's 200 members of Parliament are elected by proportional representation.

National Museum and Olympic Stadium

A short distance west of Mannerheimintie in Tempeliaukio is Taivallahti church, one of Europe's most unusual modern churches, built into the living rock. Designed by the brothers Timo and Tuomo Suomalainen, it is also used as a concert hall. Returning to Mannerheimintie, just a few hundred yards from the House of Parliament is an odd-looking edifice with a tower which gives it a church-like appearance. This is the

National Museum, which houses a large collection of ethnographical exhibits illustrating Finland's history. This area, round the shores of Töölönlahti Bay, is the site of the big new city plan designed by Alvar Aalto. Part of this is Finlandia Hall, the Concert and Congress Center, designed by him, which opened in 1971, close to the shore of the bay and not far from the National Museum. The Intercontinental Hotel is nearby, while the ultramodern City Theater, designed by Timo Penttilä, is across the bay.

Further along Mannerheimintie, not half an hour's walk from the railway station and but 10 minutes by tram, rises the imposing tower of the Olympic Stadium. One of the finest views of Helsinki can be obtained from the top of this tower. Further north still and to the east of Mannerheimintie, less than two miles from the city center, is Helsinki's fine new International Fair Center, which opened in 1975. Exhibition halls, a restaurant, cafeteria and well-planned open spaces make it a showplace of its kind.

The street leading off at right angles from Mannerheimintie, Helsinginkatu, leads to the beautiful Botanical Gardens and the Water Tower, from which there is a fine view. Nearby is Helsinki's Tivoli, or permanent amusement park, called Linnanmäki, offering top-class entertainment of universal family appeal. Continuing along this street we come to the "East End" of Helsinki where there is little to see except proof of the fact that Helsinki has indeed no slums.

If you return to Mannerheimintie and cross the street, you will find yourself in the hospital center of the capital. Actually, it is still Töölö, the biggest residential district, but in this little section are concentrated most of the city's biggest and newest hospitals.

Although it may seem a startling suggestion, you next ought to go and see the cemetery. When you get there, you will realize why it is a favorite rendezvous for a promenade, for it is a beautiful place. Marshal Mannerheim is buried in the military section. It is a custom to place candles on each grave on Christmas Eve, a moving sight.

Another place well worth visiting is Arabia. This is one of the largest pottery factories in Europe and can be visited by appointment. Although the Arabia plant is some distance out of town, a tram service runs practically to the gate.

Suomenlinna

For a complete change of scene you will enjoy a visit to the fortress of Suomenlinna. It is built on a series of islands, and the entire Finnish army assisted in its construction, which began in 1748. Under the protection of this fortification, Helsinki first began to develop and flourish. Once called the Gibraltar of the North, it was indeed impregnable, never having been taken by assault. Twice, however, it was surrendered without a fight, first to the Russians in the war of 1808–1809, and then during Finland's war of independence when the German Baltic Division, assisted by the Finnish Civic Guard, captured the city of Helsinki. During the Crimean War a combined British and French fleet bombarded the fortress and the fires caused by the cannonade convinced the army that the fortress could not withstand modern artillery fire.

Yet Suomenlinna is more than an ancient military monument with several museums; its parks and gardens are lovely, especially in the spring. One of the forts near the historic King's Gate has an outstanding restaurant. Bearing the historic name of Walhalla, it has been changed as little as possible. Over the next years, this group of islands is being further developed into an all-purpose center for cultural and leisure activities. It includes the new and expanding Nordic Arts Center, focussing on exhibitions and the promotion and exchange of ideas on Scandinavian art.

Seurasaari, an island linked by bridge to the mainland, is another good spot to visit. It houses a delightful open-air museum which brings together houses, ranging from simple huts with turf roofs to lovely wooden villas furnished with original furniture, transported from various parts of the country. The President's residence is nearby.

A short distance from Helsinki is the famous Tapiola Garden City, situated in the forests and close to the sea. In addition to its exceptional architectural interest, it has some good restaurants and leisure facilities. If you are interested in imaginative architecture, it is worth browsing around almost any of the Helsinki suburbs.

•

PRACTICAL INFORMATION FOR HELSINKI

 HOTELS. During the peak summer months reservations are necessary to avoid disappointment. There is a Hotel Booking Service in the railway station for hotel and private accommodations, open: mid-May to mid-Sept., weekdays 9–9, Sat., 9–7, Sun., 12–7; mid-Sept. to mid-May, weekdays, 9–6, closed Sat., Sun. Unless otherwise stated, all the hotels listed below are open all the year, have licensed restaurants and can offer some or, in many cases, all rooms with bath or shower. The price categories (E), (M) and (I) are explained in the section "Practical Information for Finland". In most cases, hotel restaurants in the (E) and (M) categories have music and dancing on some or most evenings, and several in these categories offer roulette, though maximum stakes are 5 Fmk and you are not likely to win a fortune! The majority of establishments also have sauna baths. Otherwise, special facilities, such as nightclubs or sports amenities have been indicated for each hotel.

Expensive

Dipoli Strand, new, in garden suburb of Otaniemi, 9 km. from center; 213 rooms, most with sea view, sports facilities.

Helsinki, Hallituskatu 12, centrally located, newly renovated, 85 rooms, disco.

Hesperia, Mannerheimintie 50, 285 rooms, pool, nightclub.

Inter-Continental, Mannerheimintie 46, probably Helsinki's plushest, 468 rooms, pool, nightclub.

Kalastajatorppa, Kalastajatorpantie 2, in glorious seashore situation and linked by underground passage-way with famous nightclub of same name; 235 rooms, pool, tennis, boating, fishing.

Klaus Kurki, Bulevardi 2, 75 rooms.

Korpilampi (Forest Lake), in Espoo, 14 miles northwest of city, very new congress hotel in lovely forest setting, 162 rooms, pool, tennis, boating, fishing, nightclub.

Marski, Mannerheimintie 10, centrally located, 162 rooms, nightclub.

Merihotelli, Hakaniemenranta 4, 87 rooms, pool, disco.

Olympia, L. Brahenkatu 2, 101 rooms, disco, pool.

Palace, Eteläranta 10, with stunning view over the South Harbor, 59 rooms.

Presidentti, E. Rautatiekatu 4, new in 1980, central, 500 rooms, several restaurants, pool, nightclub, all-night café.

Rantasipi, near airport, new in 1981, 176 rooms. Excellent for transit stopovers, with shuttle service to airport.

Seurahuone, Kaivokatu 12, central location opposite railway station, 76 rooms, nightclub, disco, elegant Café Socis.

Tapiola Garden, in the garden suburb of Tapiola, 82 rooms, pool.

Torni, Yrjönkatu 26, 158 rooms, recently renovated, several restaurants with different specialties.

Vaakuna, Asema-aukio 2, central location on main railway station square, 290 rooms.

Moderate

Aurora, Helsinginkatu 50, 75 rooms, unlicensed restaurant.
Dipoli Summer Hotel, as above, 363 rooms.

Espoo, 8 miles from city, 94 rooms, rooftop pool.

Finn, Kalevankatu 3B, 28 rooms, no restaurant.

Haaga, Nuijamiestentie 10, not so central, part of the Hotel and Restaurant College, 40 rooms, pool, tennis.

Helka, P. Rautatienkatu 23, 101 rooms, unlicensed restaurant.

Hospiz, Vuorikatu 17b, 141 rooms, unlicensed restaurant.

Martta, Uudenmaankatu 24, 44 rooms, unlicensed cafeteria.

Ursula, Paasivuorenkatu 1, not so central, 43 rooms, cafeteria.

Inexpensive

Academica, Hietaniemenkatu 14, summer only, 217 rooms, pool, disco, tennis.

Kesä Hospiz, Paraistentie 19, 71 rooms, unlicensed restaurant, summer only.

Kustaa Vaasa, Vaasankatu 10, summer only, 90 rooms.

Mercur, Ruusulankatu 5, summer only, 50 rooms.

Satakuntatalo, Lapinrinne 1, summer only, 64 rooms.

Cheapest accommodation is in boarding houses such as *Clairet,* It. Teatterikuja 3; *Erottajanpuisto,* Uudenmaankatu 9; *Lönnrot,* Lonnrotinkatu 16; *Omapohja,* It. Teatterikuja 3; *Pensionat Regina,* Puistokatu 9.

 RESTAURANTS. You will meet Swedish smörgåsbord, with Finnish variations, as well as foreign specialties from most parts of the world in Helsinki's restaurants. The problem of tipping takes care of itself as 14% is automatically added to your check (15% on weekends and holidays), though you may leave a little extra if you have good service. Note that *table d'hôte* meals served between fixed hours work out very much more cheaply than eating *à la carte.* Menus are available in English in many places nowadays, and English is widely spoken. Roulette is played in several top category restaurants, and music is often provided. Those listed below are fully licensed for drinks unless otherwise stated.

Expensive

Adlon, Fabianinkatu 14, smart and with floorshow.

Bellevue, Rahapajankatu 3, Russian style.

Fen Kuan, Eerikinkatu 14, Oriental cuisine.

Fennia, Mikonkatu 16, floorshow.

Havis Amanda, Unioninkatu 23, by the South Harbor; two sections of which one specializes in fish.

Kaivohuone, in attractive location in Kaivopuisto Park looking out to the Harbor; floorshow.

Kalastajatorppa (Fisherman's Cottage), Kalastajatorpantie 2, a famous showpiece, beautifully situated near the seashore, but bearing little resemblance to the original fisherman's cottage! Floorshow. See also under *Hotels.*

Karl Konig, Mikonkatu 4, subdued, sophisticated setting, below ground.

Katajanokka Casino, Laivastokatu 1, in fine seashore location.

Kulosaari Casino, Hopeasalmenpolku 1, pleasantly placed on island of same name, but accessible by road.

Mestaritalli, Toivo Kuulan puisto, formerly stables, now an elegant restaurant in a seashore park.

Motti, Töölöntorinkatu 2, has some unusual items on the menu.

Savoy, Eteläesplanadi 14, a favorite lunch place for Finland's tycoons. Designed by Alvar Aalto.

Svenska Klubben, Maurinkatu 6, intimate manorial atmosphere in listed historic house by North Harbor.

Walhalla, on fortress island of Suomenlinna, reached by short ferry journey from South Harbor. You dine in the authentic 18th-century atmosphere of a fortress never taken by storm, in a setting of ancient ramparts and flowering lilac bushes—one of the memorable sights of Helsinki.

Moderate

Agora Tea Room, Unioninkatu 30. Especially for tea enthusiasts.

Café Socis, in Seurahuone hotel, elegant rendezvous, lunch (M), coffee and cakes (E).

El' Greco, Eteläesplanadi 22, Greek food.

Esplanadikappeli, in the Esplanade near the South Harbor, recently renovated with several sections including open-air summer restaurant.

Happy Days, Pohjoisesplanadi 2, adjoining Swedish Theater, with several restaurants of various price levels and types.

Karelia, Käpylänkuja 1, Karelian specialties.

Kultainen Orava, Siltawsaarenkatu 18.

Parrilla Espanola, Eerikinkatu 4, Spanish food.

Perho, Mechelininkatu 7, run by the Helsinki Hotel and Restaurant College and recently renovated. Excellent value.

Punainen Hattu, Keskuskatu 7, intimate atmosphere.

Troikka, Caloniuksenkatu 3, one of a chain of three small eating places, specializing in excellent Russian food.

Tullinpuomi, Mannerheimintie 118.

Välskarin Kellari, Hallituskatu 3. Intimate cellar atmosphere in the "Whitehall" of Helsinki.

Wanha Manala, Töölönkatu 3, Finnish specialties.

Wellamo, Vyökatu 9, small, intimate, rustic atmosphere, good food if you like garlic.

White Lady, Mannerheimintie 93, elegant.

Inexpensive

Carrols, self-service hamburger restaurants at Mannerheimitie 19, in the City Passage, and in Puotinharju Shopping Center; disposable plates and cups; good value.

Chez Marius, Mikonkatu 1, French cuisine, beer and wine only.

Davy's, Fredrikinkatu 22, good tavern-style pizzeria.

Eliel, in the railway station. Genuine *art nouveau* style. Self-service.

Groovy, Ruoholahdenkatu 4, good jazz restaurant.

Kasvisravintola, Korkeavuorenkatu 3, self-service vegetarian restaurant.

Kellarikrouvi, P. Makasiininkatu 6, cozy wine cellar atmosphere.

Pizzeria Rivoli, Albertinkatu 38, Italian food.

Säkkipilli, Kalevankatu 2. Cozy English atmosphere.

The Old Baker's, Mannerheimintie 12.

Tuuliviiri, Eteläranta, beer and wine only.

Vanhan Kellari, Mannerheimintie 3, in cellar of Old Students' House.

Voudin Grilli, Torivoudintie 1, beer and wine only.

Many modern and attractive cafés *(kahvila* or *baari),* dotted about town, offer refreshments and sometimes hot meals, as well as coffee, cakes, etc. Among several chains of cafés and low-priced restaurants are: *Fazer* and *Go-Inn.* A selection of English-style pubs includes *Angleterre* (M), Fredrikinkatu 47; *Annan Pub* (M), I. Roobertinkatu 16; *Richard's Pub* (M), Rikhardinkatu 4; and *St. Urho's Pub* (M), Museokatu 10.

ENTERTAINMENT. The solid façade of the old-established *National Theater* is a dominant feature of the railway station square. It incorporates a later annexe designed by Heikki and Kaija Siren for the modern and well-equipped *Pieninäyttämö (Little Theater)*. Here plays are given in Finnish, whereas at *Svenska Teatern* or the *Swedish Theater,* a familiar landmark where the Esplanade meets Mannerheimintie, performances are in Swedish as the name implies. The ultra-modern *City Theater,* Eläintarhantie, near Töölönlahti Bay, opened only a few years ago, and even more recent is the splendid Aalto designed *Finlandia Hall,* Concert and Congress Center, on Mannerheimintie. The *National Opera* in Bulevardi offers performances of international and Finnish operas and ballets.

The Finns are enthusiastic theatergoers and, though the theaters themselves are closed in summer, they are replaced by summer theaters of various kinds. Among them are the *Helsinki Summer Theater* on Mustikkamaa island and in the minor auditorium of the City Theater; *Ryhmäteatteri* on Suomenlinna island; *Student Theater* at Seurasaari; *Töölönranta Summer Theater* at Töölölahti Bay; *Summer Theater* in Central Park, in the grounds of Laakso riding field; and *Operetta Theater* at the Rowing Stadium.

Musical performances are also held in a number of attractive settings in summer, such as organ recitals on Sunday evenings in the *Lutheran Cathedral,* concerts in *Temppeliaukio Church* and the *House of Nobility,* and open-air concerts of various kinds in *several parks.*

Moviegoers can choose from numerous *cinemas;* all films are shown in their original language.

Linnamäki amusement park is Helsinki's Tivoli, with the Peacock Theater, side shows, open-air dancing, etc. in summer (closed Mon.) Recent innovations are the Monorail sightseeing train and the jungle train.

The *Helsinki Festival* for two weeks at the end of August and beginning of September is a major event, combining all kinds of cultural events.

WHAT TO SEE. In the center of the city, the South Harbor and, behind it, the Cathedral-dominated Senate Square in neo-classical Empire style, are very pleasing indeed on the eye. There are also delightful views to be had of the city and archipelago from the **Stadium Tower,** Eläintarha, lift, 9 A.M. –8 P.M. weekdays, 9 A.M.–5 P.M. Sat., Sun.; **Tähtitorninmäki,** Observatory Hill Park; and **Seurasaari** Island. The morning (7–1) open-air markets for vegetables, fish, and other foodstuffs are colorful spots: at the Market Place, by the South Harbor, and Hietalahti, Hakaniemi, and Töölö markets. The following opening times of museums, etc. apply to summer, check with the Helsinki Tourist Office for other seasons.

Atheneum Art Gallery, Railway Square. Mainly paintings, sculpture, drawings, etc., by Finnish artists; also foreign and old masters. Mon.-Fri. 9–5 (except Wed. 9–8), Sat., Sun. 11–5.

Parliament Building, Mannerheimintie. Shown to visotors Mon.-Fri. at 2, Sat. at 11, Sun. at 12 and 1 (except when Parliament meets and holidays). Public admitted to gallery during full session.

Helsinki City Museum, Mannerheimintie, opposite National Museum. Art, furniture, archives illustrating history of city. 12–4, Thursday 12–8 (free).

National Museum, Mannerheimintie 34. Three sections: prehistoric, historic, ethnographic. 11–4 Tues. also 6–9; Sun. 11–4. Closed on Mon. in winter. Free on Tues.

Burgher's House, Kristianinkatu 12. Oldest wooden house in Helsinki (1817). 12–4, Thurs. 12–8 (free), closed Sat.

Helsinki City Art Museum, Tamminiementie 6, near Seurasaari. Finnish and French art from 20th century.

Gallen-Kallela Museum, Leppävaara, Tarvaspää, reached by bus from platform 31B at the bus station (to Leppävaara) or No. 4 tram to Munkkiniemi, then pleasant 1–1½ mile walk. The home and works of one of Finland's greatest painters in charming surroundings. Tue.-Thurs. 10–8, Fri.-Sun. 10–5.

City Conservatories, Eläintarha Park; 12–3, Sun. 1–3. Winter garden. Free.

Museum of Finnish Architecture, Kasarmikatu 24. Daily, 10–4.

Museum of Applied Art, Korkeavuorenkatu 23. Development of design. Tues.–Fri. 11–5, Sat.–Sun. 11–4.

Mannerheim Museum, in Kaivopuisto at Kalliolinnantie 14. Home of Marshal Mannerheim, containing his collected trophies. Fri., Sat., 11–3,Sun., 11–4.

National Maritime Museum, Hylkysaari island, ferry 10 min. from Market Square. Recently opened and specialized maritime history museum. Daily 10–3.

Open-Air Museum, Seurasaari Island. Farm and manor buildings. 11.30–5.30 daily. 11.30–7 Wed. (free).

Suomenlinna, frequent ferry service from Etaläsatama-South Harbor. Fortifications on series of islands, currently being restored and developed into a multi-purpose center; Nordic Arts center, museums, summer restaurants, summer theater, guided tours. Museums open daily, 11–5.

Korkeasaari Zoo, reached by ferry from North Harbor, or by footbridge from Mustikkamaa island, which is accessible by road. Weekdays 10–9 (June-July), closing earlier in other months.

Old Town (Vanhakaupunki). Original site of city founded in 1550. Tram 6 (Arabia).

Cathedral. Senate Square, 9–7, Sun. 12–7.

Temppeliaukio Church, Lutherinkatu 3, beautifully carved out of living rock. Daily 10–9, except Sun. 12–3, 6–9.

Uspensky Cathedral (Orthodox), Kanavakatu 1. Mon.–Fri. 10–4.

Arabia pottery factory may be visited by arrangement. (See *Shopping* for showrooms.)

 SIGHTSEEING. In summer, daily buses from Simonkatu 1 tour the city at 10 and 2 (2½ hours). There is a combined city and suburbs tour at 11 A.M. (3½ hours) including lunch, and a lunch or dinner tour, including traditional Karelian meal. Sightseeing trips by boat leave from the South and North Harbors for both the eastern and western sections of Helsinki's archipelago. Some include a lunch stop ashore. Several of the travel agencies already listed have a variety of arrangements in and around Helsinki. There is also winter sightseeing daily.

The No. 3T tram, which describes a figure eight through and around the city center, provides a commentary in several languages in summer on main points of interest. A free descriptive folder, with map, is obtainable on the tram. From the City Tourist Office or any public transport ticket office (but not on board vehicles) you can buy a 24-hour Tourist Ticket (22 Fmk) entitling you to unlimited travel on all central buses and trams.

Or you can walk. The Helsinki City Tourist Office have prepared an excellent series of texts outlining various itineraries in and around the center that can be followed on foot, with points of interest indicated.

Their office at Pohjoisesplanadi 19 can provide a considerable variety of leaflets on different aspects of the city, free of charge, as well as information on sightseeing, cultural and leisure activities.

A free one-hour film on Helsinki, three times weekly in summer (English language 3 P.M.) is shown at the Nordia cinema, Yrjönkatu and Simonkatu.

EXCURSIONS. When you've had a glimpse of Helsinki's chief attractions, you will want to visit some of the main places of interest in the immediate environs of the capital. Hvitträsk, with its lovely lake and the former studio-home of three leading Finnish architects is one suggestion. Another short excursion is to Ainola, near Järvenpää, the lovely home of Sibelius, now open to the public. The composer is buried in the grounds. Among other trips that can be made in one day, there are three you won't want to miss; to Porvoo (Borgå), to Hanko, and to Hämeenlinna, combined with Aulanko. You can travel to Porvoo by boat in 3 hours, returning by bus; or go both ways by boat.

 TRANSPORTATION. A new facility introduced in 1983 is the Helsinki Card, valid 2 days (45 Fmk) or 3 days (60 Fmk), reduction for children, and available from the Helsinki Tourist Office or Hotel Booking Service in the rail station. This entitles you to unlimited travel on city public transport, free entry to many museums, reductions on sightseeing tours and in many shops, saunas, cafés, restaurants and places of entertainment.

The first section of Helsinki's splendid new subway has recently opened; it goes from the main rail station northeast to Itäkeskus, there linking with buses to the outer suburbs. (Same fare and transfer system as tram/bus below.)

A bus or tram ride costs 4.10 Fmk (slight reduction on multi-ride tickets) allowing transfers within a one-hour period. A tourist ticket valid for 24 hours for unlimited travel costs 22 Fmk. The 3T tram, with commentary in several languages in summer, follows a figure-eight circuit right around the city center.

Regular ferries link the South and North Harbors with island sights, and there are sightseeing excursions by boat throughout summer.

Taxis charge a 9.40 Fmk minimum, and a surcharge of 3 Fmk is added after 6 P.M. and at weekends. The fare increases according to the length of the journey, the amount of luggage, and number of people. No tips are necessary or expected.

The airport is situated at Seutula, north of the city. Airline buses depart from behind the Inter-Continental Hotel, at Töölönkatu 21, but there is also a cheaper, local bus service from the railway station.

 CAMPING. Best site, both for tents and caravans, is Rastila, 13 km east of the center, open from mid-May to mid-Sept; excellent modern facilities.

 SPORTS. Helsinki has quite a bit to offer. You may swim at Uunisaari, an island opposite the residential and diplomatic district of Kaivopuisto; at the sandy beach of Hietaranta; on the island of Seurasaari (accessible on foot); at Mustikkamaa; farther out on the island of Pihlajasaari; at the Swimming Stadium; or at Kumpula open-air pool. Nearly all hotels have saunas, but also recommended and inexpensive are the saunas attached to swimming halls listed in the leaflet "Helsinki Tourist Information". There is a good 18-hole *golf* course at Tali Manor, 7 km from the city center. Other sports catered for are *tennis, riding, squash, archery, water skiing, windsurfing, flying* and *parachuting.*

In winter, you can *ski* in the heart of the city through the parks, as some Helsinki-ites do on their way to work! Or anywhere in the surrounding countryside. More specifically, Nuuksionpää, north-west of the city by bus offers good terrain or, further afield, the ridges of Hyvinkää can be reached by bus or train. Also *ice skating* at numerous public rinks in Helsinki.

 SHOPPING. Prices may not be low, but quality is high and so is the standard of design of most Finnish products. If you haven't much time to shop around, your best bet is to go to one of the big stores, of which the best known is *Stockmann's,* founded in 1862 and still going very strong. Here you may glean some idea of the craftwork for which Finland is famed. It also has an export service department to forward your goods. Helsinki's latest department store, *Aleksi 13,* Aleksanterinkatu and Mikonkatu, is very central.

Another source for discovering some of the best in Finnish design products is the permanent exhibition at the *Finnish Design Center,* Kasarmikatu 19.

Two big marketing groups with a nationwide network are SOK with their *Sokos* stores and hypermarkets, and E Marketing with their *Centrum* and *EKA-Market* (cut price) department stores.

If you are a bookworm, *Academic Book Store* is Scandinavia's biggest at Keskuskatu 1. Nearby, at Vanha Yliopilastalo (Old Students' House), entrance from Aleksanterinkatu, is another famous bookshop: *Suomalainen Kirjakauppa.*

For a selection of small shops, go to the *Station Tunnel* (linking the station with the City Center complex opposite), or *Hakaniemi Market Hall,* where 50 shops above the covered food market in Hämeentie offer interesting variety. One of Helsinki's latest attractive shopping precincts is Kaivopiha, off Mannerheimintie and linked to the railway station. A smaller one, Agora, is off Unioninkatu near the South Harbor, and others are burgeoning.

Some of the shops listed below have several branches; the main or most central addresses are given.

Ceramics and Crystal. This visit may bring to your attention the china and faience of *Arabia* (ceramics factory), one of the largest of its kind in the world, and the artists, Kaj Franck, Kyllikki Salmenhaara, Schilkin, Bryk, and Kaipiainen, who were responsible for many of its most original conceptions. The artshop is at Pohjoisesplanadi 25, which also displays Nuutajärvi glass.

Another must on Pohjoisesplanadi is *Anu Pentik,* who has her studio near the borders of Lapland and is known for her ceramics and leather goods.

Of Finnish glass, the best bears the names of Nuutajärvi, Riihimäki, or Iittala, including heavy glass pieces with flowing lines, smoke-colored sets and art crystal. Among the craftsmen who design contemporary works are Timo Sarpaneva, Tapio Wirkkala, Göran Hongell and Yrjö Rosola (his wood sculptures are also acclaimed.)

Textiles and Fashions. Hand-woven textiles, especially the classic *ryijy* rugs, are an excellent buy, and traditional patterns and weaves are sold along with those more modern in feeling. Several Finns have achieved prominence in international exhibitions, among them Dora Jung, Uhra Simberg-Ehrström, Marjatta Metsovaara, Kristi Ilvessalo and Eva Brummer. All home textiles, particularly the richly figured wall hangings, may be recommended.

Try *Neovius* at Olavinkatu 1 for a wonderful selection of *ryijy* rugs.

Marimekko, with several branches, designs and makes ladies' and children's clothes of heavy cotton material printed in rich colors. The main shop is at Pohjoisesplanadi 31; almost next door is another well-known name in Finnish fashion: *Vuokko Fabrics* at No. 25.

To the list above must be added *Vokki-Virkki,* Merikannontie 3; *Poppana,* Liisankatu 19; (fine wool fashions) *Arola,* Kalevankatu 4; (hand-knitted goods) *Kapteenska,* Fabianinkatu 4; (hand-printed cottons and silks) *Peterzens,* Korkeavuorenkatu 17. Then there's *Inva,* a very special shop at Mannerheimintie 20, where the war-crippled market their goods.

Design. Finland is young in spirit: modern architecture seems to grow naturally out of such soil. So it is hardly surprising to find extraordinarily fine designs in all fields of industrial art. *Artek,* at Keskuskatu 3, specialize in the wonderfully different furniture of Alvar Aalto, famous for his use of plywood.

Other specialists in new Finnish furniture are *Bitco,* Kluuvikatu 1, and *Haimi,* Eerikinkatu 11. Also for design ware, try *Rake,* Bulevardi 2, and *Tallberg* in Aleksanterinkatu 21.

The *Aarikka* boutiques at Pohjoisesplanadi 27 and Eteläesplanadi 8 concentrate on artist Kaija Aarikka's wooden buttons and costume jewelry, as well as textiles and silver designed by her.

Jewelry. Most unusual ornaments in bronze, silver or gold are the so-called Kalevala brooches. These have been fashioned in the traditional motifs handed down through the centuries from the time of the *Kalevala,* the national epic saga that has inspired much of Finnish art.

Try *Kalevala Koru* and *Lahjavakka* at Unioninkatu 25, pioneers in modern jewelry using Finnish precious stones and with typical handicrafts.

For truly handsome modern jewelry, visit the *Galerie Björn Weckström,* Unioninkatu 30, or *Lindroos,* Aleksanterinkatu 48.

Miscellany. Some other purely Finnish items may also interest you as gifts to take home or to use during your trip. One is a pair of warm reindeer slippers, skillfully sewn. Another is the native sheath knife (called *puukko*), its enameled handle gilded with special patterns. For Finnish candles in all their glorious colors, go to *Desico,* Tehtaankatu 5 or *Kynttilapaja Haaranen,* Uudenmaankatu 42. There's all a sauna needs at the *Sauna Shop,* Mannerheimintie 22–24.

Furs and Sporting Goods. You'll want to investigate furs in Helsinki. Perhaps a scarf or cape, or merely the pelts, will appeal to you more than the full-length fashions. Try *Turkistuottajat,* who have an auction at Martinkyläntie 40 (in the suburb of Vantaa); *Ali Fur,* Erottaja 1–3; *Polar Turkis,* Yrjönkatu 1; or *Fur-Lyx,* Eteläesplanadi 22; Grunstein, Iso Roobertinkatu 20–22; *Rahikainen,* Kasarmikatu 48.

In the sports line is *Renlund,* Mikonkatu 7 and *Tallberg,* Aleksanterinkatu 21. Since the Finns themselves are keen on athletic activity, you are assured of finding equipment ideally adapted to local conditions. Cross-country ski equipment is very reasonable.

 CLOSING TIMES. Normal Helsinki shop hours are 8.30 A.M.-5 P.M. Mondays to Fridays, 8.30 A.M. - 2 P.M. on Saturdays. In Helsinki, department stores are also open to 8 P.M. on Mondays and Fridays. Shops on the railway station are also open in the evening, and the very wide variety of shops situated in the Station Tunnel (an underground passageway linking the station with the City Center complex opposite) are open from 10 A.M.-10 P.M. on weekdays, 12–10 P.M. on Sundays. These include a good selection of those souvenirs you forgot to buy during the day.

THE SOUTH COAST

The Cradle of Finnish Culture

Anyone with a weakness for islands will find a magic world of them stretching along Finland's coastline. There, in the Gulf of Finland and the Baltic, over 30,000 islands form a magnificent archipelago. Westward from Turku ride the rugged but fascinating Åland Islands group, forming a province of their own. Turku, the former capital, was also the main gateway through which cultural influences reached Finland over the centuries. The coastal district of Porvoo, east of Helsinki, is another area stuffed with history and cultural associations.

In this section, where two place names are given for a center, the second is the Swedish one and it indicates that there is a substantial Swedish-speaking element in the population. An exception is the Åland archipelago, where the population is entirely Swedish-speaking and therefore preference has been given to Swedish names.

Exploring the South Coast

Thirty-one miles east of Helsinki and on the coast lies Porvoo (Borgå), one of the oldest towns in Finland. It was only Helsinki's privileged position, plus the usual run of fires and wars, that kept Porvoo from growing into a great port. The major landmark of Porvoo Cathedral dates from the 15th century and it is famous as the setting for the first meeting of the Finnish Diet, called by Czar Alexander I in 1809, at which he proclaimed Finland an autonomous Grand Duchy. Today it is thought of as a town of poets and painters, for it has been the home of many of Finland's most famous names in the realm of arts and letters; the colorful wooden houses and shady alleys of the old district are enchanting. The greatest of Porvoo's sons was J. L. Runeberg, the national poet, whose home, kept as it was when he lived in it, stands at the corner of Runeberginkatu and Aleksanterinkatu in the new part of town. Also worth seeing are the old Town Hall, now a historical museum, and the Ville Vallgren Museum housed in typical 18th-century buildings.

Loviisa comes next, a rather charming summer resort; a special feature is its open-air theater with revolving auditorium, on a smaller scale to the famous one at Tampere.

Farther east are the two islands of Kotka and Hovinsaari, at the mouth of the Kymi river. Kotka was practically unknown until the naval battles of Ruotsinsalmi fought off its shore in 1789 and 1790 revealed its suitability as a harbor. (There is an open-air museum to the battle on Varissaari (Fort Elisabeth) reached by boat.) The Russians also saw the Kotka area as an excellent place to build frontier fortifications against attacks by land or sea from the west. Work on the fortifications was begun in 1791, and at the same time the fortress of Kyminlinna was built on the northern end of Hovinsaari. In 1855, during the Crimean War, a British naval force bombarded the island, landed on the shore, and fortifications and garrison buildings were destroyed. Ten years later, thriving sawmill industry brought it back to life, and today Kotka is Finland's largest export harbor for timber.

West of Helsinki

Hvitträsk, 28 km west of Helsinki, was the home of famous Finnish architects Eliel Saarinen, Armas Lindgren and Herman Gesellius. Today it is a museum, with an excellent restaurant attached, beautifully situated above Hvitträsk lake. There are Stone Age traces in the vicinity.

Next comes Tammisaari (Ekenäs). Predominantly Swedish-speaking, Tammisaari has little of historical interest, although like most towns along Finland's south coast, it, too, can produce a cannon ball that was fired at it by the British fleet during the time of the Crimean War. But it is a pretty town, with narrow old streets, and the drive to it from the capital is a pleasant one. The forests here are more of the broad-leaved variety, as opposed to the vast majority of Finland's forests, which are of pine and fir. Tammisaari also goes in for the cultivation of what the foresters term exotic plants and trees, and it is interesting to find oak trees here, some of the very few in Finland. An excursion from Tammisaari is to the ruins of medieval Raasepori (Raseborg) Castle, about 10 miles east.

An hour's drive farther to the west is the popular seaside resort of Hanko (Hangö), with its long stretch of sandy beach. This very popular sailing center was once a major launching point for emigrants to the U.S.A., Canada and Australia.

Turku, the old Capital

Finland's oldest city, founded in the 13th century, and its capital until 1812, Turku is situated on both banks of the Aura river. With a population of 165,000, it is the country's third largest city and is sometimes called "the cradle of Finnish culture". Commercially its great importance lies in the fact that its harbor is the most easily kept open throughout the winter. In fact, the very word, *turku*, means trading post. It is also widely known for its shipyards. It has both Finnish and Swedish Universities, the new buildings of the Finnish one being well worth a visit.

Called Åbo by the Swedish-speaking Finns, Turku is the center of the southwest part of the country, whose land is fertile and winters are milder. With a cathedral over 700 years old, the city is still the seat of the Archbishop of Finland. Although gutted by fire in 1827, the cathedral has been completely restored. In the choir can be seen R. W. Ekman's frescos portraying Bishop Henry (an Englishman) baptizing the heathen Finns, and Mikael Agricola offering the Finnish translation of the New Testament to Gustav Vasa of Sweden.

Where the Aura river flows into the sea stands Turku Castle, the city's second most important historical monument. The oldest part of the fortress was built at the end of the 13th century, whereas the newer part dates back to the 16th century. Once a prison, it has been attractively restored and contains today the Historical Museum, with collections of furniture, portraits, arms and implements covering 400 years.

Among the unusual features of Turku is the Handicraft Museum. A group of wooden houses that survived the 1827 fire, it contains over a score of small shops of that period. The comb-maker, the weaver, and the potter still ply their trades using equipment and techniques that date back a century and a half. In summer, visitors may also try their hand under expert guidance. Notable, too, is the Resurrection Chapel, one of the outstanding creations of modern Finnish architecture. Also well worth visiting in Turku are the Sibelius Museum and the rather new Wäinö Aaltonen Museum, the latter devoted to the works of Finland's great sculptor and additionally featuring changing exhibitions of contemporary art. Another recent addition to the banks of the River Aura is the striking modern theater.

Besides several old churches erected during the Middle Ages not far outside the city, there is the Ruissalo National Park, located on an island though accessible by road; it has the largest oak woods in the country. There is also a pleasant sandy beach, modern accommodations and good sports facilities.

But one of the greatest attractions in the vicinity of Turku is the beach at the coastal resort of Naantali (Nådendal), where the President of Finland has his summer residence. Finland's oldest known author, Jöns Budde, was a monk in the 15th-century monastery whose chapel now serves as the church. There are water-bus trips on certain summer evenings from Turku to Naantali. Other good excursions from Turku include: a watercoach trip along the Archipelago Route from Turku to Uusikaupunki, taking 6 hours each way; and the Tour of Seven

Churches which lasts 6 hours, covering some of the delightful medieval churches of the area.

From Turku there are air and sea connections to the Åland (Ahvenanmaa) islands, where rural calm combines with fine coastal scenery. In all, there are over 6,500 islands and skerries, a handful of them inhabited by a total population of 22,000. Virtually all of them are Swedish-speaking and the Ålanders are very proud of their largely autonomous status. Nearly half the population lives in the pleasant little capital of Mariehamn (Maarianhamina) which straddles a narrow peninsula, its two harbors linked by the shady main avenues of Norra Esplanadgatan and Storagatan. The Maritime Museum near the main harbor is well worth visiting for the islands have a very long seafaring tradition; nearby is the splendid four-masted barque *Pommern*.

Åland is particularly well organized for cycling and fishing packages, motor tours (you can go island-hopping on the network of car or passenger ferries), farmhouse holidays and self-catering cottages—2,000 of them scattered about the islands. These are marvelous sailing waters though, as yet, only a few yachts are available for rent.

There is much of historic interest for the archipelago has been inhabited since prehistoric times. Some of the medieval stone churches on the islands are particularly well preserved, notably those of Jomala (7 km north of Mariehamn), Finström (25 km north), Hammarland (21 km northwest), Eckerö (37 km northwest), Sund (25 km northeast) and Lemland (13 km southeast). Also of interest are the scattered ruins of a big naval fortress built by the Russians in the early 19th century and only half completed when it was blasted out of existence by Anglo-French forces during the Crimean War in 1854. These are at Bomarsund, about 35 km northeast of Mariehamn and, only 10 km away, is Kastelholm Castle built by the Swedes in the 14th century, though considerably damaged. The castle is currently being completely restored, a process which will take several years though parts of it, including the museum, can be visited. Very close is the excellent open-air museum of Jan Karlsgården, a collection of farm buildings from the mid-19th century. In the vicinity is a new golf course. In prehistoric times, the Åland isles were—relatively speaking—heavily populated, as shown by traces of no less than 10,000 settlements, graves and strongholds from antiquity, though they are mostly difficult to find. One of the largest Viking cemeteries is near the 13th century ruins of Lemböte chapel in the parish of Lemland.

PRACTICAL INFORMATION FOR THE SOUTH COAST

WHEN TO COME. With its appeal for water sports enthusiasts, summer is the time, with July being the busiest month.

WHAT TO SEE. The islands; Turku with its ancient cathedral, castle, folk museum and contrasting modernities, and several medieval country churches in the area; the medieval cloister church, the summer residence of the President of Finland at Naantali; pretty, old-world Porvoo; the combination of rural calm, nautical pleasures and little old churches on the Åland islands.

Hanko and Tammisaari are main seaside centers on the south coast, but the whole coast is unspoilt and offers wonderful bathing, especially off rocks. For an off-beat holiday, Kaunissaari (see Kotka) is delightful, traffic-free and has some gorgeous sandy beaches.

HOW TO GET ABOUT. Helsinki is linked eastwards to Porvoo by boat and bus, and further east by bus (rail routes are a bit long-winded); westwards to Turku by air, bus and rail, and thence by boat and air to Mariehamn in the Åland islands. Also several shipping services from the southwest coast to the Åland islands, and daily sea and air services between Turku and Stockholm. Islands near Helsinki are reached by ferry from the South Harbor, opposite the Empress Stone and from the North Harbor behind the City Guard House, near the President's Palace. Many of the islands off Turku near the mainland are linked by bridges and causeways and may be reached directly by road.

HOTELS AND RESTAURANTS. Unless otherwise stated, all the hotels listed below are open all the year, have licensed restaurants and can offer some or all rooms with bath or shower. As in Helsinki, most hotel restaurants in the (E) and (M) categories have music and dancing on some or all evenings, and many in these categories offer roulette, with maximum stakes of 5 Fmk. The majority of establishments also have sauna baths. Otherwise, special facilities, such as nightclubs or sports amenities, have been indicated for each hotel. In addition to those having swimming pools, many hotels in lake or coastal areas are situated near the shore. The price categories (E), (M) and (I) are explained in the section "Practical Information for Finland", as are the same categories for those non-hotel restaurants listed separately under larger centers. In the latter case, (I) restaurants are usually licensed for beer and wine only.

The development of holiday villages and other forms of self-catering accommodation has been widespread over recent years, and addresses for further information on these are given under "Useful Addresses" at the end of this section.

HAMINA. Near Kotka. *Seurahuone* (upper M), 12 rooms; *Hamina* (M), 11 rooms without bath or shower.

HANKO (HANGÖ). Bathing and sailing resort. *Regatta* (upper M), 33 rooms.

Restaurant: *Casino* (E), traditional style, summer only.

KOTKA. Major seaport with nearby bathing. *Seurahuone* (M range), 50 rooms, disco; *Kymen Motelli* (upper M), 104 rooms, pool; *Ruotsinsalmi* (M), 24 rooms; *Koskisoppi,* summer hotel (M), 75 rooms.

Restaurants: *Itämeri* (E); *Kotkan Klubi* (E); *Fennia* (M); *Meriniemi,* summer only (M); *Mesikämmen* (M); *Puistogrilli* (I).

One hour by motorboat away is lovely Kaunissaari island with rooms (I) in fishermen's houses and meals available at *Kaunissaari restaurant.*

LOHJA. Small inland town, west of Helsinki. *Laurinportti* (M-I), 16 rooms.

LOVIISA (LOVISA). South coast town. *Skandinavia* (M), 21 rooms, pool; *Zilton* (M), 12 rooms.

MARIEHAMN (MAARIANHAMINA). Cozy capital of the Åland islands. *Arkipelag* (E-M), 86 rooms, pools, nightclub, disco; *Adlon* (E), 54 rooms, pool; *Cikada* (E-M), 60 rooms, unlicensed restaurant, pool; *Passat* (upper M), modern apartments with kitchen, no restaurant, pool, opposite *Pommern* (M range), 45 rooms, cafeteria; *Park* (M range), 47 rooms, pool; *Savoy* (E), 45 rooms, unlicensed restaurant, pool; *Esplanad* (M-I), 28 rooms, summer only. Also several boarding houses (M-I), offering half board.

Restaurants with dancing at several of the hotels and also at the *Sabina* (E); disco *Galleri* near Arkipelag hotel.

NAANTALI. Attractive small coastal town, near Turku. *Kultainen Aurinko* (M), 29 rooms, pool.

Restaurants: *Kaivohuone,* summer only (E); *Tavastin Kilta* (E); *Merenrantaravintola,* summer only (M).

PARAINEN (PARGAS). Small coastal tourist center, near Turku. *Airisto Congress and Tourist Center* (M-I), 50 rooms, sports facilities, summer only.

PORVOO (BORGÅ). Delightful old coastal town, east of Helsinki. *Seurahovi* (E), 32 rooms. A few miles southwest of town in lovely seashore setting, *Haikko Manor Hotel and Congress Center* (E), 138 rooms in converted old manor house, superbly furnished, pools, extensive sports facilities, health treatment, disco.

Restaurant: *Wanha Laamanni* (E). New restaurant near the center of town, 18th-century décor, excellent food: highly recommended.

SALO. Small inland town between Turku and Helsinki. *Kaupunginhotelli* (M), 35 rooms, disco, sports facilities.

TAMMISAARI (EKENÄS). Attractive south coast center. *Marine* (M-I), 24 rooms, cafeteria.

Restaurants: *Knipan,* summer only, on the water (E); Gnägget (M), cozy "stable" atmosphere; *Lindholms* (M); *Svenska Klubben* (M).

TURKU (ABO). Major sea port and interesting former capital of Finland. *Rantasipi Turku Congress Center* (E), Pispalantie 7, newest, 150 rooms, pools, disco; *Marina Palace* (E), Linnankatu 32, attractive riverside position, 188 rooms, pool, nightclub; *Hamburger Bors* (E), Kauppiaskatu 6, recently renovated, 160 rooms, pool, nightclub, popular beer garden; *Maakunta* (E), Humalistonkatu 7, 159 rooms, disco; *Seurahuone* (E), Humalistonkatu 2, 63 rooms, night club; *Henrik* (M); Yliopistonkatu 29a, 77 rooms, unlicensed restaurant; *Turku* (upper M), Eerikinkatu 30, 36 rooms; *Ikituuri Summer Hotel* (I), Pispalantie 7, 600 rooms in modern student complex, pools, disco; *Domus Aboensis* (I), Piispankatu 10, 72 rooms, summer hotel, cafeteria only.

About 5 km out of town in lovely park-like setting, *Rantasipi Ruissalo* (E), 136 rooms, pool, sports facilities including golf, disco.

Restaurants: *Brahen Kellari* (E), Puolalankatu 1; *Pietari* (E), Brahenkatu 1; *Samppalinna* (E), Samppalinnanpuisto, summer only; *Le Pirate* (E-M), Läntinen Rantakatu, on a boat in the river; *Turku Castle Restaurant* (E); *Hämeenportti* (M), Hämeenkatu 7; *Jarrita* (M), Martinkatu 1, Spanish décor and food (also Finnish), intimate atmosphere; *Pinella* (M), Porthanin puisto, traditional style, good atmosphere, openair section in summer; *Pippurimylly* (M), Stålarminkatu 2; *Kultainen Hirvi* (I), It. Pitkäkatu 12–14; *Hiivari* (I), Rauhankatu 10; *Tammio* (I), Konstansankatu 4.

SPORTS. Åland islands, Naantali, Hanko and Kaunissaari island are popular seaside spots. There is good swimming and fishing throughout the archipelagos, and sailing especially in the Åland islands, in the Turku area and at Hanko. Water-skiing is practised at Hanko, Lohja, Mariehamn, Naantali and Turku, and windsurfing facilities are increasing; riding at Hamina, Hanko, Kotka, Lohja, Loviisa, Mariehamn, Porvoo, Tammisaari and Turku; and a golf course in Åland and near Turku. Cycle hire and cycling routes are organized in the Åland islands and in the Tammisaari-Hanko areas.

USEFUL ADDRESSES. Tourist information Hanko: Bulevarden 15; Kotka: Keskuskatu 13; Lohja: Laurinkatu 37–39; Loviisa: Brandensteinsgatan; Mariehamn: Norra Espalanadgatan 1; Naantali: Tuulensuunkatu 19; Porvoo: Rauhankatu 20; Tammisaari: Skillnadsgatan 16; Turku: Käsityöläiskatu 4.

Holiday villages (for the Åland islands): Ålands Turistförening, Norra Esplanadgatan 1, Mariehamn and Sand-Strands Turistbyrå, Torggatan 15, Mariehamn; (for the Hanko district): Turistföreningen Sydväst, Skillnadsgatan 16, Tammissari; (for the Turku area): Varsinais-Suomi Travel Association, L. Rantakatu 13, Turku,

There are one or more **travel agencies** in most centers, and **youth hostels** and **campsites** throughout the area.

THE CENTRAL PROVINCES

Way of Poets and Pioneers

Romanticists sometimes speak of "the land of a thousand lakes", but they don't even come close. Actually there are something like 60,000 of them, or nearly a tenth of the Finnish countryside. Almost all the rest of the land is covered with forests. In the midst of all this, the Finns have somehow managed to find space for their cities, homes and farms. Yet though they have built well and solidly, though they have bent the land to their will, Nature is still triumphant. And indeed the magnificent and sometimes wild country Finland possesses is perhaps its most notable attraction. As you sit by your train or bus window, you will at times be startled by the variety of scenery which passes in review. At other times the face of the country will seem the same. But no matter where you travel, you will feel overwhelmed by the beauty and magnitude of the natural surroundings.

Since one of the greatest attractions this nation offers the visitor is the opportunity to come really close to nature, you would be wise to allow a little time to savor the true delight of life outdoors. If you have but a few hours to spare, slip away from your hotel and just walk around.

Exploring the Central Provinces

If you only have time for a brief trip into the Finnish countryside, you could do far worse than head for Aulanko. In the middle of a national park of great natural beauty, Hotel Aulanko is one of Finland's showpieces. Here you can indulge your athletic whims, wander through the spacious park, or swim in the lake nearby. An observation tower in the grounds provides a magnificent and extensive view.

There are a number of sights to be seen in the vicinity. The town of Hämeenlinna, the birthplace of Jean Sibelius, boasts a castle, the oldest part of which probably dates from the crusades which Birger Jarl led into Finland in 1249. Six miles away on the road to Tampere is Hattula Church, built of stone about the year 1250. The few remaining old country churches in Finland are well worth visiting because of their unique interior decoration, dominated by paintings covering the walls and ceilings. Artists of those days had a firm belief in all the horrors of hell fire, and spared no pains in depicting their beliefs with the brush. Hattula Church has some fine wood carvings.

Even closer to Helsinki is Hyvinkää, with its forested ridges, and one of Finland's most fascinating museums, the Railway Museum which dates back to the 1870s. Among the exhibits are the two Imperial carriages used by the Russian czar.

Tampere, the Weaving Wonderland

Almost every book, pamphlet, brochure, and guide will inform you that Tampere, the country's second largest city, is Finland's Manchester. Many of these sources omit mention of the fact that this city combines industry with some very beautiful scenery. In fact, Tampere bears little resemblance to Manchester's gloom.

From about the year 1000, this part of Finland was a base from which traders and hunters set out on their expeditions to northern Finland and even to Lapland. But it was not until 1779 that a Swedish king actually founded the town of Tampere. Some 41 years later a Scotsman by the name of James Finlayson came to the infant city and established a factory for spinning cotton. This was perhaps the beginning of "big business" in Finland. The firm of Finlayson exists today and is still one of the country's leading industrial enterprises.

Artful location is the secret of Tampere's 400 factories. An isthmus less than a mile wide at its narrowest point separates the lakes Näsijärvi and Pyhäjärvi, and at one spot the Tammerkoski Rapids provide an outlet for the waters of one to cascade through to the other. Called the "Mother of Tampere", these rapids provide the power on which the town's livelihood depends. Their natural beauty has been preserved in spite of the factories on either bank, and the well-designed public buildings of the city grouped around them enhance their general effect. Also in the heart of town is Hämeensilta bridge with its four statues by the well-known sculptor Wäinö Aaltonen.

The high ridge of Pyynikki forms a natural park near the center of town, and on its top is an outlook tower commanding a view of the surrounding countryside. Not far away, the even higher, modern observation tower of Näsineula soars above the lake, forest and town, topped by a revolving restaurant. The same building houses the first planetarium in Scandinavia and a well-planned aquarium. From these towers you can fully appreciate the truly amazing contrasts between the industry humming at your feet and the quiet lakes stretching out to meet the horizon. At one moment you are in the midst of a busy city, at the next you are confronted with a seeming wilderness. At the foot of this Pyynikki Ridge is the Pyynikki Open Air Theater with its revolving auditorium which can be moved even with a full load of spectators to face any one of the sets, ready prepared by nature.

A number of museums include a pleasantly-situated provincial museum, a good art gallery, the charming Haihara Doll Museum just outside town, and the Lenin Museum (it was in Tampere that Lenin and Stalin first met in 1905!). Most of the buildings in Tampere itself, including the cathedral, are comparatively modern. The latter was completed in 1907, but it houses some of the best known masterpieces of Finnish art, including Magnus Enckell's fresco, *The Resurrection*, and two works by Hugo Simberg, *Wounded Angel* and *Garden of Death*. Another modern building is the startling Kaleva Church, which was designed by Reima and Raili Pietilä. Just outside of town, there are one or two fine 15th-century characteristic small stone churches.

The "Poets' Way" boat tour along Lake Näsijärvi, north of Tampere, passes through the agricultural parish of Ruovesi where J. L. Runeberg, Finland's national poet, used to live. At Petoniemi Mansion he collected the material for his famous *Tales of Ensign Stål*. Not far away, artist Akseli Gallen-Kallela built himself a castle-like building in Kalevalan style. Shortly before the boat docks at Virrat you pass through the straits of Visuvesi, a place where many artists and writers today spend their summers. Not far north of Virrat is Ähtäri where Finland's first wildlife park has been established in a beautiful setting, with a holiday village, a good hotel and recreation facilities.

The center of a region considered by some to be even more beautiful than the "Poets' Way", Kangasala, southeast of Tampere, was immortalized in Z. Topelius' poem, *A Summer Day at Kangasala*. (The poem has been set to music and is one of the loveliest of many haunting Finnish songs.) It lies on one of the routes of the Finnish Silver Line, through Lakes Roine and Vanajavesi to Aulanko and Hämeenlinna.

Along the way, the modern water bus passes by Valkeakoski, a town typical of the many Finnish industrial communities which are set in idyllic surroundings. Here a plant of the great United Paper Mills combine provides practically the only livelihood. Here and there across the country, sometimes in the middle of a forest, but always on a waterway, you will find similar towns. Each has a factory and an old church, and around these two poles cluster the mill employees' dwellings. The factory provides recreation grounds, clubhouses, indoor tennis courts and gymnasiums, and supplies fresh vegetables from the firm's greenhouses all through the winter. Other places of interest along the Silver Line route include the Iittala glass factory and museum, and the home and studio of the sculptor Emil Wikström.

Lahti, Gateway to Central Finland

Let's look now at the center of the country, starting with a short trip to the modern town of Lahti. Located at the southern end of one of Finland's largest lake systems, Vesijärvi-Päijänne, this community is now the sixth biggest town in the country, with rapidly expanding industries. Its proudest possessions are the City Hall, designed by Eliel Saarinen, a model secondary school, a modern concert hall, and the ski jump. The town is also noted for the nearby athletic academy of Vierumäki, possessing an international reputation and an unsurpassed location.

Lahti is better known, however, for winter sports. Good enough, in fact, to have been selected for the 1958 World Ski Championships. In general, Finland is comparatively flat, but running across the country is the very prominent Salpausselkä Ridge formed during the Glacial Age. Where this crosses the town boundaries, it has given its name to winter games which attract thousands of Finns and many foreigners every March.

At the northern end of Lake Päijänne lies Jyväskylä. Known as a cultural center and containing a high school of pedagogy, Jyväskylä was the first to establish a secondary school that used Finnish as the language of instruction and now has its own university. This brings up an interesting point. The schools of Finland may conduct their classes in either Finnish or Swedish, both of which share equal status guaranteed by law. Whichever school a child attends, he must learn the second official language of the country in addition to any other foreign tongues, included in the syllabus. Today, English is the most popular, and in many schools, is compulsory. German or French ranks next. Like the inhabitants of all small nations, the unfortunate Finns have to spend a lot of time learning to decline and conjugate. Not far from Jyväskylä is Säynätsalo with its well-known civic center designed by Aalto.

Jyväskylä is also an important woodworking center for it is right in the forested heart of Finland. The whole region and Viitasaari to the north is being developed as a holiday area. Delightful holiday villages in log cabin style have been built in several places. The idea is to provide accommodation for 10,000 in the area over the years, and if this sounds a lot you must remember that this is a vast region, deeply forested and lake-strewn. The holiday villages offer sports facilities as well—and also a good opportunity to probe deep into Finland's "off-the-beaten-track". Jyväskylä's annual Arts Festival in summer has become a major event, and the town is also important as a starting point for the boat trip down Lake Päijänne, the second largest in Finland. During the early part of the journey south to Lahti, the scenery is wildly beautiful, with forest-covered ridges and completely uninhabited rocky shores. The landscape grows milder and more serene as you travel south, and numerous villas are scattered along the banks or built on the many islands that cut up the lake throughout its 70-mile length.

Should you weary during your tour, there are cabins available where you may lie down and take a short nap. Simple but wholesome food is served on all the boats, which are also licensed for beer and wine. A hydrofoil service covers the same trip in three hours instead of nine, but it is naturally not so tranquil. If you're traveling between Lahti and Jyväskylä by car, the eastern route is the more beautiful and takes you through Sysmä, near which is the delightful Suvi-Pinx open-air art exhibition (summer only) in a beautiful forest setting. It has a restaurant and amusements for children.

Saimaa Lake District

Now that we have explored some of the more interesting parts of central Finland, let's move on eastwards to the region known as the Saimaa Lake system. It is in this area that many of the most beautiful places in the country are concentrated, and it is here that some of the most interesting pages of Finnish history have been written. It might be a good idea to adopt Savonlinna as your new headquarters. It is an attractive lakeside resort also noted as a watering place and is a terminus of the Saimaa lake steamers. The healing baths are to be found in the Casino Park. The latter is on one of the many islands, all linked by bridges, which, together with a cape jutting out into the lake, constitute the town of Savonlinna. Besides its location and its baths, Savonlinna's outstanding attraction is the fortress of Olavinlinna, Finland's finest medieval castle and one of the best-preserved historical monuments in Scandinavia. Still surrounded by the water that formed such an essential part of its defensive strength centuries ago, it is in the eastern part of the old section of town.

A Danish-born knight built this fortress with the object of providing a bastion for the eastern frontier of the then kingdom of Sweden-Finland to assist in repulsing attacks and invasions from the east. Apart from the important role it played in the wars of those days, Olavinlinna Castle helped to protect and support the Finnish colonists who began to develop the land for several miles around. During the numerous wars of the 18th century it changed hands repeatedly, but it lost its military significance when Finland became a Grand Duchy of Russia. The fortress is open from 8.30 to 6 in summer, 10 to 3 in winter.

In recent years the main courtyard has been the setting for operatic and theatrical performances, and an Opera Festival is held here lasting three weeks in July. From mid-June onwards there also occur other events such as the annual Operatic Course, Savonlinna Music Days and a Music Summer Seminar, so the town becomes a veritable musical mecca for a month or so each summer. Arts and crafts are also strongly featured in studios and exhibitions around town in summer, including a special Opexpo near the castle during the festival.

Of special interest, too, is the *Salama,* a steam schooner, built in 1874, shipwrecked in 1898 and raised from the lake in 1971. Very well preserved, she has been turned into a museum showing the history and development of lake traffic, including the fascinating floating timber trains which are still a common summer sight on Saimaa today.

Until recently Savonlinna was the central hub of a network of regular lake traffic leaving for and arriving from the four points of the Saimaa compass each morning and evening. Some of these regular schedules have been replaced by sightseeing cruises, but the quaysides of Savonlinna still present a lively scene with the daily to-ing and fro-ing of these venerable vessels.

A short distance from Savonlinna is the famous ridge of Punkaharju; five miles long, it rises between the lakes and at some points is no more than 25 feet wide though it manages to accommodate both a road and railway. A leisure and art center has been created in this area. Nearby, Punkaharju's National Hotel, originally built in 1845 as a gamekeeper's lodge by Czar Nicholas I and subsequently enlarged, has been restored as a restful oasis in which to stay or simply enjoy a meal. At Kerimäki, 23 km east of Savonlinna, is the world's largest wooden church from the 1840s, holding 5,000 people. Both areas offer good and expanding water sports facilities, and some particularly well equipped camp sites and holiday villages.

You can either continue farther to the north, or start your return, still a leisurely one, towards the capital, and in most directions you can still travel by boat. Helsinki-bound, the steamer runs through the Saimaa lake system to Lappeenranta. This is a lively resort and town on the southern shores of Saimaa and, from here, trips are available on the Saimaa Canal, re-opened a few years ago. The canal crosses into the Soviet Union to Viipuri (Viborg), but for the moment this route, which leads eventually to Leningrad via the Gulf of Finland, is not open to non-Scandinavian visitors. The old fortress area of Lappeenranta is of particular interest. A half-hour drive from here is Imatra whose magnificent rapids, tamed and diverted to help power the considerable local industry, are released as a tourist attraction on certain Sundays each summer. Other possibilities from Savonlinna are to take a ship in the opposite direction northwest to Kuopio, or train or bus northeast to Joensuu. These routes pick their way through or beside an amazingly long and immensely intricate system of lakes, canals and narrow channels, all part of the Saimaa network, Finland's largest lake system.

Joensuu and Koli

Joensuu is the only town of any size in the vast area known as North Karelia. Its chief claim to distinction is a town hall which, like the one at Lahti, was designed by Eliel Saarinen. Our objective, however, is Koli on the western shore of Lake Pielinen (Pielisjärvi), nearly 40 miles due north of Joensuu. By boat, three times a week, the journey takes a leisurely six to seven hours, but you can also go by train to Vuonislahti, on the lake's eastern shore, and take a motorboat across to Koli. Alternatively, there is a bus service from Joensuu to Koli.

As we mentioned earlier, Finland is relatively flat; thus, in comparison with the hills found in most parts of the country, Koli is considered a mountain. This is its great appeal. From the rocky summit of Ukko-Koli more than a thousand feet up, there are some of the most magnificent views to be found anywhere. There is a recently modernized tourist hotel near the hill top and holiday villages on the lake shore.

Much has been done for the visitor to Koli in the way of well-marked footpaths and tracks for the hiker and other facilities. On the Pielisjoki river the canoeing is excellent. But it is for winter sports that this region is particularly noted.

Kuopio

From Kuopio there are almost daily monastery cruises to the Orthodox convent of Lintula and monastery of Uusi-Valamo, which removed to these remote parts from Lake Ladoga when that region of Karelia was ceded to Russia. Kuopio itself is an interesting town and excellent ski center. It has an Orthodox as well as a Lutheran Cathedral. Housed in a modern building on the outskirts of town is a museum whose collections from Orthodox Karelia must be unique in the western world. Kuopio's market place is a colorful spot. The slender tower on Puijo hill offers superb views—and a revolving restaurant.

Farther north still, you come into the wilderness landscapes of Kainuu, with Kajaani as the main (and only!) town. It has 17th-century castle ruins and a town hall designed by Engel; but the region's chief claims for attention are its scenery and amenities for outdoor activities —especially for enthusiasts of fishing or canoeing or, in winter, cross-country skiing.

PRACTICAL INFORMATION FOR THE CENTRAL
PROVINCES

 WHEN TO COME. The interior of Finland can be seen to advantage any time from May to September, but the best season for touring the Lake District is from the beginning of June to the end of August, when delightful cruises can be made through the labyrinthine waterways. For winter sports, you should time your visit for the period from the beginning of January to the middle of March.

 WHAT TO SEE. Scenic: the lakes of Näsijärvi and Pyhäjärvi (Tampere region); Vesijärvi-Päijänne (between Lahti and Jyväskylä); the great watery labyrinth of Saimaa in the east; Lake Pielinen (north of Joensuu); Aulanko National Park, near Hämeenlinna; the rapids of Imatra; Väinölanniemi peninsula and park at Kuopio; the Koli hill district rising from immense lakescapes, north of Joensuu; the wild forestlands of central Finland, now blossoming with attractive holiday villages (main center Jyväskylä with excellent sports facilities and fine modern architecture); the wilderness country of Kainuu region surrounding Lake Oulujärvi.

Interesting buildings: Olavinlinna Fortress at Savonlinna; 13th-century Häme Castle at Hämeenlinna, and nearby Hattula Church; the 17th-century castle ruins at Kajaani; Kuopio's Orthodox Cathedral with its unique collection; ruins of the rampart and fortifications in the old section of Lappeenranta; modern Lahti, "the most American of Finnish cities"; Tampere's Art Gallery, Provincial Museum, modern aquarium and planetarium, Hämeensilta Bridge, early 20th-century cathedral, ultra modern Kaleva Church and many modern buildings. Also in Tampere, Pyynikki Park and its open air theater with unique revolving auditorium. Many modern churches, such as at Hyvinkää and Lauritsala (near Imatra).

 HOW TO GET ABOUT. The best way to see this region is to combine transport by train, plane, bus or car, and boat. A number of excursions are offered utilizing several of these services. To use Tampere (2 hours by train and 40 minutes by air from Helsinki) as a starting point: "The Poet's Way", an 8-hour boat trip along the length of Lake Näsijärvi to Virrat; "The Silver Line", an 8-hour trip by motorboat from Tampere to Aulanko and Hämeenlinna; an alternative route with a bus trip from Tampere to Kaivanto to begin with, takes 5 hours; then by train from Hämeenlinna to Helsinki (1¼ hours). Motorists can have their cars driven to the terminus while they take the lake trip, for a moderate fee.

Päijänne Lake. From Lahti (about 1½ hours by train from Helsinki), a 10½ hour steamer trip along Päijänne lake to Jyväskylä (also direct air connections with Tampere, and Helsinki). The trip between Lahti and Jyväskylä can also be made by fast hydrofoil boat in 3 hours. Regular motorboat service as well between Lahti and Heinola (4 hours).

Saimaa Lake System. There are various all-in tours combining lake with bus, rail and air travel in this region. Or you can cruise for a weekend or more, sleeping and eating on board one of the lake ships. Or stop off in port to pick up another steamer another day. Savonlinna (45 mins. by air, 6 hrs. by train from Helsinki) is at the heart of the Saimaa lake system and from here you can radiate in most directions. One attractive possibility would be by lake ship in 11 hours along Lake Haukivesi via the Heinävesi route to Lake Kallavesi and Kuopio (6 hours by rail, 40 mins. by air from Helsinki); there are rail and air connections from Kuopio to Kajaani. Cruises on the Saimaa Lake System are run by a number of firms—latest details from Finnish Tourist Board offices.

From Lappeenranta (3½ hours by rail, ½ hour by air from Helsinki), lake cruises on Saimaa including cruises to Savonlinna (8–9 hours). The Saimaa Canal (reached from Lappeenranta), now largely in Soviet territory, has been re-opened and boat trips are arranged without visa on the Finnish section; cruises through to Viborg and Leningrad are not currently available to non-Scandinavian visitors.

From Joensuu (6–7 hours by train, 40 mins. by air from Helsinki) to Vuonis-lahti by train (2½ hours), then by motorboat (50 minutes) across Lake Pielinen (Pielisjärvi) to Koli, returning to Joensuu by bus (2 hours); from there by bus to Savonlinna.

MOTORING. As a result of extensive road building schemes, main roads are comparable to those elsewhere, but it's best to avoid the secondary ones during April, October and November. However, you will encounter beautiful scenery all along the way, following these two itineraries:

Eastward to the Lake District: Depart Helsinki-Porvoo-Loviisa-Kotka-Hamina-Lappeenranta-Imatra-Punkaharju-Savonlinna-Mikkeli-Heinola-Lahti-return Helsinki. Distance, about 480 miles (763 km).

Northward via Tampere: Depart Helsinki-Hämeenlinna-Tampere-Jyväskylä-Kuopio-Kajaani-Joensuu-Savonlinna-Lahti-Helsinki. Distance about 820 miles (1,350 km).

HOTELS AND RESTAURANTS. Unless otherwise stated, all the hotels listed below are open all the year, have licensed restaurants and can offer some or all rooms with bath or shower. In most cases, hotel restaurants in the (E) and (M) categories have music and dancing on some or most evenings, and many in these categories offer roulette. The majority of establishments also have sauna baths. Otherwise, special facilities, such as nightclubs or sports amenities, have been indicated for each hotel. In addition to those having swimming pools, many hotels in the lake areas are situated near the shore. The price categories (E), (M) and (I) are explained in the section "Practical Information for Finland", as are the same categories for those non-hotel restaurants listed separately under larger centers. In the latter case, (I) restaurants are usually licensed for beer and wine only.

The development of holiday villages and other forms of self-catering accommodation has been widespread over recent years, and addresses for further information on these are given under "Useful Addresses" at the end of this section.

ÄHTÄRI. Finland's first wildlife park. *Mesikämmen* (E), 103 rooms, pool, disco, sports facilities.

HÄMEENLINNA. Sibelius' birthplace and with other cultural associations. *Cumulus* (E), 60 rooms, pool; *Vouti* (E), 41 rooms.

A short distance from town, *Rantasipi Aulanko* (E), set in beautiful park, 233 rooms, pool, extensive sports facilities including golf, nightclub. Well worth a day's visit if you can't stay longer.

Restaurants: *Linnanvouti* (E); *Kultainen Orava* (M); *Pop Hälläpyörä* (M); *Paukero* (M); *Papukaija Pub* (I).

HEINOLA. Lakeside town and resort. *Seurahuone* (M), 27 rooms, sports facilities.

HYVINKÄÄ. Small town amidst forested ridges; summer and winter resort. *Rantasipi Hyvinkää* (E), 190 rooms, pools, tennis, nightclub, disco; *Hopealyhty* (M), 27 rooms, pools.

Restaurants: *Stefan* (E); *Teho* (E); *Tinapub* (M); *Eila Airola* (I).

IISALMI. On routes north through central Finland. *Seurahuone* (E), 50 rooms; *Koljonvirta* (upper M), 44 rooms.

IMATRA. Industrial center with famous rapids. *Imatran Valtionhotelli* (E), 62 rooms, pool, disco, located by the rapids (only seen in full flood on summer Sundays); *Imatra* (E), 34 rooms, pool; *Niskahovi* (M), 50 rooms.

JOENSUU. Lake resort and industrial town. *Kimmel* (E), 129 rooms, pool, disco; *Karelia* (E), 34 rooms; *Pohjois Karjala* (M), 49 rooms; *Wanha Jokela* (I), 13 rooms; *Wiiri Summer Hotel* (I), 40 rooms without bath or shower, unlicensed cafeteria.

Restaurants: *Teatteriravintola (E); Shemeikka* (E); *Wienitär* (M); *Puikkari* (M); *Virvatuli* (I).

JYVÄSKYLÄ. University and industrial town in heart of lakes and forests. *Cumulus* (E), 200 rooms, pool; *Jyväshovi* (E), 121 rooms, pool, disco; *Raatihotelli* (E), 80 rooms, pool; *Milton* (M), 35 rooms; *Seurahuone* (M), 21 rooms; *Amis* (I), summer hotel, 92 rooms without bath or shower, unlicensed cafeteria; *Rentukka* (I), summer hotel, 136 rooms, disco.

On Laajavuori hill, just outside town, *Rantasipi Laajavuori* (E), 176 rooms, pool, extensive summer and winter sports facilities, nightclub, in particularly fine setting.

Restaurants: *Katinhäntä* (E), intimate, gracious atmosphere; *Kantakrouvi* (M); *Ilokivi* (M); *Mörssäri* (M); *Priimus* (M), good value in hotel and restaurant school; *Katrilli* (M-I), lunch only, clean, cozy; *Pikantti* (I), self-service.

KAJAANI. Interesting regional capital of Kainuu district. *Valjus* (E), 31 rooms, pool; *Vanha Välskäri* (E-M), 37 rooms, pool; *Seurahuone* (E), 34 rooms; *Kajaani* (upper M), 70 rooms, pool.

Restaurants: *Kellari-Kievari* (M), *Kuukkeli* (M); *Sampola-Kievari* (I).

KOLI. Small tourist center in beautiful, hilly lake and forest setting. *Loma-Koli Tourist Center* (M), 36 rooms, summer and winter sports facilities; *Koli* (upper M), 42 rooms, pool, splendid views.

KUHMOINEN. On main route in central Finland, *Eurooppa* 4 (M), motel, 29 rooms, sports facilities.

KUOPIO. Lake resort, ski-ing center and industrial town. *Kuopio* (E), 24 rooms; *Atlas* (E-upper M), 40 rooms; *Cumulus* (E), 134 rooms, pool; *Iso Valkeinen* (E), motel, 100 rooms, pool, sports facilities; *Puijonsarvi* (E), 61 rooms, nightclub; *Kalla* (M), 37 rooms; *Savonia Summer Hotel* (lower M), 26 rooms, pool.

Hospitsi (I), 27 rooms without bath or shower, unlicensed restaurant; *Tekma* (I), summer hotel, 78 rooms without bath or shower.

Restaurants: *Peräniemen Kasino* (E), summer only; *Puijon Torniravintola* (E), revolving restaurant on top of tower; *Henry's Pub* (M): *Kummeli* (M); *Puhvetti* (I); *Sampo* (I), fish specialties, shabby but excellent value; *Taverna Traviata* (I).

LAHTI. Lake resort, major ski-ing center and industrial town. *Lahden Seurahuone* (E), 119 rooms, pool, nightclub, long gastronomic tradition; *Valtakulma* (E), 75 rooms; *Tallukka* (E), 145 rooms, pool, boating, angling, nightclub; *Jukola* (M), 40 rooms; *Lahti* (M), 87 rooms; *Messilä Manor Hotel* (M), a few km from town, 33 rooms, pool, extensive sports facilities, arts and crafts center; *Musta Kissa* (M), 67 rooms.

Mukkulan Summer Hotel (I), outside town, 80 rooms, sports facilities.

Restaurants: *Kommodori* (E); *El Toro* (M), Spanish style and food (also Finnish); *Hoijakka* (M); *Nelonen* (M); *Taverna* (M); *Takkatupa* (I); *Tillikka* (I); *Tunneli* (I).

At *Messilä* (see Hotels), 8-course turn-of-the-century style dinners are a weekly feature.

LAPPEENRANTA. Major lake resort with some industry. *Cumulus* (E), 95 rooms, pool; *Lappeenranta* (E-M), 40 rooms, sports facilities; *Patria* (E-M), 58 rooms, disco; *Viikinkihovi* (E), 28 rooms, pool; *Hospiz* (M), 32 rooms, unlicensed restaurant; *Karelia-Park* (I), summer hotel, 120 rooms.

Restaurants: *Casa Nostra* (E), good Italian food; *Kasino* (E), traditional style, near harbor, summer only; *Kolme Lyhtyä* (M); *Willikissa* (M); *Adriano Bar* (I); *Repsikka* (I); *Sirmakka* (I).

Pappilan kahvila (I) is an attractive coffee house in the fortress area with Orthodox music and specialties.

MIKKELI. Lakeside and industrial town. *Cumulus* (E), 115 rooms, pool, new; *Rantasipi Varsavuori* (E), 98 rooms, pool, boating, angling; *Kaleva* (M), 34 rooms; *Nuijamies* (M), 40 rooms, disco; *Pillinki* (M), 13 rooms, disco; *Tekuila* (M-I), summer hotel, 69 rooms, cafeteria only.

Restaurants: *Teatteri Holvi* (E); *Kestikievari* (M); *Suur-Savo* (M); *Kahveri* (I); *Särvinsoppi* (I).

PUNKAHARJU. Ridge and beauty spot near Savonlinna. *Valtionhotelli* (National Hotel) (E-M), 31 rooms, beautifully restored 19th century building in lovely situation, sports facilities.

SAVONLINNA. Major lake resort with medieval castle. *Casino* (E), 79 rooms, pool, sports facilities, nightclub, health treatment; *Seurahuone* (E-M), 32 rooms, disco; *Tott* (E-M), 43 rooms, roof terrace restaurant, disco; *Vuorilinna* (E-M), 150 rooms, pool, sports facilities; *Kyrönsalmi* (M), 46 rooms, unlicensed cafeteria; *Malakias* (M), summer hotel, 220 rooms.

Restaurants: *Kasino* (E), turn-of-century style, summer only; *Rauhalinna* (E), charming turn-of-century castle-like villa, 16 km from town (4 km by boat); *Linnantupa* (Castle Tavern) (M), in the castle; *Majakka* (M), unpretentious but good food; *Hopeasalmi* restaurant ship (I), in the harbor; *Musta Pässi* (I) beer tavern; *Savo* (I), tavern-style (with sauna!).

SOTKAMO. In north central district of Kainuu. A few km away, *Tulikettu* (E-M), 37 rooms, pool, sports facilities. *Vuokatti Holiday and Sports Center* (M), 35 rooms without bath or shower, pool, extensive summer and winter sports facilities.

SYSMÄ. Small, inexpensive lake and forest resort. *Uoti* (M), 8 rooms; *Ilolan Kartano* (I), 27 rooms, summer weekends only, sports facilities.

TAMPERE. Finland's second city, major industrial town and lake-side center. *Cumulus* (E), newest, Koskikatu 5, 231 rooms, pool; *Grand Hotel Tammer* (E), Satakunnankatu 13, 90 rooms, pool, nightclub. *Jäähovi* (E), Sammonvaltatie 2, motel, 72 rooms, pool; *Kaupunginhotelli* (E), Hämeenkatu 11, 83 rooms; *Rosendahl* (E), Pyynikintie 13, 213 rooms, pool, sports facilities, nightclub.

Victoria (upper M), Itsenäisyydenkatu 1, 100 rooms, pool, disco; *Domus* (I), Pellervonkatu 9, summer hotel, 200 rooms, pool, disco.

Summer Hotel Rasti (I), Itsenäisyydenkatu 1, 94 rooms without bath or shower, pool, disco.

Some kilometres out of town, a new and growing holiday complex in a delightful setting includes the *Maisa* (M), 62 rooms with shower, sports facilities.

Restaurants: *Cabare Oscar* (E), Kirkkokatu 10; *Hämeensilta* (E), Hämeenkatu 13; *Laterna* (E), Puutarhakatu 11, Russian style; *Näsinneula* (E), Särkänniemi, revolving restaurant on top of great tower; *Rustholli* (E-M), Aitolahti, on lakeside 8 km from center, excellent cold table with regional specialties; *Sorsapuiston Grilli* (E), Sorsapuisto 1, excellent food including Baltic herring specialties in pleasant atmosphere; *Tiiliholvi* (E), Kauppakatu 10; *Kaijakka* (M), Laukontori; *Merirosvo* (M), Särkänniemi, splendid Baltic herring dishes; *Ohranjyvä* (M), Näsilinnankatu 15, intimate atmosphere; *Pirkanhovi* (M), Sukkavartaankatu 9.

Antika (I), Väinölänkatu 1; *Uintikeskuksen ravintola* (I), by swimming hall 2–3 km from center, home-made food, good value.

VARKAUS. Industrial and lakeside town. *Taipale* (E), 45 rooms, pool, disco; *Keskus-Hotelli* (M), 56 rooms.

Restaurants: *Kaupunginkellari* (M); *Oskar's Pub* (M); *Onni-Manni* (M).

VIITASAARI. Forest and lake center, central Finland. *Pihkuri* (M range), 24 rooms, sports facilities, disco; *Rantasipi Ruuponsaari* (M), 55 rooms, pool, sports facilities, disco.

 SPORTS. Water sports and **hiking** are the principal Lake District activities, though the increasing popularity of riding has considerably widened the possibilities of enjoying the scenery from horseback. Facilities for various sports are available as follows. **Riding** in nearly all centers. **Golf** at Hämeenlinna, Jyväskylä, Kuopio, Lahti, Lappeenranta, Mikkeli, Tampere. **Sailing:** Flotilla sailing on the Saimaa lake system is arranged by the Nautic Center, Karhusaari, Espoo 10, near Helsinki; sailing boats may also be rented in Lappeenranta. **Water skiing:** Hämeenlinna, Jyväskylä, Kajaani, Kuopio, Lappeenranta, Savonlinna, Sotkamo, Tampere. **Windsurfing:** Hämeenlinna, Imatra, Joensuu, Jyväskylä, Kajaani, Kuopio, Lahti, Lappeenranta, Lieksa, Mikkeli,

Savonlinna, Sotkamo, Tampere, Varkaus, Virrat. **Canoeing:** Hämeenlinna, Joensuu, Jyväskylä, Kajaani, Kuopio, Lahti, Lappeenranta, Lieksa, Mikkeli, Savonlinna, Sotkamo, Tampere, Varkaus. **Gliding** at Hyvinkää, Imatra, Hämeenlinna, Jyväskylä, Kajaani, Kuopio, Lahti, Lappeenranta, Mikkeli. Cycle hire and marked **cycling** routes are to be found in several areas, including Jyväskylä and Lappeenranta.

WINTER SPORTS. Cross-country skiing is the great winter pastime and, at the other end of the scale, ski jumping is very popular. The number of ski lifts has also increased in recent years. During January, skiers enjoy 6–7 hours of daylight, 9 hours in February and 12 in March. Ski instruction and the hire of equipment are available in most of the principal centers listed below.

Aulanko: wooded hills with varied terrain, ski lift, ski-joring.

Hyvinkää: ski lift, ski jumps, slalom, trails through wooded, hilly terrain.

Jyväskylä: huge ski jump, fine terrain and sports center on Laajavuori hill, ski lifts, slalom.

Kalpalinna (near Aulanko and 50 miles north of Helsinki): several ski lifts, slalom slopes.

Koli: at over 1,000 feet, with slalom track, ski lift and excellent varied terrain.

Kuopio: a popular center in hilly terrain, with ski lifts, jump and runs on 700-foot Puijo Hill.

Lahti: south Finland's top center for international events, excellent ski jumps, trails and runs in varied terrain of wooded ridges; also very good facilities at nearby Hollola.

Tampere: good cross-country terrain, ski lifts; also good facilities at Ellivuori, 20 miles to the west.

Vuokatti (reached from Kajaani): main training center for skiers, especially noted for its cross-country courses, but also with ski lifts, ski jumps, slalom slopes.

USEFUL ADDRESSES. Tourist information offices: Hämeenlinna: Raatihuoneenkatu 13: Heinola: Kauppakatu 5; Hyvinkää: Hämeenkatu 3D; Imatra: Keskusliikenneasema; Järvenpää: Mannilantie 4; Joensuu: Koskikatu 1; Jyväskylä: Vapaudenkatu 38; Kajaani: Pohjolankatu 21B; Kuopio: Haapaniemenkatu 17; Lahti: Torikatu 3B; Lappeenranta: Valtakatu 23; Mikkeli: Hallituskatu 3a; Savonlinna: Olavinkatu 35; Tampere: Aleksis Kivenkatu 14; Varkaus: Ahlströminkatu 11.

Holiday villages (for Hämeenlinna district): Kanta-Hämeen Tourist Office, Raatihuoneenkatu 13; (for the Jyväskylä district): Keski Suomi-Loma Suomi, Vapaudenkatu 38; (for Kuopio district): Kuopion Matkailupalvelu, Haapaniemenkatu 17; (for Lahti district): City Tourist Office, Town Hall; (for Lappeenranta district): Lappeenranta City Tourist Office, Valtakatu 23; (for Tampere district): Pirkanmaan Matkailuyhdistys, Aleksis Kivenkatu 14B.

Most centers have one or more **travel agencies,** and **youth hostels** and **campsites** are to be found throughout the region.

OSTROBOTHNIA

Rural Plains to Forested Ravines

The flatlands of Ostrobothnia are the least visited by tourists, with some reason since they lack that primeval wilderness quality with which so much of the rest of Finland is endowed. Yet there is quite a lot of interest, especially if you want to get to grips with Finnish history and, not least, if you have a taste for huge sandy beaches that you can enjoy with very little interference from other humanity. The coastal towns vary from charming backwaters to busy bustling places, but most of them have played their part in one way or another in shaping Finland's destiny at some time. The land itself, by the way, has noticeably risen over the centuries so that quite a few harbors are now some miles from the modern nucleus of the towns.

Much of the hinterland is agricultural and nearly all of it flat with one notable exception. That is the north-eastern part of the region, close by the Soviet border, where there is as wild and rugged an area as you could wish to meet in the vicinity of Kuusamo.

As many of the coastal towns have a substantially Swedish-speaking population, the Swedish name is also given where appropriate in this section. It is, incidentally, from this province that so many Finns have emigrated to the United States.

Coast and Plains

You may find yourself entering Ostrobothnia either from Turku to the south or from Tampere and the neighboring province of Häme to the southeast. Almost due west of Tampere on the coast is Pori, the biggest industrial town and harbor on the Gulf of Bothnia, and famous for its annual Jazz Festival. This is one of the places where the retreat of the sea is most noticeable. About twelve miles away, the long beach at Yyteri is a favorite summer resort—the sands are really superb and there are all kinds of sports facilities as well as a splendid hotel there. The old fishing communities of Reposaari, an island accessible by road, are other points of interest about 20 miles away.

Or you may come into Ostrobothnia further north, taking in on the way Finland's first wild-life park at Ähteri, due north of Tampere and on the boundary of the two provinces. Your first major coastal town then is likely to be Vaasa (Vasa) and, on the way, you will observe how the country begins to flatten out and finally becomes a succession of rolling plains. There is open country in northern Finland too, but nowhere the cultivation that can be seen here. The whole landscape takes on a new aspect, one unlike any in the other regions of Finland: even the houses are different, generally two-storied.

Vaasa is an important port, with regular passenger service across to Swedish ports. After the disastrous fire of 1852 (a few interesting buildings of Old Vaasa can still be seen) the town was moved nearer the sea and given a Russian name. During the 1918 war of independence Vaasa became the capital of "White" Finland, the country's official government having moved there from "Red" Helsinki, and to commemorate the event the city was allowed to include Finland's Cross of Liberty in its coat of arms. In fact, South Ostrobothnia seems to have taken a prominent part in Finnish politics on several occasions. Besides being the site of a Russian defeat in 1808–9, the parish of Lapua is the place where the anti-Communist Lapua Movement originated in 1930. Spreading quickly all over the country, it reached a climax in the so-called Peasants' March, when 12,000 men from all over the country gathered in the capital and forced Parliament to declare Communism illegal.

The plains of Ostrobothnia are strewn with the battlefields of one or another of the numerous wars that the Finns have fought, first against the Swedes, then against the Russians, and for a brief while even among themselves. The coastal scenery is lovely, and there is good sailing in the Gulf of Bothnia. Apart from Vaasa, there are only two other cities of any size in the province: Kokkola (Gamlakarleby) and Pietarsaari (Jakobstad), lying on the coast to the north of Vaasa. Pietarsaari is an attractive place with strong associations with the national poet Runeberg and has an active, modern trade center. Among the smaller coastal towns, Kristiinankaupunki and Uusikaarlepyy are both charming, with a good crop of ancient wooden houses. For beaches, go to Kalajoki where the sands are truly glorious and there are good amenities in the way of accommodation and sports facilities, set amidst the dunes.

Kokkola has one sight of particular interest to English visitors. On the banks of the small stream which runs through town is the English Park, and here in a small building is an English pinnace captured during the Crimean War when a landing was attempted near here in 1854. One British officer and eight seamen fell in the engagement, and they are buried in the Maaria Cemetery just outside the city. A memorial to this small battle stands on Halkokari Point in the old harbor.

Bothnian Gulf to Bear Country

Towards the top of the Gulf of Bothnia is the lively northern university town of Oulu. Originally a fur- and salmon-trading port, it became one of the major tar export harbors of the world in the last century and is today a busy industrial center. You can find out about the historic tar trade at the fascinating Turkansaari outdoor museum and try out regional specialties at the museum's cafe. Oulu's excellent modern buildings include a fine theater facing ancient warehouses by the harbor, and there are pleasant parks, a colorful market and plenty of cultural activities.

For complete contrasts with the rest of Ostrobothnia, you must turn northeast to the rugged ravines and forested hills that lie just north of Kuusamo, including the fell district of Rukatunturi and Oulanka National Park. It's an area of gorge-like valleys where you have the opportunity to experience the thrills of shooting the rapids. The fishing is particularly good in these parts, and so is the walking, with marked trails to follow such as the 80 km-long Bear's Tour. It's quite appropriately named, too, though these denizens of the wild are rarely to be seen.

PRACTICAL INFORMATION FOR
OSTROBOTHNIA

WHEN TO COME. In summer for the sightseeing or bathing pleasures of the coast. The Kuusamo and Oulanka National Park areas are popular both for summer and winter sports.

WHAT TO SEE. Scenic: the wilderness areas in the northeast near Kuusamo are the tops; the sand dunes and beaches of Yyteri, near Pori, and Kalajoki; attractive island-strewn coastal scenery around Pietarsaari and Kokkola. **Interesting buildings:** lovely old wooden houses of Kristiinankaupunki, including museum, church and customs house; museums, art collections and several buildings of Old Vaasa; old wooden houses from the 17th-18th centuries in Uusikaarlepyy; Runeberg's cottage and school in Pietarsaari, and the old parish church; English Park and its captured British vessel at Kokkola; the old market place of Kalajoki; in Pori, the strange Gothic-style mausoleum erected by a businessman for his daughter.

HOW TO GET ABOUT. The railway system sends branches to serve the coast, but bus routes are more comprehensive and give delightful glimpses of coastal and rural scenery. The area is well served by internal flights. Pietarsaari is linked by sea and Vaasa by air and sea with Swedish ports across the Gulf of Bothnia.

HOTELS AND RESTAURANTS. Unless otherwise stated, all the hotels listed below are open all the year, have licensed restaurants and can offer some or all rooms with bath or shower. In most cases, hotel restaurants in the (E) and (M) categories have music and dancing on some or most evenings, and many in these categories offer roulette. The majority of establishments also have sauna baths. Otherwise, special facilities, such as nightclubs or sports amenities, have been indicated for each hotel. In addition to those having swimming pools, many hotels in lake or coastal areas are situated near the shore. The price categories (E), (M) and (I) are explained in the section "Practical Information for Finland", as are the same categories for those non-hotel restaurants listed separately under larger centers. In the latter case (I) restaurants are usually licensed for beer and wine only.

The development of holiday villages and other forms of self-catering accommodation has been widespread over recent years, and addresses for further information on these are given under "Useful Addresses" at the end of this section.

KALAJOKI. Small bathing resort with superb sandy beaches. *Rantakalla* (M), 35 rooms, pool, good sports facilities.

KAUSTINEN. Small village best known for its annual folk festival. *Marjaana* (M), motel, 10 rooms, pool, disco.

KOKKOLA. Town near shores of Gulf of Bothnia. *Vaakuna* (E), 71 rooms, pool, nightclub, disco; *Milton* (upper M), 45 rooms; *Grand Hotel* (M), 42 rooms, unlicensed restaurant, extensive sports facilities; *Seurahuone* (M), 62 rooms.

KUUSAMO. Small town near wild fell and forest country not far from Arctic Circle; summer hiking and winter sports center. *Kuusamo* (E-M), 67 rooms, pool, boating, angling, nightclub, disco; *Otsola* (M), 40 rooms, disco. *Kitkapirtti* (I), motel, 8 rooms, boating, fishing.
About 25 km away, *Rantasipi Rukahovi* (E-upper M), 78 rooms, pool, angling, and possibilities of excursions in the wild surrounding fell country of Rukatunturi.

OULU. Important northern port on Gulf of Bothnia, industrial and university city. *Cumulus* (E), 207 rooms, pool, new; *Vaakuna* (E), 217 rooms, pool, boating, fishing, nightclub, disco; *Arina* (E), 64 rooms; *Tulli-Hotelli* (M), 29 rooms, disco; *Hospiz* (M), 27 rooms, unlicensed restaurant.
Välkkylä (I), summer only, 120 rooms, pool, disco; *Otokylä* (I), summer only, 88 rooms, disco; *Oulas* (I), 29 rooms, unlicensed restaurant.
Restaurants: *Albert* (E); *Hovinarri* (E); *Zivago* (E); *Botnia-Pub* (M); *Haarikka* (M); *Merikulma* (M); *Myllytulli* (M); *Reidar* (M); *Lintula* (M); *Peikonpesä* (M).

PIETARSAARI (JAKOBSTAD). Attractive small coastal town and birthplace of national poet Runeberg. *Pool* (E), 40 rooms, pool; *Kaupunginhotelli* (E), 58 rooms, disco.

PORI. Major port on Gulf of Bothnia, industrial center near excellent beaches. *Juhana Herttua* (E), 55 rooms; *Satakunta* (E), 63 rooms; *Karhun Kruunu* (upper M), 57 rooms; *Cumulus* (E), 54 rooms, pool; *Otava* (M), 22 rooms. *Tekunkorpi* (I), summer only, 32 rooms, cafeteria only.
About 20 km away, by the splendid sandy beaches of Yyteri, *Rantasipi Yyteri* (E), 113 rooms, pool, extensive sports facilities including golf, nightclub.
Restaurants: *Itäpuisto* (E); *Monttu* (E); *Punapaula* (M); *Selkämeri* (M); *Jussikka* (I); *Sarkka* (I).

RUKATUNTURI. See Kuusamo.

SEINÄJOKI. Inland town, east of Vaasa. *Rantasipi Sorsanpesä* (E), 90 rooms, pool, disco; *Aapo* (E), 50 rooms; *Cumulus* (E), 71 rooms, pool, disco. *Lakeuden Seurahuone* (M), 14 rooms without bath or shower, disco.

VAASA (VASA). Major west coast port and historic town. *Waskia* (E), 186 rooms, pool, boating, fishing, nightclub; *Central* (E), 145 rooms, pool; *Fenno* (E), 102 rooms; *Coronet* (E), 52 rooms; *Astor* (I), 26 rooms; *Tekla* (I), 58 rooms, unlicensed restaurant, tennis.
Restaurants: *Birra* (E-M); *Centrum* (E-M); *Ernst* (E); *Fondis* (E); *Elite* (M); *Reimari* (M); *Sekstantti* (M); *Koti* (I).

228   FINLAND

SPORTS. Sea bathing and some water sports are the main outdoor activities of the coastal area, the **bathing** being particularly good from the splendid sandy beaches of Yyteri, near Pori, and Kalajoki. **Walking, fishing** and **shooting the rapids** are the specialties of the Kuusamo area. Other amenities are: **riding** at Kokkola, Oulu, Pietarsaari, Pori, Seinäjoki, Vaasa; **golf** at Kokkola, Oulu, Pietarsaari, Pori, Seinäjoki, Vaasa; **water skiing** at Kalajoki, Kokkola, Kuusamo, Oulu, Pietarsaari, Seinäjoki; **Windsurfing** Kalajoki, Kokkola, Oulu, Pietarsaari, Pori, Seinäjoki, Vaasa; **gliding** at Kokkola, Pori.

WINTER SPORTS. The Rukatunturi fells north of Kuusamo provide the major facilities of the region, with three ski lifts, ski jump, marked trails through varied terrain and fishing through the ice.

USEFUL ADDRESSES. Tourist information offices: Kokkola: Pitkänsillankatu 39; Kuusamo: Kaiterantie 22; Oulu: Kirkkokatu 2; Pietarsaari: Rådhusgatan 5; Pori: Antinkatu 5; Vaasa: Town Hall.

Holiday villages: Keski-Pohjanmaa Tourist Office, Pitkänsillankatu 39, Kokkola; Botnia Tourist, Hovioikeudenpuistikko 11, Vaasa; Kuusamon Lomat, Kitkantie 20, Kuusamo.

There are one or more **travel agencies** in most centers, and **youth hostels** and **campsites** throughout the area.

FINNISH LAPLAND

Adventure among Forest Wilds

Lapland is a twofold miracle, a product of man and nature working in close harmony. Nature fashioned a wilderness of endless forests and great silences. Man set out to make it habitable and bend the land to his will. So often the human footstep has obliterated all that came before, but here man has walked gently and left the virgin solitude of this country almost unspoiled. Now easily accessible by plane, train or bus, this Arctic outpost offers comfortable hotels and modern amenities, yet you won't have to go very far to find yourself in an almost primordial solitude. Small wonder that this country has so many romantic traditions.

Exploring Finnish Lapland

The oldest traces of human habitation in Finland have been found in Lapland, and hoards of Danish, English and even Arabian coins indicate trade activities many centuries ago. The origins of the Lapps themselves are lost in the mists of history. There are only some 2,500 pure Lapps still living here; the remainder of the provinces' population of some 220,000 are Finns. Until the 1930s, Lapland was still largely unexploited, still a region where any trip was an expedition of exploration. Then the Canadian-owned Petsamo Nickel Company (now in

Soviet hands) completed the great road which connects Rovaniemi
with the Arctic Sea. Building activities increased along this route (later
to be known as the Arctic Highway), the land was turned and sown,
and a few hotels were built to cater to the increasing numbers of
visitors.

Next came World War II with the Soviet Union still the enemy. In
September, 1944, in conformity with the terms of the Armistice Treaty
with their foe, the Finns started to drive out the considerable number
of German troops then stationed in Lapland. Methodical to the last,
they retreated destroying all they could. The capital Rovaniemi was
levelled; almost every farmhouse, cottage and cattle-shed was burned
down or blown up.

Barely giving the ruins time to cease smoking, the Finns started back
again in a few weeks to create modern communities out of the desolation. Certain areas of Lapland had to be ceded to the Soviet Union (the
Arctic coastline, Petsamo, and part of the Salla district on the east
frontier), but their inhabitants were settled within the new boundaries.
They included some 250 Skolt Lapps, a unique Lapp tribe, who were
settled at Sevettijärvi on the northern shores of Lake Inari.

Along the Arctic Highway

To get down to rather more practical details for the intending visitor,
let us find a base in Lapland itself from which we can explore the
country. The southernmost town of the province, Kemi, is somewhat
south of the Arctic Circle on the coast of the Gulf of Bothnia. But
practically on the Arctic Circle is the "Gateway to Lapland", Rovaniemi, the administrative hub and communications center of the province
where the Ounas and Kemi rivers meet.

In the process of post-World War II rebuilding, Rovaniemi's population shot up from 8,000 to its present 30,000, so don't expect to arrive
in a backwoods shanty town. This modern city on the edge of the
wilderness comes as a surprise to most people with its excellent architecture and amenities—quite a lot of it, including the layout of the
town, the work of Alvar Aalto. Note especially Lappia Hall, the brand
new concert and congress center which also houses the Lapland Provincial Museum, the world's northernmost professional theater, and
the Library, both beautifully designed by Aalto.

Quite a lot of light industry has come to Rovaniemi, too, and with
all the varied amenities it has to offer, it attracts visitors from all over
the province on business or pleasure, for health or further education,
or simply because it has the best selection of shops of anywhere on or
north of the Arctic Circle. Among other places to visit here are the
modern church with its impressive mural, and various museum collections devoted to the region and its different features.

Local sightseeing also includes summer trips on the Kemi river and
year-round ones to Pohtimolampi (28 km.) where the Sports and Excursions Center features the world's only reindeer-driving school.

But interesting though it is, Rovaniemi is by no means typical of
Lapland and to explore the province you have two main alternatives.
The first is to take the Arctic Highway from Rovaniemi to Ivalo, the

main artery of central and northern Lapland and, like other roads in the region, an important post-bus route. Five miles from Rovaniemi, on the Arctic Circle, is a shop and café where mail is postmarked with a special Arctic Circle stamp. At Sodankylä is an ancient wooden church under which mysterious mummies were discovered. The nearby fells have been developed into a holiday area; and at Vuotso, further north, you can even try your hand at goldwashing for an hour, a day or several days under expert guidance at Tankavaara, about ½ km east of the Highway; there is now an interesting Gold Museum here, with a restaurant and self-catering accommodation.

Only a little further north you come to the expanding tourist center of Saariselkä, with a varied range of accommodation from which to embark on lone or guided trips into the true wilderness. The sprawling small township of Ivalo (airport) is a main center for northern Lapland with a top class hotel and all the amenities of a modern community.

The huge island-studded expanses of Lake Inari, north of Ivalo, offer endless possibilities for wilderness exploration, and the village of Inari on its southwest shore is a good center from which to radiate in almost any direction. It has a charming modern church and sightseeing cruises on the lake are arranged in summer. West of it lies the Lemmenjoki (River of Love) where there is a small holiday village from which wilderness treks or boat trips are organized, including into a remote goldwashing district where a few hardy souls are still trying their luck.

In recent years, a growing number of small holiday villages have blossomed on or near the Arctic Highway near Inari and to the north of it, usually with a small restaurant and shop attached. Amenities are simple, but the situations are often magnificent and bring you very close to the true pulse of Lapland. Usually there will be a boat at your disposal, fishing possibilities and the experience of preparing your own sauna. From Kaamanen, north of Inari, a side road leads to Sevettijärvi, home of the Skolt Lapps, and eventually into Norway.

Further north still is Utsjoki, a most straggling village on the Norwegian border. This is the country's northernmost parish in which you can travel by boat on the Teno river—famed for its salmon waters and called Finland's most beautiful river. Should you wish to take a trip into Norway, you can drive over the border at Nuorgam northeast of Utsjoki, or from Karigasniemi over the Norweign Arctic Highway, eventually returning into Finland at Kilpisjärvi in the far northwest, though this is a very long detour. However, Utsjoki and Karigasniemi are now also linked by a minor road following the Teno river, a road which continues further south still along the border with Norway to Angell from which you can return east to Inari, so that there are now several round-trip possibilities of various lengths.

To the Three Countries Boundary

The other alternative from Rovaniemi is to head via Kittilä or Pello and the Tornio valley into western Lapland, reaching right up to the meeting point with Norway and Sweden near Kilpisjärvi. The fells are higher and the scenery more impressive on this side of Lapland, and the fell group of Pallastunturi and the villages of Enontekiö and Kilpisjärvi are particularly recommended. A superb wilderness trail, about 60 miles long, links Pallastunturi and Enontekiö across the fells, with unattended huts along the way in which to overnight. Enontekiö straggles along a lake shore and from it a road leads to Kautokeino in Norway, eventually linking up with the rest of the Norwegian road network. The road from Muonio to Kilpisjärvi, paralleling the Swedish border, is known as the Way of the Four Winds (after the four points of the male Lapp headgear). Along this route, Karesuvanto is well placed for excursions into the wilderness and trips over into Sweden. From Kilpisjärvi itself, a popular excursion is to the simple granite Stone of the Three Countries, marking the boundary of Sweden, Norway and Finland. There are marvelous views for those with energy to climb Saana fell, looming over Kilpisjärvi and, to the northwest, rise more fells including the highest in Finland, Haltia at over 4,000 feet.

The Wild and Not-so-Wild

But what are those special features that draw some people back to Lapland again and again? It is difficult to put your finger on them for they are made up of many factors as intangible as the Northern Lights that send their flickering veils of color weaving across the winter sky. If you can take the intense but dry cold, winter is a fascinating time in Lapland, not only for the Northern Lights, but for experiences such as the unique reindeer round-ups.

From December to March, reindeer owners round up their herds all over the Lapland map, and collect them in their thousands into huge corrals. Sometimes dressed in their colorful costumes, the Lapps and also many Finns lasso the reindeer in true Wild West fashion, recognizing their own animals by brand marks on the ear. Once sorted into individual herds, they are counted, some selected for slaughter and the rest go free again. The round-ups are also attended by many buyers, for reindeer meat is considered quite a delicacy not only for eating locally, but for "export" to the south and even abroad.

To get to some of the remoter round-ups you may have to travel by taxi plane, though other corrals are near the road, especially around Ivalo, Inari and Enontekiö. Most Lapps and northern Finns get there on skis or by one of those motorized sledges which rather sadly have almost entirely replaced the much more attractive (and silent) reindeer —drawn *pulkka* (a kind of boat-shaped sleigh on one runner). In southern Lapland especially, an increasing number of round-ups occur in the fall. Finding out exactly when and where a round-up is taking place is not easy, for much depends on the whims of the weather and the reindeer, so you must check locally. The information offices in Rovaniemi, however, will be able to give some guidance.

A few words should be said about the Lapps—a proud, sensitive and intelligent people some of whom, with justification, resent the attitude of those visitors who regard them as a tourist attraction put there for their benefit. Remember this is their country and they have an ancient culture, language and customs of their own. Modern influences (and intermarriage) have rather regrettably changed many aspects of their traditional way of life; for example, the attractive costumes are less frequently seen, except on festive occasions. The young especially have been affected by the changes and many of them are far more interested in becoming teachers, lawyers or engineers than breeding reindeer or hunting from their remote homesteads. Yet others have found profit from selling souvenirs to the tourists. But most prefer to go about their daily life minding their own business. The Lady Day Church Festival in Enontekiö in March and Easter Church Festival in Inari are particularly colorful events, attended by many Lapps in their most brilliant costumes, and usually featuring reindeer racing or lassoing competitions.

Of other winter attractions such as skiing, reindeer safaris and dog sledge tours, more has been said under "Winter Sports" at the end of this section. Summer has the blessing of daylight up to 24 hours long, and often beautiful weather to go with it, but beware of the mosquitoes. In the fall—usually early September—the colors are quite fabulous.

So the new and the old intermingle in this remote northern corner of Europe. The new Lapland is a place of modern techniques in which careful management is gradually driving back the wilderness and creating cornfields beyond the Arctic Circle. The forests are being exploited and managed with expert care, and light industry and hydro-electric projects have added their mark to the Lapland map. Yet goldwashers still wash the gravel of the Lemmenjoki river, cut off from the world except for occasional visitors and the aircraft that swoop down with their mail and provisions, and the rhythm of the seasons still governs the life of all those connected with reindeer. And the experienced traveler who would like to roam through the wilds for days on end without meeting a fellow human being can still do so without any problem at all. Be warned, however, that climatic conditions change rapidly and often unpredictably, especially on those lonely Arctic fells. Always seek and heed local advice, and tell your hotel or friends where you are heading and how long you intend to be away. An attractive alternative is provided by organized canoeing trips with nights in huts or tents in the wilderness.

Details of the many facilities and types of holiday in the region are given in the annually revised brochure 'Finnish Lapland' produced by Lapland Travel in Rovaniemi and available from Finnish Tourist Board offices.

PRACTICAL INFORMATION FOR FINNISH
LAPLAND

 WHEN TO COME. As with the rest of Finland, there are two Laplands: the white, frozen and cold country of winter, and the warmer, color-rich summer "Land of the Midnight Sun". The great attractions of the former are winter sports-from Jan. to end Apr.-and the Northern Lights. This is also the time of the impressive reindeer round-ups. The attractions of the summer season are the possibilities offered for hiking tours and fishing, and for viewing the Midnight Sun from about end May-mid-July. In September, the fall colors are unbelievably beautiful; they are known as "*ruska*" in Finnish.

 HOW TO GET ABOUT. Rovaniemi, the "Gateway to Lapland", is 11 hours by train from Helsinki, but the same distance can be covered by 1½ hours by plane. A quickie "Tour to the Land of the Midnight Sun" can be made by air from Helsinki lasting about 15 hours, during which you cover almost the whole of Finland. But that's all too brief. Ivalo may be reached from Rovaniemi by air, but the principal means of transportation north of the Arctic Circle is by bus; Rovaniemi-Ivalo (6 hours) Ivalo—Inari (1 hour) Rovaniemi-Pallastunturi (6 hours); Pallastunturi-Kilpisjärvi (6 hours) Kilpisjärvi-Tornio-Kemi (13 hours)—from Kemi it is 9 hours by train to Helsinki, 1 by air. You can also put yourself and your car on an overnight sleeper train from Helsinki to Oulu and Rovaniemi, and from Turku and Tampere to Rovaniemi. Small planes can be hired for private charter in several centers.

 MOTORING. Note the car-sleeper trains mentioned above. If you are driving, avoid northern Finland around late May when the spring thaw makes some roads impassable. Or at least check conditions in advance. You will find filling stations in most places, but it is a good idea to keep the tank topped up because of the distances involved.

We suggest the following route in the north: Kemi-Tornio, then up the Tornio and Muonio river valleys to Pello-Kolari-Muonio (side detour to Pallastunturi)—Karesuvanto-Kilpisjärvi, 340 miles (548 km). You could then cross north Norway, returning south through Finnish Lapland via Utsjoki-Inari-Ivalo-Sodankylä to Rovaniemi. New minor roads increasingly penetrate into remoter areas if you want to get further off the beaten track. Menesjärvi and Sevettijärvi are two suggestions, using Inari as your launching point. A new road continues from Sevettijärvi to Norway, and from Menesjärvi across central Lapland to Kittilä from which you can travel north to Kilpisjärvi or south to Rovaniemi. Another minor road follows the Norwegian border from Angell via Karigasniemi to Utsjoki, offering alternative circuits in northern Finnish Lapland.

HOTELS AND RESTAURANTS. Unless otherwise stated, all the hotels listed below are open all the year, have licensed restaurants and can offer some or all rooms with bath or shower. In most cases, hotel restaurants in the (E) and (M) categories have music and dancing on some or most evenings. The majority of establishments also have sauna baths. Otherwise, special facilities, such as nightclubs or sports amenities, have been indicated for each hotel. In addition to those having swimming pools, many hotels in lake or coastal areas are situated near the shore. The price categories (E), (M) and (I) are explained in the section "Practical Information for Finland".

For self-catering accommodations, contact *Lapland Travel,* Pohjanpuistikko 2, Rovaniemi. From the same address you can get details of Lappi à la Carte, three gourmet routes through the province featuring traditional dishes.

ÄKÄSLOMPOLO. Fell center near Kolari near Swedish border. *Äkäs-Hotelli* (E-M), 60 rooms, pool, angling, skiing; *Akäskero* (M-I), 11 rooms.

ENONTEKIÖ. Lakeside village in western fell district. *Hetta Tourist Hotel* (lower M), 16 rooms, boating, fishing, skiing; *Jussan Tupa* (M), 34 rooms, pool, boating, fishing.

INARI. Pleasant village by huge lake of same name in northern Lapland. Riverside *Inari Tourist Hotel* (lower M), 22 rooms without bath or shower, boating. Several small, simple holiday villages to the north include: *Kaamasen Kievari,* simple huts, restaurant serving excellent local specialties; *Muotkan Ruoktu,* cafeteria; *Neljän tuulentupa,* accommodation in 3- or 4-bed rooms in main buildings, pleasant café and restaurant; *Kiellatupa,* modern, 3- or 4-bed rooms in main buildings. West of Inari is *Lemmenjoen Lomamajat* in a fine riverside wilderness setting up the Lemmenjoki river, cafeteria, shop, fishing.

IVALO. Main village and communication center in northern Lapland. *Ivalo* (E), new, 61 rooms, pool; *Ivalo Tourist Hotel* (lower M), 37 rooms without bath or shower, unlicensed restaurant.

KARESUVANTO. Village near Swedish border, northwest Lapland. *Ratkin* (M), 26 rooms, attractive local style, angling.

KEMI. Port and industrial center on far north of Gulf of Bothnia. *Cumulus* (E), 120 rooms, pool; *Merihovi* (E), 51 rooms; *Nestor* (M), 22 rooms without bath or shower, disco; *Reissumies* (M), 14 rooms, motel, beer and wine only.

KILPISJÄRVI. Beautiful situation by lake and beneath fells in far northwest, near borders with Sweden and Norway. *Kilpisjärvi Tourist Hotel* (M), 35 rooms, boating, angling; *Saananmaja* (I), 13 rooms, unlicensed restaurant, angling.
Also excellent *Hiking Center,* 27 rooms without bath or shower, boating, angling, skiing.

KITTILÄ. Main village at road junction in west central Lapland. In nearby fells, *Levitunturi* (E), 82 rooms, winter and summer sports facilities.

LAANILA. See Saariselkä.

MUONIO. Main village near western fell districts, near Swedish border. *Muonio* (M), 13 rooms; *Olostunturi* (M), a short distance from village at foot of fell, 35 rooms, pool, skiing.

PALLASTUNTURI. Splendid group of western fells. *Pallastunturi Tourist Hotel* (M), 49 rooms, skiing, in beautiful lone setting.

PYHÄTUNTURI. Fine group of southern fells north of Kemijärvi. *Kultakero* (M range), 50 rooms, pool, angling, skiing, in grand wilderness setting.

ROVANIEMI. Modern capital of Lapland province; winter sports center. *Rantasipi Pohjanhovi* (E), 214 rooms, pool, tennis, angling, disco; *Polar* (E), 53 rooms, nightclub, pool.
Ounasvaara (upper M), hilltop position on outskirts of town, 39 rooms, skiing; *Lapinportti* (E-M), 18 rooms, pool; *City-Hotelli* (M range), 66 rooms, beer and wine only; *Oppipoika* (M-I), 15 rooms, pool, partly summer only.
Domus Arctica (I), summer only, 140 rooms; *Rovaniemen Ammatti-Koulun Summer Hotel* (I), 36 rooms, unlicensed, cafeteria.
Restaurants: *Hartsuherra* (E), modern, attractive; *Lapinpoika* (M), excellent cold table, intimate atmosphere; *Iisakki* (M); *Haarikka* (I); *Kesäpaikka-Summerplace,* by the river, light meals.

SAARISELKÄ. Expanding tourist and walking center with modern facilities near virgin wilderness area east of the Arctic Highway; guided hiking trips and gold-panning excursions to old gold workings in the area. *Riekonkieppi* (E), 103 rooms; *Saariselkä Recreation Center* (E-I), wide range of accommodation from top class to dormitory, several restaurants, amusement arcade; *Laanihovi* (M), 20 rooms without bath or shower. Well equipped holiday villages in the area include *Kelohovi* and *Kakslauttanen*.

SODANKYLÄ. Main village on major route north. *Kantakievari* (E-M), 53 rooms, pool. *Kantakievari Luosto* (E-M), 7 rooms, skiing, situated in nearby Luostotunturi fell district.

SUOMUTUNTURI. Fell district on the Arctic Circle, near Kemijärvi. *Suommu* (E-M), 62 rooms, Lapp-style restaurant astride the Arctic Circle, pool, boating, angling, skiing.

TANKAVAARA. Gold-washing center near Arctic Highway. Simple self-catering accommodation, attractive restaurant.

TORNIO. On Swedish border at northern tip of Gulf of Bothnia. *Kaupunginhotelli* (E), 76 rooms, pool, angling.

UTSJOKI. Village in northernmost fell district by Norwegian border. *Utsjoki Tourist Hotel* (M), 31 rooms, angling.

SPORTS. The vast wild areas around Kuusamo, Kemijärvi, Salla, Sodanyklä, Kittilä, Muonio, Enontekiö, Kilpisjärvi, Inari, and Utsjoki are ideal for **hiking** through the forests or scrub wilderness of the fells: although having little to boast of in height, except in the northwest, they are scenically memorable. Reindeer are a common sight, especially during July and August, the hottest part of summer, when they gather on the baretopped fells. Lapp communities inhabit the sparsely populated Enontekiö-Inari-Utsjoki areas. There are well-marked trails, along which refuge huts are always open for use free, and guided hikes or canoeing trips are arranged from a number of centers. Well-known fell areas are: Pallastunturi National Park, Saariselkä fells in eastern Lapland, Kilpisjärvi district, Utsjoki district, Pyhätunturi in the Kemijärvi district. At Tankavaara near Vuotso, you can go goldwashing, and other gold-panning excursions are organized to the old gold workings, for example, along the Ivalo river. Mosquitoes and midges, though non-malarial, are pests in summer, so take a good supply of insect repellent.

There is good **fishing** in all lakes and rivers of Lapland, with salmon heading the list, also sea trout, forel, river trout, char, laveret, pike. **Loggers' competitions** are held in summer at one or two places, which vary each year. There is **riding** at Kemi, Kemijärvi and Rovaniemi, and **windsurfing** in Inari, Pyhätunturi, Rovaniemi and Suomutunturi. And now you can even go sailing north of the Arctic Circle; details on all these activities from Lapland Travel, Pohjanpuistikko 2, Rovaniemi.

WINTER SPORTS. Depending how far north of the Arctic Circle you go, the sun doesn't rise for anything up to several weeks around mid-winter. Don't imagine it is pitch dark, though. There is reflected light from the sun invisible below the horizon during the middle hours of the day, and a luminosity drawn from the ever-present snow. Among the great beauties of the Lapland winter, too, are the displays of Northern Lights. For skiing, however, the best time to come is March, with 12 hours of daylight, or April, with 16 hours. A word of warning: don't expect the range of sophisticated amenities associated with the better-known European sports centers. Here you will find modern comfortable accommodation, and you will get a great deal of exercise, for to ski down a hill in most places you must first climb to the top of it. Or you may prefer cross-country skiing (it doesn't have to be far!) which is a wonderful way of experiencing these far northern landscapes. For downhill enthusiasts, however, an increasing number of ski lifts is being built.

Other winter activities include the possibility to test your skill at the world's only reindeer-driving school, at Pohtimolampi, near Rovaniemi. In quite a few centers, rides by reindeer-drawn sleigh are arranged, and in a few places, notably Rovaniemi, motorized sledges can be rented. Reindeer safaris provide an unforgettable experience but are expensive. Dog-sledge tours are a more recent innovation. Or you can try your hand at fishing through the ice of a frozen lake.

The following are some of the centers for skiing in Finnish Lapland:

Rovaniemi, with 2 ski lifts, 2 ski jumps, slalom slopes and the site of the annual Ounasvaara Winter Games held on the slopes of Ounasvaara Hill on the outskirts of town.

Pallastunturi, one ski lift, a favorite skiing area in western Lapland.

Kilpisjärvi, in the far northwest, with varied terrain catering for experts and novices.

Kaunispää south of Ivalo, one ski lift.

Phyätunturi, north of Kemijärvi, three ski lifts and very varied terrain.

Suomutunturi, southeast of Kemijärvi, with ski lift, right on the Arctic Circle.

Luostotunturi, near Sodankylä, with Finland's longest ski lift.

Levitunturi, north of Kittilä, two ski lifts.

Olostunturi, near Muonio, one ski lift.

238 FINLAND

USEFUL ADDRESSES. Tourist information offices: Ivalo: Bus station, Piiskuntie; Kemi: Town Hall; Rovaniemi: City Tourist Office, Aallonkatu 2, or Lapland Travel, Pohjanpuistikko 2; Tornio: City Tourist Office, Välikatu 3.

ICELAND

PRELUDE TO ICELAND

Europe's Newest, and Oldest, Republic

Floating damply in the North Atlantic, Iceland has long been both a scenic and a social curiosity. Beneath the icy glaciers that cover a substantial amount of its surface, churning cauldrons of volcanic lava and super-heated steam have burst forth in more than a hundred recorded eruptions. Indeed, one such crater looms so ominously that stout-hearted Vikings mistook it for the entrance to the netherworld. Frogs, snakes and other reptiles never existed here, although once there was a unique breed of man-sized penguins—they disappeared in a cloud of hissing smoke when their nesting grounds blew up.

Surrounded by such bewildering phenomena, it is hardly astonishing that the daily life of the people should be equally unusual. Icelandic men and women have traditions and customs which are understandable only when interpreted in terms of their isolation and environment. Inhabitants of the Arctic Circle isle of Grimsey, for example, have become champion chess players through hundreds of sunless winters spent separated from their compatriots on the mainland. Per capita, moreover, a greater number of books are written, printed, bought and read in Iceland than anywhere else in the world.

A Bit of History

Historically speaking, this largely barren island has a past stretching back to the year 874, when the first Norse colonists arrived. Although Irish monks in search of solitude apparently had settled in parts of Iceland at least a half-century earlier, they either fled or were enslaved when the Norwegians, princely refugees from the tyranny of Harold Fairhair at home, came ashore and settled down. Prosperity was their lot at first. They multiplied and in 930 established the first parliament (today the world's oldest surviving legislature) and first republic north of the Alps. Forests melted before the ax, the sod was turned with primitive ploughs, sheep roamed the uplands, fish thronged river, lake and bay, and the skalds sang eulogies of the pagan gods.

But success came too easily. Icelandic chieftain Erik the Red had to flee from his enemies (and in doing so discovered Greenland and found-ed the Icelandic settlement); his son Leif discovered in his flight a country called Vinland, now established as the northern part of the United States. Meanwhile quarrels, feuds and power struggles con-tinued to usurp the place of patient toil. By the beginning of the 13th century there was general civil war. Fratricidal strife continued for more than fifty years, periodically stirred up by the Norwegian king who hoped to claim Iceland; his success came in 1264 when he stepped in as "arbiter" and sovereign.

This sea of troubles was destined to mount ever higher. By the end of the 14th century, Iceland had been absorbed, with Norway and Sweden, into a Danish union. Here it remained for nearly 600 years. Royal officials replaced the rebellious chieftains; the Black Death, the struggles of the Reformation, smallpox, leprosy and starvation suc-ceeded one another, while furious volcanic eruptions, particularly in the 16th and 17th centuries, periodically buried farm and village under suffocating blankets of volcanic ash.

Not before the 19th century did Icelandic nationalism emerge in opposition to the oppressive Danish trade monopolies. Soon the move-ment gained momentum. Partial home rule came in 1904, and full sovereignty under the Danish King in 1918. Then, when Denmark was invaded by Germany in 1940, Britain occupied undefended Iceland to keep it from falling into the hands of the Axis. A year later American forces replaced the British (and built Keflavik airport), and on June 17, 1944, Iceland severed its remaining ties with Copenhagen to become a republic once more, a reversion to the past.

Of Language and Literature

Alone among the world's myriad tongues, modern Icelandic has changed so little since pagan times that reading the ancient sagas presents no more of a problem for the present-day Icelander than do Shakespeare's works for the average Englishman or American. Swed-ish, Danish and Norwegian have all developed from the same stem, of course, but Icelandic bears about the same relationship to them as Anglo-Saxon does to English, and it's an exceptional Scandinavian who can make his way through Icelandic literature without the aid of dictionary and grammar. Even at this late date, Icelandic retains two peculiar letters of the alphabet which long ago disappeared from the other northern languages. One looks like a *b* combined with a *p* and is pronounced like the *th* in *thin;* the other, pronounced like a *d,* resembles a lazy *d* with a horizontal line drawn through the stem. Both look formidable on first acquaintance but yield to a little persistent lisping and buzzing.

The reputation of Icelandic literature rests solidly on three traditions: skaldic poetry, sagas and the Eddas. The first of these, skaldic poetry, was borrowed from the Norwegian and subsequently polished into an esoteric art long after the original inventors had given it up as hopeless. Imagine a poem constructed according to rigid rules of rhyme, alliteration, meter, stress, and so on. Next imagine a series of super-metaphors or euphemisms (called *"kenningar"*) so intricate that, like ladies' legs during the Victorian era, they could be discussed at length without ever being named. Combine everything and the result is skaldic poetry, read today more for curiosity than for content. Sagas, on the other hand, were straightforward, red-blooded, fast-moving tales of battles, gods and heroes. The facts rather than the form received the extra polishing, and a saga monger with any pretensions at all could be counted on to outwear the most persistent audience, even at a time when feasts went on for weeks. The Eddas, by way of contrast, are anthologies of poems, proverbs, myths, history and rules for poetry-making. The important ones were written by a many-sided genius named Snorri Sturluson around the year 1200. Snorri also dashed off the Norwegian national saga or *Heimskringla,* an ofttimes imaginative pageant of events from the mythological origins of the world down to the royal Norse family.

The Women of Iceland

In addition to its literary achievements, Icelandic has had a novel effect on matrimony and the position of women. In Iceland the custom persists of giving children the *first* instead of the *last* name of their father. Thus Magnus, the son of Svein, becomes Magnus Sveinsson, and Gudrun, the daughter of Einar, is known as Gudrun Einarsdottir. What's more, Gudrun keeps her maiden name even after she marries, but her children will bear her husband's name.

Iceland has the world's first freely elected woman head of state: President Vigdis Finnbogadottir was elected in 1980 for four years.

The modern Icelandic housewife is adept at various domestic crafts, learned at home and then perfected still further in one of the many women's schools and colleges, all of which stress these skills. Women travellers may well be interested in visiting some of these admirable institutions, for many of them have wonderful collections of tapestries, both sewn and woven, home-spun upholstery materials, etc. Among the best known is: *Husmaedraskoli Reykjavikur,* or Reykjavik Household School. Then there is the Teachers' College for Women, which trains women to become teachers in the various household schools of the country. In the country districts the most noteworthy are the women's schools at Blönduos, Akureyri, Langamyri, and Laugar, all of which are located in northern Iceland. Those who travel to the northeastern district must visit the school at Hallormsstadur. In the summertime, like so many of the larger school-houses in the country districts, it is turned into a hotel for visitors. There are 17 of such summer hotels scattered about the country, most of them modern and often with naturally heated warm-water swimming pools.

A not inconsiderable number of older women still wear the graceful national costume, which consists of a long, full black skirt and a black bodice, embroidered in gold and laced with gold cord over a colored blouse. An apron, worn as an ornamental panel, is usually of the same material as the blouse. Their hair is done up in two long braids which are looped up behind, and on their heads they wear small black velvet caps, with long black tassels, which are bound by two- or three-inch rings of gold or silver. Many of the younger women treasure the beautiful embroidered costumes worn by their mothers or grandmothers, but do not wear them except on a gala occasion.

Unusual features of Icelandic life are by no means limited to language peculiarities. Besides chess and books, singing has long been a favorite pastime. Even today the influence of medieval church music is revealed by the use of some harmonies long ago superseded elsewhere. Choral groups are numerous and active—again there are more per capita than in any other country—and part of the explanation seems to be that until relatively recently, musical instruments were comparatively unknown. Singing developed naturally from ballad and saga recitals, and the tradition persists.

Fish and More Fish

From the economic point of view, fish are the country's mainstay. Though grains are extensively cultivated, and in spite of the fact that every citizen has four sheep to his name and a one-third interest in a cow, Iceland barely produces enough to feed itself. With a scant one per cent of the land under cultivation, everything must be imported. The only commodity available for export is fish, and about 75% of Iceland's foreign trade (it used to be more) is based on fish products. Per fisherman, the annual catch amounts to something like *290 tons,* another world record.

Some years ago overfishing began to show its disastrous effects and Iceland's declared policy on fisheries jurisdiction was a desperate measure to protect spawning stock for future reproduction within a 200-mile fishing limit. More than that, it was designed to protect the jobs of the one in seven of Iceland's work force who are employed in the fishing industry. Thus, for example, the herring's virtual disappearance after 1968 led to strict conservation measures which have happily paid dividends; herring stocks have begun to recuperate to the point where some villages can relive the "herring adventure" for a short time each year.

In recent years Iceland has increasingly been exploiting her remarkable energy resources, both hydro-electric and thermal, an almost limitless supply of which awaits harnessing.

PRACTICAL INFORMATION FOR ICELAND

WHAT IT WILL COST. There is no such thing as a "cheap visit" to Iceland at the present time. World inflation and the necessity to import most consumer items have brought the cost of living to a very high level, and there is no expectation that it will go down. Note that in 1981 Iceland adjusted its currency to New Krona (locally abbreviated to Nkr.), where 1 new krona equals 100 old kronur, and new bank notes and coins were introduced.

The following prices are subject to Iceland's somewhat horrific rate of inflation which, however, is compensated for by frequent adjustments in her rates of exchange. Because of this, it is wise not to convert your money into Krona until you need to.

Accommodation Rates. Hotel prices are quoted by the Icelandic Tourist Board in US$, and the cost per person in a double room with bath or shower, excluding breakfast, depending on category, ranges from $32–70 in Reykjavik, $21–37 elsewhere. Particularly good value is the chain of 17 Edda Hotels operated by Iceland Tourist Bureau, mostly adapted from modern boarding schools into summer hotels.

Least expensive are guest houses and private homes; bed and breakfast in the former costs from $21. Also good value is farmhouse accommodation.

There are half a dozen youth hostels (at Reykjavik, Akureyri and elsewhere), and a score of other places where cheap accommodation is available for those with their own sleeping bags, charge $5 per night, plus $2 if sheet and blanket are required.

Restaurant Prices. Meals are expensive, but tourist menus are becoming more widely available and bring costs down. For an expensive meal (E) count from 300 Ikr. and up, moderate (M) 135–185 Ikr., inexpensive (I), 65–160 Ikr. Attractive small restaurants are now adding more variety to Reykjavik's gastronomic scene.

Some other costs: Cinema (moderate seat) 45 Ikr.; theatre (moderate seat) 90 Ikr.; coffee in snack bar 18 Ikr.; beer (very mild only available) 25 Ikr. in snack bar, 30 Ikr. in moderate restaurant; bottle of wine in moderate restaurant 200 Ikr.; bus to Keflavik airport (about 45 min.) £3; airport tax (international) £8, (domestic) 50p.

A Typical Day for One Person

Room with breakfast in moderate hotel	485 Ikr.
Lunch, moderate, with coffee	135
Dinner, moderate, with coffee	285
Taxi (say 5 km)	90
Cinema ticket (middle range)	45
2 coffees, popular cafe	36
Miscellaneous	75
	1,151 Ikr.

TIPPING. Hotels and restaurants usually include in the bill both a service charge of 15% and a sales tax of 23.5%. Extra tipping is not expected. Taxi drivers, hairdressers, and washroom attendants are not tipped.

 WHEN TO COME. Iceland's climate is as varied as her history. Though the Gulf Stream keeps average temperatures unexpectedly mild—warmer in winter than New York for instance—it's a "hot" summer when the mercury climbs over 70°F. (21°C.) and the wise visitor provides himself with a stout raincoat as well as extra sweaters and scarves. In Reykjavik it may rain, shine, drizzle, snow, shine all during the same day. Although it is obvious that good weather cannot be guaranteed, the best time to visit is from mid-June to the beginning of September. There is continuous daylight for 24 hours from the end of May until the beginning of August, and in northern Iceland the Midnight Sun hovers so close to the horizon that twilight never has a chance to fade into dawn. The end of August marks the first appearance of the Aurora Borealis, or Northern Lights.

  WHAT TO SEE. In Reykjavik, the National Theater, the University, the National Museum, Arbaer (the Folk Museum), the view from the observation platform in the steeple of Hallgrims Church, and the famous pond in the town center.

There are a number of excellent art and sculpture exhibitions (see *Museums and Sights*). Look out especially for the works of Asgrimur Jonsson, Einar Jonsson and Asmundur Sveinsson. The Arni Magnusson Manuscript Museum at Arnagardi, Sudurgotu, houses a unique and superb collection, a must for anyone interested in the Icelandic sagas and other early manuscripts. Finally, a dip in the natural hot water of the open-air pools is extremely pleasant, whatever the weather.

Shorter trips from Reykjavik include the impressive hot springs' area of Krisuvik. The popular full-day Golden Circle tour out of Reykjavik includes three major sights: the magnificent Gullfoss waterfall; the famous Great Geysir area, bubbling and steaming with hot springs, mud pools and geysirs, of which Strokkur (the world's most active) is likely to spout several times up to a height of 100 feet; the Thingvellir, site of Iceland's ancient Parliament in a starkly dramatic volcanic setting.

Another full-day trip east of Reykjavik is to the Thjorsardalur Valley, overlooked by Mount Hekla, one of the world's most famous volcanoes; in this area you visit the Viking Age farm manor at Stöng, an evocative place associated with one of the most famous sagas.

Further east still, and really needing two days, is the lovely oasis of Skaftafjell National Park beneath the massive icy bulk of Vatnajökull, Europe's greatest ice cap—a spectacular area. Indeed, beyond Vatnajökull, the heavily indented east coast is scenically magnificent too; it can be visited on a day trip by air from Reykjavik, but for those with time provides one of many highlights on a round tour of Iceland. The small east coast town of Höfn in particular has become a good center from which to explore the outlying glaciers of Vatnajökull and make trips to Skaftafjell.

In the west of Iceland, the Snaefellsnes Peninsula was Jules Verne's choice for the starting point of his *Journey to the Center of the Earth;* this area also has particularly strong associations with many of the sagas. Off the south coast are the rugged Westmann Islands which leapt into the world headlines a few years back with the eruption of Helgafjell overlooking the small town of Heimaey. Though many houses were permanently buried under lava, the islanders are now back to normal living; tourists are not only welcome, but will marvel at the energy and courage that has revived this thriving community. There are day trips to the islands from Reykjavik, which usually also include views of Surtsey, the island which burst into being in 1963, though only scientists on research projects may land there. The fantastic cliffs and nesting colonies of many sea birds are other special features of the Westmann Islands.

In the north, Akureyri—Iceland's second "city"—has a fine position near the head of a fjord, and from here you can easily visit the strange volcanic land-scapes around Lake Myvatn, a mecca for bird-watching enthusiasts. Dettifoss, Europe's most powerful waterfall, is to the north-east. This area is often visited on many of the overland tours into Iceland's grandiose if uninhabited interior whose gravel deserts, lava fields, mountains and ice caps will leave indelible memories with those with a spirit of adventure and a taste for incredible scenery.

HOW TO GET ABOUT. *Icelandair* (Flugleidir) flies on the domestic routes which link about a dozen of the island's main towns and villages, as well as the West-mann Islands and also runs summer excursions to Greenland. Other transport is by bus, and this air-bus combination provides daily services to most of the towns and places of interest, Reykjavik and Akurey-ri being the chief airports.

There are no railways in Iceland, but a comprehensive network of bus services reaches to all communities and, though the road may often seem rough, they take you through superb scenery. There are a number of special runabout bus tickets in Iceland which give either unlimited travel or a circular tour. They last from 1 week to 1 month, and cost between $150 and $250.

At Reykjavik Airport air taxis can be hired and there are also daily sightsee-ing flights by private firms. There are shipping services to ports around the coasts and to the Westmann Islands, details of which can be obtained in Reyk-javik.

Motoring: Apart from the asphalt roads through and around the towns, and the one stretch of highway between Keflavik and Reykjavik, motoring can be a hazardous exercise, often along lava track or dirt and gravel surfaces: best use local hired cars rather than subject one's own vehicle to the wear, tear and volcanic dust. The "road" around Iceland is now completed, but it can hardly be called a highway, in the best sense of the word. One motors—and arrives—eventually, and seldom without some minor excitement en route, such as the disappearance of the road under a small river, which wasn't there the day before—but it is a fascinating exercise. On the whole, you must be prepared to handle small repairs and maintenance yourself though there are a few small garages. Fuel service stations are few and far between. You drive on the right. An international driving license is necessary.

Car hire is available through several companies (see *Useful Addresses*). Note that fly-drive arrangements ex-UK also exist, with rates from £310 for 6 days including 600 Km.; these can be combined with camping arrangements to provide one of the cheapest ways of visiting Iceland (see *Tours* below).

TOURS. All the areas mentioned under "What to See" can be visited on organized trips out of Reykjavik and, in some cases, Akureyri. For details contact Reykjavik Excursions at Hotel Loftleidir or at Gimli, Laekjargata 3; this company is jointly owned by Icelandair and all the major travel agencies in the city. Among the latter, offering tours of longer duration, are: *Gudmundur Jonasson Tours,* Borgartuni 34; *Ulfar Jacobsen Tourist Bureau,* Austurstraeti 9; and *Urval,* Posthusstraeti 9. All in Reykjavik. These possibilities include grand-circle tours of the whole of Iceland, farmhouse holidays, pony trekking, highland safaris through the uninhabited interior, walking and naturalist holidays, sea angling, and special Saga tours covering many of the sites associated with Iceland's famous sagas. There are also fabulous one- or four-day trips to Greenland, and professional study tours of all kinds.

Many of these, as well as fly-drive arrangements are marketed ex-UK by a number of operators including the following:

Destination Iceland (Twickenham Travel), 84 Hampton Rd., Twickenham, Middlesex.

Finlandia Travel Agency, 49 Whitcomb St., London WC2.

Fred Olsen Travel, 11 Conduit St., London W1R OLS.

Dick Phillips, Whitehall House, Nenthead, Alston, Cumbria CA9 3PS.

Regent Holidays, 66 Regent St., Shanklin, Isle of Wight, PO37 7AE.

Scantours, 8 Spring Gdns, Trafalgar Square, London SW1.

Sonic World, 8 The Boulevard, Crawley, W. Sussex RH10 1XX.

Waymark Holidays, 295 Lillie Rd., London SW6.

YHA Travel, 14 Southampton St., London WC2E 7HY.

Economically, your best bet is to combine camping, youth hostels or guest house accommodation with fly-drive or bus travel. All camping equipment can be hired if required: e.g. tent rentals are from £2–2.50 per day according to size (2–5 persons), sleeping bag 50p, double-burner gas stove £1, set of pots and pans £1 for 4.

 CAMPING. Over a score of camp sites have been created in Iceland, and a list of these, with their amenities, can be obtained from the *Iceland Tourist Board.* Most of them are fairly basic, but usually provide camp toilets and running water, in a few cases hot water and electrical outlets. The site at Reykjavik is well placed next to the swimming pool and sports stadium; in Akureyri, it is adjacent to an open air swimming pool near the town center. Charges are about 30 Ikr. per night or less.

Where there is no site, tents may be pitched in any suitable spot, except for cultivated ground or fenced-in areas. If near a farm, permission should be obtained and this is usually readily granted.

Where camping is prohibited, such as in parts of a national park, signs are displayed reading *Tjaldstaedi bönnud.* In other places areas have been marked out for camping, frequently marked *Tjaldstaedi,* and no special permission is then necessary. In some areas international signs are posted.

As no firewood or other fuel is to be found in Iceland, and it is forbidden by law to use the scant scrub found in some areas, campers should bring along paraffin or gas stoves for cooking and heating. Supplies of paraffin are available at gas stations and a few stores in Reykjavik, and at gas stations in Keflavik, Hafnarfjördur, Akureyri and Husavik. Propane gas is sold at Shell gas stations in Reykjavik and at the larger Shell gas stations throughout the country. Butane gas and Camping Gaz are available in Reykjavik (at Solvholsgata 1), and at most co-operative stores throughout the country.

Camping equipment can be rented only in Reykjavik and advance reservations are advisable. For rates see *Tours* above.

SPORTS. Hiking through the extensive uninhabited interior and **mountaineering** are two of the favorite pastimes. A leaflet *Climbing and Ski-ing in Iceland*, obtainable from the *Iceland Tourist Board*, gives excellent guidance on some of the best areas and advice on equipment and guides. No expedition should be undertaken lightly and certainly never without advising local people where you are going, and in many cases taking guides.

Also available from the *Iceland Tourist Board* are leaflets on salmon and trout fishing and one called *The Viking Horse*. There is some of the best salmon and trout **fishing** in Europe; and sea angling for cod, haddock, etc., at Grindavik, and halibut fishing in Breidafjördur. Reindeer **hunting** in Aug. and Sept., and wild goose shooting from Aug. 20-Nov. 20.

Icelandic ponies can be hired in most places for those who want to get in a spot of **riding.** These sturdy steeds are direct descendants of those brought over by the Vikings and ideally suited to the rough terrain. Riding possibilities range from a few hours from a number of centers, to much longer treks with a guide, staying at hotels, hostels or camping.

There are ten **golf courses**—mostly 9 holes—including an 18-hole one near Reykjavik. **Swimming**—don't shudder, remember this is the land of hot springs —is possible in the waters of those springs, at Reykjavik's outdoor pool on Sundlaugavegur, indoor pool on Baronsstigur and at the outdoor pool, Sundlaug Vesturbaejar, on Hofsvallagata.

There is enough snow most winters for **skiing,** and most of the population gets out into it. There are a few ski-ing centers, notably near Akureyri in the north and, in summer, in the Kerlingarfjöll mountains in remote south central Iceland, about 125 miles from Reykjavik. The latter are best explored from the little valley of Askard where weekly courses are arranged (hostel and camping facilities).

GASTRONOMY. As befits Denmark's former Atlantic offshoot, Icelandic cuisine is a mixture of Scandinavian and Continental, with heavy emphasis on vegetables, for the natural steam that this geyser-filled country produces is used to heat greenhouses, among other things. Iceland has, however, a few specialties of its own—*hangikjot* (smoked lamb), *hardfiskur* (dried fish), and *skyr* (curds). Icelandic *sild* (herring), especially in hors d'oeuvre, is delicious. A potent variant of aquavit, *brennivin,* derives its kick from the placid potato.

POSTAL RATES. Rates for postcards are 3.50 Ikr. for Europe, 7 for US; for letters 4.50 Ikr. for Europe, 8 for US.

SAGA ISLAND

Volcanos, Hot Springs and Glaciers

A glance at an atlas confirms the fact that Iceland is the second largest island in Europe—only Great Britain covers more area. Its 40,000 square miles (Kentucky size) are tucked away in the lee of Greenland, a scant 215 miles distant. Scotland lies 520 miles to the southeast, with the Faroes marking the halfway point, while almost 3,000 miles separate the capital, Reykjavik, from New York. The air age has revolutionized geography for these latter-day Vikings.

During World War II the island was a most vital link between the old and the new world, and for long, the country was an important landing place for airplanes traveling the northern transatlantic route. Advantageous rates apply for those wishing to make a short stop-over. Iceland's main international airport is at Keflavik, 29 miles from Reykjavik, the capital, whose airfield is now used for domestic flights only.

To the foreign visitor who comes to Iceland for the first time, the people may seem to be rather reserved. This is perhaps a characteristic of all islanders and not least of a small people and a nation that is only beginning to come into its own as a member of the community of free nations. But if you make the first step you will find warmth, kindness, and exceptional hospitality.

Exploring Iceland

Besides having the biggest glacier in Europe, Vatnajökull, and the most volcanos, Iceland is also provided with a truly fabulous supply of hot springs. In fact, the very name of the capital was taken from this phenomenon—*reykja* means "smoke", *vik* is the word for "bay", and the two together describe the vapor clouds that are a common sight throughout the country.

About fifty years ago, the Icelanders began to put this priceless natural resource to work for them. For many years now, most of Reykjavik has been heated by this means and the experience gained applied to many other parts of the country.

The basic principle involved has long been obvious, but it was only after considerable experimentation that the best system was hit upon. Then in the case of Reykjavik, two 10-mile-long heavily insulated pipelines were built to carry the almost boiling water from springs outside town to storage tanks inside town and thence to individual homes. The heat lost while the water is running from underground streams to the housewife's tap is amazingly small, less than 10°. Natural hot water has also been harnessed for the heating of houses and hotels in the capital, and as a result, Reykjavik is a city completely free from smoke and smog.

In the country areas natural hot springs have also been widely exploited for much the same purpose, especially for schools, and, as many of these schools are used as summer hotels, this ensures constant hot water at the disposal of tourists too. The same is true, of course, of all the greenhouses where fruits and vegetables—those that cannot be cultivated outdoors such as tomatoes, cucumbers, grapes—are grown to satisfy the home market. Flowers are also raised in these greenhouses, quite an industry in Iceland today. Country towns like Hveragerdi have been built on the basis of this expanding industry. Most excursions from Reykjavik include a visit to the greenhouses there.

From these relatively humble beginnings, the harnessing of Iceland's seemingly boundless sources of geothermal activity has proceeded apace and is now geared to power considerable industrial enterprises. The process is expensive, but the potential enormous.

Iceland's Capital

Still quite young as a town, Reykjavik is only in its earliest infancy as a modern city. In the period of a few decades, Iceland has revolutionized its whole social fabric, and nowhere else in the country are the changes wrought by this remarkable development more evident than in Reykjavik.

A sleepy fishing village of 6,000 at the turn of the century, the capital, including suburbs, now houses 118,000 of Iceland's citizens. Since the war, it has been riding the crest of a building boom. Earthquake-proof houses and apartment blocks of reinforced concrete are going up, and the city is expanding according to a carefully worked-out plan. Not least among these plans was the much challenged 1971 decision to enforce the 1924 law which forbids its citizens to keep dogs within the city limits, and the argument still rages!

Reykjavik is not only Iceland's center of government, but its cultural center as well. Among the more important buildings are the Parliament or Althing, the University, National Library, National Theater, Navigation School, National Museum, Arbaer Folk Museum where the careful, reconstructed old country houses include a turf and stone church, and the Hallgrims Church which, with a statue of Leif Eriksson, dominates a rocky plateau above the harbor. The museum of the late sculptor Einar Jonsson is worth a visit, too.

Sprawling at the southwest corner of Iceland, Reykjavik makes a good base for exploring other parts of the country. About 30 miles to the south-east is Hveragerdi, the small town famous for its hot springs and greenhouses; nowadays there is also here a modern and well-equipped Nature Cure Sanatorium providing treatment for rheumatic complaints, obesity, digestive disorders and recuperation from over-work or nervous strain.

About 35 miles to the east of the capital stretches the broad lava plain of Thingvellir, site of the first parliament and now a national park. A placid lake, Thingvallavatn, the biggest in Iceland, lends a deceptively idyllic air, for it was here that chieftains and citizens from every village and farm met each summer to make the law, here that the decision was taken around the year 1000 to lay aside pagan ways and adopt the tenets of Christianity. The speaker's rock and the hollowed-out seats reserved for the most important men can still be seen, together with the ancient fairgrounds where wrestling matches took place, weddings were contracted, and witches drowned. Nowadays Thingvellir is a favorite place for holiday-makers and the modern campers' tents in summer do, in a way, carry on the tradition of the great meeting place, but in a much more gentle form. Do not miss a stroll along the Almannagja chasm, and the magnificent view from its upper rim.

A little further out from Reykjavik, the Great Geysir, which gave a name to hot springs around the world, bubbles away with oblivious nonchalance and takes little note of the expectant crowds which gather there daily in hopes of some excitement. Geysir is getting old and cannot be relied upon to perform, but a junior geysir, Strokkur, seldom fails, throwing up boiling water to considerable heights at five-minute intervals. In the same area are small boreholes from which steam arises, as well as beautiful pools of blue water.

Twelve miles away there is more thunder, this time in the form of the deafening Gullfoss waterfall. The river Hvita plunges down a series of steps before throwing itself 90 feet into a narrow canyon. The noise—and the spray—are on a heroic scale, and towards afternoon the sun illuminates the moist air, making it in fact, as well as name, the Golden Falls. 18 miles from Geysir is Skalholt, a hallowed spot in Icelandic history. There has been a Christian Church on this site for nine centuries, and the present exquisitely simple building is the eleventh in its line. Jon Arason, last Catholic Bishop in Iceland, opposed the Reformation and was beheaded without trial at Skalholt in 1550. A plaque marks the spot.

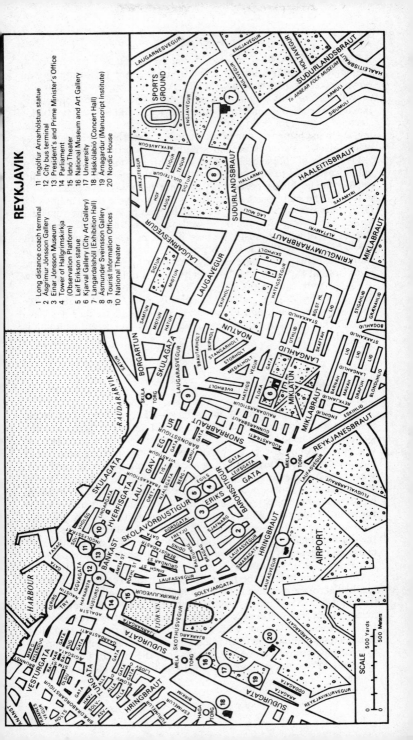

REYKJAVIK

1 Long distance coach terminal
2 Asgrimur Jonsson Gallery
3 Einar Jonsson Museum
4 Tower of Hallgrimskirkja
  (Observation Platform)
5 Leif Erikson statue
6 Kjarval Gallery (City Art Gallery)
7 Langardalshöll (Exhibition Hall)
8 Asmunder Sveinsson Gallery
9 Tourist Information Offices
10 National Theater
11 Ingólfur Arnarhólstun statue
12 City bus terminal
13 President's and Prime Minister's Office
14 Parliament
15 Idnó Theater
16 National Museum and Art Gallery
17 University
18 Háskólabíó (Concert Hall)
19 Arnagardur (Manuscript Institute)
20 Nordic House

SCALE
500 Yards
500 Meters

To ascend 5,000-foot volcanic Mount Hekla requires two full days, although by road it's only 75 miles from the capital. Getting up and down the mountain is a 10-hour undertaking in itself, but the view into, as well as from, this trouble-making giant justifies the strenuous climb. Hekla has erupted several times in recent years, and the new lava fields stretch for some miles around the crater. For those who dislike trudging, a 4-hour plane trip combines a good look at Hekla with a glimpse of the glacier, Vatnajökull, and a flight north to the Arctic Circle.

Hekla has of course been troublesome throughout Iceland's history, and it was thanks to an eruption in 1104 that the valley of Thjorsadalur, once fertile farmland, became the desolate yet impressive place that it is today. The main place of interest is Stöng, where the remains of a farm dating from Saga times were unearthed in 1939. The ruins are roofed to preserve them, and are well worth visiting if only to get an impression of what it must have been like in medieval Iceland. Nearby are very pretty waterfalls which provide an oasis of brilliant green in the black landscape. There is only one crossing place of the Thjorsa river, so that this area was until very recently difficult to get to. Now a guided tour can be taken from Reykjavik which includes Thjorsadulur valley, Stöng and the Waterfalls, and the new, impressive Burfjell power plant, and takes one to the edge of Hekla's new lava fields. There are no hotels or restaurants in the valley, but camping is allowed.

Western Iceland

The long, sometimes monotonous drive to the Snaefellsnes peninsula is worth taking, particularly if you call in at Hvalfjördur, to the whaling station at the head of the fjord. You might arrive at the same time as a whale. In that case be prepared for a strong smelling and rather bloody experience. Further north you can turn inland to visit Reykholt, where you can see the small hot pool which belonged to Snorri Sturluson, Iceland's famous poet, who recorded the Sagas. After crossing moorlands where only ponies and sheep graze you finally arrive below the snout of Snaefellsjökull, where Jules Verne set the starting point for the *Journey to the Center of the Earth*. It is a wild beautiful place, where the main attractions are the myriad seabirds nestling along the basalt cliffs, and the seals who pop up to gaze curiously at intruders. At Arnastapi is a tiny fishing village.

On the other side of the peninsula are weirdly shaped rock castles reached across a grey lavafield. By continuing on the northern side of the peninsula you'll reach Stykkisholmur. This town is popular with many sea sports fishermen who come for the halibut in Breidafjordur. It is a pleasant little place with a modern hospital run and staffed by Belgian nuns. Behind the town is a hill known as Helgafjell. According to local superstition anyone who climbs Helgafjell for the first time will be granted three wishes, provided he doesn't look back, or talk on the way up.

Southeast Iceland

In 1974 the final bridge spanning the treacherous glacier waters pouring from the tongues of the Vatnajökull was completed and now this impressive area is within reach of Reykjavik by car. It is still a long journey, but you can watch the miniature icebergs sliding impassively towards the sea while the great Skua gulls swoop overhead and across the black moving sands. Skaftafjell reserve contains Svartifoss waterfall, dropping thinly over a cliff whose sides resemble the pipes of a great organ. One can walk on the glacier tongues, but this should not be attempted without expert guidance or correct equipment. Höfn on the east coast is developing as a popular center from which to explore the extraordinary landscapes created by the outlying glaciers of Vatnajökull and the wild coastline. From here excursions are arranged to these, as well as to Skaftafjell National Park.

If you're following the southern road, stop at Skogar, a tiny settlement beside the impressive Skogafoss. You could lunch at Hotel Edda by prior arrangement, then visit the small museum consisting of turf houses brought from elsewhere in the district and re-erected. Fishing along this treacherous coast used to be from boats, and the last of these now rests in the little museum with many interesting insights into life in the not so long ago.

Westmann Islands and Surtsey

The mighty eruption of Helgafjell (Holy Mountain) at Heimaey in the Westmann Islands in 1973, with the consequent evacuation of the entire population, was a disaster for Iceland, and more particularly for the Westmanners themselves. Their main industry is fishing, and they were dependent on the safe harbor at Heimaey as well as upon the fish processing plants there. However, with the grit and determination of people long used to living on the edge of the forces of nature, the Westmanners started to dig themselves out long before the eruption ceased, removing tons of black lava dust from their buried houses and streets. Now the streets are cleared, houses repainted and rebuilt, and fishing and processing working normally, though some of the plants were damaged. But the island has six hundred meters of lava on the approaches to the harbor, and many of the houses which were nearest to the eruption are buried forever. It is an odd sensation, as one struggles upward in the ash that one has walked over someone's rooftop . . . and talking to the Westmanners as they build new houses on the other side of the town, or scrape the reluctant ground to form a new playing field, determined that they will live nowhere else, one respects and admires their tenacity.

The tradition of puffin catching has been re-started along with the fish processing, for though of little economic value puffins are used in large quantities for food. They were not affected too greatly by the eruption, but a considerable number of seabirds were lost and this has affected the task of the egg-pickers, who estimate that it will take several years for the colonies to pick up again. Egg-picking is hazardous work. Dangling from ropes, the men swing from ledge to ledge down sheer volcanic cliffs to collect eggs from the nests, often attacked fiercely by the birds. Primitive winches haul the men back up with their fragile loads. Throughout the years there have been eighteen fatal accidents and legend has it that when the nineteenth man falls to his death, the volcano Katla on the mainland will erupt. Its performance has been overdue for a while. A highlight of the Icelandic calendar is the festival held each August near Heimaey.

It is well worth taking time to visit the Westmann Islands, despite the fact that the return air flight might be cancelled by bad weather and you'll face a ten-hour sea journey instead. But if you really cannot spare more than a few hours, take a sightseeing trip from Reykjavik. A few miles from the Westmann Islands is the new volcanic island of Surtsey already several hundred feet high. Scientists work there recording the progress of nature, but lesser folk are not allowed so you must content yourself with yet another sightseeing flight.

Akureyri and the North

Iceland's second largest town, Akureyri, is an hour from Reykjavik by plane. Ranged up and down a series of irregular hills on the western side of Eyjafjördur, the town is dominated by a simple, ultra-modern Lutheran church whose twin spires accent the barren and treeless landscape. Some of the surrounding mountains reach a height of 4,500 feet and offer fine climbs and ski runs.

Near the summer Hotel Edda, you will find an interesting statue. In the old days, if a man transgressed the laws of the community, he was often banished, with his family, to the lavafields. This was virtually a death sentence for nothing could sustain life in those regions. This poignant statue, called the Outlaw, is by Einar Jonsson and depicts a man, carrying his wife and child and accompanied by his dog, walking into outlawry.

From Akureyri, you can get a boat to Grimsey, particularly interesting to seabird enthusiasts. You can also take a long, jolting bus ride into the unreal volcanic plateaux of the interior to the magnificent waterfall of Godafoss, where the local chieftain threw his pagan household gods into its foaming depths when he was converted to Christianity in 1000 A.D. The old bridge is so narrow that buses have to be accurately aligned and passengers asked to alight to lighten the load! The new bridge does away with the perils, and the excitement too. In the adjoining district is Glerardalur, a valley where petrified wood is found. The bus continues to Lake Myvatn, a birdwatcher's paradise, where vast numbers of waterfowl make their homes. One can get a guide to some of the more remote nesting areas.

Myvatn also has a specially tasty breed of trout, which feeds on the midges which give the lake its name. A few days at either of the modest hotels enable one really to enjoy this sheltered, peaceful place as well as some of the exotic natural phenomena. These include Dimmuborgir (the black castles) where the fantastic landscape is said to resemble the lunar surface more closely than anywhere else on earth, Storagja and Grotagja, two pools of natural hot water in underground caves, where one can enjoy wonderful bathing, and Namaskard, where the purple sulphur boils like a witches' cauldron in the strange red and yellow valleys.

There is another strange thing among so many—when the volcano Askja erupted two centuries ago, the lava ran directly towards the lake and the small settlement which lay beside it. But in the path of the lava stood the tiny church, and the molten mass stopped within inches of its walls. There is a new church now, but the remains of the old one can be seen, surrounded on three sides, by the old, cold lava. Farther afield are Dettifoss, Europe's largest waterfall, and the fascinating, lush national park of Asbyrgi with the curious echoing rocks of Hljodaklettar. From here you can continue to Husavik, an attractive port on the north coast, and thence back to Akureyri.

Central Iceland

The interior of Iceland is virtually uninhabited except for the odd meteorological or other scientific station. Though the Icelanders may get rather tired of having it likened to the moon, it really is very reminiscent of the science fiction imaginings most of us have of lunar landscapes: great stony deserts, extravagantly contorted lava fields, towering glaciers from which crystal-clear streams and green rivers drain across the land. The colors are superb and there is a feeling of timelessness that few other places in the world can match.

This is *not* an area where you go exploring on your own. But there are excellent overland tours escorted by experienced guides that provide unforgettable memories if you have the right adaptable temperament. You don't have to be young and hearty or tremendously energetic to enjoy these, but you do need to be an outdoor enthusiast and prepared to camp. Transport is in specially constructed buses, and tents and all necessary equipment are provided; you are usually expected to be in charge of your tent during the trip, but meals are prepared for you. Since this kind of tour tends to attract those who are interested in birds or flowers or geology, it's usually a fine meeting ground for like-minded souls of all ages and many nationalities. Overnights may be spent near a small community or in the heart of a rugged and uninhabited nowhere, perhaps on the edge of a lava field or beneath some craggy white glacier.

There are opportunities to bathe in clear, natural hot water under the open sky, peer into volcanic craters, walk amongst wild, stunning landscapes, and experience a stillness that really has been barely broken by human presence through an immeasurable eternity. One thing is certain: it all adds up to an unforgettable journey. These tours, incidentally, usually incorporate many of the more usual historic or scenic sights en route.

These, then, are the distinctive features of Iceland, a land that woos and ultimately wins all who have once stood on its gray shores and felt the rock beneath them tremble with the subterranean forces of an unseen world.

PRACTICAL INFORMATION FOR REYKJAVIK
AND REGIONS

HOTELS AND RESTAURANTS. Apart from the top hotels in Rekyjavik, Iceland's hotels are modest and simple. Breakfast is not included in the hotel price and there is a high service charge and a state tax. Somewhat less expensive accommodation is available in private homes. Students and other adventurous travelers who want to tour the countryside can usually obtain a night's lodging from $5 provided they supply their own sleeping bags. The summer hotels (university and school hostels used as tourists during the summer vacation) are moderately priced, but demand for rooms is high. For information on rates in the various categories, consult the previous chapter and the *Facts at Your Fingertips* section. Hotels listed below are rated (E) expensive, (M) moderate, and (I) inexpensive. Note that the Edda Hotels are open summer only. In country districts, restaurants are usually limited to those of hotels.

REYKJAVIK

Hotels. All (E): *Loftleidir* (at the airport) where stopover travelers are accommodated. Tropical garden restaurant, bars, heated pools; *Saga,* panoramic view from *Starlight* restaurant; *Esja; Holt,* modern; *Borg,* older but comfortable, very central, and a little less expensive.

City, no restaurant; *Hekla; Gardur,* university hostel used as summer hotel are (M).

The Guest House, Viking Guesthouse, and *private accommodation* are (I).

The *camp site* is in Sundlaugavegur, near the sports stadium and open air swimming pools. The *youth hostel* is at Laufasvegi 41.

Restaurants. There have been some welcome additions recently and there is now a small but attractive selection of eating places catering for all pockets. The price range is approximately as follows: expensive (E) from 300 Ikr.; moderate (M), 135–185 Ikr.; inexpensive (I), 65–160 Ikr. New tourist menus may lower some prices.

Arnarholl (E), new, exclusive and central, with Icelandic specialties; *Naust* (E), best known in city, with attractive nautical atmosphere; *Hlidarendi* (M), good food in pleasant setting; *Kaffivagninn* (M-I), bustling site on fish wharf, specializing in fresh fish (from sea and river); *Hornid Restaurant,* (M-I), attractive, very central, Icelandic lamb among specialties; *Kokk-Husid* (M-I), central, reasonable prices; *Laekjarbrekka* (M-I), in restored old timber house, Icelandic meat and fish specialties as well as morning and afternoon coffee snacks; *Laugaas* (M-I), popular dishes and prices, near camp site; *Torfan* (M-I), Icelandic specialties in old-world atmosphere. In addition a number of discos include *Odal, Hollywood, Thorskaffi* and *Broadway.*

NORTH ICELAND

Akureyri. *K.E.A.* (E-M), 28 rooms; *Vardborg* (M), 24 rooms; *Edda* (I), 70 rooms without bath, summer only.

Blonduos. *Edda* (M-I), 30 rooms.

Husavik. *Husavik* (M), 34 rooms.

Myvatn. *Reynihlid* (M), 44 rooms; *Reykjahlid* (M), 12 rooms without bath, summer only.

Saudarkrokur. *Maelifell* (M-I), 7 rooms.

Skagafjordur. *Varmahlid* (I), 17 rooms.

EASTERN ICELAND

Egilsstadir. *Valaskjalf* (M-I); *Egilsstadir* (I), 15 rooms without bath, summer only.

Eidar. *Edda* (I), 36 rooms without bath, summer only.

Hallormsstadir. *Edda* (I), 27 rooms without bath, summer only.

Hornafjördur. *Höfn,* Hofn (M), 40 rooms; *Edda,* Nesjaskoli (I), 36 rooms without bath, summer only.

SOUTH ICELAND

Fludir. *Summerhotel/Skjolborg* (M-I), 26 rooms.

Hvolsvöllur. *Hvolsvöllur* (M-I), 20 rooms.

Kirkjubaejarklaustur. *Edda* (M-I), 16 rooms, summer only.

Laugarvatn. *New Edda* (M-I), 27 rooms, summer only; *Edda* (I), 88 rooms without bath, summer only.

Selfoss. *Thoristun* (M), 17 rooms.

Skogar. *Edda* (I), 38 rooms without bath, summer only.

Thingvellir. *Valhöll* (M-I), 37 rooms, summer only.

Westmann Islands. *Guesthouse Heimir* (I), 22 rooms.

WESTERN ICELAND

Akranes. *Akranes* (I), 11 rooms without bath.

Isafjördur. *Isafjordur* (M), 33 rooms; *Manakaffi* (I), 15 rooms without bath; *Salvation Army Hostel* (I), 17 rooms without bath.

Reykholt. *Edda* (I), 64 rooms without bath, summer only.

Snaefellsnes. *Budir* (I), 20 rooms without bath, summer only.

Stykkisholmur. *Stykkisholmur* (M), 26 rooms.

Vatnsfjördur. *Edda,* Flokalundur (I), 32 rooms, summer only.

 **SHOPPING.** Iceland cannot qualify as a shopper's paradise, but locally made sweaters, scarves, etc., are beautiful and worth considering. So are sheepskins, ponyskins, lava ceramics or Icelandic silverware. Try the shop of the Handknitting Association of Iceland at Klapparstig. 25–27, or one of the following: Grafeldur, Thingholtsstraeti 2; Framtidin, Laugavegi 45; Rammagerdin, Hafnarstraeti 19; Thorvaldsensbazar, Austurstraeti 4.

Keflavik International Airport is particularly well stocked with duty-free goods as well as a wide variety of local food products, original Icelandic sweaters, handicrafts, etc. Unusually, you may take advantage of purchasing on arrival as well as departure.

 MUSEUMS. In Reykjavik: *Arbaer Folk Museum,* on the city outskirts, interesting and attractive collection of old buildings depicting rural life in the past; *Museum of National History, Museum of Natural History; Arni Magnusson Manuscript Museum (Stofnun Arna Magnussonar)* with splendid collection of ancient manuscripts; *National Library and Archives; Nordic House,* cultural center with exhibitions, lectures, concerts.

Art galleries and exhibition halls in Reykjavik: *Kjarvalsstadir,* Miklatun; *Asgrimur Jonsson Art Gallery,* Bergstadastraeti 74; The *ASI (Iceland Labor Federation) Art Gallery,* Grensasvegur 16; The *National Museum Oval Hall;* The *Nordic House Exhibition Hall* (basement); Sculptor *Asmundur Sveinsson,* Sigtun; and numerous exhibition halls, including *Gallery Sudurgata* and exhibition hall at Laugavegur 112.

Of note in Akureyri are: *Gallery Haholl,* the *Akureyri Folk Museum,* the *House of Nonni* (literary figure), and the *Natural History Museum.*

There are local museums in many towns and villages. In Skogar's *Folk Museum* curator Tordur Tomasson has built up a collection of local items, most still in use until recently. Also interesting is the Glaumbaer turf farm, and Vidimyri's turf church, both near Varmahlid.

 ENTERTAINMENT. Leading drama theaters are the *National Theater* and the *Reykjavik Idno Theater.* These are closed in summer, but during the tourist season there is an attractive light entertainment show in English called "Light Nights" providing an introduction to traditional Icelandic stories and folk songs. The Society of Icelandic Solo Singers also give recitals of Icelandic poetry and songs every week in July and August. *Operas* are performed on average once a year in the National Theater, and *concerts* by the Iceland Symphony Orchestra are fortnightly during the season (September to May or June) in the University Theater building (Haskolabio).

There is dancing in *Sigtun, Thorskaffi, Klubburinn, Glaesibaer, Hotel Saga, Restaurant Naust,* to name the leading ones. Discos are indicated under Reykjavik *Hotels and Restaurants.*

 USEFUL ADDRESSES. Embassies. U.S. 21 Laufasvegi; British, 49 Laufasvegi, both in Reykjavik. Tourist information: Laugavegur 3, and at the Information Tower at Laekjartorg; tourist bureau: 6 Reykjanesbraut, both in Reykjavik. Branch offices at Akureyri and at Keflavik Airport Terminal.

Travel agents. *Utsyn,* Austurstraeti 17; *Atlantic,* Hallveigarstigur 1; *Ferdamidstödin,* Adalstraeti 9; *Gudmundur Jonasson,* Borgartuni 34; *Ulfar Jacobsen,* Austurstraei 9; *Samvinn/Landsyn,* Austurstraeti 12; *Urval,* Posthusstraeti 9.

Climbing. *Icelandic Mountaineering Club* (Ferdafjelag Islands), Reykjavik.

Central Post Office. Reykjavik, on the corner of Austurstraeti and Posthusstraeti; 9–5, Saturdays 9–12.

Car hire. The two main firms are *Icelandair Car Rental* in Reykjavik, and *Akureyri Car Hire (Höldur S.F.)* in Reykjavik and Akureyri.

NORWAY

PRELUDE TO NORWAY

Land of Sea and Mountain

The sea and the mountains: these two themes, with endless variations, weave themselves into the very fabric of Norwegian life. The sea beats along a thousand miles of shoreline, ripples back into a hundred fjords, and bears forth her country's sons to the most distant corners of the earth. The sea brings warmth to an Arctic latitude, but it can be hard and cruel too. So can the mountains which divide the land, isolate one man from his brother and loom ominously over many a village huddled against barren hillsides. Yet the mountains, like the sea, are more loved than feared. Beauty, solitude, forest riches—these are the gifts to Norway.

With two such elemental forces permeating every aspect of Norwegian thought, art, history, economics and culture, it is hardly astonishing that these hardy people of the North are, above all, nature people. Their language itself has a seemingly inexhaustible fund of precise and often idyllic words to describe every kind of natural formation, whether it be of the ocean or the land. And their music and poetry, gay and haunting by turns, never strays too far from an awareness of how closely life is linked with earth, sky and water.

Even the name "nor-way," suggests the subtle fascination of a country on the outermost fringes of the globe. The Greek Pytheas was among the first to record with wonder his trip to "Ultima Thule" in the 4th century B.C., to a shore where the sun shone at midnight. Everything about this Scandinavian nation is on a unique scale. Were someone to straighten out the coast, it would reach halfway around the circumference of the earth. If you could rotate this long and narrow land on its southern tip, it would stretch across the continent of Europe clear down to Rome. If it were populated as densely as the British Isles, there would be 66,000,000 Norwegians instead of a twentieth of that number. However you look at Norway, ordinary words are inadequate.

Keeping alive has never been a simple matter in a country which is not only closer to the Pole than any other, but has few of the resources that are the basis of civilized existence. There is little soil—barely four per cent of the land is arable—and less coal and steel. Of other minerals, only a few are abundant enough to make any difference. Once again it is the mountains and the sea which, together with the character of the people themselves, play the decisive role. The discovery of oil in the North Sea is of primary economic importance for Norway. The Norwegians, famed in the past for their skill in whale-hunting, now contribute to preserving the species; it is the leviathan oil rigs anchored off their coast that concern them now. The mountains nurture forests with the hundred and one products wood gives birth to. And the waters tumbling from their heights spin the turbines that generate light, heat and power for all.

Even so, the scales dip heavily on the side favoring Nature against man. Courage, hard work, and above all, perseverance, are the decisive factors in the human equation. A lesser folk might have sought excuses or given up entirely, but the modern descendants of the Vikings are made of sterner stuff. The last war demonstrated this, if the fact required proof at all, when a gallant though hopeless resistance was followed by a united struggle against the invader. At one time, indeed, nearly 600,000 of the enemy were occupying and seeking to exploit the nation they had thought to win over so easily. Nor does everyone know that the tankers of the Norwegian merchant marine carried more than half the fuel during the Battle of Britain in the summer of 1940.

Our first principle is thus that Norway is a country of individualists who have learned to work collectively for the national good. The sailors and fishermen, the nomadic Lapps of Finnmark, the lumberjacks of the eastern valleys, the industrial workers in Oslo, all these are joined together by the Norse farmers, who provide the link between sea and mountains. For the three per cent of the land they claim as their own is scattered everywhere: on the southern plains of Jaeren, the rolling hills of Tröndelag, on the tiny islands, on steep slopes and in forest clearings.

The second principle is that this nation is an outdoor country. The capital numbers less than half a million, and only one other city, Bergen, has more than a third of Oslo's population. All the rest of the people live in much smaller towns and communities spread over an area twice the size of England and Wales. Along that tortuous coast some 150,000 islands make a paradise for the bather, fisherman, sailor or simple boat-passenger. Inland there are great regions which are essentially unpopulated, and here you can hunt for elk and reindeer, angle for salmon and trout, or camp, climb, and hike or ski for as long and as far as you please. If most Norwegians live within 20 miles of the sea, it is equally true that practically all of them dwell within sight of the mountains. And with the great outdoors at both their front and back windows, they naturally seek fresh air and blue skies whenever they can.

The final principle is that Norway and its people are pre-eminently civilized. Though Nature dominates the scene, man's work is always in the foreground. And though mountains and sea circumscribe and delimit, the Norwegians are as vitally interested in what takes place beyond their borders as in the unnoted progress they make from day to day within. As a nation they have little need of the urban amusements which distinguish more "sophisticated" countries to the south. Music, theater, the arts and learning are appreciated no less sincerely, but they are seldom allowed to soar beyond the grounds of reason and fantasy into the merely obscure. Knowledge is regarded as part of the common birthright which all men inherit, and understanding is sought as one, but never more than one, of the marks of a balanced personality.

Civilization, however, is more than a matter of books, great ideas and noble art. Here the Norwegians, in common with their Scandinavian brothers, come into their own. Pedants and theoreticians are thought to be pitiful rather than impressive, and demagogues lead an unhappy life. Instead, a sense of civic duty, a feeling of obligation towards other, less-favored men, and an affirmation of individual integrity are perhaps the distinguishing features of the Norwegian character. Nearly all Norwegians are friendly, nearly all are genuinely interested in the visitors who come to see their country, nearly all have that engaging admixture of common sense and good humor which is the leaven of their national life. They will make you feel welcome wherever you go.

PRACTICAL INFORMATION FOR NORWAY

WHAT IT WILL COST. See also *Facts at Your Fingertips* section earlier in this volume. Inflation is hitting Norway, as everywhere else, and you can expect a yearly increase of about 10 per cent. The prices outlined below are approximate and should serve to give you an idea of the costs.

Hotel prices: for a double room with bath and breakfast in Oslo, around 500 Nkr for deluxe, around 350 to 500 Nkr for an expensive hotel, around 250 to 375 Nkr for a moderate hotel and 64 Nkr per bed, in a youth hostel. Prices in Stavanger, Bergen and Trondheim are slightly lower, while in country hotels they are considerably less.

A Typical Day In Oslo Might Cost Two People:

Hotel, moderate, with breakfast	270 Nkr
Restaurant meal	140
Transportation, 2 taxis, four tram rides	75
Cinema	45
Coffee, one beer	40
Miscellaneous 10%	57
	627 Nkr

Restaurant prices: Expensive, deluxe meals are just that and cost upwards of 100 Nkr (excluding wine). An average meal costs about 70 Nkr (excluding wine). Cocktail costs 25 Nkr and beer from 20 Nkr.

Some local costs: cinema 10–20 Nkr; ladies' hairdresser 70 Nkr; man's haircut 50 Nkr; cigarettes, local variety, 17.20 Nkr.

TIPPING. The service charge on hotel bills is 10–15 per cent; more often it is already included in the bill. Where the charge is added, it covers everyone but the head porter who is paid 5 Nkr per day for services rendered. Maids and bellhops are only paid for extra services. The man who carries your bags is paid 2 Nkr per suitcase. Restaurants also almost always put the service on the bill, and you can leave the odd change to bring it up to an even crown. Tip the bar man 5%. Tip washroom and cloakroom (included in the ticket price in theaters) attendants 1.50 Nkr. Barbers, mechanics, and cinema attendants are not tipped.

WHEN TO COME. Summer in Norway lasts from early May until mid-September, May and June are considered the best months for visiting the "Fjord Country," when the thousands of fruit trees in blossom present an unforgettable sight. In the early summer the weather is also usually warm and reliable, thanks to the influence of the Gulf Stream (during June-August the mean temperature in Oslo is higher than in such places as London and San Francisco). At the North Cape, the sun does not sink below the horizon from the second week in May until the last week in July, and at Spitsbergen (Svalbard) you have the Midnight Sun from April 20 to August 24. June, July and August are popular holiday months for locals and tourists and the sea is then warmest for swimming, but some hotels are apt to be crowded. Because of the beauty of the autumn foliage, September is tops with those seeking a mountain holiday, but weather can be variable. The top winter sports season runs from Feb.-late Apr.

WHAT TO SEE. Norway is primarily an outdoor country, its attractions being its people and its scenery rather than the entertainments usually supplied by cities. To visit Norway without seeing its scenic wonders is like visiting the Grand Canyon without seeing the canyon. Since these sights are spread over a 1,100-mile length of countryside, however, the problem is *how* to see them. Where to go depends upon what you wish to see: *Fjords* are everywhere along the coastline, from the Oslo Fjord at the foot of the capital to the Kobbholm Fjord east of Kirkenes, in the Arctic, but the spectacular "Fjord Country" is that region in the west stretching from Stavanger in the south to Kristiansund in the north. *Mountains and waterfalls* are part of the fjord district, but northern Europe's mightiest mountain range is the Jotunheimen, lying between the Fjord Country and the Gudbrandsdal and Valdres valleys. *The Midnight Sun* must be viewed above the Arctic Circle, a good 700 miles north of Oslo. *Folklore* is richest in the Setesdal-Telemark district, in the regions of the Hardanger and Sogne fjords and the Valdres and Gudbrandsdal valleys.

Highlights of Norway. The Number One city is Oslo, with its Vigeland Park and its Viking ships, and Bergen, surrounded by seven beautiful mountains, is second. The Number One Trip is, of course, a visit to the fjords, where the finest and highest waterfalls in Europe drape the horizontal cliffs. The trip to the North Cape and the Midnight Sun is another classic. For a medieval town there's Trondheim—from which, as an oddity, you can go to Hell and prove it to your friends by the postmark on your cards (there's a place by that name in Norway).

Stave Churches rank high among the famous tourist attractions of Norway. They are real masterpieces of ancient architecture, with beautiful interiors, richly decorated with wood carvings, often of outstanding artistic value. The origin of the stave church is a controversial issue. Some historians believe they were rooted in the heathen cult of the Viking Age—and the frequent use of dragon heads and serpent ornaments seems to support this theory. Others say that the stave church represents the Norseman's adaptation of the Gothic.

Most stave churches were built during the 12th century or earlier. Only 32 of the original 750 stave churches remain today, and four are museums. Even Vikingland's capital city has a fine stave church—probably one of the most photographed buildings in the country—it's the famous Gol stave church at the Norwegian Folk Museum in Oslo. Bergen has the beautiful Fantoft stave church, situated 6 km from the city center, and Lillehammer is proud of the Garmo stave church, in the unique Maihaugen Museum. Other stave churches are mentioned later in this book.

HOW TO GET ABOUT. Much of the Norwegian railroad system is through beautiful countryside, and a number of express trains have coaches with large viewing windows. These serve the routes linking Oslo with Stavanger, Bergen, Åndalsnes and Trondheim, even as far north as Bodø beyond the Arctic Circle. Seat reservation is compulsory on all express trains (the fee is 10 Nkr.), and can be made up to a year in advance. The Sleeper supplement costs 125 Nkr first class, 90 Nkr second class. All main trains carry first- and second-class by day and night. Local trains are generally second-class only.

Because of the difficult mountainous terrain of the country, overall speeds are not high. If speed is your requirement use the widespread internal air service operated by SAS, Braathens and Widerōe. But if you want to see the country, take the train.

All trains in Norway are classified as *Ekspresstog* (Express), *Hurtigtog* (Fast) or *Persontog* (Slow). Mainline daytime expresses have either dining or buffet cars. Overnight trains usually carry first- and second-class sleeping cars, day coaches, but not couchettes.

Tours. The best way to get an overall look at Norway is to take one of the combined air-sea trips run by various travel agencies in conjunction with SAS, British Airways and Norwegian shipping lines. You can fly from Bergen to Kirkenes near the North Cape, and take the leisurely boat trip southward through magnificent channels and fjords, in a 7-day package tour. There is a 22-day camping trek into the Arctic Circle via the western fjords. Numerous other package possibilities exist, including one-day air or steamer excursions which cover especially the fjord country. (See tour operators in *Facts at Your Fingertips* section earlier.)

A number of reduced-rate round-trip-tours in Norway can only be purchased there. The tours, for a minimum of 3–5 days and often combining rail, bus, and steamer travel, offer a reduction over ordinary fares of 30%. There are no reductions on ordinary round trips. The Norwegian Fjord Line and Viking Line operate 3- and 6-day tours through the famous fjord country between Oslo and Bergen. (See also *Motoring* section following.)

MOTORING in Norway is very different from what it is in most other European countries. There is never a long and tedious journey to reach your destination, because you are there all the time. The scenery is constantly changing in all its breath-taking beauty. Many roads are outstanding tourist attractions on their own merit—particularly in the Fjord Country—with hairpin bends and mountain passes, smiling lakes and thundering waterfalls. There are good hotels along every major tourist route. Roads are often narrow, so you should plan to cover no more than 250 km (154 miles) per day. As filling stations may be far apart, particularly in the north and on the mountain roads, stock up.

The ideal starting point for any motoring vacation in Scandinavia is Bergen on the west coast, reached by direct flights from New York or London. Visitors should first explore the Fjord Country, then drive across the mountain ranges to Oslo and onwards to Stockholm and Copenhagen.

Starting from Bergen, there is a choice of four major routes to Oslo, each of such great scenic beauty that it is difficult to choose among them. All take in the fantastic Tokagjel canyon east of Bergen and the giant Hardanger fjord with stunning vistas of the huge Folgefonn glacier, but here they part. One route goes through the Telemark region to Oslo (538 km or 334 miles), and another across the Hardanger mountain plateau via Geilo to Oslo (489 km or 303 miles).

Two other routes from Bergen continue via Voss and the stupendous zig-zag road through Stalheim canyon to Gudvangen on the narrow Naerøy fjord—a branch of the Sogne fjord, longest and deepest in Norway. One route goes by ferry to Revsnes and then via the Tyin mountain road to Oslo (565 km or 350 miles), whereas the other route goes by ferry to Kaupanger and then along Sogne fjord and across Sognefjell mountain pass—highest in Norway at 1440m or 4690 ft—down to Otta and Oslo (735 km or 456 miles).

Any of these four routes could be covered in 2 days, but there is great scope for excursions en route, so you could easily spend 3 or 4 days on the trip. The

Telemark route is open throughout the year, because two mountain passes are now bypassed by tunnels. The other routes are blocked by snow from November to May. See the *Fjord Country* chapter for many other tours of the western fjords. Remember that any combination of two eastern valleys with one or more western fjords invariably makes a perfect itinerary.

Ambitious motoring buffs may like to drive all the way from Oslo to North Cape—a distance of 2233 km or 1383 miles, including 3 ferry crossings and several mountain passes. You drive through Trondheim, Bodø, Narvik and Tromsø, but in between every town you will experience all the scenic delights that Nature's Wonderland can offer you—fjords, rivers, waterfalls, mountains, glaciers and even Lapps with their reindeer herds.

 HOTELS. Norwegian hotels are spotlessly clean and comfortable, and the visitor receives value for his money. Inclusive pension terms are available for stays of 3 or 5 days or longer. Hotels, of course, vary in size and degree of comfort, but the hotel trade is protected by law in Norway, and every establishment calling itself a hotel must fulfill certain requirements with regard to size, standard of modern conveniences, etc. Resort hotels offering superior accommodation are called "tourist" or "mountain" hotels (*Turist* or *Höyfjell-shotell*). "Mountain" hotels must be situated at least 2,500 feet above sea level.

Norwegian hotels follow the "middle way" with respect to prices: there are few in the top luxury categories or in the very lowest category. Establishments such as mountain inns, chalets, tourist stations, hostels, and boarding houses generally come under the "pension" category. For information concerning rates in the various categories, consult the *Facts at Your Fingertips* and *What It Will Cost* sections preceding.

Note hotels strictly enforce a noon-checkout. If you want to keep your room until 1 or 2 P.M., it will mean an extra 25%, if you want to remain until 6 P.M., you must pay 50% of the full rate.

Chalets. The Norwegians are a cottage-minded people, and there are several hundred thousand privately-owned chalets, some of which are hired out when not in use. Likewise, there are a great number of cottages built for renting to visitors. Inspected chalets can be rented through *Den norske Hytteformidling,* Box 3207, Oslo 4, or through *Norsk Folke Feries Reisebyrå,* Arbeidersamfunnet-splass, Oslo 1. They also arrange rentals of cabins in the popular ski centers in winter.

The cabins generally contain kitchen, open-hearth sitting-room and from one to three bedrooms, with accommodation for 4–6 persons. The kitchen is equipped with dishes, cooking utensils, etc. A top standard cottage with mod. cons. costs between 400 and 1,300 Nkr a week during the summer. Special cottage holidays for motorists are arranged by *Danish Seaways,* Tyne Commission Quay, Tyne & Wear, NE29 6EE; and by *Norway Only,* 126 Sunbridge Rd, Bradford, W. Yorks, BD1 2SX.

 FOOD AND DRINK. Norwegian food is tasty and plentiful. The national specialty, known as the *koldtbord* (cold table) is famous for its variety of dishes, such as smoked salmon, fresh lobster, and Norwegian shrimps. The *smörbröd,* a single-decker sandwich, offers an endless variety of succulent snacks, including meat, salad, cheese, etc. Venison, ptarmigan in cream sauce, wild raspberries, cloudberries and brown trout are among the specialties.

In an effort to keep prices down, a number of restaurants and cafés offer a *feriemeny* (holiday menu) consisting of a main course and coffee for 29 Nkr or 43 Nkr, including service and tax.

Norwegian law forbids the sale of hard liquor in cities at weekends, on national holidays and on the days preceding holidays. However, licensed restaurants serve any kind of wine even when their bar is closed. Bottles of spirits can be bought at branches of the state-run Vin Monopol, but imported whiskies are very highly priced, and Norwegian brands are drinkable only if diluted with something else.

 CAMPING. Over 1,400 camping sites are scattered throughout the tourist areas of Norway, and charges for car and tent are very reasonable. The Norwegian Tourist Board offers a free folder on camp sites, listing them with 1, 2, or 3 stars according to the facilities available.

 SPORTS. Although spectator sports exist, they do not satisfy the Norwegian individualist. He must have his own skis, his own skates, and his own boat, and these he uses whenever he can and whatever his age or walk of life. A good instance of this is the annual ski marathon, which is restricted to government employees, ministers included. What other government can muster so many nimblefooted ski-wearing chief executives?

The south coast and the region around Oslo have several seaside spots where the weather is reliable and the facilities for **swimming** and other **water sports** are plentiful. Stavanger, on the west coast, has fine sandy beaches. **Sailing** is enjoyed in Norway all around the coast from Trondheim to Oslo. The capital itself, situated at the head of the picturesque island-studded Oslo Fjord, is the most important yachting center.

Norway's mountain districts are easily reached from all parts of the country. In a few hours' walk from road or railway you can reach beautiful country off the beaten track. The great mountain ranges are ideal for **hiking** and offer excellent holiday facilities. Although most—but not all—have been climbed, there is still scope for further exploratory **mountaineering.** All the popular rock climbs are well marked, thus making these ideal for parties of some experience wishing to learn guideless climbing.

Over 200 rivers provide salmon and sea-trout **fishing.** The season extends from June to September. Some of the best salmon fishing in the world can be had in these Norwegian rivers. In addition, Norway is honeycombed with several thousand lakes scattered all over the country. There is trout in practically every lake and river, even high up among the mountain ranges. The season varies according to altitude, but generally speaking there is trout fishing from end May to mid-Sept.

The Norwegian Tourist Board's inexpensive guide book *Mountain Touring in Norway* is indispensable for hikers, and anglers should get their invaluable guide *Angling in Norway.*

Salmon fishing is offered by *Fly-spesialisten,* Kronprinsesse Märthas plass 1, Oslo 1, while hunting trips are organised by *Trönderreiser,* Kongensgate 30 N-7000 Trondheim.

WINTER SPORTS. In Norway, the home of **skiing,** the whole country is a vast skiing area, with terrains to fit the abilities of expert and novice, the tastes of ski tourer and downhill runner. Ski lifts are available at all the major centers, and skis may be hired for a small fee. Prices and fares are reduced in January, when the snow also is at its best. However, there is ample snow from Christmas until the end of April, with plenty of warm sunshine and dry, inland air. The cross-country ski craze hit America a few years back and package tours from the U.S. and Canada are very popular to such traditional touring centers as Lillehammer, Voss or Geilo. Check with a travel agent or the Norwegian tourist office.

Norway is so mountainous that you can ski almost anywhere. Nevertheless, there are regions where more people congregate for this purpose than elsewhere and which, consequently, offer more facilities to visitors. Oslo—with the wooded hills of Nordmarka—is the biggest winter sports center of east Norway. Other resorts within easy reach of the capital are Kongsberg and Klekken, while Norefjell provides downhill running.

Woodland settings characterize the Telemark resorts of Bolkesjö, Morgedal, Vrådal and Vråliosen, whereas more mountainous country is found at Rjukan, Rauland and Tuddal. West Norway has developed skiing resorts at Kvamskog and Seljestad. Along the Bergen railway are such well-known resorts as Voss, Mjölfjell, and Vatnahalsen in alpine terrain; Finse, surrounded by glorious mountains; while Ustaoset and Geilo (the biggest and most popular resort), Ål, Gol, and Nesbyen, are set in more rolling country.

The top winter sports center on the Dovre railway in the Gudbrandsdal country is Lillehammer in hill country. Similar undulating terrain is found at Tretten, Espedal, Harpefoss, Vinstra, and Dombås. Oppdal offers more rugged country, Hamar is set in typical wooded terrain. The hotels in the Jotunheimen mountains—Bygdin, Tyin, Eidsbugaren, Spiterstulen and Leirvassbu—are all situated in alpine terrain. Valdres offers a great variety of skiing country: typical woodland skiing down in the valleys, and mountainous terrain at Beitostølen, Grindaheim, Nystova, Nøsen and Maristova. (See the regional chapters.)

Although skiing is the big sport, there is **curling, tobogganing,** and **skikjoring** as well, and many resorts have excellent **skating** rinks. You may even indulge in a week or two of dogsled touring on skis if the fancy strikes you. This is not for novices, but you needn't be an expert skier either.

YOUTH AT THE HELM. Tomm, Murstad's Sailing Camp at Hoyerholmen, on the Oslo Fjord near Oslo, trains boys and girls 8–15 years old in sailing, water skiing, rowing, outboarding, and life saving.

POSTAL RATES. Letters to the U.S., Canada, and the U.K. cost 3.50 Nkr for the first 20 grams; postcards cost 3 Nkr. All letters and postcards are sent by air automatically. (Postage lower to other Scandinavian countries.)

ACCESS IN NORWAY. A most valuable booklet with this title is available from 68B Castlebar Rd., Ealing, London W5. It gives a great deal of extremely handy information for the disabled or less mobile traveler. Highly recommended. The Norwegian Tourist Board has also published a list of hotels with facilities for the physically handicapped.

OSLO

The Countryside Capital

The bright, breezy and outdoorsy capital of Norway is a hospitable city of 459,000 people at the head of the Oslo Fjord. You may be surprised to know that in area it is one of the largest metropolises in the world, the city fathers having made it 27 times larger than its original size with a stroke of the pen in 1948. This is Norway's answer to all those progressive cities that have recently more than doubled their size. Here is a world capital with Nature at its very doorstep, a perfect place to adjust from the frenetic, over-sophisticated existence of some Western cities to the simpler and more wholesome values of Norwegian life.

Oslo in itself is not a city of great architecture, yet in the somewhat haphazard arrangement of streets and buildings there is an unmistakable charm. And if you really go looking, you will certainly find modern architecture that will soothe the eye. But, as every Oslo-ite says, "The surroundings!" Yes, they are magnificent, and the view of town and fjord from any of the easily-reached heights is entrancing. But do not jump to the conclusion that the first thing to do upon arrival is to rush out of town. That is only part of your curriculum—there is plenty to see and do right in Oslo before you head for the hills.

Exploring Oslo

Paradoxical as it may seem, the capital of Norway is not only the fourth largest metropolis in the world but is largely covered by forests. Both these statements, we're sure you'll agree, require a little explanation. In 1948 the citizens of Oslo indulged themselves in a bit of tongue-in-cheek deception. Some progress-minded cities like to boast about how they have doubled their size in so-and-so many years. The Oslonians, not to be outdone, decided that no half measures would suffice. At one stroke of the pen they extended the city limits in all directions, and on New Year's Day of the year just mentioned, Oslo woke up to find itself 27 times larger than it had been the night before.

As far as the forest is concerned, it is easy to see what happened. While mountains, meadows and remote farms were being swallowed up, the trees simply stayed on where they had been. Whatever your reaction to this sleight of hand may be, the fact remains that Oslo is one of the least urbanized cities anywhere. In a sense, the capital has Nature on its very doorstep. To the south are the harbor and the fjord leading down to the sea, and on all other sides are high hills and friendly valleys leading into the vast Norwegian hinterland. Thus Oslo is the gateway to Norway.

The capital is an excellent spot to begin your tour of this westernmost country of Scandinavia. Besides its natural beauty, besides being the heart of this lamb-chop-shaped nation, it provides you with a hospitable and stimulating place to stay while you are readjusting.

Readjusting? Yes, from over-sophisticated existence in the larger cities of the West to the simpler, close-to-earth customs and activities of the Norwegian people. The Anglo-Saxon visitor will have to readjust himself to many things, particularly if he intends to stay long enough to discover the real Norway. From dependence on a car to the use of his own feet; from expecting quick service wherever he goes, to a more leisurely philosophy of time; from vast crowds to vast spaces. He must even adapt himself to the practical Norse habit of undressing on the beach without benefit of a bathhouse, albeit skillfully and decently.

A sojourn in any Norwegian town will prepare you to understand and to participate in the Norseman's active love of Nature. However, Oslo offers the best example of how the whole schedule of business life is influenced by the urge to be out of doors as much as possible. Offices don't close for lunch as in the rest of Scandinavia. Instead, the Norwegian businessman or government official works straight through the day with only a short pause at his desk to eat sandwiches brought from home. Around the middle of the afternoon he has dinner, takes a nap (in winter at least) and then it's out sailing, swimming, hiking or skiing, or pottering around the garden, as the weather and the season dictate.

Preview on Deck

If you approach Norway's capital by boat, the 60-mile sail up the Oslo Fjord will be an experience you'll long remember. Near the eastern side of the fjord mouth is the island of Hankö, where in summer

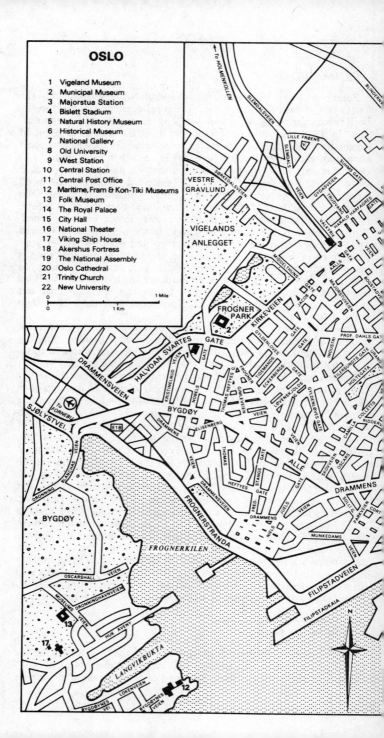

OSLO

1 Vigeland Museum
2 Municipal Museum
3 Majorstua Station
4 Bislett Stadium
5 Natural History Museum
6 Historical Museum
7 National Gallery
8 Old University
9 West Station
10 Central Station
11 Central Post Office
12 Maritime, Fram & Kon-Tiki Museums
13 Folk Museum
14 The Royal Palace
15 City Hall
16 National Theater
17 Viking Ship House
18 Akershus Fortress
19 The National Assembly
20 Oslo Cathedral
21 Trinity Church
22 New University

0 _____ 1 Mile
0 _____ 1 Km

you may catch a glimpse of white sails in one of the international regattas for which these waters are famous. Farther up the fjord, the paper mill town of Moss will be briefly visible until hidden by Jelöy Island, while on the opposite bank, connected with Moss by car ferry, lies the former naval base of Horten. Dröbak, on the east side, appears about an hour later. Just ahead is the island fortress of Oscarsborg.

Passing through the Dröbak Narrows, you have a short hour's cruise between the holiday suburbs of Oslo that line both shores of the now broadening fjord. Gaily painted summer houses are everywhere, each with its white flagpole and its little pier.

Along the western shore near the city you see the striking silhouette of a whole row of high ridges running south and ending in abrupt precipices. These are ancient lava-flows from a crater many miles inland which has now disappeared. Skaugum and Kolsås are two of the highest (about 1,200 feet) but the well-known Holmenkollen Hill dominating the head of the fjord is higher by a third. Other hills to the north and east—Vettakollen, Grefsenkollen and Ekeberg—complete the characteristic setting of Oslo by giving it a backdrop of forest and highlands on three sides. The center of the city is now at hand, and its man-made landmarks pass by in quick review. On your left: Fornebu Airport, which is Oslo's principal airport; Bygdöy peninsula, with the sharp-pitched roof of the building housing the polar expedition ship *Fram;* and then those bluntly striking twin towers of Oslo's red brick Town Hall. Just beyond, and far more rambling and romantic in form, are the stone ramparts and spires of Akershus Fortress.

On your right, just before you dock, you look down Bunde Fjord, which, though it appears to be another major waterway, is in reality a dead-end affair only 12 miles long. Just above the harbor on the west side the big gray buildings of the Merchant Marine Academy dominate the scene, while higher up in a clearing among the pines stands the white shape of Ekeberg Restaurant.

Getting Orientated

Now that you've arrived, found your hotel and have had a chance to change into your walking shoes, you'll want to get your bearings in Norway's charming capital. Perhaps the best way would be to go up to the Merchant Marine Academy, which you saw on your way into port. From the terrace in front of this buildings there is a close-up, bird's-eye view of downtown Oslo. Assuming that you could take your eyes from the small boats poking their way among the many islands below your feet, you should recognize the more important features of the city from your map, and in a few minutes you'd feel just as much at home as if you were a native son.

But you'll probably want to explore the heart of the city first, so we'll let this trip wait until you've had a chance to see a little more. Karl Johansgate is Oslo's principal street, running from the Central Station uphill to the Royal Palace. More or less halfway in between is a small green park through which sooner or later every Norwegian finds his way. Let's start here.

If we stand in Stortingsgate, the street running parallel to Karl Johansgate on the harbor side of the park, the National Theater will be immediately on our left. This is one of the focal points of the capital's cultural life, and the two statues which flank its entrance are Henrik Ibsen, the Norwegian poet and playwright, and Björnstjerne Björnson, his distinguished colleague. As you stroll around the National Theater you come to a spot which will be your point of departure for trips to the outlying section of Oslo. This is the unimpressive-looking set of stairs leading down to the underground station.

Of Kings and Commoners

Before crossing towards the Royal Palace, step up to the Kongeterrassen on the corner from Stortingsgate and Munkedammsveien. There are little open air restaurants here, but it is the statue you have come to see. The tall, slim figure gazing into the distance is King Haakon the Seventh, who was the beloved monarch of Norway for fifty years and the focal point for Norway's hopes during the Second World War. His son, the present King Olav, also has a deep hold on the affections of his people, and lives, as his father did, in the Royal Palace, known as Slottet, which is surrounded by a park. The grounds around the residence are open to anyone, and are a very pleasant oasis on a summer's day. On the rise overlooking Drammensveien, you will find a monument by Gustav Vigeland which is an allegorical commemoration of Niels Henrik Abel, Norway's mathematical genius.

The king has his own guards, and you can watch their ceremonial changing of the guard every day at 1.30. The statue on the parade is of King Carl Johan, who was a Swedish king of Norway. To the west of the palace in front of it, is a statue by Ada Madssen of Queen Maud, the English wife of King Haakon, mother of King Olav.

Continuing around the square you come to the Studenterlunden, the tree-shaded promenade along Karl Johansgate opposite the neoclassic building of the University of Oslo. Between the two symmetrical wings is the Aula, where the students gather for their matriculation exercises. The main hall is graced by Edvard Munch's haunting murals. Past this spot on the 17th of May, Constitution Day, march thousands of school children, each with his own flag, as they go up to the palace to greet the royal family.

We make our way, however, in the opposite direction. As soon as we have gone by the little band stand where programs of light music are presented during the summer, we catch sight of the Storting or Parliament directly ahead of us. Keeping this on our right we proceed down Karl Johansgate four blocks to Kongensgate, where we turn left at the traffic light and come into the busy flower market at Stortorget.

Facing you is Our Savior's, Oslo's cathedral, consecrated in 1697. Dagfin Werenskiold's bronze reliefs decorate its doors. The royal figure who stands with his back to you and arm outstretched is Christian IV, King of Denmark and Norway, who moved the ancient town farther westward so as to bring it under the protective wing of Akershus Fortress. At the same time he changed the infant city's name to Christiania, and this was the name it kept until just over a generation ago.

The Akershus Fortress

By now you're probably curious about this oft-mentioned Akershus Fortress. After one last glance at the imperial features of good King Christian, let's leave Stortorget by Kirkegate. We have now reversed our direction, and in a moment we cross Karl Johansgate again. If you pause at this intersection the Central Station comes into view to your left, but we must proceed five or six blocks more, a route which takes us through Oslo's main shopping section and brings us to the entrance of the fort.

Here the guide will give you the details about the oldest ramparts, about the palace occupied by King Håkon V during the 14th century, and of events between 1940 and 1945 when it was a German headquarters.

Close behind the stone monument which honors the memory of the Norwegian patriots who were executed within these walls, is a very interesting, factual, and unembittered Resistance Museum, with unique exhibits which give a clear picture of the years the Norwegians called "long". There is also a photograph, treasured by all the Norwegians, showing two nattily-dressed German officers saluting a knicker-clad member of the Norwegian Home Front as they surrendered the fort to him on May 11, 1945. The latest addition to the museums in the Akershus is the Defense Museum, with much to interest both the military-minded and others who wish to learn about Norway's development in the art of war.

When you've finished exploring Akershus and seen the royal mausoleums and the pleasant grounds, retrace your steps to Rådhusgate and turn left. A pleasant stroll takes you to the Rådhusplass, the vast square separating the Rådhus, or City Hall, with its bronze and granite statues, fountains and flowers, from the harbor. Just before entering the square, look to the left as you cross at the traffic lights. You will see a statue of Franklin D. Roosevelt, holding a copy of the Atlantic Charter. It is the work of Stinius Fredriksen, and was unveiled by Eleanor Roosevelt in June 1950. The martial figure pointing out to sea from the square is the naval hero, Peter Wessel Tordenskiold, admiral in the Danish/Norwegian fleet from 1715 to 1720. Time was when only the fishing boats, tied up to sell their freshly-caught shrimp (which taste marvelous if you can eat them on the spot sitting on the edge of the piers), could be found here, along with the tourist and ferry boats.

Ferry steamers connect the center of town with Bundefjord, a lovely armlet of the main Oslo Fjord, Nesodden, the large peninsula on the eastern side, lower Oslo Fjord. It's from here that you can get a boat during the summer to take you to Bygdöy, on the western side of the fjord, where the museums are. On a summer's day the area is warm with life and local color.

If you stroll across the square towards the West Station, you can walk through the gardens on the western side of the City Hall. In a moment or two you are in Fridtjof Nansen's Plass which is either the front or the back of the City Hall, depending on how you look at it. The debate as to which way the building faces has been raging for some years now, and probably always will. Ramble up the steps past the gaily painted wooden bas-reliefs and the Swans Fountain, brace yourself and go into the main hall.

Yards of Art, Sculpture by the Ton

Straight ahead on the south wall is Henrik Sørensen's 40-by-77 foot oil painting of *Work, Administration and Leisure,* a dynamic and multidetailed masterpiece in the contemporary Norwegian style of murals. On the north wall another staggeringly vast fresco confronts you. This time it's Alf Rolfsen's picturization of different phases of life and work in Norway. Similarly, on either flank are more monumental paintings and decorations competing for your attention. It is perhaps Philistine-like to state that the total area of the murals in the Rådhus has been estimated at close to 2,000 square yards. On the other hand, it would be presumptuous to attempt to sum up this much art in a line or two. Perhaps the best way of coming to terms with so overpowering an impression is to return several times, meanwhile giving your dazzled eyes a chance to refocus. Unless you do, the strong colors and bold figures of the larger works will distract you from the more engaging details that have been lavished on the various public rooms by Norway's foremost artists.

By now if your feet don't ache, your head probably does, so we suggest that you head up Universitetsgate. In a moment you are back in front of the National Theater, where any number of nearby restaurants will be glad to restore you while you reflect on all that you've seen.

Probably the most famous part of Oslo is Frogner Park. Here there are some hundred and fifty groups of statuary in bronze and granite which represent almost the entire output of one fantastic genius, Gustav Vigeland. Many are the opinions regarding the immobile people who populate this gracious park.

Judgments vary from condemnation of certain works as being a "glorification of obesity" to unanimous praise for the sympathetic studies of little children in a garden beside the bridge.

But see it all for yourself: the massive entrance gates in wrought iron, the figures on the bridge parapet, the bas-reliefs around the fountain depicting the cycle of life, and the 60-foot monolith which Vigeland meant to be the crowning achievement of his career. Wander among the statues, reach out and touch them, and then retreat to the terrace of the open-air restaurant nearby where you can sit and contemplate the total effect. Whatever else may be said, these are the sometimes tender, sometimes brutal but always honest figures of a man who loved life.

Bygdöy, Boats and Outdoor Museums

All good Norwegians put to sea at some time during their lives. Let's go down to Pipervika behind the Town Hall and do the same. The ferry-boat indicating "Til Bygdöynes og Dronningen" churns officiously across the harbor towards that steep-pitched roof on the tip of Bygdöy peninsula.

The wedge-shaped building now in front of us shelters the famous polar ship *Fram,* which took Fridtjof Nansen, Otto Sverdrup and later Roald Amundsen farther north and farther south than any other boat had been before. Inside, the vessel stands with its rigging, its thick reinforced wooden hull and all its equipment intact. Outside, you will find the stout little ship *Gjøa* that in 1903 took Amundsen to the Northwest Passage. (Incidentally, Roald Amundsen lived in a house along Bunde Fjord, once only reached by boat or on foot, and these ships lay at anchor there before their voyages. You can visit the house any day between May 15 and September 15.) The Maritime Museum is an impressive one, with an important collection of seagoing objects and navigational models, including one of the sloops which took the first Norwegian immigrants to the U.S. in 1825.

Just a harpoon's throw away is the museum building containing the even more famous Kon Tiki balsa raft. As everyone who has read the book by the same name knows, Thor Heyerdahl, a Norwegian ethnologist, used this primitive craft on his 4,300-mile trip across the Pacific from Peru to Polynesia. Heyerdahl undertook this journey in the hope of proving his theory that the southern Pacific islands were first settled from the Americas as well as from Asia. The trip was a success—only the parrot came to grief. The *Ra II,* the papyrus boat in which Heyerdahl crossed the Atlantic in 1970, has now joined the Kon Tiki here.

Some distance inland (just follow your map), is perhaps the greatest memorial to the Norwegians' seafaring tradition. This is the trio of Viking ships dating back to the 8th or 9th century. The Oseberg ship contained many treasures meant to accompany a Viking queen on her last journey. The low sides of this boat indicate that it was used primarily in sheltered water. The largest vessel is the Gokstad ship, built solidly enough to cross the Atlantic although it seems almost fragile.

Bygdöy's most impressive establishment is the immense Folk Museum. In the course of a few hours you can view a cross section of Norwegian life and culture through the ages.

To get your land legs back again, there's no better way than to explore Holmenkollen, the hill that separates Oslo from Nordmarka, its year-round outdoor playground. At Frognerseteren Station you get off and walk first to the top of Tryvannshøgda where an elevator will whisk you up the TV and tourist tower to a commanding view of Oslo and seven surrounding parishes. Then walk down the hill, stopping to enjoy the view up Bunde Fjord and down Oslo Fjord. Otherwise, follow the road down Holmenkollen Way for about 15 minutes, and you'll come to an even more spectacular place to pause and meditate. You'll find yourself just under the spot where ski jumpers launch themselves into the air after hurtling down from the top of the Holmenkollen ski jump, and you can try to imagine what it would be like to travel some 270 feet (the record) without ever touching the ground. Before leaving, take a look at the interesting ski museum and ride the elevator to the top of the jump for more views of the fjord. (The ski jump was greatly extended for the 1982 world championships).

The Old City

As yet we haven't really explored the older, more historic section of Oslo. One reason for this oversight is that very little remains. But if the site of the original settlement is today largely overgrown by a busy industrial district, at least there is another superb view awaiting us at the journey's end. At the East Station we climb aboard the Ekebergbanen. Ask the conductor for a ticket to Sjömannskolen, the Merchant Marine Academy. The electric car travels along Schweigaardsgate before it turns into Oslogate, and where it passes under the viaduct it crosses the built-in Akerselv river. About 900 years ago, King Harald the Hard founded Oslo in the area east of this underground river and between its mouth and the foot of Ekeberg on what was then the bank of the fjord. Before you've had a chance to reflect on the life of rivers, you're at St. Halvard's Square, one of the few reminders of medieval Oslo. Here is the foundation of St. Halvard's Church, together with part of the St. Olav Cloister, and the remnants of the Cross Church. Across Oslogate stands the Ladegarden, built around 1725 on the vaults of the medieval Bishop's Fortress, and the newly-restored Bishop Nicholas' Chapel dating from the 13th century. Perhaps you may wish to explore this historic spot on your way back to town. Just remember that this is the heart of Gamlebyen, abandoned after the disastrous fire of 1624 in favor of the new site selected by Christian IV on the western side of the Akers River.

The Merchant Marine Academy is a place of artistic as well as scenic interest. Inside are murals by Per Krohg, a prolific Norwegian painter whose works are not only scattered around Oslo but now will be found in the United Nations building in New York. (Unfortunately, the building is not open to the public.) Outside is a dramatic piece of sculpture by Gunnar Utsond, entitled *The Journey to Hell.* An interesting feature is the existence of five-thousand-year-old rock drawings near this spot. You will find them quite near to the main road as it turns uphill from Sjömannskolen.

From the terrace in front of the Merchant Marine Academy is perhaps the most intimate view of Oslo to be obtained from the surrounding hills. Spread out before us is the harbor, the two fjords, the old and the new towns, and ring of mountains shutting out the horizon, the peninsula of Bygdöy straight ahead and Nesodden to the left, and all the other features of metropolitan Oslo, natural and manmade. Because you are close enough to pick out individual buildings and streets, this is a good spot to visit for purposes of orientation before you begin your tour of the capital.

The number of excursions that you can make from Oslo is so limitless, that it would be impossible to describe them all. Instead, in the

Practical Information section on the next page, we have outlined three: one by tram, one by sea, and one by bus.

PRACTICAL INFORMATION FOR OSLO

 WHEN TO COME. Though the influx of visitors culminates in the summer season, Oslo more than most capital cities is a year-round resort. This is primarily due to the fact that Oslo is the foremost winter sports town of the world, where everybody from toddlers to oldsters practise their form of skiing, skating or tobogganing from January to April. Star event of the winter season is the annual Holmenkollen Ski Festival in *March,* when the skiing world flocks to this Mecca of skiers, and some 100,000 spectators watch the jumping on Holmenkollen Hill. A special race is open to visitors.

The gap between skiing, swimming and sailing is almost unnoticeable in Oslo, and you may, in fact, practise them simultaneously. *May* sees the summer season in full swing with flowering fruit trees, and the first yachts on the fjord. Constitution Day, May 17, is a day of festivities and well worth including in your Oslo itinerary, and so are the Midsummer Eve festivities, which take place on the 23rd of *June.* This is also the signal for Norwegian holiday-makers to go to the country.

July and *August* muster the greatest number of foreign visitors, although many Americans have taken advantage of the early season, with no particular events to attract them.

The first half of *September* is a very busy time for the Oslo hotels, what with old alumni streaming to the university to celebrate reunions and business life coming alive after the long summer lull. Coming alive also are the theaters, concert halls, and artistic life generally. This finds its expression in Oslo Culture Week, with special programs at theaters, concert halls, museums and cinemas. *October* can still be beautiful in Oslo.

 WHAT TO SEE. Regular city tours offered include: (a) Morning sightseeing by bus, starting from Town Hall and including the Cathedral, Munch Museum, Vigeland Park and Holmenkollen, 3 hours. (b) Afternoon sightseeing by bus including the Folk Museum, Viking Ships, *Fram,* and *Kon-Tiki,* 3 hours. (c) Sightseeing launch around the harbor leaving every hour in front of City Hall, 50 mins. There is also a 2½-hour tour 4 times daily. (d) All-day sightseeing by boat and bus. Start at Pier C.

Other excursions include a sea tour which starts out from Pipervika, behind the City Hall. Modern and comfortable sightseeing boats with English-speaking guides depart regularly from this point. If you're allergic to crowds, you'll get a more authentic picture of life in Oslo's seaside suburbs by taking one of the regular passenger ships that ply between the city and Nesodden. Travel by boat all the way out and back, or get off at Nesodden to explore, and return by a later boat.

Or you can take bus No. 36 (starts from Grønlandstorg, but best entered outside the University), to Sundvollen. For the next hour you will see some of the most magnificent scenery to be found in the Oslo region as you wind and climb your way around the precipitous edges of the crystal blue Tyri Fjord. At Sundvollen you can walk up Dronningveien, or go by car, to the top of Krokkleiva with famous views from Kongens Utsikt (the King's View), one of the most beautiful in Norway. The 36 bus also goes to Jevnaker, where you can visit

Hadeland Glass Works, the largest of its kind in Scandinavia. Founded in 1762, the work is still performed by hand craftsmen and visitors may see glassblowing, cutting and etching of crystal.

 HOW TO GET ABOUT. Street car and bus stops are indicated by round metal indicators painted blue. Schedules are posted at these stops. Fare, 7 Nkr. Yellow metal placards indicate suburban bus stops. Schedules are likewise shown here. If you are going to take trams or buses often, buy a *trikkekort,* good for 9 rides for 50 Nkr. The airport bus costs 14 Nkr. from the Central Station or Scandinavia Hotel.

The suburban areas are served by local electric trains and Underground (T-Banen). Most important of these for visitors is the Holmenkolbanen, starting underground at the National Theater. This electric train will whisk you high above the town—marvelous views en route—to Holmenkollen and Frognerseteren in some 30 minutes. Another suburban line is the Ekebergbanen, which brings you up to view point at Sjömannskolen in 15 minutes.

Taxi stands are found at the Central and West Railway Stations and at various points throughout the city. Vacant cabs may be hailed anywhere if they are more than 300 yards from a stand. You can order a cab from a central dispatching office (dial 348), but there can be up to a half-hour wait. Extra charge for more than 2 passengers and at night; no charge for luggage. Fare to the airport is around 55 Nkr, including tip.

 HOTELS. Oslo is well supplied with hotels in all price ranges. Detailed information about Oslo hotels may be found in the *Oslo Guide,* which is published annually and is available from the *Tourist Information Center* in the City Hall.

For those without reservations, the *Oslo Tourist Association* has a reservation service at the Central station. This is open until 11 P.M. but reservations can only be made in person. There is a small fee.

Deluxe

Bristol, Kristian IVgate 7, centrally located on a quiet side street; 215 beds, 156 rooms, 137 with bath. The *Bristol Grill* has first class cuisine, while *El Toro* is a Spanish restaurant with dancing and floor shows. There is also the *Leopard* grill, a night club and disco on the 2nd floor. The *Trafalgar* bar, the *Library* bar and the *Winter Garden* complete the facilities.

Continental, Stortinsgate 24/26, opposite the National Theater and with view of the Royal Palace; 318 beds, 189 rooms with all facilities. The *Annen-Etagen* is one of the most elegant restaurants in Oslo while the *Loftet* is a new beer and wine restaurant with billiards and a disco. The *Theatercafeen* is an unrivalled Oslo favorite, much frequented by journalists, actors and artists. There is also the *Tivoli* grill, a modern and inexpensive restaurant and the *Continental* bar near the lobby.

Grand, Karl Johansgate 31, on Oslo's main street and opposite Parliament and city park; 525 beds, 350 rooms most with bath or shower and all with color TV. Indoor pool, sauna and solarium. The *Speilen* restaurant is Oslo's most exclusive and has dancing; the hotel's other restaurants include the *Etoile,* a top floor restaurant with first class cuisine; the *Palmen,* a sandwich buffet much frequented by diplomats' wives, and the *Fritzner* grill, a top grade restaurant. The *Grand Café* is a famous Oslo rendezvous with murals depicting life in Oslo at the end of the 19th century. The *Bonanza* is a restaurant and night club with cowboy decor.

Holmenkollen Park, Kongevein 26, situated on a hillside overlooking the city and fjord and originally built in 1894 in old Norse style; entirely rebuilt and extended in 1981; 350 beds, 200 rooms with all facilities and most with private balcony. There is a 3-story atrium lobby, gourmet restaurant, coffee shop, bar and night club, indoor pool, whirl pool, sauna, gym, squash court, curling rink and parking for 90 cars.

Scandinavia, Holbergsgate 30, facing the Royal Palace and the park and Norway's largest hotel and tallest building; 967 beds, 476 rooms with all facilities and round the clock room service. The restaurants include the first class gourmet grill with its international menu, the *Café Royal,* which offers a spectacular smørgasbord for lunch, the *Hetland Juballong,* a night club with disco and live music. There are also two bars, an indoor pool, a shopping center. The hotel also doubles as the city air terminal.

Expensive

Ambassadeur, Camilla Collettsvei 15, near the Royal Palace; 54 beds, several suites, indoor pool, sauna.

Astoria, Akersgaten 21, near Parliament; 136 beds, popular restaurant.

Carlton Rica, Parkveien 78, in quiet west end street; 86 beds. Its Rica restaurant is famous for fine food.

KNA, Parkveien 68, run by the Royal Norwegian Automobile Club and entirely modernized in 1981; 226 beds, most rooms with bath or shower. Intimate restaurant and bar and good bistro.

Müllerhotell West, Skovveien 15, behind the Royal Palace; 59 beds, most rooms with bath; the *Coq d'Or* grill here is a popular eating place; also has bar.

Nobel, Karl Johansgate 33, on Oslo's main street; 104 beds, most rooms with bath or shower; bistro and bar.

Sara, Gunnerusgate 11/13, opposite Central rail station; 343 rooms, 92 with bath. *Crystal Garden* restaurant has both Scandinavian and international menu; *Glåmrik* pub has Viking style decor; coffee shop.

SAS Globetrotter, Fornebu park, near the airport; 273 beds, all rooms with bath or shower. Has the *Globetrotter Grill,* a smallish restaurant with an internatioal atmosphere, adjoining bar; ample parking space.

Moderate

Esso, Ramstadsletta 12/14, Høvik, 6 km W of City Hall on road E18; 115 beds, all rooms with facilities, restaurant, cafeteria, sauna, parking.

Europa, St Olavsgate 31, central; built in 1983, with 300 beds, all rooms with facilities inc. color TV and fridge. Special reductions for parents with children.

Forbunds, Holbergs plass 1, near city air terminal; 137 beds, cafeteria, unlicensed.

Norum, Bygdøy Alle 53, in west-end residential area; 90 beds, most rooms with facilities; bistro with good food.

Saga, Eilert Sundtsgate 39, in west-end; 65 beds, all rooms with facilities.

Savoy, Universitetsgate 11, near National Art Gallery; 97 beds; restaurant.

Stefan, Rosenkrantzgate 1, central; 200 beds, most rooms with bath/shower; popular restaurant, unlicensed.

Inexpensive

Anker, Storgata 55, central, June-August only, 426 beds, many rooms with 4 beds; cooking facilities, restaurant, cafeteria, supermarket.

Gyldenløve, Bogstadvei 20, 330 beds; bed and breakfast hotel, unlicensed.

Haraldsheim, Haraldsheimvei 4, one of the finest youth hostels in Scandinavia, truly international atmosphere, 6 km NE of City Hall, reached by tram or bus; 270 beds, 6 in each room; showers in corridors, cafeteria, sauna.

 RESTAURANTS. The choice of eating spots in Oslo is so great that you could happily spend a couple of weeks just sampling those at the top end of the scale alone. The deluxe hotels are home to Oslo's most elegant restaurants, but many other hotels also have excellent restaurants (see above for details). You'll find that fine food and scenery are something of a specialty in Oslo and many restaurants combine excellent eating with dramatic views.

Details of all restaurants in Oslo, including opening times, are listed in the *Oslo Guide,* available from the Oslo Tourist Information Center at the City Hall.

Expensive

Blom, Karl Johansgate 41, on Oslo's main street. Excellent food in a Bohemian atmosphere with walls decorated with humorous coats of arms of well-known personalities; popular among artists and journalists; piano music.

Caravelle, Fornebu, at Oslo airport. Overlooks the runways; international menu. Try the *Caravelle Cabin* (M) for pizzas, steaks and sandwiches. The *Caravelle Cafeteria* (M) has a large self-service counter.

Frascati, Stortingsgaten 20, opposite National Theater. French rotisserie with international menu; piano music.

Frognerseteren, Frognerseteren, on top of hill overlooking city and fjord, reached by Holmenkollen train from National Theater underground station. Old timber building in traditional Norse style with large open-hearth and Norwegian specialties; a must for all visitors to Oslo. The adjoining cafe (I) is very popular with hikers and skiiers.

Holmenkollen, Holmenkollveien 119; hillside restaurant between Holmenkollen station and the ski jump with spectacular views of the city and fjord; also has an adjoining cafeteria (I).

King George Steakhouse, Torggaten 11, on "Strøget" pedestrian alley near center. In old stable with interesting decor; the menu includes horsemeat steaks.

La Petite Cuisine chez Ben Joseph, Solligaten, in Oslo's west end. Rôtisserie with French atmosphere and cuisine; frequented by shipowners.

Najaden, Bygdøynes, 10 minutes from City Hall by ferry and located in the Norwegian Maritime Museum; unusual interiors, good food.

Regnbuen, Klingenberggate 4, centrally located; enormous hall for dining and dancing with international bands, floor show, bar and night club.

Tre Kokker, Drammensveien 30, near the Royal Palace; Norwegian style charcoal grill with outstanding food; run by Norway's top gourmet, Hroar Dege. Dancing in bar.

Moderate

Bagatelle, Bygdøy Alle 3, west of the Royal Palace; French restaurant.

Bajazzo Rica, Bygdøy Alle 5, west of the Royal Palace; restaurant during the day, disco at night; pub in the cellar.

Cheese Inn, Ruseløkkveien 3, south of the Royal Palace. Small and intimate restaurant specializing in cheese dishes (of course).

Christian, Stortorget 10, on market square; located in a department store and popular for lunch.

Cossack, Kongensgate 6; Russian and international food; with bar, dancing and disco.

Ekeberg, Kongsveien 15; reached by tram 9; magnificent views of harbor, city and fjord.

Engebret, Bankplassen 1; downtown restaurant and the oldest in Oslo; established in 1857, period interiors; famous for its seafood.

Gallagher's Steak House, Karl Johansgate 10, on Oslo's main street; restaurant with pub and pizza parlor, American-style steaks and pancakes; light music in the evenings.

Handverkeren, Rosenkrantzgate 7, opposite the Bristol Hotel; lunchtime sandwich buffet; also grill and bar.

Herregårdskroen, Frogner Park, adjoins the famous Vigeland sculpture park. Small inn in the City Museum with an open-air restaurant in summer.

The Scotsman, Karl Johansgate 17, on main street; pub and steakhouse with Scottish atmosphere and evening entertainments.

Wessels Kro, Stortingsgate 6, opposite Parliament; cozy inn that features a replica of a street in Copenhagen where the Norwegian satirist, Johann Herman Wessel, used to stroll; fish and traditional food.

Inexpensive

Den Lille Fondue, President Harbitzgate 18; Oslo's only fondue restaurant; small and intimate; music.

Kaffistova, recommended chain of coffee shops with generous helpings; check the Oslo Guide for locations.

Kurbadets Vegetarrestaurant, Akersgaten 74. Vegetarian dishes only; no alcohol and no smoking.

 ENTERTAINMENT. In Oslo the arts have been elevated to a position of unusual importance. Foremost is the *National Theater,* rich in tradition from the times of Björnson and Ibsen and still serving as guardian of classic drama and as sponsor of modern plays by Scandinavian, European, British and American authors. Performances are in Norwegian, of course, but the opportunity of seeing an Ibsen drama presented here is something you would be wise not to miss.

Amfiscenen is a small intimate theater in the same building as the National Theater. *ABC Theater* is a revue theater, and *Chat Noir* offers variety shows. *Det Norske Teatret* presents plays in the dialect of "nynorsk" (new Norwegian), and *Oslo Nye Teater* shows Norwegian and foreign plays, musicals and operettas. *Oslo Nye Dukketeater* is a puppet theater in the same building as the City Museum. Plays for children and youth are featured by Oslo Nye in the old *Centralteatret.*

The musical life of the capital is equally impressive, with concerts by the *Oslo Philharmonic Orchestra,* which has visited many cities in the USA. It is often assisted by soloists and conductors of international fame. Concerts are held in the *Oslo Concert Hall,* completed in 1977, one of the most modern of its kind, seating 1633 persons, also a chamber music hall with 300 seats. The *Norwegian Opera* with its ballet company is active from September to June.

At Oslo's numerous movies shows begin at fixed hours, usually 5, 7 and 9 P.M., and, ticket or no ticket, you will not be admitted if you arrive late. Seats are reserved at most cinemas, so it's best to order them in advance, especially on Saturdays. Tickets can be bought at the Kino Central, Karl Johansgate 35, until 4:15 P.M. After this time at the various movie houses. The films are mainly American, British and Scandinavian, with subtitles. No smoking is allowed.

Folk dancing in national costumes to the tune of Norwegian folk music is presented during the summer season at Oslo Concert Hall, including demonstration of various old Norwegian musical instruments. The *Norwegian Folk Museum* at Bygdøy also invites you to attend folk dancing displays during the summer season.

NIGHTLIFE. Several hotels and restaurants in Oslo present cabaret programs and floor shows, and the number of night spots is rising. However, they come and go as frequently as discos in Manhattan and Soho. Some are very short-lived, so always check the current *Oslo This Week* for details. Most night clubs stay open until 4 A.M.

MUSEUMS. Most cities in the world have museums of the traditional kind, and Oslo has its share—but in addition, Oslo has a series of unique musuems, which can be seen nowhere else in the world, particularly its "one man" and "one ship" museums. Opening times are changed according to season, so always consult the current *Oslo Guide*.

Akershus Castle. Built by Haakon V around 1300, rebuilt by Christian IV around 1600, subsequently restored and redecorated; it is one of Oslo's most attractive buildings. It contains the royal mausoleums, the World War II Resistance museum, and the defense museum.

Fram, Bygdøynes. The polar exploration vessel used by Nansen, Amundsen and Sverdrup on great expeditions. *Gjøa* is another vessel, used by Amundsen in the exploration of the Northwest Passage. Also at Bygdöynes, the *Kon-Tiki Museum* and *Maritime Museum* now in its new building, with ship and harbor models, fishing gear, working models. Ferry from Rådhusplass.

Henie-Onstad Art Center, Høvikodden. Excellent collection of modern art. Buses 32, 36 or 37 from Grønlands torg (more conveniently entered outside the University) and 5-min. walk from Høvik.

Historical Museum, Frederiksgate 2, consists of the University's Collection of Antiquities, with emphasis on the Viking age and medieval ecclesiastical art, the Ethnographical Museum and the Numismatic Collection; admission free.

Munch Museum, Töyen. Edvard Munch, Norway's foremost painter, bequeathed the bulk of his paintings and drawings (more than 20,000) to the city of Oslo. Selections are presented at this museum; admission free. Bus 29 from center of town, bus 20 from Majorstuen.

Museum of Applied Arts, St. Olavsgate 1. Domestic art from the Middle Ages to present times. The Baldishol Tapestry from the 1180's. European applied arts from the Renaissance onwards. Admission free.

National Gallery (Nasjonal galleriet), Universitetsgate 13. Norwegian painting, sculpture, drawing and graphic arts. Fine collection of modern French art, including works by Matisse and Cezanne, also Van Gogh and prominent Danish and Swedish painters. Admission free.

Natural History Museum, Sarsgata 1, includes several interesting sections—such as the botanical garden and conservatories; mineralogical and geological museum with one section devoted to Norway's mining industry; paleontological museum with fossil plants and animals; also the rebuilt zoological museum. Admission free. Trams 1 or 7 from city center.

Norwegian Folk Museum, Museumsveien, Bygdøy. Excellent outdoor collection of wooden buildings representing different parts of Norway. Among them a 12th–century stave church; 18th–century town; Henrik Ibsen's study and rich indoor collections. Bus 30 from Wessels Plass.

Norwegian Maritime Museum, Bygdøynes. Norwegian maritime traditions throughout the ages.

Norwegian Technical Museum, (closed during transfer to new premises). Hydraulic machinery, communications, aviation, electricity, X-rays, radio. Large model railway.

Oslo City Hall (Rådhuset). Built 1933–50. Lavishly decorated by Norway's leading painters and sculptors. Admission free.

Oslo Cathedral, Stortorvet. Built 1699, exterior restoration 1849–50, interior restoration 1949–50. Impressive ceiling decorations by Hugo Lous Mohr; admission free.

Ski Museum, Holmenkollen. Contains skis from the earliest time and polar equipment of Nansen and Amundsen. Holmenkollen electric railway from National Theater to Holmenkollen station.

Vigeland Sculpture Park and Museum, Frogner Park and Nobelgate 2. The park comprises 150 sculpture groups, culminating in 60-foot granite monolith; admission free; tram 2 to Frogner Park. The museum contains many of Vigeland's original works; admission free; tram 2 to Frogner Plass.

Viking Ships, Huk Aveny 35 Bygdøy. The Oseberg, Gokstad, and Tune ships, all found near the Oslo Fjord, are the most remarkable relics of the Viking age. Unique collection of household articles, etc. Bus 30 from Wessels Plass, near the Parliament, also (summer) ferry from Rådhusplass.

 SHOPPING. In Norway as well as in the other Scandinavian coutries you will find continuity with the peasant heritage in handicraft—ceramics and textile weaving, wood carving and decorative painting. It is easy to see why strong individualistic traditions developed in isolated areas where the people observed the beautiful color and form of their natural surroundings. Self expression was so strongly reinforced by resourcefulness that the subsequent foreign influxes were reinterpreted and absorbed into the native creative culture. You may find it has all the more distinctive appeal, and certainly flavor, for its unselfconscious strength and simplicity.

Arts and Crafts. *Forum,* Rosenkrantzgate 7 (opposite the Bristol Hotel), is a good place to start, especially if your time is limited. It is a permanent sales exhibition of contemporary Norwegian arts and crafts. Each item on display must first be accepted by a jury.

A similar establishment is *Norway Designs,* Stortingsgate 28 (entrance from Roald Amundsengate), the capital's largest center for the exhibition and sale of top quality Norwegian applied art, with special facilities for export.

For the most indigenous Norwegian handicraft try *Husfliden* (Norwegian Association for Home Arts and Crafts), Möllergate 4, near the cathedral. A non-profit organization for preserving and continuing the traditions of Norwegian handicrafts and rustic culture, it offers a wide range of home industry products including the well-known knitted sweaters, woven tapestries, dolls in national costumes, woodcarvings, ceramics etc.

Heimen at Kristian Augustsgate 14, has handknitted sweaters and mittens, and should you care to see authentic Norwegian costumes—each valley has its own—this shop makes them to order.

William Schmidt, Karl Johansgate 41, is an excellent gift shop specializing in beautiful ski pullovers.

There are many new galleries springing up all over Oslo now. Complete lists to date are available from the Tourist Office.

Pewter, Ceramics and Crystal. A great Norwegian specialty is its pewter-ware: sugar bowls and creamers, all sizes of trays and bowls, candlesticks and pitchers. With a light-finish technique, Gunnar Havstad has created the best contemporary works, whereas the Groseth pewter bears the marks of the heavy sandstone presses that formed them after the old English manner.

Tinnboden, Tordenskioldsgate 7, has a good selection, as well as a splendid array of dolls in colorful regional dresses. Also *Småkunst,* Tordenskioldsgate 6.

These ceramics are perhaps more primitive than those you have found in Denmark and Sweden—the plates and bowls often thicker and embellished with peasant figures and symbols of the life they know. Norway's best known porcelain factory is Porsgrund. Also outstanding are the pottery works at Egersund and Stavanger, and the Hadelands glass company. Since their production, though of top quality, cannot incorporate all the vigorous ideas of young creative innovators, the works of individual craftsmen are equally numerous. Originality and taste are the rule in even the most common art glass, ceramics, and porcelain.

Arts and Crafts Center in Basarhallene, behind the cathedral, is worth looking into for all of the above.

For the very best in crystal and glass etching be sure to go by *Christiania Glasmagasin,* Stortorget 10. In the glass department here you will find distinguished modern glassware, amusing cocktail glasses, and exquisite art glass in a range of delectable hues.

Silver. It would be a pity not to buy something of the world-famous enamel on silver that is perhaps most appealing of all. You may have seen the gold-washed silver demi-tasse or dessert spoons in the home of one of your friends. The coffee spoons and those for jelly are generally adorned with abstract designs whose handsome black outlines set them off. The dessert spoons are more often made dainty by a web of fine ridges underneath the enamel. The bold cuff links and ash trays of these firms enjoy great masculine popularity, or you might choose one of the very lovely cocktail sets.

Metal work is an ancient craft in Norway: even in the most isolated homes you will commonly find a handwrought silver coffee set or tankards decorated in the ornamental tradition of the country. The contemporary silver designs, however, are usually quite simple, sometimes to the point of severity, but always graceful and sturdy. Along with these modern patterns are sold unique serving pieces, with highly decorated latticework handles and odd-shaped bowls, distinctly Norwegian in feeling and appeal. Delicate silver filigree buttons and bracelets enjoy an all-time popularity with natives and visitors alike.

David Andersen, Karl Johansgate 20, has traditional and modern patterns. This firm makes the world famous "David Andersen Enamel."

J. Tostrup, at number 25 on the same street, features somewhat more modern pieces, particularly those of Arne Korsmo and his wife.

Just off this street, at Övre Slotsgate 12, is *N. M. Thune,* also a first class silversmith. Others are: *Tv. Marthinsen,* Karl Johansgate 19, and *Heyerdahls,* Fridthof Nansens pl.

Among silver factories, the best known is the *Marthinsen Sölvvarefabrikk.* Its creations can be found in jewelry shops throughout the country. But coming up fast in popularity are the exquisite works of the *Juhls,* made in their Lapland workshops at Kautokeino; both traditional Lappish and modern designs.

Antiques and Furniture. For the antique-lover, *Kaare Berntsen,* Universitetsgate 12, should prove a happy hunting-ground. If you have been fascinated by some of the old household furnishings you saw at Bygdøy, site of Oslo's open air museum, here you will find authentic examples for sale, along with a most extensive collection of antique silver ornaments.

Though the Norwegian economy has not yet been able to foster a widespread market for modern furniture, functional designs and light woods are preferred, and the industry has attained high standards.

Tannum, Stortingsgate 28, has interesting examples of this.

Furs and Sporting Goods. All kinds of fur pelts are nurtured in Norway, including mink, seal, and fox. The firm of *Pels-Backer,* Kongensgate 31, has long been famed for its furs. Almost every kind of fur is displayed here, and you can be assured of beautiful cut and superior craftsmanship. Pride of place, perhaps, goes to the Norwegian *Saga* mink.

Thorkildsen, N. Slottsgate 9, also have luxurious pelts.

In Oslo again the sports lover comes into his own. *Gresvig Sports Shop,* Storgata 20 and Haakon VII gate, also *Christiania Glasmagasin* at Stortorget 10, are probably the best in town and, in this sportsman's paradise, that means a lot. The Norwegian packsacks mentioned previously, flies for your fishing rod—or the rod itself—skis, any kind of sports equipment for use during your trek through the countryside or for shipment home (which *Gresvig's* will happily and efficiently handle for you) are featured here.

Norway's famous ski jumper, *Sigmund Ruud,* has a shop at Kirkeveien 57.

Miscellany. Everyday needs can be filled at the *Steen og Strøm* department store. As for clothes, *Molstad* on Kongensgate has been busy since 1883.

GUIDES. Multi-lingual guides can be hired from the *Oslo Guide Service, Oslo Tourist Information* in the City Hall (seaside entrance). Guides are licensed.

WINTER SPORTS. The season runs from Christmas to the end of March. There is fine skiing country with marked trails in the hills around the city. Floodlit trails can be found in Nordmarka, Lillomarka and Østmarka (some are specially marked for handicapped or blind people). Excellent communications to all starting points from town center. There are several ski lodges run by Skiforeningen (Ski Association) in Nordmarka. Slalom hills and ski lifts at Tryvannskleiva, Grefsenkollen, Kirkerudbakken, Ingierkollen, Rödkleiva. Tobogganing at Korketrekkeren Hill; skating and curling rinks; icefishing is allowed on the lakes and Oslo Fjord, on marked trails you can follow without risk.

OTHER SPORTS. The Oslo Fjord is teeming with white sails in summer afternoons, and **yachting** regattas take place early and late in the season, though the winds are not reliable enough for international events. No arrangement exists for the renting of yachts though visiting yachtsmen are offered harbor facilities by the Royal Norwegian Yacht Club at Dronningen. Boats and sailing dinghies can be rented from Asker and Baerum Boat Rental, Hvalstad.

The Bogstad golf course, 6 miles from the town center, enjoys unrivalled surroundings, and offers extremely good **golfing** (18 holes) from May to October.

Tennis-playing visitors may hire courts at Frogner Stadium.

Horse racing and trotting are regular events of the summer season with weekly race-days from May to November (no trotting in July) with totalisators at Övrevoll Race Course and Bjerke Trotting Track.

Beaches and swimming pools. There are many fine bathing beaches on both sides of the fjord, reached by bus from the City Hall. Ingierstrand, Katten, Hvervenbukta, Ljanskollen and Bestemorstranda are situated on the east side, reached by bus 75. Rolfstangen near Fornebu airport on the west side is reached by bus 31. Langøyene are two adjoining islands with sandy beach, owned by Oslo municipality. Take ferry from pier 4. Water temperatures average 68°F or 20°C during July and August. The most popular open-air swimming pool is situated in Frogner park, close to the Vigeland sculpture park.

Good trout fishing is offered in the vast open country around Oslo. Fishing permits are on sale in sports shops and in the chalets of Kobberhaughytta, Kikutstua, and Lövliseter, where fishermen may be accommodated.

CAMPING. *Bogstad Camp and Tourist Center,* Bogstad, 6 miles from the town center, close to the golf course, is undoubtedly one of Europe's finest camping sites, with a capacity of 1,000 cars and equipped with all modern amenities. Beautiful surroundings overlooking the Bogstad Lake—popular bathing place—and forested hills. There are also 20 self-contained 4-person chalets at budget prices which have been "winterized" and are well placed near skiing runs. Bogstad Camping is reached by bus 41 from the National Theater. It is open all the year.

Ekeberg Camping is also a favorite site, 3 km from the city center, with magnificent views of the city. It is reached by bus 24 or tram 9. Open from June 20 to Aug 20.

USEFUL ADDRESSES. Embassies: U.S., Drammens- veien 18; Canada, Oscarsgate 20; Britain, Thomas Hef- tyesgate 8.

Tourist Information: Oslo Travel Information Office, in the City Hall (seaside entrance); billeting office at Central railroad station.

City Air Terminal at Scandinavia Hotel, Holbergsgate 30; SAS booking office at Ruseløkkveien 6 and in Scandinavia Hotel.

Travel Agents: Bennett Reisebureau A/S, Karl Johansgate 35; Berg-Hansen Reisebureau A/S, Tollbugata 27; Thos Cook & Son Ltd, Tollbugata 27; Folkef- erie, Arbeidersamfunnets plass 1; KNA's Turistbureau A/S, Parkveien 68; Erik Myhre Reisebyrå A/S, Nedre Vollgate 19; NAF's Reisebyrå A/S, Storgata 2; NSB Reisebyrå, Stortingsgata 28; Fred Olsen Reisebyrå, Prinsensgate 2b; Winge Reisebureau A/S, Karl Johansgate 33.

Central Post Office, Dronningensgate 18, open 8 A.M.-6 P.M. Central telegraph office, Kongensgate 21.

Norwegian Youth Hostels Assoc., Dronningensgate 26.

Norwegian Skiing Assoc., Skippergaten 40.

Royal Norwegian Automobile Club (KNA), Parkveien 68.

Norwegian Automobile Assoc., Storgate 2.

Car Hire: Avis, Munkedamsveien 27 and at Fornebu airport; Kjøles Car Rental A/S (Hertz), General Birchsgate 16 and at Grand Hotel and Fornebu airport; Scandinavia Car Rental (Eurocar), Fredensborgveien 33 and at For- nebu airport.

THE OSLO FJORD DISTRICT

Of Vikings, Whalers and Twisting Valleys

Östfold is that section of Norway lying between the Oslo Fjord and the Swedish border. A part of the greater Oslo region, its major towns of Moss, Fredrikstad, Sarpsborg, and Halden are all points on the main rail line to the capital. At the same time Östfold also belongs economically to the forest and lumber district of eastern Norway and to the great valley of Österdal, whose river Glomma flows through Sarpsborg to empty into the fjord just beyond Fredrikstad. It is a small section of the country, rich in history and modern industry. On the west side of the Oslo Fjord is located another small district, the opposite number of Östfold, quite logically called Vestfold.

Exploring the Oslo Fjord District

By leaving Oslo's Central Station some morning on a southbound express you will reach Moss in about an hour (if the wind's right, you'll know it by the smell!). Formerly known for its tremendous distillery, the town has now both paper and pulp and other types of industries. It is also the eastern terminus of the cross-fjord Horten-Moss ferry which links Östfold and Vestfold. Unless you intend to cross on this ferry, stay aboard the train another half-hour, then descend at Fredrikstad. Here is a thriving industrial town which converts animal and vegetable oil into many useful products, cans first-class anchovies, exports lumber, etc., yet is at the same time filled with historical monuments. Across the Glomma river in the New Town there is a super–cafeteria, part of Scandinavia's biggest food center—"Stabburet."

The fortified Old Town, with its earthen and stone ramparts, built in the 17th century as a protection against the Swedes, is fully worth wandering about, both on top of the walls and down among the ancient buildings. Particularly fascinating is the great stone fortress of Kongsten standing alone beyond the ramparts as an outpost to meet the first waves of attackers.

East of Fredrikstad, road 110 runs in the direction of Halden. This road—also known as the Antiquity Road—is only 10 miles long but takes visitors back 3000 years. Along it can be seen some of Norway's finest prehistoric finds, notably rock carvings and grave mounds, very clearly marked.

Home of the internationally-known Borregaard Paper Mills, Sarpsborg has had a long and checkered history since its founding in 1016 by St. Olav. Like Fredrikstad, it was burned many times during the conflicts with Sweden, but with the expansion of its paper industry in recent decades Sarpsborg is now a thriving and stable industrial town. Sarpsborg's great attraction is the waterfall which the Glomma River forms in the middle of the town. This 64-feet waterfall is always impressive and simply marvellous at flood periods. Visitors interested in history might browse around the grounds of the Borgarsyssel Museum, where the ruins of St. Nikolas Church are found, or if it happens to be a Sunday, visit the charming Hafslund Manor, impressive as any castle.

Stay overnight at Halden and devote the next morning to visiting the Fredriksten Fortress, constructed on a steep hill in the town. The views over the border country and the tales told by the guide about sieges and sorties during the 17th and 18th centuries will amply reward one for the effort expended.

Vestfold, Home of the Vikings

Even smaller than its eastern twin, Vestfold has many links with the Oslo region as well as a thriving industrial life of its own which included until 1968 that unique occupation, Antarctic whaling. Historically Vestfold, like southern Norway, has had more contacts with Denmark than with Sweden, but what will stir the imagination most of all are the traces of Viking kings and seafarers to be found there. This district has no clear-cut boundary such as the Swedish border provides for Östfold, but merges into the mountain district of Telemark.

The first half hour of the journey takes one as far as Drammen on the same main line that leads to Kristiansand and Stavanger.

The scenery is interesing but not spectacular; and it demonstrates, moreover, how quickly one gets from Oslo to the land of farms, forests and bare rock. And if you are wondering why more Norwegian railroads haven't been laid down in duplicate, the answer is easily seen on this 30-mile stretch to Drammen which has just been made doubletrack at staggering costs. Here you can see some of the difficulties that Norwegian railroad engineers encounter all over the country: steep up and down grades, cuts through solid rocks and tunnels . . . tunnels. In fact the Norwegian State Railways on the Oslo-Drammen run has blasted Norway's longest tunnel (10.8 km) through the mountains to open the double track. The sisyphean job was completed in 1973. After the tunnel is passed there is a view over the valley and across Drams Fjord to the lumber, paper and shipping town of Drammen, sixth largest city in Norway. Located at the mouth of the large timber-floating river, Drammen has the same strategic location as Fredrikstad on the other side of the Oslo Fjord, albeit without any walled town or fortress. The "Corkscrew Road" tunnelled through the mountain to the top of the Bragernes Hill is a unique attraction.

The Vestfold express branches off here and inside an hour we pass through long, narrow Holmestrand, squeezed in between fjord and hillside, and Skoppum, from where the bus runs to the former naval base (also car-ferry) town of Horten. A short ride beyond brings Töns-berg which the inhabitants proudly claim as Norway's oldest town, founded in the year 870. The hill rising steeply beside the railway station demands a visit even though all that is left of the extensive fortress, castle and abbey which once crowned it are some ruined foundations. The outlook tower on top is of modern construction, erected in 1870 to commemorate the 1,000th anniversary of Tönsberg's founding, and it offers a panorama comparable in sweep to that from Frognerseteren in Oslo.

Because of the passages both to the Oslo Fjord eastwards and to the open sea southwards you can see at once why Tönsberg was a strategic place, not only for the old Viking chieftains and raiders but also for shipping. From the sailing ships of the 18th and 19th centuries there has been a steady peaceful development to today's fleet of cargo liners and oil tankers which has won Tönsberg fourth place among shipping ports in Norway.

Looking back north along the railway from the Millenium Tower, one can almost locate Borre, site of many ancient Viking burial mounds; while much nearer Tönsberg is another famous site: Oseberg, where one of the Viking ships now at Bygdøy was found. You should really have a guide or Norwegian friend along to point out other historic spots, such as Ramnes, where rival pretenders to the throne fought decisive battles in the 12th century, and the old manor house at Jarlsberg, the seat of Norway's last family of nobility. Hereditary titles were abolished by parliament early in the 19th century, but Count Wedel Jarlsberg was permitted to keep his distinction until he died in 1893.

Don't forget to look southwards also, for in that direction you can see the start of famous recreational territory: the islands of Nötteröy, Tjöme, and Hvasser, which are the holiday haunts of thousands of Oslo-ites each summer. The tip of the island of Tjöme is the "End of the World" (Verdens Ende), facing the waves of the Skagerrak.

Sandefjord and the World's Largest Mammal

Next stop is the picturesque town of Sandefjord, which was once the main base for the Norwegian whaling fleet. Sven Foyn, a native of

Tönsberg, invented the explosive harpoon, but it was the skippers from Sandefjord who developed the business of Antarctic whaling to its recent level. The sight of the huge floating factories—up to 25,000 tons—and of their dozens of attending whale-catchers, tiny 200-tonners, used to be a fascinating and instructive sight. The great era of Antarctic whaling, nevertheless, has come to an end. With Japanese and Russian whalers joining the Norwegians after the last war, the whales are becoming fewer and fewer, and Sandefjord has withdrawn from the great hunt. However, in compensation, Sandefjord has acquired Norway's fifth largest merchant fleet. By all means visit the Whaling Museum given to the town by the local "whale king", Consul Lars Christensen.

An interesting side-trip by taxi from Sandefjord is to Gokstad Mound where another of the Viking ships at Bygdøy was found in 1880. Only a grass-covered mound can be seen there now, but it will give some idea of the magnitude and pomp of medieval Viking burials.

Larvik is another of Vestfold's busy ports but it combines this with important lumbering activities, lying as it does at the mouth of another great timber-floating river: the Lågen from Numedal Valley. Walk up to the little park on the height near the harbor for a splendid view. Larvik is also important for motorists, since the car-ferry plies from here to Frederikshavn, Denmark. Other claims to fame are having one of Norway's very rare beech forests and being the home of the well-known Farris mineral water springs.

PRACTICAL INFORMATION FOR THE OSLO FJORD DISTRICT

WHEN TO COME. The summer season generally extends from May to September, but all town hotels are open throughout the year, and so are the roads. Two outstanding events take place in July—the national regatta at Horten and the international yachting races at Hankø in the outer Oslo fjord.

WHAT TO SEE. In Östfold, the fortified Old Town of Fredrikstad is a perfect piece of "canned" history, and so is the Fredriksten Fortress of Halden. In Vestfold, the former naval base of Stavern exudes 18th-century charm, and at Horten you'll find the Preus Photographic Museum, unique of its kind and a must for camera enthusiasts.

HOW TO GET ABOUT. There are good train services from Oslo down both sides of the Oslo fjord—on the west side to Drammen, Tønsberg, Sandefjord and Larvik, and on the east side to Moss, Fredrikstad, Sarpsborg and Halden. It is possible to do a one-day round trip to either of these areas, allowing an hour or two in any one of the towns. There is a 40 minutes ferry crossing by car ferry between Moss and Horten.

MOTORING. Comfortable 1 or 2 day trips can be made on either side of the fjord—and indeed both sides can be included even in one day, making a complete round trip. Stop-overs on the west side should be made at Sandefjord, Tønsberg or Larvik, and on the east side at Moss, Fredrikstad, Sarpsborg or Halden.

HOTELS. The only resort hotel of international standing is the *Hankö,* the rest are modest family hotels. But in this district, as in other places, it is perfectly feasible to stay in modern town hotels and enjoy swimming on the neighboring beaches. The town hotels are mostly unpretentious, but the *Grand* at Larvik, the *Klubben* at Tönsberg, and the *Park* at Sandefjord are among the best in Norway. Some of the seaside resort hotels offer reduced terms before and after the peak season.

DRAMMEN (Buskerud). *Park* (M), Gamle Kirkeplass, 202 beds, most rooms with facilities, restaurant; *Drammen Youth Hostel* (I), Korsvegen 62, 140 beds.

FREDRIKSTAD (Østfold). *City Hotel* (M), 208 beds, 50 rooms with bath, restaurant; *Victoria Hotel* (M), 82 beds, most rooms with facilities; *Fredrikstad Motel* (I), 140 beds, swimming.

HALDEN (Østfold). *Park* (M), 84 beds, restaurant; *Halden Youth Hostel* (I), 40 beds.

HANKØ (Østfold), famous yachting center, summer only. *Hankø New Fjord Hotel* (M), 140 beds, most rooms with facilities, restaurant; *Hankø Seilerkro* (I), 14 beds.

LARVIK (Vestfold). *Grand* (M), overlooking fjord, 222 beds in 117 rooms, most with facilities, restaurant; *Holms Motel* (I), 144 beds, cafeteria.

MOSS (Østfold). *Moss Hotel* (M), 96 beds, outstanding restaurant; *Refsnes Gods* (M), on Jeløy island, 90 beds, 30 rooms with bath, charming; *Moss Youth Hostel* (I), 64 beds.

SANDEFJORD (Vestfold). *Park* (E), overlooking harbor, one of Norway's best hotels, 273 beds, all rooms with facilities, restaurant, bar, swimming, saunas; *Atlantic* (M), 60 beds, some rooms with bath.

SARPSBORG (Østfold), industrial town with spectacular waterfall. *Saga* (M), 120 beds, all rooms with facilities; *St Olav* (M), 143 beds, 25 rooms with bath; *Tuneheimen Youth Hostel* (I), 63 beds.

TØNSBERG (Vestfold). *Klubben* (E), 175 beds, all rooms with facilities, restaurant; *Grand* (M), 80 beds, some rooms with facilities; *Tønsberg Youth Hostel* (I), 48 beds.

CAMPING. There are good campsites in the vicinity of most towns on both sides of the Oslo Fjord, particularly along the main road in Østfold from Sweden to Oslo.

 SPORTS. Swimming everywhere outside the Dröbak Narrows is pleasant in crystal-clear and surprisingly warm water (averaging 68°F. throughout the season). The bathing beaches at Ula are particularly good.

Sailing and boating are in evidence everywhere; the waters of the outer Oslo Fjord, with the mixture of open stretches and sheltered channels, are ideal for this activity. A sailing school with first-class instructors is run by the Hankö Hotel. **Fishing** from a boat—or with a spinning-rod from the rocks—is a popular sport, best early (May) and late (September) in the season.

TELEMARK AND THE SOUTH COAST

A Land Fit for Heroes

The Telemark district, whose name has become a part of the skier's lore, is among Norway's most beautiful and most interesting. Winding valleys, precipitous gorges, silvery lakes, snow-covered mountains, pastoral farmlands with their ancient stave churches—all present an unforgettable picture of contrasts and surprises. Dotting the islands and inlets of the South Coast—aptly called Norway's "Summer Smile"—are delightful resorts a holiday paradise, ideal for exploring or just basking in the sun. Telemark is well served by public transport—as described below—but the best way of seeing this remarkable area is to go by car.

Exploring Telemark and the South Coast

The Vestfold express takes you from Oslo via Larvik to the end of the line at Skien. Besides serving as terminus, Skien is also the beginning of another rail line to Oslo via Kongsberg and Drammen if you want to return to the capital by another route. Even more important, however, is Skien's position as a main gateway to Telemark for no eager

299

tourist should leave Norway without at least a glimpse of that ruggedly charming mountain district.

First, though, look at the city from Brekke Park on the inevitable high ridge back of Höyer's Hotel, where not only a fine outdoor Folk Museum is located but also an excellent collection of Ibseniana. For Henrik Ibsen was born in Skien in 1828 and grew up on Venstöp farm (now an Ibsen memorial), 3 miles from the town center, and in Snipetorget 27.

The classic approach to Telemark from Skien is the Bandak Canal. The charming old ship *Victoria* makes the journey from Skien to Dalen in one day, by lock and lake through the province of Telemark.

Leaving Skien at 8:30 sharp you have got 65 glorious miles in front of you, out of which 60 stay quiet, the rest are streams, canals and locks. *Victoria* is in no particular hurry to get you to Dalen. There is too much to show: the park-like lower Telemark, manor houses and timber industry at Ulefoss, winding streams, locks and narrows between Lake Norsjø and Lake Kviteseidvatn and wild Lake Bandak with precipitous mountain sides. While the boat is negotiating the locks you may stroll along the canal path, visit the local shop, chat with the locals—in fact imbibe the peaceful charm which is the very essence of this water excursion.

If this does not appeal, you may board a morning bus from Skien and skirt Lake Norsjø, passing through Ulefoss, with its manor houses on the hills and timber industry along the river en route to Bö, one of the famous districts of Telemark. We might well make the Lifjell Hotel, in the hills above the station, our first stay, for the view from there is probably Telemark's most panoramic, which is saying quite a lot. Bö is the traffic hub of central Telemark. Travelers direct from Oslo alight from the express trains at this junction and board the buses of the efficient West Telemark Bus Company for a ride along the silvery bank of Lake Seljord to the village of Seljord, with its medieval church and wealth of local tradition, thereafter continuing to Brunkeberg crossroads. The main bus line continues straight west from Brunkeberg, heading for the Hardanger Fjord. En route it passes through the steep valley of Morgedal, famous as the cradle of modern skiing.

But our aim is to ramble about a bit in Telemark, in the general direction of Dalen. Thus we catch an afternoon bus from Brunkeberg (a study of timetables is important when dealing with criss-cross Telemark), and wind down a "vistaful" road to Kviteseid and across the hills to Vrådal. This resort is located at an altitude of about 1,000 feet, and anyone wanting a quiet stay, with fishing and rowing, on a beautiful mountain-fringed lake, should stop here for a few days.

You can proceed southward by bus from Vrådal along Lake Nisser to Nelaug, and reach Arendal on the South Coast by train from there. But that's another trip. Our route takes us along another beautiful lake, the Vråvatn, to Vråliosen and across the mountains, but if traveling by car make a short detour to Skafså to visit Anne Grimsdalen's sculpture museum, before hairpinning down to Dalen, with a breathtaking view of Lake Bandak. Dalen, formerly the tourist pivot of Telemark, is today the center of the gigantic Tokke hydro-electric scheme which involves great areas of Telemark; the power station of Dalen (Tokke I) yields 400,000 kilowatts, and has few competitors in Europe.

If you decide to explore Dalen more closely, you should take a taxi up the north wall of Lake Bandak the 5 miles to Eidsborg for a most impressive hairpin climb from the water's edge up to the mountains. Here is a small but ancient stave church. Visit the old building close to it, which has been turned into a local museum and boasts the oldest washing-machine in the world, invented a couple of centuries ago by an imaginative Telemark farmer. From Dalen you can also go by taxi to another of the wonders of Telemark, the Ravnejuvet ravine, dropping some 1,000 feet into the valley of Tokke and having peculiar air currents that bring papers—and even such heavier objects as bushes—thrown down into it back over the brink. Throw in your banknotes and they will return to you.

From Dalen we travel along the Tokke Valley to Åmot, where the beautiful Hyllandsfoss Falls disappeared into the Tokke project, and head for the village of Rauland.

Culture and Sabotage

Located 3,300 feet above sea level, the Rauland Hotel is your best base of operations to combine fishing, hunting, or hiking with a study of the genuine rural culture of Telemark. From the hilltop near the hotel one can see far across Lake Mösvatn into the wild Hardanger plateau and, in the opposite direction, many of the mountain summits of Telemark. Southeast lies Lake Totak and Rauland village—15 minutes by car—with a concentration of more *stabburs,* farm buildings, etc., than can be found anywhere except in the Oslo Folk Museum. But here they have the added charm of completely natural surroundings and are still in use. Beyond Lake Totak the horizon is formed by a long row of peaks running north-south: the mountains guarding the approach to Setesdal valley.

Rauland was the home of the late Dyre Vaa, the sculptor who designed the Swans Fountain in the courtyard of the Oslo Rådhus. (Incidentally, some of his latest efforts in "modern painting" are displayed on the walls of the hotel salons.) One of the most famous country fiddlers in Norway, Myllargutten (The Miller Boy), lived at the west end of Totak, and either the hotel manager or local guides can tell you any number of stories and legends about him and the "old days" in Rauland.

Whatever the complications in choosing your route to Rauland, there is one best way out: the bus trip along the edge of Lake Mösvatn and down to Rjukan. As you cut across this southeast corner of the Hardanger plateau you are again on historic ground. In a solitary hut not far from the mountain hotel, the Norwegian leader of the famous Linge Company of saboteurs, Major Leif Tronstad, was killed in early 1945. And during the winter of 1943 this whole area was the scene of dramatic actions by the Norwegian underground against the Vemork Plant of Norsk Hydro where "heavy water" was produced by the Nazis for their atomic bomb experiments in Germany. Thus, when the bus halts at the Skinnerbu stop on Lake Mösvatn near the big dam, you may have time to buy postcards at the mountain chalet run by one of the saboteurs.

Beyond the dam the road enters a canyon which grows steadily deeper and with more precipitous walls until, in a hairpin swing, it brings you right opposite Vemork, scene of the daring coup now so widely known through the film reconstruction, *Heroes of Telemark.* In spite of the thousands of Nazi soldiers guarding the entire valley, Norwegian saboteurs climbed down into this steep-sided, snow-filled gulch on a bright moonlit night to set off dynamite charges that destroyed the heavy-water plant.

Cable Car Views of Rjukan

Still further down the canyon is the electric power and industrial town of Rjukan, squeezed in between the river and cliffs, while overhead towers the great peak of Mount Gausta, almost 6,000 feet high. Small wonder that the sun does not shine at the bottom for five months of the year. However, the inhabitants of Rjukan can quickly get up into the sunshine on the northern rim of the canyon by means of a cable car that rises over 1,600 feet in a trajectory of 3,000 feet. Don't miss taking a ride on this *Krossobane:* there are magnificent views down the narrow valley and of Mount Gausta.

From Rjukan you have two glorious ways of leaving Telemark, each with its particular attractions. One is by bus around the head of Lake Tinnsjö and across more mountains with farms and *stabburs* to Bolkesjö and then to Kongsberg. An important junction on the main Oslo-Stavanger railway, Kongsberg, an old silver mining town and still the seat of the Royal Norwegian Mint, is today famous for its remarkable 18th-century church, its Mining Museum and the miniature train taking visitors down into the old mines, 1,122 feet below the surface.

The other way out is by bus from Rjukan to Mel, and by train-ferry down nearly the entire length of Lake Tinnsjö: a wild, roadless district much like Bandak. At Tinnoset the train takes to dry land once again, pauses briefly at the industrial town of Notodden and then joins the main railway at Hjuksebö Junction below Kongsberg. For an appropriate leave-taking of Telemark, stop over at Notodden long enough to take a bus or taxi the few miles to Heddal and see that largest of Norwegian stave churches.

Exploring the South Coast

The south coast railroad from Oslo to Kristiansand and onwards to Stavanger, forces its way through crevasses and along lakes and rivers as far as Kristiansand; then there is no alternative but to go right through the mountains, bridging the rivers in vast spans of concrete and steel. Thus you will become acquainted with some of Europe's largest rail tunnels and airiest bridges, and a wild and desolate interior, but the south coast itself will still escape you—unless you take the sidetracks to Kragerø, Arendal and Flekkefjord.

Therefore our suggestion is that you should go by bus, (or car), starting in Porsgrunn (which we presume you have reached via Oslo).

However, by bus it is a question of detours if you wish to imbibe the atmosphere of Kragerø and Risør, resuming travel by a later bus. Anybody might be tempted to stay over in Kragerø until the next day, for here is a picturesqueness that has inspired generations of painters to haunt the little town and its many islands. In any case, reserve a few hours to wander through the narrow and winding streets in the old part of Kragerø.

Risør is even more romantic than Kragerø, with its stately patrician houses from the early 19th century lining the harbor. Don't worry about the winding streets of little Tvedestrand, your bus will take you right into them. We suggest you "jump ship" in Tvedestrand, leave the through-service bus to find its own way to Arendal, and enter the coastal bus which will take you to Arendal via Flosta.

Once known as "Little Venice," Arendal's canals have been turned into wide streets, but it still retains its beautiful harbor. The town is a center for holiday-makers and offers interesting boat trips among the skerries and on the delta of the River Nid.

Despite nature's charm on the south coast and despite the bustle of modern industry and communications there is a slight atmosphere of sadness about Sörlandet (the "south land"), a hint of bygone and better days. For all of these small towns and hamlets had their heyday when sailing ships were the masters of the sea. These were the times that brought the small white cottages and the large white mansion houses into being—the times described in Jonas Lie's novels, when skippers and pilots were the heroes and their wives the heroines.

You can recapture a bit of this spirit, if you stay in Arendal, by taking a trip to the large island of Tromøy and visiting the old church of the same name: and by crossing over to little Merdøy Island, where a typical skipper's home has been taken over unchanged, forming a part of the Aust-Agder Museum, and kept exactly as it was in its owner's day.

Between Arendal and Grimstad you may be tempted to step off the bus in Fevik and entrust yourself to the Strand Hotel there, facing the Skagerak from a bathing beach position. Grimstad brings back the history of both sailing ships and Ibsen, for it was here that the great dramatist served as a druggist's apprentice and began writing his first lyrics.

Lillesand, further on, will delight your eye not only by its fine mansion houses, but also by its location behind a complicated maze of channels and skerries. This is where you should finally abandon your bus—if the weather is fine—and lodge at the intimate Hotel Norge, because we suggest you investigate those skerries which are the essence of the south coast.

Kristiansand, Capital of Sörlandet

You can take the south coast railway for a dramatic but comfortable and quick ride to Stavanger, or continue to rough it along the highroad. One bus service links up with the other, and there is no doubt about it, you will reach Stavanger in the end, especially if you have been provident enough to supply yourself with the latest Norwegian timetable (*Rutebok for Norge*). Moreover, you will have had a marvellous time, if you are the type of adventurer and Norway-lover that we suspect. You will probably fall in love with Mandal's narrow streets which are lined with 18th- and 19th-century houses. You will be thrilled by the view of Kvinesdal and the Fedafjord, almost scared by the wildness of Jøssingfjord, and amazed at the number of fishing vessels in the harbor of Egersund. Your last surprise on the journey will probably be that mountainous Norway contains a stretch of flat farming land the size of Jaeren, south of Stavanger.

But now let's assume that, having decided to make the journey to Stavanger another time, you have stayed overnight in Kristiansand. Formerly the arch-enemy of the other southern towns, because of its founding by the Danish king in 1641 with special royal privileges, Kristiansand has now made peace with them and is a respected industrial leader.

Kristiansand is the capital of Sörlandet, and offers good shopping facilities. Take a stroll through the old–world Kvadratur area, the checker–board plan of streets between the harbor on two sides and the Otra River on the third, the old fortress of Christiansholm, the cathedral. An exceedingly visible but non-cultural landmark is the tall chimney of the nickel-refining plant on the east side of the harbor approach, claimed to be the highest stack in Europe. Despite the regularity of the old part of the city, there are many delightful houses of typical southern Norway style and neatness, but most of them are jammed so tightly against each other that there is no place for the little garden in front. Apparently Kristiansand has always been crowded, for Gabriel Scott quotes a visitor in 1799 as having said that if a man absent-mindedly smoked his pipe by his own open window, he might easily happen to spit into a neighbor's parlor.

The Otra River, which flows into the sea at Kristiansand, provides the clue for our next move: namely, to follow it upstream about 100 miles through Setesdal to its source. The charming narrow-gauged Setesdal Railway runs no more, except as a hobby train along a 3-mile track on summer week-ends. Therefore, we enter a morning bus at Kristiansand in the direction of Setesdalen. The first two hours are uneventful. Whereas the old railway criss-crossed the foaming Otra and clung to it like a stamp, the Setesdal highway, to begin with, roams about the provinces miles away from the lively river. At Haegeland, river contact is once more established and we advise you to discontinue your morning nap. At Evje a wide flat area suddenly appears and, sure enough, here is Evje-*moen,* or the military training ground, for there are not too many places in upland Norway where naturally level drilling grounds are available.

Byglandsfjord, former terminus of the Setesdal Line, is reached in 2½ hours. The Otra is quite logically called Byglandsfjord at this point, for it's now a lake a mile wide in places and at least 25 miles in rambling length. We are now entering the real Setesdal, that formerly most isolated and inaccessible of all Norwegian valleys, and the one which still bears many traces of its erstwhile quaint manners and culture.

Cliffs and Cutthroats of Setesdal

In olden days its inhabitants were not the most peaceful and lawabiding of citizens—witness the "Robbers' Hole" (Tjuvehola) in the mountain side just beyond the hamlet of Byglandsfjord, where thieves used to waylay farmers returning from town and relieve them of their purchases and leftover cash. And not far beyond there, we have the most dramatic evidence conceivable of how natural barriers for ages cut off Setesdal, not only from the outside world, but from itself. Just above the water's edge the road runs through a 600-yard tunnel blasted out of a cliff which, before the highway engineers came along, rose perpendicularly from the lake without offering even enough foothold for a mountain climber.

Byglandsfjord is the undisputed central point in lower Setesdal, as well as a convenient stopping place for tourists. However, another couple of hours will bring you to Valle which, in our opinion, is the most rewarding part of all Setesdal. Spend a day or two in Valle, try trout fishing in the river (permission must be obtained), and go walking among the remarkable old farms that line the lower, moderately sloping hillsides. This will enable you to see more closely the unusual outfit that a few older men still wear while working in the fields. It consists of a white shirt and black trousers that give a remarkably dressed up appearance to men pitching hay; an appearance partly comprised, however, by the very battered and narrowrimmed black felt hat which completes the costume. Some elderly women may also be seen in the fields raking hay and hanging it up to dry on racks in their distinctive attire: black woolen stockings, white woolen skirt with black edgings, white blouse, black bolero or red jacket; while the older ones also wear a curious scarf-like headgear which shades their eyes like a bonnet in front and hangs down at back like a pigtail.

Yet these working clothes in Setesdal are nothing compared to the Sunday and festive costumes. The women put on black skirts and blouses over the white ones for church-going, while for weddings they add a bright red skirt, also over the previous foundation. The men change to black trousers with a heavy piece of leather reinforcing the seat and with gaily colored cuffs, and wear a heavy pullover with decorations in front and at the wrists to match the trouser cuffs. But again all this pales in contrast to what the bride and groom must don for their wedding! To the basic festive outfit are added embroideries, silver, ornaments and a bridal crown, said to be worth at least a thousand dollars. However, everyone can afford it in this valley, for helpful neighbors each lend a certain item, or else the young couple can rent a complete set of finery from the local "Housewives Association" just as one hires a dress suit in a city.

Hikes and Hideouts

The history of Setesdal is as interesting as its costumes, yet one would need to be something of a hiker to appreciate it at first hand. At Valle begins the old "Skin Trail", so called because it took the peasants westward over the mountains to the nearest tax-collector's office where they paid in skins, a 2-day journey that was extremely unpopular with the inhabitants. East from Valle the energetic tourist can take a 2-hour hike along the road leading to the mountain farms or *seters* where the cattle graze in summer and where *seter*-maidens make cheese. Or he can follow the "Bishop's Trail" into Telemark, along which church officials made their way in olden times on their not too frequent visits to the "stubborn devils" in Setesdal.

Indeed, the valley's parishioners were so averse to change in the early days of the Reformation that they killed or drove out more than one of the new Lutheran priests. Tax-collectors and sheriffs were equally disliked, and some natives carried on feuds with the royal officials which remind one of the encounters between American hillbillies and revenue officers.

Such a famous local character was "Bad Aasmund", and you should not miss a visit to his hideout 6 miles up the valley from Valle. He tangled with the law four centuries ago, fled to Holland, returned after many years but just in time—according to the legends—to abduct his former fiancée as she was about to be married to a persistent farmer she didn't like. Again outlawed, "Bad Aasmund" lived with his bride in the farm at Rygnestad, taking refuge in a stoutly fortified *stabbur* or *loft* whenever the sheriff was so rash as to put in a decidedly apprehensive appearance.

However, the gentleman apparently didn't call very often, for Aasmund was as handy with a bow and arrow as Robin Hood, and the massive logs of his *loft* still stand there today as impregnable as ever. But strangely enough, after all the glamorous days of adventure and rebellion, the bad man settled down, and in later life became a sheriff and tax-collector himself.

The bus ride north from Valle to Bykle and Hovden is perhaps the most exciting part of the trip. The road climbs steeply, now running close to the rushing torrent Otra, now hugging the valley walls. Like all other mountain highways in Norway, this one has its share of curves with the customary steep slope or even precipice on the outside edge. Low cement parapets or large stones are set up along this edge as guard-rails and there is usually room for two vehicles to pass. Nevertheless, the tourist driving his own car should exercise particular caution at such points and make his presence known by sounding the horn before entering a blind curve.

Near Bykle you will see another dramatic reminder of former hardships in communication: the Byklestigen or Bykle-ladder. This is a narrow path cut across the face of a cliff, which used to be the only way people could get from the lower valley to Bykle. Supplies had to be carried on their own backs, for not even pack-horses were able to negotiate Byklestigen. A full-width roadway has been carved out at the bottom of the rock wall along the river, so the distance which formerly took hours of toil is now made in a few minutes.

An hour later you are at Hovden, where there is easy access to both mountain lakes and rivers, in case you are a fisherman. (By the way, the source of the Otra River lies up in one of these lakes.) Hovden is also the end of the Setesdal bus line and here we change to another bus whose ultimate destination is Odda on the Sör Fjord.

You may think that you've seen everything in the way of wild scenery by this time but there is still much more in store, thanks to our *northbound* route. The great advantage of traveling up-stream through Setesdal rather than down is that one can thus enjoy the natural crescendo of change from miniature Sörlandet up through the ever-higher, ever-shifting Setesdal to something even more magnificent but as yet unknown, which you sense lies right ahead.

And sure enough, just beyond Hovden comes another climax. There's a long straight piece of road ahead bordered on either side by a forest of dwarf birches which grow smaller and sparser for each mile. Beyond and above them on all sides rises a vast mountain plateau with snow patches here and there on the heights. This is the great central massif of the Hardangervidda: thousands of square miles of heath, lakes and mountain peaks.

The bus follows this road for many minutes but then, just as you think you are reaching these highlands, a deep, broad valley appears a thousand feet below with the familiar pattern of cultivated fields and green meadows with golden hay drying on the racks. This is Haukeligrend village, an important road junction. If the purpose has been only to discover Telemark and the South Coast, this is where we turn east and take a bus that will bring us through the winding valleys of Telemark to Bö, and from there by train to Oslo. If you wish to wander farther afield, the direction to follow is westward across the mountain passes to Hardanger. Magnificent scenery and stupendous hairpin curves await you along this route—the high mountains around Haukeliseter, the steep and winding ascent into Röldal with its pilgrim stave church, the unsurpassed view of Lake Röldal from the mountain road to Seljestad, the Seljestad Gorge and the view of the Folgefonn Glacier. Without a doubt, this can be an immensely impressive journey.

PRACTICAL INFORMATION FOR TELEMARK
AND THE SOUTH COAST

 WHEN TO COME. Telemark is a two-season region with winter sports from Christmas until after Easter. Spring tours in the lower parts of Telemark can be readily undertaken in early May, but the more mountainous parts should not be visited before early June. From then on it is straight going until the end of September. The South Coast is the Norwegian Riviera, but unlike its southern counterpart, is not visited in the early season. Here the season extends from the middle of June to the middle of September.

 WHAT TO SEE. The highlights of Telemark include the lakes of Bandak, Fyresvatn, and Tinnsjö; the views from Lifjell, Nutheim (across Flatdal), Brunkeberg, and Bolkesjö; the majestic Mount Gausta and the stupendous Vestfjord valley at Rjukan; the old farms at Rauland and the stave churches of Heddal and Eidsborg.

No such inventory can be made up for the South Coast, where the charm is everywhere—in the white-painted towns and fishing villages, and the tang of sea and tar. Yet the principal towns of Kristiansand and Arendal, and the small towns of Tvedestrand, Grimstad (with Ibseniana), Lillesand (with Hamsuniana), Flekkefjord, Farsund, Mandal, and the villages of Lyngör, Brekkestö, NyHellesund and Loshamn, represent the typical South Coast charm and tradition.

Inland is the striking Setesdal valley, featuring the remarkable Rygnestad loft.

 HOW TO GET ABOUT. From Oslo, Sørlandsbanen railroads runs through Kongsberg, Kristiansand and Egersund to Stavanger, with branches to Arendal and Flekkefjord. In addition, connecting bus services go from the main line to other towns and villages, both on the coast and inland, generally connecting with the trains. Fastest trains to Kristiansand take between 4½ and 5 hours. Several services daily to Kristiansand with the majority running through to Stavanger or with good connections.

 MOTORING. A tour of Telemark and the south coast can be easily made from Oslo following the suggested itinerary or with variants, depending upon one's choice of scenery. At least 7 days are recommended in order to provide for excursions and stop-overs.

Depart   Oslo-Drammen-Kongsberg-Bolkesjö-Rjukan-Haukeligrend-down Setesdal Valley to Kjetså–Mandal–Farsund–Kvinesdal–Flekkefjord, and return via Kristiansand–Arendal–Larvik–Sandefjord–Tönsberg–return Oslo, about 1,352 Km.

HOTELS AND RESTAURANTS. The majority of Telemark hostelries are in the moderate price category. Since they are for the most part "tourist" or "mountain" hotels, you can rest assured that they will automatically reach the high standards of equipment, service, and food required by law.

ARENDAL (Aust Agder). *Phønix* (E), 150 beds, restaurant, bar, dancing, disco; *Central* (M), 65 beds, restaurant.

BØ (Telemark). *Bø Hotel* (M), 150 beds; *Lifjell* (M), situated below Mt Lifjell, 120 beds; *Grivi Youth Hostel* (I), 134 beds.

BOLKESJØ (Telemark). *Bolkesjø* (E), built in 1881, rebuilt and enlarged, old interiors preserved, fine views of Telemark, 238 beds, all rooms with bath or shower, restaurant; *Uppigard* (M), 60 beds.

BYGLANDSFJORD (Aust Agder). *Revsnes* (M), 84 beds, most rooms with facilities.

DALEN (Telemark). *Bandak* (M), 24 rooms, 3 with bath; *Dalen Youth Hostel* (I), 70 beds.

FARSUND (Vest-Agder). *Farsund Fjord Hotel* (E), 108 beds, all rooms with bath/shower.

FEVIK (Aust Agder). *Strand* (E), 86 beds, most rooms with bath, restaurant, sea view, sandy beach.

FLEKKERFJORD (Vest-Agder). *Maritim* (E), 96 beds, all rooms with bath/shower; *Grand* (M), 33 beds, most with bath/shower; *Bondeheimen* (I), 19 beds.

GRIMSTAD (Aust Agder). *Müllerhotell Helmershus* (M), 70 beds, all rooms with bath or shower; *Grimstad Youth Hostel* (I), 21 beds.

HOVDEN (Aust Agder). *Hovden Apartment Hotel* (E), weekly rental, 300 beds; *Hovden Mountain Hotel* (M), 180 beds, all rooms with bath or shower.

KONGSBERG (Buskerud). *Grand* (M), 166 beds, 64 rooms with bath; *Gyldenløve* (M), 110 beds, 12 rooms with bath; *Kongsberg Youth Hostel* (I), 90 beds.

KRAGERØ (Telemark). *Victoria* (M), 22 rooms, 6 with bath; *Kragerø Youth Hostel* (I), 100 beds.

KRISTIANSAND (Vest-Agder). *Caledonien* (E), Vestre Strandgate 7, 400 beds, all rooms with facilities, restaurants; *Christian Quart* (E), Markensgate 39, 230 beds, all rooms with facilities, restaurant; *Evenbye's Ernst* (E), Rädhusgate 2, many rooms with bath, restaurant; *Fregatten Rica* (M), Dronningensgate 66, 110 beds, most with bath, restaurant; *Metropole* (M), Dronningensgate 8, 21 beds; *Norge* (M), Dronningensgate 5, 140 beds, all rooms with bath/shower, restaurant; *Vestre Rooms* (M), Vestre Strandgate 28, 32 beds, no meals; *Bondeheimen* (I), Kirkegate 15, 64 beds; *Roligheden Youth Hostel* (I), 135 beds.

KVINESDAL (Vest-Agder). *Utsikten* (M), 69 beds, all rooms with bath/shower; *Alfarheim* (I), 20 beds.

MANDAL (Vest-Agder), adjoining popular Sjøsanden sandy beach; *Solborg* (M), 102 beds, 40 rooms with facilities, restaurant, swimming, sauna, sightseeing boat; *Bondeheimen* (I), 30 beds, some with shower; *Mandal Youth Hostel* (I), 48 beds.

MORGEDAL (Telemark). *Morgedal* (M), 130 beds in 70 rooms, all with bath/shower.

RAULAND (Telemark), 3300 ft. *Rauland Mountain Hotel* (M), 70 rooms, 23 with bath.

RJUKAN (Telemark). *Rjukan Hotel* (M), 60 beds, all rooms with bath/shower; *Skinnarbu* (M), 110 beds; *Rjukan Fjellstue* (I), 140 beds; *Rjukan Youth Hostel* (I), 88 beds.

The Gaustablikk holiday center is situated 15 km SW of Rjukan, access by road throughout the year, 3180 ft, views of Mt Gausta. *Gaustablikk Mountain Hotel* (M), 165 beds, all rooms with shower or toilet; *Kvitåvatn Fjellstoge* (I), 108 beds in family rooms.

SKIEN (Telemark). *Ibsen Hotel* (E), 238 beds, all rooms with bath/shower, restaurants, swimming; *Müllerhotell Høyer* (M), 130 beds, 35 rooms with bath; *Skien Sportell* (M), 52 beds, all rooms with shower.

VALLE (Aust Agder). *Valle Motel* (M), 160 beds, all rooms with shower; *Bergtun* (M), 23 beds.

VRÅDAL (Telemark). *Straand* (M), 130 beds, most rooms with facilities, dining room, cafeteria, swimming, sauna; *Vrådal* (M), 58 rooms, 30 with bath.

VRÅLIOSEN (Telemark). *Vråliosen* (M), 56 beds, 2 rooms with bath.

CAMPING, HOSTELS. The south coast camping sites have a tendency to overcrowding, as they are mostly on or near beaches of pure white sand; very popular are the Mandal and Kristiansand sites, and those between Arendal and Grimstad. West of Mandal there is more elbow-room, especially if you make for the sites off the beaten track.

SPORTS. In summer there is quite good *fishing* in the mountains of western Telemark, very good on the Hardanger Plateau. *Hiking* from chalet to chalet on the Hardanger Plateau is another attraction. The South Coast offers *swimming* from the cliffs or lovely beaches (best are Sjösanden near Mandal, Hamresanden near Kristiansand, and the beach at Fevik), *boating* among the skerries, and *fishing* in the sounds. The mountain lakes of Setesdal hold plenty of sleek trout.

Telemark, the cradle of skiing, is today one of Norway's most popular winter sports areas. The principal resorts are Bø, Bolkesjø, Morgedal, Rauland, Rjukan, Vrådal and Vråliosen. The season extends from Christmas until after

The magnificent view over the Næröydal
Valley in Norway

Alesund, nestling like a toy town
between sea and mountain

An old Viking house at Lofthus in Norway

The fine Renaissance castle at Kalmar in
Sweden; and some old timbered houses in
Ystad

Easter. Most hotels have ski lifts of various types, and they employ their own ski instructors.

LANGUAGE/30

For the Business or Vacationing International Traveler

In 24 languages! A basic language course on 2 cassettes and a phrase book . . . Only $14.95 ea. + shipping

Nothing flatters people more than to hear visitors try to speak their language and LANGUAGE/30, used by thousands of satisfied travelers, gets you speaking the basics quickly and easily. Each LANGUAGE/30 course offers:

- approximately 1½ hours of guided practice in greetings, asking questions and general conversation
- special section on social customs and etiquette

Order yours today. Languages available:

ARABIC	GREEK	JAPANESE	RUSSIAN
CHINESE	HEBREW	KOREAN	SERBO-CROATIAN
DANISH	HINDI	NORWEGIAN	SPANISH
DUTCH	INDONESIAN	PERSIAN	SWAHILI
FRENCH	ITALIAN	PORTUGUESE	SWEDISH
GERMAN	TURKISH	VIETNAMESE	TAGALOG

To order send $14.95 per course + shipping $2.00 1st course, $1 ea. add. course. In Canada $3 1st course, $2.00 ea. add. course. NY and CA residents add state sales tax. Outside USA and Canada $14.95 (U.S.) + air mail shipping: $8 for 1st course, $5 ea. add. course. MasterCard, VISA and Am. Express card users give brand, account number (all digits), expiration date and signature.
SEND TO: FODOR'S, Dept. LC 760, 2 Park Ave., NY 10016-5677, USA.

THE FJORD COUNTRY

Wonders and Waterfalls

Norway's Fjord Country provides one of the world's unique travel experiences. The fjords tell different things to different people, with their awesome power and majesty, their changing moods. More likely than not, however, the visitor will recall something more, something of the atmosphere of quiet beauty. Whether it might be on the banks of one of the fjord's famous salmon or trout streams, or rowing in the shadow of a thousand-foot rock face, or relaxing with a pot of good coffee and pleasant company on some fjord farm, there will always be that element of tranquil calm. There's a peace in these parts which will give one the satisfaction that comes only to those who have found what they are seeking.

Exploring the Fjord Country

Conspicuously located in downtown Stavanger, only a stone's throw from the busy wharves with their hundreds of larger and smaller craft, is a monument to Alexander L. Kielland, the city's literary light and chronicler. With a good view from his pedestal, he stands there somewhat critically appraising the scene before him. Today it's certainly not the same town which he so vividly described some eighty or ninety years ago. But neither has it acquired the impersonal self-absorbed air which one might expect in the fishcanning capital of the world as well as one of the headquarters of Norway's North Sea oil fleet.

The new Stavanger of modern buildings, bustling traffic and great waterfront factories has emerged from the familiar, flat sardine can; and the man who turned the key bringing about this change was the former broom peddler, Christian Bjelland. Bjelland was the founder of Stavanger's canning industry, which each year probably exports more canned foods than any other city on the globe. It's an interesting spot in which to spend some time. With a population of over 86,000, Stavanger is the fourth largest city in Norway, and the oldest in this part of the country. It was founded in 1100, and boasts a stately Anglo–Norman cathedral well over 800 years old.

Every visitor to Stavanger should walk around the older quarters with their picturesque alleyways, old style wooden structures and cobblestone streets. The venerable Kongsgaard school, as well as Ledaal–the old Kielland estate which is now public property–and the royal residence in Stavanger, should also be seen. Like so many Norwegian cities, Stavanger appears to be in a period of transition when the old must adjust itself to the demands of the times, while the new, in turn, must temper its urge to tear down and modernize. Stavanger has often been called the city with the many churches and has long enjoyed an active highly individualist spiritual life. One of its streets, Berglandsgate, is lined practically solid on both sides with a spectrum of churches, chapels and missions representing a large number of dissenting faiths and groups.

The Ryfylke fjords north and east of Stavanger form the southernmost part of the Fjord Country. Stavanger is well suited for its part as port of entry to this district, because the "White Fleet", consisting of low-slung, speedy craft known as "sea buses", provides swift and comfortable transport for both passengers and cars to the surrounding fjords. You may stay in Stavanger's fine hotels and make daily excursions on the ships of the "White Fleet" even to the most distant fjords of Ryfylke and return to your base in the afternoon. Stavanger is also the western terminus for the South Norway Railway, which skirts the whole of the southern coast.

The visitor should also make it a point to visit the Lyse Fjord. This trip should be made if for no other reason than to see the fjord's "cliff-dweller" communities, where farms cling to narrow ledges hundreds of feet above the sea.

Though Stavanger has been primarily oriented towards the sea, it has more recently recognized its role as the gate to what has become one of Norway's leading agricultural counties. Stretching southward along the coast is a huge glacial moraine known as Jaeren. Flat and stony, it is probably the largest expanse of level ground to be found in all of Norway. But it is practically without harbors, nor is there much fishing. The inhabitants were therefore forced to turn to farming at an early date, and the district's hundreds of miles of stone fences stand today as monuments to centuries of back-breaking labor.

Once freed from stones, however, the soil was capable of growing crops of all kinds. There is little if any snow here, the climate is mild and the growing season long. Today, Jaeren is the country's leading producer of eggs and wool. For the vacationer, the district's wide sandy beaches and mild sunny weather provide just the antidote for over-wrought city nerves. Stavanger is also Norway's new "oil city", serving as a base for the oil rigs in the North Sea. Many American oil experts are now residents of Stavanger, which even has an American school.

The "Discovery Route"

The "Discovery Route" is the classic route through the Ryfylke fjords to Hardanger and Bergen, with traditions dating back to the days of the pony cart. Thanks to the "White Fleet" and modern buses, this time-honored route has become popular lately.

The fjord boat leaves Stavanger early in the morning for Jelsa at the entrance to the Sand Fjord, where your bus is waiting. It takes you via Sand, along the famous Suldalslågen salmon river to Solheimsvik, where a ferry will bring you across Lake Suldal to Nesflaten. The journey then leads through the narrow and rugged Bratlandsdal Valley, where the road is hewn from the steep mountainside. At Breifonn you join the main Telemark road from Oslo to Bergen. Years ago it was blocked by snow every winter, but by means of huge tunnels, the road now goes straight through the impeding mountains.

At Breifonn you change to another bus, which takes the zig-zag road to the Seljestad mountain pass (now bypassed in tunnel) with fine views of Lake Røldal and the Breifonn Glacier. Descending on the Seljestad side, the bus will make a short stop at the Låtefoss waterfall, tumbling down the mountainside in a double avalanche and gently spraying the road. The Discovery Route terminates in Odda, the industrial center at the very head of the Sør Fjord—a branch of the mighty Hardanger Fjord.

Of all the popular spots in Hardanger, most of the visitor's en-thusiasm is probably reserved for the Sör Fjord. This fjord arm extends from Utne, almost due south to Odda, its east shore a continuous sweep of orchards—in springtime an undulating sea of white and pink blos-soms. This setting, with its old farms, orchards, green plots and eternal mountains, has provided inspiration for great works of art, literature and music during the resurgence of national romanticism in the last century. Paintings of Adolf Tidemand and Hans Gude, songs like Ole Bull's *Seter Maiden's Sunday,* and many of Grieg's melodies had their origin in this part of the Hardanger Fjord. Visitors to Sör Fjord should not fail to see the old farm community at Aga on the west shore. The old buildings preserved here in their natural setting have retained an air of antiquity which no outdoor museum can match. A rather narrow road on the left of Sör Fjord leads through Aga to the charming resort of Utne.

Out of the Sör Fjord and continuing almost due east, the Eid Fjord comprises the eastern extremity of the Hardanger Fjord, pushing in-land almost to the very base of the Hardangerjöklen, a high-lying glacier. Eidfjord village, at the head of this fjord arm, has for centuries been a junction point between eastern and western Norway. From the earliest times, travelers on foot, horseback or on skis have followed this natural declivity down from the Hardanger plateau. Today, one of the main east-west highways follows this route through the magnificent Måbödal valley, passing by the well-known waterfall, the Vöringfoss.

It is time now to look around for some of those renowned Hardanger beauty spots in which to relax. We have already passed the peaceful villages of Röldal and Seljestad, and on the eastern shore of the Sör Fjord there is the district of Ullensvang, with more fruit trees than any other Norwegian community, with a medieval church on a romantic point in the fjord, waterfalls draping the cliffs, the Folgefonn glacier capping the mountains across the fjord, and Edvard Grieg's studio hut. Exuding the same charm is lovely Utne on the point between the main fjord and Sör Fjord, Ulvik nestling at the head of its own little fjord and with terraced farms climbing the steep hills. Granvin, terminal of the Hardanger Railway (a branch of the Bergen Line) is also an unforgettable resort.

Continuing from Odda along Sør Fjord, we ferry across the Hardanger Fjord from Kinsarvik to Kvanndal, and ride along the northern shores of the mighty main fjord. The highroad takes us across the Fyksesund bridge, spanning the 755-foot gap of that imposing offshoot of the Hardanger Fjord, and along it we ride into the charming villages of Öystese and Norheimsund, both famous Hardanger resorts.

From Norheimsund we have the choice of two roads to Bergen. The main route takes us through another of those wild canyons—the Tokagjel Gorge—and across the mountain moors of Kvamskogen to the "Capital of the Fjords". The other route, narrower but no less interesting, continues along the Hardanger Fjord to the smiling district of Strandebarm, another flourishing Hardanger resort, and via Mundheim westwards to Bergen.

Waterways to Haugesund

Hydrofoil boats have been introduced between Stavanger and Bergen making the trip to Haugesund in 75 minutes and Bergen in less than 4 hours. However, the more leisurely way of going by ferry to Kopervik and bus to Haugesund fits in better with most itineraries. Haugesund, built, it is said, on a foundation of herring bones, is a major shipping center.

Just north of the city is King Harald's Column, a monument raised on the burial mound where the Viking King Harald the Fairhaired is believed to lie. The column was dedicated in 1872, presumably 1000 years after the battle of Hafrs Fjord, when Norway was united into a single kingdom. This historic battleground is located a short distance southwest of Stavanger.

Across the channel from Haugesund is the level, treeless island of Karmöy, the site of one of King Harald's favorite estates. A wealth of archeological finds have verified the island's importance during Viking times, when its strategic position controlled an important section of the country's coastal waterways.

Northward by boat or northeast from Haugesund via Highway E76 the destination is the same. By highway, one enters the back door, by boat the wide-open front door of Hardanger, loveliest of the fjords. Going by road a dilemma arises. By following Highway E76 all the way we travel along one of the finest fjordside roads hewn into the vertical wall of the Åkrafjord. By branching left at Håland, however, we include such gems as the villages of Skånevik and Rosendal, with modern hotels. Rosendal estate, which became a barony in 1678, has a history going right back to the days of the ancient Norse king, Håkon Håkonsson. The main building dates from the 1650's and is one of the most beautiful in all Norway, while the Rosendal Gardens are a sight long to be remembered. Estate and gardens were deeded to the University of Oslo in 1927 and the property is now being operated as an experimental farm.

While Hardanger is a tourist's paradise from early spring to late fall, one is in the habit of thinking of this fjord in terms of blossomtime. For Hardanger is the richest orchard district in Norway, with fruit trees often forming a seemingly endless border between fjord edge and the snow-capped mountains.

Northward to Sogne Fjord

Sailing northward from Bergen, we keep pretty well within the island fringe that provides a good sheltered waterway along much of the Norwegian coast. Inland the mountains rise range upon range, but along the coast the land is scraped and bare—nothing but smooth rounded stones with an occasional farm wherever a handful of soil made it possible. These weathered, rocky islands were evidently former mountain tops, and even farther inland the mountains seem rounded and worn. In fact only a few peaks in these parts protruded above the vast ice field that covered this whole fjord district in the Ice Age. When this huge blanket began to slip from east to west, it ground off the mountain tops and chiseled a series of deep valleys extending westward to the sea.

Then followed a period of indecision while the coastline rose and fell, finally sinking until the tops of former peaks had been turned into islands, and long fingers of sea water had been sent probing into the innermost recesses of the valleys—in the case of the Sogne Fjord, a good 130 miles. In the latter, the present sea level is halfway up the former valley wall, and the water is 3,700 feet deep at one point. Here in the fjord country people are now living a couple of thousand feet above what was the valley floor some millions of years ago. Hence the fjords, and so much for a second-hand geography lesson.

Bypassing a little spot called Eivindvik, about three quarters of the way up the coast between Bergen and the mouth of the Sogne Fjord, you may notice two old stone crosses on the shore. It seems that these fjord districts were popular spots with the chieftains and clan leaders, most of whom preferred the rough, bald coastal tracts to the more protected and fertile inner fjords, a preference based on tactical rather than personal considerations. By establishing himself at a strategic point on the island-protected waterway which extends along a good length of the Norwegian coast, a chief who used foresight could secure himself a little Norwegian Gibraltar. Back in those early days, the landed peasants, clansmen and chieftains from the fjord districts used to meet somewhere in this section for their Gula Parliament, the laws of which have served as a model for the parliament of Iceland. Its location, as well as the stone crosses, suggest that Eivindvik was the site of this ancient legislative body.

Rounding the corner and swinging eastward into the Sogne Fjord, some interesting changes take place. As you push deeper into the fjord, the strip of land between the water's edge and the mountain wall becomes broader and greener. There are more farms, and the bald, naked rocks of the outer coast disappear. By the time Lavik is passed, you can begin to get an insight into the true fjord country.

Lavik sits just inside the outer Sogne Fjord, where the main highway leading northward to Sunn Fjord and Nord Fjord connects with a side road leading to the aluminum center of Höyanger. Thanks to quantities of cheap hydro-electric power, bauxite can be shipped in and processed into aluminum more cheaply here than in any other part of the world. The same is being done at Årdal, all the way at the end of the fjord. Höyanger itself is one of the best planned industrial towns on the globe. High, and near the top of one of the two peaks between which the town nestles, fumes pour out of a hole in the mountain side. This is smoke from the factories far below, led to the mountain top through a tunnel which functions as a gigantic smokestack. Here mountain breezes carry it away so that none of it ever reaches the town.

About halfway up the fjord at Balestrand begins the true fjord country. For generations this has been the most famous tourist region in Sogne. Here the harsh and bare landscape of the coast and outer fjord has gradually been building up to something surprising and exciting. By the time you push as far inland as Balestrand the world is new, and the inner Sogne lies before you. Here it's the magnitude that impresses. Towering snowcapped mountains drop 4,000 feet into a fjord often no wider than a city block. Against a background like this, a tourist steamer can look as insignificant as a water bug. In many places there's no shore at all; the perpendicular mountain faces continue right down beneath the water for hundreds, thousands of feet, and even the largest boats can slip along these rock walls at hand-shaking distance without worrying about where the bottom is.

From Balestrand, the long, narrow Fjaerlands Fjord probes northward towards Jostedalsbreen, Norway's mighty glacier. A short distance inland from Fjaerland, at the fjord's head, are the Suphelle and Böyum glaciers. Resembling a massive waterfall, the slow forward movement of the glacier pushes ice over the precipice and adds to the glittering blue-white wall along one side of the valley.

Second only to the magnitude of Norway's longest and mightiest fjord, it is the color and the ordered neatness of man's contribution to the scene that makes inner Sogne an event of discovery. Although the mountains are sheer and push to the very heavens, rivers and streams have built up sizeable deltas between mountain and sea. There are green, well-kept fields, separated by fences of a million stones plucked from the land, and orchards of fruit trees turning a whole fjord rim into a single great orchard. It is easy to see why farming is the major source of livelihood here.

Like many of the innermost fjord communities on the Norwegian coast, this district enjoys an inland climate even though it is located on salt water. Moisture-laden clouds sweeping in from the ocean are deflected skyward by the mountains farther out towards the coast and drop their rain there. Here there are clear skies, sunshine, and often enough dryness to necessitate irrigation. Fjord-ends and narrow valleys cuddled between these huge bastions of sheer rock are actually natural greenhouses. Rock walls absorb the heat from the sun during the daylight hours and radiate it after sundown. Crops are heavy, the fruit is the finest in Norway and even tobacco may be grown.

Four Fingers of the Sogne Fjord

About two-thirds of the way along its length the Sogne Fjord becomes undecided, and before it makes up its mind has branched off in four different directions. The southernmost finger worms due south past Aurland and finally lodges fast between two mountain peaks at Flåm. From that point an electric spur line carries visitors up 3,000 feet in 45 minutes to Myrdal on the Oslo-Bergen railway. The next, and shortest, of these fingers comes to rest at Laerdal, near which is the famed Borgund Stave Church. This is one of the most interesting and best preserved of these early medieval edifices. Constructed of hewn timber and roofed and sided with long round-tipped shingles, the church dates from the middle 12th century and presents an amazing insight into the period when Norway was newly Christianized. Crosses vie with dragons, reflecting a charming indecision on the part of the builders as to just what would do proper justice to their new-found faith. Standing there on the earth floor of that gloomy interior, with the scent of century-old wood smoke and tar in his nostrils, the visitor can't help but hear gruff and probably faltering voices intoning the strange new chants to the Church of Rome. Notice the worn round hole in one wall; this was the lepers' hole, through which the afflicted who stood outside could hear the priest.

Continuing northward, the third of these four fjord fingers was once probably longer than it is now. Millenniums ago a huge glacial dump was deposited about midway up this fjord valley, forming what is now a large fresh-water lake. Here at Årdal is one of Norway's largest aluminum factories based on hydro-electric power from Tyin Lake, some 3,000 feet above the plant, and the Jotunheim Mountains. The water drops that full distance through underground conduits to a turbine-generator room blasted out of solid rock deep in the mountain. From outside, there is little in the diminutive tunnel entrance to suggest that you are looking at one of Norway's mightiest power plants.

The fourth and longest of these fingers of the Sogne Fjord, known as the Luster Fjord, extends almost due north, terminating between the Jotunheim range to the east and the Jostedal Glacier to the west. What this scenery may lack in wild grandeur it makes up for in pastoral beauty and neatness, but if you sidetrack to Nigard glacier (a "tongue" of the massive Jostedal) you'll find all the spectacle you could wish for. Guides wait at the ice tip which is reached by boat across the glacier lake, twice a day in summer. Remember to wear sensible clothing. The

Urnes Stave Church dating from 1070 and probably the oldest of its kind in Norway, is an easier excursion from Sogndal via Solvorn, across Luster Fjord. From Fortun, at the end of this fjord, a highway climbs over Jotunheimen to Lom in Ottadal.

Going to the Sogne Fjord by boat is only one of the methods—though certainly one of the best—to probe its wonders. Another way of approach from Bergen is by railway to Myrdal and down the stupendous Flåm Line, one of the most remarkable pieces of railway engineering in the world. From Flåm a tourist steamer plies daily to Balestrand and Fjaerland on the northern shores.

Another star-spangled route (because of Nature's beauty and Americans' predilection) is the one from Voss by bus via Stalheim—a true eyrie overlooking the Naeröydal valley with rainbow-dancing waterfalls and sugarloaf mountains—and out to the finest piece of fjord scenery belonging to Sogne, the Naeröyfjord, often not more than 1,600 feet across, with mountains towering to 3,000 feet and more on both sides, and sprinkled with waterfalls. By an ingenious system of connections (boarding one boat from another in mid-fjord) not only Laerdal but Balestrand and other important places on the northern shore are reached.

The straightest approach to the Sogne Fjord is a variation of this latter route, branching off at Vinje from the main road, and crossing the mountain plateau before gently unwinding itself down to the village of Vik, with its characteristic stave church. From Vangsnes, where Emperor Wilhelm II of Germany saw fit to erect a Viking monument of gigantic dimensions, there is a ferry across the fjord to Balestrand, the central point.

The Nord Fjord and the Geiranger Fjord

Exploring the Nord Fjord can again be done by fjord steamer from Bergen or by choosing one of the scenic overland routes from the Sogne Fjord area, such as the one from Lavik via beautiful Lake Jölster, which at Moskog is joined by the route across the Gaularfjell Mountains from Balestrand. The most impressive of these routes, however, is the Sognefjell road, which climbs in magnificent curves from the head of the Luster Fjord to the high mountains of Jotunheimen and Norway's highest mountain pass 4,690 feet to descend into the romantic Böverdal valley. At the village of Lom you turn westward again, climbing to the mountain plateau at Grotli. Here there is a choice of two routes, the one heading northwest to Geiranger, and the other one southwest to Nord Fjord. By choosing the second, you will more or less complete a circuit around the mightiest glacier of the European continent, Jostedalsbreen.

By steamer, you continue on from Sogne Fjord to Målöy and Nordfjordeid. As at Årdal, a glacial moraine has filled in the natural fjord valley, separating Nordfjordeid from Hornindal Lake by a barrier of land about a mile wide. Much of this is cultivated, but these lush fields represent generations of work.

At Loen you may follow the Loen valley up to a long, narrow lake where blue-white glaciers overhang the valley walls. It is here that subterranean rumblings have twice preceded natural catastrophes when a part of the mountain has crashed down into the lake. From the road, you will notice Loen Lake practically filled in at one point; whole communities have simply disappeared here in the course of minutes. At the extreme end of the valley the road peters out amid a moraine at the foot of cliffs whose walls are laced with glacial brooks.

There are many who regard Nord Fjord as the most beautiful of Norway's fjord districts. It is more gentle, probably a bit more willing and every bit as colorful, but at the same time just a little more secretive and reserved than the other districts we explored. There seems to linger something of the old days of trolls and giants and a strain of that mystery which in Grieg's music belittles the man who believes only what he sees.

In Geiranger the mountains tower upward for thousands of feet straight out of a channel so narrow that the boat seems barely to squeeze through. Yet here, high on what appears to be a notch on the mountain face, people actually lived and farmed a generation ago on the few hundred square yards of soil that Nature has scattered in this niche.

The road to Geiranger from Nordfjord worms its way upward via a series of switchbacks to a height of over 3,000 feet. After some twenty bends there is a stop at Videseter to enjoy the view of one of the world's wildest valleys—the Hjelledal. As you progress upward, you enter a strange, new world—the roof of Norway, a vastness of snowcapped peaks, lakes, stone and more stone. From Djupvasshytta a private toll road leads upwards another 1,500 feet to the top of Mount Dalsnibba, from whose peak it is possible to see for more than a hundred miles.

The spectacular "Eagle Road" with its unforgettable view of the Seven Sisters waterfalls, zigzags from Geiranger to Eidsdal. Stop at the "Eagle's Turn" to take in one of the outstanding views of the fjord country. From the village of Eidsdal there is a ferry across the fjord to Linge, where the road leads on to Valldal. Here you may notice the zig-zag stripe in the mountain wall—this was the sea monster that Norway's holy king, St. Olav, smashed against that cliff when it tried to oppose his landing in Valldal some 900 years ago. The "Trolls' Path" (Trollstigveien), between Valldal and Åndalsnes, is a giant among Norway's serpentine roads, coming down the vertical cliff-face in 11 unbelievably audacious bends, among majestic mountains—the "King", the "Queen", and the "Bishop" (all of which challenge the rock climber)—with the 500-foot Stigfoss fall and fantastic views thrown into the bargain.

Another wonderful route runs north from Geiranger. You go by ferry on the Geiranger Fjord past the Seven Sisters waterfalls to Hellesylt, where you take a bus for a breathtaking ride high above the Sunnylvs Fjord, via Stranda and Sykkylven to Ålesund.

"Top of the Fjord Country"

Thus we have arrived at the "Top of the Fjord Country", a title aptly applied to the northernmost fjords of Vestlandet as it indicates both their geographical position and their striking character. It is doubtful whether there are many areas of this size where Nature has concentrated such an abundance of magnificent scenery as in the county of Möre and Romsdal. It comprises such fjords as the Geiranger Fjord—the very quintessence of fjords—the Hjörund Fjord, magnificent nave of a Gothic Cathedral, the Romsdal Fjord surrounded by alpine peaks, and the Sunndalsfjord, a water-filled canyon among towering cliffs. There are valleys of almost supernatural grandeur and beauty—the Innerdal, Eikesdal, and Norangsdal; waterfalls among the world's highest, such as the Mardalsfoss of Eikesdal, with an uninterrupted fall of 975 feet, followed by one of 722 feet, the total measuring 2,150 feet and appearing from the valley in spring as one unbroken whole; mountains like the wild formations of Trollheimen, the vertical cliffs of Sunndal, the unruly sea of alpine peaks in Sunmöre, and the "troll" pinnacles of Romsdal. Åndalsnes and Geiranger are the main resorts, second come Ørsta, Hellesylt, Stranda and Öye.

The three towns of the "Top of the Fjord Country" are tourist attractions in their own right. The *klipp*-fish town of Kristiansund, built out on islands facing the sea, connected by bridges and ferry boats, and almost totally rebuilt in colorful architecture after World War II, is extremely pleasing to the modern eye. In the ocean outside lies the island of Grip, Norway's smallest community, until it was incorporated into Kristiansund, clustering round an old stave church. The sea has taken its toll of the Grip people; after the catastrophes of 1640 and 1802 only the church remained. No wonder that the surrounding skerries have such names as "Devils", "Man Killer", and "Hard Skull". As late as 1897, Grip was without both franchise and taxation.

The residential town of Molde is known for its panorama that takes in the 87 snow-crowned peaks of the Romsdal mountains. This is a typical resort town, offering a host of interesting excursions, fishing in sea and lake, mountaineering and other activities and an annual and highly popular jazz festival.

The biggest town of Möre and Romsdal, Ålesund, has its own "Acropolis" with no temple but with a restaurant and a stadium on top and a view of ocean, fjords, and mountains that rivals the view from Flöyen, Bergen. The fjord flights starting from Oslo offered by the Braathen SAFE Airline are something very much out of the ordinary walks of life and travel. Just south of Ålesund is the island of Runde, Norway's southernmost bird sanctuary, with 700,000 inhabitants, including some very rare species, sea-grottos and needle-shaped cliffs. About 3 miles to the east of Ålesund, at Borgund, is the open-air Sunmöre Museum comprising 30 old timber dwellings, a medieval church and the excavated sites of a Viking town.

PRACTICAL INFORMATION FOR THE FJORD
COUNTRY

WHEN TO COME. Any time from May to September. Fjord Blossom Time in Hardanger occurs round the middle of May, in Sogne two weeks later. The winter sports season runs from December to April.

WHAT TO SEE. A tall question that can only be answered by districts in this Wonderland of Nature: **Stavanger District** (the Ryfylke Fjords): The Lyse Fjord (daily excursions by fjord clipper from Stavanger), Suldal Lake and the Bratlandsdal valley, both on the "Discovery Route".

Bergen District and Hardanger Fjord: The Sör Fjord (innermost part of the Hardanger Fjord) and the Mauranger Fjord; the old Aga village and Renaissance castle of Rosendal; the Vöringfoss cataract and twin Låtefoss falls; the canyon-like valleys of Måbödal and Tokagjelet.

The Bergen Railway: The Mölster, and Finne farms at Voss; the Flåm Railway (branching off from Myrdal to the Sogne Fjord), and the main line itself, especially the mountain crossing near Finse.

The Sogne Fjord: The Naeröy, Fjaerland, and Luster fjord arms; the serpentine roads of Sognefjell, Gaularfjell, Vikefjell, and Stalheimskleiva; the icy blue off-shoots of the Jostedal Glacier at Fjaerland and Jostedalen; the Aurlandsdal and Laerdal valleys, the waterfalls of Vettifoss near Årdal, Kjosfoss, and Rjoandefoss in the Flåm Valley, the Stalheimsfoss and Sivlefoss at Stalheim; the stave churches of Borgund, Vik, Urnes, and Kaupanger.

The Sunn Fjord and the Nord Fjord: The wonderful lakes of Jölster, Olden, Loen, and Hornindal; the Kjendalsbre (Loen) and Briksdalsbre (Olden) glaciers; the Hjelledal valley; the Huldrefoss fall near Förde.

Möre and Romsdal: The Geiranger Fjord, Hjörund Fjord, and Romsdal Fjord; the valleys of Norangdal, Eikesdal, Lilledal, and Innerdalen; the serpentine roads of Geiranger (including the ascent to Mount Dalsnibba); the "Eagles' Road" (Örneveien) and "Trolls' Path" (Trollstigveien); the Rauma Railway (through the Romsdal valley); the waterfalls Mardalsfoss of Eikesdal, Brudeslöret, the Seven Sisters, and Storseterfoss of Geiranger, the Stigfoss of Romsdal and many more; the bird rocks and sea-grottos at Runde, and the island of Grip off Kristiansund.

HOW TO GET ABOUT. If coming from Oslo you can travel by train to Stavanger (about 8 hours), to Bergen (6–8 hours) and to Åndalsnes (7–8 hours) with both day and overnight services. These places are connected by air with the capital either directly, or via nearby airports with onward bus connections. And the internal air services go to a number of other small towns in the region.

Getting about in this large area is a matter of judicious combination of ferries, buses and trains, allowing you to reach even the smallest community. There are express coastal boat services from Bergen to the Sognefjord as well as the daily "trunk route" ship service to the Far North. Coastal ferries to the south link

Bergen with Haugesund and Stavanger (plus other places en route) with both express and local services. Both hydrofoils and catamarans are used on some of these. As the whole system is somewhat complicated, you should enquire locally about those routes of particular interest. Apart from one of two summer "specials", they all operate through the year.

MOTORING. The coastal road from Oslo to Stavanger and many mountain roads (among which the Haukeli, Valdres-Fillefjell, Romsdal, and Sunndal roads are open all year) run into the Fjord Country. Bergen is an excellent starting point for a circuit north to Kristiansund (via Voss-Gudvangen-Balestrand, lake Jölster and the Geirangerfjord, returning by Nordfjord and the Vadheim-Bergen ferry: about 757 miles) or south to Stavanger along the "Discovery Route" (via Röldal and Sand, returning via Haugesund). Motoring in the fjord country is by nature a leisurely affair, interrupted by spectacular trips across blue fjords. Along these winding roads and in such scenic surroundings there is little sense in covering more than 100–125 miles a day.

HOTELS AND RESTAURANTS. The Fjord Country has been popular for nearly a century so it has an impressive array of small attractive resorts and a high assortment of hotels. Most of those listed below are licensed but the smaller pensions (*gjestgiveri*) and farm-pensions sometimes are not; if it's important to you, check first. Many hotels offer reduced rates before June 15 and after August 25. For easier reference, localities are listed under the districts in which they are situated.

STAVANGER DISTRICT

BRYNE (Rogaland). *Jaeren Rica* (M), 110 beds, 51 rooms with facilities, restaurant, swimming, sauna.

HAUGESUND (Rogaland). *Saga Hotel* (E), 140 beds; *Touring Motor Hotel* (E), 175 beds; *Haugaland* (M), 37 beds; *IMI* (M), 40 beds, mission hotel, unlicenced; *Saga Maritim* (M), 92 beds; *Skeisvang Youth Hostel* (I), 60 beds.

SANDNES (Rogaland). *Holiday Motel* (M), 74 beds, 25 rooms with bath/shower; *Sandnes Motor Hotel* (M), 100 beds, all rooms with bath/shower.

SAUDA (Rogaland). *Grand* (M), 36 beds; *Kløver* (M), 38 beds, all rooms with bath/shower; *Sauda Fjord Hotel* (M), at Saudasjøen, 60 beds, good restaurant.

STAVANGER (Rogaland). *Esso Motor Hotel* (E), Eiganesvei 181, 270 beds, 153 rooms with facilities, restaurant, grill, bar; *KNA* (E), Lagardsvei 61, 210 beds, 120 rooms with bath/shower, restaurant, grill, bar; *SAS Royal Atlantic* (E), Jernbanevei 1, best hotel in town, 454 beds, 255 rooms with facilities, several restaurants and bars, dancing; *Victoria* (E), Skansegaten 1, on quay, 160 beds, 97 rooms with bath/shower, restaurant, bar; *St Svithun* (M), Klubbgate 3, 110 beds, 70 rooms with bath/shower, cafeteria, temperance hotel; *Mosvangen Youth Hostel* (I), Tjenstvoll, 120 beds.

Pensions: Bergeland Hospits (M), Vikedalsgate 1a, 40 beds; *City Hospits* (M), Madlaveien 18/20, 27 beds; *Commandør* (M), Valbergsgate 9, 92 beds, 20 rooms with bath; *Øglaend Hospits* (M), Jens Zetlitzgate 25, 15 beds; *Rex Hospits* (M), Wesselsgate 11, 20 beds; *Rogalandsheimen* (M), Musegate 18, 20 beds.

STAVANGER ENVIRONS. MADLA, *Molkeholen* (M), summer hotel (June/Aug), 162 beds, 114 rooms with bath/shower, unlicenced. **RAN-DABERG,** *Viste Strand* (E), 90 beds, 50 rooms with bath/shower, restaurant, sandy beach. **SOLA,** at airport, *Sola Strand* (M), 115 beds, 23 rooms with bath/shower, restaurant, sandy beach. **TANANGER,** *Hummeren* (M), 20 beds, 3 rooms with bath, popular restaurant.

BERGEN DISTRICT AND HARDANGER FJORD

GODØYSUND (Hordaland), a cluster of small islands, famous yachting center. *Godøysund Fjord Hotel* (M), 100 beds, 45 rooms with facilities, restaurant.

GRANVIN (Hardanger fjord), *Maeland* (M), in pleasant garden facing fjord, 60 beds, 7 rooms with bath.

KINSARVIK (Hardanger fjord), busiest ferry point in Hardanger, fine views of fjord and glacier. *Kinsarvik Fjord Hotel* (M), 140 beds, 28 rooms with bath/shower.

KVAMSKOG (Hordaland), skiing center, 1200 ft. *Ungdomsheimen* (I), Kvernavollen, popular youth center, 101 beds, cafeteria; *Kvamskog Youth Hostel* (I), Kvernavollen, 20 beds.

LEIRVIK (Hordaland), village on Stord island, bathing, boating, fishing, riding. *Grand* (M), 150 beds, 50 rooms with facilities; *Stord Motor Hotel* (M), 130 beds, all rooms with bath/shower; *Lillebø Youth Hostel* (I), 45 beds.

LOFTHUS (Hardanger fjord), famous resort in fruit growing district, facing Sør fjord and Folgefonn glacier. *Ullensvang* (E), outstanding, 250 beds, most rooms with facilities, Edvard Grieg's composing cabin in garden.

NORHEIMSUND (Hardanger fjord), resort. *Norheimsund Fjord Hotel* (M), facing fjord, 80 beds, all rooms with bath/shower; *Sandven* (M), facing fjord, 75 beds, 20 rooms with bath/shower, large restaurant used in many package tours.

ODDA (Hardanger fjord), at head of Sør fjord, industrial center with outstanding surroundings. *Hardanger* (M), 82 beds, 32 rooms with bath; *Sørfjordheimen Pension* (M), 63 beds, 10 rooms with bath; *Odda Youth Hostel* (I), 125 beds.

OS (Hordaland). *Solstrand* (E), facing fjord, one of finest hotels on west coast, 200 beds, all rooms with facilities, restaurant, swimming, sauna.

ØYSTESE (Hardanger fjord). *Hardangerfjord* (E), 170 beds, most rooms with facilities; *Øystese Fjord Hotel* (M), 49 beds, 8 rooms with bath; *Øystese Pension* (I), 15 beds; *Øystese Youth Hostel* (I), 20 beds.

ROSENDAL (Hordaland), ancient manor, medieval stone church. *Rosendal Fjord Hotel* (M), 90 beds, all rooms with facilities; *Rosendal Gjestgiveri* (I), old but well-run inn, 40 beds;

SELJESTAD (Hordaland), 980 ft., fine views of Folgefonn glacier, ski center with lifts and instructors. *Solfonn* (E), 150 beds, 64 rooms with facilities; *Seljestad* (M), 121 beds, 43 rooms with facilities.

SKÅNEVIK (Hordaland). *Skånevik Fjord Hotel* (M), 110 beds, all rooms with facilities, salmon and trout fishing.

STRANDEBARM (Hardanger fjord). *Strandebarm Vegetarhotell* (M), 63 beds, vegetarian food.

ULVIK (Hardanger fjord), fashionable resort at head of narrow Ulvik fjord. *Müllerhotell Brakanes* (E), outstanding, 200 beds, most rooms with facilities, restaurant, boats; *Bjotveit* (M), 60 beds, 4 rooms with bath, sun terrace, boats; *Strand* (M), 94 beds, 30 rooms with bath; *Ulvik Tourist Hotel* (M), 120 beds, 27 rooms with bath.

UTNE (Hardanger fjord), idyllic village, orchards, views of Folgefonn glacier. *Utne* (M), traditional style, 46 beds, 7 rooms with bath.

SOGNE FJORD

BALESTRAND, one of Norway's oldest tourist centers. *Kringsjå* (M), 55 beds, 17 rooms with bath, private ketch for fjord trips; *Kvikne* (M), 400 beds, 79 rooms with facilities; *Balestrand Youth Hostel* (I), 90 beds.

FJAERLAND, secluded fjord village, access by boat only, excursions to glaciers. *Mundal* (M), good family hotel, 75 beds, 30 rooms with bath; *Fjaerland Pension* (I), 45 beds, 6 rooms with bath.

FLÅM, terminal of railroad, descending 866m from Myrdal through a string of tunnels. *Fretheim* (M), 140 beds, all rooms with facilities, salmon and sea trout fishing, boats; *Solhammer Pension* (I), 15 beds.

HERMANSVERK. *Sognefjord* (M), 80 beds, all rooms with facilities.

LAERDAL, fjord village on famous Laerdal salmon river. *Lindstrøm* (E), 152 beds, 70 rooms with bath/shower; *Offerdal Pension* (M), 90 beds; *Laerdal Youth Hostel* (I), 45 beds.

LEIKANGER. *Leikanger Fjord Hotel* (M), 85 beds, 33 rooms with bath.

MARIFJØRA, village on Luster fjord. *Tørvis Fjord Hotel* (M), 90 beds, 20 rooms with bath.

SKJOLDEN, fjord village in fruit-growing district. *Skjolden* (M), 95 beds, 56 rooms with bath; *Skjolden Youth Hostel* (I), 48 beds.

SOGNDAL, village with orchards, salmon fishing. *Hofslund* (M), 90 beds, 87 rooms with bath; *Sogndal* (M), 190 beds, 85 rooms with bath; *Loftesnes Pension* (I), 15 beds; *Sogndal Youth Hostel* (I), 90 beds.

TURTAGRØ, 3250 ft., ideal starting point for walks into Jotunheimen mountain ranges. *Turtagrø* (M), 85 beds, 5 rooms with bath.

VIK, old churches. *Hopstock* (M), 70 beds, all rooms with bath/shower.

SUNN FJORD AND NORD FJORD

FLORØ (Sunn fjord), Norway's most westerly town, sheltered by numerous islands. *Victoria* (M), 150 beds, 42 rooms with bath.

FØRDE (Sunn fjord), at head of Førde fjord. *Sunnfjord* (E), 330 beds, most rooms with facilities, salmon and trout fishing, angling school; *Førde* (M), 120 beds, 50 rooms with bath.

JØLSTER (Sunn fjord). *Skei* (M), on lake Jølster, 102 beds, 33 rooms with bath, good trout fishing in lake, rowing boats.

LOEN (Nord fjord), a fine resort, excursions to Jostedal glacier. *Alexandra* (E), outstanding family hotel, 360 beds, all rooms with facilities, folk dancing; *Richards* (M), 43 beds, all rooms with facilities; *Loen Pension* (I), 50 beds.

MÅLØY (Nord fjord), on island connected with mainland by 1224m long bridge. *Hagens* (M), 78 beds, 30 rooms with facilities.

NORDFJORDEID (Nord fjord). *Nordfjord* (M), 110 beds, all rooms with facilities.

OLDEN (Nord fjord), excursions to Jostedal glacier. *Olden Fjord Hotel* (M), 77 beds, 36 rooms with bath; *Yris* (M), 170 beds, 59 rooms with bath; *Olden Krotell* (I), 30 beds, all rooms with bath/shower.

SANDANE (Nord fjord), folk museum, church. *Sivertsen* (M), 80 beds, 26 rooms with bath/shower; *Heimen Pension* (I), 34 beds, 17 rooms with shower.

STRYN (Nord fjord), traffic junction for regional bus services. Several inexpensive pensions. *Stryn Youth Hostel* (I), 88 beds.

VIDESETER (Nord fjord), 1970 ft., magnificent views down Hjelledal valley, glacier skiing in summer; *Videseter Mountain Hotel* (M), 57 beds, 19 rooms with facilities.

MØRE AND ROMSDAL

ÅLESUND (Sunnmøre). *Noreg* (E), Kongensgate 27, 181 beds, 44 rooms with bath; *Parken* (E), Storgaten 16, 248 beds, 138 rooms, all with facilities, large restaurant, bar, grill, sauna, whirl pool; *Scandinavia* (E), Løvenvoldgate 8, 90 beds in 63 rooms, all with facilities, restaurants; *Havly Pension* (I), Rønnebergsgate 4, 95 beds, 10 rooms with facilities.

ÅNDALSNES (Romsdal). *Grand Bellevue* (M), 100 beds, 35 rooms with bath; *Rauma Pension* (M), 20 beds; *Setnes Youth Hostel* (I), 75 beds.

GEIRANGER (Sunnmøre), fjord boat trips. *Union* (E), 190 beds, 68 rooms with bath, swimming, sauna; *Geiranger Hotel* (M), 151 beds, 70 rooms with bath, swimming; *Meroks Fjord Hotel* (M), 105 beds, 33 rooms with bath; *Utsikten Bellevue* (M), 70 beds, 12 rooms with bath.

KRISTIANSUND (Nordmøre). *Grand* (E), 225 beds, 33 rooms with bath; *Fosna* (M), 75 beds, 14 rooms with bath; *Atlanten Youth Hostel* (I), 32 beds.

MOLDE (Romsdal). *Alexandra* (E), magnificent views of fjord and mountains, 207 beds, most rooms with facilities, swimming, sauna, sun terrace; *Nobel* (M), 48 beds, 6 rooms with bath; *Romsdalsheimen* (M), 50 beds, 4 rooms with bath; *Studentheimen* (I), 232 beds, summer youth hostel.

ØRSTA (Sunnmøre). *Viking Fjord Hotel* (E), 82 beds, 44 rooms with bath, salmon fishing, deer shooting.

SUNNDALSØRA (Nordmøre), at head of Sunndal fjord. *Müllerhotell Sunndalen* (M), 115 beds, 30 rooms with bath; *Sunndalsøra Youth Hostel* (I), 30 beds.

SURNADAL (Nordmøre). *Surnadal Hotel* (M), 150 beds, 17 rooms with bath.

VOLDA (Sunnmøre). *Svendsen* (M), 20 beds, 3 rooms with bath; *Volda Tourist Hotel* (M), 48 beds, some rooms with bath.

CAMPING, HOSTELS. Youth Hostels: specially-built and modern, Stavanger and Nesflaten in the Ryfylke fjords, and Geilo, Mjölfell and Voss on the Bergen railway.

Camping sites: best at Kristiansund, Molde, Ørsta, Geiranger, Valldal, Åndalsnes. Eidsdal and Ålesund in the county of Möre and Romsdal; Stryn Loen, Bjørkelo, and Jölster in Nordfjord and Sunnfjord; Voss, Ulvik, Øvre Eidfjord, Kinsarvid, Kvanndal, Rosendal, Strandebarm and Etne in the Hardanger area; Saudasjøen, Haugesund, Stavanger, Sand, Sandeid and Egersund in the county of Rogaland.

SPORTS. Angling is a time-honored sport in the fjord country. For generations fine salmon rivers, such as the Sand, Laerdal, Åröy, Flåm, Rauma, and Sunndal have attracted sportsmen from all over the world. Oslo travel agencies *Mytravel,* N. Vollgate 19, and *Flyspesialisten,* Kronprinsesse Märthasplass 1, offer first rate salmon fishing in the fjord country. Deep sea fishing jaunts, run on the principle "no catch—no cash" on board the *Sea Queen* are a Stavanger must. *Mountaineering* is another specialty of this land of fjords and mountains. Expert rock climbing can be done from such centers as Turtagrø in Sogne; Öye, Åndalsnes, Sunndalsöra, and Innerdalen in Möre and Romsdal; and ordinary "Sunday climbing" almost everywhere. The fells of Ryfylke, the Hardangervidda mountain plateau, the Finse-Aurland-Fillefjell district, the Jotunheimen-Jostedal area, the mountains south and north of the Rauma Railway, and the Trollheimen mountains all have well-marked paths with pleasant and fully staffed chalets among them. Thus it is perfectly feasible to walk carrying a light rucksack through the Fjord Country or parts of it. *Swimming* in the fjords at the height of summer is extensively done; *waterskiing* is practised at Ulvik and Balestrand; fine beaches and bathing resorts are found near Stavanger. The honeymoon island of Godöysund, south of Bergen, is ideal for *boating* (hotel has boats).

WINTER SPORTS. A number of centers have sprung up in the Hardanger area, and in the superb skiing country along the Bergen Railway. As at other Norwegian winter sports resorts, skiing and skating equipment may be hired for a small fee. It is well to remember, too, that winter sports equipment is not very different in price from other countries, but the quality is very high. There are well-stocked sports shops in such Bergen Railway area resorts as Ål, Geilo, and Voss.

WORDS TO THE WISE
A Few Useful Travel Hints

Whether you are on holiday or have important business to do, after a flight through several time zones give your body's clock a chance to catch up. It is easy to underestimate the effects of jet-lag.

Don't carry all your cash, travellers' checks, passport etc. in the same place, spread them around a bit – and never carry your wallet in your hip pocket.

Experienced travellers travel light. Don't forget that the hand luggage you carry with you onto the plane is a vital part of your travel equipment. Make sure you have your essentials in it, not in your other baggage.

With strikes and the cost of excess baggage always in the background, you would be sensible when flying not to take more than you could comfortably carry yourself – in a pinch.

Don't leave already exposed film in your pockets or in any hand luggage while passing through airport X-ray machines. The process can sometimes fog the film and you may find a whole trip's photographs ruined. Put the film on one side while passing through.

Never make long-distance phone calls from your hotel room without checking first on the likely price. Some hotels have been known to mark up the cost of a call as much as 200%.

Several airlines will provide a cardboard carrying box for any loose items you might arrive clutching at the checking-in desk. It saves leaving a trail of last-minute purchases all the way to the plane.

You would be amazed the amount of free information that you can get from National Tourist Offices to help you plan your trip – all the way from brochures to movies.

Put a tag with your name and address on it *inside* your suitcase as well as outside. It will greatly help identification if the case goes astray.

Never leave valuables in your hotel room – put them in the hotel safe.

CENTRAL MOUNTAINS, EASTERN VALLEYS

Cradle of Liberty—Home of Giants

As each area of Norway unfolds, chapter by chapter, so the scenery that we describe becomes more and more spectacular. This chapter is no exception, and has a variety of territory to cover which will offer even more of interest when actually seen, rather than read about. In fact, the area which this chapter describes contains some scenery which can compete even with the northern parts of Norway for breathtaking things to see. In the eastern valleys holidaymakers will find a wealth of beautiful countryside, dappled with lakes, swift-flowing streams, and silent forests, while the Jotunheimen—"Home of the Giants"—mountain range is a paradise for nature lovers and hikers.

Exploring the Central Mountains and Eastern Valleys

First we shall follow the great valley of Østerdal, which runs southward parallel to the Swedish border for about 200 miles. From Trondheim we follow the bends of the Gauldal until, at 2,000 feet above sea level, we reach Röros, once the center of Norway's coppermining region.

With its heaps of slag and its many unpainted timber houses, Röros looks like a mining town, and it has had such a character since its founding three centuries ago. A dominating landmark is the town's main building in stone, the late 18th-century church, one of Norway's best examples of baroque architecture. The countryside around is nearly bare of trees; for most of the forests were cut down years ago when charcoal was the chief fuel for the smelting ovens.

Don't be frightened away by the drab side, however; Röros has many attractions. And there is the great plateau, Rörosvidda, stretching north and east to the Swedish border and inhabited by Lapps with herds of reindeer. The Röros plateau is crisscrossed by marked trails and dotted with tourist-huts, mountain farm (seter) quarters, etc., so it is quite possible—given good feet and some ambition—to walk from Lake Aursunden near Röros all the way to the Trondheim-Sweden railway, about 60 miles north. Röros also had its great writer, Johan Falkberget, who died in 1967. His novels about past and present life in this mining district have become literary classics.

Norway's longest river, the 370-mile Glomma, rises just north of Röros and meanders the entire length of the vast eastern forests to empty into the outer Oslo Fjord beyond Fredrikstad. The train from Trondheim parallels the Glomma for about half the distance, or for 6 hours. This river's chief task is to float logs downstream to the sawmills and paper factories, and the traveler also might as well follow the current. In this way you can watch the Glomma start as a mountain stream in the copper mining district, and finally develop into the mighty timber conveyor that sweeps through Elverum and Kongsvinger.

Elverum serves as junction point for the railway west to Hamar and for a main road leading east to Sweden. It is famous for the final meeting of the Norwegian Parliament in April, 1940, just before the town was destroyed by bombing. It gave King Håkon power to carry on the war outside Norway.

You are now in the region of the great forests which some writers have described as the "ocean of east Norway". Vast, undulating expanses of pine trees whose sounds and whose silence have shaped the lives of people just as the sea has on the west coast, or the long winter nights and long summer days have in Finnmark. Here are persistent influences, reflected not only in literature but in the folk customs, superstitions and tales of trolls, huldra, and other supernatural forest creatures which have been handed down for untold generations.

Gudbrandsdal

If in possession of a good walking outfit, you start out from Oslo's Central Station for the central mountains by way of Lake Mjösa and that greatest of Norwegian valleys, Gudbrandsdal, which is 200 Km long. The area is rich in traditional Norwegian arts, and folk music and dancing are both popular. Wood carving and painting are also held in high esteem.

Eidsvoll, on the south end of Mjösa, is perhaps the most resounding name in Norwegian history, for it was here that the Norwegian Constitution was framed and adopted in mid-May of the year 1814. This event marked Norway's emancipation from Danish rule and gave her that now-famous Independence Day, the 17th of May, as widely and enthusiastically celebrated as the American 4th of July. However, the main feature of the Norse celebration—as you will discover if you are in any town in May—is not shooting off fire-crackers but the huge and colorful parades of school children.

While the Eidsvoll "Cradle of Liberty" is well worth a visit for its own sake and for the excellent collections of contemporary furniture, engravings, etc., you will not be able to combine it on the same day with the absolute *must* for travelers in this area: the boat trip on Lake Mjösa. The Eidsvoll Building lies a couple of miles from the station, and since the early morning train from Oslo which connects with the steamer gives you only 10 minutes' leeway, you'll have to board her right away.

By Steamer to Lillehammer

This steamer, the old side-wheeler *Skibladner,* will probably remind you of Mark Twain and the old days on the Mississippi, for in 1976 she celebrated 120 years of service. She takes almost 6 hours to reach Lillehammer at the head of Mjösa, but dinner is served on board, and on a warm day it's a fine trip. You stop briefly at Hamar on the eastern shore, and have, both when approaching and leaving, excellent views of its hinterland of fertile farms. Hamar has the ruins of what was once an impressive stone cathedral.

From Hamar you cross the widest part of the lake, passing near Helgöy or Saints' Island, where many leading Norwegian churchmen were interned during the war because of anti-Nazi activities, and call at Gjövik on the west side. Gjövik is an active industrial town, the terminus of a railway that connects with the Valdres-bane at Eina. Side-wheeling northwards from Gjövik, you see that both shores are more rugged and forest-covered and come closer together until, just above Lillehammer, Lake Mjösa narrows into a non-navigable river, the Lågen. Here is the entrance to Gudbrandsdal.

Lillehammer is well aware of being a tourist center. Everything is available for visitors, except perhaps some of the genuine and unspoiled atmosphere that one still finds in Telemark and Setesdal. Nevertheless, Lillehammer is also a cultural center, thanks to the famous Sandvig Collection at Maihaugen, an open-air museum much like the Folk Museum in Oslo, but specializing in farm buildings, *stabburs,* water-wheels, workshops, etc., of Gudbrandsdal.

The town is also famous as having been the residence for many years of the well-known author and Nobel prize winner Sigrid Undset; while the Nansen School, Norway's only "academy of humanism", was founded here in 1939. And at Aulestad, a few miles northwest of Lillehammer, in Östre Gausdal Valley, stands the former home of the great 19th-century poet, Björnstjerne Björnson, author of the Norwegian national anthem.

Throughout most of this stretch the valley of Gudbrandsdal has nearly the same topographical pattern: fertile fields on the level ground on either side of the river, patches of cleared farmlands on the wide sloping hillsides, sometimes way up to the first shoulders, but intermingled with wooded patches. Beyond the forests on top begin those *seter* highlands and mountains so prized by skiers in winter and hikers in summer.

Across Dovrefjell and from Otta to Vågå and Lom

If you are making the journey between Trondheim and Oslo by car, you will be certain to travel over the impressive Dovrefjell plateau and, sooner or later, arrive at Dovregubbens Hall, a delightful place at which to stop and have coffee. Take a look at the quaint, but entirely natural trolls formed by the trees. Legend has it that every stone, every tree in Norway has its own troll or fairy and who are we to argue?

Just beyond Otta, you skirt the Rondane Mountains and adjacent hiking areas that extend clear to Österdalen. At Dombås, the railway divides in two lines: the Rauma-bane to Åndalsnes, and the Dovrebane which crosses over the Dovre Mountains to Trondheim. In between the forking rail lines and beyond are the trails and huts of three other upland Norwegian playgrounds: the Romsdal Alps, Trollheimen, and Dovre.

For our purposes, however, it's best to leave the train at Otta, 2 hours above Lillehammer, and change to a westbound bus. This vehicle will soon bring you to Lake Vågå and the village of Vågå in the midst of a district as interesting as Telemark and with an abundance of grass-roofed timber houses and *stabburs*. It is also a region abounding in legends and folklore, for the surrounding mountains have sheltered many a strange monster or giant.

A tale is told, for example, about Johannes Blessom, a native of Vågå, who had to spend considerable time in Copenhagen because of a lawsuit, but who kept pining away for his native hills. He was walking the streets in the Danish capital on Christmas Eve when a stranger driving a horse and sleigh accosted him and asked if he wanted to go home. Blessom said yes, and in an instant he was whirled through the air and shortly afterwards deposited on the ground just outside his own farm in Norway. The stranger then drove full speed into a mountainside which opened in a blaze of light to let him enter, for he was, of course, the Jutul or Vågå-giant.

There is an interesting stave church at Vågå, and another at Lom, one hour farther west, at both of which you can take a quick look while the bus has a rest-stop. At Lom two possibilities open up: to continue westwards to Grotli and the notorious zig-zag descent to Geiranger, or to branch off southwest on the Sognefjell highway which crosses part of Jotunheimen. This time suppose you take the latter road up Böverdal Valley as far as Elvesaeter.

Aerial Vistas over the Jotunheimen

Next morning step aboard the jeep or truck that makes the daily ascent from Böverdal to a tourist hut called Juvass-hytta. The rough ride up a very rocky trail will certainly lead you to suspect that altitude is being gained—but you will be thoroughly amazed to learn that

Juvass-hytta is over 5,500 feet above the sea. Stay overnight to get acclimatized and then join the forenoon promenade of roped-together guests and guide across Styggebreen Glacier and up to the summit of Galdhöpiggen, Norway's highest rock peak at 8,181 feet.

Once on top, and with good visibility, you will agree that this is the place to look at Jotunheimen. On every hand there stretches an overwhelming ocean of cliffs and deep valleys, peaks and glaciers: a sight as spectacular as anything to be seen in Norway.

From Galdhöpiggen you can make the same sort of survey of this part of the world as you did of the Oslo region from Kolsås. Your compass and the detailed maps of Jotunheimen will show you, for example, the location of Mount Glittertind, whose thick snowcovering on top gives it a 40-foot margin over your vantage point; or of the many other peaks on all sides. When you tire of mountain identification, turn to the N.T.C.'s general map of trails and huts and plan what to do next.

There's the 3-hour descent to Spiterstulen in the valley between the two rival peaks and from there a long walk to Gjendebu on Lake Gjende; 7 hours by land or 8 if you choose the route over Memuru Glacier. Or you can do it the really hard way by toiling from Spiterstulen up over Glittertind and down to the hut at Glitterheim (7 hours) and then—preferably another day—cross the eastern edge of Memuru Glacier to reach Memurubu (9 hours). Either way you arrive in one of the most famous parts of Giant-Land.

This is the Gjende country, haunt of both historical and legendary characters. For instance, Jo Gjende himself, the mighty reindeer hunter and mountain philosopher who served as guide to many visiting sportsmen and alpinists during the last century, and whose exploits are part of the modern saga of Jotunheimen. Then, of course, there is the Peer Gynt of folklore and the one in Ibsen's great drama, both of whom were well acquainted with these hills.

By all means take the hike from Memurubu to Gjendesheim, allegedly a 5-hour jaunt, via the famous Besseggen or Edge of Bess. This brings you along that scenic but narrow pinnacle path where you can look down on one side to Lake Bess and 2,000 feet on the other to Lake Gjende. But there's plenty of room for your feet, and if dizzy, just think of Peer Gynt, who claimed to have ridden this path one night at top speed on the back of a reindeer.

Safely down at Gjendesheim, you will find many alternatives lying in wait. The trail east to Sikkilsdalseter (4 hours) and the bus down to Vinstra in Gudbrandsdal; or the trail or bus southwards to Bygdin, whence you can continue all the way by bus to Fagernes. From there the Valdres Railway can take you either to its junction with the Bergens-bane at Roa, or all the way to Oslo.

If this Besseggen excursion sounds too strenuous, a boat plies from Memurubu to both Gjendesheim and Gjendebu at opposite ends of the lake. From the latter hut you can elect the 2-day trip to Leirvassbu and Skogadalsböen, which in turn provides possibilities too numerous to describe here. Suffice it to say that from Skogadalsböen you can proceed to the Sogne Fjord either west via Turtagrø and by bus on the cross-mountain highway from Lom, or south all the way by foot through Vetti (900-foot Vettisfoss waterfall) to Upper Årdal. Inveterate alpinists, who naturally snort at such tame hiking, may seek their thrills by climbing about in the Hurrungene Range, that chaos of pinnacles and precipices which lies between the Vetti trail and the road to Sogne Fjord. Upper Årdal is the site of one of Norway's newest aluminum processing plants.

But in planning your route through the Home of the Giants, keep two points in mind. First, that at least 20 per cent must be added to the times given in the trail maps for the various journeys from hut to hut; and even more if you intend to proceed leisurely, take photographs, etc. Second, that ropes and guides are necessary when crossing glaciers as on many of the longer routes. That boaster, Peer Gynt, may have performed reckless deeds in his imagination, but real mountaineers like Jo Gjende never took foolhardy chances.

Valdres and Hallingdal

Let's say that after criss-crossing Jotunheimen we have decided to end up in Årdal, ferry to Revsnes (Laerdal), and wind our way back to Oslo via Valdres. The first part of our bus ride is as wild as they come, up through the canyon-like Laerdal valley to the village of Borgund, where the best-preserved of Norway's stave churches is in perfect keeping with the stern surroundings; and across the high fells of Fillefjell, where the hostels (now modern resorts) date back to medieval times.

The first part of Valdres to greet us, Lake Vangsmjösi, is surrounded by fierce mountains, making it reminiscent of the West Country we have just left. But hardly is the lake left before the smiling, open, farm-dotted Valdres landscape—lakes, silvery rivers, ancient farms on sloping hillsides—arrives to keep us company all the way down to the railhead at Fagernes. The Valdres Express—as it proudly used to call itself in posters all over Norway during the late '20s—is not exactly flying along. It is more of a "Berg und Thalbahn", which climbs painstakingly to the top of a pass to rattle triumphantly down into the following valley, repeating this process on diminishing scales time and again before reaching Oslo. But all the charm of Norway's railways is here to feel and enjoy for those who are not speed maniacs; the open hospitality and friendliness of the conductors, the somewhat inexplicable halts; the breathtaking scenery, the peace that follows from gentle travel through generous landscapes in good company.

From Fagernes, instead of returning by the Valdres Railway, we might have entered a bus that would have brought us to an even more scenic line—the Bergen Railway—at Gol in the Hallingdal. The most spectacular part of that railway lies west of Gol—that part which leads across the high mountains to the fjord country. If one includes the Flåm Railway into the bargain, it is indeed doubtful whether there is anything in the way of railroads to match it in Europe. East of Gol the railway follows impulsive Hallingdal valley, where abrupt changes of scenery and the funniest mountains crop up at every swerve and squiggle of the snake-like train. Now put these east and west parts of the Bergen Railway together, and the whole magnificent Oslo-Bergen run is complete, giving a cross-section of Norway that is hard to beat. Sixty busy years in the business of hauling tourists across the mountains have in no way diminished the spell of this spectacular line.

PRACTICAL INFORMATION FOR CENTRAL
MOUNTAINS AND EASTERN VALLEYS

 WHEN TO COME. The summer season here lasts from early May to the end of September. In the higher regions the season is shorter—from the middle of June to the middle of September. The winter season begins at Christmas and lasts till after Easter.

 WHAT TO SEE. Österdal Valley: Open-air museum at Elverum; the Jutulhogget canyon near Barkald station. **Gudbrandsdal Valley:** The Maihaugen Collections of old farms at Lillehammer; paddlesteamer *Skibladner* on Lake Mjösa; the Hunderfoss dam and Ringebu stave church; cauldrons of Espedal; Lom stave church; old farms in Vågå (Håkenstad) and Heidal (Bjöl-stad).

Jotunheimen Mountains: View from Galdhöpiggen; Lake Gjende, Lake Tyin, and Lake Bygdin; the Sognefjell road with views of the Fanaråki ridge and Skagastöl peaks.

Valley of Valdres: View from the Tonsåsen ridge; scenery around Fagernes; Lake Vangsmjösi; the stave churches at Lomen, Hedal, Hegge, Hurum, and Reinli.

Hallingdal: Lake Kröderen; the Hemsedal; Mount Hallingskarvet seen from Ustaoset; the Geilo chair lift; mountain villages and farms, and the Torpo stave church.

Numedal: the stave churches of Nore and Uvdal; Nore hydro-electric power station.

 HOW TO GET ABOUT. Getting about is fairly simple as the main valleys are served efficiently by railways. The Röros Railway runs through the entire length of forest-clad Österdal; the Dovre Railway covers the Gudbrandsdal both with express and express special trains and night trains; the same services are effected by the Bergen Railway through the Hallingdal; the Valdres Railway charmingly deals with that province, and even the Numedal has its little railway running between Kongsberg and Rödberg. If you want to get from one valley across to the next one, have a look at the map, pick out the connecting roads, and at those junctions of roads and railway you will find buses waiting to perform exactly the service you desire.

 MOTORING. The combination of beautiful scenery, excellent accommodation, and varied excursion possibilities, makes touring this area by car especially rewarding. We suggest three itineraries covering the highlights:

Gudbrandsdal—Jotunheimen—Valdres: Take E6 from Oslo via Lillehammer to Otta, then drive via Lom across the Sognefjell mountain pass—highest in Norway, elevation 1440m or 4690 ft—and down to Kaupanger on the Sogne Fjord. Ferry across the fjord to Revsnes, then drive via Fagernes to Oslo. Distance 858 km or 532 miles.

Hallingdal—Numedal: From Oslo via Gol to Geilo, then southwards across the Dagali mountain plateau to Kongsberg, and return via Drammen to Oslo. Distance 490 km or 304 miles.

Valdres—Dovre—Østerdal: From Oslo via Hønefoss to Fagernes, then across the mountain ranges to Lillehammer and on to Hjerkinn on the Dovre mountain plateau, down to Atna in the Østerdal valley, and finally via Elverum and Hamar to Oslo. Distance 885 km or 552 miles.

 HOTELS. This area, particularly in the mountains lining the Gudbrandsdal valley, boasts the finest group of resort hotels in Norway. Resorts are so numerous that we list only the best known. Some open only for the summer and winter seasons, others all the year.

BEITOSTØLEN (Oppland), 2970 ft, ski touring area, ski lifts, ski school. *Beito Mountain Hotel* (M), 300 beds, all rooms with facilities; *Beitostølen Mountain Hotel* (M), 175 beds, 80 rooms, all with shower and toilet.

BØVERDALEN (Oppland), romantic entrance to Jotunheimen, good skiing area. *Elveseter* (M), 2290 ft, 140 beds, 47 rooms with bath/shower; *Røisheim* (M), 1690 ft, 38 beds, some rooms with bath; *Spiterstulen Lodge* (M), 3610 ft, situated between the two highest peaks in Norway, Galdhøpiggen and Glittertind, 120 beds, some rooms with bath; *Leirvassbu Fjellstue* (I), 4890 ft, access by jeep from Elveseter, 195 beds, many rooms with shower; *Bøverdalen Youth Hostel* (I), 40 beds.

BYGDIN (Oppland), 3490 ft. *Bygdin Mountain Hotel* (M), 56 rooms, 14 with bath.

DOMBÅS (Oppland), 2160 ft, good ski touring. *Dombås* (M), 271 beds, many rooms with bath; *Dovrefjell* (M), 165 beds, most rooms with bath or shower; *Dombås Youth Hostel* (I), 85 beds.

ELVERUM (Hedmark). *Elgstua Pension* (M), 45 beds; *Dano Kro* (I), 32 beds.

ESPEDALEN (Oppland), 985 to 3050 ft, popular for ski touring. *Dalseter Mountain Hotel* (M), 154 beds, most rooms with facilities; *Espedalen Fjellstue* (M), 70 beds; *Ruten Fjellstue* (M), 60 beds; *Strand Fjellstue* (M), 43 beds.

FAGERNES (Oppland), 1180 ft, ski touring. *Fagernes Tourist Hotel* (M), 240 beds, all rooms with facilities, swimming.

GJØVIK (Oppland), facing lake Mjøsa. *Strand* (E), Strandgate 15, 150 beds, most rooms with facilities, swimming, sauna; *Grand* (M), Jernbanegate 5, 48 beds, some rooms with bath; *Hovdetun Youth Hostel* (I), 156 beds.

GRINDAHEIM (Oppland). *Grindaheim Tourist Hotel* (M), 98 beds, 38 rooms with bath/shower.

HAMAR (Hedmark). *Victoria* (E), 200 beds, all rooms with facilities, sauna; *Astoria* (M), 125 beds, all rooms with facilities; *Olrud* (M), 360 beds, all rooms with bath/shower; *Hamar Youth Hostel* (I), 97 beds.

HARPEFOSS (Oppland), 730 to 3050 ft, popular skiing area. *Golå Mountain Hotel* (M), 66 beds, all rooms with facilities, sauna; *Wadahl Mountain Hotel* (M), 150 beds, 90 rooms with facilities, swimming, sauna; *Grøntuva Gjestgiveri* (I), 38 beds.

HØVRINGEN (Oppland), 3120 ft, ideal terrain for ski touring. *Høvringen Hotel* (M), 56 rooms, 31 with bath; *Høvringen Fjellstue* (I), 19 beds.

LILLEHAMMER (Oppland), 590 ft, probably Norway's largest tourist resort, on hillside overlooking lake Mjøsa, grand terrain for ski touring, many ski lifts, ski school, marked trails, skating rink. *Victoria Rica* (E), 180 beds, 93 rooms with facilities; *Breiseth* (M), 80 beds, some rooms with bath; *Kronen* (M), 130 beds, all rooms with bath/shower, sauna; *Lillehammer Sommerhotell* (M), 300 beds, all rooms with shower, summer only (June/Aug); *Lillehammer Tourist Hotel* (M), 260 beds, most rooms with facilities, swimming, sauna; *Oppland* (M), 160 beds, many rooms with bath, swimming, sauna; *Bellevue Sportell* (I), 140 beds; *Birkebeiner Youth Hostel* (I), 88 beds; *Langseth* (I), 85 beds.

LILLEHAMMER ENVIRONS. The vast mountain plateau (about 2800 ft) beyond the town and lake has been highly developed for winter sports. There are three modern resorts, reached by bus from Lillehammer rail station. **HORNSJØ:** *Hornsjø Mountain Hotel* (M), 401 beds, most rooms with bath/shower, swimming, sauna. **NORDSETER:** *Frimos Tourist Center* (M), 113 beds, some rooms with shower; *Nevra Mountain Hotel* (M), 130 beds, most rooms with facilities, swimming; *Nordseter Fjellstue* (M), 60 beds, sauna; *Nordseter Mountain Hotel* (M), 83 beds, all rooms with facilities, sauna. **SJUSJØEN:** *Sjusjøen Mountain Hotel* (E), 120 beds, most rooms with facilities, swimming, sauna; *Sjusjøen Panorama Hotel* (E), 100 beds, all rooms with facilities, sauna; *Fjellheimen Mountain Center* (I), 65 beds, sauna; *Rustad Fjellstue* (I), 83 beds, sauna; *Sjusjøen Fjellstue* (I), 120 beds, sauna.

LOM (Oppland), 1250 ft. *Fossheim* (M), traditional Norse style, 140 beds, 54 rooms with bath/shower.

MARISTOVA (Oppland), 2740 ft. *Maristuen Mountain Center* (E) (original 1790 inn now a museum), 20 apartments, each for 4–5 persons, restaurant, supermarket, swimming, ski school, marked trails for ski touring.

NOREFJELL (Buskerud), 2740 ft, Oslo's nearest mountain resort, wonderful view of lake Krøderen. *Fjellhvil* (M), 98 beds, many rooms with bath, sauna; *Norefjell Mountain Center* (M), 80 beds, some rooms with bath, sauna.

NYSTOVA (Oppland), 3309 ft, popular for ski touring. *Nystuen Mountain Hotel* (M), 115 beds, all rooms with facilities.

OTTA (Oppland), 950 ft. *Otta Tourist Hotel* (M), 189 beds, all rooms with facilities, swimming, sauna; *Rondane Mountain Hotel* (M), 130 beds, 35 rooms with bath/shower, swimming, sauna.

TRETTEN (Oppland), fine skiing terrain, 2640 ft. *Gausdal* (E), 200 beds, 55 rooms with bath, swimming, sauna; *Skeikampen* (M), 113 beds, 45 rooms with bath, swimming, sauna.

VÅGÅMO (Oppland), mountain village, stave church, old farms. *Villa* (M), 120 beds, all rooms with facilities, sauna.

VINSTRA (Oppland), fine views. *Fefor* (M), 3050 ft, 221 beds, 45 rooms with bath, sauna, swimming, ski lift.

SPORTS. Sports play an important part in the holiday life of this region. *Fishing* comes first. The lakes and rivers are too many to be mentioned. The best fishing in lakes and rivers above 1,500 feet is available after June 15, and above 2,500 feet after July 15. Mountain *hiking* comes second. The Jotunheimen mountain ranges are the finest in northern Europe, with more than 200 peaks above 6,500 feet, glaciers, wild valleys, and mountain lakes of great beauty. The other famous mountain area is the Rondane mountains. Both Jotunheimen and Rondane are perfectly organized from the hiker's point of view, with cairned routes between the staffed chalets. The chalets open at the end of June. (Remember to get a copy of the Norway Travel Association guide book "Mountain Touring in Norway".) The best period for walking would be in July and August. The many first class resort hotels of the Eastern Valleys offer good *tennis, boating* and *bathing* in pools or nearby lakes. Some offer *riding* also.

WINTER SPORTS. This is excellent *skiing* country, with plenty of snow and terrain to suit every degree of skill—nursery slopes for beginners, downhill and slalom runs for experts, and ski touring. Skis can be hired at most of the resorts. Many resorts have their own skating rinks which are floodlit at night, and *sleigh* rides by the light of pitchpine torches are an added feature.

USEFUL ADDRESSES. Tourist information; At Fagernes, Geilo; Gjøvik, Hamar; Lillehammer; Otta, Vinstra.

Youth Hostels: Many throughout Eastern Valleys; best those at Geilo and Gjövik (Hovdeheimen), exceptionally fine ones at Hamar and Lillehammer (Birkebeinern). In the Central Mountains, the excellent chalets run by the touring clubs serve the same purpose.

Camping: Best sites are at Hamar, Lillehammer, Tretten, Ringebu, Otta and Kvam in the Gudbrandsdal area; Gjøvik, Biristrand, Fagernes and Bessheim in the Valdres-Jotunheim district; Elverum, Tynset and Röros in the Østerdal area.

BERGEN, CAPITAL OF WEST LAND

City of Quays and Grieg

Walking along the quay of Olav Kyrre's old town at night, you will see the thousands of lights that mark the houses, streets and highways as they follow the valleys and shores, now concentrated in narrow belts, now spreading out widely. Meanwhile, out in the fjords, heading north and south and west, are other lights. Those are the fishing boats, cargo liners, and passenger ships to which Bergen mainly owes its position as Norway's second city and capital of Vestlandet.

Bergensers do not suffer from any inferiority complex and particularly not as far as the capital of Norway is concerned. They point out that Bergen was an important commercial and military center when Oslo was still a village, and further, that until as late as the 1830s their town had the larger population. (Today Oslo has just over twice as many people as Bergen.) But they are especially proud of their cultural achievements and point to the great playwright Ludvig Holberg, the National Theater founder in 1859 (which they claim to be the first in Norway), their symphony orchestra, organized way back in 1765, and their annual International Festival.

Exploring Bergen

The steepest thousand-foot mountain in the world is surely Bergen's own Flöyen. A visitor once made this remark about the most renowned of the seven hills among which Bergen has grown up. But he must have been inspired by a native, for the words reflect perfectly the pride, independence and not-too-carefully-hidden superiority complex which mark the true Bergenser. In any case, let's jump on the funicular which leaves the head of Vetrlids-almenning every 30 minutes, ride up those lofty thousand feet, and have a bird's-eye view of this westernmost city in Norway.

Flöyen is a perfect place from which to plan our sightseeing, since the whole city is spread out below like a relief-map. (But bring a conventional map along for reference.) We see how Bergen stretches out in an elongated form running roughly from north to south, bounded for the most part by the fjord on one side and steep mountain slopes on the other. Sandviken, with its old warehouses at the seashore and contrasting new villa sections, is the most northern part, Paradis and Fjösanger the most southern; while farthest to the west are the industrial sections of Laksevåg and others along the Pudde Fjord. The central part in between is of most interest to us, and we shall descend for a look. Almost underfoot, and near the octagonal but somewhat lopsided lake called Lille Lungegårdsvann, lies the railway station.

Continuing our round-up from the air, we turn to the right bank of the central harbor, where the original town was founded by Olav Kyrre in 1070. There is the age-old fish market and, farther inland, Maria Church, which dates from about 1100, easily recognizable by its square twin steeples. Near the waterfront are the old warehouses of Hanseatic times, while beyond medieval Håkon's Hall, a long pier juts out into the fjord. That is Skoltegrunds-quay, where the Newcastle steamers dock. Directly opposite, on the southwest side of Vågen as the inner harbor is called, we see the park on Nordnes Point and back towards town, more of that complex pattern of wharves, warehouses, cottages, office buildings, narrow lanes and wide fire-prevention avenues or *almenninger,* which is the unmistakable trademark of Bergen.

Now the funicular lowers us swiftly down the inclined railway, which is so steep that one involuntarily shivers a bit. There's no reason for alarm, since every existing safety device is installed on the car, and the trackgripping brakes work automatically in case of emergency. We reach the bottom in a few minutes and walk down the Vetrlids-almenning into the midst of history.

First, a pause at the well-known fish market—Torget—at the inner end of Vågen, to observe or photograph the thousand-year-old scene of thrifty housewives negotiating for their daily supply of fish with the men who caught them a few hours ago. Then we pass by two short blocks of modern buildings and arrive at that world-famous monument to medieval life and trade, the old warehouses of the Hanseatic period in the 14th and 15th centuries.

Bryggen

"Yes, it used to be called Tyskebryggen, or the German Quay," admits the cicerone, "but by unanimous vote at the first meeting of the city council after the liberation, we decided to call it Bryggen, or The Quay." And, as if by way of further explanation, he looks down the waterfront towards the restored Bergenhus Fortress and Håkon's Hall, Bergen's most prized examples of 13th-century architecture.

The old wooden warehouses, long and narrow, jammed so closely against each other that air and daylight can enter only through tiny slits, are both the acme of picturesqueness and a working model of life in bygone times. They are still used for storage and for offices, and wares are still hauled up by hand pulleys from the narrow planked alleyways to the lofts above. The Hanseatic Museum and the old Schötstuene, in nearby Engelsgaarden, complete the medieval picture with their collections of ancient documents, coins, furniture, etc.

Nevertheless, this quarter is not equally reverenced by all Bergensers. Our friend can tell us that a good-sized fraction of the public, including a few town-planners, look on it more as a rat-ridden firetrap than as a sacred memorial. Some of them urge that the best preserved warehouses be dismantled and transplanted elsewhere in a kind of Bergen Folk Museum. Others say that these buildings are unpleasant reminders of a previous period of national downfall and of occupation by an enemy, so why preserve them? And they frankly bemoan the fact that a north gale was blowing that night in January, 1916, when the central town was burned down; an east wind would perhaps have taken care of Tyskebryggen as well. This school of thought had no regrets when, in July of 1955, part of the Quay was devastated by fire.

Fire has been the greatest enemy of Bergen and has harried it far longer than the Hansa ever did. As in old Oslo, fate seemed to decree that some careless person would let his house catch fire every 50 or 100 years, with the result that whole areas would be destroyed. But whereas Oslo was simply abandoned after the fire of 1624 and rebuilt on a new site, the citizens of Bergen had to rebuild on the old foundations. As they learned from each catastrophe, the town planning became more safety-conscious, until after 1916 the present series of broad streets was developed in addition to the old crosstown *almenninger* at regular intervals. Today, it is said that in the main business section streets occupy almost as much area as the buildings.

Ferry and Fortress

We take the little ferry which plies from near the Rosenkrantz Tower across to the middle of Nordnes, and walk out to the point. Here there is much of interest: another old fortress called Frederiksberg, a beautiful park, the Nordnes bathing establishment, and a fascinating Aquarium. From the south side of the point we have a good view down Pudde Fjord to Laksevåg and the other modern industrial suburbs which have spread out along the narrow stretch between shore and steep mountainside. Just north of Laksevåg the Naval Academy is located at Gravdal.

On top of Sydnes Hill is the former Bergens Museum, where Fridtjof Nansen worked as an assistant before making his astounding trip across Greenland on skis, and where the meteorologist Vilhelm Bjerknes first worked out his now internationally known methods of weather forecasting. The museum is at present part of the new University of Bergen, which was created in 1948. The Graduate School of Business Administration is very appropriately located in Bergen, for this is the city with the longest and strongest traditions in commerce and trade, yet also one of the most progressive business centers in Norway. It has its new and monumental headquarters at Helleveien in the northern outskirts of Bergen.

Famous Sons

If you bring up the subject of Vigeland and the sculpture-park in Oslo, our man from Bergen admits that there is nothing like it here, "not even in the Fish Market!". But he says it with such a glint in his eye that it's hard to know whether he's bragging or complaining. At least until he starts to point out how many well-placed statues there are in Bergen. In the City Park is Edvard Grieg, for example; and on the steps of the National Theater, Björnstjerne Björnson, who was its director for a time. This statue, by the way, is the work of Vigeland. But our guide's favorite is obviously sculptor Stephen Sinding's highly original likeness in bronze of Ole Bull. For here is the giant violinist standing on some rocks beside a waterfall, right in the heart of Norwegian nature, yet transplanted to the center of Bergen.

Many famous men have come from Bergen, like the painter I. C. Dahl, and the statesman Christian Michelsen, who was Prime Minister in 1905 when Norway finally succeeded in breaking out of the union with Sweden. But unquestionably the greatest is that trio: Ludvig Holberg, Ole Bull and Edvard Grieg. And while Holberg lived his adult life in Copenhagen, both the violinist and the composer not only claimed Bergen as home but actually lived there even after they had achieved fame. Consequently, we can visit their homes, Ole Bull's at Lysöya, and Grieg's Troldhaugen, which has now become a museum. Situated in a beautiful natural part at Hop, five miles from Bergen, Troldhaugen (whose name means "hill of trolls") has become a Norwegian national shrine. Grieg's studio, his piano, his notes, are all to be seen.

No mention of famous sons can omit those who in every generation have taken the initiative in maintaining or improving Bergen's economy. Such pillars of society range from the untold numbers of fishermen and skippers, like those in Revold's murals in the Stock Exchange, to scores of organizers of great shipping, canning and manufacturing concerns. It was they who created Bergen when the town was almost entirely dependent on sea communications with the rest of Norway; that is until the railway to Oslo was cut through the barricade of mountains and opened for traffic in 1909. And today the sea is still the only connection with many parts of Vestlandet, though since the Flesland airport, 12 miles away, was opened Bergen has been on both domestic and international air routes communicating with places as widely diverse as Bangkok and Vancouver. It is this mixture of remoteness and integration into the modern world which gives Norway its peculiar fascination.

PRACTICAL INFORMATION FOR BERGEN

 WHEN TO COME. The period between May 1 and the end of September is the best time for a visit, and especially during the 17-day (end of May to mid-June) Bergen International Festival. This greatest of Scandinavian cultural events presents annually scores of orchestral concerts, stage and ballet performances, folklore events and open-air shows, starring famous international singers and musicians, with concerts of Grieg's music in his home. (Details and tickets from PO Box 183–5001, Bergen.)

 WHAT TO SEE. Bergen is one of the most attractive towns in northern Europe, and certainly one of the most interesting places in Norway. Musts are the view from Flöyen, the fish market, Bryggen with the Hanseatic Museum and Schötstuene, Bergenhus Fortress and Håkon Hall, the Maria Church, Old Bergen, the new Aquarium at Nordnes, and most famous of all, Grieg's house Troldhaugen, at Hop, and Fantoft Stave Church at Paradis. A ramble through the streets gives you the historic atmosphere.

Details of opening times are listed in the *Bergen Guide,* available free at the Tourist Office in the city square.

Bergenhus Fortress with Håkon Hall. Norway's most valuable medieval secular memorial (under restoration). The Håkon Hall is a royal hall erected in the mid-13th century. The Rosenkrantz Tower also at Bergenhus has a medieval origin, but the present exterior dates from 1567.

Mariakirken (St. Mary's Church). One of the most remarkable churches of Norway and the oldest edifice in Bergen, built in the first half of the 12th century.

Hanseatic Museum, Finnegården. In one of the old houses of Bryggen. Shows the merchant's office and living-room, the room of his employees, and the warehouses.

Bryggen (The Quay). The wooden houses date from the period after the fire of 1702. However, the buildings then erected were faithful copies of those destroyed, and accordingly form an excellent illustration of Norwegian medieval architecture.

Schötstuene, opposite Mariakirken. The common or club rooms of the Hanseatic merchants, still in use for social gatherings.

Gamle Bergen (Old Bergen). Modern town planning often involves the pulling down of old houses. Some of the most characteristic ones are moved to Old Bergen, where they become parts of a little town, complete with streets, marketplace and alleys.

Rasmus Meyer's Collections, by Lille Lungegårds Lake. Choice selection of Norwegian paintings and the interior of Bergen homes.

Bergen University has a number of museums on its premises at Sydneshaugen; the best is probably the Maritime, with models, prints, etc. from Viking days to the 20th century.

Troldhaugen, Hop, outside Bergen. Victorian villa home of Edvard and Nina Grieg, preserved in its original state. During the Bergen Festival intimate concerts are given here.

Fantoft Stave Church, Paradis. One of the unique wooden medieval churches, probably from about 1150, moved from Fortun in Sogne in 1883.

Fishery Museum, Nordahl Brunsgate 9. Central museum of Norwegian fisheries.

Aquarium, at Nordnes, opened 1960, beautifully arranged, it is the most modern of its kind in Europe.

HOW TO GET ABOUT. The best way to get around Bergen is on foot. You take the funicular to Flöyen. Buses cover the town and surroundings fairly well. Taxis are plentiful.

HOTELS. The overcrowding that has plagued the Bergen hotel scene has eased, and there is space for visitors all year round. However, it is always wise to make reservations ahead especially at festival times.

Norge (L), Ole Bulls plass 4, 498 beds, all rooms with facilities incl. piped music/radio, 15 suites, several restaurants and bars, Garden Room with nightly dancing June/Aug.

SAS Royal (L), Bryggen, opened in Feb 1982 on site of old warehouses ravaged by fire 9 times since 1170. The houses were rebuilt each time in the same style and SAS has incorporated this ancient architecture in the hotel, which makes it one of the most interesting in Europe. 500 beds in 265 rooms, all with facilities incl. piped music/radio, swimming, exhibition of Hanseatic artifacts unearthed during construction.

Ambassadeur (E), Vestre Torvgate 9, 57 beds, all rooms with facilities, dining room and pizzeria.

Neptun (E), Walckendorffsgate 8, 195 beds, all rooms with facilities.

Orion (E), Bradbenken 3, 250 beds, 110 rooms with facilities, dining room, disco bar.

Rosenkrantz (E), Rosenkrantzgate 7, 155 beds, 88 rooms with bath, restaurant.

Terminus (E), Kong Oscarsgate 71, 225 beds, 116 rooms with bath, temperance hotel, restaurant.

Bergen Apartment (M), Haakonsgate 2, 2 km from station; 59 beds, all rooms with facilities.

Bergen Center (formerly *Bristol*) (M), Markevei 2, on city square, 100 beds, 65 rooms; bed and breakfast hotel.

Esso Motor Hotel (M), Kokstad near Flesland airport, new in 1982; 300 beds in 175 rooms, all with facilities; restaurant, taverna, indoor pool, sauna, ample parking.

Gjestehuset Rica (M), Vestre Torggate 20a, central location; 36 beds.

Skogens (M), Haakonsgate 27; 50 beds, 2 rooms with bath.

Slottsgarden Rica (M), Sandbrogate 3, 1 km from station; 57 beds, 21 rooms with bath/shower, restaurant, grill.

Strand (M), Strandkaien 2/4, facing harbor; 100 beds, 15 rooms with bath; dining room.

Toms (M), C Sundtsgate 52, 1 1/2 km from station; 78 beds, all rooms with facilities inc. refrigerator; dining room.

RESTAURANTS. Bergen's "vista-vision" restaurants, *Bellevue* and *Fløyen,* provide magnificent views of the city and the fjord beyond. In town are a number of fashionable restaurants, particularly in the two luxury hotels (*Norge* and *SAS Royal*). The following restaurants can also be recommended.

Bellevue (E), Bellevuebakken 9, on hillside overlooking city and fjord, in charming 17th century manor, silver, crystal and tablecloth, good food and personalized service.

Bryggen Tracteursted (M), Bryggestredet, in Hanseatic surroundings. You may buy live fish from the fish market and ask the chef to prepare it any way you want it!

Bryggestuen Restaurant (M), Bryggen 6, popular for morning coffee and light lunch.

Chianti (M), Strømgaten 8, at central bus station, specialty spaghetti and fish, dancing daily except Mon.

Excellent (M), Torvgaten 1a, grill, specialty sea food, Show Boat dancing every eve.

Fløyen Restaurant (M), Fløyen, at top of funicular, famous view of city and fjord, grill, open-air restaurant in summer, dancing.

Grand Cafe (M), Olav Kyrresgate 11, opposite Norge Hotel, specialty Chinese food and—in season—boiled cod, pavement cafe during summer.

Holbergstuen (M), Torvalmenning 6, will serve fish any way you want it, popular meeting place.

Holms Discosteak House (M), Kong Oscarsgate 45, grill, dancing on weekdays.

Villa Amorini (M), Rasmus Meyers Allé 5, new, good food.

Wesselstuen (M), Engen 14, pot luck and fish, much frequented any time of day, favorite haunt of the bergensers.

 SIGHTSEEING AND EXCURSIONS. There are any number of coach tours lasting from 1½ to 3 hours, with all departures from the tourist office at Torgalmenning. The longer ones take in Grieg's Troldhaugen and/or Fantoft Stave Church. There is a "Fana Folklore" excursion making an evening visit to Fana where you meet the people and hear hymns played on the organ of the 800-year-old church (which once was believed to heal the sick). There is a traditional Norwegian meal and folk dancing in national costume in which visitors are invited to participate. There are daily tours to the fjord district, fjord sightseeing boat rides and fishing trips on Wednesdays. You can take a trip to the top of Mt. Flöyen on the funicular, or go by cablecar to Mt. Ulriken, but choose clear days for these.

 SHOPPING. If you are going to Bergen, you might wish to hold back on furs till you have been to *Brandt's,* the shop which is perhaps among the best in Norway for serving the overseas visitor. Prices for export are reasonable, though your own customs man may not be when you return home, so check with your consulate before making a large purchase.

We must also mention the handwrought silver of *Theodor Olsen,* to be found here in his own shop. *Prydkunst Hjertholm,* Torgalmenning 8, has a good assortment of pewter and textiles. *Husfliden,* Vagsalmenning, and Østre Skostredet, is best for authentic homemade arts and crafts. The art of *rosemaling*

continues to flourish in western Norway, and the names of Peder Rød and Knut Hovden should be remembered.

SPORTS. Local amenities include a *golf* course, *tennis* courts, a *harness racing* track, *rowing, yachting,* and *boating* clubs. The surrounding countryside is ideal for *hiking* and there is trout and salmon *fishing.* Kvamskog, only some 2 hours by bus, is Bergen's "back door" *skiing* resort. Other well-known centers lie in the magnificent skiing country alongside the Bergen Railway, which runs cross-country to Oslo—a 2–3 hour journey.

CAMPING. For a town of its size, Bergen is not too well provided with facilities, but there are organized sites south and north of Bergen. The best are Lone Camping and Grimen Camping, respectively 12 and 10 miles out on road E68.

USEFUL ADDRESSES Consulate: British, Strandgaten 17. **Tourist information:** Slottsgaten 1; kiosk on city square.

HOTELS ALONG THE BERGEN RAILROAD

ÅL (Buskerud), 1430 to 3610 ft. *Bergsjø* (M), 25 km by bus from station, 140 beds, most rooms with facilities, swimming, sauna, solarium, trout fishing, ptarmigan shooting (Sept), fine skiing terrain, ski lift, ski school; *Sundre* (I), 48 beds, some rooms with bath/shower.

FINSE (Hordaland), 4010 ft, magnificent surroundings of mountains and glaciers. This is where Captain Scott trained for his South Pole expedition in 1911; and later both *Scott of the Antarctic* and *The Empire Strikes Back* were shot here. The skiing season lasts until May, but you can ascend the glacier on skis in mid-summer! *Finse Hotel* (M), 19 rooms, all with facilities, swimming; *Finse 1222* (I), 90 rooms, restaurant, disco, sauna.

GEILO (Buskerud), 2625 ft, renowned tourist center and ski resort, varied terrain, ski lifts, ski school, skating rink. *Bardøla* (E), 180 beds, 95 rooms with facilities, swimming, sauna, resident orchestra; *Holms* (E), one of the most famous resort hotels in Norway, 140 beds, all rooms with facilities; *Vestlia* (E), 146 beds, all rooms with facilities, swimming; *Geilo Apartment Hotel* (M), 30 apartments, each for 4 persons; *Geilo Hotel* (M), 145 beds, all rooms with bath/shower; *Highland* (M), 174 beds, most rooms with facilities; *Ustedalen* (M), 100 beds, all rooms with facilities; *Geilo Youth Hostel* (I), 200 beds, comfortable.

GOL (Buskerud), 680 ft, ski center, lift, marked trails. *Eidsgaard* (M), 60 rooms; *Pers* (M), 270 beds, all rooms with facilities, swimming; *Gol Youth Hostel* (I), 40 beds.

MJØLFJELL (Hordaland), 2340 ft, grand area for ski touring. *Mjølfjell Youth Hostel* (I), 6 km from station, 140 beds, sauna, all meals, popular.

OPPHEIM (Hordaland), 26 km by bus from Voss, 1090 ft, good skiing country, chairlift. *Oppheim* (M), 94 beds, some rooms with bath; *Vossestølen* (I), 48 beds, 13 rooms with bath.

STALHEIM (Hordaland), 35 km by bus from Voss, overlooking the Nerøy valley. Zig-zag road now bypassed by giant tunnel, opened 1980, but hairpin bends still there in summer for venturesome motorists. *Stalheim* (E), outstanding, 212 beds, all rooms with facilities, souvenir shop with local arts and crafts, museum.

USTAOSET (Buskerud), 3250 ft, views of Mt Hallingskarvet, good ski touring. *Ustaoset Mountain Hotel* (M), 147 beds, all rooms with facilities; *Ustaoset Motel* (I), 50 beds.

VATNAHALSEN (Sogn), on Flåm railroad, 2790 ft, good skiing terrain. *Vatnahalsen* (M), 80 beds, many rooms with bath.

VOSS (Hordaland), 180 ft, large village facing lake Vang, educational center of the province. St Olav stone cross from 1023, Finneloftet, built around 1250, Norway's oldest nonecclesiastical timber building. Voss Folk Museum, ancient farmhouses at Mølster and Nesheim. Voss church, completed 1277 with 7 ft thick walls. Cablecar to mountain top with panoramic restaurant. *Fleischer* (M), 122 beds, all rooms with facilities, swimming, sauna; *Jarl* (M), 130 beds, 35 rooms with facilities, sauna; *Kringsjå Pension* (M), 34 beds, all rooms with facilities; *Park* (M), 96 beds, all rooms with facilities; *Vossevangen* (M), 130 beds, 45 rooms with bath/shower; *Nøring Pension* (I), 45 beds; *Rondo Pension* (I), 45 beds, 10 rooms with bath; *Voss Youth Hostel* (I), facing lake Vang, special facilities for handicapped, 220 beds, cafeteria.

HEALTH ON THE MOVE

While we don't suggest that you turn into a traveling hypochondriac, here are a few points to consider for making sure your holiday isn't spoiled by avoidable health upsets.

Flight Planning

Sleep well before you leave

Plan to arrive at your normal bedtime

Go easy on the food and alcohol on board

Wear loose comfortable clothes

Wrap yourself in a blanket to sleep—the body temperature drops

Take it easy for 24 hours after arrival (especially after a big time change): no important meetings immediately

Montezuma's Revenge and Allied Ills

Be wary of shellfish, icecream, salads and unwashed fruit

Drinking-water can be deadly—avoid village pumps

Make sure food is well-cooked—avoid any that has been left on display

Shun restaurants with flies

Bottled mineral water is usually safe—as is Coke and Pepsi

A good treatment for diarrhea is *Kaomycin* (an antibiotic with kaopectate) every four hours—or take *Lomotil* plus *Neomycin; Entero-Vioform* is no longer recommended

Mosquitos can be more serious than vampire bats; malaria can be prevented by regular dosage with *Proguanil* or *Paludrine—Chloroquine* is best for treatment

Hot Tips

Never wear nylon in the heat—cotton is best

Keep your intake of fluids going with plenty of salt

Go easy on sunbathing for the first few days

Always use a good quality cream or lotion

If you have heat prostration—*don't drive*

ANCIENT TRONDHEIM AND DISTRICT

Stronghold of Crown and Church

A glance at the map will show you that Trondheim is situated more or less where Norway's long tadpole-like tail joins the rounded body which is usually described as South Norway, and it is not surprising that the Viking kings should have chosen this site for their first capital. From the sheltered waters of the land-locked Trondheim Fjord their longboats would sail out on raids that carried them west to the coast of America and east to the shores of the Byzantine Empire.

Norwegian towns have a disconcerting habit of reverting to their former names, but you may rest assured that Trondheim has now made up its mind as to what it wants to be called. This city was once the capital of Norway under the name of Nidaros, and when the Norwegian people were seized 40 years ago with a burning desire to toss aside newfangled names of a mere 300 years' standing, the authorities in Oslo (then Christiania) decided to change Trondheim back to Nidaros. However, they were reckoning without the proverbial obstinacy of the Trönder, and Trondheim it remains to this day.

Exploring Trondheim and District

Trondheim is a delightful city, possibly the only one in Norway with a genuine air of the medieval about it. King Olav Tryggvason founded the town in the 10th century on the southern shores of the fjord of the same name, where the Nid River runs into the sea. Just before the river pours its waters into the fjord, it makes an abrupt loop, so that the triangle of land on which Trondheim stands is surrounded on two sides by the river and on one side by the sea, and is thus a sort of peninsula connected to the mainland by a narrow strip. A number of bridges cross the Nid River to modern suburbs, but the essential Trondheim is to be found north and west of the Nid.

The cathedral occupies an imposing position to the south. From it a broad avenue runs straight through the central part of the old town to the statue of King Olav in the marketplace.

Sitting at home, you may imagine that a visit to Trondheim would resemble one of Amundsen's polar explorations, but the climate is essentially continental, with surprisingly warm summers. Furthermore, Trondheim is not only a cultural and industrial center, but the hub of a large agricultural district which in some years actually exports hay to the British Isles. Trondheim is also an excellent winter sports center, and it is not surprising that in recent years local skiers and skaters have created almost a monopoly of championships in Norwegian winter sports.

Cathedral, Capital and Court

In the Middle Ages Trondheim enjoyed a European reputation when the great Nidaros Cathedral was raised as a shrine to Saint Olav, King of Norway and one of the greatest figures from the Saga Age. King Olav's shrine was visited by pilgrims from every Christian land in the world, and a chain of inns or hostels was built all the way from Oslo in the south, through the broad-bosomed Gudbrandsdal, over the mighty back of Mount Dovre and down to the Gothic cathedral by the banks of the Nid River. This cathedral, now almost completely restored, still stands in all its pristine glory, and it is not only the pride of the citizens, but Trondheim's chief claim to fame. The architecture bears clear marks of the influence of the English Gothic style and it is probable that English masons assisted in its erection.

When the cathedral was built, Trondheim was the undisputed capital of Norway: here the king had his court and here the ecclesiastical dignitaries had their seat. On the little island of Munkholmen, which lies like a cruiser at anchor in the bay, you can still see the ruins of an old monastery, bringing to mind Longfellow's own description of the island in his poem *The Saga of King Olaf,* where he says, "At Nidarholm the priests are all singing."

King Haakon VII of Norway was crowned here in 1906, but formal coronations are no longer a part of the ceremonies of state in Norway. Still, it is interesting to know that it was here that all Norway's kings—including Canute, King of Denmark, Norway and England—were elected by the old Norse *tings,* the 10th-century forerunners of the modern Norwegian Storting, or Parliament.

Like most Norwegian towns, Trondheim has from time to time suffered devastating fires, but in one respect Trondheim was more fortunate than either Oslo or Bergen. In the 17th century, after most of the residential quarters had been razed to the ground, a town-planning scheme was carried out by Johan Cicignon, a Norwegian of French extraction, who replaced many of the narrow twisting streets with broad avenues. To this canny "foreigner" the people of Trondheim owe the spacious layout of their town. Some people may consider it a little too spacious for its size, though the narrow streets which survived the fire contrast charmingly with the well-planned, orderly alleys and streets of Cicignon.

Other Notable Buildings

The Stiftsgården, or royal residence, used by the King whenever he visits Trondheim, is a magnificent structure in late baroque style dating from 1775. Incidentally, this is the second largest wooden building in Scandinavia, and doubtless provides the local firemen with an oversize headache. The largest, Singsaker Studenthjem, also belongs to Trondheim. The Bishop's Palace, only a stone's throw from the cathedral, is another interesting relic of the medieval days when Trondheim had some 16 churches and two monasteries. From the nearby market place the statue of King Olav Tryggvason, Carlyle's "wildly beautifullest" king, surveys the town he founded in the year 997.

In the Folk Museum you will find an excellent collection of buildings, customs and implements illustrating the life in Trondheim and surrounding districts in medieval times. The Kunstforeningen Art Gallery, with a fine collection of paintings by representative Norwegian artists, and the Fortress of Kristiansten, which in the old heroic days guarded Trondheim from the landward side, are also both worth a visit. The latter is situated on a rocky eminence to the east of the city, where it commands a magnificent view of the fjord and of Munkholmen.

On another rise overlooking Trondheim Fjord is Ringve. The estate dates from the 1600s but was given to the city, as a music center, by the will of the last owner, who was responsible for acquiring many of the fine and rare instruments including a magnificent harpsichord once housed at Versailles.

Trondheim, in common with Bergen, has older cultural traditions than Oslo, which both cities regard as somewhat of an interloper, or at best an upstart. While Bergen glories in a Philharmonic Orchestra which is the third oldest in the world, antedating its counterpart in Vienna by a good 70 years, Trondheim has a number of societies which make their opposite numbers in Oslo mere striplings by comparison. Chief among these is the Videnskapsselskapet, or Academy of Sciences, which has been running ever since the 18th century.

Trondheim is also the site of Norway's Tekniske Høgskole, where Norway's architects and engineers receive their training. This institute is now part of the university, and in the course of time a student milieu has grown up in the town unlike that of any other Norwegian city. The

University of Bergen, founded in 1948, is as yet only an infant in arms, while the students at the University of Oslo tend to be swallowed up in the capital and have little chance of giving it the stamp of a university town. Not so Trondheim, where the students have their own special societies, clubs and restaurants, and put on a musical revue every other year that is not only traditional, but a box-office success as well.

The Tröndelag Provinces

Few parts of Norway are so varied in their scenery as the twin counties of North Tröndelag and South Tröndelag, of which Trondheim is the capital. Apart from the agricultural districts, there are vast forests, rivers and waterfalls, fjords and mountains.

These provinces are also unusually rich in historical mementos, including such sights as the old ting-place at Frosta, where representatives from eight counties met regularly to pass laws and mete out justice from 940 A.D. right up to the 16th century. No place in Norwegian history is better known than the battlefield of Stiklestad, where St. Olav met his death in 1030 A.D., and where the church was built, on the very spot he was slain, a hundred years after the battle. The Reformation proved a stirring time for Tröndelag, the citadel of Roman Catholicism in the north. Olav Engelbriktsson, last archbishop of Norway, held out in his fortified castle of Steinvikholm (interesting ruins) before fleeing the country. Austråt Castle, at the mouth of the Trondheim Fjord, has been described as the most original building of the Norwegian Renaissance, and in the 17th century the copper-mining town of Röros was founded. Röros is a favorite excursion from Trondheim by rail or road, as this remarkable little town, immortalized in the great novels of Johan Falkberget, has retained its original appearance right down to the present. The old mines were closed in 1978, but have now been re-opened as a unique museum. There are guided tours throughout the year to the Olav mine.

The other great resort of Tröndelag is the mountain village of Oppdal on the Dovre Railway. At Oppdal, some of Norway's longest lifts whisk the visitor up to the Troll Eye Restaurant, 3,400 feet above sea level, from where there is a superb panorama of the surrounding mountains.

If you have a sense of the macabre, you might go to Hell—quite literally. Hell in this case is not a roaring inferno where sinister-looking gentlemen will chase you around with pitchforks, but a charming little railway station not more than half an hour by train from Trondheim. You will have the satisfaction of being able to buy a round-trip ticket, and you should not miss the opportunity of mailing a letter or two and taking advantage of the unique postmark.

PRACTICAL INFORMATION FOR TRONDHEIM AND DISTRICT

WHEN TO COME. The summer season lasts from May to September, but the Trondheim district can be visited all year round: September and October for the huntsman, for the skier from December to the end of April. Historical plays are enacted yearly at Stiklestad in the last week of July.

WHAT TO SEE. The principal sights include: Trondheim with the Nidaros Cathedral; Röros with its old copper mines; Oppdal with its alpine character; Austråt Castle at the mouth of the Trondheim Fjord; the battlefield and church at Stiklestad; the Frosta *ting*-place; the village of Hell; rock drawings at Hegra; and Ringve's Music Museum.

HOW TO GET ABOUT. Trondheim is reached by train, plane, and road from Oslo, and Stockholm is only 514 miles away via the newest inter-Scandinavian motor route. Traveling within the Trondheim district is easy as the Nordland Railway goes through the entire length of North Tröndelag, and the Dovre and Röros Railways through South Tröndelag. The rest is covered by bus routes. A ferry from Trondheim across the fjord links up with roads and bus routes on the west side of the fjord.

MOTORING. The long North Cape road (E 6), crosses the Tröndelag (Trondheim region), and when traveling from the south towards Trondheim, it is worth branching off west at Berkåk to traverse the picturesque and wild Orkdal valley (via Lökken and Orkanger), about 52 miles. Other scenic and interesting routes include: from Trondheim along the fjord to Orkanger and across the hills to Sunde on the coast, then by ferry to Hitra island with superb sea-fishing and picturesque fishing villages. From Hitra, another ferry crosses to the island of Frøya. From Trondheim by ferry to Rörvik, along the coastal road and past lake Gjölavatn (Stone Age paintings) and Austråt (Renaissance chateau) to Örland (about 55 miles).

HOTELS AND RESTAURANTS. Most visitors to Norway inevitably make the acquaintance of either Bergen or Oslo. Although both these towns are charming starting points for any exploration of Norway, there is a third—Trondheim—which has ancient claims to being included in any triumvirate of Norwegian towns, and has good hotels, and a variety of restaurants.

LEVANGER (Nord-Tröndelag), area rich in archeological finds. *Backlund* (M), 120 beds, most rooms with bath; *IMI* (I), bed and breakfast only, mission hotel; *Levanger Youth Hostel* (I), 48 beds.

MERÅKER (Nord-Trøndelag), folk museum, old copper mines, skiing, chairlift. *Meråker Inn* (M), 85 beds, some rooms with bath.

NAMSOS (Nord-Trøndelag), small mountain in center of town, Namdal folk museum. *Grand Hotel Bondeheimen* (M), 77 beds, 10 rooms with bath; *Namsen Motel* (M), 60 beds, all rooms with bath/shower.

OPPDAL (Sør-Trøndelag), 1790 ft, popular ski resort with all facilities, curling, skating. *Hovd Inn Sportell* (M), 94 beds, all rooms with facilities, swimming, sauna; *Nor Tourist Hotel* (M), 50 rooms, 18 with bath; *Oppdal Tourist Hotel* (M), 90 beds, most rooms with facilities, swimming, sauna; *Oppdal Hotel* (I), 60 beds; *Turistheimen* (I), youth hostel, 48 beds, cafeteria.

ORKANGER (Sør-Trøndelag). *Bårdshaug Herregård* (E), converted manor, 117 beds, many rooms with bath, swimming, sauna.

RØROS (Sør-Trøndelag). *Bergstadens Tourist Hotel* (E), 156 beds, all rooms with facilities, swimming, sauna; *Røros Tourist Hotel* (M), 209 beds, all rooms with facilities, swimming, sauna; *Røros Youth Hostel* (I), 120 beds.

STEINKJER (Nord-Trøndelag), folk museum, burial mounds, salmon fishing. *Grand* (E), 170 beds, most rooms with facilities, sauna, restaurant.

TRONDHEIM *Ambassadeur* (E), Elvegate 18, 85 beds, all rooms with facilities, roof terrace.

Astoria (E), Nordregate 24, 103 beds, most rooms with facilities, restaurant, bistro, dancing bar.

Britannia (E), Dronningensgate 5, 180 beds, all rooms with facilities, excellent Palm Garden restaurant, breakfast/lunch restaurant, bar.

Larssens (E), Ths Angellsgate 10, 50 beds, most with facilities, restaurant.

Nye Sentrum (E), Olav Tryggvasonsgate 5, 98 beds, most rooms with facilities, restaurant and cafeteria.

Prinsen (E), Kongensgate 30, 110 beds, 70 rooms with facilities, excellent Coq d'Or restaurant, bistro, cafeteria, grill, wine lodge, beer garden.

Dronningen Bed & Breakfast (M), Dronningensgate 26, 53 beds, some rooms with bath/shower, Den Gamle Cafe restaurant.

Esso Motor Hotel (M), Brøsetveien 186, 300 beds, all rooms with facilities, sauna, restaurant, bar.

Gildevangen (M), Søndregate 22b, 71 beds, some rooms with bath/shower, dining rooms and cafeteria, unlicenced.

IMI (M), Kongensgate 26, mission hotel, 120 beds, dining room, unlicenced.

Neptun (M), Ths Angellsgate 10B, 60 beds with facilities, bistro.

Norrøna Misjonshospits (M), Ths Angellsgate 20, mission hotel, 35 beds, cafeteria, unlicenced.

Phoenix (M), Munkegate 26, 120 beds, most rooms with facilities, restaurant, bar, dancing, open-air restaurant in summer.

Trønderheimen (M), Kongensgate 15, 77 beds, some rooms with bath/shower, dining room, cafeteria.

Singsaker Sommerhotell (I), Rogersgate 1, summer only (June 15-Aug 15), 200 beds, some rooms with bath/shower, sauna, restaurant.

Trondheim Youth Hostel (I), Weidemannsvei 41, 200 beds, cafeteria.

RESTAURANTS. The most elegant restaurants in Trondheim are found in the leading hotels, such as *Britannia* and *Prinsen* described above, but in addition the following restaurants can be recommended.

Bajazzo Rica (M), Søndregate 15, grill, dancing, disco, billiards, night club.

Benito (M), Vår Fruegate 4, Italian food, wine lodge.

Braseriet (M), Nordregate 11, pizzeria, disco, open-air cafe in summer.

Cavalero (M), Kongensgate 3, restaurant, grill, bar.

China House (M), Søndregate 17, Chinese food, closed Mon.

Daniel (M), Tinghusplass 1, steakhouse and grill.

Erichsen (M), Kongensgate 3, lunch and dinner, bar.

Galleyen (M), Dronningensgate 12, all-night restaurant, dancing.

Grenaderen (M), Kongsgården, music, open-air restaurant in summer.

Krovertens Hus (M), Nordregate 23, new and different restaurant.

Kunstnerkroen (M), Prinsensgate 38, intimate artistic restaurant with music, dancing, bar.

Landlord Pub (M), Prinsensgate 40, English pub.

Naustloftet (M), Prinsensgate 42, seafood restaurant, bar.

Peppe's Pizza Pub (M), Kjøpmannsgate 25, American pizza parlor in old warehouse.

 SPORTS. Outdoor life is the chief attraction. **Swimming** in the Trondheim Fjord may be chilly, but is popular with the Trönders themselves. Excellent trout and salmon **fishing** is within reach; in the Namsen, Gaula, Nea, Orkla, and Stjördal rivers. The mountains of Snasa and Namdal in the north, and Sylene in the south, also provide good angling. Elk **hunting** in the Snåsa forests is the best in Norway, and the coastal islands, especially Hitra, are the haunt of red deer. Ptarmigan, a game bird similar to grouse, can be shot during September and October.

Mountaineering and **hiking** in the Trollheimen and Sylene districts, where there are trails and charming chalets.

Trondheim is one of the few towns to boast a **golf course** (9 holes), which is situated at an elevation of 700 ft, overlooking the cathedral city and the fjord. Famous for its annual Midnight Sun Golf Tournament.

 WINTER SPORTS. On the outskirts of town, Trondheim, much the same as Oslo, has its own private stretch of skiing country, Bymarka. Easily reached from the center of town by bus or train (20 minutes), it is a sportsman's paradise. **Skistua,** opposite the Gråkallen ski jump, is the center. Ski lift and ski trails in all directions.

Other centers include Meråker, Oppdal and Røros, as described above.

 USEFUL ADDRESSES. Tourist information: Trondheim Travel Association, Kongensgate 7.

Camping: Best sites are those at Trondheim, Malvik, Lundamo, Hembre, Stjørdalshalsen, Steinkjer, Kvam (Lake Snåsa), Overhalla and Namsskogan.

WAY TO THE NORTH

Folklore, Finnmark and the Midnight Sun

Norway's main problem was how to care for tourists, not how to attract them. This is still true of northern Norway. From Steinkjer at latitude 64° on up towards the Arctic Ocean, it's just one feast of scenic beauty after another, and the whole, incredible northern outdoors is lit up by both the noonday and the midnight sun. From the moment you pull away from the quay and head out of the Trondheim Fjord, you know that a new kind of adventure has begun.

Exploring North Norway

The great charm of the express steamer trip is seeing the sights when they appear, no matter how awkward the hour. The 800-foot stone mountain, Torghatten, for example, is passed about 1 A.M., and there's enough light to observe the famous hole clear through the rock about halfway up and a good 500 feet long. Geologists talk about the action of waves washing out this tunnel when the shoreline was much higher, but local folklore has a far more colorful explanation which we'll come to shortly. At 4 A.M. you pass the Seven Sisters—seven snow-covered peaks, each more jagged than the last.

If you're breakfasting around eight, you'll have to stop and run out on deck when the approach to Hestmannen or The Horseman is an-

360

nounced. Not just because the silhouette of this rocky island, from a certain point, looks remarkably like a horse and rider, but because he is the clue to Torghatten. It seems that Hestmannen, quite some time ago, was enamored of the Leka-Maiden near Rörvik, but she paid no attention to him. Whereupon the enraged Horseman shot a long-distance arrow at her, only to have it intercepted by Torg who threw his hat in the way; hence the great hole. To top things off, when the sun rose, everyone involved in the affair was turned into stone, including the Seven Sisters, who fled with the Leka-Maiden.

At the north end of the petrified Hestmannen you encounter something far more stimulating to the imagination than folklore, though quite invisible. This is the imaginary parallel of 66° 32′ North of the Arctic Circle, and once it is crossed, you are in that much-advertised, much-described Land of the Midnight Sun. The coastal express boat calls at the little village of Ørnes, and overland excursions are arranged by bus via the Saltstraumen *maelstrom* (or whirlpool) to Bodø.

After a forenoon among the ever-present islands you dock at Bodø where you stay for a couple of hours.

By engaging a cab, you may even have time to combine looking across the Salt Fjord south of Bodø towards the spot where the notorious Saltstraumen churns and eddies during each change of tide, with a quick trip to the Rønvik Restaurant two miles north of town. From here there's a panorama of rock masses, islands, valleys and fjords that will open the eyes of the most scenery-satiated traveler.

There would also be a fine view of the Midnight Sun from Rønvik if you stayed there long enough, but by midnight the *hurtig-rute* is steaming through Raft Sound in the Lofoten Islands. In fact, by supper time you are close upon the "Lofot-Wall", as the Norwegians so aptly describe the jagged series of mountain peaks of this island-chain.

Catch as Catch Can

First it's Stamsund at 7 P.M., one of the largest of the many fishing ports and shipping centers in the Lofotens, where the scenery consists of boats, warehouses, rocky shores covered with wooden racks for drying codfish, and steep snow-covered mountains in the not-distant background. About two hours later it's Svolvaer, largest town of the islands and with the same sights, only more of them.

Svolvaer is also the fishing capital of the north during the cod season each winter in February and March. Furthermore, it is already something of a tourist center at that time, since many hardy travelers each winter take advantage of special excursions by boat to witness this fantastic spectacle. Thousands of craft of all kinds engage in fishing with all kinds of gear. But there's plenty of fish for everyone, no matter what his apparatus, and all return loaded to the gunwales. On shore the activity is equally hectic, for all these tons of cod must be cleaned and processed; fillets are sent away for deep-freezing, livers for stewing, roe for canning and the split cod is hung up to dry into *törr-fisk*.

"But some places they don't bother with such drying contrivances," says the friendly captain. "Near Kristiansund, for example, the cod are just spread out on the bare rocks along the shore. We've got plenty of those, you know. That's why around there, they're called *klipp-fisk,* for *klipp* means cliff."

"Where's that Midnight Sun?" you'll sooner or later ask. The answer will be disappointing. Throughout June and most of July there is plenty of twilight, or rather a combined sunset and sunrise effect, but there are too many islands and mountain walls for you to see the sun when it approaches the horizon at midnight. So, after looking at the wildest parts of the Lofot Wall—Digermulen Mountain and the narrow Raft Sound which you sail through after leaving Svolvaer—you may as well turn in for some much-needed sleep. Of course, if you are troubled with insomnia you'll find plenty to look at all night while the steamer winds among the Vesterålen Islands, which in contrast to the Lofotens, are amazingly flat.

Before breakfast the second full day from Trondheim, you can go ashore in Harstad for an hour and a half. Not only is this an important fish-canning and shipping town, but it can show, a couple of miles north, the curious fortified church of Trondenes. Built in the 13th century, this edifice has stone walls over eight feet thick and is one of the very few church-fortresses in Norway.

At Tromsö, the capital of Troms Province and the largest city above the Arctic Circle, the Midnight Sun is still elusive because of those ever-present mountains to the north. In any case, you can get a good night's rest and look at the sights next day. These include the longest bridge in Northern Europe spanning the Tromsö Sound, the gondola lift to Storsteinen, the Tromsdalen Church, the Observatory for Northern Lights—which devotes the long Arctic night to studying the Aurora Borealis—and another well-known scientific institution, the Tromsö Arctic Museum.

If you don't want to go on an expedition for your polar bear, you can meet one in the street in Tromsö itself, but stuffed into immobility. You'll find others, the alive kind, at the zoo, together with seals and otters. But don't wander too far, at 6 P.M. that next *hurtig-rute* leaves with you on board, according to our plan. And this night is your first real chance for a look at the sun, weather permitting, for here's an open space northward between the two islands of Vannöy and Arnöy which the steamer should cross around midnight.

At about 4.30 A.M., the steamer reaches Hammerfest. Again there's an hour for sightseeing, and this time you are in the northernmost city in the world. (By the way, Hammerfest was also the first town in Norway to install electric lights: in 1891). Climb the 300-foot hill just behind the town for a good look at this plucky little community and its not-too-friendly natural environment. Not only was it completely razed in late 1944 by the retreating Nazis, who applied scorched earth destruction to almost all of Finnmark Province, but it has also been damaged repeatedly by avalanches. Yet in spite of all handicaps the town was rebuilt, and one of its most impressive sights is the church with its tall tower shaped like an elongated Lapp tent or *kåta.*

Fish export is the main industry of Hammerfest, together with tourist trade in normal times, and here you will see another of the deep-freezing plants which have revolutionized the processing of fish in these parts. Fresh frozen fillets are rapidly replacing the age-old dried *klipp-*

fisk and *stokk-fisk* as export items, and are bringing a correspondingly new year-round prosperity to communities which formerly suffered much from seasonal unemployment.

The North Cape

On leaving Hammerfest, you have only 24 hours left of the four-day cruise from Trondheim, but most of them will be spent on the very top of Norway. The steamer crosses several stretches of water that open directly north of the Arctic Ocean, and on approaching the big island of Mageröy, it may be that you'll head into this "Ice-Sea" as the natives call it. You will sail right by that famous chunk of rock, the North Cape.

There's not much to see except a cliff of blackish granite, either from the water or on top, but if your life ambition has been to follow the example of King Oscar II of Norway and Sweden, who climbed this northernmost piece of Europe in 1873, you can do so. The ships call at Skarsvåg, from where buses are run to North Cape to save a really steep 1,000-foot climb. Perhaps the best idea is to step off the ship at Honningsvåg and take an evening bus to North Cape across arctic Mageröy (literally Meager Island). The North Cape Hall will greet you upon arrival with a panorama window offering a sweeping view, and perhaps the Midnight Sun hanging above the Arctic Ocean for good measure.

The road itself was opened by King Olav (then Prince) in 1956. It leads past a Lapp encampment at Nordmannset and offers magnificent views of the Cape itself. Honningsvåg is connected by an auto-ferry with Kåfjord, the nearest point on the mainland.

The steamer now crosses the mouths of three vast fjords—Porsanger, Lakse, and Tana—all of which cut far south into the mainland, and call at some fishing villages. But the main event after the North Cape is passing the enormous bird-rock of Svaerholtklubben on the tip of the peninsula between Porsanger Fjord and Lakse Fjord. Midnight will again find you with an unobstructed view to the north so, weather permitting, you'll have another chance to watch the sun toy with the horizon as it passes without interruption from setting to rising.

By 2.30 A.M. there'll be an opportunity to walk around the historic fortress of Vardöhus at Vardö, the easternmost town in Norway. The most ancient part of the stronghold, now long disappeared, was constructed in the early 1300s, while the present ramparts, shaped like an eight-pointed star, date from the 1730s.

Depending on which day of the week it is, the express steamer may or may not call at Vadsö, the administrative capital of Finnmark. This town is located on the upper edge of the wide Varanger Fjord which, unlike the previous three, cuts westward instead of south. In any case, early in the morning next day, you will reach the end station of the North Norway *hurtig-rute:* the important mining town of Kirkenes.

Between Allied bombing raids and Nazi earth-scorching, both Kirkenes and the Syd-Varanger iron mines were almost totally wrecked at the end of World War II. Today, the huge plant in Kirkenes produces by magnetic separation about 1 million tons of iron-ore concentrate annually.

Many interesting side-trips can be made from Kirkenes. First of all, a visit to the iron mines a few miles from town which, being open-pit affairs, can be seen just by looking at them from the road. Then there's the road south along the Pasvik River which forms most of the boundary between Norway and Soviet Russia. The 40-mile drive to Skogfoss, for example, will provide a good view of the friendly scenery—birch trees, green fields and rolling hills—which is astonishingly different from the stern rockiness of the North Cape country. And you can also have a glimpse of the land on the other shore, behind the Iron Curtain. Incidentally, it's forbidden to carry cameras into this area near the border, a regulation strictly enforced by Norwegian guards.

From Kirkenes you have two new ways of returning to Trondheim: swiftly and spectacularly by plane with landings at Lakselv, Alta, Bardufoss and Bodø; or slowly and fascinatingly by bus or car, "slowly" meaning in this case exactly three days to either Tromsö or Narvik, with two overnight stops. And while the plane trip presents a wonderful bird's-eye view of the top of Norway, the slower route overland is more rewarding.

Finnmark by Bus

You leave Kirkenes after early breakfast and drive along the lower side of Varanger Fjord to Tana bridge. Then the new road runs alongside the River Tana into Lapp country. The Tana is a long and interesting river, famous for heavy salmon. It also forms the border between Norway and Finland over a long distance. The road leaves Tana river at Karasjok, one of the largest Lapp villages on the Finnmark mountain plateau, and the day's journey ends at Lakselv on the Lakse Fjord.

Of the many things which impress you on this tour, probably the most remarkable is the tremendous differences between the rocky bareness of the Arctic coast, and the mildness and fertility of inland Finnmark. Here are farms with pastures as green as any you saw in western Norway, with healthy-looking cows, goats and sheep. True enough, little grain will ripen in this far north, even with 24 hours of sunshine during part of the summer, but potatoes and other root crops give a good yield.

Another striking characteristic is that everything up here is new: houses, barns, boats, piers, even the telegraph poles. All is new for the simple reason that the Nazis burned everything in 1944; hence any manmade structure dates from 1946 or later. But in between the villages, one can drive for scores of miles without seeing a habitation and sometimes without even meeting another vehicle.

Next morning you leave Lakselv for another day of scenic beauty. At Skaidi, you may make a detour to Hammerfest, but the main road continues southwards along Repparfjord salmon river to Alta on the Alta Fjord. The Alta River is one of the world's best salmon waters, and millionaires have been competing throughout the last century for fishing rights.

From Alta a highway runs about 80 miles south to Kautokeino, a village chiefly inhabited by Lapps. This is a side-trip which can be made the year round and will let you see the semi-nomads in their own setting rather than as a tourist attraction on the side of the road. There are a number of souvenir shops in the village, as well as the atelier of Regine and Frank Juhls whose design jewelry has become famous outside Norway too. There are designs based on traditional Lappish jewelry as well as modern ones. Even if you don't intend buying any jewelry go and visit Juhls' atelier.

The Arctic Highway continues along several fjords, also across the Kvenangen peninsula, on to Sørkjosen in Troms county, where you spend the night.

Troms by Bus

The third day you have a pleasant change in routine by riding the ferry straight across Lyngen Fjord instead of following around its shores, or you may go by the new road along the eastern side of the fjord. This may also be your introduction to the custom in North Norway of allowing bus-passengers to help support the ferry company, even though they have already paid for their through ticket by bus. (It seems that this arrangement simplifies bookkeeping for the bus companies.)

Soon you are speeding nearly south along the west shore of Lyngen Fjord to Nordkjosbotn, at the south end of still another fjord, this time an old acquaintance called Bals Fjord, which stretches more or less north for 40 miles to Tromsö.

Olsborg is a hamlet consisting of a small inn, a service station and a few houses, in the picturesque district bordering the Målselv River. This part of Troms Province was colonized 150 years ago by pioneers from the eastern valleys in lower Norway, and today is a thriving agricultural district with solid houses and barns, and, in good years, a harvest of grain beyond the needs of the inhabitants.

In the afternoon the bus passes the sprawling Bardufoss Airport and climbs over a 1,400-foot pass. Here there is a good view out to sea, or rather towards the Vågs Fjord through which you sailed after leaving Harstad. Then it's down to sea level again at Bjerkvik in the midst of both spectacular and historic country, for here are many scenes of battle from World War II. Within an hour you will have crossed the magnificent new bridge across Rombaken Fjord and entered Narvik in Nordland county.

Nordland by Bus and Train

Narvik is a name that awakes a response in most travelers, whether from the Continent or from English-speaking lands. For here occurred the great naval engagement in the Ofot Fjord in April, 1940, when the Germans seized Narvik, and the ensuing campaign in which Norwegian troops, aided by British, French and Polish detachments, inflicted the first defeat of World War II upon the Nazi military machine by recapturing the town, so General Fleischer of Norway was the first field commander to defeat Hitler in battle. Narvik was, of course, a much sought-after prize because of its importance as the shipping port for the valuable iron ore from the Swedish mines located a short way over the border at Kiruna. The town has been rebuilt and is a pleasant place. While you are there, take a look at the small museum which commemorates the action with a model reconstruction.

Besides the economic importance of Narvik, it can well stand on its own feet as a tourist center in competition with any part of Norway for its panorama of fjords with rows of snow-topped peaks in the background. During the Midnight Sun season, the combination sunset-sunrises enhance the scene with those incredible color and light effects you have now seen so many times. However, for a really breathtaking view of all this the cable railway (Fjellheisen) will carry you from the town to the Fagerness mountain plateau—well, go and look for yourself.

Ore-Train Route

The best way to combine economic studies with sightseeing is to ride the ore-carrying railway up to the mines and back, or at least as far as Björnefjell on the Norwegian-Swedish border. You can ride the regular passenger trains up and back, about one hour each way, returning in time to have dinner in Narvik and spend the evening looking around the town. As at Kirkenes there is great activity in Narvik. Ore trains run day and night, unloading their valuable contents at the tremendous quay installations where several freighters are always tied up having their holds filled, while out in the fjord are others waiting their turn. Along the streets at night and in the cafés you'll see and hear the sailors of a dozen nationalities; all of which adds to the impression of a busy cosmopolitan port.

The fourth and final day of the bus journey provides even more scenic variation and grandeur than before. Now begins a really amphibious part of the journey which we'll summarize as follows: first, a mixed run of 50 miles on dry land and a 40-minute cruise across a genuine fjord, Tys Fjord. Again there's a pleasant 20-mile dry run to Innhavet. Here you can look out over the Sag Fjord towards Svolvaer and the Lofoten Islands. But your day has only begun; moreover, you find that the stages are now getting longer. Thus it's 44 miles over rising and falling land to Bonåsjöen, a 15-minute sail across Leirfjord, and then a mere 30 miles to Fauske. At this far-inland port town you must make up your mind whether to return to Bodø—due west of here on the Skjerstad Fjord—for a closer look at the Saltstraumen *maelstrom* or to continue southward.

Fauske is your junction for the Nordlandsbane to Trondheim or Bodø, if that is your destination. Hardy travelers may want to take the night express that same evening to Trondheim. But a better plan is to take this train to Lönsdal only, spend a night or a couple of days there in magnificent mountain scenery, with a Lapp encampment, excellent trout fishing, and the wildly luxurious Junkerdal valley close at hand, and continue by day train. Whatever you do, about a half-hour from

Lönsdal there will be a long blast on the locomotive's whistle. Nothing to cause alarm—it merely marks the crossing of the Arctic Circle.

Mo-i-Rana is only a brief stop for the summer expresses, but it's a fascinating place for anyone wishing to combine hiking, glacier-exploration, etc., with the study of the Norwegian kind of industrialization based on abundant hydro-electric power. The largest electric-process steel mill in Scandinavia was built by the Norwegian Government, partly financed by American contributions to the European Recovery Program which released Norwegian capital for this project.

The afternoon brings you mile after mile down the long narrow handle of Norway, with stops every half-hour or so at the most important places. There's Grong, junction for the side-line to Namsos, and Steinkjer, scene of crushing air attacks upon the British Expeditionary Force which, in 1940, was trying to make its way south from Namsos.

You are now in sight of the upper end of the Trondheim Fjord, and back in North Tröndelag province. The express next stops at Verdal, where it's possible for those who are historically inclined to alight and make the brief side-trip by bus or taxi to Stiklestad, catching a local train afterwards to Trondheim.

Spitsbergen

Although it's highly unlikely you'll spend any time on the inhospitable archipelago which comprises Spitsbergen, a number of cruise ships do call in at Longyear, its administrative center. Since the treaty of 1920, Spitsbergen has been recognized as Norwegian territory but Russia still mines coal there and there is a sizeable Russian community. For the visitor, however, it's the sheer magnificence of the icy wastes which provide the attraction, especially in good weather. The icefloes provide a glimpse of a world far removed from everyday surroundings. Walking trips of 4 or 11 days were introduced in 1982. Programs are available from the Norwegian Tourist Board.

PRACTICAL INFORMATION FOR THE NORTH

 WHEN TO COME. The Midnight Sun is visible at the North Cape from May 14 to July 30, but this is only one of the marvels of the north. June, July, and August are the best months—though motorists must observe that some of the Finnmark mountain crossings may not be open before June 1. The Lofoten cod fishing is a great event, best visited in March, when the trip can be combined with skiing in the Narvik district.

 WHAT TO SEE. Nordland: The striking mountain formations of Torghatten, Seven Sisters, Hestmannen, and Rödöylöven (Red Island Lion) are seen from the coastal express steamer. Off the beaten track are some of the world's most remarkable peaks: Reka on the Langöy Island in Vesterålen, and Tilthorn and Stetind between Fauske and Narvik. Fjords and narrows include the Skjomen Fjord near Narvik, the Saltstraumen Eddy near Bodø, and the Raftsund (in the coastal express fairway) north of Svolvaer. The Lofoten Isles with alpine peaks rising directly from the sea, the bird sanctuaries at Röst (reached by local steamer from Bodø or Reine), the "maelstrom" Moskenestraumen of literary fame is passed on the way to Röst. Near Mo are a couple of very interesting grottos, and the Svartisen glaciers. The Junkerdal valley near Lönsdal should not be missed, nor the Midnight Sun view at Bodø.

Troms: Here the famous sights include the Lyngen Fjord and Lyngen Alps, the valleys of Spansdal, Signaldal with the Otertind peak, and the Reisdal with the Mollius waterfall. Another spectacular waterfall is the salmon-filled Malangsfoss.

Finnmark: The bird sanctuaries of Hjelmsöy and Svaerholt (both passed on the coastal steamer), the greatest—Syltefjordstauren—is off the beaten track west of Vardö. Finnkjerka—the most elegant sea-cliff of Norway—seen from the steamer near Kjöllefjord. The Öksfjord Glacier. The Lapp villages of Karasjok and Kautokeino. The picturesque fortress of Vardöhus. And, of course, the goal of all travelers, the North Cape.

 HOW TO GET ABOUT. The enormous distances of North Norway demand time. Chief means of transport is the daily year-round service maintained by the fine **coastal express steamers,** sailing from Bergen to Kirkenes and back in 11 days and calling at important coastal places en route.

From Trondheim, the **North Norway Railway** (Nordlandsbanen) will take you to Fauske and Bodø north of the Arctic Circle in a day. On top of that comes a one day bus ride to Narvik, two days to Tromsö, and four days to reach Kirkenes on this longest **bus** line in Europe, called Nord-Norge-Bussen.

Narvik can be reached **by train** from Stockholm (25 hours), and Narvik is an excellent place to enter the North Cape Bus for a ride to Kirkenes. Return by coastal steamer or plane, as time and purse allow.

By plane one can go from Oslo to Bodø (1½ hrs), Tromsö (3 hrs) and Bardufoss (3 hrs), Alta (4½ hrs), Lakselv (6 hrs), and Kirkenes (7 hrs).

Two mountain passages on Highway 6 in Finnmark get blocked by snow every winter. The bus company plays safe and stops this route on October 15th. SAS and Wideroe flights and coastal steamer services are operated all the year.

MOTORING. Norway's Number One highway—E6— will take you from Oslo and right across the Artic Circle to Kirkenes near the Soviet Russian frontier. It is also the gateway to North Cape, but since the road distance from Oslo to North Cape is 2233 km or 1383 miles, there are few people who can afford the time to do it. Many prefer to travel by air to one of the northern-most towns and rent a car there. The distance from North Cape to Tromsø is 484km (299 miles), Narvik 750 (464) and Bodø 925 (572). The return trip can be made via Finland or Sweden or by coastal steamer—but in the latter case it is essential to have reservations long in advance.

HOTELS. It is advisable to plan any trip north of Trondheim well in advance in view of the limited accom-modations. Generally speaking, the best hotels in North Norway are found in the towns, which are in themselves sufficiently small and picturesque to provide a resort atmosphere. In Finnmark there are several inns along the Arctic Highway, which cater to the in-transit tourist. The best known of these inns are located in Alta, Ifjord, Skaidi, and Lakselv. The best inns and hotels along the Arctic Highway in Troms are found in Kvaenangsfjell, Sørkjosen, Olderdalen, Lyngseid, Nordkjosbotn, Olsborg and Gratangen. Fine inns along the Arctic Highway in Nordland at Innhavet, Rognan and Majavatn.

ALTA (Finnmark), salmon fishing in river Alta. *Alta Hotel* (M), 120 beds, all rooms with bath/shower; *Altafjord Vertshus* (M), 117 beds, many rooms with shower, sauna; *Alta Youth Hostel* (I), 52 beds.

BARDU (Troms). *Bardu Motor Hotel* (M), 78 beds, all rooms with facilities; *Bardu Gjestgiveri* (I), 50 beds, some rooms with bath/shower.

BODØ (Nordland), excursion to Saltstraumen maelstrom, 33 km from town. *SAS Royal* (E), Storgaten 2, 290 beds, all rooms with facilities; *Grand* (M), Storgaten 3, 91 rooms, many with bath/shower; *SAS Norrøna* (M), Storgaten 4, 200 beds, most rooms with facilities; *Flatvold Youth Hostel* (I), Rønvik-krysset, 132 beds; *Rønvikfjell restaurant* (M), outstanding views of ocean and mountains.

FAUSKE (Nordland). *Fauske Hotel* (M), 100 beds; *Fauske Youth Hostel* (I), 114 beds.

GRATANGEN (Troms). *Gratangen Turiststasjon* (M), 43 rooms, 3 with bath, sauna.

HAMMERFEST (Finnmark). *Brassica Pension* (M), 30 beds; *Finnmarksbo Pension* (M), 32 beds; *Grand Rica* (M), 120 beds, many rooms with bath/shower; *Hammerfest Youth Hostel* (I), 56 beds.

HARSTAD (Troms). *Grand* (E), Strandgate 9, 115 beds, most rooms with facilities; *Viking Nordic* (M), Fjordgate 2, 160 beds, all rooms with facilities, swimming, sauna; *Stangnes Youth Hostel* (I), Plassenvei 27, 90 beds.

HONNINGSVÅG (Finnmark), small town on Magerøy island, situated 2110 km from North Pole. *SAS Nordkapp Hotel* (E), 250 beds, all rooms with facilities, restaurant, cafeteria. *Havly Pension* (M), 57 beds, some rooms with shower; *NAF Nordkapp Youth Hostel* (I), at North Cape, 34 km from town, 40 beds.

KARASJOK (Finnmark), Lapp village, 30,000 reindeer, Lapp museum, Karasjok library has world's greatest collection of literature on Lapps. *Karasjok Gjestgiveri* (M), 66 beds, sauna; *Karasjok Tourist Center* (I), 65 beds, sauna; *Karasjok Youth Hostel* (I), 12 beds.

KAUTOKEINO (Finnmark), Lapp village on Finnmark mountain plateau, famous Easter race by Lapps and reindeer on ice-bound river; *Kautokeino Tourist Hotel* (M), 96 beds, all rooms with facilities, sauna; *Kautokeino Youth Hostel* (I), 56 beds, modern.

KIRKENES (Finnmark), 50 km from Soviet frontier, large iron ore mines at Bjørnevatn, 11 km from Kirkenes. *Kirkenes Rica Tourist Hotel* (E), 117 beds, many rooms with facilities, sauna.

LØNSDAL (Nordland), 1670 ft, situated near "Arctic Circle" on Saltfjell mountain plateau, good ski touring. *Polarsirkelen Rica Mountain Hotel* (M), 90 beds, most rooms with facilities, sauna.

MÅLSELV (Troms). *Olsborg Gjestgiveri* (M), Moen. *Rundhaug Hotel* (M), Bakkehaug, 46 beds.

MO I RANA (Nordland). *Holmen* (M), 50 beds, all rooms with bath/shower, grill, cafeteria, swimming; *Meyergården* (M), 250 beds, most rooms with facilities; *Fageråsen Youth Hostel* (I), 64 beds.

MOSJØEN (Nordland), salmon fishing in river Vefsna, folk museum. *Fru Haugans* (M), 120 beds, 38 rooms with bath/shower; *Lyngengården* (M), 50 beds, 17 rooms with bath/shower; *Mosjøen Youth Hostel* (I), in Sandvik folk high school, 140 beds, swimming, sauna.

NARVIK (Nordland), major export harbor for iron ore from Sweden, chairlift to top of Fagernesfjell at 1970 ft, grand skiing terrain. *Grand Royal Hotel* (E), Kongensgate 64, 230 beds, 118 rooms with bath/shower and radio, restaurant, bars; *Nordstjernen Pension* (M), Kongensgate 26, 55 beds, some rooms with bath/shower; *Victoria Royal Hotel* (M), Dronningensgate 56, 78 beds, most rooms with facilities; *Breidablikk Gjestgiveri* (I), Tore Hundsgate 41, 48 beds; *Malm Pension* (I), Frydenlundsgate 28, 50 beds, some rooms with bath/shower; *Nordkalotten Youth Hostel* (I), Havnegate 3, 110 beds, modern and popular.

NORTH CAPE (Finnmark), northermost point in Europe at 71 10' 21", on mountain plateau with 1013 ft sheer precipice into Arctic Ocean, Midnight Sun from May 14 to July 30; *Nordkapphallen* restaurant and cafeteria with post office, expensive car park, no camping.

SKAIDI (Finnmark), salmon fishing in Repparfjord and Skaidi rivers. *Repparfjord Tourist Hotel* (M), 104 beds, most rooms with bath/shower, sauna; *Repparfjord Youth Center* (I), Kvalsund, 85 beds; *Skaidi Gjestehus* (I), 54 beds, sauna.

SØRKJOSEN (Troms). *Sørkjos Hotel* (M), 80 beds, some rooms with bath/shower, swimming, sauna.

SORTLAND (Nordland), on Langøy island in Vesterålen. *Sortland Nordic Hotel* (E), 120 beds, most rooms with facilities.

STAMSUND (Nordland), on Vestvågøy island in the Lofotens. *SAS Lofoten Hotel* (M), 56 beds, most rooms with facilities, swimming, sauna; *Justad Rorbu Youth Hostel* (I), in fishermen's dwelling, 50 beds, primitive.

SVOLVAER (Nordland), on Austvågøy island in the Lofotens. *Lofoten Nordic Hotel* (M), 98 beds, all rooms with facilities; *Vita-Nova Motel* (M), 80 beds, some rooms with bath/shower; *Svolvaer Youth Hostel* (I), 150 beds.

TROMSØ (Troms), on island in a narrow sound, hemmed in by mountains, connected with mainland by 1036m long bridge, Arctic museum, aquarium, Northern Lights observatory, whaling station at Skjelnan, chairlift to top of Storsteinen. *Grand Nordic Hotel* (E), Storgate 44, 300 beds, all rooms with facilities; *SAS Royal Hotel* (E), Sjøgate 10, 370 beds, all rooms with facilities; *Tromsø Hotel* (E), new in 1982, 46 rooms, all with bath, TV, radio, and telephone; *Saga Hotel* (M), Rich Withs plass 2, 100 beds, all rooms with facilities; *Tromsø Youth Hostel* (I), Øvre Breivang, 64 beds.

VADSØ (Finnmark), on Varanger fjord, town museum, Esbensen manor is only remaining patrician building left in Finnmark, airship tower used by Amundsen's "Norge" in 1926 and Nobile's "Italia" in 1928. *Vadsø Hotel* (M), 99 beds, most rooms with facilities.

VARDØ (Finnmark), on an island; now connected with the mainland by a new 2800m tunnel, completed in 1982. Vardøhus octagonal fortress built in 1737, Vardø museum, Reinøya island with large bird sanctuaries. *Vardø Hotel* (E), 86 beds, all rooms with facilities, sauna.

 SPORTS. Fishing is *the* pastime in North Norway. The salmon rivers are famous, particularly those in Finnmark, where you may fish for a trifling fee: star attractions are the world famous Alta River in Finnmark and the Malangsfoss in Troms, where salmon is a certainty. The trout fishing on the Finnmark mountain plateau is fabulous, but includes a bit of walking.

The mountains of Lyngen, Lofoten, and the Narvik district lend themselves to strenuous *rock climbing*. Here there is still scope for exploring new routes. *Hiking* in the mountains of North Norway is only for the experienced, as the trails are seldom marked and staffed huts are few and far between.

Boats can be rented for trips on the Reisa, Karasjokka, Kautokeino, and Tana rivers. There's excellent *skiing* in March, preferably around Narvik (Narvik and Gratangen 1,000 feet), and Lönsdal (1,700 feet), south of Bodø.

Lofoten Islands Shanty Hire. Fishermen's shanties, built on the waterside, can be rented from about 490 to 770 Nkr per night (6–8 bunks). Accommodation is basic and meant for the adventurous who seek the world's best sea-fishing off Europe's wildest coastal scenery. Visitors must bring camping type equipment, sleeping bags, etc.: only bunks and mattresses, primitive furniture is provided. Boats can be hired. Information from Nordland Turisttrafikkomité (see below).

USEFUL ADDRESSES. Tourist Information. On **Nordland:** Nordland Turisttrafikkomité, Torggate 1, 8000 Bodø. On **Troms:** Troms Turisttrafikkomité, Parkgate 18, 9000 Troms. On **Finnmark:** Turisttrafikkomité for Finnmark, 9510 Elvebakken.

Youth Hostels: Plentiful, especially on the Finnmark plateau where the State's mountain chalets receive hostellers. Specially built hostel in Tromsö; a large one open year round in Narvik; the one in Harstad has been termed Europe's most original

Camping: The best sites are found at Kirkenes, Hammerfest, Alta, Kunes, Tromso, Harstad, Narvik, Bodø, Nesna and Mo.

SWEDEN

PRELUDE TO SWEDEN

Land of Lakes and Forests

Sweden is the largest of the Scandinavian countries in both population and size—over eight million people on 173,000 square miles of land and water. Its elongated shape, a jocular American visitor once remarked, makes it about as long as the Mississippi River—and just about as wide. Its greatest length, north to south is 978 miles, practically touching the European continent proper at Denmark and stretching north to well beyond the Arctic Circle. The greatest width is 310 miles.

Dozens of visitors have attempted to describe Sweden in a few words. An Englishman once said it was a country of forests and lakes, in which the cities, mostly along the coasts, form small beachheads. The columnist Marquis Childs called it the land of the "middle way", largely because of its program of social reform, and another author, Hudson Strode, had something of the same thing in mind when he named it "model for a world". Again, it has been described as a "modern democracy on ancient foundations", "champion of peace", "land of outdoor life", and more. All of these catch-phrases say something, and something of importance, about Sweden, but none of them tell more than a partial truth. For Sweden, despite a homogeneous population, an ancient tradition, and a highly organized society, is a country of contrasts.

375

Take the geography alone. The fertile, often treeless plains of the southernmost province, Scania (or Skåne, to use the Swedish name), granary of Sweden, give no hint of the northern wilderness where, beyond the Arctic Circle, nomadic Lapps still follow their reindeer herds. The highly cultivated, highly cultured life in many of the cities is a far cry from the hut of the lumberjack in the deep forests. The fully mechanized industries—among the most productive anywhere in the world—compete with an old tradition of fine handicraft, and a hand-loom is not unusual even in city dwellings. Church membership is theoretically 100 per cent, yet only a fraction of the population attends services regularly. You can't summarize it in ten words.

Sweden is probably best known for her social reform program and her successful efforts to remain at peace in a precarious world. Relations with the United States and England have been good almost without exception, and there are strong ties with both countries. The close contact between England and Sweden—which may have reached its first peak in the Viking Era—is reflected in hundreds of words of common origin. Here are some Swedish words, which mean exactly what they do in English: *arm, hand, man, son, hare, finger.* Swedish has borrowed many English words in recent years. In the newspapers you will find *lockout, handicap, jeep, good will, knockout, okay, all right,* and the like—perhaps particularly sports and technical terms.

In three years of posing the question to hundreds of Swedes all over the country, I have still to meet one who does not have a relative in the United States. This is not peculiar, since Sweden lost about one-fifth of her population in the great emigration wave to America, which reached its peak about the turn of the century or a little earlier. At one time, Swedes were pulling up stakes and moving out at the rate of 1,000 per week, and "America fever" is still a recognized entry in the dictionary. Those who return to Sweden for another look—after perhaps 50 years or more in America—and the children and grandchildren of those who sailed out earlier, find a country vastly changed. The great wave of emigration and the need to put a stop to it, if the country were to survive, undoubtedly played a part in the peaceful social revolution of the last decades.

You will find the Swedes themselves somewhat reserved but friendly. Most of them welcome visitors from abroad; they have a great curiosity about the rest of the world and its inhabitants. Somehow they often find it easier to converse with strangers than with each other. And don't worry about the language, you'll get along with English anywhere—perhaps combined with a little sign language now and again—and you'll be amazed at the number of people who handle English with a fluency that bespeaks years of intimacy. Particularly in public places, don't ever assume you're not being understood, because the chances are ten to one someone is getting every word. After all, the Swede sitting across from you in the train compartment may have spent five years with Uncle Ole on a farm in Minnesota, or be a graduate of Harvard or Oxford.

PRACTICAL INFORMATION FOR SWEDEN

WHAT WILL IT COST. See the *Facts at Your Fingertips* section earlier in this volume for general information and specific hotel rates. As everywhere in Scandinavia, costs are rising, and a 10% inflation may be expected for 1984. Sweden has some hotels of international deluxe standard, and outside of Stockholm and Gothenburg there is plenty of good and moderate accommodation.

Some local costs: SEK: Cigarettes, English or American 10–14; laundering a shirt 11; pressing a dress 45; dry cleaning, man's suit 58; dress 50; man's haircut 40; manicure 35; entertainment, opera 30–75, theater 30–75, cinema 25–35.

A Typical Day for One Person.

Hotel, moderate, one meal and breakfast, service included	300SEK
Restaurant meal	60
Transportation, 2 taxis, 4 trams or buses	75
Entertainment, entrance fees	40
Beer	15
Coffee, tea	15
Miscellaneous, 10%	45
	550SEK

By using hotel checks and looking for tourist menus, this sum can be reduced during summer months.

Average restaurant prices (in SEK): Breakfast 16–25; expensive lunch or dinner, 70 and up; moderate meal 30–60; inexpensive 25–35; wine: glass 15+, carafe 30–40; beer: glass 6–15 (there are different strengths of beer); cocktail 23+; coffee 5–8; service 13%.

Note: In the Central Station restaurants at Stockholm, Gothenburg and Malmö, you can have as much breakfast as you can eat for 30 SEK.

TIPPING. Not necessary to tip in hotels and restaurants, as service charge is included. Taxi drivers expect a 10–15% tip, as do hairdressers and barbers. Cloakroom attendants charge 3–4 SEK per coat. Rail porters charge: 6 SEK for the first two items of baggage, 4 for each one thereafter.

WHEN TO COME. From the standpoint of summer weather, the best time to come is from late May through August. July is the Swedes' vacation month—there's a mass exodus of Stockholmers from Stockholm and a mass influx of people from elsewhere into Stockholm. You can never depend on the weather, of course, but even early May, September, and October do offer some distinct advantages. You get beautiful sunny days, if a shade on the brisk side, and you also find it easier to get hotel accommodations.

For winter sports—from Christmas to the beginning of June, depending upon the region you select. Except for Lapland, the peak season is generally February-March. You won't need floodlighting if you go to Lapland for skiing under the Midnight Sun. In the second half of May the Svenska Mässan International Trade Fair is held at Gothenburg.

 WHAT TO SEE. Sweden's majestic capital of Stockholm is the *must* among cities, and the great port of Gothenburg (Göteborg) is worth a visit also. The two are connected by the Göta Canal, running the whole breadth of the country, which provides a wonderful trip, but, since it is a slow one, an excursion only for those with about three days to spare. The medieval city of Visby, one of the great centers of the Middle Ages, is another top sight in Sweden. Sweden also has Midnight Sun trips—by air, train or bus.

Also well worth visiting are Uppsala, with the largest cathedral in Scandinavia; Sigtuna, which is famous for many old buildings, especially St. Olaf's Church ruin, which was also a fortress; Gripsholm Castle and Skokloster Castle, both one-day excursions from Stockholm; the château country of Scania (Skåne); the folklore province of Dalarna; and for relaxation, what is probably the Number One resort of Sweden, Båstad.

 HOW TO GET ABOUT. An efficient **railway** network operated by the Swedish State Railways (SJ) makes all parts of the country readily accessible. Circular tour tickets at a somewhat reduced rate offer a variety of attractive itineraries.

There are also daily **air** services within Sweden, maintained by SAS and Linjeflyg AB (LIN). SAS-RESO operate roundtrip "Midnight Sun" flights from Stockholm to Kiruna from mid-June to mid-July. Check on discounts for youngsters, senior citizens, accompanying spouse, or on certain flights at the airline office.

Private planes can be hired at several airports in Sweden, e.g. at Bromma-Stockholm (Crownair-Flygtjänst-Swedair), Gothenburg (Kungsair), Malmö (Malmros Aviation AB) and Umeå (Laplandsflyg).

In summer regular **boat** services ply from Gothenburg and Stockholm to the islands of the archipelagos; to the islands of Gotland and Öland (also inter-island services) and to Ven in Öresund. There are cruises by pleasure steamer on the famous Göta Canal, on the Dalslands and Kinda Canals, and on several inland waterways.

The Swedish State Railways operate a large network of **buses** all over Sweden. In addition to the regular traffic there is a network service of express coaches over longer distances. In northernmost Sweden the Post Office has a network of coach services. These coaches, which deliver mail in outlying parts, are modern and comfortable.

As a rule, only the main roads in sparsely-populated Sweden are paved. You will find them, however, extremely well-engineered. Because of the distances between points of interest (except in the south) and the sandy or gravelly condition of the secondary roads, Sweden is not too well-suited for touring by bicycle. Suggestions for bike tours and maps are available at local tourist offices.

TOURS The 2-day *Swedish Crystal Tour* links Stockholm with Copenhagen, and visits the famous glassworks in the province of Småland. You fly to Kalmar, overnight at the Stadshotellet in Växjö, continue by bus to Malmö and then by hydrofoil to Copenhagen.

Bus tours over the "Top of Europe" (Norway, Sweden and Finland north of the Arctic Circle) are operated regularly by the Swedish State Railways and RESO, Luleå. The extensive *North Cape Tour,* which departs from the northern town of Luleå twice weekly from mid-June to mid-August, is an 8-day excursion into the country above the Arctic Circle, from the desolate tundra-like wilderness in Finnish Lapp territory to the awe-inspiring fjord scenery of the Norwegian Atlantic coast, ending at Narvik in Norway. The RESO tour is a 7-day excursion which departs from the mining city of Kiruna every day from mid-June until the beginning of August. The Dala bus runs daily Gothenburg-Mora (in the province of Dalarna) and returns from June 1 to Aug. 31.

HOTELS. Most towns have a centrally located hotel booking office *(Hotellcentral* or *Rumsförmedling).* In almost every provincial town you will encounter a "Grand Hotell", "Stora Hotellet" or "Stadshotellet", and you may rest assured that they are invariably good. Advance reservations are recommended in hotels and motels, particularly in the larger towns, during the high season (May 15 to Sept. 30). A 15 per cent service charge is included in the price of the room. Many hotels include breakfast in the rate.

Several chains of hotels and restaurants operate in Stockholm and throughout the country, catering at different price levels. Two well-known state supported companies have useful "initial" names—SARA and RESO.

There are good pensions in all parts of the country as well as comfortable resort hotels often open all year round, that are especially prepared to cater to foreign visitors. At seaside resorts on the west coast in Bohuslän, you may rent rooms in a fisherman's cottage and take your meals at a restaurant; accommodation is clean, if primitive.

Motels: *Esso Petroleum Co.* runs 53 top modern motor hotels and 32 tavernas with motels from Malmö in the south to Luleå in northern Sweden. 15% of the rooms are smoke-free. Other fuel companies also run motels and motor hotels: *OK* (13), *BP* (17) and *Shell* (4). *MHF* (The Union of Temperance Drivers of Sweden) have six excellent motor hotels.

FOOD AND DRINK. The Swedish *smörgåsbord,* someone once said, is often abused in spelling, pronunciation and preparation. *Smörgåsbordet* is a large table usually placed in the middle of the dining room and easily accessible to all guests. It is literally groaning under a large number of delicacies, and you help yourself—as often as you like—to whatever you fancy. To appreciate it properly, however, the various dishes should be eaten in proper succession and not helter-skelter. Traditionally, the order goes something like this: pickled herring (possibly more than one kind) with a boiled potato; a couple more fish courses, probably cold smoked salmon, fried Baltic Sea herring, and sardines in oil; the meats, liver paste, boiled ham, sliced beef, not uncommonly smoked reindeer; a salad, fruit and/or vegetable; and finally the cheeses. Bread and butter is served throughout.

Many of the items that appear in the *smörgåsbord* may be familiar to you. Some of the appetizers which you may not have tasted, and which are recommended, are herring on ice with chives and sour cream sauce, fried Baltic Sea herring, smoked eel (delicious, really), smoked reindeer (likewise), and the Swedish Chantilly-type cheese, milder and firmer than its French cousin.

And finally you end up with a dessert such as fruit salad or pastry. A main dish after the *smörgåsbord* is optional (you are unlikely to need one)! and costs extra.

Other national dishes are crayfish, in season from August to September and the occasion for a rash of informal parties, preferably outdoors; pea soup and pork, followed by pancakes, traditional Thursday supper from autumn through spring; and in November, particularly in southern Sweden, goose.

Generally, the Swedes do better with fish than they do with meat. If you like good, tender beef, stick to the *à la carte* menu.

Practically everything in the way of wines and liquors is regularly available at the better restaurants and bars, even the latest cocktail, although any kind of mixed drink seems somehow out of place in this land where liquor is traditionally drunk straight (neat) with no nonsense, thank you.

Quite another matter is the question of drinking hours. Before noon (1 P.M. on Sundays) you're doomed to soft drinks (not even wine or beer), unless you buy your own bottle at one of the state-owned liquor shops, which open at 9 A.M. (closed Saturdays and Sundays). At midnight everything is put away again except at the "nightclubs" that are allowed to stay open until 2 or 3 A.M.

Anyhow, if you're going to eat Swedish, order snaps and beer or table water with the *smörgåsbord*. *Snaps* is the collective name for *aquavit* or *brännvin*, Swedish liquor made under a variety of brand names and with flavors varying from practically tasteless to sweetly spiced. Recommended brands: Skåne, Herrgårds, and O. P. Andersson. Swedish beers are good—made in a variety of light and dark qualities and strengths.

A special tourist menu at SEK 36 is available at many restaurants; half price for children under 12. Summer only.

 **ENTERTAINMENT.** Stockholm has pretty well cornered the market in this category, having added a number of "nightclubs" to its varied musical and dramatic fare. A great number of recently opened clubs, discotheques and pubs is part of the new "Swinging Stockholm". Other towns are following suit. Gothenburg, in addition, offers concerts, drama, and entertainment in Liseberg Park in summer, while Malmö is justifiably proud of its modern City Theater.

 SPORTS. In addition to a long coastline and many islands, Sweden has 96,000 lakes, so it is no wonder that **sailing** is everyman's sport. The principal sailing places are Sandhamn and Saltsjöbaden (in the Stockholm archipelago), Gothenburg, Marstrand and Hälsingborg (west coast). Selected seaside spots: near Hälsingborg, the entrance from Denmark, are the popular resorts of Mölle and Båstad, the latter being one of the most fashionable seaside spots in Sweden, with golf course and fine tennis courts. Torekov, farther north, is an attractive little fishing village. Also popular are Tylösand (sand beaches) near Halmstad, and Marstrand (rock bathing) outside Gothenburg. Snäckgärdsbaden, outside Visby on the Isle of Gotland, is a popular Baltic resort.

Popular **golf** courses are located at Båstad, Falsterbo, Mölle (in the south), Djursholm, Drottningholm, Kevinge, Lidingö and Saltsjöbaden (near Stockholm), Hovås (near Gothenburg), and Kronholmen (on the isle of Gotland), Tylösand (near Halmstad on the west coast), and Rättvik (in Dalarna). Most towns and tourist resorts have **tennis courts.** Sweden has about 600 well-equipped **camping** sites. The mountains in the north, in Jämtland, Härjedalen and Lapland, are ideal for **hiking** excursions. August and September is the best time for a visit there, as the midges are not as prevalent as in mid-summer, and the cloudberries *(hjortron)*, like yellow blackberries, are ripe for gathering.

Hunting is excellent, with an abundance of moose, deer, and willow grouse. Sweden claims that her moose areas in Jämtland and Norrland produce the best trophies in that country and the largest in Europe. The open season usually begins on the second Monday of September in north Sweden; in other parts of Sweden the equivalent date is the second Monday in October, and the open season lasts only from two to six days. The Jämtland/Härjedalen area, 350 miles north of Stockholm, may be reached in 9 hours by train. The Jämtland Harjedalen Tourist Association arranges special journeys for moose hunts. The Norrland province is 750 miles north of Stockholm. Its hub for big game hunts is Luleå, which is best reached by air. Willow grouse shooting with a gun dog is thrilling. One of the best spots is near Kiruna, where experienced guides with dogs are available. The season runs from Sept. 1–30. A smart act is to hunt feather-footed grouse for the first five days and then join a moose hunt. Licenses and permits are required. Organized hunting trips are arranged by Mr. P. Mariassy, Grevgatan 28, II, Stockholm, or Sverek, S-17193 Solna.

Sweden's wealth of lakes, streams, mountain reservoirs, and coastal waters offer fine and varied **fishing**. For salmon fishing with a rod, the Mörrum River and the Ätran in the south are the best places in spring and September. Fly fishing for salmon trout is popular in the rivers and streams in Norrland, where hotels and boardinghouses often have their own fishing waters. Fishing tours are arranged in the province of Jämtland by Jämtland Tourist Association, Rådhusplan, Östersund. For fishing in the mountain regions of Lapland apply to Nordkalottresor, Box 242, 95123 Luleå and to Västerbotten Tourist Office, Box 317, 5–90107, Umeå. Pike and perch are caught on the east coast and in the lakes. On the west coast you can spin for cod, tuna (mid-Aug. through Sept.) and other deep-sea fish.

 WINTER SPORTS. Mountains run like a backbone along the Norwegian frontier all the way to the Arctic Circle and beyond. The four provinces of this area are the **skiing** regions par excellence of Sweden. Dalarna, the southernmost province, is nearest to Stockholm and its mountains are lower than in the other provinces. Next, going northward, is Härjedalen, smallest of the provinces and least accessible. Jåmtland is probably the top skiing region because of its accessibility and better accommodations. There are two reasons why Lapland has not nosed out Jåmtland for first place: distance from Stockholm and the lateness with which the season starts. For beginners, the Dalarna resorts are best; for experts, and long distance enthusiasts, Lapland and Jämtland. (More detailed information on facilities is given in the regional practical information sections.) **Cross country skiing** or **ski touring** is very popular in Sweden and most communities have ski trails. Many of them are lit up during the night.

Curling is played fairly extensively—there are 38 clubs in Sweden. The Swedes, like the Norwegians, prefer speed **skating** to figure skating, but do not practise it quite so assiduously. **Ice hockey** is played, and the Swedes are the champions at the Scandinavian game of bandy, which differs from hockey in that it is played with a ball instead of a puck.

In probably no other country in the world is one of those most thrilling ice sports so well developed as in Sweden—**sail skating**, and its grown-up brother, **ice yachting.** Conditions in southern Sweden are perfect for it—large lakes, which provide wide unbroken expanses of ice. Other winter sports include trotting races on ice, fishing through the ice, and sleigh rides, usually scheduled for moonlit nights and enlivened by the glare of flaming torches.

 MEET THE SWEDES. There are many Americans who go to Sweden to trace their ancestry. They are advised before departure to contact one of the following organizations: *Emigrantregister,* Norra Strandgatan 4, Box 331, 65105 Karlstad, or *The Emigrant Institute,* Box 36, 351 03 Växjö.

There are many gatherings of Americans of Swedish descent during the summer months. A list of events is available at the tourist office in New York or from Einar Jagemar, Vasaorder of America, Solvagen 20, 292 00 Karlshamn.

Contact with Swedes and their families can be arranged through *Friends Overseas,* 68–04 Dartmouth St., Forest Hills, N.Y. 11375.

 HINTS FOR BUSINESSMEN. With the introduction of "flextime" in Sweden, it is advisable not to make appointments after 4 P.M., as most staff leave their offices anytime after 3.30 P.M., as long as they make up the total number of hours on a monthly basis.

There are many secretarial services available for temporary help; ask at your hotel reception desk.

You might find it useful to visit the Federation of Swedish Industries at Storgatan 19, tel. (08) 63 50 20. The federation has 3,000 member companies. At the same address is the Swedish Export Council, tel. (08) 63 05 80, which assists its 1,700 members in the field of export.

 CHILDREN. This is a good country in which to travel with children as there are many facilities provided for them, such as reduced rates in hotels for those under 12, children's menus in restaurants and baby-sitting services in hotels. The STF chalets and youth hostels usually have rooms with 2–4 beds suitable for families with children.

The Swedish Touring Club (STF) arranges canoeing tours in south Lapland and in Värmland-Dalsland for boys and girls 13–16 years old. Riding courses and riding camps for children and young people are arranged in the summer at several places in Sweden. *Ridfrämjandet* (the Society for the Promotion of Riding), Östermalmsgatan 80, Stockholm, publishes annually a list of such courses and camps.

 POSTAL RATES. Airmail letters to the U.S. and Canada cost 3.20 SEK, Aerograms 2.70 SEK. Airmail postcards cost 2.40 SEK. Letters and postcards to European destinations always go by air and cost 2.70 SEK and 2 SEK respectively.

Telex is available in bigger cities and costs 20 SEK plus 11.75 per minute to the U.S.

Cables. To U.S. and Canada, 3.75 SEK per word and to Britain 1.50 per word. A basic fee of 20 SEK is always charged.

CAMPING. It is best to use the regular camping sites (about 600) listed in *Camping-Boken* (with explanations in English), obtainable from any bookshop. Charges vary according to standard from 25–40 SEK per night per car and tent (no extra charge for persons). A camping card is required at a number of the large camping sites in Sweden. The card is issued by *Sveriges Campingvärdars Riksförbund* (SCR) and costs 10 SEK. It can be obtained at the first camping site to be visited. The *Camping-Boken* can be obtained by sending a 50 SEK international money order or bank check to Camping, Swedish Touristboard, Box 7473, S-103 93 Stockholm. It will be airmailed to overseas buyers.

GO AS YOU PLEASE. Car rental companies usually have special rates during summer months and during weekends. It pays to shop around. Recreational vehicles (Motor Homes) can be rented. Write to Kennil Marketing, Box 223, S-44125 Alingsäs.

STOCKHOLM

Open Nature and City Planning

Stockholm, Sweden's capital, has been called the most beautiful city in the world. This is open to debate, but few will deny that it is a handsome and civilized capital with a natural setting that would be hard to beat anywhere. When it was founded as a fortress on a little stone island where Lake Mälar reaches the Baltic, nobody cared much about natural beauty. It was protection the founders were after, military defense. But around the year 1250, the fortress became a town, and the town, spreading to nearby islands and finally to the mainland, became a city. And, though Nature remained the same, men's opinion of it changed, and Stockholm delights the tourist today with its openness, its space, its vistas over a great expanse of water. Of course it's been called the "Venice of the North", but that happens sooner or later to any northern city with more water than can be supplied by a fire hydrant.

Stockholm's beauty has been jealously guarded by the city fathers. The town is full of parks, tree-lined squares and boulevards, playgrounds, wading pools and other amenities of urban life, and the building codes are extremely strict. There is even a municipal "Beauty Council" to judge the esthetic qualities of proposed buildings. Nature and city planning have thus combined to create a pleasing metropolis, and it is hard to realize as you gaze out over the water from a table on the Strömparterren terrace that you are in the heart of a bustling metropolis, a town that has grown from less than 100,000 inhabitants to over a million in the space of a century.

Since the early Fifties, increasing urbanization and traffic demands have caused extensive replanning and rebuilding. First came the two huge satellite city centers of Vällingby to the west and Farsta to the south, connected by a subway (T-bana). Next came the wholesale rebuilding of a vast area in the heart of the city (from the Hötorget market place to "Sergels Torg"). Rows of tall buildings line the squares and neighboring streets; they house offices, department stores, shops and banks. New suburbs are Kista and Husby.

June, July and August are the best months to visit this capital. Then you have the best weather and the greatest variety of sight-seeing facilities. Bring a reasonably warm coat along. What most people would call a mild summer day is apt to be announced in the Stockholm papers as a heat wave. In May or October the weather is brisker, but so is the normal life of Stockholm.

Exploring Stockholm

Local patriots of other towns included, nobody denies that a unique, civilized beauty is one of the principal attractions of this northern capital. A benevolent Nature provided the foundations. Military rather than esthetic considerations dictated the choice of a site for the ancient fortress. But the bays and channels of the lake and the sea remained largely as Nature left them. It is because of these expanses of water that Stockholm gives a striking impression of openness and space.

From the vantage point of the terrace below the House of Parliament or Riksdag, you see in front of you a bronze statue by Carl Milles, the "Sun Singer". In the water below you, fishermen endlessly raise and lower the hoop nets attached to a long, hand-cranked crane on the back of their rowboats. It is a summer afternoon. Farther down the channel you see a row of buildings, four, five, six stories, red awnings flung to the sun. It is hard to realize in this peaceful setting that you are sitting in the very heart of Greater Stockholm, a metropolis of over a million people, a thriving industrial town, political and administrative capital of a modern nation, publishing and cultural center, and much more.

From a military standpoint, the choice of site was successful, and the city has only once been occupied by a foreign power (in 1520). Furthermore, it was spared the artillery barrages and bombings of two World Wars. Its historical treasures are intact, and its physical appearance is one of judicious, orderly growth.

Finally, wise city fathers have done their part to add to the loveliness of the "Queen of Lake Mälar", as Stockholm is sometimes called. Her parks are extensive—one of them embraces most of a large island which was once a royal preserve. Urns of flowers are placed at strategic points in the downtown districts, and changed with the season as different species blossom. Trees are planted in squares along streets and boulevards. There are roomy playgrounds for children, often with wading pools.

It is not surprising that much of the traffic in and out of the city, freight and passenger, moves by boat. Boat is the only means of transportation to many of the islands of the archipelago, on the Baltic Sea side, posing a real problem when some of the channels freeze in the winter time. The development of the helicopter has been literally a live-saver for the independent dwellers of these skerries. On the western side is Lake Mälar, twisting and winding a third of the way across the country. Here there is regular passenger and freight service during the summer time. Although the city apparently sits firmly on the coast, you can thus travel east and west, north and south by boat from Stockholm.

History and Growth

The earliest origins of Stockholm are largely unknown. Perhaps the first somewhat reliable report is a Viking saga, which, as all Viking sagas should, ends in violence. It seems that Agne, a warrior king of the Ynglinga dynasty, had been off on a visit to Finland. There, among other treasures, he had acquired a chieftain's daughter named Skjalf, by the effective if crude device of cutting down her father. Coming home, he stopped on the shore of an island which is now a part of Stockholm, to drink the health of his new bride and a proper toast to his late father-in-law. The mead flowed freely, Agne slept, Skjalf freed her fellow Finnish prisoners, and they hanged Agne. Then the Finns safely sailed home. The place was subsequently called Agnefit, or Agne Strand.

The first written mention of Stockholm in preserved chronicles gives the date 1252. Tradition—and some historical evidence—has it that a powerful regent named Birger Jarl here founded a fortified castle and city, locking off the entrance to Lake Mälar and the region around it. Certain it is that a castle of substance appeared during the 13th century, the beginnings of the Great Church (dedicated to St. Nicholas, patron of shipping), and the first monasteries.

From these dim beginnings the history of the city can be divided into four fairly distinct epochs: the erratic, confused first centuries; the arrival of King Gustav Vasa, who made Stockholm a capital beginning in 1523; King Gustavus Adolphus, who made it the heart of an empire a century later; and the modern era.

After the time of Birger Jarl the Swedish nation, still unorganized, groped its way forward. Up to this time Stockholm had not been the capital; the latest city to enjoy the favor had been Sigtuna. The real physical heart of Sweden remained uncertain. Nevertheless, Magnus Eriksson, a king of some importance, was crowned here in 1336. Toward the end of the century Sweden, Norway, and Denmark were united under one ruler. A period of confusion and revolt followed. Stockholm continued to be a commercial center, with monopoly trading rights for much of the territory around.

On Midsummer's Eve, 1523, when King Gustav Vasa returned from his victorious uprising for Swedish independence from the union (and from a Danish king), the real history of Stockholm began. Vasa was a powerful figure, sometimes called the George Washington of Sweden, and, although he moved from castle to castle throughout the country, his treasure chamber was in the old Stockholm Royal Palace. Succeeding kings tended in the same direction, making Stockholm more and more important.

Under Gustavus Adolphus, a great organizer as well as a military leader, who reigned from 1611 to 1632, the city became a capital in fact as well as name. Sweden had already begun to engage in political machinations and wars on the Continent and in Russia. It was partly his need to keep his military forces at top efficiency, his need for tax money, for supplies and for men that led Gustavus to concentrate the administration of the country in Stockholm. When he died on the battlefield of Lützen in 1632, Protestantism had been saved, Sweden had become an empire and Stockholm was its capital.

Prosperity and population grew accordingly. Gustavus himself, in a farewell address of 1630, had told the citizens of Sweden's cities that he hoped "your small cottages may become large stone houses". Many of them did. From a population of perhaps 3,000 when Gustav Vasa came home victorious, the number of inhabitants had grown to some 9,000 by the time Gustavus Adolphus fell, and rose to perhaps 35,000 by 1660. Meanwhile, the wars continued. Fortunately for Stockholm, they were fought on foreign soil. This did not, however, diminish the importance of the city, for it functioned as the capital even during the long absence of hero King Charles XII, who spent almost his entire reign in the field—losing much of what Gustavus Adolphus had won.

Rulers came and went, political battles were fought, won, and lost. But the building of Stockholm went on, sometimes in the hands of eminent architects like Nicodemus Tessin and his son, who are responsible for both the Royal Palace and Drottningholm Palace, as well as many other buildings which still stand. In the 18th century, Stockholm began to attract scientists and scholars, to share the spotlight with Lund and Uppsala as a center of learning. Gustav III (assassinated in 1792), a dilettante who could put on steel gauntlets when required, did much to make Stockholm a cultural, musical, and dramatic capital.

In 1850 Stockholm was still a quiet town. It had many of the stately buildings which even now give it its characteristic profile, but it numbered less than 100,000 people—a peaceful administrative center, perhaps dreaming of past glories. The first municipal cleaning department was established in 1859, the first waterworks in 1861, and gaslights had arrived but a few years earlier. As late as 1860, Drottninggatan, the most prominent commercial street, had no sidewalks. But the same year the first train arrived from Södertälje, 25 miles away. Modern communications had been born. The new era had begun.

Modern Development

The last 100 years of Stockholm's history are the story of a peaceful revolution, of industrialization, and of the remaking of a government from a monarchy with four estates in the parliament—nobles, clergy, farmers, as well as burghers—into a full parliamentary democracy with a king at its head. As the country has progressed and grown, Stockholm has progressed and grown with it. You will see the physical evidence wherever you go—the squat Parliament House on the site of one-time

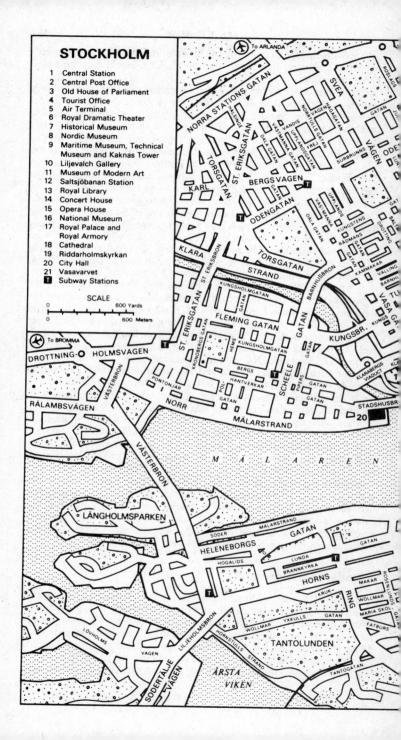

STOCKHOLM

1 Central Station
2 Central Post Office
3 Old House of Parliament
4 Tourist Office
5 Air Terminal
6 Royal Dramatic Theater
7 Historical Museum
8 Nordic Museum
9 Maritime Museum, Technical
   Museum and Kaknas Tower
10 Liljevalch Gallery
11 Museum of Modern Art
12 Saltsjöbanan Station
13 Royal Library
14 Concert House
15 Opera House
16 National Museum
17 Royal Palace and
   Royal Armory
18 Cathedral
19 Riddarholmskyrkan
20 City Hall
21 Vasavarvet
▉ T Subway Stations

SCALE

0 ———————— 600 Yards
0 ———————— 600 Meters

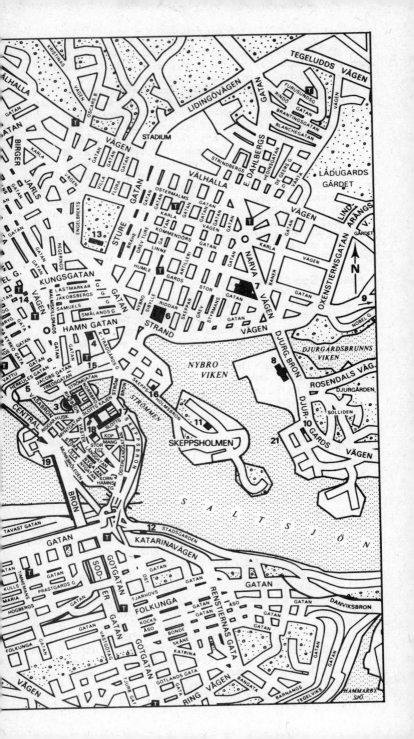

royal stables; the City Hall, an architectural masterpiece, raising its three-crowned tower above the waters of Lake Mälar, the tangible expression of a democratic city government; the extensive development in postwar years that has so rapidly changed and expanded the city. The two huge satellite centers of Vällingby to the west and Farsta to the south are connected by subway (T-bana), and were the first modern project. A vast area in the center of Stockholm has already been rebuilt: from the Hötorget market place to the Sergels Torg area.

This has resulted in a vast business and shopping district. Hundreds upon hundreds of modern apartment buildings rise toward the sky everywhere, balconies against the sun, all to house a population which now reaches over a million. As one writer has remarked, Stockholm as a city is principally a creation of the Swedish governmental power. This is largely true. But it is also true that Sweden is a democracy, ruled by the people. If Stockholm is thus the heart of a government, it is also the heart of a free people. It is this which speaks to you through the ages when you examine its dignified beauty.

How to See Stockholm

If Stockholm's island geography poses communication problems, it has the advantage of dividing the city neatly into sections and of making it possible to know easily where you are.

The city between the bridges. This consists of the Old Town, site of the Royal Palace and center of the city and nation, and its adjoining islands, Riddarholmen (The Isle of Knights), and Helgeandsholmen (Island of the Holy Spirit).

Södermalm. As the name implies, this is the southern section, across the bridge leading from the Old Town.

Norrmalm. North of the Old Town, the financial and business heart of the city. The new building construction from Hötorget to Klara-bergsgatan, which forms the new commercial center of Stockholm, constitutes the most important part of the redevelopment of Nedre Norrmalm (Lower Norrmalm).

Kungsholmen. A large island west of Norrmalm, site of the Town Hall and most of the offices of the city government.

Östermalm. East of Norrmalm, largely residential, many embassies and consulates.

Djurgården. The huge island which is mostly park, projecting east toward the Baltic Sea in the channels between Östermalm and Söder-malm. Here are concentrated museums, including Skansen, the open-air museum, amusement parks, restaurants.

Regardless of how long you intend to stay or how thoroughly you expect to see the city, begin by one or more boat excursions. Nothing else can give you a quick idea of the unique nature of Stockholm.

Let's take as a starting point the south of the large downtown park known as the Royal Gardens (Kungsträdgården), just across the rush-ing channel from the Royal Palace. It's an unmistakable point, easy to find. Immediately beside you is the striking profile of the statue of King Charles XII, arm raised and pointing east; behind him stretches the long park; to his right the unmistakable solid stone of the Royal Opera

House, a block or so to his left the familiar façade of the Grand Hotel; and across the water the dominating walls of the palace. Furthermore, just at the water's edge at both sides of the bridge there are kiosks that serve as starting points for some of the boat and bus excursions which show you the city.

Suppose you choose the one-hour trip around Djurgården—here are some of the things you'll see. You pull out from the quay, turn under the low bridge, head up past the Grand Hotel at the left, and at the end of the point—the last main building—is the National Gallery, the biggest gallery of paintings in Sweden. You turn under another bridge and on the little island on your right lies the Museum of Modern Art. You travel along with Strandvägen on your left, a lovely boulevard, soon approaching the island of Djurgården on your right. The imposing building with all the spires is the Nordiska Museum. Down the bay, on the left, a group of museums, to the right, the unspoiled beauty of Djurgården. Into a narrow canal, pastoral beauty on both sides. The end of the canal opens onto the broad main shipping channel—you will probably see sailboats, passenger and freight ships, and small passenger steamers heading for islands of the archipelago. Around the tip of the island, and the southern bluffs now rise up on your left, topped by towering apartment buildings. All along the shores of the island you will see pleasure boats, ships, and cruisers of all sizes, from rowboats to palatial yachts, at their berths. On the right, Prince Eugen's "Waldemarsudde" comes into view. He was a brother of Gustav V, and was known as the "Painter Prince" for his indisputable artistic talent, and when he died he left his lovely home and its many art treasures to the Swedish people. The mansion, adjacent art gallery, and gardens are open to the public. The flags of Skansen, the outdoor museum, rise up on the bluff way above, and you see the profile of Gröna Lund's Tivoli amusement park. Then, as you near your starting point again, Skeppsbron, a long quay where Baltic Sea shipping ties up with narrow lanes of the Old Town in the background, is on your left, followed by the garden side of the Royal Palace.

One method of sightseeing surpasses all others; most of the points of interest in the city are within relatively close range of each other, and the best way to see them is by walking or a combination of walking and brief bus or taxi hops. Pick out something which appeals to you from the list of suggestions below, take two or three hours in the morning or afternoon for a relaxed stroll, stopping where you are most interested. Even if you're not interested in details, you'll get the flavor of Stockholm's special charm.

Finally, the T-line, the subway, is not only an excellent way of getting about but fascinating in itself, with some of the stations like painted caves.

Royal Palace

The huge Stockholm Royal Palace is notable among royal seats for the freedom with which you can move around it. During the daytime, the entrance to the inner courtyard is open, and anyone may pass through freely. If you have legitimate business with some official of the court, you can often drive right in and park your car in the courtyard.

If you begin a look around the palace and the Old Town, from our traditional starting place below the statue of Charles XII, you move up along the waterfront, with the Royal Opera on your right, until you come to a bridge, which leads directly to the palace. The bridge spans an island on which, to your right, is the House of Parliament, a ponderous stone structure from around the turn of the century. Behind it is the old building of the Bank of Sweden, the national bank and the oldest existing bank in the world, founded in 1656. The bank moved to new quarters at Sergels Torg in 1975. In the old building there are now offices for members of parliament.

Directly in front of you is the palace in its most familiar profile. Actually this is the back; the intended front faces in the opposite direction. You will see for yourself when you get around to the other side, the south façade, that sculptures and reliefs break the otherwise simple and clean lines.

Palaces Old and New

The palace is not old, as palaces go, but the site is. It was here that Stockholm was born. The original palace, the Three Crowns, burned down one night in 1697, with the exception of the northern wing of today's palace. A new palace on the old site was ordered immediately. Three generations of Sweden's most famous architectural dynasty had an important part in its creation—Nicodemus Tessin the Elder planned the exterior and began the interior decoration, which was continued by his son, Tessin the Younger, and grandson, Carl Gustav Tessin. The whole project took more than 60 years, and was not completed until 1760. The building consists basically of a perfect square—enclosing a large court—with two wings sticking out on the east side and another on the west.

A number of interiors are open to the public. You may be interested in the Hall of State, which contains the king's silver throne. The Chapel Royal in the same wing has, among other impressive historical and artistic treasures, pews saved from the old palace. If you have time, look in on the Apartments of State, the Apartments of King Oscar II and Queen Sophie, and the Guest Apartments, notable for the furnishings and extremely fine Gobelin tapestries. There's also a palace museum, with bits of the previous palace, other historical finds, and the collection of classical sculpture brought from Italy by King Gustav III in the 1780's. The Royal Treasury, in the old vaults, can now be visited.

The Great Church

Diagonally across the street from the south side of the palace, and intimately associated with it, is the Great Church, the Stockholm cathedral and, in a sense, the national church. You would hardly guess from the well-kept exterior that it is believed to be the oldest building in the city, dating from about 1250. Many Swedish kings have been crowned here (until Gustav V gave up the custom when he ascended the throne in 1907), and it is still used for solemn celebrations attended by the king. There are a number of art treasures, of which perhaps the oldest, best known, and most distinguished is the statue carved in wood of St. George and the Dragon by Bernt Notke of Lübeck, which was presented to the church in 1489 to commemorate a Swedish victory over the Danes some 18 years earlier. A sound and light show is performed here for a few weeks during summer.

The Old Town

You're in the Old Town now, and there are several ways of continuing your look about. Here are two good suggestions immediately at hand. The first is to walk downhill on the lane called Storkyrkobrinken, to the right of the main entrance of the Great Church as you come out. This lane, like practically all those of the Old Town, follows the same route it did in the Middle Ages. Everywhere around you are buildings centuries old, living history. At the base of the hill you step out in a little square called Riddarhustorget. The two dominating buildings, across the square from where you enter, both date from the 17th century. One is Riddarhuset, House of the Nobility, in which you will find the crests of Swedish noble families. The white palace to its right was once a private possession, became the city courthouse in the 18th century, and is now occupied by the Supreme Court. There are over 300 shops and 40 restaurants and cafés in the old town.

Riddarholm Church

Students and lovers of history in particular will want to continue over the bridge across the canal and railway tracks to Riddarholm Church, the weathered red brick and openwork spire of which are clearly visible something over a hundred yards away. This is the Swedish Pantheon, burial place of Swedish kings for about four centuries. The most famous figures buried here are King Gustavus Adolphus, hero of the Thirty Years' War, and Charles XII (in Swedish, Karl XII), who is renowned for his signal victories over the Russian and Continental armies, with inferior forces, until the tide turned against him and he fell in Norway in 1718. Two medieval kings, Magnus Ladulås, who died in 1290, and Karl Knutson Bonde, some 180 years later, are also buried here. The latest king to be put to rest was Gustav V, on November 9, 1950. Except for the funeral of a king, the church has not been used for services for a long time. The sarcophagi of the various rulers, usually embellished with their monograms, are clearly visible in the small chapels given over to the various dynasties. The church building itself is interesting as the second oldest structure in Stockholm. It is a former monastery church completed about 1290, with many additions since.

Take 5 minutes to continue past the church down to the quay on Lake Mälar. It's well worth it. You get a fine view of the lake, the magnificent arches of the West Bridge in the distance, the southern heights, and above all the imposing profile of the Town Hall, which appears to be almost floating on the water. At the quay you may see one of the Göta Canal ships.

Swedish Academy

The second alternative to continuing your stroll from the Great Church is to turn left as you come out of the main entrance and walk up Trångsund to a little square called Stortorget, the oldest square in Stockholm. The dominating building, on the north side, is the Stock Exchange. This is also the headquarters of the Swedish Academy, which awards the Nobel Prize in literature. The other buildings are also old; note the tall, narrow, red merchant house and its sculptured portal from the 17th century.

Yard-wide Lane

The Old Town is the perfect kind of place to wander around without any decided aim, looking at the old portals, poking about in crowded antique shops, savoring the Bohemian atmosphere and the sense of age, peeking into doll-sized courtyards, making your way through curving, narrow lanes. There is little auto traffic, and the passages are too narrow to provide both streets and sidewalks. Go along Skomakaregatan to the German Church (Tyska Kyrkan), turn right for a few yards, then left again on Prästgatan. Keep your eyes open as you near the end of Prästgatan, on the right you will see one of the narrowest thoroughfares in the world. It is called Mårten Trotzigs Gränd (*gränd* means lane), and leads down to Västerlånggatan. It is scarcely a yard wide, half of it is a stairway, yet it is a public thoroughfare maintained and lighted by the city.

Katarina Elevator

It's only a couple of short blocks from here to the south end of the Old Town. You should really stroll on to that point. Above you are the southern heights, connected with the Old Town by an intricate cloverleaf of bridges and streets at about four levels, called Slussen. Katarina elevator—you see it poking up all by itself on the other side of the channel—takes you up to a platform with a fine view of Stockholm.

Skansen's Multiple Charms

The outdoor establishment Skansen is unlike anything anywhere else. It is situated in a beautiful, natural island park. It contains a museum, but it is not only a museum; it contains a zoo, but it is much more than a zoological garden; there are restaurants, an open-air theater, concerts and popular celebrations, folk dancing and public dancing, and coffee shops and workshops.

For a person with limited time, Skansen is the perfect place to get something of an idea of the culture and traditions of other parts of Sweden. Whole estates, stone buildings, farm houses, other structures have been moved here bodily from all parts of the country. There is an

18th-century church, still used for divine services and not infrequently for weddings. Other buildings are in use, too. Geese cackle near the entrance to the farm houses from southern Sweden; glass blowers blow glass—you can help blow it if you want to—in the old-time glass blower's hut. "Miss Skansen" conducts guided tours through Skansen starting from Seglora Church daily, at 11 A.M., 1, 3 and 5 P.M. during the summer months.

You can easily spend a whole day, or afternoon and evening, profitably at Skansen. Starting from the statue of Charles XII across the channel from the palace, you walk down the length of the park, turn right to a square called Norrmalmstorg, and from there a bus (No. 47) delivers you in front of the main gate in about 10 minutes. If you prefer to walk, continue across the square and a block beyond to the long, quayside boulevard called Strandvägen, and follow it to the first bridge on the right. Cross the bridge and continue on the boulevard until you see the sign "Skansen" over the main entrance. It takes about 30 or 40 minutes to make the walk at a casual pace, and it's a popular promenade route, particularly on Sundays.

Nordiska Museum

Three other museums on Djurgården are particularly recommended. The Nordiska Museum contains the most complete collection of objects illustrating the progress of civilization in Sweden since 1500, and some that are unique. The exhibits also contain some magnificent specimens of rural art, particularly in the form of fabrics, national costumes, and rugs, and there is a truly lovely collection of bridal crowns, the beautiful silver and gold, sometimes bejeweled, coronets of the kind still worn by Swedish brides. Located on the route to Skansen, just after you cross the bridge.

The Wasa

Also on the route to Skansen, just below the Liljevalch's Art Gallery you will find the salvaged 17th-century man-of-war *Wasa.* On August 10, 1628, the *Wasa,* with full complement, heeled over and sank in Stockholm's harbor on her maiden voyage. The ship was rediscovered in 1956, and in May 1961 she was raised and tugged into dry dock. The complex task of restoration continues; in the meantime the ship is kept in a high-humidity atmosphere and the hull is continually sprayed with a special compound to prevent warping. Visitors can clamber all round the ship, there is a museum and a film of the *Wasa* re-birth. Well worth a visit.

Waldemarsudde

Prince Eugen's "Waldemarsudde", former home of "the Painter Prince", brother of the late King Gustav V, was bequeathed to the people on the prince's death. The many paintings, some by Eugen himself, constitute a fine collection of Swedish art, and the mansion, art gallery, and beautiful grounds are well worth seeing. You reach Waldemarsudde by taking bus 47 from Norrmalmstorg.

Treasures of the City Hall

The Stockholm City Hall, one of the great architectural works of the 20th century, is another appropriate excursion that you can manage in a couple of hours—more if you like. Starting at the statue of Charles XII, turn to the right and merely follow the waterfront until you arrive at its massive portal. The distance is less than a mile.

Superlatives have not been lacking in describing the structure. It has sometimes been called "the most beautiful building of this century in Europe". This opinion is not unanimous, of course; some people have reacted violently against it, but even this sharp reaction is a measure of the strength of the total impression. The building was completed and dedicated in 1923, and has become a symbol of the city. It is the seat of the city council and central administration.

The most significant characteristic of the City Hall is the way the architect, the late Ragnar Östberg, was able to synthesize almost diametrically opposed styles into a harmonious whole. The tower and the handcut brick of the walls derive directly from the massive castle architecture of 16th-century Sweden, the loggia opening on the garden transports you to classic Rome and Greece, elsewhere you will detect an Oriental, almost Moorish influence. Don't miss:

The Golden Hall. Here mosaics, one of the oldest known artistic techniques, have been used to cover the high walls with symbolic pictures in the modern style—a remarkable combination.

The Blue Hall. There's nothing blue about it, except the sky visible through the windows ranged around the top of the walls. It is an inside court which would do justice to any palace.

The Prince's Gallery. Large murals by Prince Eugen.

The Terrace. A formal garden practically sitting on the water of Lake Målar—with beautiful views: in front of you the Old Town and the southern heights, in back of you the loggia and the massive walls of the City Hall rising above it.

The Tower. Rises 348 feet, its lantern topped by three crowns, Sweden's national emblem. At noon and 6 P.M. the carillon within plays the medieval war song of the Swedes at the Battle of Brunkeberg in 1471. For an excellent view of Stockholm and surroundings: elevator. The adjoining Maiden Tower is surmounted by a bronze St. George and the Dragon.

Other Sights

Depending on the amount of time you have available and your special interests, there are many other places and institutions well worth a visit. Among the dozens of museums, these are particularly recommended: The National Museum, just a few doors down the quay from the Grand Hotel, with the largest collection of paintings and sculpture by Swedish and foreign artists.

A few minutes' walk from here is the Museum of Modern Art, on Skeppesholmen Island. Here, too, is the Museum of Far East Antiquities, with a fine collection displayed in a 17th-century building.

The National Museum of Antiquities, on Östermalm at Narvavägen 17; in addition to a veritable mass of historical finds dating well back into the Stone Age, it houses the Royal Cabinet of Coins.

The Biological Museum on Djurgården gives you a comprehensive picture of the fauna of Scandinavia, and the Thiel Art Gallery has a fine collection of Scandinavian and French art from the period 1890 to 1910.

On the northern side of Djurgården, at Kaknäs, is Stockholm's latest tourist attraction, the 500-ft-high Kaknäs Tower (see "Practical Information for Stockholm").

Music and Markets

The Concert Hall, at Hötorget, is the center of Stockholm's musical life. The building, designed by Ivar Tengbom, was completed in 1926. In front is Carl Milles' huge sculptured group of Orpheus calling up the spirits. It is in this hall that the awarding of the Nobel Prizes takes place.

It's well worth your while to get to one of the market squares fairly early in the day— 9:00 A.M. will do—which are masses of color whatever the season of the year. One is just in front of the Concert House, another on Östermalm. Flowers, fresh fruits and vegetables are the principal stock in trade. Look in at the indoor markets which adjoin these squares—there you can fill your whole grocery basket from the little shops of independent dealers, and have a snack in one of the small restaurants. This is a unique aspect of Stockholm life. Incidentally, the outdoor markets operate right through the winter.

Housing and Hospitals

As you move around Stockholm you'll notice new housing developments everywhere. This is one of the expressions of Swedish government policies which have most interested foreign observers. The developments not only reflect national housing policy, they are striking exponents of architectural innovations and modern city planning. The latter is applied in Stockholm perhaps as much as in any city in the world, and co-ordinated plans must be approved in some detail by the city authorities before new areas may be opened up. The city itself, in fact, owns much of the land, which is let on long-term leases to builders and building associations.

Even a casual stroll through one development will give you some idea of how space is efficiently utilized, how shopping centers are provided, and of other community arrangements.

Low-cost medical care is another field of the Swedish social security program which has aroused widespread interest. Two large and modern hospitals which are well worth seeing, even from the outside, are Söder Hospital and the Karolinska Hospital, both with a capacity of 1,600 beds. There is a college of medicine at the latter hospital, and it is the faculty of this institution which awards the Nobel Prize in medicine.

At City's Edge

Immediately outside the city limits of Stockholm proper are a number of popular attractions which you can reach within an hour by public transportation, or half an hour by car.

Carl Milles

The sculptor Carl Milles, who was perhaps better known as an inhabitant of Cranbrook, Michigan, had his permanent home on the island of Lidingö, a Stockholm suburb, where he collected not only some of his own best works but other outstanding pieces from several eras and countries. It was here that he died in September 1955, still hard at work at the age of 80.

Drottningholm

The royal palace of Drottningholm is located on a little island in Lake Mälar—the name means "Queen's Island"—a few miles from Stockholm. The trip is a pleasant experience, particularly by boat. If you have seen Versailles, you will be reminded of it at once when you arrive at Drottningholm, for it was clearly inspired by the French style. The palace was built by Nicodemus Tessin the Elder, and his son, Tessin the Younger, completed the gardens in the style of Le Nôtre.

Drottningholm is one of the most delightful of European palaces, embracing, as it does, all that was best in the art of living practiced by mid-18th-century royalty. In the grounds, a kind of Trianon, is the China Palace, conceived in Chinoiserie terms, a lovely little palace, hidden in the trees, where the royal family could relax and entertain their friends. Also in the grounds is the Theater. This fascinating building slumbered like the Sleeping Beauty undisturbed for well over a century, the settings and stage machinery of the 18th century in perfect condition and working order. It now houses a theater museum and delightful productions of baroque opera are once again staged in the auditorium that saw the efforts of Gustavus III to create a Swedish Golden Age. The Royal Family occupies one wing at the palace.

Haga Palace

Haga Palace, formerly the home of the late Crown Prince Gustav Adolf, is located only a few minutes from downtown, right on the city limits of Stockholm. A more interesting building located on the same grounds is Haga Pavilion. It is a miniature summer palace built by Gustav III (late 18th century), exquisitely furnished.

Saltsjöbaden

The resort of Saltsjöbaden is a residential suburb the year round. During the summer it is a rendezvous for yachtsmen and motorboat enthusiasts, and the harbor is excellent. In winter there is skating, skate-sailing, iceboating, and skiing. The modern Stockholm observatory is located here. You can reach Saltsjöbaden from Slussen on an electric train. In the same general direction, but to the north, is Gustavsberg, where the noted ceramics works may be visited in groups by previous appointment.

PRACTICAL INFORMATION FOR STOCKHOLM

 HOTELS. It's essential to reserve rooms well in advance during the summer months. If you arrive in Stockholm without a reservation, consult the Hotellcentralen in the underground Central Station. This joint room booking service is open Mon-Fri 8 A.M.–9 P.M., Sat 8 A.M.–5 P.M., Sun, 1 P.M.–9 P.M., June to September. During the rest of the year it is open weekdays from 8.30 A.M.–4.45 P.M., Sundays from 2 to 11 P.M. A charge is made for each room reserved. In general, Stockholm hotels are comfortable, but prices are high.

For information about low-priced packages at weekends and during summer months, write to *Destination Stockholm,* Stora Hoparegränd 5, S-11130 Stockholm. Six first-class hotels have a joint booking service. Tel. 08–7305895. Telex 12278.

First Class Superior

Amaranten, Kungsholmsgatan 31; 415 rooms with bath or shower, restaurants, cocktail lounge, nightclub, sauna and garage, subway (SARA).

Anglais, Humlegårdsgatan 23; 299 rooms with bath. Front rooms face park. Restaurant, cocktail bar, grill, garage.

Continental, Klara Vattugränd 4; 207 rooms with bath. Restaurant, café, snack bar. A RESO hotel. Opposite rail station and air terminal.

Diplomat, Strandvägen 7C; 115 rooms, 93 with bath, on waterfront.

Grand, S. Blasieholmshamnen 8; 350 rooms, all with bath. Only front rooms have view. Central, a landmark; restaurant, winter garden, SAS office.

Grand Hotel Saltsjöbaden, in suburban resort of Saltsjöbaden; 105 rooms, Castlelike building in delightful landscaped grounds. Waterfront location, sauna, restaurant.

M/S Mälardrottningen (Queen of Lake Mälaren), Riddarholmen; 64 cabins, café, restaurant on a rebuilt luxury yacht dating originally from 1924.

Park Hotel, Karlavagen 43; 205 rooms with bath. Garden café, restaurant, garage.

Reisen, Skeppsbron 12–14; 120 rooms with bath. Restaurant. A SARA hotel built behind the façade of three 17th-century houses. Two saunas, garage.

Sheraton-Stockholm, Tegelbacken 6; 476 rooms with bath. Restaurant, cocktail lounge, garage; next to air terminal. Stockholm's most popular hotel.

Star Hotel Arlanda, 300 rooms. Restaurant, bar, sauna, pool, library, cinema, nightclub. Soundproof. Tennis court. Bus 5 min. from Arlanda airport.

Strand, Nybrokajen; 153 rooms. Central and convenient, on waterfront. Nightclub (closed July), casino.

First Class Reasonable

Aston, Mariatorget 3; 70 rooms, most with bath.

Birger Jarl, Tulegatan 8; 250 rooms with bath or shower. Unlicensed. Connected with church with English service on Suns.

Carlton, Kungsgatan 57; 150 rooms. Centrally located, near the Concert House and shopping district. Restaurant.

Castle, H Riddargatan 14; 30 rooms, 26 baths. Some rooms high-priced for category.

Eden, Sturegatan 10; 50 rooms, 30 with bath, quiet, with terrace restaurant.

Esplanade, Strandvägen 7A. 33 rooms. Breakfast only. Newly renovated. Centrally located.

Hotel City, Slöjdgatan 7; 300 rooms, many smoke free rooms, restaurant unlicensed, run by Salvation Army.

Lady Hamilton, Storkyrkobrinken 5. 35 rooms, genuine Swedish rural style. Near Royal Palace. Unique.

Lord Nelson, Västerlånggatan 22, right in the middle of the Old Town. 31 rooms. Nautical atmosphere.

Mornington, Nybrogatan 53. 123 rooms. Central.

Palace, St. Eriksgaten 115; 218 rooms, 182 with bath. Near the Haga air terminal. Also has reasonable motel rooms and 6 suites. Garage.

Sjöfartshotellet (RESO), Katarinavägen 26; 184 rooms with bath. Restaurant, garage.

Moderate

Adlon, Vasagatan 42; 64 rooms, 30 with bath.

Alexandra, Magnus Ladulasgatan 4; 90 rooms with bath or shower.

August Strindberg, Tegnerlunden 38, 19 rooms in 1890 building, no elevator. Central.

Bromma (RESO), Brommaplan; 139 rooms with bath. 10 minutes by subway from down-town shopping area. Restaurant, garage.

Flamingo, Centralvägen 20, Solna (10 minutes outside center); 128 rooms, most with bath. Restaurant, grill room, cocktail bar.

Flyghotellet, Brommaplan; 68 rooms with bath. Subway 10 min. to center.

Hotel Kom, Döbelnsgatan 17–19; 63 rooms, 150 double. Open May-Dec.

Karelia, Birger Jarlsgatan 35, 77 rooms, new 1982.

Kristineberg, Hjalmar Söderbergsväg 10; 146 rooms, 4 baths. Pleasant restaurant, informal atmosphere. Suitable for motorists.

Merc Hotel, Bromma, near Alvik subway station; 71 rooms.

Regent, Drottninggatan 10, third floor. 19 rooms without bath. Central.

Savoy, Bryggargatan 12B, 54 rooms, 7 baths. Breakfast only.

Stockholm, Norrmalmstorg 1; 108 rooms, 54 with bath. Breakfast only.

Tegnerlunden, Tegnerlunden 8; 73 rooms with shower.

Terminus, Vasagatan 20; 134 rooms, 94 with bath. Opposite main station and air terminal. Restaurant.

Summer Hotels

Jerum, Studentbacken 21; 120 rooms, all with showers.

Frescati, Professorsslingan 13–15, in Stockholm's new "university town", 154 rooms, all with showers. For self—service guests, well-equipped kitchens on each floor, self-service restaurant fully licensed.

For students and others on a low budget there are the following youth hostels: the 100 year-old sailing ship **af Chapman;** a 150-bed hostel behind it, with a fine view (42 SEK); the **M/S Manfiskaren,** a ship built in 1865; the **YMCA** (KFUM) hostel for interrail tourists at Kista (Jyllandsgatan 16, Spångor; 40 SEK); and youth hostels in the archipelago at Karlsholmen and Gällnö.

Motels

Esso Motor Hotels at Kungens Kurva, south of Stockholm, 275 rooms with bath or shower, and at Ulriksdal, north of city on E4, 215 rooms with bath or shower. The bus from Arlanda airport stops here on request.

Esso Scandic Hotel, Täby, north of the City; 124 rooms, new 1982.

Gyllene Ratten, Lotta Svärds Gränd, Hägersten; 109 rooms, 4 miles south-west on E4. Cafeteria-restaurant.

RESTAURANTS. Since restaurants play such an important part in Stockholm life, a fairly extensive list is given here. All have liquor licenses, unless otherwise specified. Some of the downtown establishments close for three or four weeks during the summer. Several of the hotel chains also manage quick-snack and cafeteria places.

Note: All below-listed restaurants are moderately expensive to very expensive, unless otherwise indicated.

Aurora, Munkbron 15, located in a beautiful 300-year-old house in the Old Town with pleasant small rooms in vaults. Excellent food. (SARA).

Bacchi Wapen, Järntorgsgatan, 5. International cuisine, good throughout. Located on a medieval lane in the Old Town, cozy cellar vaults. They produce a good steak. Music.

Bäckahästen, Hamngatan 2. Modern decor, open air service in summer. Good food, large portions.

Brända Tomten, Stureplan 13 (ICA). Good food at reasonable prices. Period décor. Quick lunches served in cellar.

Cafe De Paris, Sturegatan 29, excellent food and elegant interior. Few tables.

Cattelin, Stora Gråmunkegrand 8, seafood specialties.

Colibri, corner Drottninggatan and Adolf Fredriks Kyrkogata. Specialty: plank steak.

Coq Blanc, Regeringsgatan 111, good food.

Coq Roti, Sturegatan 19, a gourmet restaurant run by two good professionals.

Daily News Café, Hamngatan 27, in Sverigehuset. Good food.

Den Gyldene Freden, Österlånggatan 51. Medieval cellars, historical traditions, atmosphere, lute singers some evenings. Oldest restaurant in Sweden.

Djurgårdsbrunns Wärdshus, a few minutes from downtown by taxi or bus. An inn overlooking a meadow and canal, with pleasure boats passing almost constantly in the summertime.

Fem Små Hus, Nygränd 10, is charming, in the Old Town. Its name means "five small houses". Very good food.

Frascati, Storgatan 6, specializes in fish dishes. Very good. Closed Sun.

Galejan, Nybrogatan 31, next to old market hall Östermalmshallen, popular.

Garbo, at Blekingegatan 32, where Great Garbo was born.

Göta Källare, Götgatan 54–56 (SARA). Good food, reasonable.

Grand Hotel, S. Blasieholmsh. 8. You go here for the view as much as for the food. Terrace opposite Royal Palace, indoor winter garden. *Smörgåsbord.*

Grenadjären, Erik Dahlbergsg. 41–43. A cozy, friendly restaurant a little off the beaten track in a section of town called Gärdet. Pleasant summer garden. Closed in July.

Kaknäs, The restaurant on top of the tower at Kaknäs, Djurgården has a magnificent view.

Kejsaren, Holländargatan 1, Chinese food.

Konstnärshuset, Smålandsgatan 7. Good food and drinks in intimate surroundings in the heart of town. Murals by Swedish artists.

Maxim's, Drottninggatan 81, popular restaurant, pub, nightclub.

NK Department Store, a shopper's favorite, open-air terrace lunching in summer. Very good.

Operakällaren, in the Opera House. Same management as Riche and Stallmästargården. The Grill retains its cozy atmosphere, and the snack bar. *Bakfickan,* is recommended for quick meals. Fairly expensive, or moderate—all depending.

Östergök, Kommendorsgatan 46, for steak, fish, and pizza. Very popular, closed Suns.

Restaurant Gourmet, Tegnergatan 10, with annex. One of the best French gourmet places in town.

Riche and Teatergrillen, Birger Jarlsgatan 4. The Riche side has a cocktail lounge, good food, good drinks, and music. The Teatergrillen, or Theater Grill, is more intimate and lives upto its name in attracting some of the theater crowd. Steaks among the best in town. Teatergrillen closed July.

Solliden, Skansen. On the heights of Stockholm's favorite pleasure grounds, ten minutes from the center of town, this large establishment overlooks city and harbor. Occasional fireworks in summer. (SARA).

Stadshuskällaren, in City Hall basement (SARA). Popular with municipal people. Caters for official banquets and receptions.

Stallmästargården, Norrtull near Haga and the air terminal for Arlanda, old inn with historical traditions, modern management. Coffee in the court, a lovely garden, after a good meal on a summer evening can be a delightful experience. Same management as Riche, thus good food, including *Smörgåsbord.* Music.

Stortorgskällaren, Stortorget 7, charming medieval cellar in the Old Town near Royal Palace. Also a fish restaurant.

Strand, in the Strand Hotel, Nybrokajen 9. *Maritime,* specializing in fish.

Sturehof, Stureplan. An unpretentious restaurant, fairly large, which makes good fish its business. One part of the restaurant is converted into a pub in old English style. Located in the heart of town.

Ulriksdals Värdshus, in fine park near Ulriksdal Palace, 10 mins. by car or bus from city. Old Swedish inn with famed smörgåsbord and food. Bus 540 from Humlegårdsgatan.

Quick Snacks

For sandwiches and inexpensive cafeteria lunches, try *Cassi Grill,* Narvavägen 30; *Ziba Grill,* Gamla Brogatan 40, *Corallo,* Grev Turegatan 8. Many big department stores have cafeterias and tea-rooms: *Tempo, Åhléns, Skomans.* Hamburger places *McDonald* and *Clock.*

In the business and shopping district at Hötorget you may try *Sandelius* in the 3rd skyscraper. Other restaurants in the town centre are *Gladalaxen,* Gallerian Shopping Centre; *Albertina,* Drottninggatan; *Lillafaalstaff,* Sveavagen; *Cafe Stockholm,* Regeringsgatan; *Chez Charles,* Klarabagsgatan (Hotel Continental); *Carlton Inn,* Kungsgatan 57; *Pizzeria Piazza Opera,* Gustaf Adolfs Torg 20, *Wallonen,* Kungsgatan 56; *Monte Carlo,* corner Sveavågen/Kungsgatan.

 SHOPPING. The *Scandinavian Taxfree* scheme enables you to have *part* of the sales tax on purchases refunded on departure. Over 900 shops participate.Check the rules. You need special receipts to present at a special desk at the airport, harbor or on board ship. **Department Stores** We would suggest you make your first stop in Stockholm at the *Nordiska Kompaniet,* fondly known as *N.K.,* situated at Hamngatan 18–20. This store has the best features off Neiman-Marcus and Harrods rolled into one, plus a few specialties of its own. A tour of *N.K.,* through its rows of gleaming crystal, cases of silver and stainless steel, shelves of ceramics, stacks of textiles, woven and knitted articles, its leather goods and gowns, will explain the harmonious decoration of even the poorest homes and the stunning décor of the Swedish women who plan them. We can think of no quicker way one might become oriented towards the finest on the local market. You will find, in addition to gifts, everything from a city map to a shampoo and set, all within *N.K.*'s doors. Accepts most credit cards. The Swedish word for sale is *REA.*

Another exclusive department store is *Sörmans,* Biblioteksgatan 11, near Stureplan. For an equally extensive but less luxurious offering at lower prices, try *P.U.B.,* the popular department store, housed in two buildings, the old one at Hötorget, and the new in a glass-walled building at the corner of Kungsgatan and Drottninggatan.

Another block down the street is *Åhléns,* a fine department store. *Harald Löfberg,* Kungsgatan 58 and 64–66 specializes in quality household linen. In the new city center from Hötorget to Sergels Torg you will find a hundred shops, and opposite *N.K.*'s a new shopping arcade, called *Gallerian.*

Porcelain, Pottery, Glass. Because some of the best porcelain, textile, furniture and stainless steel companies have their own shops in Stockholm, you may wish to survey their larger selection before making your purchase. High on this list are Gustavsberg's lovely faïence pieces. The versatile Stig Lindberg has executed a distinctive line of bow-shaped bowls and ingenious sets of nesting candlesticks. Birger Jarlsgatan 2 is the address of *Gustavsberg's Utställning.*

If it's a glaze you desire, drop in at the *Arabia-Rörstrand Center,* Norrlandsgatan 2. Pioneering in fantastic oven temperatures, Carl Harry Stålhane has created a select group of stoneware for the connoisseur—for instance, a vase with atomic overtones, brightly speckled with a uranium compound.

Elsewhere china and pottery are almost invariably found together with the crystal for which Sweden is even more famous. Keep in mind the names of *Orrefors,* whose master artists are Simon Gate and Edward Hald, and of *Kosta* crystal (since 1741). These big two in the Swedish crystal industry have transformed their trade into a highly decorative art in the past 50 years. A thousand imaginative varieties of some of the world's finest crystal will be yours at *Nordiska Kristallmagasinet,* Kungsgatan 9. *Aveny,* Kungsgatan 41, *Svenskt Glas,* Birger Jarlsgatan 8, and *Peter Casselryd,* Storholmsgatan 5 (Skärholmen shopping center). should also be high on your list for glass.

Handicrafts. *Hemslöjdsförbundet,* Sturegatan 29, is a sales organization for handicraft societies all over Sweden with display rooms, but wholesale business only.

Svensk Hemslöjd, Sveavägen 44, concentrate in a delightful way on everyday pottery, knitted goods, hand-woven textiles and wood-carving, handwrought copper and pewter pieces. The firm also produces furniture, rugs and textiles of eminent quality and design.

Stockholms Läns och Stads Hemslöjdsförening (Stockholm County and City Handicraft Association), Drottninggatan 18–20, specializes in handicraft of Stockholm origin.

For ladies' wear of handwoven textiles visit *Hjalmarsdotter* at Nybrogatan 20.

De Fyras Bod, Birger Jarlsgatan 12 is a center for native arts and crafts by handicapped artists: handwoven linen tablecloths, handloomed rugs, wrought iron, etc.

Handarbetets Vänner (Friends of Needlework) is state-supported and has its weaving school, workshops for tapestries and embroideries, display room and shop at Djurgårdsslätten 82–84.

The well-known Dalarna workshop *Klockargårdens Hemslöjd* has a branch at Kungsgatan 64.

For all kinds of original ideas in interior decoration, your delight will be *Svenskt Tenn,* Strandvägen 5A. *Konsthantverkana* at Mäster Samuelsgatan 2–8 has a permanent exhibition of the best in Swedish arts and crafts.

Carl Malmsten and Elsa Gullberg introduced in the '30s the simple forms and functional grace now so universally admired. *Malmsten*'s own shop is at Strandvägen 5B.

Nordiska Galleriet exhibits the latest furniture at Nybrogatan 11.

Silver and Steel. Don't overlook the handsome displays of Swedish stainless steel (*Gense* is a name to look for). As one who has taken steel table and hollowware out of the kitchen and used it to set a gleaming dinner table, *Studio Swedish Crystal,* Tegelbacken 6, should be added to your shopping list. You will be tempted by everything from water pitchers to scissors, all combining high-grade steel with sleek, practical designs.

Simplicity of execution in metal work naturally carries over to the medium of silver. *Atelier Borgila* is at Sturegatan 24 and *Rey Urban* at Sibyllegatan 49.

Claes Gierta at Drottninggatan 77 has superb handwork. If you find nothing here that appeals, then try the shop of *W. A. Bolin* at Sturegatan 12, or *C. F. Carlman,* Biblioteksgatan 2, both of whom are purveyors of the Swedish Crown jewelry.

C. G. Hallberg has goods that are highly prized and shops all over the country. Several shops in Stockholm: at Drottninggatan 59, Psturegatan 6.

Accessories. Sweden is also noted for its leather goods, fashioned with native simplicity using the best imported materials.

Excellent value in price and quality for handbags and travel accessories can be found at *Walls Väskor,* Kungsgatan 23. See *Joh. Palmgren's* outstanding saddlery work and hand-made travel luggage at Sibyllegatan 7.

Other good bargains are reindeer gloves: try *Sahlgrens Handskaffär,* Sergelgatan 11.

Suede jackets and coats can be found in the big stores and at *Nya Malung* in Gallerian.

The big department store *MEA,* Hamngatan 3 at Norrmalmstorg, has a very fine stock of leather coats, jackets, hats, etc. for both men and women.

Furs and Sporting Goods. And do remember furs while in Stockholm. For top quality, the luxurious shops of *Ivan Petersson* at Birger Jarlsgatan 6, *Gunnar Christell,* Kommendörsgatan 27, and *Rune Landert,* Nybrogatan 29, will cater to your taste.

Wasa Päls, has an enormous store at Vasagatan 11 with a big assortment of furs of all kinds and prices.

As for sporting goods, *Georg A. Bastman,* Nybrogatan 1, who specializes in fishing equipment, can be counted on to prepare you for any outing you may plan.

Art. Lovers of modern art will find a good selection at *Galleri Heland,* Kungsträdgården 3, including sculpture and the graphic arts. *Konst-Salongen Samlaren,* Birger Jarlsgatan 1, has Swedish and international works; *Gallerie Pierre,* Nybrogatan 1 specializes in French graphics.

 DANCING, NIGHTCLUBS. The hotels and restaurants that have dancing do not have it every evening, so if you want to dine and dance you had better check the papers first, or ask the hotel clerk. There are a couple of public ballrooms, serving only soft drinks, and refreshments. Open-air dancing, folk dances and modern, at *Skansen* and in the amusement park, *Gröna Lund,* Djurgården, in summer.

For details of all entertainment, ask for *This Week in Stockholm,* published by the Stockholm Information Service.

All of the "nightclubs" are really restaurants licensed to stay open until 3 A.M. This simply means that you can drink another couple of hours while watching a floor show.

Long-established is *Bacchi,* Järntorgsgatan 5, popular with the expense account set.

Others include *Club Opera,* Operakajen 9; *Strand,* Nybrokajen; *Strömsborg* on Strömsborg island; *Ambassadeur,* Kungsgatan 18; *Baldakinen,* Barnhusgatan 12–14; *Grand Hotel Royal,* Blasieholmen; *Ritz,* Medborgarplatsen; *Cindy,* in the Amaranten Hotel.

Youngsters favor the many clubs and "cellars" such as *Underground,* under the square at Sergelstorg; *Gamlingen,* Helga Lekamensgränd 10 (membership required).

Several English-style pubs are a feature of "Swinging Stockholm": *Engelen,* Kornhamnstorg 59B; the *Old Bowler,* Surbrunnsgatan 33; *Stampen,* Gråmunkegränd 7; *Stinsen,* Klarabergsgatan 56; *Sturehof,* Stureplan; *Tennstopet,* Dalagatan-Odengatan; the *Tudor Arms,* Grevgatan 31.

 ENTERTAINMENT. Stockholm offers visitors a variegated theater and musical life, a large number of moving picture theaters, several amusement parks, and a surprising amount of good music. Its two centers are the *Royal Opera House* and the *Stockholm Concert House.* The Royal Opera, located just across the bridge from the Royal Palace, has a season running from mid-August until about June 10. Ballet Festival, first week of June.

The concert season lasts from about the middle of September to about the middle of May. The Stockholm Concert Association Orchestra is in regular service at the Concert House and is fully up to international standards. But perhaps of even greater interest is a veritable parade of top international virtuosos and guest conductors, representing the cream of European, British, and American talent.

Several theaters specialize in light opera—playing classics and modern musicals. It's great fun hearing and seeing a familiar perennial in a strange theater and a strange language. Season: Sept.-mid-June.

The *Royal Dramatic Theater*—birthplace of the careers of Greta Garbo and Ingrid Bergman—actually consists of two theaters, one for major performances and a smaller one for those of more limited public interest. A number of the plays presented here and at other Stockholm theaters are hits still running in New York or London. Season: Sept.-May.

Particularly recommended is the *Court Theater* of Drottningholm Palace, a few minutes to a half hour from downtown Stockholm by car or bus (or 50 minutes by boat). This is an 18th-century theater which was somehow lost sight of, closed up for years, and when reopened a few decades ago found to be in its original shape. The repertoire consists almost entirely of operas and ballets contemporary with the theater, in other words, of works written for that kind of stage. Seeing a performance there is a unique theater event. Performances during May, June, July, August and September, 2 to 4 evenings per week.

Every day during the summer concerts and other kinds of entertainment are held in the open-air at *Skansen:* displays of folk-dancing and folk-music; chamber music recitals in period costume in a manor house; children's theater every Sat. and Sun.

Between June 15 and end of August the Park Committee of the Stockholm City Council arranges free concerts in the city's many parks. In *Kungsträdgården* (Royal Garden) there are daily gramophone concerts and three evenings a week at least, free entertainment on the outdoor stage, often featuring leading variety artists.

The *Gröna Lund* amusement park on Djurgården (bus 47 or ferry from Räntmästaretrappan and Nybroplan) is open May through Sept., 7 to midnight on weekdays and 1 to midnight on Sundays. Daily open-air performances with

Swedish and foreign artists: restaurants, theaters, dance halls and traditional Tivoli amusements.

In some parks, open-air theater and ballet performances are given.

Cinema—English and American movies dominate, usually are shown in English with Swedish subtitles, and often are released at the same time as they appear in London or New York.

  MUSEUMS. National Museum of Fine Arts, near Grand Hotel; Swedish State collections of paintings, sculptures, etc., by Swedish and foreign artists; Tues 10–9, Wed–Sun 10–4, closed Mon.

Museum of Modern Art and Photography, on Skeppsholmen Island, Swedish State collections of 20th-century sculpture and paintings; one of the most interesting and progressive in the world; with temporary exhibitions all through the year, Tue-Fri 11–9, Sat/Sun 11–5, closed Mon.

Skansen, Djurgården; world famous open-air museum, situated on a height from which an excellent view of the city is obtained (described p. 393); 8 A.M. –11:30 P.M., buildings open summer 11–5 (reduced schedule winter); bus 47 and 44, ferry from Slussen, in the summer ferry from Nybroplan, too.

National Museum of Antiquities and Royal Cabinet of Coins, at corner of Narvavägen-Linnégatan; collections illustrating Sweden's history, from prehistoric times and the Middle Ages, and including the world's biggest coin; daily 11–4. Bus 41, 44 and 69 to Linnégatan, bus 47 to Djurgårdsbron, underground and bus 42 and 54 to Karlaplan.

Nordic Museum, Djurgården; large and varied collections of objects showing the progress of civilization in Sweden from the 16th century onwards; 10–4, Sundays 12–5, closed Mon. Sept–May; bus 47 and 44.

Royal Armory; Swedish State's collections of historical objects, such as costumes, arms and armory of Swedish kings, princes and other prominent persons from 16th-cent. on; 10–4, Suns. 11–4, closed Mon. Sept–April. (In the Royal Palace.)

Mediterranean Museum, Cypriot and Egyptian collections, 11–4 daily.

Waldemarsudde, Djurgården; former residence of the late Prince Eugen; paintings and sculptures; Sun. 11–5, weekdays (except Mon.) 11–4, in summer; Tue/Thurs evenings 7–9. Bus 47.

Thiel Art Gallery, Djurgården near Blockhusudden, private collection of Scandinavian and French art from around 1900; 12–4, Sun., 1–4.

Millesgården, Lidingö; former residence of the Swedish-American sculptor Carl Milles now belonging to the public. May to Oct. 15, 10–5 daily; closed in winter; by the subway to Ropsten, then bus 30.

Liljevalch Art Gallery, Djurgårdsvägen; temporary exhibitions; 11–5, Tues. evenings also 5–9. Bus 47 and 67, ferry from Slussen.

The Ethnographical Museum, Djurgårdsbrunnsvägen 34. Tue–Fri 11–4, Sat/Sun 12–4, closed Mon. Collections from Third World cultures.

Hallwyl Museum, Hamngatan 4; patrician home containing fine collections of painting, sculpture, furniture, ceramics, arms, etc.; not more than 10 visitors at a time; 12–3, closed Mon.

Swedish Museum of Natural History, Frescati; one of the finest natural science museums in Europe; weekdays 10–4, Sun. 11–5. Buses from Jarlaplan.

The National Museum of Science and Technology, in Museivägen, Norra Djurgården; collections include models of machines, illustrating development of technical engineering and industry; 10–4, Sat. and Sun. 12–4. Bus 69.

Stockholm City Museum, at Södermalmstorg in the old Town Hall (17th cent.); collections illustrating history of Stockholm including model of the former palaces of "Three Crowns" and "Non Pareil"; 11–5. Underground to Slussen, buses 43, 46, 48, 53, 55 and 59.

Museum of Far East Antiquities on Skeppsholmen. Outstanding collection, mostly Chinese. 12–4. Tues. evenings till 9. Closed Mons.

The Museum of Music, Sibyllegatan 2. Open daily 11–4, except Mon. Situated in a building dating from 1640. Concerts.

The Museum of Dance, Laboratoriegatan 10. 12–4, closed Mon.

The Toy Museum, Mariatorget 1 c. Closed Mondays. One of the biggest toy museums in Europe with more than 9,000 pieces. 12–4.

National Maritime Museum, Djurgårdsbrunnsvägen, Norra Djurgården; collections illustrating history of Swedish Navy and merchant marine. Daily 11–5. Bus 69.

Wasa, at Alkärret, Djurgårdsvägen. This Swedish man-of-war sank in 1628 on her maiden voyage and was raised in 1961. Restoration is presently taking place, and the "Wasa Dockyard" will function as a temporary exhibition ground; in summer, daily 10–7; in winter, daily, 10–5. Films every hour. Guided tours around the ship in the summer between the films, in the winter after the film at 10 and 12, 2 and 4.

 ROYAL PALACES, OTHER PLACES OF INTER-EST. Royal Palace; featuring nine major attractions: Three stately apartments, The Treasury, The Royal Armoury, The Hall of State, The Palace Church, The Palace Museum, and Gustav III Museum of Antiquities. 11–2, closed Mon.; changing of guard in west courtyard at noon, every weekday during summer, 1 P.M. Sundays.

The Hall of State and the Palace Church, in Royal Palace; May–Sept daily 12–3; Oct Sat/Sun 12–3.

Rosendal Palace, Djurgården; now a museum; in summer, 1–3 P.M., Mon. closed.

Gustav III Pavilion, Haga Park, near Brunnsviken; May–Aug 12–3, Sept. Sat/Sun 1–3. Mon. closed. Bus 515 to the Airport Terminal at Haga (short walk through the park).

Sturehov, a typical Swedish mansion from the 18th century, Sundays 1–4, reach by car, road E4 (south), get off at Botkyrka towards Vällinge, or by boat from Klara Mälarstrand. Wed., Sat. and Sun. at 10 and 11.

The Kaknäs Tower, Djurgården, daily 9–midnight, is reached by bus 69 from Norrmalmstorg. More than 500 ft. high, the fastest elevators in Europe take you up to the terrace where you get a unique view of Stockholm. Tape records guide you in four languages.

Drottningholm Palace, on island in Lake Mälar; magnificent 17th-century French-style building and gardens, notable interior; also **Theater Museum** and **"China Palace";** guided tours of all buildings every hour, May-Aug. 11–4, Sundays 1–4, Sept 1–3; fountains play daily 1–6; underground to Brommaplan, change to Mälaröarna buses (any line). In the summer, boat from Klara Mälarstrand weekdays at 11, 1 and 3, Sun. every hour, 11–6.

City Hall; guided tours weekdays 10 A.M. sharp; Sundays 10 (free) and 12; tower 11–3 in summer.

Royal Library, Humlegården; Sweden's national library; rich collections of books and manuscripts; free.

Royal Treasury, in the vaults of the old Royal Palace. Jewelry and regalia of Swedish royalty. The crown, scepter, orb and key of 1561 are still regarded as the principal emblems of the state. Open daily 11–3.

Cathedral, near Royal Palace; daily 9.30–7. Sound and light performances in summer.

Riddarholm Church, on Riddarholm Island; burial place of kings of Sweden; in summer 10–3, Sun. 1–3.

Engelbrekt Church, near Karlavägen; daily 10–6; bus 46, 50, 53 or 61.

Saltsjöbaden, year-round resort; train from Saltsjöbanan Station at Slussen, in about 20 minutes.

Gustavsberg, ceramics works; bus from Borgmästaregatan, 35 mins., or by boat (ask Tourist Office for schedule).

If you are interested in modern housing developments, the following areas are recommended: Danviksklippan, bus 53, skyscraper-type apartments overlooking city from the south; Torsvikplatån, "star"-type apartment houses, by underground to the end of line (Ropsten) then by bus over Lidingö bridge; Vällingby, Farsta and Skärholmen, underground from T-centralen. Newest developments are at Kista, Husby, and Akalla.

 SIGHTSEEING. In summer a number of round-trip tours may be made. **By air:** from Bromma Airport. **By boat:** within the harbor reaches, "Under the bridges", "Harbor and Canal tour", "Wasa tour", etc., on *Waxholm* boats, from Strömkajen/Grand Hotel, Mälartorget/Old Town, Strandvägen/Nybroplan (by *Tourist Sightseeing*); City Hall bridge (by *Forsman*). 20–25 boats operate from Stockholm to the islands in the Baltic and Lake Malaren. On most lunch is served. A few of the boats have steam engines. Enquire at the Tourist Office, or the information office outside the Grand Hotel. **By bus:** within the city and to the outskirts; from Karl XII's Torg, Gustav Adolfs Torg, Norrmalmstorg. **By train:** to the archipelago; from Saltsjöbanan Station at Slussen. There are escorted **walking** tours of the Old Town every evening from the end of May until mid-September at 6:30 P.M. For information, inquire: Tourist Information Bureau, Sverigehuset, Kungsträdgården or travel bureaus. **Guides** Authorized multilingual guides may be hired through the Tourist Information Office, tel: 227000; travel bureaus, and hotels. Book well in advance.

 TRANSPORTATION. The basic subway, tram, and bus fare of 4 SEK., for journeys within one zone, entitles you to unlimited transfers within an hour of the time the ticket is punched. An additional fare is payable for journeys into the suburbs, and on night lines after midnight. There are one-day cards for unlimited travel within the city limit at 15 SEK. A three-day card valid for the whole country is 50 SEK. Discount cards (20 coupons) at 50 SEK are also available. Youth under 16 and retired people travel at half fare. If you plan to use the subways or buses frequently it is advisable to buy a special discount card saving 33% of your travel costs. A monthly ticket for 120 SEK is a real bargain. Senior citizens pay only half. At most of the subway stations you find interesting works of art. A folder in Swedish is available at the station at T-Centralen (exit Drottninggatan). This is no doubt the world's longest art exhibition.

For a taxi, call 15–00–00; also available for sightseeing and excursions, and English-speaking drivers will be supplied on request. The sign *"Ledig"* indicates that a cab is free for hire. Ask for a "tourist taxi".

AIRPORT. Stockholm's airport is *Arlanda,* 25 miles north of the city. Coaches leave for Arlanda from Vasagatan 6–12, where they also put down arriving passengers (fare 25 SEK). The terminal is within walking distance of the subway (T-banan), Central Station, Sheraton, Continental and Terminus hotels. A limo-service is available. Ask the air hostess or your hotel for details.

 WATER SPORTS. Among the outdoor **swimming** facilities are the beaches at Rålambshov and Långholmen (the water is clean and unpolluted); Erstaviken, 25 minutes by train on Saltsjöbanan line from Slussen (change at Igelboda for "Erstaviksbadet"); Flaten Lake, 5 miles southeast of Stockholm (bus from corner of Ringvägen-Götgatan). There are also large open-air pools at Vanadislunden opposite Sveavägen, buses 52 and 61, and the new Eriksdalsbadet pool, underground to Ringvägen or bus 73, 90, 91.

Boats for **rowing** can be hired during the summer at Rålambshov Pier, Smedsuddsvägen, in Kungsholmen; at the pier below Eriksdalslunden at Årstaviken; at Kvarnviken in Blackeberg. **Motor boats** can be hired from Charter Boat, Norr Mälarstrand 64. The boats are of the Chris-Craft 26 Super Future type and are well-equipped, including water skis, fishing tackle, etc. **Fishing** is allowed in various localities in the Stockholm archipelago. A special permit is required, (unless you prefer to fish from the bridges), obtainable from the Tourist Information office in Sweden House.

 CAMPING. Official sites are located at Farstanäset (Södertörn), Bredäng, 6 miles south of town, and at Ängby by the bathing beaches. Other sites for tourists are at Finnhamn, Fjärdlång (Dalarö), Grinda, Galö (Handen), Kalmarsand (Bålsta) Rösjöbadet (Sollentuna), and Ellsboda (Bogesund near Vaxholm).

 GOLF AND TENNIS. Golfing enthusiasts have a choice of fourteen 18-hole courses. Among the best are: Stockholm Golf Club, Kevinge, train from Östra Station or bus from Jarlaplan; Djursholms Golf Club, Eddavägen Station, train from Östra Station; Drottningholm Golf Club, bus from St. Eriksgatan; Lidingö Golf Club, Sticklinge, underground to Ropsten thence bus; Saltsjöbaden Golf Club, Tattby Station, train from Saltsjöbanan Station, Slussen (change at Igelboda); on Värmdö, at Hemmestavik (bus from Borgmästaregatan) where Sweden's first Country Club recently opened.

There are a number of indoor **tennis** courts as well as outdoor courts at: Hjorthagen, in Jägmästargatan; Smedslätten, in Gustav Adolfs Park; South Ängby, in Färjestadsvägen; Enskede, Mälarhöjden, and Ålvsjö sports grounds.

 WINTER SPORTS. There are a number of **ski** trails in the vicinity of Stockholm and in the Södertörn and Roslagen areas. The track at Nacka is floodlit for night skiing. Both Fiskartorpet and Hammarby have slalom runs, lifts, and ski jumps. For **ice skating,** there are the Stadium, Östermalm Sports Ground, Tennis Stadium, and Johanneshov Rink at Sandstuvägen; many parks including central Kungsträdgården have winter rinks.

TELEPHONES. The telephone system in Sweden is completely automatic. There are English-speaking operators to help. The charge is the same whether the phone is red or green. Charges are lower to the USA and Canada on Sundays, and between 10 P.M. and 10 A.M. If you want to know what is going on in Stockholm dial 22–18–40 (all year round, 8 A.M. to 12 P.M.), and "Miss Tourist" will tell you in English about the day's chief events.

USEFUL ADDRESSES. Embassies: Britain, Skarpögatan 6; Canada, Tegelbacken 4; U.S.A., Strandvägen 101.

Tourist Information: Sverigehuset, Kungsträdgården; Hotell contralen, Central station.

Travel bureaus: Nyman & Schultz/Nordisk Resebureau, Stureplan 6; Resespecialisterna Resebureau AB, Birger Jarlsgatan 32; RESO, Västmannagatan 2, Hamngatan 31, Katarinavägen 7 and Kungsgatan 3; Swedish State Railways travel bureaus (Cook's/Wagons Lits representative) at Vasagatan 22, Hamngatan 18–20, and at Hantverkargatan 25–27; Skandinavisk Resebyrå, Kungsgatan 31; Svea Resebureau, Sveavägen 34; Swedish Touring Club - STF Resebyrå, Vasagatan 48.

Motoring: Royal Automobile Club (KAK), and Swedish Automobile Association (M), Sturegatan 32.

Car hire: City Biluthyrning, Klarabergsgatan 33; Avis, Sveavägen 61; Hertz, Drottninggatan 25; Freys Hyrverk (car with driver), Gumshornsgatan 5.

Post office: Central, Vasagatan 28–34, Mon.-Fri. 8 A.M.-8 P.M., Sat. 9 A.M.-3 P.M., Sun. 9 A.M.-11 A.M. Other post offices in Stockholm are usually open Mon.-Fri. 8.30–6.30, Sat. 8.30–1. Closed on Sundays. For *philatelists* there is a special office on Vasagatan opposite the central post office, open Mon. 8.30–3 and 4.30 P.M.-6.30 P.M. Tues.-Fri. 8.30–3, Sat. (Sept.-May) 8.30–1 P.M.

Youth Hostels: Swedish Touring Club, Vasagatan 48.

Stockholm Student Reception Service, SSRS, Körsbärsvägen 2, gives information about hotels, rooms, tourist and student activities.

STOCKHOLM ENVIRONS, DALARNA AND GOTLAND

The Capital as an Excursion Center

Stockholm is, in a literal sense, two-faced. It turns at one and the same time to two diametrically opposed worlds which have really only one thing in common—water. To the east the world is harsh, rough, rugged, primeval and its water is the treacherous salt water of the sea. To the west the world is friendly, civilized, the cradle of an ancient culture, and its water is the sweet water shed by farmland and forest. The former is the Stockholm Archipelago, the latter the valley of the sprawling, multi-armed Lake Mälar.

The Swedes have given the archipelago a name which is both romantic and descriptive, Skärgården, or Garden of Skerries. There are thousands of them, large and small, some wooded, some rocky, some even cultivated, separated by broad and narrow channels, indented by bays —in short, a unique seascape. The archipelago has supported a small and hardy farming and fishing population for centuries, living out quiet lives almost unnoticed until a few decades ago. Now the skerries are also a summer playground. And one of the great joys is convenience: you can get well out into the archipelago and back in a few hours.

Exploring the Stockholm Environs

Here are some of the principal summer resorts and sights, of which several are only an hour or so from Stockholm.

Sandhamn. Yachting center at the extreme eastern edge of the skerries, on the open Baltic Sea. Sandhamn's original importance was as a pilot station, but it is now also a popular summer resort because of its sandy beaches and good sailing facilities. The Royal Swedish Yacht Club has a clubhouse here and arranges a number of international races in the July-August regatta season. Daily boat connections from Stockholm. A package tour including round trip to Sandhamn, bed and breakfast is available for SEK 175.

Vaxholm. Characterized by an ancient fortress guarding the channel into Stockholm. (The German Field-Marshal von Moltke is said to have laughed on only two occasions in his life—one of them was at the sight of Vaxholm Fortress.) The fortress is now open as a museum showing the military defense of Stockholm over the centuries. Vaxholm is a small but progressive town with good tennis courts and bathing.

Tyresö Castle. An ancient estate southeast of Stockholm, only 40 minutes from Ringvägen, (bus No. 10). The estate has belonged to some of Sweden's outstanding noble families since the Middle Ages. Its last owner willed it to the Nordiska Museum in 1930. Interesting art, including 18th-century French paintings.

Nynäshamn. A seaside town. Good beaches. Port of departure for steamers to the Baltic Sea island of Gotland.

Here is an important note: *Some parts of the archipelago are defense zones, closed to foreigners.* These zones presumably contain military installations. To avoid possible inconvenience, check before starting. If you put ashore at a strange point, look for the presence of a sign which might indicate that it is a prohibited area. They are posted in several languages, including English. If, for any reason, you wish to enter one of the zones—it may be quite possible that some Swedish friend or acquaintance of yours has a summer cottage within one—you can apply to the "Kustartilleri-stationen" in Vaxholm. The regulations are fairly strict, and there is no guarantee that such an application will always be approved.

Lake Mälar, Birka and Uppsala

The valley of Lake Mälar might be called the cradle of the modern Swedish nation. Other regions of the country were undoubtedly settled earlier—but it was this region, during the last thousand years or so, that has furnished evolving Sweden its capitals and its political center of gravity. The oldest capital was presumably Birka, on the island of Björkö, about two hours by boat from Tegelbacken below the City Hall. Birka developed as a commercial center where the trade routes between Russia and the West crossed during the Viking Age (800–1000 A.D.), and it was here, in 829, that Christianity was preached in Sweden for the first time.

Birka was, unfortunately, wiped out completely in the 11th century, and nothing now remains to tell of its one-time significance except burial mounds and traces of the old fortifications, half-hidden in the birch groves. (The name Björkö means 'Birch Island'). At the highest point of the island there is a large cross to the memory of St. Ansgar, the first Christian missionary to undertake the perilous and slowgoing task of making converts out of Vikings. The complete process took centuries.

A thousand years of history, including a century when Sweden was one of the great world powers, is open to inspection here in a large, lovely valley. Many delightful excursions in and around the area can be completed in less than a day.

Uppsala can be placed on Lake Mälar only with the help of a little generosity and a canal, for it does not rest on the lake proper. Uppsala, old and new, has been a silent witness of 1,500 years of known history— as a heathen religious capital, as a political capital, as a Christian center and educational stronghold. Nearly 1,000 years have passed since Viking kings made their last sacrifices to Thor and Freya, but four huge burial mounds in Gamla (old) Uppsala, 3 miles north of town, testify to the power these gods once exercised over the hard-fighting, hard-drinking men and women of the North. In three of the mounds bones were found that are conjectured to be those of pre-Christian kings. The fourth mound was used as a rostrum. Where the present village church stands, a pagan temple roofed and walled with sheets of gold once attracted the international set of 1,000 years ago.

Uppsala has lost its importance as a political capital, but it is still the seat of the Archbishop of Sweden and, as the site of the oldest university in Scandinavia, an important European educational and scientific center.

Walpurgis Eve, April 30, is a national holiday, and is celebrated throughout the country with bonfires, but the most colorful observances are in the university cities of Uppsala and Lund. It is the national welcome to spring, a herald of longer days and more light after the dark winter months. Undoubtedly an ancient holiday, taken over from the heathens, it has presumably been celebrated for thousands of years.

The celebration continues all day, reaching a climax at darkness, when the student body proceeds in a torch-lit parade to a point on the height near the castle. There, with the graceful silhouette of 700-year-old Uppsala Cathedral thrusting up its twin spires in the background, the president of the students' association pronounces a traditional welcome speech to spring, and the thousands of student voices rise up in impressive song. Festivities then continue at student houses and the restaurants. If you have friends who are members or can swing it some other way, try to angle an invitation to one of the "nations", or student clubs, for their dinner, supper, and dancing. If that's impossible get a reservation at one of the restaurants.

Cathedral, Castle and Codex

Whatever time of year you come to Uppsala, however, there are a number of things well worth seeing. Uppsala Cathedral is perhaps the most impressive religious structure in Scandinavia, as well as the largest. You might begin your look at Uppsala there. It's only about a 15-minute walk from the railway station, and a pleasant stroll. The cathedral dominates the city, so you can't miss it.

Uppsala Cathedral is mentioned in written records as early as about 1285, but it was a long time building and wasn't ready for dedication until 1435. This structure succeeded an earlier, more modest church in Old Uppsala. The spires are almost 400 feet high, and said to be exactly as high as the church is long.

Aside from the Gothic architecture generally, note the following: the monumental sarcophagus back of the main altar, containing the remains of King Gustav Vasa (1496 or 1497–1560), founder of the modern Swedish kingdom, and two of his wives; the silver coffin nearby supposed to contain the remains of St. Erik, Sweden's patron saint (who died in the 12th century); and the collection of church silver and vestments. The latter includes exquisite items, among other things a red cloth-of-gold dress worn by Union Queen Margareta. It is more than 600 years old.

Near the cathedral you will find the principal university buildings. Take a look in the library, Carolina Rediviva, the largest in Sweden. It has a million or so printed volumes and almost 20,000 hand-illuminated medieval manuscripts. The most valuable treasure is the famous *Codex Argenteus*, the Silver Bible from the 5th century which is the only extant book written in pure Gothic. Capital letters are illuminated in gold, the rest in silver.

The huge red castle was begun by King Gustav Vasa about 1550 and it was here that Queen Kristina, daughter of Gustavus Adolphus, laid down her crown in 1654 in one of the most touching scenes in the nation's history. The event took place in the impressive Hall of State, which is open to the public. The castle now serves as the residence of the provincial governor and headquarters of the provincial government.

Among the other principal sights in or near Uppsala are:

The home of Carl von Linné (Linnaeus), beloved botanist known as the "flower king", who died in 1778, at Svartbäcksgatan 27. The house, grounds, and gardens are preserved much as Linné left them, and a number of his personal possessions are exhibited.

Old Uppsala, the oldest known political and religious center of the Kingdom of Svea, predecessor of the Swedish realm. This was the principal shrine of the Sveas, with a sacrificial well and a grove regarded as holy. The three huge burial mounds date from about 500 A.D., and contain the remains of the kings of the Yngling dynasty. The flat-topped mound nearby is supposed to be a judgment and election site from those early days. Christianity finally conquered even this powerful stronghold, and a church was built on the ruins of the heathen temple, about 1125 A.D. The present massive structure was built something over a hundred years later, includes walls of the first church and, the archeologists say, parts of the old heathen structure. You can inspect the latter by descending a trapdoor through the floor between two of the pews. Old Uppsala is only 2 miles from Uppsala, and there is regular bus service from the center of town. Enter the bus marked "Gamla Uppsala".

Sigtuna, Skokloster and Gripsholm Castles

Sigtuna was founded about the year 1000 by Sweden's first Christian king, Olof Skötkonung, and for a time it was the chief political and religious center of the country. Sigtuna is located north of Stockholm, a little more than half way to Uppsala. It is not on the main railway line; you change to a bus in Märsta. A visit to Sigtuna can suitably be combined with an outing to Uppsala.

The Sigtuna sun rose rapidly and sank rapidly. Bearing witness to its brief age of glory are the ruins of the first stone edifices erected in Sweden, pre-Norman churches dedicated to St. Per, St. Olof, and St. Lars. These were also fortresses, designed as much with an eye to defense as to the glorification of God. They overlooked a thriving community for nearly 200 years, during which the first Swedish coins were minted and Anglo-Saxon missionaries pushed the conversion of the Swedes.

Despite the stone churches, the city was more or less destroyed in 1187 by Vikings from across the Baltic, but lived on, thanks partly to the Dominican Monastery. The Reformation delivered a new blow, the monasteries were closed, and Sigtuna sank into obscurity. In modern times it has begun to flourish again as an educational and religious center.

You will find Sigtuna more idyllic than exciting. Note the charm of its narrow main street—Stora Gatan—which is said to follow its original route of 950 years ago and is known as the oldest street in Sweden. The layers of earth here have furnished the archeologists with a wealth of finds, from which they have reconstructed the life of various centuries. Maria Church, once the Dominican Monastery church was one of the first brick churches in the whole Lake Mälar valley, but only a few ruins remain of the monastery itself. St. Olof's Church gives you a good idea of the military aspects of early church architecture—it dates from about 1050. The construction material was rough granite blocks, the windows are mere loopholes, and the entrance just large enough to admit one person at a time.

On the heights overlooking the city you will find the modern institutions which have given new life to Sigtuna. One is the Sigtuna Foundation, sponsored by the Swedish Church, which includes a continuation college for adults, a chapel, and a guest house—the latter popular among authors as a good place to work. The others are the Sigtuna Academy and the Humanistic Academy, both boarding schools, and the College for Laymen, for instruction in volunteer parish work. Note also the unique little 18th-century Town Hall—supposed to be the smallest in the country—and a number of rune stones. About 10 miles northeast of Sigtuna lies Skokloster Castle.

Skokloster has recently been sold to the Swedish State. It has the richest collection of art treasures from the Swedish Imperial Era, and its display of weapons is outstanding.

The castle was built between 1654 and 1679 by Carl Gustaf Wrangel, one of Gustavus Adolphus' best-known field marshals. When he died it went to a relative, Count Nils Brahe, and was passed on from one Brahe to another until the family died out about 20 years ago. It then came into the hands of a related family, the von Essens. For the most part the furniture, paintings, and tapestries antedate the Thirty Years' War. The library contains some 30,000 volumes. A motor museum is the last private owner's contribution to his forefathers' collection, and there is now a hotel and vacation center in the grounds.

A pleasant place for a short excursion from Stockholm is Sturehov, 14 miles west of the city. This is an old mansion and estate belonging to the city of Stockholm and used for civic entertainment, but it is also open to the public. The mansion is an exceptionally fine example of 18th-century Swedish architecture and interior design, and contains about a dozen porcelain stoves from the famous Marieberg factory, apart from many other treasures.

Gripsholm Castle is an ideal day-excursion by boat from Stockholm. You ride 3 pleasant hours through the beautiful scenery of Lake Mälar, stop in Gripsholm long enough for an inspection of the old castle and a good lunch, and get back to Stockholm by early evening. As a castle site, Gripsholm dates back to some time in the 1300s but the present towered structure was begun about 1535 on the orders of King Gustav Vasa. Fully restored, livable and well maintained—after a period as a state prison—Gripsholm today is an outstanding museum, with a large and fine collection of historical portraits.

In the castle, note particularly the little theater. It, like Drottningholm Theater, owes its existence to drama-loving King Gustav III, and has been preserved in its original condition. Although much smaller, in the opinion of many it is vastly more beautiful and full of atmosphere than its counterpart at Drottningholm. Nearby is the prison tower, where the tragic King Erik XIV (whom Strindberg made the central figure of one of his most powerful dramas) was held captive after his dethronement. The collection of portraits was begun by King Gustav Vasa himself in the 16th century, and now numbers nearly 3,000 paintings, with emphasis on Swedish royalty but with a number of royal figures from other lands.

In the courtyards note particularly the rune stones, among the best preserved to be found, and the artfully designed bronze cannons, war booty from the Swedish wars with Russia centuries ago. (Incidentally, the Soviet government has made unsuccessful efforts to get them returned to Russia. The Swedes, however, seem inclined to keep these memories of days when inferior Swedish forces often licked the tar out of the Czar's finest.)

The adjoining city of Mariefred boasts less than 3,000 inhabitants and is one of the smallest cities in Sweden. The church is from the 17th century, the Town Hall from the 18th. There is a two-mile-long narrow-gauge railway with steam engines and cars dating from the beginning of this century. This is in operation daily from June 23 to August 18 and on Sundays from the beginning of May until the end of October.

Idylls of Dalarna

The province of Dalarna is perhaps Sweden's most traditional tourist attraction. It is rich in what is often called local color—ancient traditions, national costumes and bright peasant dresses, rural fiddlers and dances, a unique popular art and handicrafts. It has been a favorite holiday region for both Swedes and visitors abroad for decades.

The very names of the province tell you quite a bit about it. Dalarna means literally "The Valleys", and is utterly appropriate. There are both river and lake valleys, usually clad in the year-round greenery of the fir forests. Dalecarlia is presumably an Anglicized form of *Dalkarl* —man of Dalarna—and the men of Dalarna have played a unique part in the nation's history.

It was these freedom-loving men of Dalarna who had such a great role in the wars of liberation in the 15th and 16th centuries, who rallied around the standard of King Gustav Vasa and followed him to eventual freedom. It was also the men of Dalarna who were the last of the Swedes to accept the Stockholm government, which they thought was getting too big. Many of the independent men of Dalarna have traveled in or emigrated to far parts of the globe, and there were whole villages deserted in the great wave of emigration to the United States.

Side by side with this ancient rural culture, industry began here many centuries ago, and the province can be said to contain the nation's oldest industrial center. Even during Viking times primitive weapons were hammered out of the iron ore found in swamps, and before the year 1300 rolled around there was a share company digging the copper treasure out of the mine in the city of Falun. It is Stora Kopparbergs Bergslags Aktiebolag, still thriving and presumed to be the oldest corporation in continuous operation in the world.

From a casual look at this city of some 34,000 inhabitants you would hardly suspect its importance in the history of Europe and, consequently, of our whole western culture. But the Falun copper mine was what financed Sweden's imperialistic adventures of a few centuries ago, including the highly successful campaigns of Gustavus Adolphus. And his part in the eventual victory of Protestantism in the Thirty Years War was of decisive significance in the march of events for centuries to come.

The big hole has not yielded copper in commercial quantities for decades, but it is still a source of iron pyrites and other ores. It is from here that the basic ingredients are taken for the red paint which traditionally glows from most of the rural buildings throughout the nation. When the copper ran out, the corporation, Stora Kopparberg, was still vigorous enough, despite its five centuries or more of age, to move into new fields and capture a new position of importance in the economy of the world. It has huge holdings in forests, water power, and iron ores, is the largest private producer of hydroelectric power in the country, and its various plants make everything from sheet steel to newsprint paper. The main offices, which include an excellent library and archives illuminating principally the history of the company and the local region, are located in Falun, just off the main square. A little over 10 miles away, by a good highway (bus service), is Borlänge, site of the Domnarvet Steel Plant, one of the company's principal factories. It is the largest steel plant in Sweden.

The open pit of the copper mine may not look terribly impressive from the standpoint of pure size to anyone who has seen, let us say, the huge open pits of the Mesabi ore range in northern Minnesota. It had its origin in a catastrophic cave-in that occurred in 1687. In the old days, the miners would first build a fire on the rock, cool it with water after the rock was hot, then chip out the ore-bearing stone with crowbars and picks. Right at the edge of the pit is the Mine Museum, illustrating the history of the mine and the city. Of particular interest, and unique, are the huge copper coins from the 17th and 18th centuries. The very largest coin ever minted so far as is known, was one of these models, measuring 12 by 28 inches and weighing some 40 pounds. Those were the days when paper money would have been a sensation. Parts of the old mine are now open to visitors.

Other sights include the two old churches; Kristine, on the main square, from the 17th century, is remarkably ornate for a church which is not a cathedral. The provincial museum, Dala Fornsal, has good collections.

Midsummer Eve and Lake Siljan

Starting from Falun and traveling by car or bus, you can make a round trip tour north to the city of Mora, about 60 miles away, circling Lake Siljan and visiting a number of the traditionally famous resort towns en route. It is in this Lake Siljan region that the ancient Swedish festival of Midsummer Eve, celebrated during the weekend closest to June 23, perhaps has its strongest traditional roots, and is most colorful. The observance begins in late afternoon, with the raising of what is still called a Maypole, in late June, usually decorated with some kind of symbol at the top and clad from top to bottom with green branches and wild flowers. Then there is dancing around the pole, in national costumes, usually with the whole family joining in. Dancing continues all night, preferably in the open air, at pavilions or on platforms specially erected for the purpose. There is no real darkness at this season of the year, only a few hours of a strange, exhilarating dusk.

Your first main stop on this circular tour of Lake Siljan will probably be Leksand, a community dating from well before the Christian era. The lovely church is built on the site of the old heathen temple and is one of the oldest in the province. Visit it any Sunday for a sight of people attending services in the old national costumes characteristic of Leksand; quite a few folk still wear them.

Leksand boasts one annual event not duplicated anywhere else in the world—the church boat races in July. The boats, designed like small versions of Viking ships and accommodating about ten seats of oars plus room for passengers, were once commonly used by the people of the parishes around Lake Siljan for going to church. The tradition is preserved in the annual race, with crews from the various parishes competing. The event draws nationwide attention.

Another Leksand event is *The Road to Heaven,* an open-air miracle play based on provincial traditions, with folk music and folk dancing. It runs for about ten days in July. By all means try to hear an orchestra of fiddlers—their traditional music is unique. You may find it somewhat related to the bagpipe—strangely enough—but considerably more pleasing to the uninitiated ear. Or listen to some discs in a music shop.

As you travel these routes, note the old and picturesque buildings, some of them concentrated into villages. They represent a highly developed rural culture, and many of the interiors are exquisite samples of an unusual popular art. The semi-primitive paintings of Dalarna are justly famous; for example, you will find traditional Biblical figures staring out at you in countenances and clothes resembling those of a Dalarna farmer more often than a formal picture of, say, the Angel Gabriel.

Among the best places to get a good idea of these arts and crafts are two stops a little farther along the route. The first is Tällberg, a resort with a magnificent natural site, where you will find the home of the late Swedish artist, Gustaf Ankarcrona, now a museum with a number of works of rustic artists; and the second, Rättvik. Rättvik has a "Gammelgård", an old Dalecarlian farmstead, richly adorned with rustic peasant paintings. Performances by folklore musicians and folk dancers are twice-weekly features during July until mid-August. The old church, known as "The Kneeling Bride", is beautifully located on a point in Lake Siljan.

Gustavus Vasa's Appeal at Mora

Mora is one of the most interesting provincial towns in Sweden. First of all, it was the home of the painter Anders Zorn, which means the Zorn Museum (with much of Zorn's best as well as other works of art), his quaint home—also a museum—and Zorn's Gammelgård, a collection of some 40 timber buildings as much as 600 years old. The latter is the seat of the study of wooden architecture in Sweden. Mora means the statue of King Gustavus Vasa by Zorn, and a statue of Zorn by Christian Eriksson. Mora means history: here is where the population finally rallied to the cause of freedom behind Gustavus Vasa in the decisive war of liberation. Mora means winter sports, opening as it does on the snow regions of the northern part of the province.

Don't miss the Zorn Museum. Sweden's most famous painter is classified as an impressionist, but it is his lush use of color in his portraits of the local people that give him his greatest appeal. Some of the comely young maids of Dalarna as portrayed by him—in varying stages of undress—are inimitable.

The church dates from the Middle Ages and is well worth seeing. The statue on the mound across the street is that of Gustavus Vasa, erected on the spot where he is supposed to have delivered a speech to incite the population to fight for liberation from the Danes. They didn't react at once, and subsequent events gave rise, of all things, to what is now the major annual skiing race in Sweden. Sweden was still technically a part of the Scandinavian Union, under a Danish king, at this time. It seems that in the year 1521, after a number of narrow escapes from the Danish bailiffs and soldiers who didn't care for his liberation ideas, Vasa had made a last appeal to the traditionally freedom-loving Dalecarlians. But even they were tired of the years of fighting, and the only course open to Vasa was to flee over the mountains to Norway. Once he departed, however, the men of Dalarna got to thinking it over and talking it over, and changed their minds. They sent a couple of their fastest skiers after Vasa with the word, and they caught up with the future King at Sälen, 55 miles west and a little north.

Every year, usually on the first Sunday in March, crosscountry skiers from Sweden and from abroad race the same route in reverse, from Sälen to Mora. The event draws 8,000 competitors and tens of thousands of spectators both from Sweden and abroad.

You'll find memories of Vasa here and there throughout the region. A mile or two from town is a cellar in which he is supposed to have hidden from the Danes. A small building has been erected over it, containing two or three large interesting paintings representing scenes from Vasa's career.

Visby and the Isle of Gotland

If you choose to visit Visby—the "City of Ruins and Roses" on the storied isle of Gotland in the Baltic Sea—during the off-season, say early November, you will find the short flight from Stockholm unforgettable. The sunset will provide one of those incredible displays of color that are to be found only in this part of the world.

At the Visby airport, you will be amazed to see a bed of red, red roses, in this northern corner of the world, still blooming. According to the inhabitants, roses are sometimes to be seen blooming in even December and January. Whatever the season, the red has a special brilliance resulting from the composition of the soil.

You feel something in the very atmosphere of Visby, a sense of the Middle Ages living on into the 20th century. Looping around the city is the magnificent wall, completely embracing it on all but the sea side. And everywhere are buildings centuries old, some of them well preserved, others, particularly the churches, in a gaunt state of disrepair that adds to their charm. Try, if you can, to see the view from the Powder Tower in the moonlight. This tower, serving as one of the main anchors of the wall, near the sea on the north side of town, is perhaps the oldest of the watch towers that rise up at intervals along the medieval wall.

The history of the island of Gotland, and the capital city Visby, goes back thousands of years, and its earth has yielded treasures speaking eloquently of contacts with the Minoan, Greek, and Roman cultures. But the Golden Age arrived in the 12th century, when Visby and Gotland dominated the trade of northern and western Europe and the town could undoubtedly be classed as one of the major cities of the world. Wealth followed wealth, and within the confines of the city wall alone, itself a magnificent structure from every standpoint, the rich merchants erected no less than 17 churches. Outside of the city, farmer-merchants built parish churches more like small cathedrals than rural houses of worship. On the whole island, measuring only about 30 by 80 miles, there are approximately 100 churches still intact and in use today, which date from this great commercial era.

Trade routes shifted. War parties ravaged. The first of a series of major catastrophes took place in 1361, when the island and city fell to Danish King Valdemar Atterdag. The decline had set in with a vengeance. The island was variously occupied by Baltic powers during the succeeding century and more, until 1645, when it was definitely sealed into the Swedish kingdom.

Today, the island is a vacation paradise *par excellence*. There is no lack of sights in the traditional meaning. See the churches and medieval merchant palaces of Visby—St. Nicholas, St. Clemens, the Church of the Holy Spirit, St. Catarina, and a half dozen more—and the wall. *Walk* to see Visby—pick up a map and an English guidebook at the travel bureau in Burmeister House, itself a historic building near the harbor—and wander. Wherever you go, you can't go wrong. Don't miss the museum, particularly the impressive picture stones, which antedate the Viking rune stones. There are other remarkable finds on display, too—coins and jewelry from many centuries, religious art (note particularly the gentle loveliness of the Öja Madonna, a medieval wood sculpture), and ancient weapons unearthed from the scenes of battles for this once flourishing island.

If you happen to be in Visby at the end of July or in early August don't miss the pageant opera "Petrus de Dacia" performed in the ruin of St. Nicholas Church.

Justice cannot be done to the cultural history of Visby and Gotland in anything smaller than a book. The names of the masters who designed and decorated these churches have been lost to history, but scientists have been able to identify and classify a few of them by characteristic features of their styles as they recur in various works. Among the dozens of rural churches well worth visiting in the vicinity of Visby, the following have been selected more or less at random—there are many others.

Rural Churches

Barlingbro, dating from the 13th century, with vault paintings, stained glass windows, remarkable 12th-century font.

Dalhem, one of the 16 largest rural religious edifices, construction begun about 1200 or somewhat earlier, an exquisite example of Gotland church architecture.

Gothem, one of Gotland's most impressive country churches, mainly built during the 13th century, with notable series of paintings of that period.

Grötlingbo, a 14th-century church with stone sculpture and stained glass: note the 12th-century reliefs on the façade.

Tingstäde, another of the 16 largest, a puzzle of six building periods from 1169 to 1300 or so. Note the general proportions, the stained-glass windows, and murals from the 14th century.

Roma Cloister Church, the massive ruins from a Cistercian monastery founded in 1164. The ruins are sufficiently well preserved to give a good picture of the architecture and construction.

Öja, decorated with paintings and containing a famous Holy Rood from the late 13th century.

There are a number of other sights well worth your time. Among them are curious rock formations along the coasts, including the "Old Man of Hoburgen" at the southern tip of the island; and two island bird refuges off the coast south of Visby, Stora and Lilla Karlsö. The bird population consists to a large extent of guillemots, which look like penguins. Visits to these refuges are permitted only in company with a recognized guide, and the easiest way to see them is to join a conducted tour from Visby.

PRACTICAL INFORMATION FOR THE ENVIRONS
OF STOCKHOLM

 WHEN TO COME. The vacation period reaches its summer peak in July and August, its winter peak in Dalarna comes in February and March. For special events at other times of the year, go to Mora for the cross-country ski race, usually the first Sunday in March; to Uppsala on April 30, Walpurgis Eve; to Dalarna for midsummer Eve festivities on the weekend closest to June 23.

 WHAT TO SEE. In the archipelago: the castles at Vax-holm and Tyresö. In the valley of Lake Mälar: Grip-sholm Castle and its portrait gallery, the 17th-century castle (with its Motor Museum) of Skokloster, Sigtuna, with its rune stones and House of Antiquities.

At Uppsala: the university, cathedral, castle and burial mounds in Gamla Uppsala.

In Dalarna: Falun copper mine, the open-air museum "Gammelgården" at Rättvik, and Anders Zorn memorabilia at Mora.

On Gotland: Visby, containing the richest medieval remains in Sweden; the medieval churches of Anga, Barlingbro, Dalhem, Endre, Gothem, Lärbro, and Väskinde, among others; the bird sanctuary of Stora Karlsö.

 HOW TO GET ABOUT. One way, but not the least expensive, to see the archipelago is by chartered cruiser (Taxi-Båt). In summer scheduled water-bus services ply to most points of the archipelago from Stockholm: *em-barking* at Klara Strand (near City Hall) for Gripsholm Castle and Drottning-holm Castle; at Munkbron (Old Town) for Skokloster Castle; at Strömkajen (near Grand Hotel) for Sandhamn, Husarö, Möja and Vaxholm; at Slussen for Sandhamn (bus with boat connection); from Central Station by train, bus and coach to Utö.

To Visby, it is a 5-hour night trip by comfortable motorship from the port of Nynäshamn (an hour or so by train or car from Stockholm). You can leave Stockholm one evening and arrive back by midnight next day, leaving Visby about 5 P.M. via the connection Visby-Nynäshamn or Visby-Södertälje. There are also day services between Visby and Nynäshamn in both directions every day from mid-June to mid-August. By air, Visby may be reached by daily flights from Stockholm in less than an hour.

There are 3,000 bikes for hire at Gotland; inquire at the tourist bureau.

A day trip to Mariehamn on the Åland Islands (Finland) provides a wonderful boat journey through the Stockholm archipelago: the fare is under 50 Skr roundtrip.

MOTORING. If you have your car with you in Sweden, by all means bring it along to Gotland. The car ferries alternate on the routes Nynäshamn-Visby (5 hours), Södertälje-Visby (6 hours), Västervik-Visby (3 hours 45 min.), Oskarshamn-Visby (4 hours and 40 min.), Oskarshamn-Klintehamn (4 hours) and Klintehamn-Grankullavik/Öland (3 hours).

A tour of the Uppsala-Lake Siljan-Lake Mälar areas can be made following this itinerary:

First day: Depart Stockholm-(Sigtuna)-Uppsala-Gävle-Sandviken-Falun-Leksand-Bergsäng hills route (Tällberg) to Rättvik-Mora returning to Leksand. Distance, about 272 miles (438 km).

Second day: Leksand-Grangärde-Örebro-Eskilstuna-Strängnäs-Mariefred, Gripsholm Castle-return Stockholm. Distance, about 279 miles (449 km).

Husbyringen is a scenic 35-mile route in Dalarna. It starts at Husby some 13 miles north of Hedemora and runs over Långshyttan-Sifhytteå-Stjärnsund-Kloster. Along this route you will find many remains of past industrial activity as well as many thriving modern industries. Hotel and inns along the route; numerous opportunities for fishing pike, perch and trout.

 SPORTS. Sailing, swimming, and **boating** are the principal activities at the lake and seaside resorts.

Skiing is concentrated in Dalarna, with the season normally running from Christmas through March, into April in the northern centers. Dalarna resorts include Falun, only 150 miles from Stockholm. Even nearer: Fagersta, in the southern part of the province, and Borlänge which both offer good skiing not far from the capital. In the center of the province, grouped about Lake Siljan, are its principal resorts, all of which have slalom runs and skating rinks, and from which sleighing parties are organized, while ski trails lead to chalets in the surrounding mountains. The largest are Leksand, Tällberg, Rättvik, and Mora, the terminus of the Vasa Ski Race. The start of the race, Sälen, has ski lifts, and its Högfjälls Hotel is one of the few fashionable establishments in a country which doesn't much mix society and sports. In the north are Älvdalen and Grövelsjön, tucked against the Norwegian border, in the highest region of this province, where there are many fine runs and some peaks above the tree line, but much less abrupt and better suited to beginners than the higher stretches of Lapland. The latter (2,676 feet) has a slalom run dropping 574 feet in a length of 2,034 feet.

Southern Sweden is the center of **sail-skating** and **ice-yachting.** Farthest north for this sport is Uppsala, which manages to be on Lake Mälar by grace of a canal; on the lake are Eskilstuna, Västerås, and Enköping, all of which have clubs and just east of the lake Stockholm has two, one for skate-sailing and one for ice-yachting: its suburb, Djursholm, has another. Farther south, Nynäshamn and Norrköping, are also sail-skating centers.

 HOTELS AND RESTAURANTS. You'll find the hotel standards good, with luxury the exception. Inexpensive boarding-houses also exist practically everywhere. Many resort hotels also offer demi-pension rates (breakfast and dinner), and advantageous pension rates for a stay of 3 days or more.

BORLÄNGE. Hotels: *Brage,* 94 rooms, most with bath. A SARA hotel. *Gylle Wärdshus,* 32 rooms with bath or shower. Moderate.

FALUN. Hotels: *Grand,* Åsgatan 18–20, has 70 good-sized rooms, 38 with bath; near main square; moderate. *Ritz,* 38 rooms; inexpensive to moderate. *Esso Motor Hotel,* 85 rooms with bath or shower.
Restaurant: *Lilla Gormet,* fully licensed.

INSJÖN. Hotel: *Sätergläntans Gästhem,* 27 rooms, 2 baths, inexpensive to moderate pension rates. Pension: *Turisthotellet,* 67 rooms, inexpensive rates include service.

LEKSAND. Among the inexpensive hostelries are *Korstäppan,* 44 rooms, in a romantic turn-of-century setting, and *Turisthemmet "Tre Kullor",* 40 rooms.

LUDVIKA. Hotels: *Stadshotellet,* 33 rooms, inexpensive, fully licensed. *Star Hotel,* 66 rooms, nightclub; moderate.

MORA. Hotels: *Mora,* Strandgatan 12 in center of town opposite a park, 80 rooms, 20 with bath, fully licensed, moderate; its older annex *Gustaf Vasa,* is inexpensive, *Siljan,* 29 rooms, 8 with bath, moderate. *Esso Motor Hotel,* 47 rooms with bath or shower, moderate.

NYNÄSHAMN. Hotel *Nynäshamn,* 16 rooms, moderate.

RÄTTVIK. Hotels: *Lerdalshöjden,* 82 rooms, fully licensed, moderate. *Turisthemmet,* 23 rooms, is inexpensive.
Motels. *OK Motor Hotel,* 32 rooms with bath; *MHF Motel Tre Hästar,* 36 rooms, half with bath or shower. Swimming pool.

SÄLEN. Hotels: *Wärdshuset Gammelgården,* 22 rooms, 12 with shower in annex, moderate, *Lindvallen,* 22 rooms, inexpensive, cottages.

SIGTUNA. Hotel: *Stadshotellet,* 23 rooms, moderate, good, fully-licensed restaurants.

SILJANSNÄS. *Hotel Siljansnäs,* 38 rooms, most with bath, comfortable holiday hotel. Also cottages. Barn dancing. Pool. Moderate.

SKOKLOSTER. The grounds of the castle now house a vacation complex with a 73-room hotel, restaurant, water sports, fishing. Moderate.

SÖDERTÄLJE. *Esso Motor Hotel,* Verkstadsvägen 151, off E4, 112 rooms with bath.

TÄLLBERG. Hotels: *Green,* 75-rooms, all with bath. Charming atmosphere, beautifully located. Swimming pool, good cuisine. First class reasonable.
Dalecarlia, 75 rooms, 19 with bath, lodge-type hostelry overlooking Lake Siljan, landscaped grounds, terrace, fully licensed, moderate.
Also moderate are *Siljansgården,* 46 rooms, half with bath, 34-room *Tällbergsgården. Långbergsgården,* 30 rooms, 5 with bath and *Akerblads,* 41 rooms.

UPPSALA. Hotels: *Gillet,* 170 rooms, 95 with bath, near cathedral; cheerful décor, moderate to first class reasonable. *Uplandia,* 106 rooms with bath. First class reasonable. *Hörnan,* 35 rooms, inexpensive.

Motels: *Esso Motor Hotel,* Gamla Uppsalagatan 48, 125 rooms with bath or shower.

Restaurants: *Flustret,* Flustre Parken at west end of Västra Ågatan; continental and Swedish dishes, outdoor garden. Also good, fully licensed, are restaurants *Gillet* and *Valthornet,* Gottsunda (ICA). *Glunten,* Drottninggatan 5, is cozy. *Francis Drake* is at Kungsängsgatan 20.

VAXHOLM. Hotel: *Vaxholm,* 32 rooms, most with bath. First class reasonable.

VISBY. Hotels: First class is *Visby Hotel,* just off square, near quay; 94 rooms, half with bath; fully licensed, open all year. *Snäck,* 102 rooms, first class, new 1982. *Fritidsbyn Kneippbyn,* 36 rooms, inexpensive.

Restaurant: *Gutekällaren,* fully licensed.

YOUTH HOSTELS abound in the area; **Camping** among many sites are those at Avesta, Borlänge, Hedemora, Leksand, Malung, Orsa, Rättvik, Älvdalen, all in Dalarna; on Gotland, at Tofta and Visby; also at Eskilstuna, Katrineholm, Nynäshamn, Uppsala, Öregrund and Östhammar.

SWEDEN'S SOUTHLAND

Breadbasket, Battlefield and Summer Playground

Southern Sweden is a world of its own, clearly distinguished from the rest of Sweden by its geography, culture, and history.

Scania (the Swedish name is Skåne, pronounced "scone-eh"), the southernmost province, is known as the "granary of Sweden". It occupies a more or less rectangular area, including the almost square peninsula that forms the southern tip of the country and supports no less than one-eighth of the whole Swedish population. It is a comparatively small province of beautifully fertile plains, sand beaches, scores of castles and châteaux, thriving farms, medieval churches, and summer resorts.

East of the northern end of Scania is the province of Blekinge, called "Sweden's garden", occupying another southern coastal reach extending to the east coast. North of the western part of Scania, ranging along the west coast of Sweden, is the province of Halland, a rolling country of heaths and ridges rising above the beaches. Halland faces the Kattegat (the southeastern part of the North Sea), and contributed its full share of the Viking forces which once struck terror into the populations of many countries. It still produces its share of modern sea captains.

428

There is an old tradition that while the Lord was busy making Scania into the fertile garden that it is today, the devil sneaked past him farther north, and made the province of Småland. The result was harsh, unyielding, unfriendly country of stone and woods and more stone. When the Lord caught up with Satan and saw what had happened he said, "All right, it's too late to do anything about the land . . . so I'm going to make the people." He did, and He made them so tough and stubborn and resilient and long-lived that they carved a true civilization out of their sparse heritage. There is still a folk saying that you can deposit a son of the province of Småland on a barren stone island with only an ax in his hands and he'll manage—and have a garden going before long.

Whatever the validity of the legend, it is true that Småland is vastly different from the other three provinces of southern Sweden. It is a good deal larger and is noted particularly for its glass industries, as well as furniture and other wood products, and its great historic region with Kalmar at the center.

Skåne, Blekinge, and Halland also form a natural historical group of provinces; they were actually the last incorporations of territory into what constitutes the present-day Swedish kingdom. The time was 1658. These southern provinces had been part of Denmark for centuries (and thus the medieval architecture is Danish). Sweden and Denmark had been fighting intermittently for generations. Karl X (anglicized as Charles X), a king and general of parts, whatever his faults, was off in Poland on one of the many indecisive Swedish attempts for a reckoning with that country. This looked to the Danes like a perfect opportunity for a reckoning with the Swedes. But when the Danish fleet arrived at Danzig to fall on the Swedish rear, the Swedes were moving overland at top speed toward Denmark. After two bold, unprecedented marches across the ice of the sounds separating the Danish islands, the Swedish army of 12,000 battle-hardened men faced an almost undefended Copenhagen. Although Sweden was also at war with Poland and Russia, Karl X was in a position almost to name his own terms. They were so rough that one of the Danish commissioners, preparing to sign this historic Peace of Roskilde, complained, "If only I didn't know how to write!".

By virtue of that treaty Sweden achieved natural southern boundaries—the coasts of the Baltic Sea—for the first time in its history, and acquired the rich territory which now nurtures one-fourth of the population. But the marks of long association with Denmark and its Continental culture live on in the language, the architecture, the way of life.

Exploring Sweden's Southland

Let's say that you have arrived in Helsingborg from the Danish side by ferry. In front of you stretches a long, comparatively narrow square, dominated at the far end, on the height, by a medieval tower stronghold known as Kärnan (the Keep). The surviving center tower, built to provide living quarters and defend the medieval castle of Helsingborg, is the most remarkable relic of its kind in the north. The interior, which may be visited, is divided into several floors, containing medieval kitchen fittings, a chapel, etc. From the top you have a magnificent view of the coast, the Sound, and the Danish shore.

A thousand years ago, this city was an important European capital. Today it is a thriving industrial town of some 101,000 inhabitants, the eighth largest city in Sweden. For centuries Helsingborg and its Danish neighbor across the Sound, Elsinore (Helsingør), only about 3 miles away, controlled all shipping traffic in and out of the Baltic Sea.

In Södra Storgatan are St. Mary's Church, built in the 13th century and rebuilt during the 15th century, with an interesting triptych and magnificent late Renaissance pulpit, and the Town Museum, containing exhibits depicting the early history of Helsingborg. Take time to visit Fredriksdals Friluftmuseum, an 18th-century mansion set in a lovely old park around which old Scanian farmhouses and buildings have been set up to form an open-air museum. During summer there are performances in the attractive open-air theater.

About 3 miles north of the city—bus to Pålsjöbaden, then a half-hour walk along the Sound—is Sofiero Castle, summer residence of the King, built in 1865 in Dutch Renaissance style. The grounds are open to the public (enter by northern gate near gardener's lodge).

North Along the Coast

If you proceed north from Helsingborg, you come immediately into a region of summer resorts stretching along a promontory. One of the main resort towns is Mölle, near the end of the peninsula, which looks out upon the south end of the Kattegat. Proceeding back along the north shore of this peninsula, you arrive in Ängelholm, a small and charming city at least 500 years old, which has become a popular summer resort.

Only some of the main stops can be mentioned here. As you continue north along the coast, the next in line will be Båstad, perhaps the most fashionable of the summer resorts in this region. It is frequented throughout the summer by the international set, and ambassadors and ministers of several countries may sometimes be in residence there at the same time. The principal attractions include the natural beauty of the region (known for its flowers and fruit orchards), 18-hole golf course, and several tennis courts. International tennis tournaments every year at the beginning of July.

Recommended is a visit to the Norrviken Gardens, two miles northwest of Båstad. They comprise a number of gardens of various styles, agreeably laid out in varied grounds and each one in character with the landscape's lines, perspectives and vistas. Just east of Båstad is Malen, with an interesting sepulchral mound from the 11th century B.C. It has been excavated and restored so that you can enter and study the stones set up in the form of a ship.

Don't miss Torekov, a little fishing village on the point of a peninsula about 6 miles due west of Båstad, which was recently discovered by summer visitors. Despite a too generous influx of summer folks in July and August, many of whom have built or bought their own homes, the community remains an authentic part of this coastal region. There is a tiny but interesting museum—not a few of whose treasures have been gathered from ships wrecked in the treacherous waters off the point. The days here are serene and rhythmical with the pulse of an ancient way of life, a life close to the sea. Just off the coast is an island—Hallands Väderö—a national reserve known for its flora and bird life.

Continuing north from Båstad, you cross almost at once into Halland, another of the provinces acquired by Sweden in the fantastically profitable peace of 1658. By this time you will have noticed the changing nature of the landscape, the way ridges billow up in more pronounced fashion from the coast. In back of them are broad heaths unique to this part of Sweden. This whole coastal province is another section of the long vacation playground of the west coast.

Halmstad, port, provincial capital, summer resort, is an industrial center with a population of some 46,000. It once was an important meeting point for the armies and negotiators of the Scandinavian governments, in peace and war. The town is some 600 years old on its present site, and the oldest building is the church, a Gothic structure from the 14th century. From an architectural point of view the modern buildings of the Town Hall, the theater and the library are well worth a visit. Miniland, near Halmstad, represents Sweden in miniature (scale 1:25). Nearby Tylösand is a popular summer resort.

Falkenberg, known for its salmon fishing, is an idyllic little city popular amoung vacationers. It is supposed to have been moved from a nearby site about 700 years ago. There is a minor industry. The outstanding sight is the stately bridge over the Ätran River, which dates from about 1750.

Varberg, port, industrial center, and summer resort, is also an old town, an embattled fortress in the Scandinavian wars. The old fortress has parts from the 13th century. The museum is one of the largest in the province: its collection includes the world's only known fully preserved medieval costumes.

South to Lund and Malmö

If you start south from Helsingborg, the first coastal town of any size will be Landskrona, a modern industrial and shipping center with some 35,000 inhabitants. The 17th-century fortifications surrounding Landskrona Castle are reputed to be the best preserved relics of their kind in Europe. From here the main route leads inland, and you are soon in historic Lund.

Lund was once the religious capital of a region which stretched from Iceland to Finland, over which the Roman Catholic archbishop resident here held more or less absolute sway in matters of faith. The city was founded almost a thousand years ago by the Danish King Canute the Great, and during its early burst of prosperity could boast a score of churches and a half-dozen monasteries. The Reformation changed all that. But the founding of Lund University in the 1660s, after the province became part of Sweden, brought new intellectual prosperity, and the arrival of the railroads, not quite a century ago, brought industrial prosperity. The population is about 80,000, and enrollment at the university and high schools about 20,000. The most colorful students' events are Walpurgis Eve, April 30, and the carnival in mid-May every four years.

The principal sight is the cathedral, whose construction was begun about 1080, a massive structure and one of the few churches in this part of the world in Romanesque style. There are a number of medieval treasures, of which the most notable is the huge, ornate, intricate astronomical clock that still plays daily at noon. This remarkable instrument, several yards high, will tell you practically everything about the position of the heavenly bodies and time except the date of your own birthday. The intricate mechanism and the beautifully carved figures which go into action when the clock plays make a fascinating sight. Nor should you miss Lund's Museum of Cultural History, the Archive for Decorative Art, and the Art Gallery.

Less than 19 miles southwest of Lund is the city of Malmö, the largest in southern Sweden and, with a population of 244,000, the third largest in the whole country. Malmö is the small but opulent capital of a small but opulent province, and a sense of well-being strikes you as soon as you set foot there.

In addition to the usual historical sights offered by most Swedish cities, Malmö distinguishes itself by having also a top-flight modern one—the City Theater. It is surprising that this comparatively small city has been able to build and maintain such an imposing stage. It was completed in 1944, seats 1,700 persons (other theaters in Malmö are the Intima, in the same location, and the NYA Theater, Amiralsg 35). If you have a chance to see an operetta or musical comedy here, by all means do so.

The impressive statue on the central square is that of Karl X—the king who acquired this part of the country for Sweden. Just off the square (look for the steeple and follow your eyes) you will find St. Peter's Church, a brick structure from shortly after 1300. It is the largest Gothic church in south Sweden.

The plains, the gently rolling hills and fields of the province of Skåne are broken every few miles by lovely castles, which have given this part of Sweden the name of the "Chateau Country". Usually they are surrounded by lovely grounds, often by moats, and they add a graceful note to travels through this region. Here, perhaps more than anywhere else in Sweden, these huge estates have remained in the hands of the original families, and they date from many centuries and many architectural periods. Some of them contain invaluable treasures of art and culture, and a few are open to the public.

Only 20 miles from Malmö, on a tiny peninsula projecting out from the very southwest corner of Sweden, are the idyllic little twin cities of Falsterbo and Skanör. Once important towns, they now are villages which still enjoy city rights, as well as being very popular summer resorts.

Continuing on from Malmö, you can make your way to Ystad, a medieval city on the southern coast. If you are driving, you might go by way of Torup Castle, a typical example of the square fortified stronghold, built about 1550. Ystad, perhaps more than any other city on the Swedish mainland, has preserved its medieval character, with winding, narrow streets and hundreds of half-timbered houses from four or five different centuries. Perhaps the principal ancient monument is St. Maria Church, begun shortly after 1200 as a basilica in Romanesque style, but with additions from several centuries. An historical curiosity is a half-timbered house (at Stora Västergatan 6) supposed to have been occupied by King Charles VII during two brief visits in Ystad shortly before and after 1700. Do see the old Franciscan monastery and its museum. Ystad has become a popular summer resort town.

Up Sweden's East Coast

Turning north again, along the east coast of Skåne, you may want to have a look at Simrishamn, a charming village with a pronounced medieval atmosphere, a favorite haunt for painters because of its clear air. Still farther north you find little Kivik, center of an orchard region, boasting an ancient royal grave which the scientists say dates from 1400 B.C. The Kivik grave is a huge, rounded mound of boulders and stones, and the crypt itself contains interesting picture stones.

In Maglehem, a few miles farther on your route north (and on the railway line), is to be found one of the most exquisite old churches in the whole region. It's an outstanding example of the architecture which prevailed here during the Danish era, with the massive white walls and stepped gables that you have been seeing everywhere in the province. Most of the interiors had been plastered over through the passage of the centuries, but thanks in great measure to the initiative of the local pastor, Erik Söderberg, who had devoted years to this labor of love, magnificent wall paintings have been brought out from as far back as the 14th century. There are a great many medieval churches in Sweden of which more than 150 are to be found in the province of Scania.

The next main town on this route is Kristianstad, founded in 1614 by Danish King Christian IV as a border fortress against Sweden. The Church, the Holy Trinity, is a typical example of Christian's building style. Not far from here is Bäckaskog Castle, and from here you can proceed to Kalmar by traveling east through the province of Blekinge, then north along the Baltic coast.

The province of Blekinge shares Skäne's and Halland's long association with Denmark, but the geography is considerably different. You will find fertile valleys and coastal regions—origin of the name "Garden of Sweden"—alternating with wooded heights, and a few miles north of the coast the landscape gives a hint of the rocks and woods of Småland across the border.

Sölvesborg, according to legend, was founded in 700 A.D. by a seagoing king named Sölve. Today it is a small port supported also by industry. The principal sights are the old castle, which played an important part in the Swedish-Danish feuds, and the church begun in the 13th century and constructed in Gothic style.

Karlshamn, a port which accommodates ocean-going vessels, is an idyllic coastal town. The Kastellet, or fortress, overlooking the channel into the harbor, was started by Karl X to defend the province of Blekinge from the Danes, who had just yielded it up to him. The elevators for grains and oilseeds are said to be the largest such concentration in Europe.

Ronneby was well known to vacationers of a couple of generations past for its mineral wells. The rebuilt resort hotel is still operating, and is set in an unusually beautiful park. The principal sight is a so-called fortress church, built probably in the 13th century.

Karlskrona was until recently the home port of the Swedish fleet, and the naval station still dominates the city. Well worth visiting is the Shipyard Museum (Varvsmuseet) in what was formerly the sailors' barracks. Its rich, in many ways unique, collections give a manyfaceted picture of the history of the Swedish navy, with special reference to its traditions in connection with Karlskrona. Two churches, the Holy Trinity and Frederik's, were planned by the outstanding architect Nicodemus Tessin. The city was founded in the 17th century.

Kalmar, a Name to Reckon With

You can see at a glance why Kalmar was once called "the Lock and Key of Sweden", and why it played an historic role in Scandinavian history before the airplane added a third dimension to warfare. The magnificent Renaissance castle—the earliest parts of which date from the 12th century—was also a mighty fortress, dominating the sound which separates the mainland from the island of Öland. When Kalmar began its age of greatness, the southern border of Sweden was only a few miles south—on the then Danish province of Blekinge. The long narrow island lying parallel to the mainland and thus forming a narrow channel completed the strategic picture: whoever controlled Kalmar controlled traffic along the coast north to Stockholm.

The importance of Kalmar is reflected in the name Kalmar Union (an agreement signed here in 1397), an ill-starred attempt to unite Scandinavia under one ruler. It limped along for more than a century of intermittent civil wars before it was formally dissolved by Swedish independence under Gustav Vasa in 1523. It was this great king who made Kalmar Castle what it is today—with its courts and battlements, its moat, its round towers. But even this powerful stronghold could not prevent the destruction and ravaging of the city in the recurring Danish-Swedish wars. The city was practically wiped out in the so-called Kalmar War of 1611–13. Fire again destroyed the town in 1647, and, with the Peace of Roskilde, the region lost some of its strategic importance. The decline had begun. Today Kalmar is the commerical and administrative center for southeastern Småland, a port and tourist attraction.

The principal sight is, of course, the castle. (*Note:* it closes at 4 P.M.) You get a good picture of the integrated life of a whole royal establishment as it functioned centuries ago, from the king's bedroom to the huge kitchens. Note especially the Castle Chapel, a charming little place of worship in rococo and Renaissance, which is still used for divine services (Sundays at 10 A.M.). The grim dungeon is a curiosity —it was cunningly placed below the surface level of the nearby sea— thus making attempts to tunnel out impossible. Prisoners sometimes survived for years in this dingy, damp hole. The castle also contains the extensive collections of the Kalmar Museum.

You will find the city itself rich in atmosphere and structures from the 17th and 18th centuries, when the present city was largely laid out and constructed. In particular see the cathedral (designed by Nicodemus Tessin the Elder and built about 1675). Not far from here is a smaller square (Lilla Torget), with the residence of the provincial governor, originally from 1674. It was the scene of a footnote to history —the French King Louis XVIII lived here briefly in exile shortly after 1800.

A Kingdom of Crystal

In Kalmar you are only an hour or two from some of the finest glass works in the world—Orrefors, Kosta, Boda, Strömbergshyttan. Exquisite pieces by famed designers from these factories are found in exclusive shops almost all over the world. But don't look for something that resembles an industrial region. The plants are scattered in the wooded wilderness of Småland, communities of a few hundred people built around the factory. From these isolated, unprepossessing villages go regular shipments to London and Paris, New York's Fifth Avenue, the cities of South America; special orders start on their way addressed to kings and emperors, presidents and ministers, tycoons and simple lovers of beautiful things.

You'll have no trouble getting in and having a look around: they are accustomed to visitors. Nevertheless, it's a good idea to call up in advance, thus making sure that the plant is operating on the given day and that you can be shown around. Important hint: the best crystal, the fancy and intricate pieces, is usually made in the mornings. (There are shops where glass of inferior design or quality and the first-class pieces are sold at good prices.) The finished pieces are normally sold through regular retail channels, and you'll have to do your buying at one of the shops to be found in almost every city. Even so, however, you save substantially in comparison with prices in other countries. Conducted tours are arranged round most of the glassworks.

Orrefors is the best-known Swedish glass maker, probably produces the greatest variety, and the quality and design are, of course, unsurpassed. The community of Orrefors is located about an hour west and a little north of Kalmar (train connections). It's so unpretentious you'll pass right through it if you're not looking.

Watching the skilled craftsmen of Orrefors (or one of the other plants) is almost like a slow dance—with the pieces of red hot glass being carried back and forth, passed from hand to hand, as they are blown and shaped by trained, sensitive muscles. The basic procedure and the tools are said not to have changed appreciably in 2,000 years. It seems peculiar, but the glass is actually cut with shears in its molten state—like scissors cutting tough taffy. The designing and engraving processes are also fascinating—and the finished product is the result of unusual teamwork, from the designer to the craftsman to the finisher. (Many of the pieces get no further treatment after leaving the blower and shaper, however.) One of the special attractions of Orrefors is a magnificent display of various pieces made through the years, ranging in value up to thousands of kronor.

Borgholm and the Isle of Öland

This long, narrow island is unique in several respects—and not least among them is the number of former citizens of the U.S.A. who dwell there. Öland was distinguished not only by the number of people who emigrated—the best figures indicate that of all the people alive today born on the island more than half are or have been in the U.S.—but by the number who came back. The latter figure is placed at 5,000, or nearly a fifth of the island's population today. It is said that practically every household contains someone who has been in the States for a few years. Strangely enough, the people never traveled elsewhere to any extent. Some have seen Denmark and England en route to or from the States, others saw something of France, courtesy of the American Army in World War II. Incidentally, the story of some early Swedish emigrants to the U.S. has been masterfully told by a Swedish author, Vilhelm Moberg, in *The Emigrants, Unto a Good Land* and *Last Letter Home,* published, and made into a film, in English. It deals with a family from the mainland, only a few miles from Kalmar, and a look at it will give you an interesting sidelight on the histories of Sweden and America.

The nature of Öland is so different from the mainland that you feel almost as though you had entered another country. This, and a great profusion of old-fashioned, more or less Dutch-type windmills, give the island an unmistakable profile. With luck you may be able to count as many as 84 such windmills in a couple of hours' auto tour. You reach the island over Europe's longest bridge (6,070 meters, about 4 miles).

Öland is a tourist mecca in the summer time. The capital, Borgholm, is a town of a little more than 2,000 people, offering many holiday activities during the summer. Here are a few of the most interesting sights:

Borgholm Castle ruin, perhaps the biggest and most beautiful ruin of a castle stronghold in Sweden. It originated as a medieval fortress, was rebuilt during the 16th and 17th centuries, and ravaged by fire shortly after 1800. It overlooks the city of Borgholm from a commanding site and is most impressive by moonlight.

Solliden is one of the summer residences of the royal family. The beautiful grounds around the sparkling white mansion are open at specified hours, depending on the time of year and whether the royal family is in residence. Located on the outskirts of Borgholm, within easy walking distance.

Gråborg Fortress. Only the massive stone walls, as much as 25 feet high and 25 feet thick, remain of this onetime stronghold, probably from about 500 A.D. This must have been a gigantic establishment at one time, for the walls enclose an area some 250 yards long and 190 yards wide.

At Eketorp there are excavations. A "Viking Village" is being built.

Much of Öland is covered by a huge, treeless steppe known as the Alvar, a limestone plateau without counterpart in northern Europe. It gives a sense of peace bordering on quiet desolation.

PRACTICAL INFORMATION FOR SWEDEN'S
SOUTHLAND

 WHEN TO COME. This refreshingly unspoiled holiday land can be enjoyed all summer, from June to October. Plan to come in June for the famous Sunlit Nights, or in August when transportation and accommodation are uncrowded. Even in September you'll find the water warm enough for swimming and the landscape at its colorful best.

 HOW TO GET ABOUT. Southern Sweden is linked with Denmark by boat via: Malmö-Copenhagen (1½ hours), Limhamn-Dragör (55 minutes), Landskrona-Tuborg (1¼ hours), Helsingborg-Elsinore (25 minutes), Varberg-Grenå (4½ hours) and Gothenburg-Frederikshavn (3¾ hours). Traffic is heavy on all runs, and the ferries carry cars and international trains. From Stockholm, Malmö is 6 hours by train, 10¼ hours by bus; Helsingborg 5 hours by train and 9 hours by bus. By air, Malmö is a mere 25 mins. from Copenhagen (4 flights daily); daily flights from Stockholm to Malmö (1 hr.). Local flights run between Malmö and Visby. There are bus services on all major roads; the express bus Malmö-Kalmar along scenic Highway E66 takes 7 hours (183 miles).

A hydrofoil service operates between Malmö and Copenhagen, with regular trips taking only 35 minutes.

 MOTORING. If you are driving from Stockholm and Helsingborg is your goal, follow Highway E4 all the way (363 miles or 584 km); from there, Highway E6 leads into Malmö. A more scenic route to Malmö from Stockholm follows Highway E4 to Norrköping, then swings off on the mainly coastal Highway 15. The circular tours suggested represent only a few of the circuits that can be made from centers in this area.

From Helsingborg. *North:* Vegeholm-Ängelholm-Torekov-Båstad-Helsingborg. Distance, 78 miles (130 km), *South and east:* Landskrona-Trolleholm-Trollenäs-Eslöv-Skarhult-Bosjökloster-Höör-Billinge-Knutstorp-Duveke- Helsingborg. Distance, 102 miles (170 km).

From Malmö. Lund-Svenstorps Castle-Örtofta Castle-Kävlinge-Borgeby-Bjärred-Malmö. Distance, about 41 miles (65 km). *South:* Torups Castle-Skabersjo Castle-Mänstorp Ruin-Vellinge-Kämpinge-Falsterbo-Höllviknäs-Vellinge-Malmö. Distance, about 50 miles (80 km.).

From Växjö. Circuit *"Tracing the Emigrants":* Hovmantorp-Kosta (glassworks)-Ljuder-Algutsboda-Långasjö-Rävemåla-Älmeboda-Linneryd-Ingelstad--Växjö. Distance, about 93 miles (155 km.).

 WHAT TO SEE. Halland: Lagaholm Castle ruins and Old Town (Gamleby) at Laholm; old castle and gate, modern town hall and Carl Milles' "Europa and the Bull" fountain at Halmstad; 18th-century stone bridges at Falkenberg, the ancient fortress at the holiday resort of Varberg.

Skåne: Kärnan tower, open-air museum (Friluftsmuseum), and St. Mary's Church at Helsingborg; Malmöhus Castle and museum, Renaissance buildings and City Theater at Malmö; university and cathedral at Lund; Norrviken Gardens at Båstad; the half-timbered houses of Ystad, Kristianstad, and Simrishamn; among the many country churches, those of Gårdstånga, St. Olof, Fjälie, and Vä.

Småland: Kalmar Castle and cathedral; the glassworks of Orrefors, Kosta, and others; Växjö's Glass Museum; House of Emigrants (Utvandrarnas Hus); country churches of Askeryd, Hagby, Lannaskede, and Dädesjö, among many others. The *Öland Bridge*, the longest bridge in Europe.

Blekinge: Swedish Baroque churches by the Tessins and Erik Dahlberg, Shipyard Museum, at Karlskrona; 12th-century Holy Cross Church at Ronneby; ramparts of old castle at Karlshamn.

Öland: Borgholm Castle ruins; the 5th-century circular fortifications at Ismanstorp and Gråborg; the old village of Långlöt; Solliden, royal summer residence; the Alvar steppe; windmills. There is the "Viking Village" at Eketorp.

 CASTLES AND MANORS OF SKÅNE. The hundreds of castles, chateaux, and manor houses, of every size, type, and age, constitute the great tourist attraction of Sweden's "Chateau Country". Among the oldest are Glimmingehus and Torup—quadrangular, thick-walled strongholds of the medieval type, built to withstand long sieges. Belonging to the great castle-building age of the 16th century are Vittskövle, Skarhult, Trolle-Ljungby, and Bosjökloster, while others, such as Trolleholm, Wrams-Gunnarstorp, and Knutstorp, bear the distinctive architectural marks of successive post-16th century reconstructions. Thousands come every year as well to visit their lovely formal gardens and parks.

Most of the chateaux are still inhabited and cannot be visited except by special arrangement, often requiring personal contact. The best way to get more than a simple exterior view is to join an organized tour. These guided tours originate in most of the major towns in Skåne during the summer season, but Malmö offers the greatest variety. However, Bosjökloster at Lake Ringsjön, Christinehof in eastern and Svaneholm in southern Skåne, Bäckaskog near Kristianstad, Snogeholm near Sjöbo and Bjärsjölagard near Hörby—all with catering facilities and Bäckaskog—are regularly open to the public. Inquire at any travel bureau.

 HOTELS AND RESTAURANTS. Because of its many tourist attractions and the popularity of its summer holiday resorts, this region is one of Sweden's best-equipped from the point of view of hotel accommodation. Remember, too, that resort hotels have advantageous pension rates for stays of 3 days or longer. For fine provincial cuisine—salmon and eel dishes are a specialty —in an authentic atmosphere, stop at some of the old country inns for a meal or two. Try those at Höör, Margretetorp, Skivarp, Broby and Östarp.

ÄNGELHOLM. Hotels: *Continental,* 14 rooms and *Tre Hjärtan* at Angelholms Havsbad, 26 rooms, both inexpensive. At the beach, *Klitterhus,* restaurant.

Motel: *Ängelholms Motel,* 16 rooms with bath or shower.

BÅSTAD-MALEN. Hotels: *Båstad,* moderate to first class reasonable, a few of its 25 rooms with bath. *Malens Havsbad,* 160 rooms, some of them with bath or shower; swimming pool with temperate salt water and special pools for children; tennis, minigolf. *Riviera Hotel and Restaurant,* 52 rooms, moderate. *Hemmeslövs Herrgårdenspensionat* can offer 200 beds, swimming pool and skating rink. Dancing every night.

Pensions: *Lassens, Enehall, Furuhem* and *Möllers,* all moderate, licensed for wine and beer.

BORGHOLM. Hotel: *Strand,* 66 rooms, and *Borgholm,* 22 rooms, moderate.

FALKENBERG. Hotels: *Strandbaden,* 73 room (a few with bath), music, terrace restaurant with sea view, *Grand,* 54 rooms, 15 with bath, music, both SARA and first class reasonable. *MHF Motel Tre Hästar,* 47 rooms with shower.

HALMSTAD. Hotels: *Hallandia,* 92 rooms with bath, *Mårtensson,* 85 rooms, 50 baths, first class reasonable to moderate; *Grand,* 46 rooms, 12 with bath, moderate; *Simlångdalens Gästgivargård,* small inn with superb cuisine.
Restaurant: *Norre Kavaljeren (SARA).*

HELSINGBORG. Hotels: *Grand,* 76 rooms, 43 with bath, large rooms; *Mollberg,* 65 rooms, 15 with bath. Sweden's oldest hotel but completely modernized; *Högvakten,* 36 rooms, 21 with bath or shower. All central, on Stortorget, first class reasonable. *Villa Vingård,* 28 rooms, 12 baths, moderate.
Motels: *Esso Motor Hotel,* 180 rooms with bath or shower, MHF *Motels Tre Hästar,* Ängelholmsvägen 35 on Hwy E4, 1½ miles north of Central Station, 43 rooms; and at Fleninge, 6 miles northeast on Hwy E4, with 24 rooms. Both these motels have all rooms with bath or shower. *Hälsingborgs Stadsmotell,* Hantverkaregatan 11, 26 rooms with bath.
Restaurants: *Mollberg,* Stortorget 18, very good. *Parapeten,* on mole protecting ferry harbor, dancing. *Spisen,* S. Kyrkogatan 9, good, moderate.

KALMAR. Hotels: *Stadshotellet,* on picturesque main square, 80 rooms, most with bath; restaurant, dancing, bar, moderate. *Frimurare-hotellet,* 35 rooms, 7 with bath, inexpensive. *Witt,* 110 rooms, recent. In the same building, the restaurant *Wittens Wärdshus.* Dancing.
Esso Motor Hotel, Dragonvägen, 50 rooms with bath or shower. *Kalmarsund Hotel,* Fiskaregatan 5, 85 rooms, quiet, new 1982.
Restaurant: *Teaterkällaren,* alfresco service. *Byttan,* near the castle. Summer only.

KARLSHAMN. Hotel: *Stadshotellet,* 52 rooms, 20 with bath. Motel: *Esso Motor Hotel* on Hwy 15/29, 39 rooms with bath or shower.

KARLSKRONA. Hotel: *Stadshotellet* (SARA), 89 rooms, most with bath. First class reasonable. *Frimurarehotellet,* 43 rooms, 9 with bath (SARA). *O.K. Motor Hotel,* 48 rooms with shower, at Ronnebyvägen.

LUND. Hotels: *Lundia,* 55 rooms with bath, near Central station, first class reasonable. *Sparta,* 150 rooms with bath, open June 1-Aug. 31.
Restaurants: *Storkällaren, Akademiska Föreningens Restaurant Chrougen* and its pub *Tua,* Sandgatan; *Stäket,* Stora Södergatan 6.

MALMÖ.

HOTELS

First class superior

Savoy, Norra Vallg. 62, 100 rooms with bath, traditional comfort, excellent grill; near rail station.

Kramer, Stortorget 7, 110 rooms, 85 with bath, charming, traditional or period furnishings.

First class reasonable

Garden Hotel, Baltzarsgatan 20, 173 rooms; near air terminal, ferries, station.

Scandinavia, Drottningsgatan 1, 181 rooms with bath, licensed restaurant.

Skylina Hotel, Bisittargatan 2, 270 rooms, luxury standard at low cost.

St. Jörgen Hotel, Stora Nygatan 35 (RESO), 304 rooms with bath.

Hotel Winn, Jörgen Kocksgatan 3 (SARA), 100 rooms. Very modern.

Moderate

Teaterhotellet, Rönngatan 3-Fersens väg 20, 46 rooms.

Strand Hotel, Strandgatan 50, 24 rooms with bath, recommended for families.

Alexandra Hotel, Sallerupsvägen 5, 72 rooms, modern.

Esso Motor Hotels, on E6, at Arlöv, 76 rooms, and at Segesvängen, 158 rooms with bath or shower.

Jägersro Motel, Jägerrovagen 160D, 160 rooms.

Inexpensive

Sjöfartshotellet, Citadelsvägen 4, 64 rooms.

Hembygden, Isak Slaktaresgatan 7, 26 rooms.

RESTAURANTS

Savoy in hotel of same name, one of Sweden's top restaurants with outstanding French cuisine, a culinary institution of international fame.

Kronprinsen, Mariedalsvägen 32, a high quality restaurant with excellent food and international variety show.

Översten, Regementsg. 52, on the 26th floor, overlooking half of Skåne and parts of Denmark, very good food, charming bar.

Kockskakrogen, Frans Suellsg. 3 by Stortorget, a vaulted cellar from the 16th century, beautifully furnished, very good food. All expensive.

SARA manages a number of good restaurants: **Rådhuskälleren,** in the City Hall. **Teaterrestaurangen** in a wing of the city theater and **Tröls Jins Kru,** Karlskronaplan 4, genuine Skåne dishes in regional surroundings. **Falstaff Steakhouse,** Baltzarsgatan 25, one of the best restaurants for steak. **Carolus,** Östergatan 12, in Caroli City, **Olga's Restaurant** in Pildamspark. Moderate expensive.

MÖLLE. Hotels: *Grand,* 40 rooms, tennis, swimming, moderate. Inexpensive: *Turisthotellet,* 32 rooms.

MÖRRUM. Hotel: *Walhalla,* 25 rooms, inexpensive.

RONNEBY. Hotels: *Ronneby Brunn,* 354 rooms, all with bath; dancing, beautiful park, tennis court, swimming pool, modernized, new wing, moderate.

(RESO). *Grand,* Järnvägsgatan 11 (opposite railway station), 19 rooms, a few with bath, inexpensive.

TYLÖSAND Hotel: *Tylösands Havsbad,* 200 rooms, modern, tennis, dancing, first class reasonable to moderate.

VARBERG. Hotels: *Stadshotellet,* (SARA), 48 rooms, modern, moderate; *Varbergs Hotell,* 30 rooms, inexpensive.
Restaurants: *Coq d'Or, Gillets Restaurant, Societsrestaurangen* (summer only).

VÄXJÖ. Hotel: Stadshotellet (SARA), Kungsgatan, 118 rooms, 77 with bath. *Esso Motor Hotel,* Mörnersväg, 39 rooms with bath or shower.

YSTAD. Hotels: *Ystads Saltsjöbad* (RESO). 112 rooms; tennis, sandy beach, dancing. Well-directed, moderate.

SHOPPING. You should find time to visit the excellent shops in Malmö and Helsingborg. This province is fast developing, both economically and touristically.
    In Malmö the foremost feature is the imposing permanent exhibition of Swedish design called *FORM Design Center* at Lilla Torg; it includes a gift shop. *Nordiska Kompaniet* is the leading shop in Malmö, at Stora Nygatan 50. Has a fine display of glass and porcelain, silver and jewelry, carpets, furniture, linen, men's and women's wear, gift shop and grocery store.
    In town, *Silverberg* has a fine show of glass and furniture at Baltzarsgatan 35.
    Charlotte Weibull, Lilla Torg 5, produces charming dolls in authentic Swedish costumes. Gift shop and exhibition of old costumes. *Malmöhus Hemslöjd* has a shop in Malmö at Kalendegatan 9, in Kristianstad, Storg. 43 and in Österlen, Ingelstorp Klockaregård in Glemmingebro. Exhibitions of exquisite handworks and textiles.
    Baltzar AB Boutique, Baltzarsgatan 31, exclusive, men's wear, Boutiques: *La Parisienne, Amorella* and *Margot.* A good fur shop is *Mattsons Päls,* N. Vallgatan 98.
    In Helsingborg you should have a look round the well-known glass and china store *Duka,* Söderg. 22 and Kullagatan 23. *Emil Palmgren,* Kullagatan 6, is a good shop in the same line. Fashionable boutique EVA and department store *Reflex* AB have Swedish and foreign clothing.
    In Landskrona, the exclusive and exotic store *Sia Lustgården* AB, N. Kyrkogr 9 in the city center. Porcelain, china and glassware, tea.

SPORTS. There are fine sandy beaches at Falsterbo, Mölle, Tylösand, Ängelholm, Malen, Mellbystrand Skrea, Ystad, Åhus, and on the isle of Öland. Most resort hotels have **tennis** courts, and **golf** may be played at several places. 18-hole courses at Båstad, Falkenberg, Falsterbo, Halmstad, Helsingborg, Kalmar, Lund and Mölle.
    Good salmon **fishing** in the Mörrum River, with the season from April-May until September 30. It is advisable to order fishing cards in advance if you come during April or May. Write Hotel Walhalla, Mörrum. Good salmon fishing also in the Ätran River at Falkenberg. Sea-fishing tours are arranged from Helsingborg, Falkenberg and Varberg.
    There's a good **horseracing** track near Malmö, at Jägersro, where the Swedish Derby, usually about mid July, draws a big, international crowd.

CAMPING. Well-equipped sites at Helsingborg, Landskrona, Malmö, Torekov, Trelleborg, Ystad, Jönköping, Kalmar, Västervik, Karlskrona, Karlshamn, Falkenberg, Halmstad, Ljungskile, Tylösand and many others.

USEFUL ADDRESSES. Consulate: British, Lilla Nygatan 11, Malmö. **Tourist Information:** Most of the towns have local Tourist Offices and room booking services; Helsingborg, Hamntorget, tel. 042-120310; Malmö, Hamngatan 1, tel 333-02.

Foreign exchange office: Hamngatan 1, Malmö.

Motoring: (Malmö) Royal Swedish Automobile Club, (KAK), and Swedish Automobile Association, Skeppsbron 2.

Car repair: Centralgaragets verkstad, Baltzarsgatan 14, Malmö, open 24 hours a day, tel. 766-00.

GOTHENBURG

Gateway to Northern Europe

It is only proper to approach Gothenburg (or Göteborg) by the sea, for at heart it is a product of the oceans and the ships that sail them. Shipping, shipbuilding and fishing set their stamp on this region long before the age of the Vikings. You never get far from the maritime influence, and the harbor bustles (as does Europe's newest airport here, Landvetter).

A classic example of honesty, modesty and frankness once was found in a shipping company's guide to Gothenburg. "Gothenburg is by no means a Tourist Mecca," it read, "but it has its points." This is to certify that it does have its points, and plenty of them. Actually, Gothenburg is a gateway to the entire world, with regular freight services and frequent passenger connections to all the Seven Seas. If you come to Scandinavia with one of the Swedish lines—Sessan Torline from Germany, England or Holland, or with Stena Line from Germany—Gothenburg is your first Scandinavian port of call. And the city is the ideal place to begin a round trip tour of Scandinavia, since it occupies almost the exact center of a triangle of which the capitals of Stockholm, Oslo, and Copenhagen are the points.

Exploring Gothenburg

An intangible air, perceptible enough almost to be held in your hands, distinguishes Gothenburg from Stockholm. Many attribute it to centuries of close relations with Great Britain, birthplace of the Anglo-Saxon tradition of freedom. It has even been called "Little London". The residents are fully conscious of this pronounced attraction westward. Others attribute it to the physical nature of the city, with its broad avenues, its huge, sprawling harbor, its comparatively great geographical area for a city of some 450,000 people. Finally, age has something to do with this sensation. Gothenburg is young, officially born in 1621, when parts of Stockholm's Old Town looked about as they do now. There is something of a friendly rivalry between the cities.

A great Swedish king, Gustavus Adolphus, the "Lion of the North", gave Gothenburg its charter in 1621. He called in Dutch builders, and the canals and architecture will show the strength of their influence. The town soon began to play a part in history. Karl X summoned the parliament to meet there in 1659–60, in Kronhuset, the oldest building extant, and there his son was crowned Karl XI after Karl X's death. Scotsmen and Germans had by this time settled in the town in considerable numbers.

As early as 1699 the British community formed an association for mutual support. The influx of Scots and Englishmen continued through the 18th and 19th centuries, and they and their descendants have had a decisive importance in the commercial and cultural development of the city. Many of the finest old families of Gothenburg have typically English names.

At one time Gothenburg enjoyed a thriving trade with the East Indies, as evidenced by the old factory building in the Norra Hamngatan, which now houses the Ethnographical, Archeological, and Historical museums. However, the city's first great commercial impetus resulted from Napoleon's continental blockade in 1806, when its port became the principal depot of British trade with northern Europe.

The opening of the Trollhätte Canal shortly after 1800, connecting Gothenburg by water with huge Lake Vänern and the rich forest and iron products of the region around the lake, offered a new commercial stimulus. Before the middle of the century the first shipbuilding yard was turning out sailing vessels, and industrializing was under way. Today Gothenburg is the headquarters of many industries, including the world-wide SKF ballbearing empire; AB Volvo, Scandinavia's largest maker of automobiles; three hyper-modern shipyards; and the Hasselblad camera factory. About one third of the population gets its living from industry. Incidentally, Gothenburg is one of the few remaining cities with streetcars.

After 54 years of service, Torslanda is now being replaced by Göteborg-Landvetter Airport—a facility of international standards which both commerce and tourists have been eagerly awaiting. Landvetter provides West Sweden with access to very large aircraft with direct lines to other countries. This new airport has a capacity that will meet the requirements of the regions for many years. With its location close to Highway 40, the new airport is easy to reach from all the towns in West Sweden. Signposts marked with the airport symbol clearly show the way from the roads in the vicinity.

City Highlights

You must really see the harbor to appreciate it. There are 14 miles of quays, 200 cranes that sometimes seem to rise up like steel forests, and the warehouse and customs sheds cover more than 1½ million square feet. Gothenburg is the home port of 40 per cent of the Swedish merchant fleet—better than 4 million tons of shipping—and handles a third of the country's imports and a quarter of the exports. During the summer there are boat tours that take you around the harbor and entrance.

Skandiahamnen is the new port for container and roll-on/roll-off traffic which partly came into use in 1966 and is now in full operation. Here you find the terminals of Tor Line, Atlantic Container Line and other shipping companies.

Gothenburg's Fish Harbor, one of the largest in Scandinavia, opened in 1910. Its early morning fish auction, at which wholesalers publicly bid for cod, catfish, sole, herring, and occasionally even whale, has become something of a tourist attraction.

Trädgårdsföreningen, site of the magnificent gardens of the horticultural society, begins right across the square from the Central Station. The Palm House is an impressive example of what you can grow in a northern climate with the help of heat and glass. Flowers by the acre, beautifully tended lawns.

Götaplatsen is an impressive square (near the Park Avenue Hotel) which might be described as the cultural heart of Gothenburg. In the center is the famed "Poseidon" fountain by Milles. The columned building which rises up above the broad steps at the end of the square—and dominates it—is the Art Gallery. As you face the art museum, the building on the left is the modern City Theater, the one on the right the Concert Hall. If you climb the steps leading up to the museum, you get a fine view of the wide boulevard Kungsportsavenyen, with the profile of downtown Gothenburg in the distance. This square is notable as an expression of modern architecture, as impressive as older and better-known counterparts elsewhere in Europe.

Liseberg Amusement Park is only a few minutes from downtown by streetcar or taxi, a walk of only 15 minutes or so from the Park Avenue Hotel. This is one of the best, neatest, and best-run amusement parks in existence—partly because of beautiful gardens that you don't ordinarily find in this kind of establishment. There are several restaurants, open-air concerts, variety theater, and wide range of the usual carnival attractions.

Among other sights are the Sailor's Tower, near the Maritime Museum, a tall monument to seamen who lost their lives in World War I, from which you have an excellent view of the harbor and city; Masthugget Church, a striking modern edifice on an impressive site overlooking the city; Guldeheden, a housing development with an unusually pleasant central square; and the huge natural park, Slottss-kogen.

There are several good museums with fine, often unique, collections. Anyone interested in shipping should by all means see the Maritime Museum between Karl Johansgatan and route E3.

Gothenburg Environs

In the neighboring industrial town of Mölndal, only a short distance away, is the delightful 18th-century mansion of Gunnebo. It is a good example of architecture and landscaping of a period that combined the best of French and English influence. The house was designed by C. W. Carlberg, who also designed the furniture in 1796. John Hall, a merchant of British origin, was the first owner of Gunnebo. It is now the property of Mölndal community. During the summer visitors are shown around in the early afternoon; there are hourly buses to Mölndal and Gunnebo from Nils Ericsonsplatsen (behind the Central Station).

Särö, a bit farther south, by bus, is known for its thriving foliage and oak trees, which grow right at the edge of the sea. On the route to Särö is the beautifully situated Hovås golf course.

On a day tour to the south of Gothenburg, visit Fjärås Bräcka (20 miles), an ice-age sand ridge that divides Lake Lygnern from the sea. From the top there is a splendid view over this coastal area, and on the slopes are Iron Age and Viking graveyards.

Only a few minutes away lies the impressive turn-of-the-century Tjolöholm Palace, now open to the public—hourly tours every day during summer and on weekends in winter—and there is also a "stable" cafeteria, a horse carriage museum, and a park.

A few miles east of Tjolöholm is the tiny, picturesque village of Eskhult, now an open-air museum.

To the east of Gothenburg is a large, hilly forest-and-lake area. Visit the 19th-century Nääs manor house on route E3 (20 miles from Gothenburg; hourly tours in the summer). In the outbuildings there are stables, restaurant, coffee shop and several exhibition shops selling traditional Swedish products—textiles, wood, furniture, antiques and souvenirs.

Nearby is the medieval Öijared chapel, in the middle of a 45-hole golf course. Further northeast is the Anten-Gräfsnäs Line (see p. 26).

The coast north of Gothenburg (Bohuslän province) is the beginning of fjord country, with its dozens of fishing villages and thousands of islands. Marstrand, one of the main sailing centers on the west coast, bustles with life in the summer, beneath the 300-years-old Carlsten castle. Frequent boat trips into the archipelago for fishing, swimming and regatta-viewing.

Forty minutes from Gothenburg by car lies the former fishing village of Stenungsund, today Sweden's busy petrochemical center. Just outside, the mighty Tjörn bridges span the fjord—the breathtaking view will give you a strong incentive to explore.

PRACTICAL INFORMATION FOR GOTHENBURG

WHEN TO COME. Gothenburg is essentially a summer town when it comes to pleasure visits, May to September, possibly October if the autumn is pleasant. The winter weather can be as bleak as in any town with a maritime climate—windy, wet, sometimes broken by a brief-lived snowfall. This is not to say you may not enjoy a winter visit—in the opinion of many the musical life is superior to that of Stockholm, and the theaters are second to none.

HOW TO GET ABOUT. Gothenburg is about 4½ hours by express train from Stockholm, Oslo, and Copenhagen, or a little under an hour by air. There are good communications to Helsinki direct by air or via Stockholm by train and boat. The best ways to get a look at Gothenburg's attractions are to explore them yourself with map and guidebook (available in any bookshop and some newspaper kiosks), or to take the conducted boat and bus tours, which operate from May to September. Buses leave from Kungsportsplatsen in the city center at regular intervals. There are one- and two-hour trips and regional 5–6 hour tours. English-speaking guides on most tours. There are trips around the harbor and canals by boat (about 1 hour) from Kungsportsbron, in the center of town; and at Lilla Bommen (close to Nordstan) starts a tour through the entire harbor to the fascinating 17th-century Elfborg fortress. It is advisable to buy a tourist ticket for 10 kroner which is valid for 24 hours on all buses and trams. These tourist tickets are sold in the tramway kiosk and during the summer also by conductors.

For something different, *Inter-Holiday,* Lilla Kungsg. 1, operate "midnight sun" flights to the far north.

HOTELS. Gothenburg is fairly well supplied with accommodation in all categories, but it is always a good idea to reserve ahead. If you happen to find yourself without a room, you can contact the Room Booking Service of the city's Tourist Office, Kungsportsplatsen 2, tel. 13-59-92 or 13-60-28, open June 1-Aug. 31 daily 9 A.M.-8 P.M.; Sept. 1-May 31 Monday through Friday 9–5, Saturday 9–1. Room Booking Service is also available at Airport Terminal, Nordstan Mon-Fri. 10 A.M.-6 P.M. all year.

Luxurious

Park Avenue, Kungsportsavenyen 36–38; 320 rooms all with private bath. Considered by many to be Sweden's finest. All double rooms have balconies, 3-room suites on top floor individually furnished. Panorama lounge on top floor. Three restaurants: *Belle Avenue, Tidbit,* and *Lorensberg,* the last with dancing and floorshow.

Europa, Kopmansgatan, 400 rooms, all with bath; swimming pool. An efficient sound insulation eliminates annoying street noises. *Stork* nightclub (SARA).

First Class Superior

Opalen, Engelbrektsgatan 73, 230 rooms with bath or shower; well-known dancing restaurant *Amorinen.* RESO hotel.

Rubinen, Kungsportsavenyen 24, 189 rooms, 180 with bath. RESO hotel.

Scandinavia, Kustgatan 10, 323 rooms with bath.

Victors, Skeppsbroplatsen 1, 38 rooms, most exclusive. Restaurant.

Windsor, Kungsportsavenyen 6, 83 rooms with bath; quiet, secluded atmosphere. Excellent restaurant.

Ramada, Gamla Tingstadsgatan 1, Hisings Backa, 135 rooms with bath.

First Class Reasonable

Carl Johan, Karl Johansgatan 66–70, 151 rooms with bath or shower.

Eggers, Drottningtorget 1, 88 rooms, 22 with bath; casino and dancing.

Tre Konor, N. Kustbanegatan 15, 172 rooms, most with bath, has nightclub.

Moderate

Frälsningsarméns Hotel Ritz, Burggrevegatan 25, 104 rooms, 32 with shower, no restaurant, Salvation Army.

Kung Karl, Nils Ericsongatan 23, 80 rooms, 30 baths, at station, television in most rooms.

Partille, on outskirts, route E3, 38 rooms with shower.

Excelsior, Karl Gustavsgatan 9, 60 rooms, some with bath or shower.

Royal, Drottningatan 67, 71 rooms, 3 baths, no restaurant.

Lorensberg, Berzeliigatan 15, 60 rooms;

Heden, Sten Sturegatan, 106 rooms.

MOTELS: Esso Motor Hotels at Mölndal on E6, just south of center, 99 rooms with bath, and at Backadalsgatan, off E6, north of center, 144 rooms with bath.

OK Motorhotell on E3, 118 rooms with bath, on Kaggeledsgatan.

Hallarna, Partihandelstorget, 111 rooms with bath or shower.

YOUTH HOSTEL: Ostkupan Mejerigatan 2. 3 km from city center, bus 64 from railway station or tram 5 to St. Sigfridsplan. 150 beds. 50 SEK.

Private Rooms are also available—apply to the Tourist Office, Kungsportsplatsen 2.

RESTAURANTS. Gothenburg has a number of restaurants offering good and varied food. Its specialty, however, is fish, fresh from the sea and ingeniously prepared. Ask the headwaiter what's best for the day. Below-listed restaurants are moderately expensive unless otherwise indicated. The Tourist Office regularly publishes a list of budget-price restaurants.

Henriksberg, Stigbergsgatan 7, with magnificent view of the harbor, nautical décor and seafood specialties, terrace dining in summer. Expensive. Old-fashioned maritime atmosphere. Closed Sat., Sun. (SARA).

Fiskekrogen (SARA), Lilla Torget 1, excellent for lunch and fish dishes. Dancing.

Golden Days, Södra Hamngatan 31, cozy atmosphere.

White Corner, Vasagatan 43, is the address for good meals, steak house, cafeteria and a pub in English style. **Hunters Pub,** Östra Hamngatan 30.

Liseberg, the amusement park, has several restaurants. You can dine in the open as you watch the lighted fountain and the outdoor performances of variety artists. Open Apr.–Sept.

Räkan, Lorensbergsgatan 16, behind Hotel Rubinen. Here you get your shrimp to your table in small fishing boats you control by radio. In the basement there is usually dancing.

For an inexpensive meal or quick snack, try the **Mac Sweden** chain or one of the many pizza restaurants (which also offer other dishes), or department store cafeterias.

 SHOPPING. For the traveler with a little time at Gothenburg, it will be well spent at the *NK* department store at Östra Hamngatan 42. Best for ladies wear is *Gillblads,* Kungsgatan 44.

If what you wish is some specialty shop, there is the *Almedahlsmagasinet* at Korsgatan 13 with—among other things—exquisite linen seldom seen elsewhere. *Bohusslöjd,* Kungsportsavenyen 25, specializes in the famous Bohus knitwear and in handicrafts from Bohuslän province. *Klockargårdens Hemslöjd,* Korsgatan 3, has a good choice of products from their Dalarna workshop.

The silversmiths *Högberg & Co.,* have an exclusive boutique at Engelbrektsgatan 32 (opposite Park Avenue Hotel). *Artium,* Korsgatan 13 and Kungsportsavenyen 31–35 have decorative Swedish crystal. *Josephssons',* two shops on corner of Kyrkogatan and Korsgatan, specializes in traditional and modern styles of glass, china and stainless steel, while *Irma's Konsthandel,* Kyrkogatan 38 is well stocked with all Swedish arts and crafts.

Nordstan is the biggest shopping center in Sweden. Near the rail station, it has a tourist office, air terminal, hotel, cinemas, 24-hour pharmacy, and, together with the nearby, enclosed shopping malls *Kompassen,* Fredsgatan, and *Citypassagen,* Södra Hamngatan, it offers a great variety of specialized shops.

 ENTERTAINMENT. Several hotels and restaurants have dancing 2 to 6 nights a week. *Valand,* Vasagatan 41, *Krokodil, Ambassadeur,* Norra Hamngatan 24–28 and *Liseberg* Amusement Park, offer cabaret and night-club attractions. *Lorensberg* (in Hotel Park Avenue) and *Trägår'n* have floorshows. There are also several pop clubs and discotheques. The theater and musical life of Gothenburg during the main season is concentrated around four principal institutions, the City Theater, the Stora (Great) Theater, the Folkteatern, and the Concert Hall (Konserthuset). For details of all entertainment, ask for "Göteborg denna vecks" (This week in Gothenburg).

The *City Theater,* municipally supported, as the name implies, ranks with the Royal Dramatic Theater in Stockholm in the world of the legitimate stage. It has produced a number of stars, and members of the permanent company are often to be seen starring in Swedish films.

The *Stora Theater* presents operas, operettas, and musical comedies of a quality which draws critics from all over Sweden to opening nights.

The *Symphony Orchestra* is among the very best in this part of the world. When it comes to the City Theater and the Concert Hall, the magnificent modern buildings add much to the pleasure of the performances.

There are plenty of good cinemas with English and American films predominating.

  MUSEUMS AND OTHER PLACES OF INTEREST. *Art Gallery,* Götaplatsen, has excellent collections of Dutch and Italian masters, French Impressionists, 19th and 20th-century sculpture, and Swedish painting and sculpture from 18th century to present: Tues.-Sat. 11–4, Sundays 12–4.

Röhss Museum of Arts and Crafts, Vasagatan 37–39, displays Swedish and foreign furniture, glass, ceramics, textiles, etc., also Oriental collections; Tues.-Sat. 11–4, Sundays 12–4.

Museum of Industry, Götaplatsen, features articles produced by industrial concerns in and around the city; Tues.-Sat. 11–4; Sun. 12–4.

Maritime Museum, Varvsparken, is devoted to history of merchant shipping, fishing, Swedish navy; 10–6 weekdays in summer, Sundays 11–4; winter schedule, weekdays 10–4, Sun. 11–4. *Aquarium,* in same building, illustrates aquatic life of Scandinavian lakes and coastal waters; same hours.

Military Museum, in Kronan Fortress, displays arms and uniforms; 1–3, Sundays 12–3.

Theater Museum, Lorensberg, illustrates theatrical history of city from 1780 to present; Tues.-Sun. 11–4.

Ethnographical Museum, Norra Hamngatan 12, displays valuable collections of pre-Columbian Peruvian textiles and of South American Indian cultures among others; Tues.-Sun. 11–4.

Archeological Museum, in same building, contains primarily prehistoric finds from west of Sweden, same hours.

Historical Museum, in same building, history of Gothenburg and west of Sweden; same hours.

Natural History Museum, Slottsskogen, zoological, entomological, and mineralogical collections; same hours.

Botanical Gardens, south of Slottsskogen Park, rock garden, herbarium hothouses; 9 A.M. to sunset.

Elfsborg Fortress. This historical fortress dating from 1670 is well worth visiting. There are regular boat trips from Lilla Bommen, at Östra Nordstan, Jun. 1-Aug. 31, which includes harbor sightseeing. There is a cafeteria in the fortress.

The Crown House (Kronhuset). A visit to this 17th-century building is an enjoyable adventure. Stroll in the cobbled courtyard, visit the shops, or have coffee and cake.

Svenska Mässan, Skånegatan 26, is the ground for fairs and exhibitions, including the annual international Swedish Industries Fair in mid-May. Also permanent exhibitions such as **Building Center** with more than 260 exhibitors of building products, and **Swedish Export** *Exhibition* with about 130 exhibitors. The office of the **World Trade Center** is at Östra Hamngatan 26 (Östra Nordstan).

 SPORTS. There are more than a dozen **swimming** spots around Gothenburg and in the environs of Mölndal, Kungälv and Marstrand. Valhallabadet has an indoor pool in summer, also an outdoor pool.

Golf—18 holes—at the Gothenburg Golf Club links. Hovås, 15 min. by bus from Linnéplatsen; also at Delsjön, 18 holes, at Albatross, 18 holes, and at Öijared, two 18-hole and one 9-hole link. Four other courses within 30 minutes by car.

Horseracing and **trotting** at Åbyfältet, Mölndal, 15 min. by tramline 4. **Football, speedway, skating** at Ullevi, one of the most modern sports stadiums in the world.

Athletics at legendary Slottsskogsvallen. *Scandinavium* is the largest indoor arena in Scandinavia. It can seat 14,000 people.

USEFUL ADDRESSES. Consulates: Britain, Gögatan 15; Ireland, Kyrkogatan 4; South Africa, Postgatan 2; U.S.A. Södra Hamngatan 53.

Tourist information: Tourist Office Kungsportsplatsen 2, also makes "Sweden At Home" arrangements; Swedish Touring Club (STF), Östra Larmgatan 15–21, 41107 Gothenburg. Also bookings for cottages *(stuga)* all over Sweden.

Travel bureau: Nyman & Schultz, Norra Hamngatan 18. Booking office for cottages: Inter Holiday Lilla Kungsgatan 2, 411 08 Gothenburg.

Motoring: Royal Swedish Automobile Club (KAK), Park Avenue Hotel, Swedish Automobile Association (M), Södra Vägen 3–5.

Car hire: Scandinavia Car Rental, Västra Hamngatan 13; Hertz, Engelbrektsgatan 73 (Hotel Opalen); Avis, Västra Larmgatan 7.

Car pilots: Park Avenue Hotel.

Youth Hostels: Apply to the Swedish Touring Club or the Tourist Office (addresses above).

Camping: Sites at Askim, Kärralund (open all year, 12 camping cottages), and Lilleby Havsbad.

Church services: English, St. Andrew's, Hvitfeldtsplatsen; Roman Catholic, Kristus Konungens, Parkgatan 14.

THE LAKE DISTRICT

Home of the Goths

To the north and east of Gothenburg spreads a broad region known as Sweden's lake district, containing thousands of small lakes, medium-sized lakes, and two of the largest lakes in Europe, Vättern and Vänern. The Göta Canal, a blue ribbon stretching across Sweden, combines some of them with rivers and with manmade channels and locks to create a water route from Gothenburg to Stockholm.

This part of the world, ancient home of the Goths, has been settled for some 4,000 years or more, and has a number of historic sights setting exclamation points to its variegated natural beauty. Each of the region's provinces has its own history and traditions and its own distinct character.

Exploring the Lake District

North and slightly west of Gothenburg stretches the province of Bohuslän, a coastal and island summer playground among the most popular in Sweden—a part of the famed west coast. It was more or less discovered by the royal family. Prince Vilhelm, brother of the late king, wrote with much great feeling about Bohuslän, beginning with a visit there in the '90s with his father, King Gustav V. "So the ocean, the ships, and the rocky islands form the trinity that characterizes Bohuslän," Vilhelm writes in *This Land of Sweden,* "A name that sounds good to all seafaring folk, for it bespeaks a coast peopled by strong men and sturdy objects, an archipelago formed of gneiss and granite and water which eternally stretches foamy arms after life."

Proceeding north from Gothenburg, you come to Kungälv, which was a commercial center before the year 1000. It is overlooked by a huge medieval stronghold, Bohus Fortress, built by the Norwegians in 1308. Kungälv is a sea of flowers during apple blossom time.

The island city of Marstrand was also built by the Norwegians, some time during the 13th century. This was the favorite west coast summer resort of King Oskar II, who died in 1907, and the resort hotel emits something of a turn-of-the-century air. It is still a popular summer resort. There is an interesting 17th-century fortress overlooking the city—Karlsten—used as a prison during the 18th and 19th centuries. The church is from the 14th century.

Lysekil is a popular and reasonably typical example of the villages along the west coast which have become Meccas for summer vacationers. It rests on the mouth of a long fjord, protected from sea and wind by cliffs.

On the other side of the fjord is Fiskebäckskil, another popular summering place. Farther inland, roughly northeast, is the city of Uddevalla, the biggest municipality in this region (population, over 36,000). Uddevalla as a city leaves much to be desired in its appeal to the eye, but is a good overnight halt. The principal industries are textiles, paper, wood processing, and shipbuilding.

Along the coast north of Lysekil are a whole row of villages familiar to west coast vacationers and to the painters and sailors who haunt this region in the summer time—Smögen (a singularly picturesque fishing village), Bovallstrand, Fjällbacka, Grebbestad, and many more. At the very north end of the province, just below the border to Norway, is Strömstad, the northern anchor of the Bohuslän vacation region, so to speak. The city has old traditions both as a port and military objective and as a summer resort. In addition, Strömstad offers you interesting excursions. The best from a historical point of view is to Fredriksten Fortress, just over the Norwegian border at Halden, where King Charles XII fell in 1718. This whole region was bitterly contested for centuries in the Scandinavian wars.

Västergötland

The name of Västergötland means, literally, "the western land of the Goths"—as contrasted with Östergötland, or the eastern land of the same people. The Swedish Goths apparently originated on the continent of Europe. They were thus at least distant cousins of the barbarians who overran the Roman Empire and made the name Goth a synonym for "one who is rude or uncivilized". Some investigators think this region of Sweden was the first home of the Goths. Others believe that Östergötland should have the dubious honor of having spawned all branches of this people. Certain it is, however, that Västergötland was one of the first regions of Sweden to be settled in the wake of retreating glacial ice. Giant sepulchers have been uncovered from the late Stone Age, about 2500 to 2000 B.C., and so-called gallery graves from the age following.

Geographically, the province is rich in coastline, although it can boast only the small but important piece on the ocean which includes Gothenburg. In the northwest it has some 90 miles of the shore of Lake Vänern, the largest fresh-water sea in Western Europe, and to the southeast it has Lake Vättern, not so wide but almost as long. The scenery varies from wooded mountains with rare flora, to the fertile plain around the city of Skara.

Lidköping is a city of some 19,000 people at the inner end of a bay of Lake Vänern, on the southeast shore. It is the oldest city on the lake (its charter was granted in 1446), and is proud of the Rörstrand Porcelain works where 18th-century faience and modern ceramics are made side by side. The principal sight in the city proper is the Old Courthouse, once the hunting lodge of Magnus Gabriel de la Gardie, a powerful politician, noble, and controversial figure from the time of Queen Christina, King Karl X, and his son and successor, Karl XI.

De la Gardie was responsible for an even more impressive structure, however—Läckö Castle. It lies about 15 miles north of Lidköping on a beautiful road leading to the end of Kålland peninsula. Actually, the oldest parts of the structure date from 1298, when the building was begun as the residence of the bishop of Skara. De la Gardie—during his brief period of power in the 17th century—made it largely what it is today. Few of the 200-plus rooms are now furnished, but don't miss the chapel, the Hall of Knights, and the guest room prepared for King Karl XI. By one of the ironies of history, it was this king who deprived De la Gardie not only of the Läckö earldom but of most of his other holdings, in a great program of reform reducing the property and power of the nobility. Every summer an exhibition is put on at the castle, which is always worth seeing.

Across the bay to the east from Läckö Castle you see the bold outlines of Kinnekulle, one of the unique "table mountains" of this region. To reach it you will have to retrace your route to Lidköping and move up to Kinnekulle on the eastern side of the bay. Kinnekulle (sounds approximately like "chin-eh-culeh") is notable for two things —the view from its top and the millions of years of geological history it lays open to the naked eye. The process was a complicated one—in brief, Kinnekulle and the other table mountains are masses of sub-surface igneous rock which forced themselves up through fissures in the sedimentary rock when this country was still one big sea. When the sea went out and time went to work, the less resistant sedimentary rock was eaten away, but the more durable igneous rock—battered and weather-beaten though it be—still stands. You can study the various layers and get an idea of the whole process at Kinnekulle, besides enjoying the far-flung view.

Moving south and west from Lidköping, you find yourself, after about 15 miles of travel through charming country, in the city of Skara, one of the oldest in the country. It was ravaged by war and burned several times, and the only surviving building of any real age is the cathedral. It was founded about the middle of the 11th century, and is probably the second oldest church in Sweden (oldest—Lund Cathedral). Successive reconstructions and additions have mixed the styles—it was originally Romanesque, changed into Gothic, and its exterior is now largely a product of the last century, in traditional high Gothic style.

Skara became a religious center early in medieval times, and has been an educational center ever since 1641, when one of the first higher institutions of learning in Sweden was established here. Its history goes back to at least 829.

Don't miss Varnhem Abbey Church, ten miles or so east of Skara, perhaps the best preserved monastic building in Sweden. It is, furthermore, the outstanding example of the Cistercian Order's considerable building activities in Sweden (well before the Reformation, of course). The Varnhem Abbey Church, started about 1250, is notable—aside from its age and architecture—as the burial place of four medieval kings, Magnus Gabriel de la Gardie (builder of Läckö Castle), and Birger Jarl, founder of Stockholm.

Östergötland and Lake Vättern

The land of eastern Goths, or Östergötland, is a country between two coasts, as different as an imaginative nature could make them. The western coast is formed by Lake Vättern, a long, narrow inland sea around which nestle some of the nation's most treasured natural and historical sights. The east coast is on the Baltic Sea, comparatively harsh and unyielding, but just as beautiful in a bolder fashion. Between are some of the most fertile farmlands and finest estates in the entire country. Linköping, an ancient religious, administrative, and cultural center, lies in almost the exact middle of this luxuriant plain. Norrköping, sometimes inaccurately called a twin city of Linköping, is a modern industrial center forming the northeast anchor of the province on the Baltic Coast.

This whole area can be divided roughly into two regions for purposes of a visit, the east coast of Lake Vättern, ranging from Jönköping at the southern tip, north as far as the medieval city of Vadstena, and the Linköping-Norrköping area.

Lake Vättern is the second largest lake in Sweden, and its surface area of about 750 square miles ranks it among the major inland seas in Europe. It stretches almost due north and south for nearly a hundred miles, but its greatest width is less than 25 miles. Around its shores, particularly on the eastern side, lived an ancient culture.

If you approach Lake Vättern from Gothenburg or from the south, your starting point will be Jönköping, at the very southernmost tip of the lake. Jönköping's greatest claim to fame is perhaps as the central stronghold of the Swedish Match Company, a great international enterprise. It was here, about 100 years ago, that the history of one of our most commonplace daily necessities, the safety match, began to be written. The Swedish Match Company still operates a factory and makes its headquarters in Jönköping. There is a museum in the old factory illustrating the history of manufacturing safety matches.

Jönköping is an important administrative center—besides serving as the residence of the provincial governor, it is the seat of the Göta Court of Appeals for southern Sweden. This is the second oldest appeals court in Sweden, and you can see its distinguished building, from about 1650, on the main square. Several of the other buildings, including nearby Christina Church, are from roughly the same period.

Proceeding now along the lake shore, first east and then north, the first main town is Huskvarna, only 4 miles away. It is comparatively young and owes its existence principally to an arms factory moved there shortly before 1700. The factory is still turning out weapons—in newer quarters, of course—and there are other ultramodern plants turning out sewing machines, sporting rifles, chain saws, moped motors, refrigerators, deep-freezers. Specially trained guides show visitors round the factory.

Gränna and Historic Visingsö

The next main point of interest is Gränna and, if you are spending any time in this region, you might make this your headquarters. Stay at the Gyllene Uttern (Golden Otter) Inn, situated about 200 feet above Vättern, with a magnificent view of the lake and surroundings (including the isle of Visingsö).

Gränna is never more beautiful than when the fruit trees blossom. You'll see signs along the road advertising *Polkagrisar*—meaning literally "polka pigs"—a kind of red and white striped peppermint candy for which Gränna is famous in Sweden. Do try them, fresh from the hands of the maker.

This little community is the birthplace of a famous polar explorer, and there are two museums devoted to his memory near the site of the house where he was born. His name was S. A. André—and he tried to reach the North Pole by air in 1897. He and two companions started by balloon from an island near Spitsbergen, and disappeared silently into history. More than three decades later the remains of the ill-fated expedition were discovered on White Island, not far from Spitsbergen, and so well-preserved that not only could the diaries be read but the films could be developed.

André was buried in Stockholm with great honors, but the record of his premature tragic death in the cause of science is to be found in the interesting exhibits of the André and Vitö museums in Gränna. See also the ruins of the castle built by Count Per M. Brahe some 300 years ago on road E4. The view is magnificent.

As you look out upon Lake Vättern from Gränna you see a long, narrow island resting peacefully 4 miles across the water. This island, Visingsö, played a role in history up to about 1725. Today there are about a thousand inhabitants, mostly farmers. There is regular boat service (several crossings a day) to the island from Gränna, and you can easily arrange tranportation on the island to see the sights. The principal one is the ruins of Visingsborg Castle, built around 1550, and last used as a prison for captives taken in Charles XII's wars with Russia, before it burned shortly after 1700. See also the Brahe Church, the 12th-century Kumlaby Church (with interesting murals), the remains of the tower and walls of the medieval castle on the southern extremity of the island. It won't take you long to get around, the whole island is only about 10 miles long.

Proceeding north again from Gränna to Vadstena, you come first to Omberg, a national park containing Mount Omberg. There are interesting caves near the shore, but the principal attraction is the broad view from the crown of Mount Omberg, "eight cities, 30 churches, and four provinces".

From Vadstena to Norrköping

Vadstena, the next stop, has all the natural beauties of this region plus unique historical memories. To a great extent Vadstena is the physical reflection of the long and strange life of St. Birgitta (or Bridget), high-born (shortly after 1300) daughter of the royal Folkunga dynasty, mistress of a great estate and mother of eight children, religious mystic, and founder of the Roman Catholic Birgittine Order for women. Birgitta received her instructions from God in the form of visions, which led to the founding of the order in Vadstena. About 1350 she made the strenuous journey to Rome to get the papal blessing and died there in 1373 after a pilgrimage to Jerusalem. Her remains were returned home for burial in the church she designed for Vadstena.

You can easily visit Vadstena on foot. The church is an architectural jewel, begun shortly after 1350 and requiring some 70 years in the building. Aside from the noble Catholic architecture, note particularly the triumphal crucifix, the so-called Lovely Madonna, the Maria triptych at the high altar, the Birgittine triptych showing St. Birgitta presenting her revelations to two cardinals, and—behind the high altar —the lovely coffin containing the recently authenticated relics of the saint and one of her daughters. Also behind the high altar are the confessional stalls once used by the nuns.

Ironically enough, King Gustav Vasa, whose reformation dealt a death-blow to Catholicism in Sweden, chose Vadstena for one of his great fortified castles. The castle is still framed by its protecting moat, but a massive outer wall has disappeared. Construction was begun by King Gustav Vasa about 1540 and the place was used for some time by him and his descendants, but by about 1700 had ceased to be occupied as a royal seat. Note the wedding room (so-called because Gustav Vasa took his 16-year-old bride here about 1550), the small Hall of State, and the chapel.

If you have time, take a look at the interesting old house of Mårten Skinnare (Martin the Tanner) from about 1550, located not far from the church. Theater lovers will be interested in another nearby building, the theater, opened about 1825. It is said to be the oldest provincial theater in the country, and gives you a good idea of what life on the boards was like over a century ago.

Note: Vadstena has acquired quite a reputation within Sweden for its hand-made laces. It will be worth your while at least to have a look at them in one of the shops. Not far from Vadstena are the ruins of the first monastery in Sweden, Alvastra, founded in 1143. Nearby Skänninge is a community at least 1,000 years old, which is mentioned in the text of a 10th-century rune stone. Its Church of Our Lady dates from the late 13th century.

Linköping is smaller than Norrköping but vastly more interesting for a pleasure visit. It is an ancient seat of religion and learning, in the middle of a fertile agricultural region. In recent years, a growing industry (most notably aircraft and the SAAB automobile) has forced the idyllic to give ground. Even the cathedral—unhesitatingly called the most beautiful in Sweden by its highly partisan admirers—harmoniously combines both old and new.

You can't miss the cathedral. It is located a block from the central square, where you ought also to study the Milles fountain. It was erected to the memory of the great Folkunga dynasty of the Middle Ages (Birger Jarl, King Magnus Ladulås, St. Birgitta), and shows the progenitor, Folke Filbyter, searching for his lost grandson on a weary horse. Man and beast have traveled together for so long that the sculptor has portrayed them as one living being. The dynasty originated in this area. The oldest part of the cathedral dates from the 12th century, but was really not completed until shortly after 1500, a building period of more than 300 years. The steeple was added only about 75 years ago. Of particular interest are the triumphal crucifix and the baptismal font of the 14th and 15th centuries, the modern altar painting by Henrik Sörensen, and the modern tapestries behind. They are by Märta Afzelius, on a theme from the Creation.

If you have any interest in museums, you ought by all means to see the Provincial and City Museum in Linköping. Examine it as much for the application of modern architectural and display techniques as for the valuable collections.

Seven miles from Linköping you will find Vreta Cloister, once a thriving establishment of the Cistercian Order. The cloister church, still preserved, was dedicated about 1290 by no less a personage than King Magnus Ladulås himself. The baptismal font of Gotland stone was fashioned before 1300. Several notables, from medieval times on, are buried here. The nunnery itself has fallen into ruins, but you can see fragments of the old walls. The conducted bus excursions from Linköping include both Vreta and some historic manor houses.

Norrköping, fourth largest city in Sweden, is notable principally for its industries—largely textiles and wood products. It is one of the major east coast ports. A comparatively young town, the oldest building, Hedvig's Church, is from about 1675. Incidentally Norrköping and Linköping share a full-time professional theater company of high quality, which is particularly remarkable in terms of the relatively small population of the two municipalities. Norrköping is located on a bay of the Baltic Sea, Bråviken, leading out to the archipelago. At the mouth of the bay is Arkösund, a coastal community popular with summer sailors. Kolmårdens Djurpark, 15 miles north of Norrköping on Highway E4, is a new zoo and recreation ground with camping site, bathing beach and a swimming pool, cableway. There is a regular boat service from Norrköping to the zoo, and the park is open all year round.

Building the Göta Canal

A bountiful Nature in this country of almost 100,000 lakes and rivers provided much of the route ready-made, but man had to do his full share before it was possible to travel between Stockholm and Gothenburg by water. The builders were not interested in tourists—for them the canal was a straight-out commercial freight proposition, of tremendous importance for the country's future. No less than 65 locks were required, as well as miles of channels to connect the lakes and rivers. The result was a waterway which tremendously facilitated the movement of freight within and across the country.

In 1800 the Trollhätte Canal connecting huge Lake Vänern with Gothenburg and the North Sea was completed and soon demonstrated its value. Then, in 1808–9, Baltzar von Platen, a military man and ranking government official, advocated the bold plan of continuing on from Lake Vänern to Lake Vättern and across to the Baltic Sea. It is a tribute to the leaders of the country in an era when the whole outlook for the future of the nation was as dismal as it had ever been, that they boldly appropriated 2,400,000 *dalers* to begin the project. It was a tremendous piece of work, and during the years of building ran into constant obstacles and required some five times the original financial appropriation. A masterful piece of hard-headed Swedish logic was applied to overcome one of them. The farmers of one region had refused to sell their land for the right of way. The representative of the canal company asked, "Did you ever see water run uphill?" Nobody could answer in the affirmative. "Well, then," he said, "when this idiot von Platen fails, too, you'll get the land back." The farmers signed. But von Platen *did* make water "run uphill", and it has been doing so in the Göta Canal ever since. Von Platen was never able to take the trip himself: he died shortly before his great dream was realized and the canal opened to traffic. You will find his grave and a statue of him in the city of Motala, on Lake Vättern, one of the cities along the route.

Some of the high points have already been described: Bohus Fortress, Trolhättan Falls, Läckö Castle, Vadstena. You can take it easy, seeing the various sights as thoroughly or superficially as suits you, enjoying the company of your 50-odd fellow passengers. You come in intimate contact with the countryside—here and there the grass alongside the narrow channel and the overhanging trees actually brush the rails and decks. You also see an almost unlimited variety of drawbridges.

You come out on the island-strewn Baltic Sea just south of Norrköping, and follow the coast north for a way before turning into the Södertälje Canal. The canal carries you into Lake Mälar, which brings you, via the beautiful channel from the west, right to the heart of Stockholm. You tie up at Riddarholmen—rested, full of fresh air, and with a real mental image of the heart of Sweden.

Värmland

Perhaps no other region of Sweden has been so romanticized as the province of Värmland. Sweden's greatest authoress, Selma Lagerlöf, made it a national legend in *The Saga of Gösta Berling,* and there is a widely sung, melancholy, hauntingly beautiful song titled *Song of Värmland.* It is often an anticlimax to visit a region which has been sung in song and story, Värmland will not disappoint you.

Don't be deceived by the endless woods and the idyllic nature of the landscape. The woods, the rivers, and the iron ore of the ground actually make this a leading industrial region, with ultra-modern factories dotted here and there in pleasant, comparatively small towns. The wood and iron ore industries have centuries-old traditions, and the old semi-rural culture was based to some extent on them.

Karlstad is the provincial capital and seat of the diocese, with some 53,000 inhabitants. The oldest building is the cathedral, built between 1723 and 1730. There is a comparatively large harbor on Lake Vänern which has direct connections with the ocean through the Trolhätte Canal.

The origins of Karlstad are lost in antiquity, but because of destructive fires the city hardly looks old. It has apparently been the capital of this region from the beginning of time and was formerly known as Tingvalla, after the *ting,* or meetings of the legislature, which were held here. When Duke Karl issued it a charter in 1584, he also gave it a name. Karlstad means "the city of Karl".

Värmland is cut by rivers and long narrow lakes, running roughly north to south (with a slight bias of the southern end of the axis to the east). The largest of these, and the best known, is the Fryken chain consisting of three lakes. The most popular sightseeing route is the Fryken Valley.

A tour along the following lines can be managed easily in one day by car. During the summer season, you will find guided bus tours to the principal points of interest. Take the main road north along the beautiful Klar River (in the spring full of timber being floated down to factories) about 25 miles to Ransäter, where you will find a rural museum, a lookout tower, and the home where Erik Gustaf Geijer, a national literary great, was born in 1783. A few miles farther on you come to Munkfors, site of one of the major steel plants of the Uddeholm Corporation. It will give you an idea of the highly-developed quality steel industry of this part of the world. Just north of Munkfors, turn off to the right on the road to Sunnemo. It brings you down to the narrow lake called Lidsjön, and a ferry that accommodates two cars. The crossing takes only five minutes or so. The Sunnemo church is a little known exquisite rural parish church, utterly charming in its modest expression in wood of the people's religious feeling. Note the individual carved shingles.

From here you proceed north again along Råda Lake to Uddeholm, a deceivingly peaceful village of 500 souls or so. You'd never know by looking at it, but this is the main headquarters of a huge international corporation. Prince Vilhelm once said of it that you could imagine it as the site of a sanatorium, a children's home, a vacation home—in short, anything except what it is. It is truly peaceful. But inside some of the unprepossessing buildings, direct telephone and teletype lines keep Uddeholm in constant touch with its far-flung empire, with its many plants producing iron and steel, wood products, chemicals, and paper, with its sales organization in two hemispheres. The Uddeholm Corporation descends in a direct line from a 17th-century ironworks, and today it is perhaps the largest private employer in Sweden.

Selma Lagerlöf's Home

Because the roads due west may not be too good, your best bet is to continue around the north end of the lake, then turn due south again and make your way back to Munkfors. But here, instead of returning directly to Karlstad, you can cut almost due west (to the right) to Sunne, which brings you into the very heart of the Selma Lagerlöf country. It's only 34 miles south of here to Mårbacka, her ancestral home, now a public museum maintained largely as she left it at the time of her death in 1940. You are better advised to go back to Sunne from Mårbacka, cross over to the west side of the Fryken Lakes, and turn south towards Karlstad again. Only a couple of miles below Sunne you reach famed Rottneros, the "Ekeby" of the Lagerlöf book, a truly fine example of the old culture of the landed gentry. The buildings themselves are stately, and the grounds, overlooking the lake, are well kept. About ten miles before you reach Karlstad, near Kil, is the Apertin Manor House. It's worth a look, but, since it is privately owned, don't expect to get inside without special arrangements. The same thing applies to Rottneros, although the public is permitted to wander freely through the grounds.

The city of Filipstad, about 40 miles from Karlstad, has a special interest for Americans. It is the home ground of John Ericsson, whose iron-clad ship, the *Monitor,* meant victory at sea for the North in America's War Between the States. Ericsson's place in history would have been assured had he never seen America, however, for he contributed a number of major inventions to the exploding technological progress of the 19th century. Because of his contribution to American national unity, his body was delivered to Sweden in 1890 by the United States Navy, and buried with great pomp. You will find his tomb, and a memorial statue, in this idyllic little city where he grew up. The population is now something over 7,000, and there is a varied industry. The peaceful appearance of the city belies its industrial and commercial importance, however, and it is perhaps never more beautiful than in the spring, when the high waters of the Skiller River go rushing through the heart of the town, almost on a level with the sidewalks.

Dalsland and Its Canal

The province of Dalsland is for lovers of the outdoors. It is shaped in the form of a huge, irregular wedge, with Bohuslän and Norway forming the western border, Lake Vänern the eastern, and the province of Värmland the northern.

Actually, the most beautiful part of Dalsland is perhaps not the coastal regions but the deep forests and lakes of the western and northern areas. The principal tourist centers are Bengtsfors, the northwest anchor of the lovely Dalsland Canal; Ed, on the road to Norway; and Åmål, the principal city.

The Dalsland Canal, built in 1860 under the direction of Nils Ericsson, brother of John Ericsson of U.S. Civil War fame links up a 169-mile waterway with no less than 29 locks. You can travel by boat from Köpmannebro on the shores of Lake Vänern up through the whole of northern Dalsland, over the aqueduct at Håverud, and on by the way of Värmland lakes to the Norwegian border.

PRACTICAL INFORMATION FOR THE LAKE DISTRICT

WHEN TO COME. From May to September is a good time to visit this region, but a lot depends what you wish to do. If the seaside is the big attraction, it is well to know that many of the hostelries there do not open until mid-June and close the end of August. If your goal is the Göta Canal or Dalsland Canal trip, you must schedule your visit from about the first of June to the first of September, the period during which the cruises operate.

WHAT TO SEE. In addition to the veritable inland seas of Lakes Vänern and Vättern and the Göta Canal that wends its scenic way from Stockholm to Gothenburg, each province presents its own distinctive glimpse of past and present.

Bohuslän: Fortresses of Bohus at Kungälv, Karlsten at Marstrand, and Fredriksten near Strömstad. The country churches of Bokenäs, Bro, Kungälv, and Svenneby.

Västergötland: The Old Courthouse at Lidköping, and nearby Läckö Castle; the Stone Age burial place near Falköping; the 13th-century cathedral of Skara; hills of Hunneberg, Halleberg, and Kinnekulle, the latter sheltering in its pine forests and old manor houses and the ancient churches of Varnhem and Husaby; the country church of Borgstena, with its rich baroque and rococo interior, and Hedared, Sweden's only existing stave church.

Östergötland: Linköping, with its modern factories, beautiful cathedral, and "Folke Filbyter" fountain by Carl Milles; Lövstad Castle, the medieval abbey church of Vreta with its interesting cloister ruins, St. Birgitta's town of Vadstena, Omberg Hills on the shores of Lake Vättern, all near Linköping. The big city of Norrköping with a beautiful archipelago and the zoo and recreation park of Kolmården.

Småland: The island of Visingsö, with Visingsborg Castle ruins and Brahe and Kumlaby churches.

Värmland: Fryken lakes; Mårbacka, home of Selma Lagerlöf; 18th-century Apertin Manor House; the towns of Filipstad and Arvika; the churches of Sunnemo and Södra Råda.

Dalsland: Dalsland Canal; the 18th-century country churches of Fröskog and Skållerud.

HOW TO GET ABOUT. You will see a good deal of Västergötland on the main highway or railway from Gothenburg to Stockholm, as well as by way of the Göta Canal. A good idea is to plan a route that includes Lidköping, Skara, and the interesting points around them.

In **Östergötland,** the highway route between Jönköping and Vadstena (bus and rail-bus service) that winds along the eastern shore of Lake Vättern is for many people the most beautiful road in Sweden. It can very well be combined with a trip from Gothenburg to Stockholm, or from southern Sweden to Stockholm, or vice-versa. The Norrköping area of Östergötland similarly can be combined with any of the same trips, but it is close enough to Stockholm to make a convenient excursion of a day or two from that city (Linköping is about 135 miles from Stockholm, Norrköping 90 miles).

In **Värmland,** Karlstad is easily and quickly reached (4–6 hours by train) from Oslo, Gothenburg, or Stockholm. By air Karlstad is reached in about one hour from Stockholm and Gothenburg. During the summer, there are guided bus tours to the principal points of interest in Fryken valley.

You pass through the eastern regions of **Dalsland** along the Vänern shore, if you travel by road or train from Gothenburg to Karlstad; through the northern regions, on the Dalsland Canal route.

BY BOAT. Göta Canal: Few regions of the world are served up to visitors with the same graceful ease as those along the Göta Canal, well over 100 years old. You climb aboard a comfortable steamer in Stockholm or Gothenburg—for the 3-day trip (2–3 sailings weekly in each direction)—and take it easy as the heartland of Sweden moves by you. If time is limited, it is possible to take shorter daytime boat trips on the Göta Canal starting from Stockholm, Gothenburg, or interim points.

Motorists taking the 3-day trip can have their cars driven between Gothenburg and Stockholm, or vice versa, to await their arrival.

Dalsland Canal: Undoubtedly one of the most beautiful waterways in Scandinavia, passing through the most scenic parts of the province and on via Värmland to the Norwegian border (4–5 services weekly).

HOTELS AND RESTAURANTS. Accommodation in general is on the modest side. A few towns draw a more or less fashionable trade, but most of the people who inhabit this region during the summer live in cottages or aboard their sailboats. You will find comfortable cottages in the holiday villages of Vette, Kungälv and Hökensås for 600–800 kr. a week: contact *Inter Holiday,* Lilla Kungsgatan 2, 41108 Gothenburg.

ÅMÅL. Hotel: *Stadshotellet,* 27 rooms, 7 with bath, inexpensive.

ÅRJÄNG. Motel: *Esso Motor Hotel,* 40 rooms with bath, pool, sauna. New.

ARVIKA. Hotels: *Bristol,* 33 rooms, 18 baths, moderate; *Stadshotellet,* 40 rooms, moderate to inexpensive.

BENGTSFORS. Hotel: *Dalia,* comfortable, moderate resort hotel, 40 rooms, 10 baths, restaurant.

BORÅS. Hotels: *Grand,* 160 rooms with bath, best. *Stadshotellet,* 70 rooms with bath or shower; *Vävaren,* 80 rooms with bath or shower; both moderate. **Motel:** *Esso Motor Hotel,* 51 rooms with bath or shower.

ED. Hotel: *Eds Turisthotell,* 40 rooms, 2 baths, inexpensive.

ESKILSTUNA. *Esso Motor Hotel,* Strängnäsvägen, off E3, near golf course: 60 rooms with bath. *Statt,* in the center of the city, 120 rooms.(SARA.)

FALKÖPING. Hotel: *Stora Hotellet,* (SARA), 44 rooms, near town center, moderate.

FILIPSTAD. Motel: *Esso Motor Hotel,* 47 rooms.

FISKEBÄCKSKIL. Two inexpensive pensions, *Strandvillan; Rågårdsvik.*

GRÄNNA. Hotel: *Gyllene Uttern,* high above Lake Vättern, about 1½ miles south on E4, an *Esso Motor Hotel,* modern, but copied from old Swedish castle architecture, 52 rooms, 26 with bath, annex, also 2/3-room cottages, moderate. Good restaurant.

HINDÅS. Hotel: *Hindåsgården,* 68 rooms, 25 baths, inexpensive, home cooking.

JÖNKÖPING. Hotels: *Ramada-Jönköping,* 116 rooms; restaurants, bars, heated pool, solarium, comfortable. *Stora Hotellet,* 111 rooms, some with views of Lake Vättern and canal, central and very good, first class. *Grand,* 60 rooms, 10 baths, inexpensive. *Portalen,* 172 rooms. RESO hotel.
Motels: *Vätterleden* on E4, 9 miles north of Jönköping, 52 rooms with bath. *Esso Motor Hotel,* Rosenlund, 174 rooms, *MHF,* Birkagatan, 44 rooms with bath or shower.

KARLSKOGA. Hotel: *Stadshotellet,* 59 rooms, 37 baths, 3 restaurants, golf, moderate (SARA). *Rex,* 45 rooms with bath or shower.

KARLSTAD. Hotels: *Gösta Berling,* 60 rooms, 18 with bath, moderate to first class reasonable; no restaurant but next-door cafeteria. In same category: *Stadshotellet,* 165 rooms, most with bath; grill room, bar. *Grand,* 75 rooms, half with bath, restaurant. *Wåxnäs,* 38 rooms with bath, has a pleasant restaurant, steakhouse and pub. Slightly lower rates prevail at the *Ritz,* 64 rooms. *Savoy,* 60 rooms, most with bath.
Motels: *Esso Motor Hotel,* 81 rooms with bath, by lake just off E18. *OK Motorhotell,* on E18, 80 rooms with shower.
Restaurant: *Stadskällaren,* Kungsgatan, by railroad station, pleasant and good food (SARA). *Sandgrund,* has terrace, bar, dancing.

KRISTINEHAMN. Hotel: *Stadshotellet,* 40 rooms, 22 with bath, top moderate class.
Restaurant: *Kavaljeren* (SARA), new, agreeable, moderate.

KUNGÄLV. Hotel: *Fars Hatt,* 130 rooms. Heated outdoor pool. First class reasonable.

LAXÅ. on E3, southwest of town, *Esso Motor Hotel,* 42 rooms with bath or shower.

LIDKÖPING. Hotels: *Stadshotellet,* 74 rooms, 44 baths; faces shady park, has the attractive *Druvan* restaurant (SARA); *Örnen,* 22 rooms; both moderate.

LINKÖPING. Hotels: *Hotel Ekoxen,* Klostergatan 68, 117 rooms, first class. *Frimurarehotellet,* 122 rooms, restaurant, grill room, summer terrace and park;

first class reasonable. Same category, *Rally*, 100 rooms, 80 with bath, garage for 150 cars, bar, restaurant, cafeteria (SARA).

Stora Hotellet, 101 rooms, moderate. *Hotel Diplomat Roxen*, 91 rooms with bath, first class.

Inexpensive are: *Baltic*, 77 rooms; *City*, 38 rooms; *Palace*, 22 rooms.

Motels: *Esso Motor Hotel*, off E4, southwest of town, 94 rooms; *Motel Filbyter*, on E4, 2 miles north, 22 rooms.

Restaurants: *Druvan*, Platensgatan 3, nourishing, unpretentious food at moderate prices. *Tradgårdsföreningen* has open-air dining, music, dancing. *Tresnäckor* at Herrbeta on E4 is a good ICA place.

LYSEKIL. Hotel: *Lysekil*, 50 rooms, and *Strand*, 24 rooms, moderate resort hotels with some rooms higher-priced. Seawater pool.

MARSTRAND. Hotels: *Marstrand*, 45 rooms, 8 baths, exquisite and modern interior; *Sommarhotellet*, 32 rooms, restaurant, bar; *Grand*, 33 rooms, no restaurant; all moderate.

Restaurant: *Societetshuset*, summer restaurant, late 19th cent.

MOTALA. Hotels: *Stadshotellet*, 60 rooms, 25 with bath or shower; *Palace*, 56 rooms, most with bath; both moderate.

NORRKÖPING. Hotels: *Standard*, 176 rooms, (SARA). Restaurant, steakhouse, pub and cocktail bar, located opposite small park.

Motel: *Mobilen* on E4, 84 rooms with bath or shower. *Esso Motor Hotel*, 155 rooms, on E4 north of town.

Restaurants: *Druvan*, Slottsgatan 104, skip the first floor and go on to the second for a satisfying meal at moderate cost. *Nordstjärnan*, Vattengatan 12, again upstairs is best, good service and well-prepared food, moderate. (Both SARA).

ÖDESHÖG. Motel: *Vida Vättern*, 26 rooms, inexpensive.

ÖREBRO. Hotel: *Stora Hotellet*, central, excellent restaurant; well established, 120 rooms, most with bath. *Bergsmannen*, 68 rooms, half with bath. *Grev Rosen*, 73 rooms, moderate.

Motel: *Esso Motor Hotel*, southwest of town, off E3, 205 rooms.

SKARA. Hotel: *Stadshotellet*, 44 rooms, moderate. Motel: *Skara* on E3, 35 rooms with shower. Swimming pool, Shell service.

SKÖVDE. Hotel: *Billingen*, 90 rooms, most with bath or shower. Pleasant restaurant "Zum Dicken Fritz" (both SARA). *Billingehus*, 150 rooms, most with bath.

Motel: *OK Motorhotell*, 44 rooms with shower.

STRÖMSTAD. Hotels: *Laholmen*, 17 rooms, 3 baths, swimming and fishing facilities, dancing, moderate. *Stadshotellet*, 30 rooms, and *Grand*, 22 rooms, are inexpensive.

TANUMSHEDE. *Gästgiveri*, 29 rooms (and a bridal suite with circular bath tub): excellent food.

TIDAHOLM. Hotel: *Stora Hotellet,* 21 rooms, 4 baths, moderate. (SARA).

TORSBY. Hotel: *Björnidet,* 26 rooms, most with bath; restaurant.

TROLLHÄTTAN. Hotel: *Stadshotellet,* 60 rooms, most with bath, moderate. Restaurant, bar, dancing. Rooms on west side have view of Göta Canal.

Restaurant: *Minerva,* Kungsgatan 35, dining on two floors—upstairs best, moderate prices (SARA).

UDDEVALLA. Hotels: *Carlia,* 97 rooms, 31 baths. *Gvldenlöwe,* 43 rooms, *Viking,* 23 rooms. All are moderate. *Hotel Bohusgården,* 97 rooms, restaurant, panoramic view of the bay.

ULRICEHAMN. Hotels: *Esso Motor Hotel,* 60 rooms, moderate.

VADSTENA. Hotel: *Vadstena Klosters Gästhem,* 25 rooms all with bath, moderate.

VÄNERSBORG. Hotel: *Grand Hotel,* 31 rooms. *Esso Motor Hotel,* 87 rooms. **Restaurant:** *Elvan.*

 USEFUL ADDRESSES. Tourist information and room booking service: Gränna, Torget; Jönköping, Kyrkogatan 6; Karlstad, Hamngatan 22; Lidköping, Old Town Hall; Linköping, Stora Torget 1; Motala, Stora Torget; Norrköping, Central Station; Skara, Central Station; Vadstena, Town Hall; Åmål, Kungsgatan 20.

Camping: Sites at Grebbestad, Hamburgsund, Ljungskile, Marstrand, Borås, Mariestad, Linköping, Motala, Norrköping, Vadstena, Arvika, Filipstad, Åmål, many others.

NORRLAND AND LAPLAND

Winter Wonderland

The Swedish highlands, ranging from central Sweden up beyond the Arctic Circle for a distance of 500 miles or more, offer you holidays quite unlike any others anywhere. The region has been settled for centuries, its natural resources are among the most important in northern Europe, yet it is a country of open spaces, virgin wilderness, and a combination of natural beauties not to be found anywhere else in the world.

Norrland—as the entire region of northern Sweden is called—occupies half of Sweden's territory but holds only 17 per cent of its population. Modern industry already has put its stamp on parts of Norrland, with its vast resources of timber, iron ore, and water power. But the traditional peasant culture of the river valleys and coastal areas, deep-rooted in the Middle Ages, and the ageless civilization of the independent, nomadic Lapps have remained virtually unchanged.

Exploring the North

Sandwiched between Norway in the west, Jämtland in the north, the coastal provinces in the east, and Darlana in the south, Härjedalen possesses only one center of any size—Sveg, with a little over 2,000 inhabitants. Because of this—or in spite of it—Härjedalen was the first mountain province to attract visitors in the days when both tourism and skiing were in their infancy. One reason for its continued popularity with skiers is the great variety of terrain it offers, from the gentle rounded southern mountains to the originally volcanic Helag Mountains in the north. Fjällnäs, Funäsdalen, Bruksvallarna and Vemdalskalet all offer comfortable lodging and are both summer and winter resorts.

Across the Flatruet plateau in the western part of the province runs the highest road in Sweden (3,000 feet), offering a breathtaking view from its summit. On one of the cliff walls are rock paintings, almost 4,000 years old, depicting animal and human figures. Another curiosity is the "frozen sea" of the Rogen area, with its striated and pitted Ice Age boulders.

Jämtland

Östersund is on the railroad line that crosses the Scandinavian peninsula from Sundsvall, industrial center on the east coast of Sweden, to Trondheim on Norway's Atlantic coast, a fact which accounts for much of its growth in recent years. Despite its northerly clime, however, the region around Storsjön, or the Great Lake, has been settled since heathen times. The ancient capital of this region was Frösön, an island in the lake just off what is now Östersund. It was the site of a heathen sacrificial temple and the place where the *ting,* or popular council, met. The strange Viking alphabet also penetrated here, and the northernmost rune stone in Sweden is to be found on Frösön near the bridge. It was erected there by one Östman Gudfastsson about the year 1050. From the heights of Frösön you have unbelievably distant views —of the lake, the cultivated areas around the shores, and, in the west, the mountains reaching above the timberline.

Today Östersund has taken over Frösön's role as capital of the province, and has grown into a city of 26,000 inhabitants, with several industries. It is a good starting point for motor tours within the province or into Norway—the joint Swedish-Norwegian "Trondheimsleden" highway leads via Enafors and Storlien to Trondheim.

Here are some of the principal resorts in the region stretching west of Östersund:

Åre, site of a former World Ski Championship, and located in the beautiful Åre valley at the foot of Mount Åre, is popular both winter and summer. It is the largest resort in this region and also boasts a church dating from the 12th or 13th century.

Vålådalen has become known as the training center for Sweden's Olympic champions in cross country skiing and running. It is located a few miles south of Åre in a region of impressive mountains, the Snasa and Syl ranges.

Storlien, the last point in Sweden on the east-west railway line, is actually a border and customs station. It is perhaps the second largest resort center in this area.

There are a dozen or so other resorts or mountain hotels, among them Duved, Undersåker, Hålland, Ånn, Bydalen, and Anjan, all with good terrain. Farther north, in even more isolated country, are Gäddede and Jormlien. You're really in the wilderness here—observe reasonable precautions before taking off from your hotel. There are expert guides. The requirement that you notify the management of your intended route when you go out any distance is a simple precaution for your own safety. Don't laugh at it. Even if you're in perfect safety, which is likely, you'll feel awfully silly if half the population drops its other pursuits to come out looking for you.

Lapland

There is nothing more dramatic in all of Scandinavia than this region north of the Arctic Circle. It seems terribly far north, terribly distant, and it is at about the same latitude as northern Alaska. Yet it is a remarkably accessible place. You climb aboard an express train in Stockholm one afternoon, sleep soundly in a comfortable sleeper, eat in the diner, and by noon the next day you have arrived in a strange and wonderful world.

These contradictions never fail to fascinate the visitor. The region is huge—the province of Lapland covers about one fourth of Sweden's total area, but is only sparsely settled, of course. And its great beauty as a vacation region is the ease and comfort with which you reach it, without strain, special clothes or equipment, or much traveling time.

If you travel by train, the main line proceeds on or near the eastern coast, along the Gulf of Bothnia, all the way to the city of Boden. You pass through a huge industrial region—largely forest products—and magnificent natural scenery. Since this is a night train you will sleep through most of it, but the coastal cities, such as Gävle, a major port; Sundsvall, a paper and pulp center; Umeå, the cultural capital of northern Sweden; and Luleå, with a museum featuring Lapp collections and a 15th-century church, are of more than passing interest.

The whole of northern Sweden is a region of forests and huge rivers. The rivers cut eastward across country from the mountain range along the Norwegian border to the east coast of Sweden, and are used both to float logs to factories on the Baltic coast and for hydro-electric power. A trip through this region shows you why Sweden is one of the world's great producers of paper, woodpulp, and other wood products —the forests seem endless. At Boden, a northern military and industrial hub, the line makes a junction with the line going diagonally across Norrland, from Luleå on the Swedish coast to Narvik, Norway. It was built around the turn of the century to exploit the huge finds of iron ore (up to 70 per cent pure) at Gällivare and Kiruna. Narvik has become the principal shipping point, and Luleå ranks second. Up to 16,000,000 tons of ore are taken out and shipped annually via this line, and the ore trains run day and night.

North of the Arctic Circle

Keep your eyes open after you leave Boden. About 60 miles north— and a little west—you will see a line of white stones cutting squarely across the railroad tracks and a sign "Arctic Circle" in two or three languages, including English. You're now in the land of the Midnight Sun, near the legendary home of Santa Claus.

The sun never sets from the end of May until the middle of July, and if you have looked at pictures of it making its way across the horizon, let me assure you at once they are misleading. The apparent darkness in the photos, giving more of an impression of moonlight than sunlight, is caused by the filters used when shooting directly at the sun. Actually, the Midnight Sun is as bright as it is anywhere an hour or so before sunset. The whole thing has a mystical, unreal, ethereal quality—you sometimes find yourself feeling almost light headed. But well before the date when the sun actually stays above the horizon all night and well afterwards, the nights are light all night long. So if your visit must take place a week or two before or after the specific dates given, you will still enjoy the "sunlit nights" that give you approximately the same sensation.

Forty miles north of Boden you arrive in Gällivare, center of a mining region with ore reserves estimated at 400,000,000 tons. The principal mine is Malmberget, about four miles out of town. From here you can take an interesting side trip, the railway to Porjus and then by a new road to Vietas, not far from the Saltoluokta Tourist Station, and from there a motorboat trip in Sjöfallsleden, "Lapland's Blue Ribbon", the source lakes of the Big Lule River. Combined with some 12 miles walking you will, by this westbound route, finally reach the Atlantic. At Gällivare you will get the first glimpse of the Lapland mountains. Dundret (Thunder Mountain), 2,500 feet, has a convenient chair lift to its summit, and the view is well worth the trip. The midnight sun is visible in this neighborhood from June 1 to July 12.

Another 50 miles or so north on the main railway line is Kiruna, the world's biggest city. Kiruna became big enough to accommodate, shall we say, London, New York, and a few dozen other cities by incorporating the whole province within the municipality some years ago. It covers no less than 3,000 square miles. The mining town proper had a population of some 21,000, but only picked up an additional 6,000 or so people by this huge extension of its borders. The people, including the Lapps, were quick to react to the knowledge that they were living in the world's biggest city. A man we know was trying to get hold of a Lapp friend of his by telephone to a remote village. He finally succeeded in locating the man's wife, who said her husband wasn't at home: "He's out in the city with the reindeer herd."

Kiruna lies on a slope between two ore-bearing mountains with the jaw-cracking names of Kirunavaara and Luossavaara. The ore reserves are estimated at 500,000,000 tons. Mining operations are going more and more underground, but during the past decades most ore has been taken out by the open-pit method. You should try to see the biggest pit—if possible when blasting is going on. Tons of dynamite go off at one time in a huge manifestation of explosive power. From high points around Kiruna you get beautiful views—on clear days you can see the irregular contours of Kebnekasje, Sweden's highest mountain, about 50 miles away. And here in Kiruna you may see the blue and red costumes of the Lapps for the first time.

Meeting the Lapps

For a long time the Lapps were believed to be of Mongolian origin, but the latest theory now supposes they stem from somewhere in central Europe. Presumably they came to northern Scandinavia more than 1,000 years ago. They number about 8,000 in Sweden (of which only 2,000 are nomads deriving a living from the breeding of reindeer), 20,000 in Norway, 2,500 in Finland, and perhaps less than 2,000 in the Soviet Union.

The reindeer is the bone, sinew, and marrow of the economy of the nomadic Lapps of this area. (There are also forest Lapps and fishing Lapps.) Reindeer is the only domestic animal which can feed itself on the meager vegetation here beyond the Arctic Circle. The Lapps are nomads perhaps less from a restless desire to keep on the move than the necessity of following their reindeer herds from one grazing ground to another. In the winter they move down to the protected forests, east and south of the mountains, but in the spring they travel in the opposite direction for the grazing on the high slopes. The total number of reindeer in the Swedish herds has been estimated at something like 200,000.

The Lapp culture is not as primitive as many have chosen to believe —rather, it is a highly developed culture perfectly adapted to perhaps the only way of life which will mean independent survival in these northern wastes. Take just the matter of languages, for example: practically all of the Lapps are at least bi-lingual and many are fluent in three or four tongues—their own language, Swedish, Norwegian, Finnish, and possibly others. Their handicrafts make use of the horns and skins of reindeer, and their distinctive costumes, largely in red, yellow, and blue, are as functional as they are ornamental. During the war they performed invaluable services to the Allied cause by helping Norwegians and other prisoners of the Nazis escape from Norway through the mountains to Sweden.

The Lapps, as they follow their herds, live in a special type of tepee, or hut, which is called a *kåta*. They eat reindeer meat—some reindeer are milked—and about the only things a Lapp family needs from the outside world are coffee and salt. They, like other people in the North, are devoted to coffee. Some of the larger reindeer owners are wealthy. Many now move to and from the summer camps by helicopter, leaving only the young men to accompany the herds. But don't ask a Lapp how many reindeer he has. It is the measure of his wealth, and is about as rude and nosy a question as asking an acquaintance how much money he has.

The Lapps have equal status with other Swedes under the law, and some special privileges. The government provides special schools for their education, and attendance is compulsory, as it is for all the other groups. There is a special inn for Lapps in Kiruna, and you often see them on the streets. Or you may meet them on the train carrying knapsacks. Don't be patronizing—they're not "simple" people. They have produced at least one great primitive artist and some university professors. But whatever their talents, whatever their education, most of them prefer their own way of life.

Almost due east of Kiruna, about 10 or 15 miles, is Jukkasjärvi, a little village. This is a sort of semi-permanent Lapp headquarters, with a modern school, an equally modern home for aged Lapps, and an appealing old church. The structure dates from 1726, was built on the site of a previous church (1611) which was the second one in all of Lapland. Note the remarkable architecture. At the times of the great religious holidays, Lapps gather here in huge crowds, and a Lapp wedding may be a tremendous event.

To get to Jukkasjärvi you must cross the mighty Torne River. These rushing waters make a magnificent sight, and beneath the turbulent surface there are fighting game fish—including salmon, trout, and grayling.

At Kaitum, 15 miles south of Kiruna is the Kaitum Chapel consecrated in 1964 as an ecclesiastical center for Laplanders but also as a memorial to Dag Hammarskjöld.

Mount Kebnekajse, 6,965 feet above sea level, the highest mountain in Sweden, is an excursion point best reached from Kiruna. It is really in the wilderness, about 20 miles by bus, 25 by motorboat, and the last 15 by foot. (In the winter it's bus and skis; sometimes sleighs are available.) Here you literally get away from it all, but the trip is recommended only for those who are in good physical condition. From Kebnekajse the sun is visible round the clock from May 23 to July 22.

An hour or so north of Kiruna on the main railway line you approach the southern shore of Lake Torneträsk, a long, narrow body of water which extends for miles almost to the Norwegian border. This is the real wilderness, but modern communications put it right outside your window. The railroad follows the southern shore, and at the eastern end you come to one of the most popular resort regions in Lapland.

The first resort, and the best known, that you reach is Abisko. There are regular motorboat tours on Lake Torneträsk, mountain excursions during the summer season and skiing during the spring. The sun is visible round the clock from June 12 to July 4. Björkliden is a few miles farther along, also on the railway line, located near Lake Torneträsk. About 5 miles away is Låktatjåkko.

The very last resort before you cross into Norway is Riksgränsen and the little railway station also serves as the customs house. Here you can enjoy skiing by the light of the Midnight Sun, which shines from May 26 to July 18.

PRACTICAL INFORMATION FOR THE NORTH

WHEN TO COME. The Swedish highlands have their charm at all seasons of the year and offer a variety of delights to lovers of the outdoors. From Christmas to May skiing predominates. If the winters are long, the summers are brilliant—the countryside bursts into bloom, temperatures of 80–85° F (27–29°C) are not unusual, and the "sunlit nights" merge day into day with only a few hours of twilight between. In the far north, the Midnight Sun sees to it that there is no night at all from May 25 to July 15.

WHAT TO SEE. Wilderness, forests, and mountains are not the whole story. Among the other sights are: Gävle's 18th-century Court House; the prehistoric burial mounds at Högom; the Jamtli open-air museum at Östersund, one of Sweden's largest; the Jämtland waterfalls—Tännforsen, Ristafallen, and others—and the remarkable Dead Falls at Ragunda; Sweden's northernmost rune stone of Frösön Island, the fishermen's chapel at Ulvö, octagonal church at Vemdalen, and Årsunda's medieval church; the "Iron Mountain" at Kiruna; the "church town" of Gammelstad (Old Luleå); Arvidsjaur, center of the forest Lapps; and the 17th-century wooden church at Jukkasjärvi, one of the most interesting of the Lapp churches.

HOW TO GET ABOUT. Two main rail lines traverse Sweden in a south-north direction: from Stockholm near the coast to the Finnish border, and from Dalarna province through the interior to Gällivare; the Sundsvall-Trondheim and Luleå-Narvik lines cross it in an east-west direction. Secondary lines and postal buses, fanning out from the railroad stations, supplement this network and make even remote districts conveniently accessible. From Stockholm it is 7 hours to Östersund by express train, 12 to Storlien, 17 to Luleå, 20 to Kiruna, and 22½ to Abisko.

Long-distance buses link Stockholm with Funäsdalen and Härnösand, and Sundsvall with Luleå. Swedish State Railways also offer 9-day guided bus tours of the North Cape twice weekly from mid-June to mid-August, starting at Luleå and ending at Narvik in Norway. RESO operates a 7-day North Cape tour starting and ending in Kiruna daily from early June to mid-August.

If speed is essential, you can fly from Stockholm to Sundsvall in 75 minutes, to Umeå in 1 hr. 40 mins., to Luleå and Östersund in just over 2 hrs., to Kiruna in less than 4 hrs. From mid-June to mid-July, SAS/RESO operate round-trip "Midnight Sun" flights from Stockholm to Kiruna. *Inter-Holiday,* Lilla Kungsg. 1 in Gothenberg also have these flights.

If your preference is for a more leisurely route, there is a car ferry service from Vaasa in Finland to Sundsval (9 hours), Umeå (4 hours) and from Pietarsaari in Finland to Umeå and Skellefteå.

MOTORING. The most important route to northern Sweden, Highway E4, continues from Stockholm to Haparanda on the Finnish border, 681 miles (1,134 km). The main routes to the interior highlands branch off this highway at Hudiksvall: 84 via Sveg to Funäsdalen, 193 miles (322 km); Sundsvall: E75 via Östersund to Åre—186 miles (300 km)—and Storlien, so further into Norway to Trondheim; at Umeå: nos. 92, 93 and 361—the very scenic "Via Lappia"—through Storuman to Tärnaby and Hemavan, and on to Moi Rana, below the Arctic Circle; at Luleå: nos. 97 and 98 via Jokkmokk and Gällivare to Kiruna, 229 miles (381 km).

A road leading into Norway goes from Vilhelmina along the beautiful Lake Vojmsjön to Dikanäs and Kittelfjäll and via the frontier village of Skalmodal to Mosjöen in Norway (400 km).

Note that it is forbidden to take photographs near the defense areas of Sundsvall and Kalix on Highway E4, and Boden on Highway 97.

HOTELS. North, south, and west of Östersund are concentrated the Jämtland mountain resorts. These are not generally luxury establishments: they are designed principally for people who like the outdoors, and the rates are reasonable. In Lapland, you will find both modest hotels and modern, comfortable tourist hotels.

ABISKO. Abisko Turiststation, 161 rooms, 50 baths. Finnish sauna, restaurant, moderate.

ÅRE. Åregården, Diplomat, Sporthotellet, 200 rooms in all, rustic style in Åregården and Sporthotellet, moderate prices; Granen, 54 rooms, 21 baths, first class reasonable; Lundsgården, 40 rooms, 8 baths, moderate; Fjallgården, 43 rooms, 4 baths, moderate; Tott, 53 rooms, most with bath or shower, first class reasonable.

BJÖRKLIDEN. Gammelgården, modern, 35 rooms, and Fjället, 66 rooms and 80 cottages, both beautifully situated overlooking Lake Torneträsk. Owned by the Swedish State Railways.

BORGAFJÄLL. Borgafjäll, 30 rooms, moderate, chalet-type.

BRUKSVALLARNA. Several moderate to inexpensive tourist hotels: Bruksvallarnas Turiststation, 60 beds; Bruksvallsliden, 60 beds; Walles Fjällhotell, 90 beds; Ramundbergets Fjällgård, 115 rooms.

BYDALEN. Bydalens Stughotell, 38 cabins, each with 4 bunk beds; self-service but restaurant in large service building. Shops, sauna.

DUVED. Pensionat Mullfjället, 30 rooms, moderate to inexpensive. Gyllene Renen, motel, 7 rooms, inexpensive.

FJÄLLNÄS. Högfjällshotellet, 32 rooms; Göransgården, 8 rooms, inexpensive.

FUNÄSDALEN. Gästis, 33 rooms, some with bath; Wärdhuset Gronländaren, 35 rooms. Both moderate.

GÄLLIVARE. Vassara, 39 rooms, 18 baths, restaurant. Moderate.

GÄVLE. Grand-Central, 100 rooms with bath or shower, central, restaurant, first class superior; Avenue, 30 rooms; moderate.
Esso Motor Hotel, on Riks 80 west of town, 150 rooms with bath or shower. GDG Motell, Norra Rådmansgatan 38, 22 rooms, inexpensive.

HÅLLAND. Hedmans, 93 rooms, 9 baths, RESO hotel, moderate.

HAPARANDA. Stadshotellet, 41 rooms, moderate.

HÄRNÖSAND. Stadshotellet (SARA), 78 rooms with bath, first class reasonable. Centralhotellet, 17 rooms, inexpensive. Esso Motor Hotel, on E4, 52 rooms with bath or shower.
Restaurant: Nybrokälleren (SARA), Nybrogatan 5, is excellent.

HEMAVAN. Hemavans Högfjällshotell, modernized, 70 rooms, some with bath, first class reasonable. Fully licensed restaurant. Hemavans Värdshus, 14 rooms, cottages, family-run inn, mountain scenery, moderate.

KALL. Kallgården, 30 rooms, 11 baths; Permings, 24 rooms, 19 with shower. Moderate.

KIRUNA. Reso-hotel Ferrum, 112 rooms with bath or shower. The 18-room Järnvägshotellet, 26-room Kiruna, and 15-room Motel Pallia are inexpensive.
At Kebnekajse, the Mountain Station of Swedish Touring Club offers 56 beds in main building, 32 beds in annex, two cottages (together 12 beds) and five Lapp huts (kåtor) with 30 beds. Inexpensive. Meals à la carte at a self-catering bar.

LÄKTATJÅKKO. Turiststation, 15 beds, inexpensive.

LULEÅ. Savoy, 70 rooms with bath. First class reasonable. Stadshotellet, 120 rooms, most with bath; restaurant, moderate. Standard, 52 rooms, 3 baths, restaurant, inexpensive.
SAS Globetrotter Hotel, 219 rooms, solarium, pool, casino, nightclub.
Esso Motor Hotel, Bodenvägen 951, just outside town, 79 rooms with bath.

ÖSTERSUND. Östersund, Kyrkogatan 70, 60 rooms, 30 with bath, modern, central, breakfast only, moderate to slightly higher. In same category: Grand, 30 rooms, 13 with bath or shower. Zäta, 38 rooms.
Esso Motor Hotel, Krondikesvägen 97, off E75, 40 rooms, with bath or shower. Hotel Winn (SARA), 138 rooms.

RIKSGRÄNSEN. Lapplandia Turiststation, 77 rooms, 34 with bath or shower, moderate; tennis. Good skiing terrain, slalom run, ski lifts.

SKELLEFTEÅ. Malmia, Torget 2, 76 rooms with bath. Belongs to ICA. Stadshotellet (SARA), 56 rooms, 36 with bath or shower.

STORLIEN. Storliens Högfjällshotell, 318 rooms, 64 with bath; spacious and attractive modern resort complex. For winter sports: slalom hill, 3 ski lifts; for summer sports: heated outdoor pool, saddle horses, tennis, trout pool. Superior.

SÖDERHAMN. Esso Motor Hotel, 87 rooms, pool, sauna, self-service tavern.

SUNDSVALL. Strand, 115 rooms, most with bath or shower. Restaurant, grill room. A SARA hotel.
Esso Motor Hotel, 3 miles from center, 47 rooms with bath or shower.

TÄNNDALEN. Two moderate mountain hotels: **Hamrafjällets Högfjäll-shotell,** 60 rooms, half with bath, attractive, well-kept, fully licensed restaurant; **Tänndalens Turisthotell,** 95 rooms, 42 with bath or shower, fully licensed restaurant.

TÄRNABY. Tärnaby Mountain Station of Swedish Touring Club, 13 rooms, 1 bath, inexpensive. The **Tärna Turisthotell** has 30 rooms all with shower and toilet, moderate.

UMEÅ. Blå Dragonen, 73 rooms with bath or shower; casino, bowling. **Blå Aveny,** 165 rooms; casino, discothèque, sauna. **Wasa,** 52 rooms, with bath. All first class reasonable.
Esso Motor Hotel, off E4, 125 rooms.

UNDERSÅKER. Trillevallens Högfjällshotell, 34 rooms some with bath, floodlit hill for skiing practice, superior; **Köja Fjällhotel,** 58 rooms, 23 with bath or shower, ski lift, and **Renfjällsgården,** 38 rooms, both moderate; **Hosgårdens Fjällpensionat,** 22 rooms, and **Vallbogården,** 28 rooms, are inexpensive.

VEMDALSSKALET. Vemdalsskalet, 300 rooms in all including accommodation in log cabins: 26 rooms with bath or shower in main building, 8 with shower in annex, and 40 with shower in the "sports" hotel. Also 36 log cabins with shower, for 4–6 persons—guests can choose between self-service and hotel service, cook their own meals or have some or all meals in hotel. Indoor swimming pool, gym, saddle horses, trout pond. Slalom hill with three ski lifts.

 SPORTS. Many well-marked trails for **hiking** and **climbing** criss-cross the entire mountain area. Most spectacular of these is the "Royal Trail" leading from Jäckvik through the Sarek district north to Abisko. Kvikkjokk is the starting point for tours up the beautiful Tarra valley and can be conveniently reached from Jokkmokk. From Kiruna you can reach Nikkaluokta at the foot of 6,965-foot Mount Kebnekajse, Sweden's highest mountain. An extensive network of mountain huts is maintained by the Swedish Touring Club, and expeditions with guides start regularly from the various tourist stations.

Fine possibilities for trout **fishing** exist throughout the region; also char, redbelly, grayling, and salmon. Among the waterways, try the Dalälven, Ljungan, Indal, Ljusnan, and Torne rivers, and the "Ströms vattudal", 9 connecting lakes stretching northwest from Strömsund to Frostviken. Other excellent fishing centers are Saxnäs, Tärnaby, Ammarnäs, and Arvidsjaur. Fishing license fees are low; for fishing in Jämtland waters write to Jämtland Tourist Association, Rådhusplan, Östersund, and for fishing in Lapland to Norrbotten Tourist Association, Sandviksgatan 40, Luleå, or Västerbotten Tourist Assn., Länsmansvägen 5–7, Umeå.

Forests abound in game for the **hunter,** especially moose, particularly plentiful in Jämtland; open season: 4 days, usually starting the second Monday of September. Special permits are required for the import and export of rifles and ammunition, and expeditions are arranged for hunters from abroad; write to Jämtland Tourist Association, Rådhusplan, Östersund.

WINTER SPORTS. The northland is **skiing** country—slalom and cross-country. The Swedes are specialists in cross-country, with a string of Olympic titles to prove the point. Härjedalen: Smallest of Sweden's four skiing provinces, also the highest; not quite as accessible as the others but very good skiing facilities, ski lifts in most resorts, and many good hotels; season in Fjällnäs district runs from January to mid-April. Jämtland: Sweden's most frequented winter resort area, thanks to its accessibility, facilities, and fine accommodation along Stockholm-Östersund-Trondheim railway; "snow weasels" are a feature, also torchlight sleigh rides, fishing through the ice, curling; season in Åre-Storlien district from January to mid-April. Lapland: Only distance from the capital and the lateness with which its season starts prevent this area from nosing out Jämtland as Sweden's top skiing region; this is purely skiing country —no ice sports or sleighing parties; the tree line is low, so there are plenty of open slopes; latitude is the greatest asset here and spring skiing the greatest delight—this is where you enjoy the sensation of skiing in the Midnight Sun; season in the Tärna district runs from March to early May, in Abisko district from March through May.

Informality is the keynote of Swedish winter resort life. No ice bars or *apres-ski,* but plenty of good companionship, relaxing before open fires, and the opportunity of acquiring a mid-winter tan. A word of caution with respect to the latter: the late winter-spring sun here has an unsuspected power—take good sun-glasses and be careful generally about over-exposing your face and body. Here is a brief survey of the provinces with their resorts and facilities (for accommodation, see Hotels):

Härjedalen is sleigh-ride and cross-country skiing territory, with marked trails and sleeping huts enticing skiers to 2- or 3-day excursions. Its chief resorts are all clustered together, on a U-shaped road starting on the Norwegian border at *Fjällnäs* (2,400 feet) and then paralleling the Tännån River southeastward through *Hamrafjället* (2,400 feet) and *Tänndalen* (2,280 feet), after which it swings around northeastward, with *Funäsdalen* (2,175 feet) in the center of the bottom of the U and then turns northwest, with the last of the principal resorts, *Bruksvallarna* (2,550 feet) falling at about the middle of the upper line of the U. *Vemdalsskalet,* finally, lies a little apart farther eastwards and just on the border to Jämtland province. Ski lifts at Fjällnäs, Hamrafjället, Bruksvallarna, Tänndalen, Tännäs, Funäsdalen, Sveg, Lofsdalen and Vemdalsskalet.

Jämtland offers a bewildering richness of resorts. Its transportation key is *Östersund,* the main station on the Stockholm-Trondheim line, which, while not strictly a resort, can be used as a center from which to sally forth to skiing slopes in the vicinity. It has excellent skating rinks. The most easily accessible resorts are those on this rail line, which, starting from Östersund, are *Hålland* and *Undersåker,* both with ski lifts; *Åre,* the chief winter sports center of Jämtland, with an overhead cable railway; several ski lifts and skating and curling rinks; *Duved* with new chair lift; *Ånn;* and *Storlien,* the second largest resort, which has a jump, ski lifts, slalom runs, one of which drops 770 feet in a distance of 3,280, ski instructors and skating rinks.

Another important area hugs the frontier south of Storlien, which gets you into some fairly high altitudes. First comes *Blåhammarstugan* (3,559 feet).

Southeast lies *Storulvåstugan* (2,394 feet), south of that *Sylstugorna* (3,123 feet), with a ski camp built another 300 feet above it; and a little more than a mile more to the south is the province's highest peak, *Mount Sylarna* (6,779 feet). Of these resorts, Storulvåstugan has slalom runs and ski instructors on hand.

A few other resorts south of the main railway, between the border and Östersund, are worth mentioning. Farthest west, reached by road from Undersåker (on the rail line) is *Vålådalen,* a small popular resort with slalom and downhill runs, ski lift, a practice jump and a skating rink. About halfway between here and Östersund, and just about as far south of the railway, is *Bydalen,* with ski lift, and about as much farther south again, *Arådalen.* At *Hammarstrand,* some 60 miles east of Östersund, is the up-coming winter sports center with bobsleigh track, slalom run, ski lifts.

Lapland's most popular section is its farthest north, above the Arctic Circle. The entrance to this region is the iron-ore center of *Kiruna,* 124 miles north of the Arctic Circle. Kiruna is not itself a resort, but the nearby mountains provide slopes of all degrees of difficulty within easy reach, and by continuing through it on the Stockholm-Narvik railway, you pass in rapid succession through the three big winter sports centers of northern Lapland, all of which have slalom slopes, lifts, ski instructors and guides for the long excursions.

The first one reached from Kiruna is *Abisko* (1,250 feet). A chair lift takes you up to the summit of Mount Nuolja with midnight sun from May 31 to July 16. Next comes *Björkliden,* which has a ski lift. Last station on the line, practically on the Norwegian border is *Riksgränsen,* also with a ski lift; the great attraction here is not simply sliding downhill from the top of the lift, but making excursions across the spectacular broad snowfields high up in the Riksgrånsen mountains under the Midnight Sun.

A new winter sports center is developing in southern Lapland around the resorts of Hemavan and Tärnaby. Ski lifts and good accommodation, but a little awkward to reach: direct train with sleepers from Stockholm to Storuman, then by bus.

USEFUL ADDRESSES. Tourist information and room booking service: Gävle, Centralplan; Härnösand, Skeppsbron; Luleå, Storgatan 35; Umeå, Rådhustorget; Sundsvall, Esplanaden; Östersund, Rådhusplan.

Youth Hostels: plentiful in this area.

INDEX

Index

The letters H and R indicate Hotel and Restaurant listings.

GENERAL

(*See also* under each country and Practical Information sections at the end of each chapter for additional details, especially Sports.)

ATLAS OF SCANDINAVIA

SCANDINAVIA

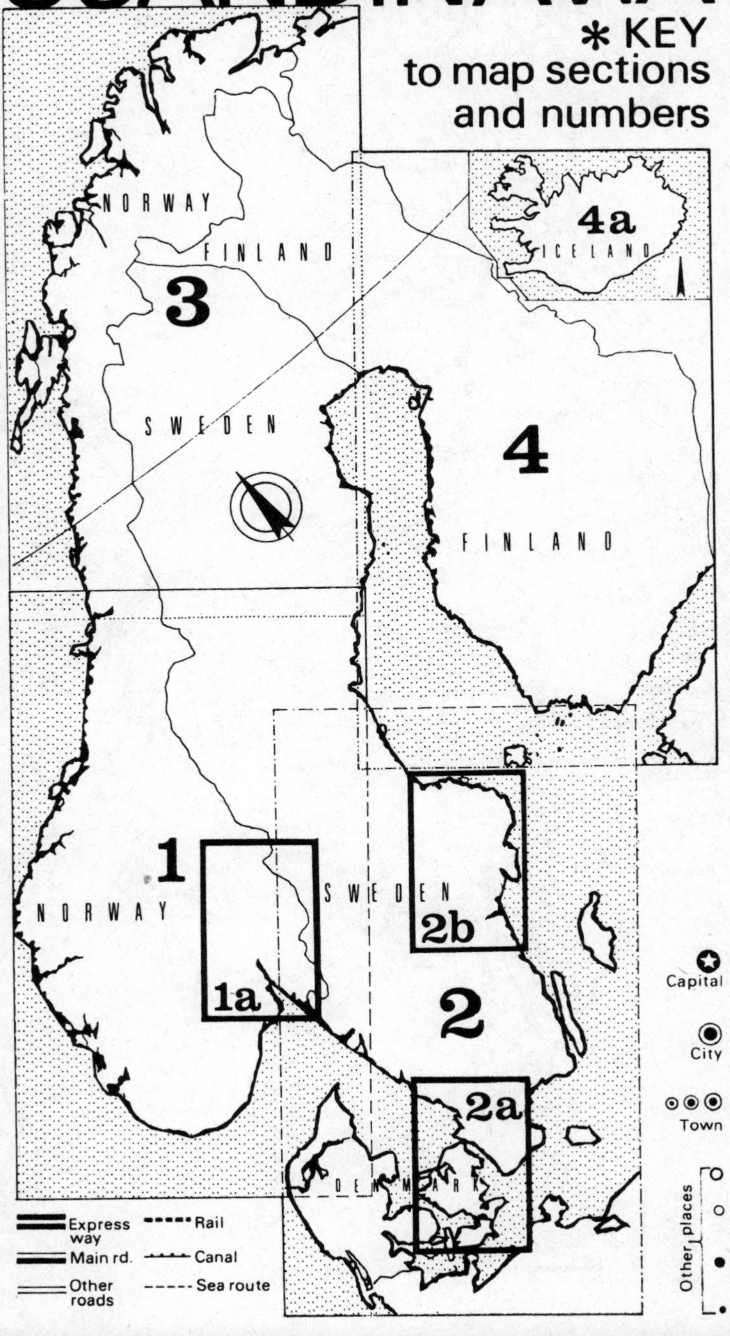

* KEY
to map sections
and numbers

NORWAY

FINLAND

3

SWEDEN

4a
ICELAND

4

FINLAND

1

NORWAY

SWEDEN

2b

1a

2

2a

DENMARK

⭐ Capital

◉ City

◎◎ Town

Other places

Express way	Rail
Main rd.	Canal
Other roads	Sea route

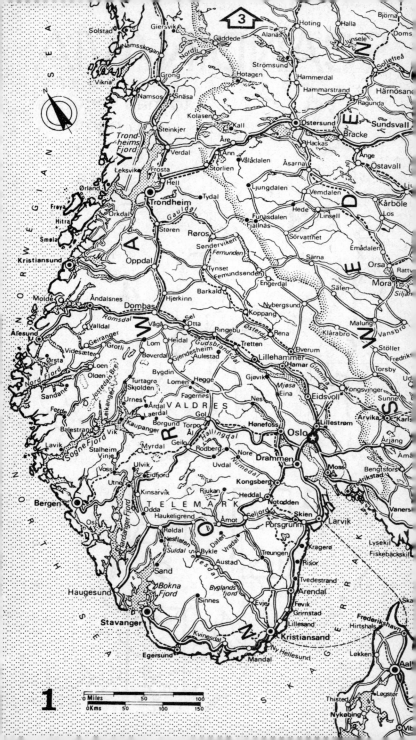

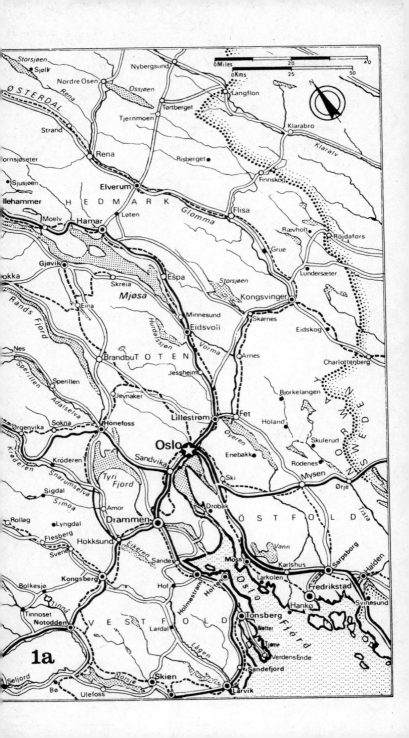

1a

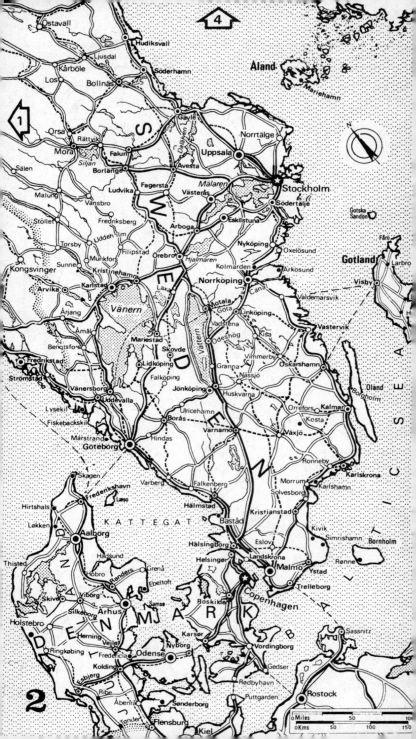

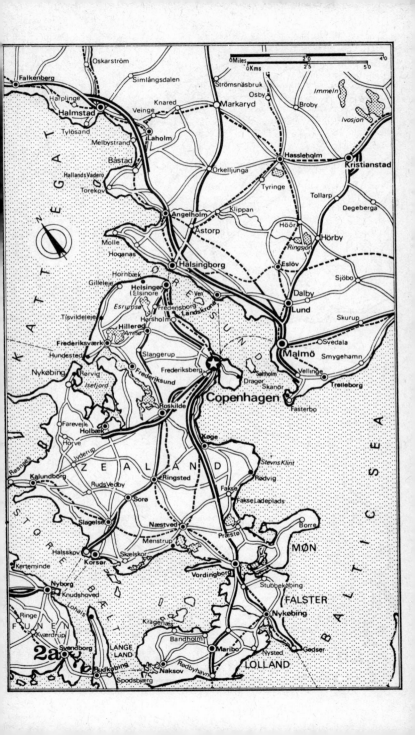

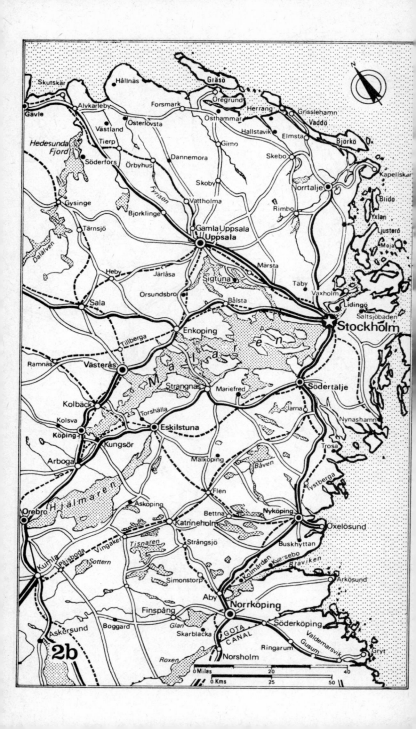